People Forced to Flee
History, Change and Challenge

People Forced to Flee

History, Change and Challenge

Great Clarendon Street, Oxford, OX2 6DP,
United Kingdom

Oxford University Press is a department of the University of Oxford.
It furthers the University's objective of excellence in research, scholarship,
and education by publishing worldwide. Oxford is a registered trade mark of
Oxford University Press in the UK and in certain other countries

First Edition published in 2022

Impression: 1

Published in the United States of America by Oxford University Press
198 Madison Avenue, New York, NY 10016, United States of America

British Library Cataloguing in Publication Data

Data available

Library of Congress Control Number: 2021953487

ISBN 978–0–19–878645–0 (hbk.)
ISBN 978–0–19–878646–7 (pbk.)

Printed in Great Britain by
Bell & Bain Ltd., Glasgow

Design by Vincent Winter Associés (VWA), Paris, France

Cover artwork: "The Sphere" © UNHCR / Younghee Lee. The Sphere allows room for
interpretation. It could be an organism, a globe or the universe. Shifting sands. The aim
is to provoke deeper thought, empathy and resonance.

Author: Ninette Kelley

Associate Editor: Preeta Law
Researchers and Analysts: Karolin Eberle and Denise Baruch-Kotulla
Research Assistant: Alexandra Holmes
Copy Editor: Michael Hunter
Assistant Copy Editor: Shannon Lee Mouillesseaux

Advisors: Ewen Macleod, Grainne O'Hara

Production Manager: Mike Walton
Production Coordinators: Françoise Jaccoud, Russell Neal
Designer: Vincent Winter Associés (VWA)
Photo Editors: VWA, Tessa Asamoah, Anne Kellner
Statisticians: Edgar Scrase, Zaruhi Mkrtchyan, Ennie Shonhiwa-Chikwanha
Graphic Designers: Younghee Lee, Eilidh Urquhart
Cartographer: Yvon Orand

Acknowledgements

In writing *People Forced to Flee – History, Change and Challenge*, I have been fortunate to work with a committed, talented team and to draw on wide expertise from within UNHCR and externally. Not least, there are the broad range of research papers and commentaries marking the 70th anniversary of the 1951 Convention relating to the Status of Refugees. A number of these authors have agreed to have their work posted on our website at (www.unhcr.org/people-forced-to-flee-book), and are indicated with an asterisk (*) below. I am also grateful to many colleagues for their comments on drafts of the book.

Within UNHCR sincere thanks go to: Allehone Abebe, Denis Alma Kuindje, Benoit d'Ansembourg, Hiroko Araki, Maria Bances del Rey, Vidjea Barathy Ramamurthy, Christian Baureder, Emily Bojovic, Veronika Burget, Jean Paul Cavalieri, Cirenia Chavez Villegas, Samuel Cheung*, Vincent Cochetel, Lisa Fergusson-Nicol, Marco Formisano, Davina Gateley Saïd*, Nathalie Antoinette Goetschi, Karen Gulick, Irina Isomova, Kerstin Jones, Elibritt Karlsen, Jasmine Ketabchi, Shaden Khallaf, Susanne Klink, Katharina Lumpp, Mai Mahmoud, Isabel Marquez, Pedro Mendes, Isabel Michal, Juan Ignacio Mondelli*, Debra Moore, Alexander Mundt, Angela Murru*, Jerome Nhan, Edward O'Dwyer, Kate O'Malley, Zeeshan Qamar, Roua Rahrah, Jennifer Roberts, Yasmine Rockenfeller, Annabelle Roig Granjon, Marian Schilperoord, Volker Schimmel, Natalie Schmidthaeussler, Salam Shahin, Rebecca Telford, Senai Terrefe, Alexander Tyler, Giuseppe Uniformi, Pieter Ventevogel, Catherine Wiesner, Michelle Yonetani, and Jeanette Zuefle. Indispensable administrative help has been provided throughout from Caroline Charmaine Torres, Jose Rodriguez Viquez, Alexandre Sarr, Ellen Joy Sibal. Special thanks to Jean-Nicolas Beuze, Sibylle Kapferer, Ewen Macleod, Grainne O'Hara and Edgar Scrase for going beyond the call of duty in their careful review and comments of previous drafts.

The World Bank and the Joint Data Center have provided considerable support for this book under the direction of Xavier Devictor, and the positive and insightful coordination of Caroline Verney Sergeant. Their thoughts and comments as well as those of the following colleagues have been invaluable: Dina Abu-Ghaida*, Alain Aeschlimann*, Michel Botzung, Ozan Cakmak*, Paola Elice*, Björn Gillsäter, Melissa Johns, Doreen Kibuka-Musoke*, Natalia Krynsky Baal*, Zara Sarzin*, Karishma Silva*, Domenico Tabasso* and Weiyi Wang*.

A range of academics, think tanks, and non-governmental organizations have provided rich and varied support. Within and alongside it, are the invaluable contributions of people with lived experience of being forcibly displaced. Sincerest thanks to: Tsion Tadesse Abebe*, Alex Aleinikoff, David Cantor, Tatiana Castillo Betancourt*, Christelle Cazabat*, Cathryn Costello*, Bina Desai*, Filippo Dionigi*, Evan Easton-Calabria*, David Scott FitzGerald, Rez Gardi*, François Gemenne*, Robert Hakiza*, Tristan Harley*, Claire Higgins, Elodie Hut*, Dragana Kaurin*, Fatima Khan*, Christa Kuntzelman*, Adam Lichtenheld*, Susan Martin, Charles Martin-Shields*, James Milner*, Vitit Muntarbhorn*, Phil Orchard*, Nandi Rayner*, Sevin Sagnic, Angela Sherwood*, Paul Spiegel, David Sulewski*, Jina Elise Swartz, Chloe Sydney*, Joseph Kofi Teye, Dzifa Torvikey, Tamara Wood*, Louisa Yasukawa*, Caroline Zickgraf* and Pascal Zigashane*.

Several interns have provided valued research help. Warm thanks to Diana Castillo Villaseñor, Liam Comer-Weaver, Danielle Douglas, Talia Gerstle, Niyonella Kamera, Johannes Lang, Kanika Mahajan, and Julie Meier. A number of students also dedicated time to writing term papers on subjects canvassed in these pages under the supervision of Peter Hoffmann and Achilles Kallergis of The New School: Isabel Arciniegas Guaneme, Ruben Cruz Valladares, Evelina Dahlgren, Emmanuel Guerisoli, Leah Guyot, Julie Kim, Jessica Matis, Eugenia Nikitina, Brooke Pascarella, Maria Julia Rivas Mor Mur, Robert Seebeck and Jodit Woldemichael.

People Forced to Flee shows how living up to humanity's ambition to improve responses to forced displacement is complex. It has never been easy to turn words honouring the spirit of the 1951 Convention into the policy and best practice that can maximize the life chances of millions of the world's most vulnerable people. To do so, and to deliver on the ambition of the Global Compact on Refugees, we need the political will of States combined with the commitment of multilateral institutions, civil society, non-governmental national and international partners, academics and those with lived forced displacement experience.

This book has been enriched by wide engagement from all of them.

NINETTE KELLEY
September 2021

Preface

by the United Nations Secretary-General

The *1951 Convention Relating to the Status of Refugees* — crafted in the wake of the horrors of the Second World War, and amid massive forced displacement — established the rights of refugees and the obligations of States towards them.

As we mark its 70th anniversary, this monumental achievement remains the foundation upon which millions of refugees find protection every day.

Today, we can find the Convention's influence across regional refugee instruments, as well as protection frameworks for internally displaced persons and those fleeing environmental damage and natural hazards.

But while this anniversary is a time to recognize accomplishments, it is not a moment for complacency.

The number of people forced to flee their homes due to conflict, violence, persecution, extremism and climate events continues to soar. In 2008, as High Commissioner for Refugees, I called attention to the unprecedented global levels of forced displacement. Since then, the number has more than doubled, reaching over 82 million forcibly displaced people today.

Most forced displacement occurs in low and middle-income countries already struggling to meet the needs of their people. Humanitarian and development assistance is growing, but so too are the demands, which too often outstrip available resources. At the same time, some parts of the wealthier world have, at times, closed their doors to people fleeing violence and persecution.

The humanitarian and development impact of forced displacement is catastrophic. But so is the human toll. We must never forget that behind each number is a story of deep personal suffering — a stark reminder of how quickly lives can be upended, and how critical it is to support people at this most vulnerable moment in their lives.

That is why this book — *People Forced to Flee: History, Change and Challenge* — is so valuable and timely.

Tracing the roots of asylum from the beginning of recorded history, this book highlights the major achievements of the last 70 years to protect and support forcibly displaced people, while exploring setbacks along the way.

The book shows the importance of sustained engagement by governments and development partners in supporting the forcibly displaced, as well as the vital role of dedicated financing instruments to assist host countries.

It showcases significant policy changes in host countries that have helped refugees access education, health services and employment, so they can build better futures for themselves while contributing to their new communities.

It outlines the increasingly close partnerships between humanitarian and development actors, including around a shared approach to data, evidence, and context and risk analysis to drive greater results on the ground.

Above all, it demonstrates the critical importance of a broad range of partners lending their comparative advantages, experience and expertise to support those people enduring forced displacement. Public and private partners are increasingly joined by civil society and faith-based partners and, most importantly, forcibly displaced persons themselves in designing and delivering solutions.

Guided by the lessons of past experience — triumphs and failures alike

— two new multilateral Compacts hold great promise to address imbalances and provide a blueprint for the future: the Global Compact on Refugees and the Global Compact for Safe, Orderly and Regular Migration. They outline critical actions to support refugees and migrants and the communities in which they live.

While the ambitions struck in the 2018 Compacts are on the path to being realized, significant challenges remain, as set out clearly in this publication.

Our task today is to build on this important work, and to gather more people to our efforts — from people already engaged in this field, to students of history, forced displacement studies and related disciplines. To them, this book will be of great value and inspiration.

But I also hope it will spur the broader community of nations to make bolder efforts on prevention, so we can address the root causes that drive so many millions of people to flee. I have set this out in more detail in *Our Common Agenda* report (www.un.org/en/content/common-agenda-report).

Let us learn from the lessons of this book, increase global support for people fleeing peril and danger, and find new ways to build safer and more under-standing communities and societies for all people.

ANTÓNIO GUTERRES

Foreword

by the United Nations High Commissioner for Refugees

Seventy years have passed since nations seeking to recover from the devastation of the Second World War drew up the landmark 1951 Convention relating to the Status of Refugees.

In that time, the Convention (along with its 1967 Protocol) has formed the basis of international protection of millions of refugees. It has been complemented by several regional treaties, such as the OAU Convention and the Cartegena Declaration, and other human rights instruments, allowing the original concepts to apply to evolving contexts.

To mark the 70th anniversary of the 1951 Convention, UNHCR is releasing *People Forced to Flee: History, Change and Challenge*, which traces the path that led to that historic moment and then follows it through seven decades up to the present day.

This book takes up the mantle of a series of publications, stretching back to 1993, that were previously entitled *The State of the World's Refugees*. In the almost ten years since the last edition, the global population of forcibly displaced people has soared, to 82.4 million at the end of 2020 and rising – almost double the number a decade ago.

The number will continue to grow so long as longstanding conflicts go unresolved and major new emergencies arise. The failure to resolve conflict has forced some refugees, often alongside migrants, to make perilous and sometimes fatal journeys in search of safety. Displacement associated with the climate emergency is adding a new dimension – one that is already a reality for millions.

Amid this torrent of challenges, every so often it is wise to take stock. This is the purpose of *People Forced to Flee*: to draw on the lessons of history in order to examine how we can improve responses to forced displacement today and tomorrow.

The task of protecting people forced to flee has always faced serious challenges. Humanitarian funding, despite the sustained generosity of governments, individuals and the private sector, has never been fully commensurate with the level of need. For many of the forcibly displaced, solutions have largely been elusive, and too often they find it hard or impossible to access the building blocks of education, health care and economic opportunity that would enable them to address and overcome their vulnerabilities.

More recently, the world has had to grapple with the COVID-19 pandemic, which has hit the most vulnerable the hardest and dealt a serious blow to development gains in many low- and middle-income countries. And while conflicts inexorably proliferate and intensify, the climate alarm is sounding ever louder. The drivers of displacement are unrelenting; the demands placed on humanitarian funding are growing.

Yet while the challenges are enormous, history has repeatedly demonstrated the potential for, and power of, positive change.

Everywhere, partnerships are evolving and expanding. In 2018, the UN General Assembly affirmed the Global Compact on Refugees, which calls for a "whole of society" approach to supporting the forcibly displaced and the communities that host them. Answering that call is a broad and diverse range of partners: refugees and internally displaced persons, local and national governments, national and international organizations, international financial institutions and development actors, academics and civil society. This book illustrates how those partnerships work and how they are making a difference.

Such thinking exemplifies the important changes that have taken place over the past several years in how the world views and responds to forced displacement, notably the wider recognition that forced displacement is both a humanitarian and a development challenge. Development actors are adding their weight through policy advice, data, evidence and analysis – as well as the largest financial support ever marshalled globally to support inclusive development, the keystone of the Sustainable Development Goals.

Underpinning these efforts are the international laws and policies that remind us of our obligations to the most vulnerable. The 1951 Convention, a living instrument working in conjunction with those laws as they have emerged and developed, has strengthened protections for people at risk of harm: women, children, people with disabilities, people with diverse sexual orientation and gender identity, and many others. The Convention and the Guiding Principles on Internal Displacement stand alongside other human rights treaties that also protect those on the move who are in need of protection.

Over the past 70 years, States have at times failed to rise to the standards set by this body of law – weakening responses to forced displacement and undermining the international solidarity. Nevertheless, those laws and treaties have been the foundation for the protection of millions of people forced to flee; they are as relevant as ever.

People Forced to Flee: History, Change and Challenge starts from the premise that transformational action is both essential and possible. It provides a detailed and an unflinching look at both the successes and the failures of the past, seeking to draw from them the elements needed to support positive, sustainable change. In that regard, it is worth noting that many of the most powerful moments in this book come from the stories of forcibly displaced people themselves – a reminder that the best way to understand and respond to their needs is to listen to their opinions, wishes, grievances, aspirations and hopes for the future.

I have been working in the field of forced displacement for more than 30 years. In that time, I have never ceased to be moved and motivated by those who put the values of altruism, compassion and solidarity at the heart of their daily lives: refugees and the internally displaced, host communities and those working alongside them. It is their example, above all, that gives us the greatest cause for optimism.

FILIPPO GRANDI

Table of Contents

Table of Contents

Data Methodology

Data on forced displacement, unless otherwise indicated, comes from UNHCR's data-base. It encompasses refugees, asylum-seekers, people internally displaced due to conflict and violence, and Venezuelans displaced abroad. In addition to the data it collects, UNHCR receives data from governments, the United Nations Relief and Works Agency for Palestine Refugees in the Near East and the Internal Displacement Monitoring Centre. Numbers are rounded to the closest hundred or thousand.

For more on UNHCR data sets, methodologies and definitions, see: UNHCR, Refugee Data Finder (www.unhcr.org/refugee-statistics/), Methodology and Data Insights sections.

Acronyms

AALCC Asian-African Legal Consultative Committee

AALCO Asian-African Legal Consultative Organization (former AALCC)

AU African Union

CARICOM Caribbean Community

CICC Coalition for the International Criminal Court

CIREFCA International Conference on Central American Refugees

CPA Comprehensive Plan of Action

DAC Development Assistance Committee (OECD)

DIHK German Chambers of Industry and Commerce

EBRD European Bank for Reconstruction and Development

ECHR European Convention on Human Rights

ECOSOC Economic and Social Council

ECOWAS Economic Community of West African States

EGRIS Expert Group on Refugee and Internally Displaced Persons Statistics

EIB European Investment Bank

ERC Emergency Relief Coordinator

EU European Union

FAO Food and Agriculture Organization

FARC Revolutionary Armed Forces of Colombia

FCDO United Kingdom Foreign, Commonwealth and Development Office

GCFF Global Concessional Financing Facility

GCR Global Compact on Refugees

GCM Global Compact for Safe, Orderly and Regular Migration

GNI Gross National Income

GNP	Gross National Product
GPFD	Global Program on Forced Displacement
HRC	Human Rights Council
IADB	Inter-American Development Bank
IASC	Inter-Agency Standing Committee
ICARA I / ICARA II	International Conferences on Assistance to Refugees in Africa
ICTR	International Criminal Tribunal for Rwanda
ICTY	International Criminal Tribunal for the Former Yugoslavia
IDA	International Development Association
IDP	Internally Displaced Person
IFC	International Finance Corporation
IFIs	International Financial Institutions
IGAD	Intergovernmental Authority on Development
IIIM	International, Impartial and Independent Mechanism on Syria
ILO	International Labour Organization
IMT	International Military Tribunal
IMTFE	International Military Tribunal for the Far East
IOM	International Organization for Migration
IPCC	United Nations Intergovernmental Panel on Climate Change
IRC	International Rescue Committee
IRMCT	International Residual Mechanism for Criminal Tribunals
IRO	International Refugee Organization
IsDB	Islamic Development Bank
ISIL	Islamic State in Iraq and the Levant
JE	Jordan Exports
MDBs	Multilateral Development Banks

Acronyms

MFU	Multilateral Framework of Understandings on Resettlement
MIGA	Multilateral Investment Guarantee Agency
MIRPS	Regional Comprehensive Protection and Solutions Framework
OAU	Organization of African Unity
OCHA	Office for the Coordination of Humanitarian Affairs
ODA	Official Development Assistance
OECD	Organisation for Economic Co-operation and Development
OECS	Organization of Eastern Caribbean States
R2P	Responsibility to Protect
RIMP	Refugee Investment and Matchmaking Platform
SDGs	Sustainable Development Goals
SIDS	Small Island Developing States
TBB	Talent Beyond Boundaries
TFD	UN Framework Convention on Climate Change Task Force on Displacement
TPS	Temporary Protection Status
UDHR	Universal Declaration of Human Rights
UNAIDS	Joint United Nations Programme on HIV/AIDS
UNDP	United Nations Development Programme
UNESCO	United Nations Educational, Scientific and Cultural Organization
UNFCCC	United Nations Framework Convention on Climate Change
UNHCR	United Nations High Commissioner for Refugees
UNICEF	United Nations Children's Fund

UNITAD   Investigative Team to Promote Accountability for Crimes
Committed by Da'esh/Islamic State in Iraq and the Levant
UNRRA   United Nations Refugee Relief Agency
UNRWA   United Nations Relief and Works Agency for Palestine
Refugees in the Near East

WBG   World Bank Group
WFP   World Food Programme
WHO   World Health Organization
WRC   Women's Refugee Commission
WWI   World War I
WWII   World War II

Introduction

Introduction

There was little sign that 17 December 2019 would be significant in Geneva. It was a typical winter day in the lakeside city. A grey mist hung low in the air, wrapping the Palais des Nations with a familiar chilling dampness. But a series of street closures was more unsual. They were in place to ease the passage of diplomats to the offices of the United Nations. Once inside, together with representatives from a broad spectrum of society, the delegates would take a positive step forward in the way the world supports refugees and the communities that host them.

Just one year earlier, United Nations member States assembled in New York and affirmed the Global Compact on Refugees.[1] It starts by recognizing that more equitable sharing of the burden and responsibility for hosting and supporting the world's refugees is urgently required.

It features a wide set of actions to meet the needs it identifies. It sets out to broaden, diversify and increase funding in support of host countries. It seeks improved reception and admission of refugees and aims to expand available solutions. Importantly, it also places refugee self-reliance as a central objective, via access to education, work, livelihoods while also improving opportunities for host communities. It recognizes the need to build on the short-term *human-itarian* responses, which suit the initial phase of a humanitarian crisis, with medium- to long-term *development* ones.

At the time of the General Assembly's endorsement, commentators were divided. Some considered the Compact a progressive achievement in a polarized world of increasingly restrictive policies and negative rhetoric towards refugees. Others felt that it did not go far enough and that, without an enforcement mechanism, it could prove to be yet another in a long line of non-binding initiatives that fade before they deliver meaningful change.[2]

It was on that otherwise unremarkable Tuesday in Geneva, at the Global Refugee Forum, that the Compact's ambitions were first tested in the form of pledges to advance and implement its broad agenda. This was not just a regular United Nations meeting of States, but a global gathering of countries, refugees, multilateral institutions, civil society, international and national non-governmental organizations, business leaders and academics coming together at a meeting called for by the Compact to assure it lived up to its promise.

Over 700 pledges were made that day. In the months that followed, there were 700 more.[3]

Multilateral development banks including the World Bank announced the largest number of development funding instruments for refugees and host communities in history. States made commitments of $2 billion. Private sector entities pledged $250 million for training and employment creation, acknowledging that refugees not only have skills that businesses need but are also a consumer market. Pledges from civil society were as diverse as the groups that made them: refugees and refugee-led organizations; faith-based groups; libraries; universities; environmental actors; sports organizations; student unions; human rights advocates; and women, children and youth groups.[4]

It was a promising start to be followed by firm commitments and implementation.[5]

People Forced to Flee: History, Change and Challenge looks at what will be needed to make the aspirations of the Global Compact on Refugees a sustained reality. Many of its core elements, as well as most of its stakeholders, are as relevant to responding to forced displacement *within* borders as *beyond* them. The book looks at improving responses for both, focusing on refugees and internally displaced persons within the mandate of the United Nations High Commissioner for Refugees (UNHCR).[6]

Statistics and details in some periods are more available for refugees than

People Forced to Flee*

1990-2020

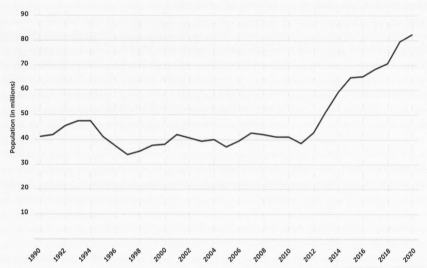

* The above includes refugees under UNHCR's mandate, asylum-seekers, internally displaced people, Venezuelans displaced abroad and Palestine refugees under the mandate of UNRWA. Data on people displaced in their own countries only became available in the early 1990s. Since then, data collection on internal displacement has steadily improved but can only be considered comprehensive at a global scale from 2008.

Forcibly Displaced Populations

2010-2020

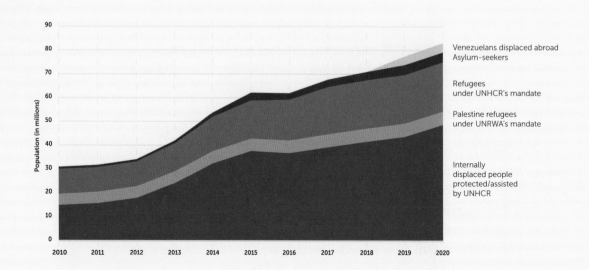

Venezuelans displaced abroad
Asylum-seekers

Refugees
under UNHCR's mandate

Palestine refugees
under UNRWA's mandate

Internally
displaced people
protected/assisted
by UNHCR

internally displaced persons, because historically refugees have been the subject of more analysis and focused support.[7]

The history and unique responses related to Palestine refugees under the mandate of the United Nations Relief and Works Agency for Palestine Refugees in the Near East are not dealt with here, although the number of Palestine refugees are included in the global number of forcibly displaced persons.[8]

As the 1951 Convention relating to the Status of Refugees (1951 Convention) reaches its 70th year, the 1961 Convention on the Reduction of Statelessness turns 60. Its history, and efforts to prevent, reduce and protect stateless persons, while not covered in this book, are reviewed in other publications and regular UNHCR updates.[9]

History

In 2013, as Syrian refugees continued to flee into Lebanon, many Lebanese opened their homes, their yards, and their fields to their neighbours. Their hospitality was not temporary, extending at times for years. When one rural Lebanese villager was asked why he continued to host dozens of Syrian refugees on his modest property, he – like many others – recalled how Syrians had helped Lebanese displaced during its 15 years of civil war (1975–1990).

Quite simply, he said: "It is a matter of history and a matter of heart."

This book takes inspiration from that powerful maxim. It looks at how responses to forced displacement can be improved by drawing from the lessons of history, the blueprint provided in the Global Compact on Refugees as well as the spirit of community and collaboration that is evident in the wide and diverse array of partners committed to the cause.

People in danger have received protection in communities beyond their own from the earliest times of recorded history. The causes — war, conflict, persecution, natural disasters and climate change — are as familiar to readers of the news as to students of the past. But, for most of recorded history, these were ad hoc responses without a unifying foundation.

That changed 70 years ago, when the international community drew up one of the most enduring documents to follow World War II. It set out the founding principles on which millions of refugees would find protection.

The 1951 Convention came after decades of failure to protect people forced to flee. It set out the obligations of States to ensure refugees the widest possible exercise of fundamental rights and freedoms.[10]

The Convention would outlive the post-World War II period, taking on global significance via its Protocol of 1967, and going on to inform international protection responses ever since. It has influenced the Guiding Principles on Internal Displacement, and helped shape international responses to protect those displaced by the adverse effects of climate change and disasters.

But, alongside the successes, there have been many failures, where States fall short of both their obligations and the spirit of the 1951 Convention. The long history of responding to people forced to flee provides important lessons for the future and reveals some persistent truths.

First – the history of global responses has an overall positive trajectory but an uneven one. Millions of forcibly displaced persons around the world have found protection and solutions. The range of people who are now recognized to fall within the 1951 Convention is broader than could have been envisaged by its framers.[11] And, the necessity to protect and resolve the forced displacement of people displaced within their countries' borders is widely recognized. Yet, alongside these developments have been continuous efforts to restrict rights, limit responsibilities, and erect barriers. Solutions to displacement remain elusive for most.

Second – while the 1951 Convention recognizes the need for international cooperation and burden-sharing, there has never been a time when they were equitably shared. The majority of forcibly displaced persons have and continue to be hosted in middle- and low-income countries, which face significant challenges in meeting the needs of their own citizens. Many high-income countries have financially supported refugee responses from afar, although not to the level of need, while also taking steps to unduly restrict the 1951 Convention's application, push back refugees at borders, and rely on other measures to intercept refugees in flight with the aim to prevent their arrival. This has undermined the international protection regime and stood in sharp contrast to their stated expression of solidarity with more impacted States.

Third – all international frameworks for responding to forced displacement recognize the right of individuals to contribute to their own well-being. Their ability to do so is too often constrained by legal or other barriers that restrict their access to work, education and health care: the necessities for dignified lives and durable solutions to displacement.

Fourth – responses to forced displacement have been too reliant on short-term humanitarian assistance, which has consistently fallen short of need. This was not intended at the time of the 1951 Convention but became the default approach as humanitarian crises increased along with the number of forcibly

Main host countries
of refugees, asylum-seekers and Venezuelans displaced abroad*

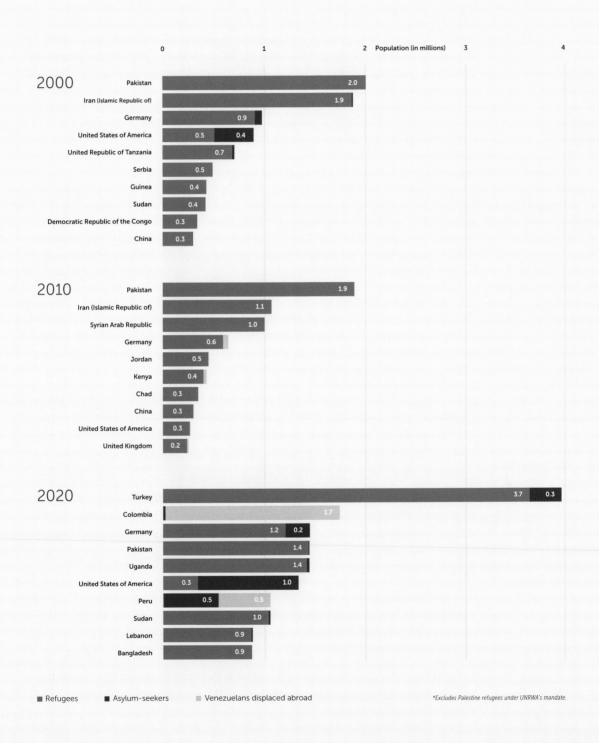

Population (in millions)

2000
Pakistan	2.0
Iran (Islamic Republic of)	1.9
Germany	0.9
United States of America	0.5 · 0.4
United Republic of Tanzania	0.7
Serbia	0.5
Guinea	0.4
Sudan	0.4
Democratic Republic of the Congo	0.3
China	0.3

2010
Pakistan	1.9
Iran (Islamic Republic of)	1.1
Syrian Arab Republic	1.0
Germany	0.6
Jordan	0.5
Kenya	0.4
Chad	0.3
China	0.3
United States of America	0.3
United Kingdom	0.2

2020
Turkey	3.7 · 0.3
Colombia	1.7
Germany	1.2 · 0.2
Pakistan	1.4
Uganda	1.4
United States of America	0.3 · 1.0
Peru	0.5 · 0.5
Sudan	1.0
Lebanon	0.9
Bangladesh	0.9

■ Refugees ■ Asylum-seekers ▪ Venezuelans displaced abroad

*Excludes Palestine refugees under UNRWA's mandate.

displaced persons. They were persistently seen as short-term phenomena, even in the face of growing evidence of their protracted nature. Too many host countries have been left without sufficient support to address the challenges to their institutions, infrastructure and economies resulting from conflict and consequent large forced displacement. And too few efforts have been made to strengthen human capital in displacement – the skills, knowledge and experience that enable individuals to realize their potential as productive members of society.

Change

Alongside those trends are positive signs of change.

There is now global recognition that improving responses to forced displacement is as much a *development* imperative as a *humanitarian* one. The explicit inclusion of refugees and other displaced people in the global Sustainable Development Goals is a long awaited step. The involvement of major development partners in forced displacement responses is evidence of this taking hold. They have introduced new funding instruments in support of the socioeconomic development of displaced and host communities. And their work is supporting policy changes in host countries for the socioeconomic inclusion of forcibly displaced persons. This could lead to positive systemic change.

More joined-up humanitarian and development approaches are also helping improve our *knowledge base*. Knowing the aggregate number of forcibly displaced people and appreciating their individual characteristics has often been limited. In some contexts, security issues have hindered access to displaced persons. Data collection tools, methodologies and capacities, until relatively recently, were not able to capture detailed information in an accurate, effective and secure manner. Because short-term humanitarian interventions dominated responses, detailed socioeconomic evidence of how forcibly displaced populations were coping over time, for good or for ill, was not prioritized. Neither was how their presence affected the socioeconomic circumstances of host communities. This is now changing for the better.

Significantly, there is greater recognition of the value of a *broader partnership base*. Humanitarian efforts targeting forcibly displaced persons are centuries older than intergovernmental humanitarian agencies. They came from national and local authorities, civil society and international charitable groups, which welcomed, protected, assisted and led advocacy and fundraising efforts. For some time, however, their work has been overshadowed by that of international institutions, which have grown in both number and size to respond to human-itarian emergencies and ever increasing levels of forced displacement. Recent emphasis on sustainable responses is bringing needed attention to the value of local response mechanisms and drawing on a broader array of partnerships than ever before.

Closely associated with this is the role of forcibly displaced persons. History reveals situations when refugees had more agency in negotiating the terms of their asylum, and freedom to become self-reliant and contribute to the communities which received them. As the number of refugees grew globally, they faced greater restrictions on their ability to do so. In the last 20 years, most major international initiatives, aimed at improving responses to forced displacement, have called for the *deeper engagement of refugees and internally displaced persons* in the design and implementation of programmes that affect their lives.[12] This call remains only partially met, but there is more momentum and effort for resolute change.

Challenge

The lessons from the past and the changes coming on stream should inform further efforts to improve. It is also the case that old and new challenges complicate the task.

Political will is necessary to sustain any efforts towards positive change. This book is full of examples of how a number of States have increased finan-cial contributions, supported new approaches, and enacted important policy changes to improve the lives of forcibly displaced persons. This is significant. But more is needed. The mobilization of timely, predictable, adequate and sustainable public and private funding called for in the Global Compact on Refugees remains a challenge, as does broadening the base beyond traditional core donors. Critical as well is the need to do more than improve lives *in displacement.* To fulfill the ambition of the 1951 Convention and the Global Compact on Refugees, States further afield, and with much more resources than most host countries, must also live up to the spirit and the letter of the international commitments and declarations they have made. This includes: improving their reception and asylum systems rather than restricting access to them; expanding refugee resettlement opportunities; and opening alternative safe and orderly pathways for refugees and migrants. These are long awaited.

Prolonged conflict and instability: In the past 20 years, global forced displacement has more than doubled with 82.4 million persons displaced at the close of 2020.[13] Many of the largest forced displacement situations are also of the longest duration. Some have lasted for generations, such as Afghanistan, Colombia, the Democratic Republic of the Congo, Myanmar, Somalia and Sudan.[14] These countries experience ongoing conflict and instability as do others that have large and protracted forcibly displaced populations, such as the Central African Republic, Ethiopia, Nigeria, South Sudan, Syria and Yemen.[15]

In these contexts, development approaches can be more difficult, depending as they do on national ownership, enabling legislation and policies, and long-term time frames. Ongoing conflict and instability can negatively affect all three.

Extremists, armed groups and criminal gangs: Persecution and violence by extremists, armed groups and criminal gangs have driven millions of people to flee their homes, and added to the complexity of forced displacement responses.

Recent years have seen the rise of the Islamic State in Iraq and the Levant (ISIL) which, for a time, controlled significant parts of Syria and Iraq. Neither its defeat in Iraq in 2017 nor in Syria in 2019 signaled the end of the group or of its offshoots and affiliates. It remains active in both countries and operates along with affiliated organizations in other parts of the Middle East, Africa and Asia.[16]

Violence perpetrated by extremists and other armed groups has continued across Africa and, together with government counter-insurgency and counter-terrorism operations, have led to substantial loss of life and human rights violations. Burkina Faso, Cameroon, Central African Republic, Chad, Democratic Republic of the Congo, Mali, Mozambique, Niger, Nigeria, Somalia and Sudan have been significantly affected.[17] In the Americas, armed guerrilla groups, paramilitary organizations, criminal gangs and drug traffickers have fuelled forced displacement within and from several countries, including Colombia,[18] El Salvador, Guatemala, and Honduras.[19]

Millions of forcibly displaced persons now live in areas under the control of non-State armed and militarized groups in conditions marked by attacks, sexual assaults, abductions, and other forms of abuse and exploitation. Humanitarian needs are acute, yet many refugees and internally displaced persons remain beyond the reach of international relief efforts, because humanitarians cannot access them safely, without the agreement of the parties controlling destinations and means of access.

The delivery of humanitarian assistance in these contexts has always been difficult, including to prevent it from directly or inadvertently benefiting those engaged in the conflict. The proliferation of extremist groups, many designated as terrorist groups, and international efforts to stop them have added to the complexity.

Counter-terrorism measures at the global, regional and national levels,[20] while important to address security threats, can adversely affect humanitarian action if not implemented with care.[21] The measures can leave humanitarian agencies open to criminal prosecution, for example, if they engage with a designated group in negotiating for access to civilian populations, and they can restrict the provision of humanitarian aid to populations in need where there may be members of a designated group living among them.

Humanitarians have sought exemptions to shield them from criminal liability where reasonable efforts have been taken to prevent the diversion of support to terrorist entities. The Security Council has recognized the difficulties and has urged States, when designing and applying counter-terrorism measures, to take into account their effect on impartial humanitarian activities.[22] This is positive, but more needs to be done.

These are all problems beyond what the programme of action in the Global Compact on Refugees can address alone. There are others too.

Climate events: The increasing frequency and intensity of extreme climate events, such as heat waves, heavy rain, drought and associated wildfires, and coastal flooding, have also contributed to increasing displacement, most of it internal.[23] Slow and sudden onset events drive hundreds of thousands of individuals from their homes each year across all continents. And, although a significant proportion has been of a temporary nature, the past decade has shown how the adverse effects of climate change and disasters can exacerbate other causes of forced displacement.

The unpredictable and extreme weather conditions around Lake Chad, a substantial source of food and income generation for bordering countries, have had catastrophic consequences – contributing to instability, conflicts and displacement, often to urban centres in the region.[24] The adverse effects of climate change, combined with conflict and instability, also contributed to forced displacement across the globe in recent years, including in Afghanistan, Ethiopia, Guatemala, Honduras, Mozambique, Nicaragua, Somalia and South Sudan.

The failure of governments to address the impacts of climate change and disasters on their communities, or the partial implementation of mitigation measures that favour one group over others, can fuel tensions and lead to

Main countries of origin

of refugees, asylum-seekers and Venezuelans displaced abroad*

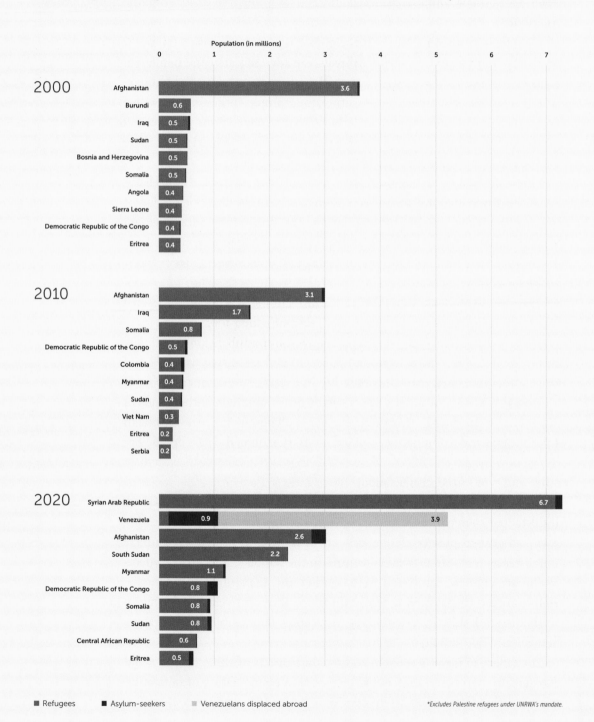

Population (in millions)

2000
- Afghanistan: 3.6
- Burundi: 0.6
- Iraq: 0.5
- Sudan: 0.5
- Bosnia and Herzegovina: 0.5
- Somalia: 0.5
- Angola: 0.4
- Sierra Leone: 0.4
- Democratic Republic of the Congo: 0.4
- Eritrea: 0.4

2010
- Afghanistan: 3.1
- Iraq: 1.7
- Somalia: 0.8
- Democratic Republic of the Congo: 0.5
- Colombia: 0.4
- Myanmar: 0.4
- Sudan: 0.4
- Viet Nam: 0.3
- Eritrea: 0.2
- Serbia: 0.2

2020
- Syrian Arab Republic: 6.7
- Venezuela: 0.9 / 3.9
- Afghanistan: 2.6
- South Sudan: 2.2
- Myanmar: 1.1
- Democratic Republic of the Congo: 0.8
- Somalia: 0.8
- Sudan: 0.8
- Central African Republic: 0.6
- Eritrea: 0.5

■ Refugees ■ Asylum-seekers ▪ Venezuelans displaced abroad

*Excludes Palestine refugees under UNRWA's mandate.

escalating violence. Disaffection with government responses, coupled with loss of livelihoods and limited opportunities, can drive people into militant groups.[25] This has been evident throughout sub-Saharan Africa and parts of Asia.[26] These challenges are predicted to increase in the coming years.

Transnational human smuggling and trafficking: War, persecution, violence and diminishing resources drive people to seek safety and better futures further from their homes. This need, coupled with efforts to deter and restrict the arrival of refugees, and limited legal means to migrate, has helped to fuel the increase in human smuggling and trafficking.

Professional transnational criminal networks now control many informal transit routes, charging increasingly high prices to move desperate people along dangerous journeys in hope of reaching safety. The higher the obstacles, the more work, contacts and money are needed to overcome them – all resources that are beyond independent smugglers but well within the purview of organized criminal syndicates.[27] The greater the surveillance measures imposed by States and the more selective their migration policies, the more these networks innovate, often by finding new and more perilous routes.[28] Risks are borne by refugees and migrants, too often at the cost of their lives.[29]

The fight against human smuggling and trafficking is an international priority for many States and emphasized as reasons for substantially increased investments in surveillance, deterrence and prosecution. But, again, it must be accompanied by more robust efforts to improve reception conditions and create more legal pathways for refugees and migrants, as promised in the Global Compact on Refugees and in another international agreement, the Global Compact for Safe, Orderly and Regular Migration, each adopted by States in 2018.[30]

COVID-19: The global pandemic has affected forced displacement in ways unforeseen in 2018. Most countries restricted access to their territories, which impeded refugees from seeking asylum. Some eventually relaxed controls to provide exceptions for asylum-seekers, but many have kept them in place.[31] In 2020, arrivals of refugees and asylum-seekers in most regions were significantly under levels that would have been expected without the pandemic. Refugee resettlement fell by close to 70 per cent.[32]

Millions of people have died because of the pandemic,[33] with countries around the world experiencing human and economic losses. COVID-19 has dealt a brutal blow, particularly to low- and middle-income countries. Although the global economy is predicted to expand by 5.6 per cent in 2021, this will be experienced unequally. The World Bank predicts that, for many emerging markets and developing economies, per capita income will likely remain below pre-pandemic levels for a protracted period.[34] Fragile and conflict-affected, low-income economies have been the hardest hit, with setbacks in previous gains in poverty reduction to be felt in the years ahead, according to the World Bank.[35]

Most of the world's forcibly displaced populations are in countries that will continue to struggle due to COVID-19 related losses for some time. These include an erosion of skills from lost work and schooling, a sharp drop in investment, higher debt burdens and greater financial vulnerabilities.[36] Adverse impacts on trade and rising food prices could aggravate matters. Overall projections suggest that, by the end of 2021, around 100 million people will "have fallen back into extreme poverty".[37] The impact continues to be particularly severe on vulnerable groups – women, children, and unskilled and informal workers.[38]

The necessity to increase humanitarian and development funding for forced displacement situations, therefore, comes at a time of heightened global need. Funding pandemic-related responses is now a common priority. Host States may be less inclined to accept loans, even on the most favourable terms, for forced displacement responses. This reinforces the importance of the emphasis in the Global Compact on Refugees on ensuring that responses to forced displacement are effective, efficient, tailored to the specific context, and of benefit to forcibly displaced and local communities. It also suggests that the advances promoted by the Compact may take longer to realize due to these additional, unforeseen challenges.

Structure of the Book

Part I: The Roots of Asylum. Refugees have received protection from others from the earliest periods of civilization. For most of history, this has been a localized response, made by those who share some affinity for those seeking their help, or who could benefit from the skills and resources that refugees could provide. Part I shows how the definitive ideals of the current international protection regime – safety, solidarity and solutions – are not new. But, the longevity of these ideals is matched by their uneven application, making the main trajectory of protection both positive and incremental. This pattern defines its history from the beginnings in ad hoc provision through its development into a broad and universal concept. Even as its ideals become established norms, their application remains imperfect.

Part II: Protecting More Broadly. The 1951 Convention set out refugees' rights and acknowledged that protecting and assisting refugees is a shared responsibility among States. Together with successive human rights instruments and regional refugee agreements, it has protected a broader group of people than initially envisaged, providing safety, solidarity and solutions for millions. But, while countries express support for the international refugee protection regime, they simultaneously limit access to it. This creates a persistent gap between commitment and practice, an area the Global Compact on Refugees seeks to address. Part II examines these tensions. It also reviews how growing levels of forced flight *within* borders, and displacement due to the adverse effects of climate change and disasters, led to multilateral protection and response mechanisms that have drawn from the 1951 Convention. Part II considers how these frameworks have helped advance protection, assistance and solutions and what is needed to address weaknesses in implementation.

Part III: Solutions – An Uneven Record. Over time, many millions of refugees and internally displaced persons have safely returned home or been accepted permanently in new communities, allowing them to forge new futures for themselves and their families. But many more have not. Part III examines the framework for solutions, the historical record, lessons learned and current efforts to improve.

Realizing a solution to displacement is a process. Solutions are not simply bestowed on forcibly displaced persons but are ones they seize, based on their calculation of what will be best for them. Solutions have a greater chance of success when they build on prior investments to help forcibly displaced persons retain and reinforce their social and economic capital in a manner that also benefits host communities.

Part IV: Improving Life Prospects. Improving lives and advancing human development for forcibly displaced persons is a global ambition, reflected in the international community's Sustainable Development Goals and the Global Compact on Refugees. However, the fact that refugees and internally displaced people should be included in development efforts does not mean that they are. Part IV looks at some of the barriers that exclude forcibly displaced persons from national development efforts, as well as positive changes that are beginning to take root.

Achieving socioeconomic inclusion and improved outcomes for host and forcibly displaced communities calls for an appreciation of the local context, including the structure of the economy, related laws and policies, economic trends and the potential for growth. It also requires information on the

People displaced internally

2010 & 2020

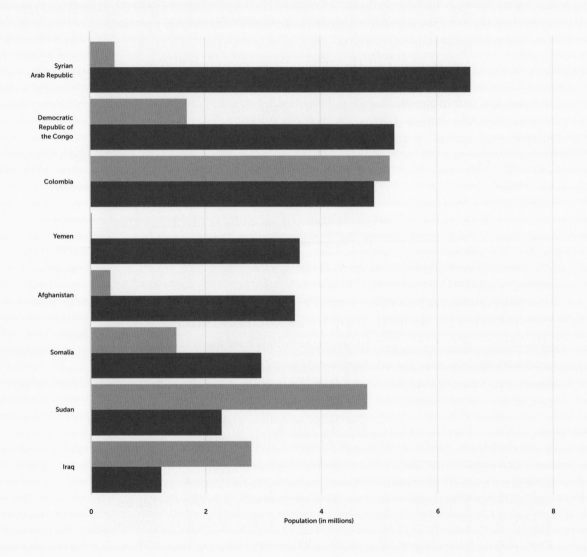

Population (in millions)

2010   2020

Source: Internal Displacement Monitoring Centre (IDMC).

economic impact of conflict and forced displacement, and the relative skills and capacities of displaced and host populations. Interventions to improve human capital in displacement – through education, health care and employment – are expanding and need to be based on reliable, context-specific data, analysis and evidence of what is feasible.

Part V: Bridging the Gap. More is needed for the Global Compact on Refugees to live up to its promise. Part V looks at efforts to expand the funding base and to improve data, evidence and analysis, which not only help build donor confidence but also effectively design, deliver and evaluate programmes. Success depends on genuine political will to secure the changes necessary for long-term solutions to be found. That shift is as significant as the challenges it aims to address – challenges which would be insurmountable without today's unprecedented and broad spectrum of expertise. Part V looks at operational approaches needed to sustain this effort, alongside the growing attempts to hold those who cause displacement – the perpetrators of serious human rights abuses – criminally liable.

Improving responses to forced displacement must be accompanied by efforts to address their root causes. Protecting human rights, preventing conflict, achieving sustainable peace and development, and promoting climate action are the core commitments of the United Nations. Efforts to improve across these areas are central to the Secretary-General's agenda.[39] The advances and setbacks of this work are reported on annually by the Secretary-General and through specific departments and agencies within the United Nations system.[40] Sadly, without significant improvements across all these fronts, we can expect a continuation of the steady annual increase in lives lost, damaged and uprooted by persecution, climate, conflict and violence.

Time will tell whether the Global Compact on Refugees marks a historic positive step that many believe it to be. The Global Refugee Forum, to be held every four years, is a mechanism to assess this periodically.[41] In the meantime, a High-Level Official's Meeting is scheduled for December 2021 in Geneva to identify progress, ongoing challenges and areas where further engagement is needed.[42]

The large and diverse number of delegates at the first Global Forum was an initial indication of progress. The positive changes these engaged actors are making are evident in the pages of this book. While the challenges are significant, they would be insurmountable without this broad coalition of partners committed to improve the lives of people forced to flee.

PART I

The Roots
of Asylum

Table of Contents

The Roots of Asylum

Human flight from harm to safety is a consistent story throughout history. Long before the right to seek asylum was formally recognized in international law in 1946,[1] persons fleeing war, conflict, territorial encroachment, and persecution received protection in communities beyond their own.

One of the earliest documented examples of a ruler providing asylum to a political refugee was in Ancient Egypt over 3,000 years ago.

Much of what we know today about the history of asylum is focused on displacement in Europe caused by religious, ethnic and political persecution and conflict. The crucible of two world wars, the European experience largely spurred the development of an international refugee regime that emerged following those global conflicts.

Even with much of the history of forced displacement unwritten or incomplete, there is enough evidence to help place current trends in a much larger historical context. Part I traces the roots of asylum leading to the emergence of an international refugee regime and highlights five consistent trends.

First – the causes of forced displacement have been relatively consistent. Key drivers have been and continue to be: climate, disasters, war, conflict and hunger; as well as persecution based on ethnicity, nationality, religion, perceived political opinion or other salient characteristics.

Second – refugees have received protection from others from the earliest periods of civilization. Yet, for most of history, this has been a localized response, made by those who share some affinity for those seeking help.

Third – people forced to flee are far from passive victims. Rather, they have been and remain central in shaping their own futures, including at times negotiating favourable terms of settlement, contributing to the growth of the communities that took them in and helping define the ideas and language of international refugee conventions of the modern period.

Fourth – voluntary and non-governmental institutions have long played an important role in the provision of protection and assistance. They have marshalled coordinated international responses even before centralized governmental or multinational ones became the norm.

Fifth – the definitive ideals of the current international protection regime – safety, solidarity and solutions – are not new. They have been evident in the human response to forced displacement for centuries before being written down.

Safety to those who are forcibly displaced.

Solidarity through support to countries confronted by large numbers of forcibly displaced populations.

Solutions through secure legal status and the ability of those who have been uprooted to move on with their lives, provide for their families, and contribute to their new communities.

But the longevity of these ideals is matched by an uneven application of them, which also dates way back from the present day, to as far as the records reach. This makes the main trajectory of asylum both positive and incremental, a pattern that defines its arc – from its beginnings in ad hoc provision through its development into a broad and universal human concept. Even as its ideals become established norms, their application remains imperfect.

Pre- and Ancient History

Two million years ago, some of the first hominins were on the move out from the African continent. Seventy thousand years ago, Homo Sapiens followed. Over the course of tens of thousands of years, they spread from Africa to the Middle East, eventually reaching Europe, Asia, Australia and the Americas to become the only surviving human species on the planet.[2] These journeys needed great innovation and adaptation. While it is not possible to know all of the factors that induced such mass migrations, physical artifacts reveal influences that remain relevant.

Climate is one of the oldest known factors. Changes in climate spurred pre-historic migrations as well as altered physical geography in ways that influenced migration routes. Glacial periods of low sea levels exposed land bridges enabling humans to move between mainland Europe and the United Kingdom, Russia and Alaska as well as South and North America, tens of thousands of years ago.[3]

Later, warmer temperatures and rising sea levels led to massive human displacement. Current estimates suggest that sea levels could rise from one third to more than one metre over the next 80 years.[4] An increase of that scale is enough to lead to the displacement of millions of people.

During the warming period around 7,500 years ago, glacial melting and consequent mounting sea levels of up to 400 meters were proportionately, if not more, consequential. When the elevated waters of the Mediterranean Sea broke through the land bridge between Bulgaria and Turkey, creating the Bosporus Strait, vast tracts of land were submerged and humans displaced to areas of Hungary, Iraq and Slovakia.[5] In Africa, rising seas led those in flooded areas to move to the southern half of the continent while increased rainfall in the Sahara and consequent formation of lakes and marshes attracted movement to northern Africa.[6]

Climate-induced forced displacement, therefore, is not a new phenomenon. As we will see in Part II, however, principles to guide State responses to it have only emerged in more recent times.

Violence and war also appear to have contributed to human forced displacement in pre-historic times. Archeologists and ethnographers have unearthed evidence to suggest that intercommunal violence and war were common between foraging communities around the world. And the causes were similar to those of today, including resource scarcity, population pressures, and the arrival of new groups in a region.[7]

Historical records of mass population movements improve over time. Archeological remnants reveal significant forced displacement between the early city-states dating back thousands of years. The pattern intensifies with the emergence of empires,[8] which continued through most of the Common Era.

At this point, asylum enters the historical record, with early records showing two clear forms of asylum, both thousands of years old.

One was provided on *holy ground*. The other was *political*.

The rights to protection, and its duration, varied between different societies. But, then as now, there was a central, common element: Flight from serious harm.

Protection within temples of worship or other sacred places was believed to come straight from deities. It was applied widely to those fearing retribution for alleged crimes and unpaid debts, as well as to those escaping active conflict. It was afforded to defeated warriors, escaped slaves, and social and political outcasts.[9] Safety depended on their physical presence within the sacred space.

Seal impression of Mursili III. © Archive of the Bogazköy/ Hattusha excavations (Deutsches Archäologisches Institut, Berlin; Photographer: P. Neve)

This tradition continues, with sanctuary still offered to refugees in places of worship today.[10]

Ancient political asylum was more analogous to international protection. It was provided by the ruler or State and generally reserved for allies of importance.

One of the first known political refugees was Mursili III, also known as Urhi-Teshub, king of the Hittite Empire which in the 13th century BCE stretched across Anatolia, present-day Turkey. During his relatively short several-year reign beginning in 1272, Urhi-Teshub battled against his uncle for the throne, and was defeated and banished to contemporary northern Syria, whereupon he fled to Egypt.

There, Ramses II granted his request for protection and refused demands for his extradition. Urhi-Teshub eventually left Egypt when his safety there was compromised by the signing of a treaty between Ramses II and his uncle. The treaty contained extradition clauses for the return of fugitives and for amnesty to be granted to them upon return.[11] Urhi-Teshub, apparently wisely, did not put the latter provision to the test. He fled Egypt and did not return home.[12]

The asylum initially provided to Urhi-Teshub has features that have been replicated over time. Asylum could be provided when politically expedient and abandoned for the same reason. Moreover, even where protections were enacted in law (such as the amnesty provision in the Hittite-Egyptian treaty), they could be abrogated in practice.

Additionally, the quality of asylum also very much depended on personal status. Urhi-Teshub was a deposed leader and the amnesty he enjoyed, albeit temporary, was more robust than that accorded to others of lesser rank and political status during the Bronze Age. Most commonly, refugees in the Ancient Near East, who were given asylum were relegated to the lowest economic ranks, some serving as mercenaries or sold as slaves.[13]

The exercise of asylum in a politically motivated manner continued in subsequent eras and was evident in Ancient Greece.[14] It was not uncommon for Greek city-states to provide refuge and special privileges to citizens from other city-states fleeing civil war and conquest. Those who benefited, tended to be from allied city-states or those who ascribed to the same political philosophy as opposed to other resident foreigners who were subject to heavy taxes and compulsory military service.[15] Refuge provided to those of shared political values would become common in the modern world.

Shared political ideology was not the only animating value for extending protection to refugees. Another motivating ideal in Ancient Greece was *humanitarianism*: "equal, unconditional compassionate concern for all fellow humans" which should be put into practice to alleviate suffering and deprivation wherever possible.[16]

This more universalistic humanitarian approach grew in prominence in the 2nd and 1st centuries BCE. Love of humanity, "philanthropia", came to be expected of good citizens. Refugees were included as those worthy of charitable treatment.[17] Thousands of years later, the right to seek asylum and the provision of asylum without discrimination are reflected in the Universal Declaration of Human Rights and the 1951 Convention relating to the Status of Refugees (1951 Convention).[18]

Examples from Athens and elsewhere in the Greek city-states, reveal that refugees who were given asylum could also be afforded opportunities to be independent and self-reliant, providing the conditions necessary for them to realize a solution to their displacement.[19] Many formed their own cities in exile, often in bordering regions or marginal regions. Others settled in urban areas and formed professional and other associations with local citizens.[20] The expectation and facilitation of their independence was consistent with Classical Athenian ideology, which considered it demeaning for men to accept charity. Athenians "strove to equip adult male refugees with the means to continue to act, even in exile, as self-sufficient, autonomous political agents".[21]

Greek drama and oratory also reveal obligations due to refugee women and children. While men were expected to be independent and self-reliant, women and children seeking refuge were assumed to be in need of assistance and support. In the classic Athenian tragic play, Suppliant Women, written by Aeschylus, the 50 daughters of Danaus, the mythical son of the King of Egypt, flee to Argos a major Greek city. They are escaping what today is commonly considered a modern claim to asylum: forced marriage. They are granted safety, "asylia", the ability to remain and be protected.[22]

Evidence of flight and finding refuge can also be found in the records of the Roman Empire, a vast empire, encompassing European, Middle Eastern and North African territories. It lasted hundreds of years becoming one of the longest imperial powers in history.

The Roman Empire was both the source of forced displacement, as well as a recipient of people fleeing war, oppression and food shortages. While scholars agree that the Empire received many thousands of foreigners, and that they came as vanquished rivals, economic migrants, allies, mercenaries, and refugees, the relative size of each is not known and the cumulative numbers disputed.[23] What is clear, however, is that like the Ancient Greeks, the treatment accorded to refugees was not uniform.

Some refugee groups were permitted to remain on reasonable terms allowing them to maintain a degree of economic and cultural autonomy. These conditions were governed by political and military considerations. Other groups could be forced to disperse, forcibly conscripted or sold into slavery.[24]

Forced displacement caused by climate, war, conflict, conquest and political dissent were features of pre-historic and ancient periods. Asylum was sought from deities in sacred temples, and from rulers. With respect to the latter, when extended, it was generally to political allies on terms that could be upended when the usefulness of the alliance ceased.

The treatment accorded depended on status as well as political affiliation, with the most favourable treatment encouraging and facilitating agency through land concessions, as well as through the rights to work, to protect one's community and to contribute to the host community. Far less favourable treatment, including death and enslavement, fell upon others in flight if they were vanquished rivals or persons who had no political cachet.

In the midst of this very mixed picture, a few glimmers of light emerge: including opportunities given to refugees to be self-sufficient, assistance provided to those with specific needs, and emergence of the humanitarian principle of impartiality in extending refuge and assistance, each of which was evident at times in Ancient Greece.

Middle Ages - Early Modern Era

A feature in the asylum narrative that emerges in this period is flight and refuge from religious persecution, which would later become a recognized basis for providing asylum in the 1951 Convention. Europe in the late 12th–17th centuries holds many examples.[25]

Beginning in the late 12th century, the Catholic Church took measures to root out heresy largely through the offices of the Inquisition. Many thousands of people suspected of heresy were persecuted, tortured and executed. In 1478, the Catholic monarchs of Spain (Isabella I of Castile and Ferdinand II of Aragon) established the Inquisition. This was followed by one of the most notorious and consequential acts against a minority faith- the Alhambra Edict of 1492.

The Edict ordered the expulsion of practicing Jews from the Kingdoms of Castile and Aragon. Those who chose not to convert were forced to leave.[26] Tens of thousands left, followed by thousands more in the mid-16th century after the installation of the Inquisition in Portugal upon its union with Spain.

Religious cleansing in Iberia also targeted Muslims. Forced to convert to Catholicism in the early 16th century, their descendants faced expulsion a century later. Hundreds of thousands fled or were expelled, many settling in North Africa.[27]

The Protestant Reformation, which posed a challenge to the Catholic Church, and the Counter Reformation that sought a Catholic resurgence of the 16th century, were marked by massive religious persecution and conflict, claiming millions of deaths and mass displacement well into the 17th century.[28]

Of the Christian refugees of the period, Huguenots fleeing persecution in France were among the first and largest number. Following the St

Bartholomew's massacre of Huguenots across France in 1572, refugee numbers increased and rose further 100 years later once the policies of toleration that had been granted to them were revoked.[29]

Although they were prohibited by law from leaving France, an estimated 200,000 Huguenots fled, accounting for close to one quarter of the French Huguenot population.[30] Accounts of their escape routes and concealed flight ring familiar today. As recounted by Susanne Lachenicht, they escaped with

Expulsion of the Moriscos, port of Denia, Spain in 1609.
La Expulsión en el Puerto de Denia, Vicente Mostre, 1613, Colección Bancaja; Photographer: Juan García Rosell/Wikimedia Commons

the "help of trafficking gangs or illegal emigration networks on board vessels… [some] packed in barrels or crates" and others fleeing on foot through mountainous regions to Swiss cantons and to Savoy.[31] Many other religious minorities, including different denominations within the Protestant and Catholic faiths, also fled religious persecution within and beyond Europe.[32]

As in Ancient Greece, many found refuge within countries of shared values. In Europe, Catholic monarchies of France, Spain, and the Habsburg dynasty received Catholic refugees while Protestants received protection in the Netherlands, England, Switzerland, Scandinavia, and Brandenburg-Prussia. Some States also extended protection to those of other religions.

The Ottoman Empire accepted non-Muslims who, while granted a large degree of autonomy, could be subject to various conditions such as extra taxes to be paid and limitations on where they could live and professions in which they could work.[33] Elsewhere, within Europe and also overseas, protection and assistance to "religious others", Lachenicht observes, depended on how useful the State considered them.[34] Admission of refugees was often viewed in these terms.

Huguenots, Catholics, Mennonites, and Jews promoted the ways they could be useful as a means of negotiating certain privileges, such as the ability

Huguenots on the road to Brandenburg. Frederick William of Brandenburg, the Great Elector, grants the right to settlement to Huguenot refugees. Potsdam Edict, 29 Oct. 1685. © akg-images

to settle collectively, administer the affairs of their community, and establish their own schools. These terms varied by group and country but could include tax concessions, exemptions from military service, and representation in State administrative offices.[35]

Concessions won, however, could depend on the contributions realized. They could be altered or restricted if expectations were not met. Jews, in particular, experienced this across Europe. Scholars describe their position as "a tolerated minority" whose position "was hardly stable, but rather ambiguous and in need of constant renegotiation".[36] Relative autonomy also came with the expectation that refugees would take care of their own communities. This included organizing poverty relief, accommodation, education and being accountable for the actions of their members.[37]

What is novel about the period is the degree to which some groups could negotiate the terms of their asylum.[38] This was due in large part because they were regarded as bringing significant economic as well as strategic advantages. For example, Jewish refugees were seen as being able to enhance commercial trade with Africa, the Americas and Asia, while the Huguenots' expertise in wine growing, silk production and manufacturing could boost these sectors.[39]

Foreigners and refugees were also important in helping consolidate frontier territories, replenish depopulated areas, and secure territory. Philip Ther observes that "as in early modern Poland and Prussia, the interests of the Ottomans lay in increasing the number of their subjects after population losses incurred in the costly conquest of Constantinople and the Balkans".[40] Lachenicht too gives many examples from the 15th through the 18th centuries of persecuted ethnic and religious minorities helping to consolidate Austrian-Hungarian, British and Russian Empires.[41]

A sustained period of cold temperatures, known as the "little ice age", and particularly harsh weather events like storms, heavy rains and droughts across the northern hemisphere during the 1600s[42] led to massive crop failures, famines and diseases. These contributed to great population losses of the period: losses which foreigners, including refugees, could help fill.

In the United Provinces of the Netherlands, receiving refugees and migrants also was important to strengthen economic and political power.[43] According to Geert Janssen, by the 17th century in the Netherlands, the arrival of many thousands of persecuted minorities contributed to the development of a new national narrative. Having fought a drawn-out struggle for independence from Catholic Spain and experienced exile, the Dutch were open to fellow Europeans fleeing persecution. Offering refuge and freedom of conscience and religion became "at the heart of Dutch identity."[44] In fact, to be a refugee from religious persecution carried such a cachet that even those who had migrated there for other reasons often cast themselves as exiles.[45]

Asylum in the Netherlands and elsewhere in Europe was not universally extended. At the same time that the Netherlands was re-imagining itself as a cosmopolitan country of tolerance, it was engaged in one of the most prolonged human trafficking exercises in history.[46] For over 200 years, the Netherlands – along with the Belgium, France, Germany, Portugal, Spain and the United Kingdom – enriched themselves and their colonial possessions through the slave trade while, at the same time, selectively providing asylum to groups or individuals within Europe.[47]

The Peace of Westphalia of 1648 largely concluded the Thirty Years of War waged within the Holy Roman Empire between Catholic- and Protestant-dominated States. By this time, securing refuge on the grounds of religious persecution was widely accepted, although the security received, and the autonomy permitted were often contingent on how beneficial the refugees could be to the State which admitted them.

The Peace of Westphalia is attributed as marking the beginning of a national legal order for among its provisions was recognition of the territorial sovereignty of States within the Empire and, by extension, the right to control their own borders. The Peace recognized the right of sovereign rulers to enter treaties (provided they were not prejudicial to the Empire), and the right of Catholics, Calvinists and Lutherans to freely worship and not be forcibly expelled.

Some consider these latter provisions as notionally bringing the concept of refugees and asylum more firmly into the modern State system.[48] It is also the case that the religious liberties were not extended to other faiths and the treaty also affirmed the sovereign right to determine the official State religion. Flight for religious freedom from Europe would continue.[49]

Modern Era

The Peace of Westphalia and the Age of Revolutions

Following the Peace of Westphalia in 1648, religious conflict in Europe began to abate. For the next two centuries, revolutionary movements and uprisings against imperial powers – often referred to as the "Age of Revolutions" – were the causes of significant refugee influxes across Europe and North America.[50]

This period marked the beginning of a recognized class of "political" refugees and prompted some of the first legislation regulating entry, treaties that prohibited the forced return – or "refoulement" – of political exiles, and the first state bureaucracies for managing refugee arrivals. As in previous centuries, the terms of their asylum were discretionary and often depended on whether they shared common values which, in the case of revolutionaries, were shared political aspirations.

In the course of the American Revolution 1775–1783, over 60,000 British loyalists, whites, blacks and indigenous Americans, along with 15,000 slaves, fled to other parts of the Empire.[51] Over half went to Canada, several thousand to England, others to the British colonies in the Caribbean and over 1,000 to Sierra Leone. British authorities rewarded them for their allegiance by providing material assistance, cash compensation and allocations of land, including the freed blacks among them. However, as Maya Jasanoff points out, many of the 15,000 slaves discovered "first-hand how slavery was preserved if not reinforced in the British Caribbean domains" and some 2,000 were taken to Canada as slaves.[52]

Nearly three times as many refugees, close to 150,000 French citizens, sought safety following the French Revolution of 1789 throughout Europe, the United States and the overseas colonies of France, Spain and the United Kingdom.[53] Those who left after 1789, or who were already abroad and failed to return, were viewed by the French authorities as being against the ideals of the revolution. Referred to as "émigrés", their properties were confiscated and their return prohibited on pain of death.[54] The émigrés were largely tolerated in European States, in part because most States had limited means to restrict their entry.

Like refugee movements of earlier periods, refugees were given agency to provide for themselves, although in Britain, they received government assistance and charity drives were encouraged. It is estimated that 40 per cent of French exiles drew from the political and social elite, including clergy and nobles, with many of the remainder being those who provided services to them, such as artisans, musicians, and domestic servants.[55] Over time, those of higher status had to find work wherever they could and many set up businesses, schools and bookstores and engaged with other refugees from revolutionary struggles.

Because they retained contacts inside France and with other French exiles, they were an important source of information to the States in which they resided[56] and, in turn, were influenced by the ideas and culture of their hosts.[57] Large numbers returned to France at the end of the reign of terror in 1799 and following the 1802 Napoleonic declaration of a wide-ranging amnesty.

Among the earliest legislative provisions regulating entry was the United Kingdom Aliens Act of 1793, passed amid fears that among the arriving French émigrés were those wishing to stoke unrest in the United Kingdom.

Ships' captains had to provide the names of all wishing to disembark, and the authorities decided who would be permitted entry, which was also conditional on registering at the place of intended residence. And, as a forerunner to modern carrier sanctions, ships' captains could be fined if they did not comply with the Act.[58] The preamble of the subsequent Act of 1798 recognized the concept of political asylum as well as the need to distinguish between those who seek refuge from "oppression and tyranny" and those who come for a "hostile purpose".[59]

Across the Atlantic, concern over foreign subversives was addressed in four bitterly contested acts passed by the United States Congress in 1798. Collectively known as the Alien and Sedition Acts, they provided for the imprisonment and deportation of foreigners considered dangerous (Alien Friends Act), or who were from a hostile nation (Alien Enemies Act), as well as made it a criminal offence to make false statements critical of the federal government (Sedition Act). The Naturalization Act imposed more stringent requirements for naturalization.[60] The legislative provisions were met with considerable opposition among Republicans and contributed to their election victory in 1800.[61] The Acts were short-lived, save for the Alien Enemies Act[62] that was used during World War II (WWII) to arrest and incarcerate resident foreigners from countries with which the United States was at war.

The Greek War of Independence from 400 years of Ottoman rule was among the bloodiest of the 19th century. Stretching over a nine-year period, it was marked by tens of thousands of deaths, huge population displacements and massive atrocities committed on both sides. Independence was secured by 1832 with the assistance of French, British and Russian intervention. By that time, the newly independent Greek territories were in ruins. The ethnic Turk population of these territories had fled to the Ottoman Empire and many thousands of Greeks were displaced internally and externally.

The majority of Greek refugees found safety in the Russian Empire among their co-religionists, supported by central, local and religious authorities and civil society.[63] Sympathetic reports favouring the Greek cause sparked public sympathy throughout Europe also due to the growing popularity of Greek politics, philosophy and art that was enjoying a revival.[64] Private charities in support of the independence movement flourished and the engagement of the non-governmental sector in assisting refugees continued to grow.

Inspired by the Greeks but not as successful, in 1830, Polish revolutionaries staged a series of uprisings against their Russian and Prussian imperial overlords. Just as French émigrés remained connected and engaged in the political future of France, so too did the Polish refugees who were concentrated mainly in western Europe, with some making their way to the United States. They were well received in France and Belgium where they were given residency permits, financial assistance and protection against deportation.[65]

The significance of the movement lay well beyond its relatively modest size of some 20,000 refugees. In exile, they maintained active political, artistic, scientific, military and social committees, nurturing the ambition for an independent Poland throughout the century. They also actively supported the national uprisings that swept Europe in 1848.[66]

The Revolutions of 1848–1849 were the largest simultaneous series of revolutions in European history. Fueled by demands for democratic reform, they erupted in Austro-Hungary, France, Italy, the Netherlands, Poland, Romania, and throughout German-speaking States. Largely unsuccessful, they

Polish refugees with their belongings.
© Smith Archive/ Alamy

resulted in many thousands of deaths and significant forced displacement.[67]

Refugees were received by the Ottoman Empire and many also were admitted to France and the United Kingdom. The welcome in France diminished due to German pressure to locate the refugees away from the border area where, as in contemporary conflicts, it was feared the refugees would launch or support cross-border raids.

German refugee involvement in uprisings in Baden and elsewhere contributed to a hardening of attitudes. Following the coup of Napoleon III and the imposition of a more authoritarian regime, France was no longer as receptive to revolutionary refugees.[68] Many moved on to Switzerland where Swiss cantons welcomed and assisted the refugees as they had the Huguenots of the 16th century. Several thousand of the fleeing refugees, who came to be known as the "Forty-Eighters", immigrated to the Unites States, with many enlisting during the American Civil War, the overwhelming majority for the Unionists.[69]

Refugees were admitted generally under regular immigration processes, and not as a distinct class of persons with internationally recognized rights to seek asylum. However, the non-return of political offenders became a feature of extradition treaties of the 19th century.[70]

In 1833, Belgium prohibited the extradition of political offenders and included this in its extradition treaty with France the next year. Other States soon followed. The Ottomans referred to these norms in refusing demands by Austro-Hungary to return Hungarian dissidents following the failed uprisings of 1848. Ahmed Cevat Pasha, who would become the Grand Vizier, later recalled that the decision was also based on Islamic principles.[71] But the fact that France and the United Kingdom promised military support if Austro-Hungary and Russia attacked, [72] could also have been decisive.

Beginning in 1843, the United States also had legal provisions to prevent the extradition of those wanted for political offenses.[73] And this protection also found expression in the first multilateral Latin American Penal Law Treaty of 1889 which recognized the right to political asylum decades before any multilateral European treaty.[74]

The 19th century also featured the beginning of government-coordinated responses to refugee arrivals. While Swiss cantons had initially taken in refugees from the 1848 revolutions, they soon became overwhelmed. Switzerland was also under pressure not to accommodate refugees near the border from where they could launch raids in support of neighbouring insurrections.

The national authorities stepped in and appointed a commissioner to redistribute the refugees internally and encourage refugees to move onward to other countries. Through both financial incentives and political pressure the number of refugees was reduced from several thousand in 1849 to some 500 persons in 1851. Those who left were asked to sign a form indicating they did so voluntarily. While the Swiss actions were consistent with past trends of restricting asylum when it was politically expedient to do so, the authorities retained asylum for high profile political dissidents who faced serious harm or death.[75]

The Ottoman Empire also was at the forefront of establishing a centralized administration for refugees. By the 1800s, the over 500-year-old Empire stretched across three continents and had taken in hundreds of thousands of refugees fleeing religious persecution and political unrest.

Non-Muslims were accorded various degrees of autonomy over religious and civil affairs.[76] As the Empire continued to fray, riven by discontent, nationalist movements and successful independence struggles in Greece and Serbia, consecutive Sultans carried out a 37-year period of reform beginning in 1839 to modernize, centralize, consolidate and unify the Empire. Measures to attract, receive and settle immigrants and refugees formed part of these efforts.

Specifically, in 1857, to attract more immigrants to land depopulated by wars, uprisings, disease and famine, an imperial decree permitted anyone to immigrate who agreed to abide by the laws of the Empire and be a subject of the Sultan.[77] The decree was published widely in European newspapers and newcomers were enticed by guarantees of citizenship, religious liberty, and free plots of agricultural land.[78] Other inducements included time-limited exemption from military service, tax concessions,[79] and the provision of cattle, farming tools, grain and temporary financial aid. Benefits were contingent on immigrants remaining in rural areas.[80]

Within years, the promotion of immigration was no longer necessary. Various groups faced persecution and expulsion from the Russian Empire in the 18th and 19th centuries leading to mass emigration into Ottoman territories. Crimean Tatars were among the largest number. Circassians too fled ethnic cleansing in the 1860s leading hundreds of thousands to flee to Ottoman areas. In the 1870s and 1880s, the Empire received other large influxes of refugees as a result of the Russian-Turkish War and rising nationalism in the Balkans.[81] Estimates suggest that by 1914 between 5 and 7 million Muslims were forcibly displaced to the Ottoman Empire within a period of some 85 years.[82]

To manage these mass influxes, the Ottomans created the Migration Commission in 1860 with a specific mandate for immigrants and refugees.[83] It marked the beginning of a series of time-limited Commissions, some with a mandate for managing specific influxes.

Broadly speaking, these State institutions were established to facilitate the smooth settlement of immigrants and refugees. This included selecting land, determining settlement locations, maintaining statistical records of arrivals and settlements, and, depending on the time and the finances at their disposal, providing transportation, in-kind support, targeted monthly allowances and mediating disputes between locals and refugees.[84] Successive administrative departments for management of refugee affairs continued into the 20th century, until the end of the Ottoman Empire.[85]

Another aspect of the Ottoman experience that remains relevant is that immigrants and refugees were encouraged to economically integrate and there was a clear legal framework for their settlement: elements that today are considered important in advancing development for refugees and their hosts.[86] In some instances, Tatar and Circassian elites were also given representation on the migrant commissions.[87]

Settlements that tended to thrive were ones where land was plentiful, with transportation links to urban areas and, importantly, where the State provided generous subsidies which enhanced social cohesion between new arrivals and local communities.[88]

By the end of the 19th century, various trends in asylum policy had emerged. Throughout Europe and the Americas, States had shown a readiness to receive and protect refugees of shared religion or political ideology. This was done through regular immigration channels that were relatively open at the time. There was no predictability regarding whether protection would be extended in all situations, the terms upon which it would be granted or its duration. This still was very dependent on State self-interest.

Refugees who received asylum were largely able to move on with their lives and build their futures, sometimes with assistance from State or voluntary associations. Centralized State administrations for the management of refugee arrivals were starting to emerge.

The 20th Century

Nationalism and forced flight

Civil unrest, national uprisings and the outbreak of World War I (WWI) within the first 15 years of the 20th century led to unprecedented levels of forced displacement from religious, ethnic and political persecution and the beginnings of an international protection regime.

The century opened with mass flight of Jewish refugees from a series of pogroms in the Russian Empire, heavily concentrated in modern-day Ukraine, Moldova and Poland. The violence perpetrated against Jews was a bellwether for what was to follow in subsequent decades. Already by the outbreak of WWI over 2 million Jewish refugees had taken flight, mostly to the United Kingdom and the United States.[89]

The rise of nationalism added further justification to the persecution of religious and ethnic minorities as newly independent States increasingly saw their development and security as contingent on a unified national identity.[90] Ethno-nationalist inspired violence was brutally on display during the Balkan

Wars of 1912–1913, which altered the map of Europe, reduced Ottoman territories on the continent and helped forge alliances that helped set the stage for WWI. Thousands died and widespread State-sponsored acts of ethnic cleansing against civil populations led to significant forced displacement and deep enmities that would explode during the Great War and in later periods.[91]

Estimates of the number of forcibly displaced due to the Balkan Wars vary between 0.5–1 million people.[92] Reception of refugees was readily extended to co-religionists. Thousands of Christians were displaced from Ottoman-held territories and their reception in Balkan States was facilitated by State and charitable institutions.[93] Muslim displacement, mostly to the remaining Ottoman territories, was significantly larger. Some 180,000 people fled to Istanbul and other towns in the first six months of 1913 alone.[94] The scale of these population transfers, large as they were, would be surpassed and their management was a motivating factor for the emergence of an international protection regime.

Within the Ottoman territories, as initial towns of refuge came under siege, many were killed or died of starvation – and thousands fled again further inland.[95] Reception of so many people in such a condensed period of time proved a challenge for the authorities, at the central and local levels. Adopting the same approach as had been taken to receive early waves of refugees, the new arrivals were assisted in relocating to the interior on vacant arable land facilitated through the provisions of tools, livestock and tax exemptions.[96]

Those remaining in cities were also encouraged to be economically self-reliant, and small business loans advanced. Funding for this enormous endeavour came from the State, local communities, and donations from all over the Muslim world.[97]

The facilitation of settlement by the State was also, more ominously, accompanied by detailed profiling efforts which, according to Peter Gatrell, helped to identify political affiliations and determine "Turkishness".[98] Moreover, lands given to the refugees were often in Anatolia which had previously been inhabited by Armenians before the purge against their community in 1896.

World War I and its Aftermath

The outbreak of WWI in 1914 marked the beginning of massive death and forced displacement across Europe and the Middle East.

At its conclusion in 1918, the conflict had claimed more than 14 million military and civilian deaths. Seven million soldiers returned home with severe disabilities.[99] Over 10 million people were driven from their homes.[100] Lands were devastated, infrastructure destroyed, and farmland rendered uncultivatable for years due to chemical contamination. Economies were broken and the loss of a large proportion of a productive generation was felt for decades.[101] The war precipitated the collapse of four Empires: Russian (1917); German (1918); Austro-Hungarian (1918); and Ottoman (1922). It brought about the

creation of new countries[102] and the birth of the Soviet Union – all of which led to further mass forced flight. It saw the emergence of the first international efforts to respond to forced displacement, the successes and failures of which informed the international protection regime that emerged in the contemporary period.

Russians accounted for the largest number of people forced to flee. Among them were hundreds of thousands who were forcibly relocated within Russia because they lived in areas of military operations or because they were minorities whose loyalties were in doubt.[103] The Russian revolution, and ongoing conflict between pro and anti-Bolshevik factions through 1923, also contributed to large displacements.[104] By that time, several million Russians were internally displaced and approximately 1 million had sought refuge elsewhere.[105]

Across Europe, millions of people fled enemy advancements. Over 2 million people in France and Belgium fled, as did 1.5 million from Austria and many hundreds of thousands throughout southern Europe.[106]

Ethnic cleansing and mass expulsions also accounted for considerable loss of life and displacement. Close to 1.5 million Armenians were killed and hundreds of thousands expelled from Turkey, reducing the centuries-old Armenian populations there by at least 50 per cent.[107] Others fled the Greco-Turkish War. By 1924, an estimated 200,000 Armenian refugees had fled to parts of Europe and the Middle East.[108]

The mass movements of refugees within and across borders, often with no assets, no immediate means of sustaining themselves and many in poor health, was challenging for State authorities fully occupied with fighting a war.

While many of the most impacted countries, like France, Italy, the Netherlands, Prussia, Russia, Serbia and the United Kingdom, instituted centralized responses, these were augmented by local and international humanitarian organizations which grew during this time. Displaced persons participated in these organizations, drawing from all sectors of society and supported by the diaspora. Ethnic and cultural groups invested heavily in supporting their displaced communities, helping reinforce loyalties to their corresponding nation-states.[109]

War-time relief work launched the careers of individuals who became leading politicians, as well as those instrumental in establishing enduring international humanitarian institutions that today remain prominent players in forced displacement situations.[110]

At the end of the war, many people who had been displaced returned to their places of origin or were absorbed in the nations of their shared ethnicity. Tens of thousands also emigrated to North America with the United States taking in close to 100,000 Russians.

There continued to be many thousands, however, with no place of permanent safety. Jews who remained or returned to Austria, Galicia, Germany, and Russia and other parts of Eastern Europe lived an uneasy existence, often denied nationality and subjected to ongoing discrimination and persecution, which increased severely over the subsequent decade.

In 1921, the Soviet Union revoked the citizenship of all Russians living abroad,[111] effectively rendering them stateless. Most remained in Europe but often with insecure status. Viewed as a social welfare burden, as well as a threat

Refugees in Antwerp during WW1. © Keasbury-Gordon Photograph Archive/Alamy

to the ethnic homogeneity of the new States, they were often denied naturalization. Without travel documents, they could not move elsewhere to join friends, family or look for employment.[112]

The emergence of an international protection regime

The plight of Russian refugees was so dire and the capacities of aid agencies stretched so thin that the circumstances led to a defining moment in response to forced displacement. For the first time, a High Commissioner was appointed

to lead the international response to the situation. Fridtjof Nansen was the League of Nations' choice and would become one of the most influential leaders of a global refugee relief effort.

Nansen was a Norwegian innovator, renowned scientist, pioneering arctic explorer, and diplomat. He was also known to be extraordinarily humble and eloquent and was initially reluctant to assume the position knowing the commitment it would entail and the scientific inquiry he would need to put on hold.[113]

Initially appointed High Commissioner for Russian Refugees, the League widened the remit of the High Commissioner in succeeding years but always in regard to specific refugee situations.[114] And, although a global mandate would come later, the efforts of the High Commissioner's Office during the inter-war period informed the mandate that would eventually be accorded to the United Nations High Commissioner for Refugees (UNHCR) following WWII.

Nansen set to work with a skeletal staff and a limited budget to facilitate the repatriation or resettlement of hundreds of thousands of Russians. Initially, he focused on repatriation and established procedures with the agreement of the Soviet Government that in key respects resemble modern protections related to return. Return was to be voluntary and to non-famine-affected areas, and returnees were to have access to Nansen representatives posted to areas of return.[115]

Returnees were also able to travel to other countries to speak to prospective returnees about conditions back home to help boost confidence for return. On the heels of the first repatriation, however, rumors spread of summary executions, and confirmed reports of disappearances dampened interest in return. The movement was altogether dealt a fatal blow in 1923 when the Government of Bulgaria was overthrown with the assistance of anti-Bolshevik Russian forces. Both the Bulgarian and the Soviet authorities refused to restart the repatriation programme.[116]

In terms of resettlement, Nansen also faced challenges for States did not distinguish between immigrants and refugees in their admission policies and refugees had to meet the same conditions for entry as other immigrants. Asylum, as in the past, was largely exercised in accordance with self-interest.

Already by the turn of the century, States had started to erect more border controls including requiring passports and/or visas, defining admissible classes, setting quotas, and imposing registration requirements upon arrival.[117] Admissibility criteria included a security dimension to exclude criminals, radicals and others suspected of being a threat to public safety. They were also a means to exclude those considered likely to become a public charge. Importantly, admission criteria and quotas were designed to give preference to the most "desirable" immigrants, often determined by race or place of origin.[118] These controls were later tightened in the 1920s and further in the 1930s as the full force of the Great Depression hit economies hard across Europe and the Americas.

Most refugees at the time did not have passports, which prevented them from being admitted to another State even when they met the admissibility criteria. Nansen successfully convinced States to agree to a special refugee travel document which permitted refugees to move between States to look for work. Subsequently known as the "Nansen Passport", its application was later extended to Armenians, Assyrians, Assyro-Chaldeans and some Turks under a new arrangement in 1928.

Importantly, the arrangements included agreed (albeit non-binding) standards of treatment in regard to recognizing the identity, good character and civil status of the bearer, the right to work, legal assistance, equality in taxation and protection from expulsion.[119] The right to a refugee travel document, as well as

Fridtjof Nansen
in New York
in 1929.
© UNHCR photo

associated standards in the Nansen Passport arrangements, would be reflected in the 1951 Convention.

Although the Nansen passport did not guarantee the bearer would receive a visa to enter a State or permanent residence to those who did, it was nonetheless significant for it allowed refugees to cross borders in search of work and provided them with a more secure legal status.[120] As Dorothy Thompson, a journalist at the time, observed: A refugee could not be assured of obtaining a work permit but "could be sure that without the Nansen certificate he would *never* get it".[121] By 1929, over 50 States were party to the arrangement.[122]

The money charged to obtain the passport was used to finance small loans to refugees. The International Labour Organization (ILO) complemented the work of the Nansen Office by matching refugees with work opportunities in other countries and monitoring conditions of work to guard against exploitation. Between 1925 and 1929, the ILO helped place over 50,000 refugees in jobs, mostly in France as elsewhere in Europe, the Americas, Asia, and the Middle East.[123]

Relief and development

The League's engagement on refugee issues further intensified following the Greco-Turkish War (1919–1922) leaving both a negative legacy of overseeing massive forced population transfers, as well as a positive one of managing the first extensive international development effort for the socioeconomic inclusion of refugees. Fridtjof Nansen and his Office were central in this effort as well.

The brutal conflict claimed tens of thousands of civilian deaths and displaced over 1.5 million people.[124] The terms of settlement provided for the denaturalization and transfer of all Greek Orthodox Christians in Turkey to Greece and all Muslims in Greece to Turkey. Transferred populations gained the citizenship of their new State of residence, while facing difficulties in transferring assets or receiving compensation for property left behind.[125] They had no right to refuse the transfer nor a right of return.[126]

Close to 1.4 million people were affected by the transfers.[127] The effects of these transfers were felt for decades. The mobility of Christians and Muslims to their former ancestral lands was tightly circumscribed until the 1990s.[128] Additionally, aside from sharing the same religion, the refugees in both countries were culturally and often linguistically different from their hosts. The newcomers were frequently perceived negatively and viewed with derision, and they themselves often felt culturally apart. Integration would be a multigenerational affair.[129]

On the Turkish side, keeping with its long tradition, the Government assumed centralized authority for the reception and settlement of new refugees, creating a new ministry for this purpose, and accepting relatively little international assistance while relying on the Turkish Red Crescent to complement its efforts. Many refugees found the lands assigned to them to be uncultivatable or were expropriated by Turkish army and police officers, compounding adjustment problems.[130]

Greece, however, welcomed international assistance, and help poured in from international charities around the world as well as from several European governments. Additional support came in the form of a multi-million-dollar loan raised and administered by the League of Nations for development initiatives aimed towards the integration of refugees.[131]

Close to doubling over the next several years, the loan was a precursor to modern-day trust funds established to support countries experiencing large refugee influxes. It was serviced by the International Financial Commission and administered by a newly created Refugee Settlement Commission under the League of Nations, with representation from the Greek Government, the League of Nations and relief organizations.[132] The scheme included land grants, settlement assistance and investments in infrastructure.

The Commission had wide-ranging autonomy to carry out its work, which was largely focused on the agricultural settlement of refugees, many on lands forcibly vacated by Muslim populations. Refugees were provided houses, livestock, seeds, agricultural machinery and tools,[133] and investments were made for the construction of roads, bridges and schools, building villages, and capacitating public health services.[134] Within a few years, crop production increased substantially. The Refugee Settlement Commission also facilitated refugee settlement and investments in industrial areas leading to an increase in industrial activity.[135]

Over 600,000 refugees were settled with the scheme bringing economic improvements and enhancing social cohesion between the refugees and host communities.[136] It marks one of the early successes of international cooperation in supporting refugees and their hosts.

A recent study on the long-term impact of the 1923 population transfer to Greece found that locations that received high concentrations of refugees, today are economically more prosperous than comparable areas in Greece that did not.[137] Among the leading factors that contributed to this higher performance were the fact that refugees were granted citizenship, permitted to settle together, provided initial financial assistance and were free to work and establish businesses helping to create favourable conditions for early industrialization and economic development that persist today.[138]

Refugees, when permitted to exercise their own agency, were able to strengthen their capacities in ways that also contributed to the broader community. The findings are consistent with the results of studies of the economic effects of more recent refugee influxes. Beyond the initial economic shock, refugees can have a net positive economic impact in the longer term.[139]

A similar loan scheme was employed to assist in the settlement of refugees in Bulgaria: These were mostly former citizens of Bulgaria forcibly displaced during the Balkan Wars and WWI. The United Kingdom, the United States and three other countries provided a loan of over £3 million. Land was provided to refugees and infrastructure improved. Some 125,000 refugees benefited.

Local communities also benefited from improved transportation, communication and health services.[140]

A more modest settlement scheme took place for Armenian refugees in the French mandated territories of Lebanon and Syria. It was supported with both grants and loans financed largely by the French Government and private organizations. The money was used to construct homes, help refugees settle in urban and agricultural areas and improve water and sanitation in settlement areas. The settlement efforts are credited with improving public works, creating jobs and benefiting refugees and the communities in which they lived.[141]

As the 1920s drew to a close, the provision of asylum remained rather ad hoc, more readily extended to those of shared ethnicity or religion or who were otherwise regarded as "desirable" on the basis of the economic contributions they could make and the cultural affinity they shared with the receiving State.

State self-interest continued to be decisive. On the other hand, by the end of the decade, the High Commissioner for Refugees could point to hard-wrought achievements that were helping to nudge international protection in a more positive direction. Many wartime refugees had voluntarily repatriated or resettled in another country with international assistance. Successful multilateral development initiatives had helped secure the economic and social inclusion of various refugees and contributed to the economic health of host communities.

Non-governmental organizations proliferated, lending substantial support to local and national relief and settlement efforts. Refugees and refugee-led organizations were active participants in advocating and designing relief and development efforts and, by 1934, they were firmly embedded in the work of the Nansen Office, serving as delegates and technical advisors and as members of the Management Committee of his Office, and holding seats on the Governing Body.[142]

The Great Depression and the Rise of Fascism

National policies, inter-State disputes, and the rise of fascism in Germany, Italy and Spain all contributed to sizable and growing refugee influxes throughout the 1930s. Efforts to forge a coordinated international response to refugees remained ad hoc and situation-specific. Adding to the challenges was the massive economic downturn of the Great Depression and the imposition of even tighter immigration restrictions across many States.

Dramatic declines in industrial production, severe losses in trade, mass unemployment, business failures and social unrest contributed to public support for tighter immigration controls. Widespread overt anti-Semitism was also at the root of resistance to assisting Jewish refugees.

Fridtjof Nansen died in 1930 and the work he steered fell to the newly established Nansen International Office within the League. For years, Nansen had advocated for a convention of common standards to be accorded to refugees. This became most urgent in the early 1930s as refugees were increasingly prosecuted, imprisoned and expelled for violating immigration and labour laws.

As Louise Holborn described the situation, refugees were caught between two sovereign wills, "the one expelling them, the other forbidding their entry". The result was high rates of vagrancy and suicides, with governments spending vast sums on enforcement but not achieving solutions.[143] The need for a more coordinated response brought several of the receiving countries to agree to the League-sponsored 1933 Convention relating to the International Status of Refugees (1933 Convention).[144]

The 1933 Convention was an important step in the road to more universal refugee protections. Positively, it was the first codification of standards of treatment towards refugees including the rights to: a Nansen certificate; not be expelled at the border or from within the country subject to limited exceptions; access to the courts; and exemptions from certain labour restrictions applied to foreigners.[145]

Refugees were to receive the most favourable treatment accorded to foreigners in regard to industrial accidents, social welfare and access to education.[146] Moreover, the role of refugees in refugee responses was also explicitly acknowledged in provisions concerning the setting up of refugee committees responsible for finding employment, coordinating assistance and collecting the fees for the Nansen certificate.[147] Refugees were also among the Committee of Experts involved in the drafting of the initial text and the negotiations among States.[148]

While impressive in its scope, the 1933 Convention faced severe limitations. It only applied to those already recognized as refugees by the League,[149] was ratified by just eight States,[150] and did not apply to two of the largest movements in Europe at that time: refugees from the Spanish Civil War and refugees from the Third Reich. It also had no bearing on the dramatic forced displacements in China.

The three-year Spanish Civil War (1936–1939) claimed 750,000 deaths both in battle and due to atrocities against civilian populations committed by both sides.[151] Over 3 million people were displaced throughout the country and over 400,000 sought safety outside.[152] The overall response to Spanish Civil

War refugees was mixed. International solidarity was evident in the humanitarian support marshalled by national and international non-governmental
agencies working inside Spain as well as in France and other countries. But
finding asylum proved to be difficult for many.

France received most of the refugees whose numbers climbed steadily from
1936 onwards. A signatory to the 1933 Convention and a country with a strong
asylum tradition, France had a relatively favourable attitude towards refugees
at the beginning of the decade. However, with the onset of the Great Depression and in a climate of political polarization and rising xenophobia, by 1937,
refugee policies became restrictive.[153]

In early 1939, on the eve of the Republican defeat in Spain, there were
some 300,000 Spanish refugees at the French border. The authorities restricted
admission, permitting one third of them to enter France.[154] Soldiers were
disarmed, and many men, along with some women and children, sent to camps
concentrated in the south. Conditions were harsh as shelter was often inadequate and those interned there also faced food shortages, disease outbreaks
and lack of adequate health care.[155]

Options to remain were extended to those qualified to join the French
Foreign Legion, who had a private sponsor or who were willing to work in
industries in need of labour.[156] Others were pressured to leave, and many did.
Overall, France provided asylum to approximately 150,000 refugees from
Spain. But a larger number, more than 250,000 persons, were compelled to
return to Spain.[157]

Latin America accepted over 30,000 Spanish refugees, two thirds of whom
were admitted to Mexico and most of the remainder to Argentina. An additional 12,000 went to countries in North Africa and over 6,000 were admitted
to the Soviet Union.[158]

A child evacuation programme, conceived as a humanitarian contribution
through the provision of temporary stay to over 30,000 children in various
countries in Europe, Mexico and the Soviet Union, did not live up to the initial
ideal. Criticized for being chaotically administered and not having sufficient
protections in place for children, including means for family tracing, its legacy
was not positive overall. Many of the evacuated children experienced extreme
hardship during their exile and upon return in Spain.[159]

The steady imposition of persecutory laws and policies after the rise of Adolf
Hitler in 1933 led to ever increasing flight from Germany. The international
response to Jewish refugees during this period marks the nadir in asylum history
of this troubled period, which the 1951 Convention was intended not to repeat.

Refugees from the Third Reich rose to 400,000 persons in the 1930s, the vast majority of whom were Jews. Revocation of citizenship, mass firings of Jewish workers, and economic boycotts accounted for the initial exodus. By 1937, over 150,000 mostly Jewish refugees had fled Germany. These numbers increased further once Germany annexed Austria and the Sudetenland and persecution extended there. Flight from Germany was accelerated following the pogroms of November 1938, which saw the country-wide rampage against Jewish homes, businesses, schools and synagogues, scores of deaths and the mass arrests of tens of thousands of Jews.[160]

While neighbouring countries, as well as those abroad, expressed their opprobrium to events in Germany, few stepped forward to provide asylum. Most did not relax their immigration restrictions and, after the horrors of the November Pogroms, many tightened them further including expanding powers of deportation and expulsion.[161]

In 1933, the League of Nations appointed an independent High Commissioner for Refugees (Jewish and others) from Germany, James G. McDonald. McDonald was a United States citizen whose long career spanned academia and the civil service. He was a specialist in foreign relations. Like Nansen, he was dedicated and committed to the refugee cause, and he worked for their admission to other countries and urged international condemnation of the persecution they experienced.[162]

His 1933 meeting with Hitler left no doubt of Hitler's intention to exterminate the Jewish population.[163] McDonald repeatedly warned world leaders of the looming tragedy to no avail. So limited were the means at his disposal, so uncompromising the position of States, and so unwilling were they to confront Germany, that McDonald resigned just two years after being appointed to the post. His letter of resignation documented the conditions prevailing within Germany and the need for international action.[164]

McDonald's relatively short tenure secured some gains. Largely with the help of voluntary organizations, he was able to assist 50,000 refugees to emigrate, most to European countries. Close to one third went to Palestine, and 10 per cent to the Americas.[165]

His successor, Sir Neil Malcolm who held the post from 1935 to 1938 was a career British Army officer, who carried out his responsibilities very differently than had Nansen and McDonald. He did not concentrate on humanitarian work or intervene in individual cases but focused on improving the legal status of refugees by engaging States.

He was known for not being one to take initiatives, but to respond to the interests of States. He was also of the view that the best solution for refugees was to emigrate with the assistance of voluntary organizations.[166] His tenure was marked with a lack of significant progress on the German refugee crisis. A travel document for German refugees was secured but limited in application to German nationals and not to the tens of thousands, mostly Jews, who had been stripped of their nationality.[167]

The 1938 Convention concerning the Status of Refugees coming from Germany that came into being in the last year of his tenure was inclusive of stateless refugees. However, its provisions were relatively weak,[168] it was signed by only six States, most with reservations to parts of it, and it was ratified by just two.[169] It reflected the poor performance of the League in regard to refugees from Germany and was soon overshadowed by the events of WWII and the genocide of those the international community largely failed to rescue during the preceding years.

The absence of States' willingness to step up and assist Jewish refugees was infamously on display at the 1938 Evian Conference. Convened by President Roosevelt and attended by 32 governments, the nine-day event was an utter failure. States were invited on the understanding that they would not be asked to change their laws and that settlement costs would be borne by private organizations. The speeches of State delegates, while acknowledging the humanitarian need and imperative of greater burden-sharing, strongly emphasized sovereignty and respect for existing immigration regulations.[170]

No meaningful outcomes were reached. States agreed to participate in a new Intergovernmental Committee on Refugees to coordinate multilateral resettlement efforts for refugees from the Third Reich; however, their ongoing unwillingness to ease restrictive immigration criteria or make other meaningful commitments rendered the work by the Intergovernmental Committee's efforts largely ineffective.[171] The Third Reich, meanwhile, was quick to point out the apparent hypocrisy of States that condemned it while themselves being unwilling to accept Jewish refugees.[172]

The League's failures in the 1930s stood in sharp contrast to the energy, commitment and accomplishments of non-governmental institutions. Despite the obstacles, at the close of the decade, close to 300,000 Jewish refugees managed to escape the Third Reich, often with the help of private institutions. The British Mandated Palestine and the United States each accounted for the resettlement of one quarter of the total. Approximately 50,000 refugees managed to reach safety in the United Kingdom, over 43,000 made it to Argentina and over 20,000 were admitted to China, concentrated in Shanghai.[173]

At the same moment – on the eve of WWII – another major displacement was in full swing, and it too illustrated the deficiencies in international action. The Japanese imperialist conquest of Manchuria (1931–1932) was a prelude to Japan's more ambitious invasion of China in 1937 and its occupation of Beijing, Shanghai and surrounding areas that summer, causing millions of citizens to flee inward. The subsequent Japanese advance west on Nanjing added to the massive number of deaths and forced flight.[174]

In a matter of months, more than 16 million people were on the move within China, a number that rose precipitously when China deliberately destroyed dikes along the Yellow River in an attempt to frustrate further Japanese advancements. Later referred to as the greatest environmental act of war in history, 1 million people died and many more were displaced.[175] The survivors were compelled to settle in other provinces and in remote areas and, by 1945, as many as 6 million people remained without a home.[176]

At the end of WWII, over 90 million people are estimated to have been forcibly displaced in China[177] – one of the greatest forced displacements in human history. Many were never able to return to their homes and it took generations before some of the most impacted cities recovered from the economic devastation caused by the conflict.

The war imposed huge economic and psychological scars, yet, as in Europe, also saw the emergence of coordinated government and voluntary responses that helped shape social service work of the future.

In Wuhan, which became the de facto capital, an impressive response to meet the needs of displaced populations was marshalled. Inspired by local individuals, the effort engaged local civil society, merchant associations, religious organizations, benevolent societies, a high-level National Relief Committee as well as the International Committee of the Red Cross. Government-led education, nutrition and health interventions would later become a model both for the Republic of China and the People's Republic of China.[178]

In Claudena Skran's history of refugees during the inter-war years, she traces the gradual expansion of the international protection regime. Positively, international cooperation did increase to the benefit of individuals and certain groups of refugees, notably through the extension of consular services, protection from expulsion, provision of humanitarian aid, settlement and emigration assistance. Refugees were increasingly seen as a specific class of persons in need of protection.[179]

The establishment of specialized agencies, like the International Labour Organization and the High Commissioner for Refugees, facilitated international cooperation and set in motion collaborative practices that could be applied elsewhere and upon which future multilateral institutions would expand and rely.

It is also the case that the inter-war period, especially during the 1930s, demonstrated the extent to which States would go in exerting their sovereign right to control their borders and deny admission to those who were not seen as advancing their economic, social or foreign policy objectives. Admissions were relaxed in times of labour shortages and preferences maintained for those who were culturally or ethnically similar. States were more likely to provide humanitarian and development assistance to host countries that were their allies and to provide refuge to those fleeing their enemies than those fleeing their friends. And, while voluntary organizations grew in size and influence throughout this period, much to the benefit of refugees, some also responded partially, reaching out to help those of shared religion or ethnicity.

World War II

WWI set the record for the largest number of deaths and displacement due to war in modern history. It was a record of relatively short duration, totally eclipsed by the mammoth consequences of WWII.

Waged across six continents, engaging more than 30 countries, over 70 million people died and tens of millions were forcibly displaced throughout its six-year duration. Six million Jews, two thirds of the Jewish population of Europe, were systematically killed. At its conclusion, borders were redrawn, mass ethnic expulsions were brokered, millions of people were returned to their countries of origin, including forcibly to situations of risk, and hundreds of thousands resettled, often continents away.

The sheer scale of the needs of displaced populations demanded a coordinated multilateral response. The war marked the beginning of more joined up responses to forced displacement and led to the 1951 Convention, which remains the foundational legal instrument of the international protection of refugees.

In Europe, tens of millions of people were killed and over 30 million civilians displaced within their countries or across borders.[180] Causes and patterns of displacement were complex. Refugees fled invading armies and persecution and were deported with many moving through several countries seeking safety.[181]

Ethnic cleansing accounted for large-scale displacement. In 1940, German forces drove out francophones, Jews, Roma and others from Alsace-Lorraine.

The next year, the Serbian minority was expelled by Croatia.[182] Following the German invasion of Poland, hundreds of thousands of people were forced out of the country.[183] In Soviet-controlled areas, ethnic minorities such as German farmers, Crimean Tatars and Chechens were also forcibly displaced and deported to Central Asia.[184] Meanwhile, over 16 million Soviet citizens were internally displaced, evacuated to the interior, many unwillingly and without the right to return.[185] Millions of prisoners of war were also displaced, many of whom had been deported to work in Germany to help feed the German war machine.

At the war's end, there were over 14 million Europeans in Allied-controlled areas "fleeing, or heading home, or searching for family members, or simply trying to survive".[186]

While most were displaced within their own countries, millions were displaced elsewhere throughout Europe and tens of thousands, mainly Eastern European refugees, were in the Middle East, Africa and Asia.[187] Thousands of Jewish refugee survivors of the Holocaust endured years in displaced persons camps in the face of no possibility of return, either because they had been stripped of their citizenship or forced to flee pogroms and persistent persecution in their home countries.[188] An additional several million foreign workers, many of them forced, and prisoners of war in Germany completed the picture of displaced persons on the continent.[189]

In Asia, a similar picture emerged. Among the legacies of the war was the first use of the atomic bomb and, as in Europe, millions of deaths, massive war crimes committed, severely damaged infrastructure, redrawn borders, and many millions of people displaced. India received hundreds of thousands of Indian workers and allies fleeing the Japanese occupation of Burma while, in Burma, tens of thousands of people were internally displaced.[190] In China, in addition to the millions of people uprooted from the Sino-Japanese conflict, close to 20 million civilians died during WWII. An estimated 7.5 million people perished from massive war-related famines in Bengal, China and Indochina during the second half of WWII.[191]

Just as borders were redrawn in Europe, so too in Asia. Imperial powers were weakened, contributing to the independence of most countries in the region within a quarter of a century after the end of WWII.[192]

While some countries achieved independence peacefully, the struggle for independence turned violent in others. The partition of British India into the two newly independent States of India and Pakistan in 1947 led to the massive population exchange of over 14.5 million people: Hindus from Pakistan to India and Muslims in the opposite direction.[193]

This displacement occurred amidst ferocious violence that claimed over half a million deaths.[194] As homes were burned, mass murders, abductions, beatings, forced conversions, rape and disfigurement were widely perpetrated. One of the most extensive population relocations in history was not a short-term displacement. Having left property and other assets behind and lacking capital, millions remained uprooted for years.[195]

Well before the conclusion of WWII, it was apparent that attending to the needs of the burgeoning number of refugees required a coordinated multilateral effort. Conceived, driven and largely funded by the United States, the United Nations Refugee Relief Agency (UNRRA) was established in 1943, representing 48 nations. Compared to previous multilateral efforts, its budget of close to $4 billion was relatively robust as was its workforce of close to 13,000 persons.[196]

UNRRA was set up to provide immediate assistance to war-affected countries and displaced populations as well as to fund development programmes in agriculture and industrial and social service sectors. Most of UNRRA's budget and efforts, however, were concentrated in Europe, excluding Germany.[197]

Working under the authority of the Supreme Headquarters of the Allied Expeditionary Forces (SHAEF) and alongside non-governmental partners, UNRRA coordinated and provided food, clothing, shelter and other forms of relief, establishing 800 camps for over 7 million displaced persons in Europe.[198]

UNRRA's work on repatriation, beyond assisting the voluntary return of millions of Germans, Italians and Austrians, proved much more controversial.[199] As a result of the agreement of the Yalta Conference,[200] the Soviet Union, United Kingdom and United States exchanged 50,000 Western Allied prisoners of war in Soviet-controlled territories and over 2 million Soviet citizens in Western Allied countries. Many among the latter were dissidents or prisoners of war and feared reprisals upon return. Their fears were not misplaced.[201]

Refugees in Europe after World War II. © UNHCR

Many returning men to the Soviet Union were interned and executed or forced to serve in the Army and later conscripted to work in mines and timber industries in Siberia. Most women returnees faced discrimination for the remainder of their lives.[202] UNRRA's engagement in this forced repatriation compromised its reputation and constituted another low point in international refugee responses.

Strong advocacy by refugees and the diaspora in the United States eventually led to the withdrawal of United States support for the forced repatriations. The discontinuation of compelled returns aggravated tensions between the democracies of the West and the Soviet republics, the former maintaining that displaced persons should not be forced to return to Communist States and the latter insisting they should.[203]

Meanwhile, within the United States, there was also mounting criticism of relief being provided to countries under Communist rule and a growing sense that United States foreign policy was no longer best served by this multilateral effort.[204] The United States withdrew its support for UNRRA in 1947 on the eve of its launch of the Marshall Plan and its $13 billion in support of reconstruction in Western Europe.

With the loss of its major donor, the mandate of UNRRA was not extended beyond its scheduled expiry in 1947. The work of UNRRA was transferred to other newly established agencies, such as the International Refugee Organization (IRO), the World Health Organization (WHO) and the Food and Agriculture Organization (FAO).

Mass expulsions were not confined to the war but also featured prominently in the negotiated terms of settlement. The Soviet border was expanded 300 kilometres into Poland, the western border of which was extended into former German lands. And as agreed by the Allies, the remaining German populations in Czechoslovakia, Hungary and Poland would be transferred to Germany.[205] Ethnic Germans were also expelled from other areas of Central and Eastern Europe.

These were often very violent movements. Germans were attacked, maimed and killed during their exodus by armed and civilian groups in revenge for German atrocities of the war.[206] Many tens of thousands died in the process from injuries, hunger and disease. Others died upon reaching Allied-controlled Germany, where food was scarce, transportation networks destroyed, water often contaminated and fuel in short supply.[207] By 1950, over 12 million ethnic Germans had fled to west Germany. Estimates place the number of deaths in this movement at between 200,000 and over 2.3 million people.[208]

Smaller yet significantly large numbers of other populations including Poles, Turks, Ukrainians and Hungarians were expelled from the Soviet Union, Bulgaria, Poland and Slovakia, respectively.[209] Meanwhile, new refugee movements of Jews fleeing pogroms in Eastern Europe[210] and defectors from the Eastern Bloc kept the refugee issue very high on the international agenda.[211]

The tensions between the West and the Soviet Bloc over refugees did not dissipate with the creation of the International Refugee Organization (IRO). Established by treaty in 1948 as a time-limited United Nations specialized agency, the IRO was mandated to help refugees and displaced persons return home or establish elsewhere and, in the interim, to provide them with material assistance.[212] The IRO Constitution excluded persons of German ethnic origin who during the war were evacuated or fled from Germany, sought refuge in Germany, as well as those who were or could be transferred there.[213] They were considered to be the responsibility of Germany.

Importantly, the IRO Constitution, passed by the United Nations General Assembly, provided that no person with valid objections should be compelled to return.[214] This reflected international condemnation of forced repatria-

Signing the 1951 Convention in Geneva. Seated, left-to-right: Margaret Kitchen, Deputy Executive Secretary; John Humphrey, Director of the Human Rights Division; Knud Larsen, Conference President; Gerrit Jan van Heuven Goedhart, High Commissioner for Refugees. © Arni/UN Archives

tions. Funded largely by the United States, with over 5,000 staff, IRO assisted over 1.5 million refugees.[215] It did not resolve the refugee situation, for there remained hundreds of thousands of refugees in Europe and millions of refugees in Asia in need and without solutions.

As discussed more in Part III, securing permanent refuge for Jewish Holocaust survivors and those fleeing pogroms was fraught. Many were temporarily assisted in displaced persons camps within zones under the control of the United Kingdom and the United States, including in former concentration camps.[216] In the months following the war, these camps were cramped, lacked proper sanitation, often encircled with barbed wire, and the shelter provided was inadequate protection against the elements. Initially, many Jews were also accommodated in camps alongside Nazi collaborators. During the mass resettlement drives to find solutions for remaining camp populations, Jewish refugees were deliberately overlooked by resettlement countries.[217]

1951 Convention Relating to the Status of Refugees

In 1941, spearheaded by President Roosevelt, allied nations signed a declaration reflecting their joint commitment to uphold human rights and justice and to work collectively to defeat their common enemies.[218] It was a foundational step in the formation of the United Nations that emerged at the conclusion of the war. The United Nations Charter was deliberated and drafted in the spring of 1945 by countries that had joined the wartime alliance and with representation from non-governmental organizations. By the end of the year, 51 nations had joined.

From the outset, its mandate was broad: to maintain international peace and security, promote respect for human rights and international law, and collectively address international problems of a social, economic and humanitarian nature.[219]

The problems faced by refugees and displaced persons featured early in the United Nations' agenda especially given the large number remaining in Europe and the controversy over the forced return of so many. Recognizing the immediate and urgent need to distinguish between genuine refugees and displaced persons on the one hand and "war criminals, quislings and traitors" on the other, early in 1946, the General Assembly referred the matter to the Economic and Social Council (ECOSOC) for consideration.[220]

This launched a four-year exercise that would culminate in the 1951 Convention. In the interim, two other significant developments advanced the protection of refugees. The first was the development of the Universal Declaration of Human Rights (UDHR). The second was the creation of the Office of the United Nations High Commissioner for Refugees with a mandate far broader than any previous specialized refugee institution.

Work on an international bill of rights came on the heels of the United Nations' creation. The aim was to give effect to the commitment of the United Nations Charter to promote universal respect for human rights for all individuals without distinction. In 1949, the UDHR was adopted with support from 48 of the 58 United Nations member States.[221] It included the right "to seek, and to enjoy in other countries asylum from persecution"; however, it did not include a specific, corresponding obligation for States to provide it. [222]

That responsibility was the focus of discussions in ECOSOC concerning a new international convention for the protection of refugees. Meanwhile, the United Nations established the Office of the United Nations High Commissioner for Refugees. Recognizing the global scope of the refugee problem, the mandate of this Office was not confined to a specific group of refugees or to a particular location.[223]

UNHCR's Statute specifies that the work of UNHCR is humanitarian, entirely non-political and dedicated to two main priorities. One is the provision of international protection to refugees. The other is seeking permanent solutions for them by assisting governments to "facilitate the voluntary repatriation of such refugees, or their assimilation within new national communities".[224] Created by the General Assembly, UNHCR remains accountable to it through ECOSOC to whom it reports annually.[225]

The Office was given a global mandate but, like High Commissioners of the inter-war period, there were no guaranteed sources of funding, beyond a limited contribution to administrative expenses through the United Nations regular budget. This was to allay the concerns of States that they only be required to finance relief efforts that they approved on a discretionary basis. Several of the same States also insisted that the term of the Office be temporary, which is why it was initially established for a three-year period.[226]

The funding constraints proved a serious and immediate problem for the first High Commissioner, Gerrit Jan van Heuven Goedhart, who was himself a refugee from the Netherlands. During the war, van Heuven Goedhart worked for the resistance, which was targeted during the German occupation. A warrant for his arrest and the capture, execution or detention of many of his colleagues prompted his eventual flight and ultimate refuge in the United Kingdom. There he became the Minister of Justice for the Government of the Netherlands in exile.

As High Commissioner, he was faced with the rather impossible task of assisting millions of refugees with an insufficient budget of just $300,000, prompting him to remark on the danger that his Office "would simply 'administer misery'".[227]

Van Heuven Goedhart moved in three ways that helped set the course for future High Commissioners. He sought voluntary contributions,[228] developed strong partnerships with non-governmental agencies and established a representational presence in countries around the world to help refugees access his Office.[229] His Office was also active in drafting the 1951 Convention.

Much of the drafting work on the 1951 Convention occurred in the Ad

Hoc Committee, established by ECOSOC in 1949.[230] The Committee was comprised of 13 governments.[231] Legal experts from within the United Nations, including the IRO, and non-governmental agencies contributed as observers. Just as many refugees in earlier periods were actively engaged in the terms of their settlement, former refugees also played an influential role in the drafting of the 1951 Convention and State negotiations.

Paul Weis was the chief drafter for the IRO and future first Director of Protection for UNHCR. Born in Austria, he was interned in the late 1930s

The High Commissioner for Refugees, Gerrit Jan van Heuven Goedhart (right), talks with Egypt's Omar Loutfi in October 1955, before a debate at the UN General Assembly. He is holding a Nansen Medal, awarded for outstanding work on behalf of refugees.
© UN photo

in Dachau concentration camp before fleeing to the United Kingdom where he became naturalized. Jacques L. Rubinstein, a member of Weis' team, was a Russian refugee and jurist who had advocated close to 25 years earlier for an international binding legal convention regarding refugees and was involved in the drafting of the 1933 Convention.[232] Also assisting Weis was Gustave Kullman, a Swiss jurist whose wife had been a Russian refugee. Their experiences helped shape their understanding of the protections needed in the 1951 Convention, including ensuring the refugee definition was inclusive of the diversity of refugee experiences, the importance of socioeconomic rights, and the necessity of non-refoulement.[233]

Others with refugee experiences contributed as government delegates and leaders of non-governmental organizations. Jacob Robinson, the chief negotiator for Israel, was a Lithuanian politician who had fled religious persecution in 1940 prior to the Soviet occupation. Rabbi Isaac Lewin represented a Jewish organization that argued persuasively for due process protections for refugees at risk of expulsion on the grounds of national security or public order.[234]

The drafting history reveals that one of the most contentious issues was whether the 1951 Convention should be wide enough to encompass present and prospective refugee situations or be confined to existing and geographically defined ones. Western countries differed in their perspectives on this, with some States changing their positions at various times in the drafting process.

Soviet bloc countries were generally hostile to the idea of the Convention, perceiving it as a means for the West to encourage defections and, in the words of one delegate, to benefit from "slave labour".[235] France and the United States wanted to limit responsibilities to refugees within Europe, while Belgium, Denmark, Egypt, Germany, Norway, Sweden were among those States who saw value in the application of the Convention to all parts of the world.[236]

In the end, the 1951 Convention had both a temporal and geographic limit, appealing to those who wanted to limit its reach. It was approved at the Conference of Plenipotentiaries in July 1951 and came into effect three years later when the requisite number of ratifications was reached. Of the 26 countries represented at the conference, 17 were from Europe, five from the Americas and three from the Middle East and one from Asia Pacific.[237]

The 1951 Convention was initially limited to those who became refugees as a result of events prior to 1951 and permitted States to further limit its application to events occurring *within Europe* prior to this time, although only four did so.[238] These significant temporal and geographic limitations were removed 15 years later, with the 1967 Protocol reflecting the widening scope of the international protection regime as did the definition of a refugee.[239]

The 1951 Convention definition was more universal, not restricted to a specific group or nationality but to persons unable or unwilling to return to their country of origin, owing to a well-founded fear of being persecuted for reasons of race, religion, nationality, political opinion or membership of a particular social group. All but the last of these grounds were familiar to the European refugee experience of the early and late modern period.[240]

The addition of particular social group was at the recommendation of Sweden and, while there is no definitive record as to the rationale, it helped to ensure that definition could be interpreted inclusively in the years to come.[241]

1951 Refugee Convention

States parties to the 1951 Convention Relating to the Status of Refugees and/or its 1967 Protocol

as of 05 October 2021

See next page

GREENLAND [DNK]

CANADA

UNITED STATES OF AMERICA

MEXICO

BAHAMAS

CUBA

HAITI

JAMAICA

BELIZE
GUATEMALA
EL SALVADOR
HONDURAS
NICARAGUA
COSTA RICA
PANAMA
ECUADOR

Caribbean Islands

BOLIVARIAN
REP. OF
VENEZUELA

COLOMBIA

GUYANA
SURINAME
FRENCH GUIANA [FRA]

PERU

BRAZIL

PLURINATIONAL
STATE
OF BOLIVIA

PARAGUAY

CHILE

ARGENTINA

URUGUAY

Pacific Islands

Caribbean Islands

DOMINICAN REPUBLIC

PUERTO RICO [USA]

ANGUILLA [GBR]

BRITISH VIRGIN
ISLANDS [GBR]

SAINT MARTIN [FRA]
SINT MAARTEN
[K. OF THE NLD]

UNITED STATES
VIRGIN ISLANDS [USA]

SABA [NLD]

SINT EUSTATIUS [NLD]

SAINT KITTS
AND NEVIS

GUADELOUPE [FRA]

SAINT VINCENT
AND THE GRENADINES

ARUBA [K. OF THE NLD]

BONAIRE [NLD]

CURAÇAO [K. OF THE NLD]

ANTIGUA
AND BARBUDA

MONTSERRAT [GBR]

DOMINICA

MARTINIQUE [FRA]

SAINT LUCIA

BARBADOS

GRENADA

TRINIDAD
AND TOBAGO

CANARY ISLANDS [ESP]

Western
Sahara

CABO VERDE

MAURITANIA

MALI

NIGER

BURKINA
FASO

SENEGAL
GAMBIA
GUINEA-BISSAU
SIERRA LEONE
LIBERIA

GUINEA

CÔTE
D'IVOIRE

NIGERIA

GHANA
TOGO
BENIN
CAMEROON
SAO TOME AND PRINCIPE
EQUATORIAL GUINEA
GABON
REPUBLIC OF THE CONGO
DEMOCRATIC REPUBLIC OF
THE CONGO
ANGOLA
BOTSWANA
NAMIBIA

The boundaries and names shown and the designations used on this map do not imply official endorsement or acceptance by the United Nations.

Final boundary between the Republic of Sudan and the Republic of South Sudan has not yet been determined.

Dotted line represents approximately the Line of Control in Jammu and Kashmir agreed upon by India and Pakistan. The final status of Jammu and Kashmir has not yet been agreed upon by the parties.

The initials in [ ] refer to the administering Power or the Power involved in a special treaty relationship.

Party to the 1951 Convention
and/or its 1967 Protocol

RUSSIAN FEDERATION

KAZAKHSTAN

UZBEKISTAN
KYRGYZSTAN
TURKMENISTAN
TAJIKISTAN

MONGOLIA

DEM.
PEOPLE'S
REP. OF KOREA

JAPAN

AFGHANISTAN

REP. OF KOREA

ISLAMIC REP.
OF IRAN

PAKISTAN

NEPAL

BHUTAN

CHINA

SAUDI ARABIA

UNITED ARAB
EMIRATES

QATAR

BAHRAIN

KUWAIT

OMAN

DJIBOUTI

INDIA

BANGLADESH

MYANMAR

TAIWAN [CHN]

HONG KONG [CHN]
MACAO [CHN]

SUDAN

ERITREA

YEMEN

LAO PEOPLE'S
DEM. REP.

VIET NAM

CAMBODIA

NORTHERN
MARIANA ISLANDS
[USA]

FEDERATION
STATES OF MICRONESIA

SOUTH
SUDAN

SOMALIA

ETHIOPIA

CHAD

CENTRAL AFRICAN REPUBLIC

UGANDA

SRI LANKA

THAILAND

BRUNEI
DARUSSALAM

PHILIPPINES

PALAU

KENYA

RWANDA

BURUNDI

MALAWI

SEYCHELLES

COMOROS

MALAYSIA

SINGAPORE

MALDIVES

INDONESIA

PAPUA
NEW
GUINEA

TIMOR LESTE

Pacific Islands

SOLOMON
ISLANDS

VANUATU

UNITED
REP. OF
TANZANIA

ZAMBIA

MADAGASCAR

MAURITIUS

REUNION [FRA]

Pacific Islands

FRENCH NEW
CALEDONIA [FRA]

ZIMBABWE

MARSHALL ISLANDS

AUSTRALIA

MOZAMBIQUE

ESWATINI

LESOTHO

SOUTH AFRICA

NAURU

KIRIBATI

TUVALU

COOK ISLANDS [NZL]

NEW ZEALAND

SAMOA

AMERICAN
SAMOA [USA]

FIJI

NIUE [NZL]

TONGA

International boundary

Undetermined
international boundary

Abyei region

Administrative line

Sources: UNHCS, UNHCR

1951 Refugee Convention

as of 05 October 2021

States parties to the 1951 Convention Relating to the Status of Refugees
and/or its 1967 Protocol

1 BOSNIA AND HERZEGOVINA
2 CROATIA
3 SERBIA*
4 MONTENEGRO
5 SLOVENIA
6 NORTH MACEDONIA
7 ALBANIA

**Party to the 1951 Convention
and/or its 1967 Protocol**

*The boundaries and names shown and the designations used on this map do not imply
official endorsement or acceptance by the United Nations.
The initials in [ ] refer to the administering Power or the Power involved in a special treaty relationship.*

* Serbia and Kosovo (S/RES/1244 (1999)).

——————— International boundary

– – – – – Undetermined
international boundary

- - - - - Administrative line

Sources: UNHCS, UNHCR

The 1951 Convention reflects the ideals of *safety, solidarity and self-reliance* for refugees, reflected at various points in history. Protection from return (refoulement) to harm for political reasons, that had long featured in extradition treaties, was expanded in the 1951 Convention, to prohibit the expulsion or return of a refugee to a territory where the person's life or freedom is threatened for reasons of race, religion, nationality, membership of a particular social group or political opinion. The only exception is on the grounds of national security or public order.[242] This principle of non-refoulement was considered so fundamental that no reservations or derogations on it were permitted and has since become a principle of international customary law.[243]

In regard to *solidarity*, the Preamble of the 1951 Convention recognizes that refugee problems are of international scope and nature. The provision of asylum can impose heavy burdens on States, necessitating "international cooperation".

As for *self-reliance*, in addition to ensuring *safety* to refugees, the 1951 Convention includes other rights important for enabling refugees to rebuild their lives, such as the provision of identification documents, access to work and freedom of movement internally and externally with State-issued travel documents.[244]

Some rights in the 1951 Convention are provided at the same level as to nationals. These rights include access to the courts, public relief, rationing, elementary education, artistic rights and industrial property, fiscal charges, labour standards and social security.[245]

In other areas, refugees are to benefit from the most favourable treatment provided to non-nationals, such as wage-earning employment and the right of association.[246] In regard to self-employment, housing, secondary and tertiary education, refugees are to be treated as favourably as possible and no less favourably than aliens generally.[247] And to ensure refugees have a stable legal status, States shall as far as possible facilitate their assimilation and naturalization.[248]

The 1951 Convention provisions, which aimed at ensuring that refugees would be able to move on with their lives, not be dependent on assistance, and contribute to their new communities, were similar to the expectations of countries and empires that had taken in groups of refugees in preceding centuries.

The 1951 Convention was a historic milestone that sets out the broadest set of rights accorded to refugees in an international instrument. And while it fell short of including an enforcement mechanism, which some commentators view as its greatest limitation, it entrenched a supervisory responsibility with UNHCR with whom signatory States agreed to cooperate.[249]

It provided a benchmark of rights and principles that would be reaffirmed by States to the present day, even though their practical adherence to the standards has been imperfect.[250] The standards would be reinforced by other international and regional instruments and national laws.[251] They would also inform the development of additional frameworks to respond to internal and climate-induced displacement discussed in Part II.

The 1951 Convention would also be the focus of much debate and reflection with some arguing that it and the 1967 Protocol did not go far enough to protect refugees or to support States that receive them, and others asserting that the 1951 Convention has proven to be an enduringly relevant and visionary instrument capable of addressing situations of modern displacement. The gaps in the provision of international protection and international cooperation, they claim, do not lie with the 1951 Convention and its Protocol, but rather in the failure of States to apply its provisions consistently and without reservation.[252]

Acknowledging the limits in the 1951 Convention, and anticipating these future debates, the President of the Conference of Plenipotentiaries, Knud Larsen, explained at the closing ceremony of the Conference, that they nevertheless achieved what was possible at the time and established "a satisfactory legal status, which would be of material assistance in promoting international collaboration in the refugee field".[253]

In the intervening 70 years, 149 countries became party to the 1951 Convention or 1967 Protocol or both, reflecting 77 per cent of the United Nations membership.[254] The 1951 Convention has been a source of protection and solutions for millions of refugees. From a historical perspective, the 1951 Convention was a singular achievement: codifying universal rights and standards of treatment afforded to refugees to enable them to live securely and rebuild their lives.

It is also the case that progress continues to be incremental and uneven. The number of forcibly displaced persons continues to substantially increase with over 82 million forcibly displaced at the end of 2020. The opportunities of forcibly displaced persons to return to their places of origin are limited particularly due to prolonged conflict. Rights set out in the 1951 Convention are not systematically honoured, limiting access to safety as well as to opportunities to become self-reliant. The vast majority of people forced to flee are in developing countries, a significant challenge borne by States with limited means and insufficient support from others.[255]

These are among the many challenges that led the United Nations General Assembly, in 2016, to commit to new ways of responding to forced displacement. The resulting Global Compact on Refugees seeks to give better effect to the Convention's core aims of ensuring safety to refugees, helping them rebuild their lives and supporting States in which they reside.

The perennial challenge – which subsequent Parts address – is how best to ensure that these aims can be met.

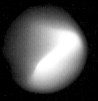

PART II

Protecting
More Broadly

Table of Contents

Protecting More Broadly

Previous page: Three South Sudanese internally displaced women walk to their family after registering their arrival with local authorities in Leer, Unity State, November 2014. © UNHCR/ Andrew McConnell

In this Part, we look at the influence of the Convention relating to the Status of Refugees (1951 Convention), beyond its roots in the realities of post-war Europe. In particular, we see how its protections have reached a much broader group of people than the drafters could have envisaged, and how it has informed subsequent regional refugee instruments. It has also inspired international frameworks for protecting internally displaced persons and those forced to flee in the context of climate change and environmental disasters. These additional State efforts have responded to growing levels of forced displacement *within* borders as well as *beyond* them, reflecting its multiple causes.

The frameworks cited above recognize the right of forcibly displaced persons to receive the protection and assistance required to overcome the vulnerabilities of displacement. They also show the necessity of genuine cooperation among States to share responsibilities and burdens equitably. Tracing these developments reveals the extent that the frameworks have widened the arc of protection. It also outlines where adherence to them has fallen short of the ideals of solidarity and inclusion necessary for forcibly displaced persons to live in dignity and achieve a better future.

Refugees

1951 Convention

The 1951 Convention outlines the rights of refugees, and the obligations of States towards them as well as towards UNHCR. States are obliged to cooperate with UNHCR in the exercise of its mandate, to provide it with information on the number and condition of refugees as well as relevant laws and regulations affecting them.[1] They are also required to cooperate with UNHCR's supervisory responsibility[2] for ensuring governments take the necessary measures to meet their obligations for people under UNHCR's mandate.[3]

As discussed in Part I, the 1951 Convention initially applied to those who became refugees due to events *before* 1951. It also allowed States to restrict its application to events *within* Europe. These limitations were lifted in the 1967 Protocol amid rising forced displacement, principally in Africa. The Protocol ensures that the Convention obligations apply to all refugee situations, regardless of where and when they arise.

Although forged from the circumstances of World War II (WWII), the 1951 Convention was intended to be of enduring nature: providing protection to refugees in varied circumstances and not confined to the post-war context. As observed in the UK House of Lords in 2003, "while its meaning does not change over time its application will".[4] And so it has broadened.[5]

International protection has been extended to those fleeing persecution by non-State agents. People have been recognized as refugees when in fear of persecution by organized gangs, traffickers and others in circumstances where the State is unable or unwilling to provide protection.[6] People fleeing disasters and famines have also been recognized as Convention refugees, when armed conflict or individual or group identity are also a source of the harm feared. And persecution on the basis of sexual orientation or gender identity has also counted.[7]

Recognition of the broad scope of international protection has come through State practice, jurisprudence and regional refugee instruments. Yet, alongside this widening scope, safety for refugees has also been withheld. Even when it has been provided, other rights are often denied. International burdens and responsibilities have not been equitably shared. How this has happened is set out in the following discussion.

Regional Refugee Frameworks

OAU Convention 1969

Africa was experiencing a steady and significant increase in forced displacement before the 1951 Convention extended beyond Europe and the events of WWII. This eventually led to a specific regional framework: the 1969 Organisation of African Unity Convention Governing Specific Aspects of Refugee Problems in Africa (OAU Convention).

The main causes of forced displacement in Africa in the 1950s were independence struggles and post-independence internal conflicts. The Algerian War of Independence was among the first. Beginning in 1954, this eight-year, bitter and violent struggle claimed over 300,000 Algerian lives. It prompted 1 million European settlers to leave and caused the mass encampment of over 1 million Algerian civilians and the flight of over 200,000 refugees to Tunisia and Morocco.[8]

Other independence struggles were to follow. Within a decade, the political map of Africa changed considerably, as the number of newly independent countries rose from a few to include most countries on the continent.[9] Many of these transitions were achieved peacefully. For others, independence was only won after years of armed conflict, many deaths and significant forced displacement.

The decolonization struggles of Angola, Guinea-Bissau and Mozambique were brutal.[10] Among the colonial powers, Portugal was particularly reluctant to "end colonization in all its forms and manifestations", as provided in the 1960 General Assembly Decolonization Resolution[11] and as intended by Articles in the United Nations Charter.[12] Aspirations for self-determination were growing. Portugal's continued denial of economic, social and political opportunities to African populations led to armed insurrection.[13]

The Portuguese Colonial War began in Angola in 1961, reaching Guinea-Bissau in 1963 and Mozambique the next year. Independence movements were met with fierce counter-insurgency measures. The conflicts continued for over a decade, marked by human rights violations and tens of thousands of deaths.[14] Hundreds of thousands of refugees fled to neighbouring countries, including Senegal, Tanzania, Zaire and Zambia.[15]

Post-independence power struggles also led to substantial forced displacement. Several thousand fled Burundi in 1965 as the Tutsi-led Government quashed a Hutu-led insurgency.[16] In neighbouring Rwanda, Tutsis fled increasingly repressive policies of the Hutu-dominated government with close to

160,000 seeking refuge principally in Burundi, DRC, Uganda.[17] Cyclical violence persisted in both countries, and refugees remained in protracted displacement. Enmities deepened and would erupt with searing violence in the 1990s engulfing Africa's Great Lakes region.[18]

Sudan was also a source of significant forced displacement in the 1960s and for reasons that would persist through many decades. Sudan gained self-government relatively early, in 1953, yet from the outset was beset with internal problems. These included difficulties in transitioning from a British- to a

Algerian refugees gather at a Red Crescent food distribution point at Oued R'man in Tunisia, in 1959.
© UNHCR/ Stanley Wright

Sudanese-dominated civil service, rising disaffection of southern Sudanese who felt left out of the political process, and a parliament that was divided along sectarian lines.[19]

Unrest in Sudan sparked a civil conflict that would continue through 1972. Violence and repression following a military coup in 1958[20] and another in 1969 resulted in significant forced displacement. By the early 1970s, up to 800,000 persons were displaced internally and some 170,000 had fled the country,[21] most to Uganda and Zaire. As with other conflicts on the continent, various exiled groups conducted insurgency efforts from neighbouring countries.[22]

Cumulatively, these independence and post-independence conflicts accounted for much of the increase in forced displacement of the period. Data collection also improved and the extent of forced displacement became increasingly visible. In 1964, half a million people were known to be refugees in Africa and, by the end of the decade, this number had almost doubled.[23]

The OAU Convention came from these circumstances and the need for a shared response across the region.[24] It is a relatively short document but an important one in the story of forced displacement. It explicitly recognizes the 1951 Convention as the "universal" refugee protection instrument.[25] States committed not to reject or return a refugee to a territory where life, liberty or integrity of the person is threatened, to act in solidarity to "lighten the burden" of other States, and to advance solutions by exerting "best endeavours" to secure the settlement of refugees and support voluntary, safe and sustainable return.[26]

The OAU Convention also broke new ground. Its broader definition of a refugee is among its enduring legacies. It explicitly included those who have fled due "to external aggression, occupation, foreign domination or events seriously disturbing public order" in either part or the whole of the country.[27] This provision was very much a product of the time, reflecting solidarity among States to support liberation movements that were still underway. It left no doubt that those fleeing under these circumstances counted as refugees.

The OAU Convention also had wider relevance. It enabled States to apply refugee status without having to decide whether the person would likely face "persecution" in the country of origin, taking the political sensitivity out of such findings.[28] In explicitly recognizing that a refugee could be fleeing from *generalized violence* rather than *individual persecution*, it allows quick applications to situations of mass forced displacement.[29] While the 1951 Convention definition can also be applied in these contexts, not all States have done so.

The OAU Convention's definition may also have significant importance in the context of climate change and natural disasters. Scholars have noted that it could cover flight from areas affected, if such events were to "seriously disturb public order".[30] And, in 2019, member States of the African Union (AU), the successor organization of the OAU, called upon the AU Commission and UNHCR to publish interpretive guidance to clarify the application of the OAU Convention refugee definition to "new causes of forced displacement, such as climate change and disasters".[31]

As one of the most widely ratified regional treaties, the OAU Convention has inspired progressive laws and policies in many African countries. It has been ratified by 48 of the 55 member States.[32] And 47 countries have national refugee legislation that is broadly in line with it.[33] Other regional instruments have drawn from its provisions, including the Cartagena Declaration in Latin America,[34] the Bangkok Principles on Status and Treatment of Refugees,[35] and

OAU Convention

States parties to the 1969 OAU Convention
Governing the Specific Aspects of Refugee Problems in Africa

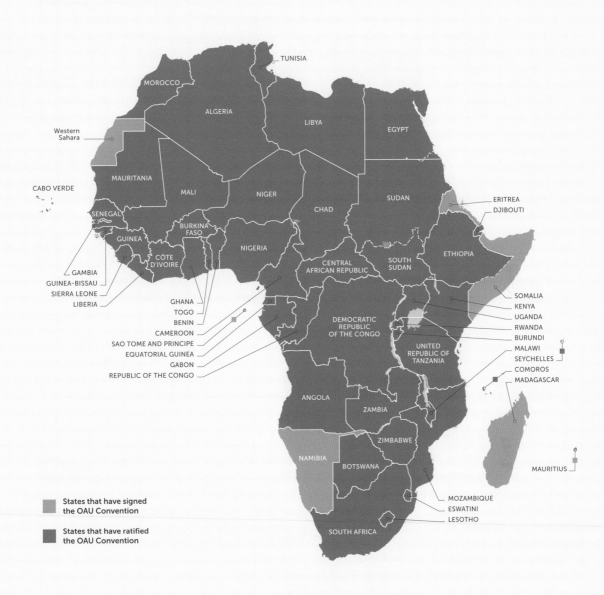

States that have signed
the OAU Convention

States that have ratified
the OAU Convention

International boundary

Undetermined
international boundary

Abyei region

Administrative line

500 km

The boundaries and names shown and the designations used on this map do not imply official endorsement or acceptance by the United Nations.
Final boundary between the Republic of Sudan and the Republic of South Sudan has not yet been determined. Final status of the Abyei area is not yet determined.

Sources: UNCS, UNHCR

the 2009 AU Kampala Convention for the protection of internally displaced persons in Africa.[36]

The OAU Convention reaffirmed the obligations of States to provide safety to refugees and made it clear that this included people fleeing individual persecution as well as serious disturbances of public order. It noted the need to find ways to alleviate suffering and provide refugees with "a better life and future".[37] It underscores the critically important non-refoulement principle, the commitment of States to settle refugees, and the imperative that returns be voluntary, safe and under conditions that are sustainable.

Since it came into force, millions of refugees have received protection in host countries throughout the continent, many for decades. Refugees arriving in large numbers have been recognized on a prima facie basis and without having to establish individual persecution.[38] African States have regularly marked successive anniversaries of the OAU Convention: recognizing its significance.[39] Deficiencies in application have been noted and areas for reform agreed.[40]

Nonetheless, the non-refoulement provision of both refugee Conventions has not been consistently observed.[41] And, while the expanded definition has led to the recognition of refugees in mass influx situations, many States also began to rely more on individual determinations rather than granting refugee status to groups on a prima facie basis. Case law on the application of the OAU Convention definition is thin, tends not to rely on the expansive grounds, and overall lacks consistency, predictability and common standards across the continent.[42]

And the OAU Convention's commitment to use best efforts to secure the settlement of refugees who are unable or unwilling to return has fallen short. As displacement numbers grew from the 1980s onwards, there was also deepening reluctance to facilitate the settlement of refugees or allow their socio-economic integration. With a few notable exceptions,[43] refugees were increasingly confined to closed camps or otherwise prohibited from moving freely, accessing services, working and engaging in income-generating activities.[44] Many African States have made reservations on 1951 Convention provisions related to rights to move freely, to work, and to access national schools.[45]

These are among the challenges addressed in the 2018 Global Compact on Refugees. Its objectives include improving refugee self-reliance as well as providing more support to States hosting large numbers of refugees.[46] Recently, some African States have shown an openness to move in this direction in line with more inclusive development approaches generally. A number have initiated policies to provide greater refugee access to national education, health services and the labour market in a manner that can improve their lives and those of the communities in which they live. These efforts are discussed more in Part IV and are encouraging. Transforming intentions into reality will depend on ongoing political will and sustained international financial and technical support to improve the lives of refugees and those who host them.

Bangkok Principles 1966

As African States were working on the OAU Convention, a related process was underway in Asia. In 1964, Egypt requested the Asian-African Legal Consultative Committee (AALCC), today known as the Asian-African Legal Consultative Organization (AALCO), to develop standards of treatment for refugees. As host to thousands of Palestine refugees since the 1948 Arab-Israeli War, Egypt also thought the issue was of broader interest given rising refugee displacement across Africa and Asia.[47]

The AALCO is a legal advisory body to its member States, today numbering 47 from Africa, Asia and the Middle East.[48] Several rank among the top refugee-hosting countries in the world. More than half are not parties to the 1951 Convention or the 1967 Protocol.[49]

The deliberations of the AALCC led to the adoption of the Bangkok Principles in 1966. They are non-binding so, while reflecting agreement between members, each State is able to decide how to apply them in practice.[50] They were amended over the years and a revised set of Principles was adopted in 2001. The refugee definition encompassed in the Principles, is fully aligned with the 1951 Convention and includes a specific reference to flight on account of ethnic origin and gender persecution, external aggression, occupation, foreign domination, or events seriously disturbing public order.[51]

The Principles include the right of non-refoulement with a requirement that any breach for reasons of national security must be effected in accordance with "due process of law".[52] The right of voluntary return includes the need for the country of origin to facilitate it by providing necessary documents, granting full rights and privileges of nationals and not penalizing returnees for having left the country. The Principles call for international responsibility and burden-sharing to support States hosting refugees, improved standards of treatment of refugees, and the provision of solutions within and outside the region.[53]

Most commentators speak favourably of the work of the AALCO, while lamenting the fact that the Principles have generally not been taken up in national laws. States do not consider themselves legally bound to them and their central tenets – burden-sharing, voluntary return and protection from refoulement – have not been systematically respected. Further, solutions to displacement have not been readily realized.[54] A number of the participating States have been among the world's largest hosting countries for decades, offering safety to hundreds of thousands of refugees. However, most restrict refugee rights and do not encourage local settlement.

Nevertheless, advocates note that the Principles are of value as a framework and that they are ready for States to apply, when there is the political will. In the meantime, they remain an important benchmark for assessing State responses.[55]

Cartagena Declaration on Refugees 1984

In Africa, mounting refugee numbers provided the main motivation for the OAU Convention. Likewise, 15 years later, escalating refugee crises in Latin America would have a similar effect.

Latin America had the first multilateral asylum provisions in the world, as noted in Part I. The 1899 International Treaty on Penal Law recognized the right to political asylum. State signatories agreed not to extradite foreigners for political crimes and to afford political refugees "inviolable asylum". They also committed to prevent refugees from committing acts within their territories that "may endanger the public peace" of the country of origin.[56] The right to claim asylum for political reasons – and not to be refouled for political crimes – was reinforced in regional Conventions over the next 80 years, leading to the so called "Latin American asylum tradition".[57]

The refugee movements of the 1970s and 1980s, however, went beyond the circumstances covered by this tradition. Conflict in Central America, for example, displaced an estimated 2 million people from El Salvador, Guatemala and Nicaragua during the 1970s and 1980s.[58] People fled from political persecution as well as from indiscriminate violence by armed insurgent and counterinsurgency forces. Many of the receiving countries in the region either were not party to the 1951 Convention or did not consider the majority of refugees at the time as falling within its provisions.[59]

The pace of displacement quickened in the late 1970s. By this time, the largely agrarian-based economies of Central America had been hard hit by a decline in foreign trade, and rising oil prices. Earthquakes in Nicaragua in 1972 and Guatemala in 1976 further aggravated matters. Economic hardship added to the list of grievances against the governing elite whose policies favoured minority landholding and international commercial interests.[60]

Nicaragua descended into civil war in 1972. In 1979, the Government of Nicaragua fell. The new Government formed by the former revolutionary Sandinista National Liberation Front was soon fighting another war against the counter-revolutionaries (the "Contras") who were backed by the United States.[61] The Contras operated out of camps in the neighbouring countries of Costa Rica and Honduras and, from there, launched attacks on rural areas within Nicaragua. Tens of thousands of civilians were forcibly displaced from their homes both internally and externally. By the mid-1980s, there were over 50,000 Nicaraguan refugees. This number would almost double by the end of the decade when the peace agreement was signed.[62]

In El Salvador, reform movements championed by the middle class as well as the rural and urban poor grew in the 1960s and 1970s. They were met with fierce repression from the security forces. The intensity of violence increased. In the late 1970s and early 1980s, over 30,000 persons were killed by State security forces, generating further support for revolutionary movements.[63] Some have estimated that the 12-year civil war led to the forced displacement of 20 per cent of the population. Close to half a million people were forcibly displaced internally and 1 million left the country until peace was negotiated in 1992.[64]

Adding to the instability of the region was ever-increasing repression within Guatemala in response to decades-old struggles against authoritarian regimes that were accused of severely disadvantaging the majority indigenous population. Armed resistance intensified in the 1970s.[65] To suppress the insurgency, Government forces decimated villages leaving 1 million people internally displaced, and over 200,000 forced to flee the country by the 1980s.[66] Most of the refugees resided in camps in inhospitable jungle areas of Mexico.[67] At the end of the decade, 90 per cent of the country lived in poverty.[68] The conflict would drag on until 1996, its 30-year trajectory constituting the longest civil war in the region.

Reception of refugees in the region was uneven, often influenced by political considerations and generally not informed by international refugee protection principles. Salvadoran refugees in border areas of Honduras became victims of attacks, disappearances and kidnappings by Salvadoran forces for which the Honduran Government had an affinity. On occasion, Honduras and Mexico forcibly pushed back Salvadoran and Guatemalan refugees respectively.[69] Very few of those who fled their countries were formally recognized as refugees by host countries.[70]

The displacement crisis in the region and the need for a unified protection-sensitive response led to the 1984 Colloquium on the International Protection of Refugees in Central America. It concluded with the Cartagena Declaration endorsed by 10 participating States.[71]

Like the OAU Convention, it affirms the principles of the 1951 Refugee Convention. It reiterates the importance of the non-refoulement principle and stresses that decisions to repatriate must be made on an individual, voluntary basis and in conditions where safety is ensured.[72] Similar to the OAU Convention and reflecting regional experience, the Cartagena Declaration calls for refugees to be located at a "reasonable distance" from the frontier. Significantly, it also endorses States' previously agreed commitments to reinforce programmes in the areas of health, education, labour and safety and with a view to ensure the "self-sufficiency of refugees".[73] It acknowledges the possibility of integrating refugees with support from the international community.[74]

The Cartagena Declaration also includes an expansive regional refugee definition. It too incorporates the 1951 Convention definition as well as specifies that refugees also include those who have fled because "their lives, security or freedom have been threatened by generalized violence, foreign aggression, internal conflicts, massive violation of human rights or other circumstances which have seriously disturbed public order".[75] This wording gives the Cartagena Declaration far-reaching potential scope.

Although the Cartagena Declaration is not a legally binding document, most countries in Latin America have incorporated its definition into their national laws, either in its entirety or with some modifications.[76] High Courts in four countries have also confirmed that compliance with the definition is mandatory in asylum proceedings.[77] In parallel, the Inter-American Court on Human Rights has affirmed the right of refugees to seek asylum, as well as the obligation of States to receive and properly assess asylum requests and not to prevent refugees from making asylum applications.[78]

The Cartagena Declaration's ten-yearly anniversaries have been celebrated with regional meetings where its provisions are reaffirmed.[79] These occasions have also launched new regional initiatives, including in regard to reception, solutions, statelessness, labour mobility and the prevention of smuggling and trafficking.[80]

This spirit of regional collaboration is an achievement of the Cartagena Declaration. But, in practice, its definition has not been consistently applied. Most asylum systems afford maximum discretion to decision makers, with limited oversight, and few guarantees for due process. This contributes to uneven decision-making and a lack of coherent jurisprudence within national systems and more broadly in the region.[81]

Over recent years, the response to the unprecedented displacement of millions of Venezuelans has further amplified the gap between aspiration and practice. Beginning around 2014, Venezuela was gripped by unrest over hyper-inflation, chronic shortages of basic goods and services, corruption, criminality and political violence. Reports of arbitrary detentions and disappearances increased. Within six years, over 5.4 million Venezuelans had left their country: the largest exodus in the history of Latin America and the Caribbean.[82]

Most States in the region have been reluctant to recognize the majority of Venezuelans as refugees, despite UNHCR's 2019 Guidance Note indicating that many are in need of international protection under the criteria contained in the Cartagena Declaration.[83] Only six States in the region have applied the expansive provisions of the Cartagena refugee definition to those who have fled Venezuela.[84] As of the end of 2020, most asylum claims remained pending and the vast majority of claims adjudicated did not recognize the applicants as refugees.[85] Brazil is the only State that has recognized Venezuelans as refugees on a prima facie basis, without the need for a detailed individual status determination.[86]

States' reluctance to accord formal refugee status to Venezuelans is primarily due to the massive scale of displacement, and concerns of more to come. As some authors observe, refugee status comes with attendant rights to social services, entailing high fiscal costs.[87] Efforts by international financial institutions to support States in providing these services is discussed further in Part IV.

While the application of the Cartagena Declaration definition has not been widely in use, many countries have provided temporary forms of stay. This has benefited some 2.7 million Venezuelans: over half of the total 4.6 million Venezuelans that are displaced on the subcontinent.[88]

Most notable in this regard is Colombia. By the end of 2020, there were some 1.7 million Venezuelans estimated in the country. About 720,000 persons had been issued Special Stay Permits.[89] The remainder did not have recognized legal status. To address this issue, in February 2021, the Government announced it would extend Temporary Protection Status (TPS) to all Venezuelans residing in the country who register with the Government within a certain period, as well as to prospective regular arrivals over the next two years. The TPS will be valid for 10 years during which time permit holders will be able to work, go to school and access health services. Within the 10-year period, they will be able to apply for permanent residency.[90]

In announcing the policy, President Duque said it was aimed at normalizing lives and to enable Venezuelans to contribute productively to Colombia. He hoped that other countries would do the same.[91] Several months later, Ecuador, host to an estimated 450,000 Venezuelans, announced a new regularization policy for Venezuelans, complemented by economic integration and labour market access.[92] These policy developments in Colombia and Ecuador are very much in keeping with the spirit of the Cartagena Declaration, and the most significant expression of its ambition in its nearly 40-year history.

In parallel, efforts to improve refugee protection systems in Central America have increased in recent years, also in line with the Cartagena Declaration and

Venezuelans cross the Tachira River to seek help in Colombia in 2019.
© UNHCR/ Vincent Tremea

commitments made in its ten-yearly anniversaries. This includes the countries of El Salvador, Guatemala and Honduras – countries whose conflicts inspired it. For the past decade, these countries have experienced exceptionally high levels of violence against civilians by criminal gangs, drug cartels and other illegal armed groups. Extortion, kidnapping, forced recruitment and extremely high rates of homicide have contributed to extensive displacement. At the end of 2020, over 850,000 persons from these countries were forcibly displaced, nearly two thirds of whom had fled across international borders.[93]

In 2017, countries of origin and receiving States adopted a comprehensive response to displacement in the region.[94] The Regional Comprehensive Protection and Solutions Framework (MIRPS) involves Belize, Costa Rica,

El Salvador, Guatemala, Honduras, Mexico and Panama. Working with humanitarian partners, the aim is to strengthen reception systems, registration, refugee status determination procedures, solutions and assistance to the most vulnerable. The challenges are considerable. Although close to 68,000 persons from El Salvador, Guatemala, Honduras and Nicaragua have been granted refugee status since 2017, at the end of 2020, pending asylum claims numbered over 500,000.[95]

Cleary the Cartagena Declaration did not transform practices throughout Latin America as quickly as may have been hoped in 1984. The path to greater consistency in practice has been slow. Although it is not a legally binding document, its refugee definition has the force of law in the 15 States that have incorporated it in their national legislation.[96] It also reflects the desire to work collectively in response to situations of displacement. This has been evident in comprehensive approaches to resolving Central American displacements in the 1990s[97] and efforts now underway in several countries to improve protection responses. It is also reflected in the responses of a number of States to the Venezuelan influx, as well as in the approach several States have taken in response to displacement in the context of climate change and disasters.[98]

Responsibility- and Burden-Sharing/Shifting

International and regional refugee protection arrangements are built on a commitment of cooperation. The foundational 1951 Convention begins with recognizing that receiving large numbers of refugees can place great burdens on States, and that responding to and resolving refugee displacement relies on "international cooperation".[99]

Over the decades, States have reiterated their commitment to more equitable burden- and responsibility-sharing in UNHCR's annual Executive Committee Conclusions and specified what it entails. It includes the provision of "emergency, financial, and technical assistance" to countries receiving large numbers of refugees.[100] It also means more than lending a hand. Each State is also required to do its part in upholding refugee protection.[101] Yet, despite the regular statements of intent, international responsibility and burden-sharing has generally fallen short.

Many high-income countries have financially supported refugee responses from afar, accepted refugees through overseas resettlement processes, established asylum systems for determining refugee claims of those that arrive at their borders, and provided integration opportunities for those that are recognized as refugees. Without their regular engagement and financial contributions, United Nations agencies, non-governmental organizations and other civil society actors working to protect and assist forcibly displaced persons would not be able to function.

And yet, these contributions continue to fall short of robust and equitable responsibility- and burden-sharing. Eighty-six per cent of the world's refugees find protection in low- and middle-income countries.[102] Resettlement from these countries to high-income countries has rarely represented more than one per cent of that.[103] The reception of large numbers of forcibly displaced persons is a humanitarian and development challenge for most host countries, and support to them has generally been unpredictable and incommensurate with need.

Humanitarian funding is generally provided on an annual basis, often tightly earmarked to specific donor priorities and falls far short of global appeals.[104] Development funding is also needed to address the fiscal impact and pressures on social services, infrastructure and the environment and to help reduce poverty overall. Using development financing in this way has only relatively recently come on stream.[105]

The absence of adequate humanitarian and development support has been a constant source of frustration for many host countries and a visible failure of international burden- and responsibility-sharing. And, while many high-income countries are consistent donors and vocal proponents of the international system to protect refugees, many of them have also instituted and expanded measures to limit the number of refugees that they accept: blocking entry to their territories; restricting admissions to their asylum processes; limiting the rights of asylum-seekers and/or interpreting the refugee definition in a restrictive manner. So, while remaining engaged in the international refugee protection regime, they also do what they can to limit their direct responsibilities towards refugees.[106]

This challenge to international cooperation is a recurring theme in international events to mark the ten-yearly anniversaries of the 1951 Convention. On its 50th anniversary,[107] more than 100 States recommitted to provide better refugee protection within the framework of international solidarity and burden-sharing.[108] This was followed by an Agenda for Protection, including steps to ensure that immigration control measures contain safeguards that allow access to international protection for those who need it.[109] Similar affirmations were made a decade later on the 60th anniversary of the 1951 Convention.[110]

Within five years, this resolve was visibly tested amidst the growing flight of Syrian refugees towards Europe.[111] They moved together with other refugees and also migrants along dangerous routes. One of the youngest people seeking safety became emblematic of the peril they faced. Three-year-old Alan Kurdi drowned on the way to Europe, and photos of him on a Turkish beach caught global attention.

His death threw new light on the lack of adequate support to host countries and the absence of cooperation within Europe, as individual States tried

An infant is carried out of a boat full of refugees and migrants arriving in Lesbos after crossing the Aegean from Turkey in 2015. © UNHCR/ Achilleas Zavallis

to block arrivals. It reflected larger systemic failures in international burden-sharing in the face of rising forced displacement, exposing risks that a lack of cooperation poses to human life and safety. To address these challenges, the United Nations Secretary-General called a meeting of the leaders of all member States to develop a more predictable and equitable way of responding to large movements of refugees and migrants.[112]

This resulted in the 2016 New York Declaration, where all 193 United Nations member States committed to do better.[113] They also agreed to the development of two Global Compacts to establish the way forward: a Global Compact on Refugees and a Global Compact for Safe, Orderly and Regular Migration. Each was affirmed by nearly all members of the United Nations in 2018.[114]

Among the many provisions in the Compacts are commitments for the safe reception of refugees and migrants and the fair adjudication of protection needs that adhere to international and regional obligations.[115] They also acknowledge the importance of strengthening efforts to prevent and combat the smuggling of persons by land, sea and air and the trafficking of persons, especially women and children. The Compacts include commitments to open additional legal pathways for refugees and other migrants to use from abroad.[116]

Well before the Global Compacts, the Agenda for Protection agreed by States in 2000, focused attention on people in need of protection in mixed movements. Subsequently, UNHCR developed advice for States for implementing protection-sensitive entry procedures: the 10-Point Plan in Action. It contains detailed guidance for ensuring entry systems respect rights and international obligations, whether at a physical border, at sea or on the territory of another State. The 10-Point Plan in Action is periodically updated, focusing on positive practice.[117]

As the following examples illustrate, however, some practices with long histories are difficult to dislodge. Newer and expanded means of access controls continue to be developed that do not have the protection safeguards envisaged in either the Global Compact on Refugees or the Global Compact for Safe, Orderly and Regular Migration. Together with other policies aimed to limit international obligations, they weaken the solidarity upon which the international protection regime is based.

Border controls

Managing borders has long been regarded as essential in the exercise of State sovereignty. After the terrorist attacks of 11 September 2001, it also became a pressing national security imperative. Long-established measures, like visas, carrier sanctions and interdictions, have been complemented by other means to intercept those who could pose a threat as well as those attempting to arrive without prior authorization.

States have the right to decide who to admit to their countries. They have a legitimate interest in seeking to prevent unauthorized entry and to combat the smuggling and trafficking of persons. The latter is even an obligation under international law.[118] However, they also have other international legal obligations, notably not to return someone to a territory where the person faces risks to life, freedom or physical integrity.[119] And, this is where many entry controls fall short. They are often applied in a manner, whether targeted or indiscriminate, that prevent refugees from claiming asylum. This exposes them to greater vulnerability and increased risks of grievous harm.

Visas and carrier sanctions

A visa authorizes the bearer to enter a country for a specific purpose and period of time. Visas are a flexible means of controlling admissions, since they generally are implemented by executive orders and do not require legislative approval or oversight.[120] Visas predate the 1951 Convention, emerging in the 19th century and have been in widespread use around the world for over 40 years,[121] as noted in Part I.

Visas can be negotiated in the context of regional or bilateral agreements between States, with visa-free travel featuring in broader geopolitical alliances.[122] Visas have been imposed in response to increased asylum claims, as a means of limiting claims from particular countries, including refugee producing ones.[123]

In law, the absence of a visa should not be used to prevent a person from seeking asylum. Under the 1951 Convention, States may not penalize refugees for unlawful arrival or presence and may not return a refugee to a place where life or freedom would be threatened.[124] To meet these obligations, a State must admit an asylum-seeker at its border or otherwise on its territory until such a determination is made.[125] However, refugees often do not reach their destination. If they do not have a visa, they can be prohibited from boarding a land, air or sea transit carrier. This pushes them to embark on perilous journeys, often facilitated by smugglers and exposing them to serious risks.

The enforcement of visa restrictions is helped by the imposition of penalties on the carriers who take people without the papers required by law. The use of carrier sanctions dates back to early American, Australian, British and Canadian immigration laws.[126] It grew during the 1980s, as increased availability of less costly travel facilitated human mobility.[127] It remains a means to stem refugee movements alongside preventing unauthorized migration.

Countries have posted their immigration officials in foreign embarkation sites to assist carriers to detect those unauthorized to enter the destination country.[128] These procedures limit the arrival of refugees and do not allow for the equitable sharing of burdens and responsibilities.

Physical barriers

Walls and other forms of physical barriers have long been used by States as a defense against enemy incursions, weapons smuggling and other forms of transnational crime. They also have been constructed and reinforced specifically to keep out refugees and asylum-seekers, and generally as part of a larger effort to restrict asylum claims from specific countries.

Between 2010 and 2012, Israel fortified its border with Egypt to restrict the arrival of refugees and migrants.[129] At the time, there were more than 50,000 refugees and asylum-seekers in Israel, most coming from Eritrea and Sudan.[130] Despite the extremely poor human rights records in places of origin, very few refugee claims were granted.[131] Eritreans were not returned to Eritrea on the basis of the non-refoulement principle. Sudanese were not returned to Sudan largely due to the absence of diplomatic relations between Sudan and Israel and the lack of agreement of Sudan to accept returnees.[132]

Border fortifications to keep out more arrivals were accompanied by other deterrence and removal policies. Beginning in 2012, mandatory detention policies for those arriving through unofficial border crossings were imposed and stiffened. By 2013, indefinite detention was imposed on those who crossed unofficially but could not be deported. Their release depended on them agreeing to leave the country.[133] The Israeli High Court of Justice held that the detention policies violated Israel's Basic Law: Human Dignity and Liberty.[134]

While detention periods were subsequently reduced, in 2015, Israel announced a plan to relocate Eritrean and Sudanese nationals to third countries. Those who refused would be detained, while those who agreed to leave voluntarily would be given $3,500. Following a series of legal cases and public protests against the relocation scheme and related detention measures, the programme was suspended in 2018.[135] By this time, around one third of Eritreans and Sudanese who were present in Israel in 2012 had left the country.[136]

The measures reduced the number of arrivals to Israel via Egypt while, at the same time, leading desperate people to try more perilous routes by sea. Others have died in attempting to scale the fence, including by shots fired by guards on both sides of the border.[137] Meanwhile, within Israel, recognition rates for asylum-seekers from Eritrea and Sudan remained low: under 2 per cent as compared to protection recognition rates of around 80–90 per cent for Eritreans and 50–60 per cent for Sudanese in the European Union.[138]

Hungary has also reinforced border barriers and enacted extremely restrictive policies to keep out foreigners in recent years with little or no distinction to accommodate people with specific protection needs. At the height of the 2015 arrivals in Europe, with hundreds of people amassing at its border, Hungary limited entry to a handful of people each day. Asylum applicants were confined to transit centres and claims and appeal procedures were terminated if people left for any reason, including for provisions such as food or other necessities.[139]

The centres were closed following a decision by the European Court of Justice that mass incarceration is unlawful and detention only permissible as a last resort, under specific circumstances following "a case-by-case" determination.[140] The Court also held that Hungary acted unlawfully in forcing people back to Serbia without observing protection principles and safeguards demanded by European law, including the right of non-refoulement.[141]

Despite the ruling, Hungary's border restrictions remain.[142] It has since enacted a law according to which asylum-seekers arriving at the border or apprehended in-country are no longer granted access to asylum procedures in Hungary. Instead, they have to express their intention to seek asylum in Hungarian embassies in Ukraine or Serbia.[143] UNHCR has noted that the failure to recognize the right to seek asylum within Hungary and to a fair determination there is in contravention of international law.[144]

And in September 2021, UNHCR and the International Organization for Migration (IOM) expressed their concern at the growing number of pushbacks of asylum-seekers and migrants along the borders of Lithuania, Latvia and Poland with Belarus. Groups of people had become stranded for weeks without assistance, exposed to the elements, and several died from hypothermia.[145]

The United States has also fortified its borders to prevent unauthorized arrivals of migrants and asylum-seekers. The completion of a wall between the United States and Mexico was a campaign promise of President Trump in the 2016 elections. During his tenure, the existing 650 miles of barriers were reinforced along the 2,000-mile southern border and an additional 80 miles of new barrier built.[146] The construction accompanied a much broader set of measures to deter refugees and migrants.

Arrivals across the southern border began to increase appreciably in 2014, corresponding to deteriorating conditions across El Salvador, Guatemala, Honduras and Venezuela. As reported by UNHCR, reasons ranged from extreme economic deprivation to persecution, with many fleeing "horrific violence by brutal gangs and in need of international protection."[147] In addition to physical barriers, the United States Department of Homeland Security issued the 2019 Migration Protection Protocols,[148] which required people seeking to enter the United States from Mexico without documents or prior authorization to remain in Mexico while they await their hearings in United States immigration courts.[149] Admissions through resettlement were also reduced by nearly 80 per cent within two years.[150]

In parallel, Mexico agreed to scale up border enforcement and take other measures to prevent asylum-seekers and migrants from reaching the United States.[151] Enforcement measures on the United States side also intensified,[152] the use of expedited processing increased,[153] detention policies broadened,[154] and criminal charges imposed on those who entered the country through unofficial border crossings.[155]

Some of these policies were discontinued in February 2021 under President Joe Biden, including the Migration Protection Protocols, but this was subject to litigation which has kept the Protocols in place.[156] Additionally, the

Border fence along the international border between the United States and Mexico at Lukeville, Arizona. 6 February 2019. © Terry Thomas/ Alamy

COVID-19-related entry restrictions continued as of September. These are being enforced under public health legislation that permits the Government to prevent the admission of individuals during public health emergencies. Under a public health order, known as Title 42, unauthorized arrivals through Canada and Mexico are denied access to United States asylum procedures.[157]

Asylum-seekers at the Mexico-United States border have been transferred by aircraft to southern Mexico. Haitians fleeing political violence and the effects of a devastating earthquake in August 2021 have been violently pushed back from the United States border and several thousands sent back to Mexico and Haiti without their protection needs assessed. UNHCR and other advocates have appealed that these restrictions be lifted and access to asylum procedures be restored.[158]

Offshore processing

Some States have taken measures to determine asylum applications in centres outside their countries, usually enforced through interdiction measures.

Australia

For several decades Australia has taken measures to restrict the right of refugees to claim asylum at its borders.[159] In the 1990s, it imposed a mandatory detention policy of all non-citizens arriving in the country without a valid visa, including asylum-seekers.[160] In 2001, faced with increased arrivals by sea, Australia introduced the "Pacific Solution" of off-shore processing.[161]

It removed those seeking to enter Australia without a visa to processing facilities located in the island nation of Nauru and on Manus Island in Papua New Guinea. Between 2001 and 2008, over 1,600 people were detained in the Nauru and Manus Island offshore processing facilities under this policy. Close to 70 per cent were found to be in need of protection and ultimately relocated to Australia or resettled in other countries.[162]

The Pacific Solution was suspended in 2007; it resumed again in 2012 when Australia received a considerable increase in asylum-seekers by boat, reaching over 20,000 in 2013.[163] Although a modest figure by international standards, the arrivals were a lightning rod of controversy, with most public opinion lining up behind politicians calling for a strict response, citing the many deaths at sea as further reason to clamp down.[164] The fact that the majority were from refugee-producing countries did not soften the position.[165] The new policy saw the transfer of 3,000 persons to Nauru and Papua New Guinea since 2013.[166] Those transferred offshore who were found to be in need of international protection were not permitted to enter Australia and durable solutions for them had to be found elsewhere.[167]

In addition to restarting offshore processing, the Government announced its "military-led border security programme" – "Operation Sovereign Borders".[168] It provides for the interdiction of persons trying to enter Australia without a visa, including refugees and asylum-seekers. They are returned to their countries of origin or places of departure. The policy has been criticized by human rights institutions, and UNHCR because it places those in need of international protection at risk of refoulement in contravention of the 1951 Convention and customary international law.[169]

In 2017, the Special Rapporteur on the Human Rights of Migrants, François Crépeau, also found Australia in breach of its international obligations. Specifically, he considered Australia responsible for the harsh conditions on Manus Island and Nauru since Australia funded the processing centres and chose the private contractors that ran them. He found high incidence of mental stress and physical suffering caused by the poor living conditions and prolonged uncertainty, and noted disturbing accounts of rape and sexual abuse of female refugees and asylum-seekers that occurred with impunity.[170]

The Special Rapporteur concluded that the offshore confinement of refugees and asylum-seekers on the islands constituted cruel, inhuman and degrading treatment or punishment contrary to international human rights law. He recommended that offshore processing be terminated, all regional processing centres in Nauru and Papua New Guinea be closed, and refugees and asylum-seekers be returned to Australia.[171]

Meanwhile the Supreme Court of Papua New Guinea found in 2016 that the detention of asylum-seekers was in breach of human rights and unconstitutional.[172] As a consequence, the Manus Island detention facility was closed and those detained there were transferred to Port Moresby.

By March 2019, all asylum-seekers and refugees had left the Nauru detention facility and were moved to the Nauruan community.[173] By the end of the following year, 900 refugees had been resettled from the islands, most to the United States.[174] As of April 2021, over 1,000 persons had been transferred to Australia.[175]

At the beginning of 2021, more than 200 of these transferred persons remained in immigration detention facilities in Australia, while others with specific vulnerabilities were permitted to reside in community detention subject to curfews and other restrictions. Others have been given temporary processing visas called bridging visas.[176] The Government maintains the position that they will not be permanently settled in Australia.

Refugees who arrived by boat who were not subject to offshore transfer arrangements were granted temporary protection visas of three- or five-year duration. While permitted to work, they are not entitled to family reunification and must periodically re-apply for the visa to remain in Australia.[177]

Extremely limited possibilities of a durable solution in Australia, thus, remain for any refugee arriving without prior authorization.

United States

Interdiction and offshore processing measures have also been used by the United States in the Caribbean. Beginning in the late 1970s and early 1980s, the number of Haitians arriving in the United States rose significantly. Growing poverty and human rights violations under the regime of Jean Claude

"Baby Doc" Duvalier contributed to the exodus.[178] American efforts to deter further arrivals, through detention and summary removals were successfully challenged in the Courts. In 1981, the Government turned to interdiction.[179]

Ships suspected of carrying unauthorized migrants or asylum-seekers to the United States were stopped by the United States Coast Guard. The provision for summary protection screening, the "manifestation of fear" test, depended on the country of origin. Cubans were asked if they had a credible fear, Haitians and other nationalities were not.[180] Eventually, United States asylum determinations were conducted at the naval base in Guantanamo Bay or sent for processing to countries in the region who had an agreement with the United States and the interception occurred in their territorial waters. While these agreements may have provisions for protection from refoulement, UNHCR and others have expressed concern about the absence of monitoring to ensure compliance.[181]

The Guantanamo facility continues to be in use. Those found in need of international protection are eligible for resettlement but not within the United States.[182] The asylum procedure there has been criticized for failing to provide access to legal counsel and the right to appeal a negative decision, having high rejection rates, and not providing residence in the United States for those found to be refugees.[183]

The Supreme Court of the United States has found the return practices at sea to be lawful. In the 1993 case of *Sale*, the Court held that non-refoulement obligations only apply to those within the territory of the United States and not to those on the high seas, even if under the control of the United States.[184] This reasoning has since been rejected in other jurisdictions, including by the Inter American Commission on Human Rights, the Court of Appeal (England and Wales) and the European Court of Human Rights.[185] The decisions of these Courts stand for the principle that there is an "overarching duty to meet standards of fairness wherever there is an exercise of state power".[186]

Europe

The 2012 decision of the European Court of Human Rights involved a case brought against Italy by several applicants from Eritrea and Somalia. They were on boats trying to reach Italy when interdicted by Italian authorities and returned to Libya.[187] The applicants claimed that they were returned to a country where they were at risk of serious harm, in contravention of the European Convention on Human Rights (ECHR), which protects against being subjected to torture, inhuman or degrading treatment.[188]

The Court found that the applicants were within the control of Italy, and therefore under its jurisdiction. It also ruled that they were at serious risk of harm in Libya due to the treatment meted out to migrants there and the lack of protection from refoulement. The Court concluded that Italy was in breach of the ECHR.[189]

The decision was important. It effectively prohibited European countries from interdicting ships and returning persons to countries where they would be at risk of torture or cruel, inhuman or degrading treatment or punishment.[190] However, it only applied to situations where States are directly exercising their control. States have sought to overcome this legal restriction by supporting other States to prevent the onward movement of asylum-seekers and un-authorized migrants. They externalize their responsibilities to others.

Externalization

Externalization policies generally involve wealthy countries providing financial incentives and support to other countries to improve border controls, increase interdictions, and otherwise prevent migrants and asylum-seekers from moving onward. This leaves many asylum-seekers in remote or dangerous places, exposed to grave human rights abuses and without an opportunity to have their claims appropriately assessed.[191]

The United States has long undertaken joint exercises with the Mexican authorities to stem the flow of migrants and asylum-seekers to the United States. It has provided billions of dollars to combat the smuggling and trafficking of people and drugs and to address root causes through improving security, good governance and economic growth across Central America and Mexico.[192] For over a decade, Australia has provided resources and trained personnel to work with Sri Lanka to prevent migrants or asylum-seekers from travelling to Australia.[193]

The European maritime States and the European Union (EU) have invested heavily in border controls in Greece[194] as well as in North Africa.[195] In 2003, Spain provided close to $400 million in aid and debt relief to Morocco in return for improved border control efforts,[196] and a further $37 million in 2021.[197] Since 2007, Morocco is reported to have received some €13 billion in development funds from the European Union also connected to tighter border controls.[198] In 2010, Italy committed $5 billion over 20 years to help Libya secure borders against the onward movement of refugees and migrants.[199]

Such efforts have picked up pace in the last decade. In 2016, the EU struck a deal with Turkey to stem arrivals of refugees and migrants travelling irregularly through and from Turkey to Greece. The European Union agreed to provide €6 billion managed by the EU Facility for Refugees in Turkey,[200] relax visa requirements for Turkish citizens, upgrade the customs union, and accelerate negotiations over Turkey's admission into the EU. The European Union also agreed to increase resettlement to the EU of Syrians residing in Turkey. In exchange, Turkey would deter asylum-seekers from entering Europe and would receive back from Greece asylum-seekers who had crossed irregularly by sea to the Greek islands from Turkey.[201]

UNHCR expressed concern regarding the apparent lack of protection safeguards. It noted that an asylum-seeker should only be returned to a third State if the country assumes responsibility for determining the claim in accordance with international standards, including respect for non-refoulement and affords those recognized full and effective access to education, work, health care and, as necessary, social assistance.[202] Turkey has not lifted the geographical restrictions of the 1951 Refugee Convention, and so does not recognize non-Europeans as qualifying for refugee status.[203] Thus, one of the consequences of the EU/Turkey agreement is that people who could be recognized as refugees under the 1951 Refugee Convention within the EU could be returned to a country where that status would not apply.

Within three years of the EU-Turkey arrangement, €3 billion were committed to projects within Turkey, and numbers of arrivals through Turkey to Europe decreased by 88 per cent.[204] The number of asylum-seekers sent back to Turkey, however, were relatively small as were the number of Syrians resettled from Turkey to the European Union.[205] Meanwhile there was little progress on the EU's other commitments towards Turkey and differences arose concerning the speed and manner of the payments.[206] Nonetheless, by and large, the agreement has had the desired effect for the EU, measured in the decrease in the arrival of asylum-seekers and migrants travelling unauthorized to the European Union across the Eastern Mediterranean Sea.[207]

Efforts have also been taken to deter the number of arrivals to the EU through the Central and Western Mediterranean routes.[208] These include support to the main countries of embarkation in North Africa including Algeria, Egypt, Libya, Morocco and Tunisia.[209]

Libya has long been a destination country for migrant workers.[210] During the regime of Muammar Ghaddafi, the use of Libya as a transit country to Europe was largely curtailed, including with support of the Italian Government.[211] The dynamic changed with the fall of Ghaddafi, and the fragmentation of the country into areas controlled by the Tripoli-based Government of National Unity (GNU) and those under various militia groups. Human smuggling, trafficking and extortion became revenue sources for rival militias and other groups. The irregular movement of people crossing from Libya to Europe increased.[212]

The number of arrivals in Europe along Central and Western Mediterranean routes grew from some 65,000 persons in 2011 to nearly 189,600 in 2016, with most landing in Italy.[213] Between 2014 and 2016, Italy received close to half a million persons arriving by sea, straining its reception capacity and generating significant public concern.[214] An initial plan to relocate 160,000 asylum-seekers from Greece and Italy to European Union member States fell far short of its target. Only about 35,000 asylum-seekers were relocated over two years. Several countries refused to participate and both France and Switzerland closed their borders with Italy to prevent onward movement.[215]

To stem the flow to Europe, the EU and some if its member States took several initiatives. One aimed at discouraging sea arrivals through laws and policies that criminalized and reduced the search and rescue capacity of private vessels.[216] As a result, there has been a significant decline in rescues by private as well as commercial vessels since 2018, given concerns of criminal prosecution should shipmasters rescue and disembark migrants in a place of safety.[217]

Their concerns seem to be borne out, as some 50 administrative and criminal proceedings were initiated between 2018 and 2020 against crew or boats and vessels have been seized.[218] These measures have been taken over the objections of UNHCR and the International Organization for Migration (IOM), given the crucial role that ships and commercial vessels have played in saving lives at sea.[219]

In parallel, some European Union member States have progressively reduced their search and rescue operations and invested over €50 million in strengthening Libya's capacities to stop unauthorized departures,[220] interdict ships in its search and rescue region[221] and return refugees and migrants to Libya.[222] Turkey too has included support to the Libyan Coast Guard as part of its broader engagement and support to training the military forces in Libya.[223]

The return to Libya is of particular concern because of the grave and widespread human rights violations that refugees and migrants experience there: arbitrary detention for undefined periods of time; torture and physical abuse; rape and other forms of sexual violence; forced labour; forced recruitment; extortion; and trafficking.[224] Refugees and migrants who are interdicted at sea and returned to Libya are transferred to Government-run detention centres which, at the end of July 2021, held around 5,400 persons.[225] Overcrowding is endemic, with torture, rape, malnutrition and the spread of infectious diseases widely reported.[226]

United Nations institutions and human rights organizations have repeatedly called for refugees and migrants not to be returned to Libya.[227] The United Nations has called for the immediate release of all refugees and migrants arbitrarily detained and for Libya to only detain persons in exceptional circumstances and subject to due process guarantees.[228]

The elaborate measures to stop unauthorized migration have been of limited effect. They have temporarily reduced arrivals at certain ports while also leading smugglers and traffickers to find alternative and often more dangerous routes.[229] So, while the number of arrivals across the Central Mediterranean to Italy and Malta declined from over 181,000 in 2016 to about 11,500 in 2019, they increased again to some 34,200 arrivals in 2020 with 955 persons reported lost at sea.[230]

As interdictions were increasing along the Central Mediterranean route, arrivals in Spain along the Western Mediterranean and the Western African routes increased from close to 8,200 persons in 2016, to some 58,600 persons in 2018.[231] To curb these flows, the EU and the Spanish Government provided additional support to Morocco to reinforce its border controls. This helped reduce the flow by almost 50 per cent in 2019 but was followed by an over eight-fold increase in arrivals to Spain's Canary Islands in 2020.[232] In 2020, 23,000 refugees and migrants landed there, departing on boats from northwest Africa and transported across the more dangerous Atlantic Ocean route. At least 480 individuals are reported to have died or gone missing in 2020 in their attempt to reach Europe through this route.[233]

Among the reasons for the relatively high volume of sea crossings are the deteriorating security situations in the Sahel, the Lake Chad Basin, the Tigray region in Ethiopia, and parts of Sudan. Many of the countries in these regions and their neighbours host millions of refugees and internally displaced persons. Yet, the burdens they bear in responding to forced displacement, and the dire circumstances that many of their populations and forcibly displaced persons face, are not as prominent in the public eye. It is the relatively small number who seek to move to Europe that capture most media and political attention.

The dangers experienced by refugees and migrants in their journeys to Europe are not confined to the last leg by sea. Well before that, all along the land routes from Sub-Saharan Africa to and through North Africa, many are subject to gross human rights violations, and transported without adequate food and water, at the cost of many lives.[234]

A more comprehensive approach is needed. This is recognized in both the Global Compact on Refugees and the Global Compact for Safe, Orderly and Regular Migration. Alternative legal pathways for migration are needed.[235] Greater efforts should be made to identify and prosecute the human traffickers that inflict so much misery on desperate people and to end impunity of collaborating State officials.[236] This must be complemented by concerted efforts to address the root causes of those who are forced to flee. It is a task far beyond the capacities of humanitarian organizations working along these routes to identify those with international protection needs, reunite families, ensure assistance to survivors of abuse, and advocate for more legal migration pathways.

Nothing short of State-led long-term efforts that reach far beyond interdiction are required.

Other deterrence measures

Many States go beyond limiting access to their asylum systems, including built-in deterrents in their design. The mandatory detention of asylum-seekers has been more widely used in the last 20 years.[237] Rights may also be limited to levels below the standards of the 1951 Convention.

Restrictive interpretations of the 1951 Refugee Convention also constitute obstacles for those in need of international protection. In Japan and the Republic of Korea, for example, recognition rates are the lowest of the 38 countries within the Organization for Economic Cooperation and Development.[238] In Japan, they average less than 1 per cent and, in South Korea, they are around 2 per cent,[239] compared to global averages of around 30 per cent.[240] Both countries have other measures for permission to remain applicable to asylum-seekers from certain countries. But these are temporary, can be easily withdrawn and are without attendant 1951 Refugee Convention rights.[241]

Recognition rates in Europe are also inconsistent, despite efforts to achieve a high-level of harmonization and compliance with international standards.[242] In 2020, for example, the percentage of Afghan asylum-seekers that were determined in need of protection ranged from 0 per cent in Bulgaria to 56 per cent in Sweden and 87 per cent in Germany. For Turkish nationals, the range was similarly stark – from 1 per cent in Bulgaria to 32 per cent in Germany and 52 per cent in Austria.[243] A report by the European Council on Refugees and Exiles (ECRE) concluded that addressing inconsistent decision-making across the EU should be a pressing priority.[244]

In March 2021, the United Kingdom put forward a legislative proposal which embodies many of the deterrence measures noted above. It was introduced to Parliament in July 2021 as the Nationality and Border Bill.[245] It aims not only to restrict access to asylum procedures, but also limit the ability of refugees to establish a claim and withholds some 1951 Convention rights from those found to be in need of international protection.

The Bill would enable the United Kingdom Border Force to stop and direct vessels out of territorial waters, including those carrying refugees and asylum-seekers. It would raise the threshold for establishing a well-founded fear of persecution, enable the removal of asylum-seekers pending the determination of their claims, and seek to establish offshore processing centres. It also proposes to penalize asylum-seekers who arrived without a visa, by only providing them with temporary status should their refugee claim be established. They would be denied the rights accorded under the 1951 Convention and be in constant risk of expulsion.[246]

UNHCR has provided extensive comments on the proposal, illustrating how its key provisions would be in violation of international law. While acknowledging the United Kingdom's contribution as a humanitarian donor, it has pointed out that this must be matched with a commensurate domestic asylum policy that abides by the letter and spirit of the 1951 Convention.[247]

Denmark has repeatedly indicated its wishes to emulate parts of the Australian model, the United States model and the EU-Turkey arrangement.[248] Although it has experienced historically low asylum applications, with some 1,400 made in 2020,[249] the Danish Government passed legislation in June 2021 which provides for the transfer of asylum-seekers to other countries outside the EU, leaving them to determine asylum claims and provide international protection to those in need.[250] In announcing the appointment of a Special Envoy for Migration to implement these reforms, the Acting Minister of Immigration, Kaare Dybvad Bek, said that Denmark wants "as few spontaneous asylum seekers as possible" in favour of helping refugees "faster and better in the surrounding areas".[251]

UNHCR has noted the various ways the plan does not comply with international law and is inconsistent with global solidarity and responsibility-sharing.[252] Given that it would shift responsibilities to other States, several potential receiving States in North Africa and the Middle East have reportedly rejected it.[253]

The Danish law and United Kingdom proposal are discouraging developments and bode ill for improved international cooperation in meeting current and future displacement challenges. These, and restrictive policies in high-income States more generally, send a powerful message to countries of far less means shouldering far more responsibilities. The international protection regime is severely weakened when countries that receive a small fraction of the world's forcibly displaced people do not take responsibility for those who arrive on their shores and, instead, take measures to shift responsibilities to others.

Measures to block the arrival of refugees and asylum-seekers are also expensive and neither address the root causes of forced displacement nor the shortcomings in national asylum systems.[254] More attention on the latter would help States manage mixed movements of refugees, asylum-seekers and migrants in ways that do not compromise protection or cooperation upon which the international protection system rests. This would also be in keeping with the provisions of the Global Compact on Refugees and the Global Compact for Safe, Orderly and Regular Migration which they have affirmed.

It is also the case that the larger the obstacles that States erect to prevent or deflect refugees, asylum-seekers and migrants, the greater the efforts of smugglers and traffickers to circumvent them and the higher the fees they charge to shepherd desperate people along ever more dangerous routes.

A combination of growing forced flight and increased barriers to stop it has transformed the human smuggling and trafficking model. As documented in the detailed account by Tinti and Reitano, what was once a "loose network of freelancers and ad hoc facilitators" is now overshadowed by professional transnational criminal networks with a great propensity to transform and innovate.[255] The higher the obstacles, the more work, contacts and money needed to overcome them – all resources that are beyond independent smugglers but well within the purview of organized criminal syndicates. The price is paid by refugees and migrants who depend on these criminal networks – and, in the worst cases, they pay with their lives.[256]

Other Forcibly Displaced People

Forced displacement is never limited to those who cross borders. Whatever the cause of flight, from conflict to the adverse effects of climate change[257] and disasters,[258] generally more people flee *within* their own country than out of it.[259]

This was very much the case during WWII, when resolving the situations of many millions of internally displaced persons and refugees was part of the work of international agencies established at that time. Yet, the 1951 Convention applied only to refugees.

Phil Orchard and others have noted, in some respects, this was a departure from previous international arrangements and practices in the inter-war period set up to respond to specific displacement situations.[260] As discussed in Part I, these efforts focused on assisting specific groups of forcibly displaced persons who lacked the protection of their country. They did not necessarily specify whether they were displaced within their own countries or outside of them.[261] The prospective scope of State obligations was a matter of debate in the meetings leading up to the adoption of the 1951 Convention. Some States supported a more expansive vision, extending protection and assistance to persons displaced within and outside their countries. The prevailing view, however, was that the Convention should be designed for those who did not have a State to protect them. The focus was on the need for *international legal protection* rather than assistance and for persons forcibly displaced *outside* their countries.[262]

The United States argued strongly for this more limited focus. Having been the principal donor of previous refugee relief operations, it was unwilling to assume disproportionate and expanding obligations. Eleanor Roosevelt, a member of the United States delegation, cautioned against "an increasing tendency to drive the UN into the field of international relief and to use its organs as the source and center of expanding appeals for relief funds".[263]

Internally displaced persons were neither included as part of the 1951 Convention nor specifically mentioned in UNHCR's Statute. Yet provisions in the Statute enable the Office to engage in "additional activities" authorized by the General Assembly and "within the limits" of available resources.[264] On this basis, UNHCR engaged in work on behalf of internally displaced persons, initially through specific requests made by the General Assembly and in later years through the annual General Assembly resolutions on the work of the Office.[265]

However, this operational mechanism was no substitute for more predictable and resourced engagement. The limits of UNHCR's abilities were more evident as the global number of forcibly displaced grew from the 1980s. UNHCR struggled to meet the needs of refugees, as part of its core mandate, and was not sufficiently resourced to extend substantial additional efforts on behalf of internally displaced persons.[266]

In 1981, the General Assembly called for a thorough review of the international community's ability to respond effectively to humanitarian crises.[267] In the same year, Prince Sadruddin Aga Khan, Special Rapporteur of the United Nations Human Rights Commission, issued a report on human rights and mass exoduses. In it he highlighted the growing scale of forced displacement including "movements within countries" and the need for a more systematic response.[268]

Two years later, in 1983, he helped establish an Independent Commission on International Humanitarian Issues to review and propose solutions to pressing humanitarian challenges. The findings of the Commission were published in 1988.[269]

In regard to forced displacement, it noted that, while the number of refugees in the world exceeded 13 million people, there were "tens of millions of other uprooted people" who were not sufficiently represented or assisted. This included those who were forced to flee *within* their own countries due to government repression, forced relocation, communal violence or environmental disasters.

The Commission observed that governments fail to protect and assist their own displaced populations either because they are complicit in the displacements or because they lack the capacity to prevent and respond. It recommended that international standards of treatment be established for "those groups of uprooted persons who do not clearly fall within the category of refugees" and a more predictable means be established for ensuring assistance to them.[270]

It would take another decade before such standards were developed.[271] It was, in part, spurred by efforts to improve the United Nation's responses to humanitarian crises more generally. In 1990, the Economic and Social Council (ECOSOC) asked the Secretary-General to conduct a system-wide review and assess the experience and capacity of organizations assisting refugees, internally displaced persons and returnees.[272] Several developments came from that review.

One was the creation of the Department of Humanitarian Affairs, which would later become the present-day Office for the Coordination of Humanitarian Affairs (OCHA). It is headed by an Emergency Relief Coordinator (ERC) reporting to the Secretary-General. The ERC also chairs the Inter-Agency Standing Committee (IASC), which was created by the UN General Assembly in 1991 as a high-level humanitarian coordination forum of United Nations and non-United Nations organizations. In internal displacement situations, the ERC, with support from OCHA and the IASC, coordinates the inter-agency efforts.[273]

Another outcome from the system-wide review was the appointment of the first Representative of the United Nations Secretary-General on the Human Rights of Internally Displaced Persons.[274] Francis Deng initially held the position and one of his first tasks was to conduct a comprehensive and consultative assessment of the scope of the problem, international and institutional responses, and the international law standards applicable to internal displacement situations.

Regarding legal standards, he concluded that a universally applicable body of principles was required to address the specific needs of internally displaced persons that drew from existing human rights and humanitarian law.[275] This was endorsed by the Human Rights Commission and the United Nations General Assembly, and development of The Guiding Principles on Internal Displacement followed.[276]

Guiding Principles on Internal Displacement

The Guiding Principles apply to the different phases of displacement: "providing protection against arbitrary displacement, access to protection and assis-

tance during displacement and guarantees during return or alternative settlement and reintegration".[277] They concern all who are forcibly displaced, whether due to "armed conflict, situations of generalized violence, violations of human rights or natural or human-made disasters".[278] A person can be considered an internally displaced person without having to show persecution on an individual basis.

The Guiding Principles begin with acknowledging that internally displaced persons are entitled to enjoy the same rights as others in the country and to equal protection of the law. This includes the right to life, dignity, liberty and

Deng Awuol (centre), has been forced to flee three times in South Sudan and is pictured here in Mingkaman, South Sudan in 2014 with wife Nycot (centre right) and his children and grandchildren. © UNHCR/ Andrew McConnell

security of the person, and the right not to be arbitrarily arrested or detained. The Principles stipulate that internally displaced persons should not be confined to camps, unless absolutely necessary, and should be able to move freely and choose their place of residence.[279]

They also recognize the right of all people not to be arbitrarily displaced.[280] In situations where displacement may be necessary, the Principles provide that the authorities must first consider other alternatives. Where no other alternative exists, adverse effects must be minimized, and relocation conducted in safety. Except in emergency circumstances, free and informed consent must be sought and access to effective remedies provided.[281] The right to family unity is also part of the Guiding Principles as is an adequate standard of living. Authorities are to provide – at a minimum and without discrimination – food, accommodation, medical services and access to education and documentation necessary for the exercise of legal rights.[282]

The Guiding Principles were not adopted through an international treaty and so are not considered binding law. However, the drafters explained that they reflected the application of existing international humanitarian and human rights law to the particular circumstances of internal displacement. In effect, they were progressively developing the law in this context.[283]

Over time, the Guiding Principles achieved considerable legal effect. They form the basis for two treaties in Africa. One was adopted in 2006 in the Great Lakes Region, obliging its members to implement the Guiding Principles.[284] The other – the African Union Convention for the Protection and Assistance of Internally Displaced Persons in Africa (Kampala Convention) – was adopted in 2009.[285]

The Guiding Principles were affirmed by States in the 2005 World Summit, which set future directions to improve international, humanitarian and security efforts.[286] The Security Council, General Assembly and Human Rights Council have also recognized their legal relevance.[287] Similar affirmations have been made in regional bodies, such as the Council of Europe and the Organization of American States.[288]

When they initially were adopted, the Guiding Principles were seen as applying existing norms in international law to the particular circumstances of internally displaced persons. Some have since suggested that, over time, they have also helped to further advance international law. For example, prior to the Guiding Principles, there was no recognized legal obligation of States to establish conditions which allow internally displaced persons to return voluntarily and safely to their former place of residence. Yet as one legal scholar has

Kampala Convention

as of 28 September 2021

States parties to the 2009 AU Convention for the Protection
and Assistance of Internally Displaced Persons in Africa
and / or the 2006 International Conference on the Great Lakes Region Protocol
on the Protection and Assistance to Internally Displaced Persons

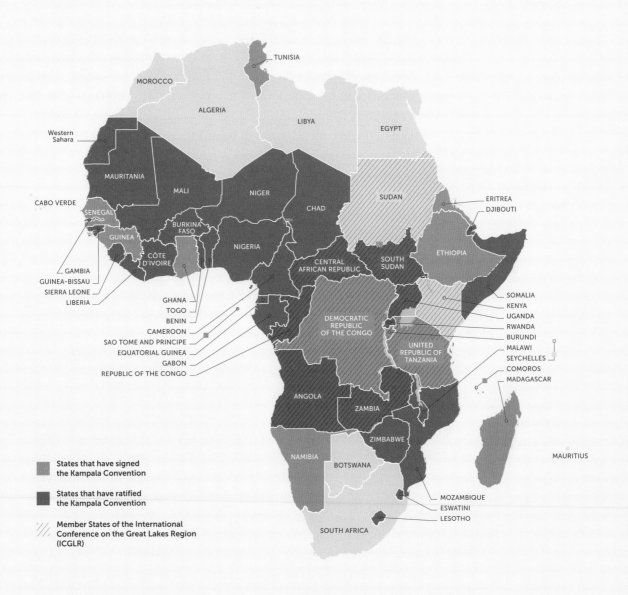

States that have signed
the Kampala Convention

States that have ratified
the Kampala Convention

Member States of the International
Conference on the Great Lakes Region
(ICGLR)

International boundary

Undetermined
international boundary

Abyei region

Administrative line

500 km

Sources: UNCS, UNHCR

observed, this responsibility, set out in Principle 28, has since been invoked by leading human rights treaty bodies in interpreting the scope of State obligations under the treaties they review. This suggests that the soft law provision is becoming hardened as the law on internal displacement develops.[289]

It has also been suggested that the Guiding Principles introduced the notion of "sovereignty as responsibility", for they recognize the primary duty and responsibility of national authorities for protecting internally displaced persons and the obligation to facilitate, and not arbitrarily inhibit, humanitarian assistance to them.[290] This responsibility is reflected in the Responsibility to Protect (R2P) principle, which is a global commitment to prevent civilian populations from genocide, war crimes, ethnic cleansing and crimes against humanity. It recognizes the right of the Security Council to permit the international community to take collective action when peaceful means have not proved effective in leading national authorities to protect their populations. It emerged following the failure of the international community to adequately respond to mass atrocities committed in Rwanda and in the former Yugoslavia during the 1990s. R2P was affirmed by all States at the United Nations World Summit in 2005.[291]

National practice

Like the refugee protection frameworks, implementation of the Guiding Principles on Internal Displacement is uneven. States that have laws and/or policies addressing internal displacement have varied records in their application. In some countries, the laws or policies themselves can be a limiting factor, including in circumstances where internally displaced persons are defined narrowly,[292] or where return is promoted as the preferred solution even in contexts where other solutions may be more desirable and attainable.[293]

Sometimes, the law meets international standards[294] but the commitment to implement it is weak. Commitments made during peace processes, for example, are not consistently met.[295] When displaced communities return to areas where their rights are not protected, this can lead to further instability and displacement.[296]

Other challenges in implementation include a lack of institutional capacity, including insufficient human and financial resources. The continuation or resumption of conflict can further exacerbate these challenges, as can situations where internally displaced persons are located in hard-to-reach places.[297] This makes efforts to implement strong policies in conflict-ridden and fragile States challenging and not necessarily due to a lack of government commitment. And, while implementation is often challenging, strong policies can provide an important foundation for humanitarian and development work, including strengthening State capacity over the longer-term.

Where there is political will and capacity, internal displacement situations have an improved chance of resolution. Political commitment and international support helped to ensure the sustainability of returns in Liberia and Sierra Leone when peace was achieved in the early 2000s.[298] Courts have played an important role in holding Governments to account for the internal displacement laws and policies they pass, many informed by the Guiding Principles.[299]

Similarly, national human rights institutions also exert influence. These are State-mandated institutions, independent of the government, with broad mandates for the protection of human rights. As documented in 2019 by the United Nations Special Rapporteur on the Rights of Internally Displaced Persons, such institutions have advanced the rights of internally displaced persons consistent with the Guiding Principles in several ways. This includes contributing to the drafting of relevant legislation and policy, monitoring and investigating the situation of internally displaced persons, providing legal assistance, issuing legal advisories and conducting trainings and awareness-raising activities.[300]

For national policies to be effective, local support is needed. Afghanistan is a case in point. In 2013, it adopted a well-articulated national policy for the return, local integration and settlement elsewhere in the country of internally displaced persons.[301] But, local opposition on issues of land rights prevented it from succeeding.[302] Niger, in contrast, adopted a national internal displacement law in 2018, developed through broad consultation involving national and local authorities, internally displaced persons and national and international experts. The passage of the law was swiftly followed by Government directives and targeted trainings to ensure implementation.[303]

These examples illustrate that, while national laws and frameworks are important steps, successful implementation depends on many factors. Government resistance to full implementation can be an insurmountable obstacle. But even when the national government is committed to respond well to internally displaced persons and to resolve situations of internal displacement, local and international support is often needed to help overcome challenges in implementation.

International coordination

There is no single United Nations agency with responsibilities and accountabilities towards internally displaced persons. Whether there should be is an issue that has been discussed many times over the years and as part of the 1990 system-wide review discussed earlier. The recommendation was that there not be a single body whose mandate would be extended to provide protection and/or assistance to internally displaced persons but that each relevant United Nations entity be responsible for the "part for which it has the best expertise" under the overall coordination of what became the Emergency Relief Coordinator (ERC).[304]

Despite the creation of the ERC and IASC, improving responses for internally displaced persons continued to be a concern the next decade. In 2005, the IASC designed the Cluster Approach to improve humanitarian coordination and delivery in internal displacement and other non-refugee humanitarian contexts. This approach has designated United Nations agencies responsible for coordinating responses in areas of their specific expertise, such as protection, food, shelter, logistics, water and sanitation in a more predictable manner. Since then, various evaluations on both the Cluster Approach and internal displacement responses point to some improvements as well as some ongoing weaknesses.[305]

On the positive side, inter-agency efforts have reduced duplication, clarified roles and responsibilities, and brought greater consistency to funding appeals. However, there are ongoing problems of leadership. There are also difficulties with strengthening national capacity, coordination, coverage and funding, while visibility of the needs of internally displaced persons and advocacy on their behalf is also insufficient.[306]

Overall, United Nations agencies have not systematically and predictably included internally displaced persons in their country operations or been adequately resourced to do so. Studies have also pointed to insufficient international efforts (development and humanitarian) to strengthen national capacities to prevent displacement, respond fully to the needs of internally displaced persons and provide solutions.[307]

In 2019, at the request of member States, the United Nations Secretary-General appointed a High-Level Panel on Internal Displacement, to focus primarily on addressing protracted situations and achieving durable solutions for internally displaced persons. The Panel issued its recommendations in September 2021. It called for greater State accountability to adopt and implement laws and policies on internal displacement, to prioritize support to their displaced citizens and to integrate internal displacement into national and local development plans.[308]

The Panel stressed the importance of engaging all relevant stakeholders including States, internally displaced persons, local communities, civil society, media, academia, private sector, international agencies, and financial institutions. It called for more regional mechanisms to improve responses to internal displacement. The Panel also made specific recommendations to encourage and support greater private sector contributions and for increased international financing to address internal displacement accompanied by greater investments in data and evidence. And to raise the level of commitment within the United Nations, the Panel recommended that work for internally displaced persons be mainstreamed throughout United Nations agencies and the United Nations Resident Coordinator at the country level. The panel also called upon the United Nations Secretary-General to appoint a Special Representative on Solutions to Internal Displacement and to report annually on positive developments and areas in need of improvement.[309]

Climate and Disaster Displacement Frameworks

Climate change and disasters have influenced human mobility throughout history.[310] Ice ages, as well as periods of warming climate and rising seas, have pushed people to move dating back tens of thousands of years.[311] Climate change has also been a pull factor – drawing people to places with favourable conditions, greater access to water, forests, grazing areas and/or more arable land.[312] These migrations may be permanent or temporary seasonal movements.

Some events, such as drought, desertification and rising sea levels, develop slowly. Others strike suddenly, including earthquakes, volcanic eruptions, or flash floods. These events are classed as disasters when they seriously disrupt the functioning of a community, overwhelming its ability to respond and to prevent loss of life or material, economic and environmental harm.[313]

Not all disasters are caused by climate change but warming temperatures are increasing the frequency and intensity of heat waves, droughts and associated wildfires, heavy rain, tropical cyclones and coastal flooding.[314] In 2020, internal displacement figures indicate that 30 million people were forced from their homes due to weather-related hazards, such as storms and floods and close to 0.7 million were displaced by geophysical hazards, such as volcanoes and earthquakes.[315] There were 11.2 million people newly displaced by conflict, that year, internally and externally.[316]

Scholars have examined the influence of climate on human mobility since the early 19th century. This focus was largely abandoned during most of the 20th century in favour of an emphasis on economic, political and social determinants.[317] As the effects of global warming became more of a concern in the 1980s, its impact on human mobility came to the fore.[318]

In 1992, the United Nations Intergovernmental Panel on Climate Change (IPCC) made some sobering projections. It anticipated that millions of people would be "displaced by shoreline erosion, coastal flooding and severe drought". Many would flee to areas unable to meet their needs, leading to "social instability in some areas". Health systems could be overwhelmed and epidemics could

Flood-affected people moving in Badin District, Sindh, Pakistan in September 2011.
© UNHCR/ Sam Phelps

"sweep through refugee camps and settlements, spilling over into surrounding communities".[319]

A few years later, Norman Myers, an Oxford environmental scientist, predicted that approximately 150 million "environmental refugees" would "rank as one of the foremost human crises of our times".[320] Other scholars, non-governmental organizations and advocacy groups, also predicted dire consequences of climate change on displacement.[321] Then, as now, water metaphors became common, with forecasts of "waves", "streams", "tides" and "floods" of migrants fleeing the adverse effects of climate change and disasters.[322]

They were not the only voices. Other academics questioned the foundations for these projections and analyses. They pointed to various factors that contribute to the decision to move. They raised the need to consider both the positive "pull" factors associated with climate change that lead people to settle in new locations as well as the "push" factors that compel displacement.[323]

In the past decade, this field of research has grown considerably and, with that, a more nuanced view of how climate change and disasters affect displacement. There is general agreement that people who move in the context of climate change and disasters often do so for a mix of reasons. As in conflict displacement, climate- and disaster-related displacement can be induced not just by the harm feared but by the absence of protection from it. Economic, family, social and political considerations can also determine when and where people move. Poor resource management, the absence of adaptation strategies, weak governance, violence and war can also contribute.[324]

Climate, displacement and development

Changes in climate affect mobility in various ways. Rising temperatures can lead to parched agricultural land, increased ocean acidity and receding freshwater lakes. Combined with other factors, such as overpopulation, poor resource management and conflict, they affect livelihoods and food security as agricultural yields fall, grazing fields diminish, and fish stocks decline. This hits poor and vulnerable populations particularly hard. Their livelihoods often depend on the threatened ecosystem and they tend to have few opportunities to adapt locally or move away from the risk.[325]

For example, Lake Chad has long been a source of water, food and income for the countries that border it: Cameroon; Chad; Niger; and Nigeria. As a result of climate change (drought and decreasing levels of water inflow from rivers and rainfall) and water mismanagement (increased extraction of water for irrigation), Lake Chad shrank by 90 per cent during the 1970s and 1980s. The region continues to be heavily affected by extreme and unpredictable climate events. The effects have been dire: loss of food sources and income-generating opportunities through fishing, agriculture and livestock farming on surrounding pastures. The dramatic decline in these resources amidst growing population pressures has contributed to instability, conflicts, and displacement, often to urban centres in the region.[326]

Climate warming – which is causing glacial melt and rising seas – threatens coastal cities and especially small island developing states (SIDS).[327] These effects will continue to worsen and be among the drivers of displacement without accelerated action to reduce greenhouse gas emissions and robust develop- ment planning at the national level.[328]

That is a central finding of the World Bank's updated Groundswell report, that examines the potential scale of internal climate migration patterns and movements to help countries plan and prepare. It builds on a previous Ground-swell report published in 2018.[329] Using the same modelling process, the report looks at likely shifts in population within countries across six regions – East Asia and the Pacific; Eastern Europe and Central Asia; Latin America; Middle East and North Africa; Sub-Saharan Africa; and South Asia – using demographic, socioeconomic and climate impact data.

The combined findings are that by 2050, as many as 216 million people – or around 3 per cent of the projected population of these regions – could be

Nigerian refugee, Hawali Oumar, fishes Lake Chad in 2016. He fled to Chad with his family after his father was killed by Boko Haram.
© UNHCR/ Oualid Khelif

forced to move within their own countries due to the slow-onset impacts of climate change.[330] Importantly, this number could be as much as 60–80 per cent lower if greenhouse gas emissions are reduced over the next two decades and countries immediately adopt adaptation strategies as part of their green, inclusive development planning.[331]

The link between climate change and *development* is clear. Most of the adverse impacts of climate change will be on poor and vulnerable popula-tions, including those whose livelihoods depend on "rain-fed agricultural, pastoral, forest, and coastal resources" as well as people in SIDS.[332] The fundamental link between climate change and development is recognized in the Sustainable Development Goals. One of the goals calls for "urgent action to combat climate change and its impacts". Related targets include improving resilience and adaptation strategies and supporting developing countries and small island states.[333]

Climate, conflict and sustaining peace

In politics, the press and public debate, it is commonly assumed that climate change provokes conflict and will be a major driver in increased forced displacement of the future. In a world of diminishing natural resources needed to sustain life, it is believed that competition for those resources will become increasingly violent, leading to ever larger numbers of persons to seek safety elsewhere.

Recent evidence on climate as a cause of conflict displacement paints a more nuanced picture.[334] While there are links between the adverse effects of climate change and conflict, they are not as direct or inevitable as widely assumed. They very much depend on context. Most research suggests that climate change aggravates, rather than causes, existing tensions.[335]

Countries that can mitigate the risks of climate change and support affected populations to adapt are more likely to avert clashes over diminishing resources. Unfortunately, the ones that are the least able to respond in this way are among the countries that are most immediately and severely affected. Many of these countries are also scenes of prolonged conflict, which further weakens the foundations needed to adapt: "institutions, essential services, infrastructure and governance".[336]

In Somalia, a 40-year period of conflict has limited the ability of authorities to manage natural resources protectively, invest in adaptation strategies and respond to sudden onset disasters.[337] That left parts of the country more vulnerable to a drought in 2010 and 2011, which affected much of the Horn of Africa. It led to water shortages, crop failures, harm to livestock, a fall in the demand for labour and increased local prices for food.[338] Hardships were exacerbated in areas of southern and central Somalia under Al-Shabaab control.

Rules imposed by Al-Shabaab intensified the hardships brought on by the drought: maintaining taxes, preventing people from travelling to receive humanitarian assistance, forcing people to move to areas under their control and restricting access to international humanitarian aid.[339] Over 160,000 Somalis fled to Kenya and over 100,000 to Ethiopia in 2011.[340] The drought, conflict and coercive policies of Al-Shabaab cumulatively contributed to mass displacement.[341]

The failure of governments to address the impact that climate change is having on their communities, or mitigation measures that favour one group over others, can fuel tensions and lead to escalating violence. Disaffection with government responses, coupled with loss of livelihoods, and limited opportunities can drive people into membership of militant groups.[342] Large areas of Africa illustrate these conditions. Pastoral livelihoods sustain over 268 million people across this region and have been under threat for decades. Pastoralists face government neglect and discrimination, insecure land rights and access to grazing lands, population pressures and poor natural resource policies.[343]

Changing weather patterns and more frequent droughts contribute to multiple knock-on effects such as diminished access to water, land degradation and rising incidence of diseases among livestock. Declining incomes, increased competition over natural resources, combined with decades of neglect and exclusion, has contributed to more frequent violence, crime, growing poverty and displacement.[344]

The Security Council has emphasized that sustained peace requires such root causes of conflict to be addressed, and for security-focused risk management strategies to include the adverse effects of climate change.[345] From a forced displacement perspective, this link is an important development affecting measures for conflict prevention and de-escalation. Advocates also hope to see climate mitigation and adaptation measures form part of future peace processes.[346]

It is also widely understood that mitigating the displacement risks associated with climate change and disasters requires a multilayered approach. *Risk mitigation* must be part of the response, for example through lowering greenhouse gases and improving resource management.

Strengthening adaptation capacities is also essential so people can remain in their areas where possible and not be compelled to leave. This can be supported through such measures as investing in human capital to facilitate diversified livelihoods and ensuring social safety nets for the most vulnerable groups. Improving infrastructure can also be important especially in urban areas that are likely to receive increased migration. In situations where local adaptation is not an option, enacting laws and policies to enable safe and dignified migration or planned relocation is necessary.[347]

Further, *engaging affected communities*, drawing on their adaptation strategies is important. Hindou Oumarou Ibrahim, an environmental activist from a pastoralist community in Chad described how indigenous communities' traditional knowledge can help. "My people don't have access to the internet, the radio, or television," she said, but they know how to interpret the signs in nature, "where the size of the fruit, the flowers, or the bird migrations, or our own cattle can tell us the information we need to find a safe place, to find food, to migrate from one place to another one".[348]

The Government of Fiji has developed planned relocation guidelines in close consultation with communities that need to move in response to climate change-related risks as well as environmental degradation, population pressures and poverty.[349] A Project Manager for a village relocation described how valuable the guidelines are, without which he would be lost: "It's like a map to help us get to the end of the process".[350]

Importantly, as many contend, the costs of mitigation and adaptation strategies should not rest on the States most affected but on those States that have been the major source of carbon emissions. This should not be seen as discretionary but rather "a responsibility of States to help prevent, reduce and remedy the dramatic externalities produced by their actions".[351]

Risk mitigation and adaptation frameworks

From 1992 to 1993, 166 States signed the United Nations Framework Convention on Climate Change (UNFCCC), which came into force in 1994.[352] Its aim is to stabilize greenhouse gas emissions, with the onus on industrialized countries, their primary source. Industrialized countries also agreed to share technology and provide additional financial support to developing countries for their risk mitigation and adaptation strategies.[353] In 2017, a dedicated UNFCCC Task Force on Displacement (TFD) was established to support States in averting, minimizing and addressing displacement in the context of climate change.[354]

The 2015 non-binding Sendai Framework on Disaster Risk Reduction focuses on sudden onset disasters.[355] It aims to reduce the risks of disasters and the associated human and financial losses over 15 years. States agree to track losses over time and mitigate them through early warning systems and measures to safeguard productive assets and critical infrastructure as well as to prevent, minimize and address displacement.

Progress is assessed through national annual voluntary reporting. While national reporting has improved over the past five years, it is often partial.[356] Reporting on the number of lives lost due to disasters is fairly common with relatively few States reporting on the economic and infrastructure losses incurred as a result of disasters. There is also no indicator under the Sendai Framework for reporting on displacement. Improving data capacities and including indicators for displacement would help improve policy measures.[357]

The Global Compact for Safe, Orderly and Regular Migration notes the importance of the work of the UNFCCC Task Force on Displacement and the Sendai Framework. It also includes objectives and actions for mitigating and responding to forced displacement in the context of sudden and slow onset events related to climate change and disasters. These include improving preparedness and adaptation strategies, regional cooperation and admission and stay arrangements for those displaced externally.[358]

Cross-border protection

The vast majority of climate-related displacement is internal displacement and is likely to remain so. Protections for internally displaced persons are discussed above under the Guiding Principles. For those who are displaced across borders due to the adverse effects of climate change and/or disasters, several international and regional frameworks may be applicable. The 1951 Refugee Convention and 1967 Protocol may offer international refugee protection in some circumstances. This largely depends on whether those who have fled face a prospective risk of persecution based on one of the 1951 Convention grounds should they be returned.[359] For example, Somali refugees who fled areas under Al-Shabaab control during the 2011 famine could fall within the 1951 Convention as refugees. They faced serious risks of persecution by Al-Shabaab had they returned, risks from which the Somali State could not protect them.

Refugees from parts of Somalia were recognized by Kenya and Ethiopia using the OAU Convention definition on a prima facie basis. These States recognized multiple serious risks facing the refugees – famine, conflict, violence, and the disruption of public order – risks against which the Somali Government was unable to provide protection.[360]

On face value, the OAU Convention and the Cartagena Declaration should also apply to situations where individuals flee events caused by the adverse effects of climate change or disaster "seriously disturbing public order" in either part or the whole of the country.[361] However, States have expressed concerns about the application in situations not affected by conflict and violence.[362] Academics, on the other hand, have argued that events "seriously disturbing public order" are not limited to human action and may include natural events.[363]

International human rights law also has provisions that can be a basis for international protection. These include the right to life, and the right not to be subjected to torture or to cruel, inhuman or degrading treatment or punishment.[364] These rights were recently invoked by a citizen of Kiribati in a complaint filed before the Human Rights Committee concerning the refusal of New Zealand to grant him refugee status.[365]

He based his claim on the grounds that he could not return to Kiribati because the effects of climate change and sea level rise threatened his life. The Human Rights Committee dismissed his claim on the basis that the risks to life were not imminent and there was time for mitigation measures to protect him. However, the Committee agreed that under international human rights law, a State could have a duty not to return a person in circumstances where environmental degradation caused an imminent risk to life.[366]

Regional free movement protocols can also be relevant in responding to forced displacement caused by climate change and disasters. For example, provisions within free movement agreements that form part of sub-regional economic integration schemes within the Americas have been used to facilitate entry and temporary residence of nationals from disaster-affected countries. In 2017, Trinidad and Tobago applied the Caribbean Community (CARICOM) free movement agreements to assist Dominicans affected by Hurricane Maria. Similar efforts were made by Antigua, Grenada, St. Lucia and St. Vincent within the Organization of Eastern Caribbean States' (OECS) free movement regime.[367]

In February 2020, the Intergovernmental Authority on Development (IGAD), comprised of eight member States in the Horn of Africa, unanimously endorsed the IGAD Free Movement Protocol.[368] Under this Protocol, citizens will be permitted to move to another member State in anticipation of a disaster, during it, or in its aftermath. They will be able to live and work for as long as return to their State of origin is not possible or reasonable.[369]

The Protocol is yet to be adopted by the IGAD Council of Ministers of Foreign Affairs, signed by IGAD Heads of State and incorporated into national laws and policies. Should these steps be taken, the Protocol has the potential to benefit all citizens from IGAD countries, including those frequently affected by drought, floods and environmental degradation. Other free movement agreements already exist in the Africa region, but those do not explicitly confer the right for persons to move to another country prior to a climate-induced disaster.[370]

Some have argued that existing international, regional and national mechanisms are important but insufficient. They are neither uniform in the degree of rights they afford, nor in the duration of protection they provide. Some advocates, therefore, have called for a new international agreement to protect those who have fled their countries due to the adverse effects of climate change and sudden or slow onset disasters.[371]

Most States have not embraced this idea.[372] Beyond the lack of State support, there are other reasons why a new protocol may not be practicable. These include the fact that the adverse effects of climate change and/or disasters are often not a sole driver of displacement and that national and regional responses may be more effective than international ones.[373]

Legal scholars have warned against using international treaties in response.[374] A dedicated international agreement may help to acknowledge a duty to accept those who must cross a border in some circumstances due to disaster. State reluctance to accept more international commitments makes an extensive treaty process a distraction, while compliance cannot be guaranteed. This argues for focusing on "more immediate, alternative and additional" migration and adaptation responses.[375]

These were among the considerations that led to the 2011 Nansen Conference on Climate Change and Displacement in the 21st Century. It grew into the Nansen Initiative on Disaster-Induced Cross-Border Displacement, which for several years worked to forge informed, consistent and effective State practice. The Initiative was chaired by the Governments of Norway and Switzerland with participation of government officials, affected populations, international organizations, academia and civil society groups.[376]

Its main achievement was the *2015 Agenda for the Protection of Cross-Border Displaced Persons in the Context of Disasters and Climate Change.*[377] Endorsed by 109 governments, it sets out policy options for governments to use in responding to displacement caused by disasters as well as the adverse effects of climate change. The Agenda focuses on three key objectives: improve data collection and knowledge; enhance humanitarian and migration measures for cross-border displacement; and strengthen risk management.[378]

In regard to addressing cross-border movements, the Agenda provides examples of promising practices from around the world, including humanitarian admission and stay programmes.[379] It also highlights how circular regular migration can provide an important means for income diversification and longer-term solutions for those confronting substantial losses of territory or livelihoods due to the adverse effects of climate change and/or disasters. The Agenda illustrates effective practices to plan relocation in a sustainable manner.[380]

The *Platform on Disaster Displacement (PDD)*[381] succeeded the Nansen Initiative in 2016. It continues the work to advance promising practices in the Agenda and is regarded as being a highly effective resource for States. Both the Nansen Initiative and the Platform on Disaster Displacement have been influential in the Americas. In 2016, Central and North American countries adopted a guide on protecting people who move externally in the context of disasters that was drafted by the Nansen Initiative.[382] It informed the related bilateral mechanisms agreed between Costa Rica and Panama to manage risks and respond to cross-border displacement.[383]

The South American Conference on Migration was similarly assisted in 2018 by the Platform and adopted its own non-binding "regional guidelines on protection and assistance of persons displaced across borders and migrants in countries affected by disasters of natural origin".[384] The Platform is also working in Asia and the Pacific to strengthen State capacities and share best practices.[385]

National laws have also been a source of protection for persons unable to return home in the aftermath of a disaster. As of 2015, at least 50 countries had received or refrained from returning individuals in the wake of tropical storms, flooding, drought, tsunamis and earthquakes.[386] The United States, for example, has provisions for affording temporary protection status to those who are unable to return home due to "an earthquake, flood, drought, epidemic or other environmental disaster".[387] The disaster must have disrupted living conditions, the home State must be temporarily unable to adequately handle the return of individuals and must have asked the United States to allow their citizens to remain.[388]

Several countries also have humanitarian and compassionate criteria for permitting foreigners to enter or remain in circumstances where they do not meet the formal criteria.[389] Canada has used such provisions for those affected by the "1998 Turkish earthquake, the 2004 Asian tsunami, the 2010 Haiti earthquake and the 2013 Typhoon Haiyan in the Philippines."[390] Similarly, following the devastation of Hurricane Mitch in 1998, several Central American States regularized the immigration status of affected migrants.[391]

The 2018 Global Compact on Migration calls for flexible "pathways for regular migration", including for people forced to migrate internationally due to sudden and slow-onset disasters. It also covers the adverse effects of climate change and environmental degradation "where adaptation in or return to their country of origin is not possible".[392] Migration avenues have already been used in these contexts. In the Pacific, for example, people affected by sudden- and slow-onset disasters have been helped to adapt through such migration pathways. Seasonal work programmes helped Pacific Islanders affected by the adverse effects of climate change to diversify their income and to send money back home. Australia and New Zealand have also granted work and education visas to Pacific Islanders, and New Zealand accepts several hundred annually as permanent residents.[393]

Trends Analysis

Strategies to mitigate and better respond to internal and external forced displacement, whether driven by conflict, climate or other disasters, depends in part on good trends analysis. Yet, tracing the trends in forced displacement over time is tricky, with difficulties relating to capacity, coordination, quality and frequency. A few are important to note here, in advance of a deeper review that follows in Part V.

Data on refugees is compiled biannually by UNHCR, drawing from its own registration data, information from its sectoral interventions and those of partners, and from States. The prime responsibility for collecting data on internal displacements rests with national authorities.[394] Yet, very few governments systematically collect and accurately report on their internally displaced populations.[395] In many cases, this is because they do not have the capacity. In some cases, it is also because they do not have the political will.[396]

Statistics provided by governments often only represent a partial dimension of the displaced population. This happens, for example, when governments define internally displaced persons narrowly: focusing on a specific group, within a specific time frame, or in a certain location.[397] Political motivations can inflate the number of forcibly displaced people, with the aim to seek ongoing international attention and assistance. Conversely, governments have been known to underrepresent their internal displacement statistics to deflect international attention, especially in circumstances where their actions are responsible for the displacement.[398]

Even when governments, international and national partner agencies do their best to present an accurate picture of forcibly displaced populations, data collection can be particularly challenging, especially in remote areas or situations of ongoing conflict. As well, forcibly displaced populations can be dispersed in rural or urban communities, not easily differentiated from local populations. Some may wish not to be identified, fearing harassment, discrimination or persecution.[399] They may also move from one displacement location to another, which makes it difficult to keep track.

Longitudinal data, collected from the same respondents over time, is infrequent and often not collected at all. This data can be especially important to identify larger trends and changes in individual circumstances over time.[400]

UNHCR updates its data on refugees through periodic verification exercises. But, by and large, most data on forcibly displaced persons is concentrated in the initial, emergency phase of displacement. The information helps in planning humanitarian responses and associated funding appeals needed to ensure the mobilization of urgent life-saving assistance. While this data is useful for the immediate response, its reliability diminishes over time. It can only capture the duration of displacement if regularly maintained.

The quality of data collected is also uneven. Data is not collected in a fully coordinated way nor using consistent methodologies to ensure it is reliable and comparable.[401] It is frequently not disaggregated to reveal specific needs and vulnerabilities or to enable comparisons with host and other populations.[402] As a result, it is not sufficient to fully inform policy options, decisions on resource allocation or to measure progress towards durable solutions.[403]

The research field further suffers from the absence of an agreed methodology for discerning causation. Surveys of populations forced to move, including in areas adversely affected by climate change and/or disasters, frequently cite livelihoods or conflict as the top drivers. Yet, as some researchers note, survey methodologies do not provide insight into possible multiple causes. Methodologies are needed to rank and better understand the different factors that influence people's decisions to move or trigger their displacement.[404]

In recent years, the United Nations has worked to improve data and analysis in forced displacement contexts. The United Nations Expert Group on Refugee and Internally Displaced Persons Statistics (EGRIS)[405] has developed an internationally agreed framework for the production and dissemination of quality statistics relating to refugees and internally displaced persons comparable between regions and countries.[406]

The work is ongoing. When complete, it will provide enhanced tools for the collection of reliable data. But improving technical data collection is not enough. As national authorities remain accountable for data on their own populations, advancing the quality of that data depends on political will, policy choices and sufficient national capacity.

According to the World Bank, "over 110 low- and middle-income countries have deficient civil registration and vital statistic systems".[407] International and national partners must support government-led efforts to improve national statistical systems. Not everything related to improving statistics can be done at once, and sequencing of strengthened capacity will often be necessary.

In the meantime, other organizations, including humanitarian agencies, will also need to work more closely together to harmonize data collection according to agreed standards. Improved reliability, comparability and quality of data will help inform policies and provide more effective protection, assistance and solutions efforts for forcibly displaced persons.

Minding the Gaps

To this day, the influence of the 1951 Convention on the international refugee protection regime is definitive. Its sustained resonance transcends the post-war period. Its interpretation has broadened over 70 years, covering people in flight from a wider range of threats. Its ideals have informed and influenced subsequent regional refugee protection instruments, reinforcing its core protections. Together, these frameworks have protected millions of people.

But, alongside this widening scope has been a trend for protection to be *with-held*. While expressing support for the international protection regime, countries have – at the same time – sought to limit access to its provisions. This creates a gap between the commitment and practice of States' responses to refugees.

It is in this gap that countries try to prevent refugees from entering to stop asylum claims. It is where nations seek to intercept refugees in flight, interrupting journeys to safety to avoid non-refoulement obligations. States have also confined refugees in ways that leave them reliant on humanitarian assistance and unable to provide for themselves – the key to a better future. Responsibility- and burden-sharing for refugees has consistently fallen short, with hosts in low- and middle-income countries carrying a disproportionate share. The future of the international refugee protection regime very much depends on countering these negative trends.

For internally displaced persons, the Guiding Principles on Internal Displacement were a major achievement, influencing the development of regional and national prevention and response frameworks for people fleeing within borders. However, like the refugee protection frameworks, implementation is uneven and international support for internally displaced persons falls considerably short of need. As will be discussed in Part III, solutions for many internally displaced persons as well as refugees have not been realized.

The world needs to learn from these shortcomings, with climate change likely to cause more forced movements. As this next challenge looms, there has already been notable progress. Twenty years ago, displacement in the context of climate change and disasters was discussed largely in alarmist terms. It was based on projections that were not well substantiated. There was relatively little emphasis on what could be done to mitigate risks, strengthen resilience and manage relocation sensitively. Since then, multilateral prevention and response frameworks have been developed to help.

However, much more work is needed to prepare for the future. Reducing greenhouse gas emissions is key. The dissemination of good practices has expanded, especially in the last five years, and in a manner that is helping States implement more effective policies. Nonetheless, the States that are the most affected are also the ones least able to mitigate and adapt to these changes. They are also not the major source of carbon emissions, which imposes an even greater obligation on wealthier States to acknowledge and remedy the harm caused on others.

From the rubble of WWII to the emerging threats that lie ahead, all protection frameworks recognize the importance of support for forcibly displaced persons to realize their potential. With it, they can strengthen their capacities and provide for themselves, contributing to their new communities. Restrictive laws and policies inhibit this. So do measures that are, at times, deliberately discriminatory.

Improved on-the-ground implementation of the expanded global ideals established in the 1951 Convention depends on many factors. State willingness is among the most dominant. State capacity is also critical: It is one thing to know what has to be done and to try to do it, but another to be able to fulfil commitments. Much more robust engagement in nationally-led efforts, underpinned by enabling policies and financial support, are required.

For responses to forced displacement to better match international intentions, a deeper understanding of its dimensions, causes and duration is needed. For this, the enhancement of data and analytical capacities needs to accelerate.

PART III

Solutions – An Uneven Record

Table of Contents

Solutions – An Uneven Record

Previous page: On a bus bound for Beirut airport in 2014, Syrian refugee Um Abdullah and her children Asmaa, 9 (left) and Louai, 3 (right), begin their journey to resettlement in Germany, with other members of their family in need of specialist medical care. © UNHCR/ Andrew McConnell

Displacement ends once a durable solution is reached.

This means more than just a safe physical presence. For a solution to be durable, a person must be able to live securely, be treated equally under the law, have a formal status, and be subject to the same rights and responsibilities of others in the community without discrimination.

This Part examines the record on achieving solutions for forcibly displaced persons and recent efforts to unlock more. It draws from what we know from contemporaneous accounts, available data, and assessments made over time.[1]

Traditionally, recognized solutions for refugees have included voluntary, safe and sustainable return to their countries, local integration in the host country, or resettlement in a third country. For internally displaced persons (IDPs), who are citizens of the State where they are displaced, solutions include sustainable voluntary return to the place of origin, or sustainable integration elsewhere in the country.

The historic record on achieving solutions for forcibly displaced persons is checkered. Over time, many millions have safely returned home or been accepted permanently in new communities, allowing them to forge new futures for themselves and their families. Many more, however, have not. The persistently high annual numbers of forcibly displaced people in need of humanitarian assistance reflect this sad reality, as more displacement situations become protracted and new situations erupt.

On too many occasions voluntary return was promoted in contexts where peace was fragile and reintegration prospects slim. Returns were followed by new displacements. Resettlement enabled only a small proportion of refugees to start new lives, some selected on the basis of their integration potential rather than on their acute needs. The record on local integration is thin: evidence points to the difficulties that internally displaced persons face in locally integrating and the legal barriers that can stand in the way of refugees doing so.

Past experience points to the need for approaches that recognize that achieving a solution to displacement is a process in which strengthening human capital during displacement is one key element. Refugees and internally displaced persons live among communities that are often poor and marginalized. Solutions have a greater chance of success when they build on prior investments to enhance the socioeconomic development of both forcibly displaced persons and local communities.

Solutions Overview

Voluntary Return

The story of forcibly displaced persons is dominated by images of flight, and subsistence living in places of immediate refuge. There is much less visibility on them returning home once conflict has abated, or when other causes of flight are gone. Some of the most moving moments in the displacement experience – returning home in safety – are rarely seen. There is good reason for this: It happens all too infrequently.

For most of the past 60 years, fewer than 10 per cent of refugees returned to their countries of origin.[2] In the last decade, this proportion has fallen generally below 5 per cent in most years. Similar data on conflict-induced internal displacement is incomplete with more extensive data collection only commencing in the 1990s for displacement and 1997 for returns.[3] But the rates of return since then have also been relatively low. For the past 20 years, annual rates of returns of internally displaced persons have mostly been less than 10 per cent of the total number.[4]

The reasons for the low return rates are clear. Conflicts that have driven people from their homes remain active. Afghanistan, Azerbaijan, Colombia, Democratic Republic of the Congo, Iraq, Somalia, and Sudan consistently generated some of the largest forcibly displaced populations in the world over the past 20 years, with the displacement from some spanning several decades.[5]

In places where the guns remain silent, other factors can prevent sustainable returns home. They can include destroyed infrastructure, the loss of roads, schools and medical facilities; the loss of property, when others live on land once owned by returnees; and ongoing fear of retribution or persecution by State or non-State actors.

Significant peace, development and humanitarian support is needed to overcome these obstacles so return can be sustainable. Support is critical in the immediate period after the peace settlement, as most returns occur within three years of the end of a conflict.[6] But it also needs to be maintained. Aid tends to fall off within a few years after a peace agreement has been formed, often at a time when governments start to demonstrate greater absorption capacities.[7]

Many returning refugees and internally displaced persons do not go to their original areas, settling elsewhere in the country. Returnees often choose urban locations, especially if they have resided in cities or towns during their displacement. Chief among the reasons are employment prospects and better access to services.[8] For those who previously lived in rural areas, loss of land or productive assets may also be decisive factors. Some who do choose to return home face security risks that either prevent them from reaching there or limit the duration of their stay, resulting in further displacement.[9]

When large numbers return to already congested and underserved areas, reintegration can be a struggle.[10] This can be further complicated if returnees have few ties to their country of origin, which is the case for many children and young people who have grown up in exile.[11]

In light of the challenges facing return, the decision to go back home is often difficult. Among the most important considerations are that the return area is safe and that there are economic opportunities to ensure a means of livelihood. Evidence shows that returnees with financial and productive assets and skills fare better upon return than those without.[12] This is why supporting training and education during displacement is important for both the immediate and longer term.

Households may not return together, with family members remaining behind either temporarily or permanently as a way to better manage risks. This occurs especially when security systems are not fully in place, access to education or medical services is not available, or there is a possibility that some family members could face greater risks upon return.

Those eligible to be conscripted may choose to remain behind rather than returning and being compelled to serve in an army that was implicated in their displacement.[13] Women and young girls may face higher risks of abuse in places of return if policing and justice systems are not effectively functioning. Individuals with employment or business in the place of refuge may choose not to return if they determine that they are better off in their current location. And those who have never known their country of citizenship—spending their entire lives in the host country—may wish to remain in the only home they have known.

Significant return can be followed by renewed displacement, often internally, especially in circumstances where the peace is fragile or conditions in return areas are so shattered that residents and returnees alike are unable to gain a foothold. Others who settle in their areas of origin can find it difficult to rebuild their lives and remain in situations of heightened vulnerability as a result of their displacement.[14]

Achieving sustainable returns is a complex task requiring peace, development and humanitarian efforts and is seldom quickly accomplished.

Resettlement

Refugees often consider being resettled as akin to winning the lottery. It is an apt analogy given that the odds are slim, and the payoff is significant in terms of the opportunity to move forward securely with their lives.

Resettlement to a third country has been a solution for only a limited number of refugees. It has provided a lifeline for over 4 million people since 1960. As a percentage of total refugees, however, it has rarely reached more than 1 per cent annually. But, unlike a lottery, being selected for resettlement is not a question of pure chance. It is a specialized and lengthy immigration process. Rez Gardi and her family were considered for resettlement while living in a refugee camp in Pakistan. She recalls how they expected to be resettled within six months. It took nine years.[15]

Resettlement countries determine how many refugees and from which regions of the world they will resettle each year. States accept referrals from UNHCR of refugees in need of resettlement, although this does not guarantee a person referred will be accepted. That is the decision of the resettlement State, based on its determination of refugee status and its own resettlement criteria.[16] The number and profile of refugees States resettle can be influenced by foreign policy considerations, labour market needs, security considerations and public support.

The annual number of refugees resettled fluctuates, but the global total has never exceeded 180,000 in a year, averaging just over 70,000 persons annually.[17] Given the limited number of resettlement places available, UNHCR relies on criteria reached in consultation with resettlement States, to help determine which refugees to refer for resettlement. The overriding consideration is to refer those who are at risk in their country of refuge or who have particular needs or vulnerabilities that cannot be appropriately addressed there.[18]

A refugee accepted for resettlement is conditionally approved subject to the results of medical and security checks. These can take many months depending on the resettlement country, which means that the length of time from the selection to arrival in the resettlement country ranges from 12 to 36 months and, in some cases, even longer.[19]

Some refugees who are not accepted by one country can be referred to another, but there are no guarantees. Many are not accepted even after multiple referrals. And, while they are informed of the odds, many refugees often hold onto hope well beyond a realistic chance of success.[20]

Resettlement has not always reflected this systematic and coordinated approach between resettlement States, UNHCR and partners in non-governmental organizations. It is a process that has evolved over the years. In the aftermath of World War II (WWII), it was primarily regarded as a useful source of European labour for resettlement States.[21] Over time, it became a solution open to refugees from all parts of the world with a specific, although not exclusive, focus on those most at risk.

Local Integration

As a durable solution to refugee displacement, local integration entails acquiring permanent legal status, generally attained through naturalization processes.[22] This recognizes refugees as full members of the community and enables them to pass on that secure legal status to their children.

Refugees who are resettled, or who are recognized as refugees through asylum processes in many States, are generally accepted permanently in their new communities. But for most refugees, including those who have lived for long periods in hosting countries, the path to permanent residency or citizenship is not open to them.

Citizenship has been afforded to a relatively small proportion of refugees over time. It has been concentrated in high-income countries that are signatories to the 1951 Convention relating to the Status of Refugees (1951 Convention) and its 1967 Protocol.[23] Traditionally, many of these countries have provided a pathway to citizenship for refugees who have been resettled or who have been recognized under an asylum process and fulfil other requirements that qualify them for citizenship.

In the past decade, 97 per cent of all naturalizations were reported from 10 countries. Of these, five are high-income countries and contributed two

An elderly Burundian refugee couple begins the process of becoming Tanzanian citizens in 2008, having arrived as refugees in 1972. © UNHCR/ Brendan Bannon

thirds of all naturalizations. Canada alone naturalized over 144,000 refugees representing 45 per cent of the total.[24]

And while naturalization of refugees has been less common in low- and middle-income countries, three examples in recent years stand out as notable exceptions. Tanzania, having been host to large numbers of refugees for many decades, naturalized over 162,000 long resident Burundian refugees, with most of the naturalizations occurring in 2009.

Meanwhile, between 2017 and 2018, Turkey naturalized over 79,000 Syrian refugees, equivalent to 25 per cent of the global total of refugee naturalizations between 2010 and 2019, while also hosting the largest refugee population in the world.[25] In Guinea-Bissau, nearly 9,000 long resident Senegalese refugees were naturalized in 2018 and 2019.[26]

Elements of Solutions

Enabling Laws and Policies

LEGAL STATUS

Recognition of legal identity and right to reside

- Residence permit
- Citizenship
- Naturalization

ECONOMIC

Legal right to

- Be employed
- Own a business
- Access financial services
- Own and sell land and property

CIVIL-POLITICAL

Participation in civil and political life

- Protection of the law and access to justice
- Security
- Civil documentation
- Freedom to move
- Political participation

SOCIAL-CULTURAL

Enjoyment of personal, family and community life

- Inclusion in education systems and health services
- Social protection
- Family unity

Short of citizenship, refugees can attain a degree of social and de facto economic integration. Even in contexts where local integration is officially not accepted, a level of informal integration especially for populations living outside camps, is widespread since most host governments do not have the capacity to prevent this from occurring.[27]

Restricting the right of refugees to work is often justified on the assumption that it protects local workers from competition. Yet, such restrictions may in fact have the opposite effect. When refugees' qualifications are not reconized and they are unable to work legally, they are pushed into the informal sector. This is where local low-skilled and frequently female labour is concentrated. When permitted to legally work, they engage across a broader range of occupations, pay taxes and make a stronger economic contribution.[28]

Refugees have faced significant resistance to any degree of local integration, especially in the context of large refugee movements with high or rising unemployment rates and scarce livelihood opportunities.[29] Refugees are frequently prohibited from moving freely, and from working or establishing a means of livelihood. Around 70 per cent of refugees face such constraints.[30]

Restrictions are motivated by several factors. Although the granting of citizenship remains a sovereign decision, some governments fear that legalizing any form of integration will bind them to conferring citizenship and, therefore, seek to avoid it. Other reasons include the perceived possible negative impact refugees may have on local economies and the potential difficulties of monitoring refugees should they be permitted to move freely.

Some States express concern that greater inclusion will lead to a withdrawal of humanitarian support, leaving them to assume greater burdens. Restrictions are often seen as necessary to deter further influxes, in the belief that providing more favourable conditions of stay will be a pull factor to new refugees, discourage those already present from returning home,[31] while also leaving countries of origin unaccountable for their own citizens.

For internally displaced persons who are citizens, integration in places of displacement or return can also be elusive. Like refugees, many are frequently poorer, with more children out of school and higher rates of unemployment than host community members. Those who have been displaced from rural to urban environments have often lost their productive assets, such as land and livestock, and may not have skills that are easily transferable to local markets.[32] Many who live in camps are often in inhospitable and remote locations, lacking infrastructure and access to markets. Challenges can be exacerbated where they do not share religious, ethnic, or kinship ties with host communities.[33]

Some governments have enacted laws and put in place policies to address the immediate needs of internally displaced persons and resolve their displacement.[34] Not all governments are committed to finding durable solutions for their displaced populations. Many are confronted with indifferent or even hostile government authorities who may have caused, contributed to, or perpetuated their displacement. Such authorities may be less inclined to pursue measures to address the vulnerabilities of internally displaced persons and achieve solutions.[35]

Normative Framework

Refugees

Durable solutions for refugees, in the form of voluntary repatriation or full integration in the host country, were the main objectives in the early years of the modern international refugee regime. In 1950, the United Nations Secretary-General Trygve Lie, set out its ambitions. At its core, he noted, were hopes for progression – from *economic integration* to *membership*.

People unable or unwilling to return would be integrated into the economic life of the country of refuge. The final result would be "integration in the national community which has given him shelter" as it is "essential for the refugee to enjoy an equitable and stable status".[36]

These alternatives, "voluntary repatriation" and "assimilation in new national communities" are reflected in the Statute of UNHCR.[37] The 1951 Convention set out progressive enjoyment of rights, with States agreeing to "as far as possible facilitate the assimilation and naturalization of refugees."[38]

Refugee repatriation

In the Universal Declaration of Human Rights, the right to return to one's country is unequivocal and for this to be a voluntary choice and in safety is definitive in the 1951 Convention. The latter prohibits States from returning a refugee to a territory where "life or freedom" would be threatened.[39] The concept was considered of such fundamental importance that no derogation from it is permissible. It was subsequently included in the 1969 Organization of African Unity Convention Governing the Specific Aspects of Refugee Problems in Africa (OAU Convention), the 1984 Cartagena Declaration, the 1966 Bangkok Principles, the 2011 updated European Union Qualification Directive, as well as the 2018 Global Compact on Refugees (GCR).[40]

Some of these instruments also set out principles that are common to organized voluntary return efforts. Among them, voluntary return is facilitated by the involvement of host countries, countries of origin and relevant international agencies.[41] Returnees are also expected to be accorded the full rights and privileges of fellow citizens and not be penalized for having left their country of origin.[42]

Refugee integration

For integration, the 1951 Convention is more equivocal. As discussed in Part I, refugees are entitled to access courts and must obey the law. But, while they have some socioeconomic rights on the same terms as nationals, they do not have full equality in this regard.[43] States can make exceptions in this area, and many have. Reservations especially apply to paid employment, equality of treatment in labour standards and social security.[44]

There is no unqualified obligation under the 1951 Convention for States to grant citizenship to refugees. Rather, they are obligated to take measures "as far as possible" to assimilate and naturalize refugees.[45] While some regional accords are more progressive on the surface, in practice, refugees often face legal barriers to integration.

The OAU Convention reflected State reticence to extend rights to local integration. It provides that States "use their best endeavours consistent with their respective legislations" to secure the settlement of refugees.[46] It is silent on the economic and social rights to be accorded, although it expressly recognizes that the 1951 Convention and the 1967 Protocol constitute "the basic and universal instrument relating to the status of refugees".[47]

The 1979 Protocol Relating to Free Movement of Persons, Residence and Establishment of the Economic Community of West African States (ECOWAS) has the potential to facilitate the integration of refugees from member States. It provides for community members to enter and reside in the territory of any member State if they possess a valid travel document and international health certificate.[48] In practice, however, refugees within ECOWAS have not systematically benefited as States have the discretion to exclude certain groups from the provisions of the Protocol. Even in the absence of these specific limitations, it affords wide and general discretion to immigration officers who have excluded refugees from benefiting.[49]

The 1984 Cartagena Declaration, adopted by Latin American States, includes specific provisions to support the "self-sufficiency of refugees" and programmes to improve their health, education, labour market access and safety.[50] On its 30th anniversary, these States went further: They committed to promote the inclusion of forcibly displaced persons in national development plans and to "multiply efforts" to guarantee the enjoyment of economic, social and cultural rights for local integration. There was also agreement to facilitate naturalization, although with qualifications. Naturalizations would be part of "a comprehensive durable solutions strategy", meaning when other solutions were also engaged, and only "in accordance with national legislation".[51]

The 2018 Global Compact on Refugees reflects States' continued sensitivity on local integration. It specifically refers to local integration through naturalization as a sovereign decision, to be "guided by their treaty obligations and human rights principles". But it also recognizes that States may opt for "other local solutions", such as interim stay, to facilitate economic, social and cultural inclusion, and that low- and middle-income countries may need support from the international community for this.[52] The Global Refugee Forum[53] is one platform where this support is pledged.[54]

Internally Displaced Persons

Internally displaced persons are entitled to all rights of citizens without discrimination. This includes the right to locally integrate in their place of refuge, elsewhere in the country or upon return to their place of origin. Nonetheless, *claiming* a right, and the ability to *exercise* it are not the same. And, as mentioned earlier, they often face significant practical problems in realizing solutions.

The 1998 Guiding Principles on Internal Displacement provide global standards for both the prevention and response to situations where forced movement arises within borders.[55] In regard to solutions, they are clear that the primary responsibility to establish conditions and means to resolve displacement lies with national authorities.

Internally displaced persons have the right to choose freely and with full information whether to remain, return or settle elsewhere in the country.[56] The Principles are also reflected in the African Union Convention for the Protection and Assistance of Internally Displaced Persons in Africa (Kampala Convention) of 2009.[57]

While both the Guiding Principles and the Kampala Convention make the right to a durable solution clear, they do not provide guidance on when a solution has been reached. In 2010, the Inter-Agency Standing Committee[58] published a Durable Solutions Framework for Internally Displaced Persons (the IASC Framework) providing some guidance in this regard.

According to the IASC Framework, a durable solution is reached when internally displaced persons "no longer have specific assistance and protection needs that are linked to their displacement" and "can enjoy their human rights without discrimination resulting from their displacement".[59] Ongoing needs linked to displacement can include: civil documentation left behind or lost in flight; employment which is not available due to discrimination or because skills are not transferable; and the absence of secure accommodation.

Factors to determine whether a durable solution has been reached are broad. They include: long-term safety and security; adequate standard of living; documentation; family reunification; and access to employment, justice and effective remedies to restore or compensate loss of land and property.[60]

Ten years on, some have argued that the breadth of the criteria accommodates ambiguity, and that the list needs to be refined to eliminate it.[61] Others have focused on tools that can help provide a context-specific means to measure the extent to which a durable solution has been reached, including qualitative long-term studies.[62]

There is also a need for greater clarity on the right of return, frequently affirmed in Security Council resolutions concerning situations of internal displacement.[63] Currently, internally displaced persons who have found a solution elsewhere in the country may still be counted as displaced if they retain an unfulfilled desire to return.[64]

The First 50 Years

Available statistics pertaining to different solutions vary. Annual statistics on refugees by country of origin, asylum, return and resettlement reach back over 60 years.[65] Annual statistics on internally displaced persons, including returns, exist only partially from the 1990s.[66] Considerable work remains to harmonize how governments define and report on internally displaced populations and how data is collected to improve accuracy discussed further in Part V.[67]

We cannot be certain of the exact number of forcibly displaced persons who have locally integrated over the decades. For refugees, UNHCR has tried to use naturalizations as a proxy.[68] The problem is that not all States have annual records on those they naturalize. Among those that do, refugees are not always distinguished from other non-citizens in the naturalization data.[69]

Over many years, solutions for refugees were perceived in a hierarchy of desirability: Voluntary repatriation was consistently described as the most preferable; local integration came next "where appropriate and feasible" followed by resettlement, when voluntary repatriation and local integration were not possible.

UNHCR's Executive Committee reflected this approach in its guidance on areas of law and policy issued through Conclusions on International Protection.[70] From 1975 and for over 30 years, its Conclusions repeatedly referred to voluntary repatriation in an unqualified manner as the "preferred solution",[71] although there was little firm evidence that all refugees viewed it in the same way.

During the first 50 years of the international protection regime, interest in solutions for refugees was commensurate with the level of refugee displacement. So, for example, the initial post-war emphasis on solving refugee situations, re-emerged in the late 1970s, as the number of refugees more than doubled during the decade.

In Africa, they rose from 1.5 million people to 5.9 million between 1975 and 1990. Among the largest refugee populations in Africa during this time were those from Angola, Ethiopia, Liberia and Mozambique.[72] In Asia, in the same period, the increase was even more dramatic: from fewer than 100,000 refugees to nearly 8.2 million mostly Afghan refugees. Refugees first started fleeing Afghanistan to neighbouring Iran and Pakistan after the fall of the monarchy in 1978. Following the Soviet invasion in 1979, their numbers increased to some 6.3 million by 1990.[73]

The wider period between the 1951 Convention and the new millennium features three patterns within the world's search for solutions for its refugees.

First, the clear preference for refugee repatriation meant that it was often favoured in situations that were far from safe or durable. The experience of this period would inform international approaches in the new millennium including a wider recognition that political stability was generally a necessary condition, although not always sufficient for sustainable return.

Second, the period also demonstrated that resettlement would likely not provide a solution for more than a limited number of refugees with specific needs. Significant multilateral efforts on resettlement were generally contingent on them serving broader geopolitical ends.

Third, in regard to local integration, the decades revealed ongoing reluctance of States hosting the majority of refugees to consider formal integration.

Focus on Return

Between the end of WWII and the new millennium, over 30 million refugees repatriated, including some 10 million who had fled to India from East Pakistan in 1971 and returned to the new State of Bangladesh in 1972.[74] The pressure to resolve forced displacement through returns to the country of origin was the main policy direction of choice for governments hosting displaced people, and it was facilitated by the international community.

The review that follows captures major returns and those that resulted in a durable solution as well as those that did not. It reveals some truths. Political stability was common to all successful repatriations. Returns to areas where the root causes of initial displacement remained unaddressed featured further flight in subsequent years. So too did returns to situations of ongoing political instability. Also, help with travel back and initial installation did not guarantee a durable solution. Nor did more robust development assistance if the country continued to experience severe internal divisions and unstable governance.

1950–1990

Middle East and North Africa

Following the massive post-WWII repatriation exercises,[75] the next significant international effort came in support of Algerian refugees. In 1958, the General Assembly requested that UNHCR support the repatriation and reintegration of over 200,000 Algerians who had fled to Tunisia and Morocco.[76] It was the first major United Nations repatriation exercise outside Europe,[77] and it defined processes and an approach that would be followed in subsequent years.

First, the return of refugees was a part of the Evian Peace Accords, and the promotion of refugee returns would become a common feature of peace agreements until the 1990s.[78]

Second, the roles and responsibilities of UNHCR, the hosting countries and Algeria were set out in a formal agreement. The use of this kind of tripartite agreement became a standard practice in subsequent years.[79]

Third, in recognition of the fact that refugees were often returning to areas devastated by conflict, UNHCR invested in initial reintegration and small-scale reconstruction programmes. These were of benefit both to returnees and settled residents of those areas. UNHCR linked the Government with United

Nations development partners.[80] A focus on the need to support development within areas of return would be part of subsequent reintegration efforts, and a lack of it among the reasons some failed.

Asia

Throughout the 1970s, many displaced populations returned home following successful independence struggles. The largest and swift-est return movement came in 1972 following the short and brutal conflict between West and East Pakistan,[81] which led to the separate States of Pakistan and Bangladesh.

Almost from its creation in 1947, Pakistan was riven by divisions between West Pakistan and East Pakistan. United in name, they were separated by over 1,000 kilometers and along ethnic lines. A Bengali nationalist movement in the East grew over the years, fueled by political, economic and social poli-cies that favoured West Pakistan and Urdu-speaking populations over East Pakistan and its majority Bengali community.

Tensions escalated in 1970 when the Awami League, based in East Pakistan, won the majority of seats in the national election which West Pakistani parties refused to recognize.[82] The arrest of the head of the Awami League, Sheikh Mujib Rahman, was followed by full-scale repression by the Pakistan Army against the Bengali population. The level of violence was particularly gruesome, generating a volume and rate of forced displacement greater than at any other time since WWII.[83] Within one year, hundreds of thousands were killed and some 10 million refugees fled mostly into India.[84]

India coordinated a massive relief operation. It set up registration systems and food rationing and provided vaccines for cholera and smallpox. Impatient with what it considered an insufficient international response, and in the face of unprecedented rates of refugee arrivals, India intervened militarily in support of the nationalists.[85] This led to the relatively quick conclusion of the war and the creation of the State of Bangladesh in 1972.

Returns to Bangladesh were immediate, with hundreds of thousands of refugees returning each day of their own accord. UNHCR received over $14 million to provide initial assistance to returnees as well as for relief and rehabilitation projects in areas of return.[86] Within four months, India announced that all but 60,000 of the 10 million refugees had returned home.[87] Both the size and speed of the return movement were rare. The relatively short duration of the conflict helped make it possible. Refugees were returning to a newly independent State where their interests dominated.[88]

There were far less auspicious circumstances for the close to 200,000 Rohingya refugees who returned to Myanmar from Bangladesh between 1978 and 1979. They had fled increasingly repressive policies of Myanmar's military government, including a massive campaign of arrests and expulsions in 1978.[89]

Bangladesh was keen to maintain good relations with Myanmar and was not willing to provide permanent residence to the refugees. The return campaign met resistance from the refugees, who feared conditions in Myanmar had not improved. In response, Bangladesh withheld food aid. The refugees' resolve

Salt Lake camp near Calcutta in 1971. It was one of 800 camps set up after some 10 million refugees fled to India amid the conflict between West and East Pakistan.
© WFP/ Trevor Page

weakened, and most returned. Ongoing persecution led to further outflows over subsequent years.

UNHCR was not a party to the return agreement. But it was later criticized for not doing more to stop it and not monitoring the situation of the returnees. Scholars have since noted that UNHCR was in a dilemma. A lack of donor countries willing to take up the cause of the Rohingya refugees meant there was little it could do. Faced with deteriorating conditions in Bangladesh, UNHCR took the view that the return would make the refugees better off.[90] The same dilemma would resurface in the 1990s regarding Rohingya refugees in Bangladesh as well as in regard to Rwandan refugees in Zaire (now Democratic Republic of the Congo) and Tanzania.[91]

UNHCR was also accused of compromising its protection mandate in its response to Thailand's efforts to resist admitting and insist on the return of Cambodian refugees in 1978 and 1979. While the plight of the Vietnamese boat people was capturing the world's attention,[92] less well known were the mass killings and deaths by starvation, disease and forced labour unravelling in Cambodia under the Khmer Rouge. The plight of Cambodians received more attention when thousands of Cambodians fled to Thailand during the 1979 Vietnamese invasion that overthrew the Khmer Rouge regime.

The refugees were considered illegal migrants and a security threat by the Thai Government and were incarcerated in camps along the Thai-Cambodian border. In 1979, Thai authorities forced 40,000 Cambodian refugees across the landmine-littered border to Cambodia amidst ongoing insecurity. Many were killed by exploding mines, others were shot trying to cross back into Thailand, while others subsequently died of exhaustion, malaria and starvation.[93]

UNHCR was criticized as being too hesitant to condemn these actions fearing that criticism would provoke harsher measures. It was seen as supportive of Thailand's efforts to promote the return of Khmer Rouge supporters, many of whom were Khmer Rouge fighters allied with Thailand's military against Vietnam. Their return prompted a swift retaliatory response from Vietnam and led to further refugee outflows from Cambodia.[94] UNHCR was accused of taking a political, rather than principled, stand – assisting a host country and ally of the West over the protection of refugees.[95]

Africa

Across Africa, many thousands of refugees returned to their countries following post-independence civil wars. Not all returns were durable. Internal conflict in subsequent years led to further displacement. Sudan was one notable example.[96] In 1972, the 17-year civil war ended and the Government was keen to welcome refugees back. It reached out to the United Nations to assist. UNHCR was charged with organizing returns, with the United Nations Development Programme (UNDP) leading development interventions needed for rehabilitation of return areas.

In what was to become standard practice in subsequent years, returns were carefully planned with the involved governments, and outreach undertaken with Sudanese opposition groups and refugees as a means of building confidence that return in safety was both possible and desirable. The President of Sudan visited hosting countries to speak with refugees and explain the amnesties for their protection. Groups of refugees were supported to return to see conditions in return areas and to report their findings to others. Within less than two years following the conclusion of the peace agreement in 1972, over 200,000 refugees had returned.[97]

Within 10 years, however, internal conflict erupted again in the south. It followed central government policies limiting the autonomy of the region. These policies declared Arabic the official language and imposed Sharia law nationally, including in areas of the south where Christianity and animism were the predominant faiths. Years of fighting and subsequent drought led to mass forced displacement and severe food insecurity.[98]

Ethiopia's experience in the 1980s also illustrated the complexity of refugee returns. Close to 900,000 Ethiopian refugees are estimated to have returned to Ethiopia between 1980 and 1989.[99] The reasons for their flight and their repatriation varied.

In 1977, Somalia launched an unsuccessful invasion of the Ogaden region of Ethiopia causing several hundred thousand refugees to flee to Somalia and Djibouti.[100] In subsequent years, many returned.[101] Initial returns from Djibouti were under considerable duress, as refugees were corralled into camps, and suffered various forms of police harassment and withholding of food assistance to compel return. After several months, and only after returnees reported back on the adequacy of the reception within Ethiopia, did the movement pick up as more refugees repatriated voluntarily.[102]

Later in the decade, over 170,000 Tigrayan refugees returned to Ethiopia having fled to Sudan during the 1983–1985 famine.[103] Their return was coordinated by the civilian wing of the Tigray People's Liberation Front (TPLF), which was engaged in an independence struggle lasting over 10 years.[104] Refugees returned to areas under rebel control, without the sanction of the Ethiopian Government. Initially, many refugees experienced great hardship for without the means for agricultural production they remained food insecure which contributed to a second famine in 1987.[105]

Despite these challenges, most returnees remained. This was in part due to the economic coping strategies of the Tigrayans. Also, within a few years of the return, the TPLF joined a coalition that overthrew the Mengistu Haile Mariam dictatorship and formed part of the Transitional Government of Ethiopia. This too contributed to the sustainability of the returns.[106]

Tensions between the Tigray region and the central government would erupt again, however, in later years, with deadly consequences. Disagreements between the regional and central governments increased in 2019 and conflict broke out again following the regional elections of 2020, which the central

Ethiopian refugees in Sudan in 1985, who fled devastating drought, crop failure and war.
© UNHCR/Marc Vanappelghem

government considered illegal. By the end of April 2021, several thousand people were killed,[107] with available information pointing to over 1 million persons forcibly displaced by the ongoing conflict.[108]

In Uganda, political instability following the ouster of Idi Amin in 1979 continued to cause significant refugee flight, mostly to Sudan. The outbreak of civil war in southern Sudan in 1983, directly affected the 200,000 Ugandan refugees that had sought shelter there.[109] Some 50,000 are estimated to have returned by 1985 to insecure and economically depressed regions.[110] Unfolding

insurgency movements, notably the violent Lord's Resistance Army (LRA), compromised security in the years to follow.

The LRA's two decade-long rebellion was characterized by war crimes, including forced child recruitment, sexual slavery and the internal forced displacement of an estimated 1.8 million civilians.[111] The refugee returns of the period exemplified how refugees were compelled to repatriate due to conflict in displacement yet returned to increasingly fragile circumstances back home.[112] The mass displacements in the region did not generate the level of international assistance required to respond to needs or their impact on host communities.

The growing number of people forcibly displaced and their assistance needs were increasingly not being matched by available support and solutions. In 1970, there were approximately 1 million refugees throughout Africa. By 1980, this figure had grown to over 4 million,[113] most of whom were not supported by international assistance.[114]

The Organization of African Unity brought the need for more international support before the General Assembly. This led to two International Conferences on Assistance to Refugees in Africa (ICARA I and ICARA II) in 1981 and 1984 respectively.

ICARA I succeeded in raising global awareness of refugees in Africa and garnered over $500 million to assist them. But the manner in which the financial contributions were made was highly political. Most donors directed funds to refugee relief in countries with which they were politically allied.[115] This meant that the allocation of the funds was not necessarily driven by the magnitude of need, nor the burden on the host country. And, while the funds enabled the mobilization and disbursement of emergency relief, ICARA I did not provide substantial benefits to host States in terms of sustained support or solutions.

The second Conference, ICARA II, in 1984 was intended to have more impact. It was to marshal international humanitarian assistance for refugees and returnees as well as to address the impact of refugees on the social and economic infrastructure of host States.[116] It appealed for both humanitarian and development funding. By all accounts, ICARA II fell short. Donors pledged just $81 million of the $352 million requested. There are several reasons for its lack of success.

An emerging and catastrophic famine engulfed parts of Africa, and particularly Ethiopia, where 8 million people were at risk of starvation. This diverted attention and humanitarian assistance from ICARA II.[117] But, even without the famine, donors seemed reluctant to invest in the development projects that host countries advanced.

They had several reservations.[118] The projects were intended to address the adverse impact of receiving refugees, yet there was no assessment quantifying the impact. This has always been difficult due to a lack of data and an agreed methodology that helps isolate the impact of receiving refugees from other contributing causes. Forty years later, the need to develop measures to determine the impact of large numbers of refugees was requested by the UN General Assembly at the time it affirmed the Global Compact on Refugees.[119]

Donors also viewed the development projects put forward by host countries as unrelated to hosting refugees and did not see their value in advancing solutions. They also questioned whether the projects were appropriately costed and whether host countries had the capacity to implement them and to sustain them over the longer term.[120]

ICARA II remains remarkable less for its achievements than its aspirations. Long before the Global Compact on Refugees, ICARA II recognized the need for humanitarian support to be accompanied by development assistance. Donor interest in having the latter be based on sound impact assessments was understandable. But it was also unrealistic for that time. Even today, with improved tools and methodologies, the task is complex as recent progress reports on 'Measuring the Impact of Hosting, Protecting and Assisting Refugees' attest.[121]

Additionally, at the time of ICARA II, government ministries responsible for development in both donor and host countries often operated separately from the ministries that responded to the management of refugee influxes and the provision of humanitarian assistance. The absence of linkages between them, also evident in certain contexts today, impeded a more integrated humanitarian and development approach.[122]

Finally, ICARA II was based on the assumption that most of the projects would be implemented through United Nations agencies with UNDP leading on the development side. Development donors, however, preferred to fund development bilaterally. This is now more firmly reflected in current approaches to unlocking more development support for host countries.[123]

1990s: A decade that stands apart

During the 1990s, the emphasis on return continued in the context of rising numbers of forcibly displaced people. What sets this decade apart from previous and subsequent ones is both the volume of returns and the fact that so many of them were neither voluntary nor sustainable.

Refugees were increasingly viewed as burdens and threats to security. Pressure on refugees to return home and on UNHCR to encourage return even in unfavourable conditions was persistently high, despite the lessons of the previous decades.

During the 1990s, over 15 million refugees returned to their countries of origin: the largest registered number in a single decade since WWII. The returns of internally displaced persons were only recorded in the latter part of the decade and reveal that almost 1.4 million conflict-induced internally displaced persons returned to their areas of origin during that time.[124] Many returnees went to areas where power struggles continued, leading to ongoing instability, insurgencies and renewed forced displacement. The lessons of the 1990s would lead to a new emphasis on safety and sustainability in the new millennium.

Asia

The Soviet withdrawal from Afghanistan in 1989, and the fall of the Afghan Government three years later, marked a period of rapid and massive refugee-led return. Over 3 million Afghans returned home during the 1990s, more than half of whom made the journey in 1992 alone.[125] However, the return movement did not signal an end to displacement. Many return areas lacked basic health and education facilities, roads and infrastructure were shattered, landmines were a constant hazard and economic opportunities thin.[126] Civil war broke out, generating new displacement, which continued following the Taliban's seizure of power in 1996.

Elsewhere, as many as 365,000 Cambodians also came home to extremely difficult circumstances.[127] Their return was part of the 1991 Paris Peace Agreements that formally ended over 15 years of conflict between Cambodia and Vietnam.[128] The returns needed speed, so refugees could participate in the 1993 elections. Coordinated by UNHCR, it was a logistically well-organized movement, and it made the deadline. Beyond that, reintegration was challenging.

The refugees lived in closed camps in Thailand for many years, unable to build skills or acquire the assets that could assist them upon return. They came back to communities where land was scarce, employment opportunities limited, and infrastructure badly damaged. Projects to support reintegration funded by UNHCR and UNDP were relatively small and not well coordinated or linked with longer-term development initiatives.[129]

But the return proved to be durable, although it took many years for returnees to be fully reintegrated. Unlike Afghanistan, there was no resumption of civil conflict following the Peace Agreement. The durability of returns owed much to relative political stability and economic growth, which were present to a greater degree than in Afghanistan.[130]

The return of Rohingya refugees to Myanmar in the 1990s proved far less durable. Myanmar's repression of the Rohingya population intensified in the 1980s. The 1982 Citizenship Law excluded Rohingya, rendering them stateless and subject to persecutory laws and policies which severely marginalized them.

In 1991, a military crackdown on the opposition also targeted Rohingya communities. Houses were confiscated, mosques burned, and cultivation destroyed. Rohingya were subjected to widespread abuse, sexual assault and forced labour. By the end of 1992, around 250,000 had fled to Bangladesh.[131] Bangladesh pushed for their repatriation, as it had done 20 years previously. But, this time, it did so with UNHCR engagement.

Although initially not a part of the agreement between Bangladesh and Myanmar, UNHCR eventually signed agreements with both countries, including provisions to permit its presence in the refugee camps to monitor that

Refugees return to Myanmar from a camp in Cox's Bazar District in Bangladesh in 1997.
© UNHCR/ Anneliese Hollmann

refugees were not coerced to return and to conduct returnee monitoring in Myanmar. Once again, UNHCR determined that returning home was preferable compared with the prospect of refugees living in underserviced, overcrowded and insecure camps. It was willing to facilitate return, including the provision of financial incentives to refugees.

The 1994 and 1995 return of over 150,000 refugees to Myanmar would come to be regarded as one of the low points in UNHCR's repatriation efforts.[132] Human rights groups reported that refugees who resisted return were beaten by the authorities, and UNHCR was criticized for not making explicit to refugees that they could refuse repatriation. Refugees were reportedly informed that conditions in Myanmar had improved, attempts to return to Bangladesh would result in their arrest and detention, and UNHCR's returnee monitoring would help safeguard their protection upon return to Myanmar. The latter, however, turned out to be limited and only in the presence of the Myanmar authorities.[133] As before, grievous repression of Rohingyas continued in Myanmar, leading to ongoing forced displacement and a much larger exodus in 2017.[134]

Middle East

In 1991, some 800,000 forcibly displaced Kurds returned to northern Iraq. They returned under the protection of the United States and members of the Allied Coalition of the Gulf War.

Iraq's invasion and annexation of Kuwait in August 1990, which led to the Gulf War, came amid ongoing internal conflicts between Kurdish nationalists and the Iraqi Government. These escalated following Iraq's defeat in Kuwait. The Government responded with an intensified military campaign against the Kurds, resulting in mass displacement. By 1991, 1.2 million people had fled to Iran.[135] Over 450,000 Kurds fled to the Turkish border and became stranded there. The Turkish Government was confronting a Kurdish separatist movement in the southeast and closed its borders to the Kurdish refugees.[136] It looked to other States to assist.

Hundreds died daily. The Security Council acted on the basis that the situation inside Iraq posed a threat to international security.[137] It passed a resolution demanding Iraq end its repression and allow immediate access by humanitarian organizations to all those in need of international assistance. It also called on the Secretary-General to use all of the resources at his disposal to address critical needs.[138]

The United States and other coalition partners then launched "Operation Provide Comfort", a military operation to secure northern Iraq and facilitate the return of the forcibly displaced Kurds. It involved: clearing out Iraqi forces; maintaining a "no fly zone"; airlifting in humanitarian assistance; and repairing infrastructure and setting up housing to support Kurdish returns.[139] Over 200,000 Kurds returned from the border with Turkey within weeks, with some 600,000 who had fled to Iran also returning in 1991.[140] But stability did not follow. Conflict between opposing Kurdish factions plunged the region into renewed civil conflict within three years.

The return of forcibly displaced Kurds stands out for several reasons. First, it was intended to further a broader military strategy in the region and it involved both humanitarian assistance and military force. Secondly, Turkey's efforts to bar admission to Kurdish refugees went largely unopposed by Western States, attributed to the fact that Turkey was a key strategic ally.[141] Finally, although the returns were conducted in safety, long-term security was not ensured as shown by the quick outbreak of new hostilities.[142]

Africa

Between 1994 and 1999, over three million people forcibly displaced from Rwanda returned home.[143] The story of their return is one of great risk and hardship and part of a broader picture of significant international failure during these years, known as the Great Lakes refugee crisis.[144]

The roots of the Rwandan displacement crisis predate the 1990s but escalated following the 1994 deaths of the Presidents of Burundi and Rwanda in a plane crash. Various conflicting allegations of Tutsi and Hutu culpability circulated. Hutu government extremists in Rwanda used the moment to set in motion a national campaign to eliminate the Tutsi population and Hutu moderates. The resulting carnage killed 800,000 Tutsis[145] and caused the flight of hundreds of thousands of refugees and was broadcast on global television. The refusal of major powers to intervene and stop the genocide remains one of the most significant United Nations security failures.

It was not the last. Within a matter of months, the Tutsi forces of the Rwandan Patriotic Front (RPF) took control of the country. Their rapid progress precipitated the return of some 700,000 Tutsi refugees.[146] It also marked a new exodus of refugees, as 2 million Hutus fled, encouraged to do so by their former government and fearing reprisals for the genocide should they remain. An additional 2 million people were internally displaced.[147]

The new Rwandan Government, anticipating that refugee insurgency groups could form in exile and destabilize the country, encouraged refugees to return to create a State in "unity and equality".[148] However, worrying reports of large-scale killings and persecution of Hutu civilians, including returnees, seriously dampened potential support for return.[149]

Over 1 million Rwandan refugees were in Zaire at the end of 1994,[150] the majority in underserviced camps in the eastern border region. The camps were controlled by deposed Hutu politicians and their supporting forces, collectively known as the "génocidaires". Camp leaders controlled the distribution of food and other relief supplies and levied taxes. They tolerated no opposition, sexually assaulted women and girls and forcibly conscripted men and boys. Cholera and other diseases proliferated, killing tens of thousands.[151]

Zairian authorities were neither willing nor able to disarm and isolate the armed groups, prosecute criminals and maintain law and order.[152] The United

Nations Security Council also did not act on appeals for a multinational contingent to protect the refugees and ensure the civilian and humanitarian nature of the refugee camps.

Complicating matters in eastern Zaire was the fact that Hutu militia were launching attacks into Rwanda. They also attacked Zairian Tutsi populations with the support of the Zairian armed forces and local ethnic

Refugees arrive in Zaire from Rwanda in 1994.
© UNHCR/J. Stjerneklar

groups. Tutsis retaliated and, with support from Rwandan forces, formed a coalition of anti-government forces under the leadership of Laurent Kabila. In their advance on the capital, they attacked the refugee camps.[153]

Over half a million Hutu refugees were driven from the camps in Goma back to Rwanda in November 1996.[154] Hundreds of thousands of refugees fled into the interior of Zaire, with tens of thousands estimated to have died there from exhaustion, lack of food and medical care. An additional several thousand refugees and Hutus from Zaire are believed to have been killed by rebel forces.[155] United Nations efforts to locate and help the dispersed refugees often failed, with just 62,000 airlifted to safety.[156] By the end of 1996, some 780,000 Rwandan refugees had fled from violence in Zaire and returned home.[157]

At the same time, pressure within Tanzania to repatriate all Rwandan refugees increased. Initial assurances by the Government that the returns would take place in an orderly and humane manner were abandoned, and more than

480,000 Rwandan refugees were forcibly returned by the Tanzanian military.[158]

The returnees did not come home to freedom. Many arrived in closed camps in insecure border regions. In 1995, over 4,000 internally displaced Hutus were killed in the Kibeho Camp alone.[159] In the following year, Amnesty International reported a significant increase in unlawful executions by the army and arbitrary killings of civilians by Hutu armed groups and of Hutu civilians by Tutsi civilians.[160]

The Great Lakes refugee crisis prompted deep reflection within the United Nations – including UNHCR – which was criticized for facilitating Hutu refugee returns that were neither voluntary nor safe.[161] UNHCR faced two dismal options[162] left available by such bleak circumstances. It opted for assisting return amid intolerable conditions within the refugee camps, increasing attacks against refugee populations in exile, and the lack of forthcoming protection from major powers.

Repatriation efforts in Mozambique around the same time were not as conflicted. Millions of Mozambican refugees and internally displaced persons moved home in relative security at the conclusion of its 17-year civil war, which began in 1977.[163] The withdrawal of Soviet and South African support led to a negotiated peace in 1992. By the end of the war, over 1 million people had been killed, 4 million were internally displaced and some 1.4 million had sought refuge in neighbouring countries.[164]

The terms of the peace agreement included the right of return and reintegration of persons that had been forced to flee. There was a guarantee of the right to equal treatment, registry on the electoral rolls, and provision for property to be restored to them.[165] A United Nations peace mission oversaw the transition.[166]

Over the course of the following four years, millions of forcibly displaced persons returned to their home areas, in what became the largest repatriation and return movements on the continent.[167] Return was by no means easy, but neither was it as fraught as in Rwanda, principally because Mozambique did not experience the same level of intracommunal conflict. The biggest threat to security came from landmines, rather than the attacks, assassinations and mass incarceration of the Rwandan experience. The success of the returns was also helped by relative political stability, and there was significant humanitarian financing which, in turn, was followed by sustained development support over subsequent years.

UNHCR assisted returnees at home and provided them with seeds and tools. There was available land and, in the years immediately following repatriation, favourable weather helped to secure sufficient food harvests. Furthermore, a return and reintegration investment budget of $100 million helped establish road and bridge construction as well as health and education facilities. A subsequent evaluation of these programmes said they established the basis for longer-term development. Nonetheless, it also found that the links they established to further such investments could be improved.[168] That objective would become a prominent ambition for return and reintegration exercises in later years.

So too would the understanding of *how* people returned home. Many family members did so in stages. Among the first to return, including for short periods, were adult men. They sought to identify economic opportunities, re-establish social contacts, set up claims to land and bring supplies across the border. Some refugees chose to remain behind to acquire more financial capital, while those who had savings and assets were able to use UNHCR's transportation assistance and return.[169]

Latin America

The return of refugees in Central America illustrated both good practice and the constraints on the support of sustainable return. As discussed in Part II, civil conflicts in El Salvador, Guatemala, Honduras and Nicaragua throughout the 1980s resulted in tens of thousands of deaths and over 2 million persons forcibly displaced.[170]

The terms of the 1987 peace agreement signed by Costa Rica, El Salvador, Guatemala, Honduras and Nicaragua included commitments to: engage in political, economic and social reforms; give urgent attention to the forcibly displaced; and facilitate, wherever possible, their voluntary repatriation, resettlement, or integration. The 1989 International Conference on Central American Refugees (CIREFCA) addressed these commitments.[171]

CIREFCA included a detailed Plan of Action, which formed the blueprint for specific humanitarian and development projects presented to donor countries for funding. It contained many progressive elements. It reaffirmed that returns had to be voluntary and supported by strengthening the capacities of civil registries to issue identity documents and civil documents relating to birth, marriage, and deaths. It recognized that initial assistance may be necessary for those wishing to return home including to equitably acquire or reclaim land.[172]

The development of projects under the Plan of Action was approached in an inclusive manner. The process engaged national and local authorities, non-governmental organizations, and displaced and host communities, with active participation of women. This approach helped the projects respond to the needs of all affected communities and contributed to national reconciliation efforts.[173]

The projects that each country submitted for funding reflected their specific circumstances and priorities. Belize, Costa Rica and Mexico submitted projects to enhance refugee self-reliance. Honduras, in contrast, focused on increasing assistance to refugees in camps. Guatemala and Nicaragua prioritized projects to facilitate the reintegration of returnees, with El Salvador focusing its projects primarily on solutions for internally displaced persons.[174]

Guatemalan refugees voluntarily returning home from Mexico start their journey in 1993.
© UNHCR/A. Serrano

CIREFCA had a five-year time frame. At its conclusion in 1994, over $422 million were raised, representing 86 per cent of the amount solicited.[175] The funding helped to support the return of refugees to El Salvador, Guatemala and Nicaragua. Available data suggests that between 1989 and 1999 just over 100,000 returned to these three countries.[176] CIREFCA is noted for having engendered a particularly collaborative approach among displaced persons, local communities, non-governmental organizations, international organizations and national governments. It would endure beyond its term.[177]

CIREFCA's focus on humanitarian assistance linked with longer-term development investments was also among the first of its kind in a forced displacement context. This helped support the sustainability of many of the efforts. It was not without its failings. Although it also aimed to find solutions for all forcibly displaced, funding disproportionately benefited recognized refugees.[178] And while funding was supposed to be contingent on projects meeting certain protection norms, much of development funding did not make this a requirement.[179]

Other problems emerged shortly after, which dampened some of its sustained impact but which were not connected with CIREFCA itself. If anything, they illustrated the kind of massive national and international political commitment that would have been needed to bring about lasting peace and security in El Salvador, Guatemala and Honduras.

The revolutions that gripped Central America were spurred by demands for socioeconomic reforms. The peace process included commitments to expand economic opportunity, improve social justice and check the arbitrary exercise of authority characteristic of old regimes. The ambitious aims were not fully realized in part because many of those who wielded power and influence during the wars, retained considerable influence thereafter.[180]

After the end of the conflicts, the causes that had stoked them persisted. Trade liberalization, relaxed labour laws, and business-friendly tax systems did not generate significant economic growth or lessen the gap in wealth distribution. Unemployment rates remained high. Insecure and poorly paid work in the informal sector grew, and social programmes were not in place to ease conditions faced by large segments of the populations in Central America.[181]

Crime also increased which led governments to resort to the authoritarian practices of the past. The number of youths leaving for the United States increased dramatically, driven by a lack of opportunity, absence of security as well as natural disasters that hit the region at the turn of the century. Among those deported back to the region were those who joined gangs during their time in the United States. Upon return, they contributed to an increase in violent crime and the expansion of transnational criminal networks in the region. Today, the region is among the most violent in the world, contributing to ongoing significant population exoduses.[182]

Violence that had besieged Central America during the 1970s would increase and lead to significant outflows in the 1980s, resuming again in large numbers 20 years later.[183] And, while this helps to explain why CIREFCA was not sufficient to address the systemic drivers, it also does not diminish its notable achievements. CIREFCA brought solutions to many thousands of displaced persons, set an important precedent for linked humanitarian and development responses, raised the profile and engagement of non-governmental organizations and led to more sensitive and effective programming for women.

Europe

The breakup of the former Yugoslavia brought ethnic cleansing and genocide once again to the continent. The conflicts in Croatia, Bosnia-Herzegovina and Kosovo[184] from 1991 to 1999 incurred the largest European wartime casualties and forced displacement since WWII. At the end of the war in Bosnia-Herzegovina in 1995, nearly half of its population of 4.4 million was displaced: nearly 1.1 million internally and 770,000 externally.[185]

The Dayton Peace Accords brought an end to the war in Bosnia-Herzegovina and created Republika Srpska, which is predominately Serbian, and the Federation, which is composed mostly of Bosnians and Croats.[186] It included provisions that all parties commit to the safe and voluntary return of refugees and displaced persons. It also called for the repeal and prevention of any laws, policies or actions inhibiting safe and secure return and reintegration. It acknowledged the right of displaced persons to return to their homes, to property restitution, and compensation for property that could not be restored. UNHCR was tasked with providing a plan for reintegration, which was to be fully facilitated by the parties to the agreement.[187]

Those who originated from areas where their group dominated were able to return in line with the aims of the plan. Circumstances for people returning to regions dominated by another group were less straightforward. They faced ongoing discrimination, harassment, unequal protection under the law and no foreseeable progress on property restitution or compensation.[188]

In Kosovo, the war ended in 1999. An estimated 1.6 million people, close to 90 per cent of the population, were forcibly displaced at some point during and after the conflict.[189] The provisions for return of those forced to flee during the conflict were part of the United Nations Security Council resolution authorizing an international civil and security presence there.[190] The return of ethnic Albanians was massive and quick. Although the security sector underwent positive reforms, ethnic tensions lingered and resolution of property disputes through the regular justice system was relatively slow.[191]

And despite efforts in support of ethnic reintegration, non-Albanian minorities faced discrimination and harassment leading 200,000 to flee Kosovo. Meanwhile, displaced Serbs were prevented from returning to their areas of origin within Kosovo.[192] More than 20 years later, thousands of people displaced by the conflict continue to have ongoing displacement-related needs.[193]

Selective Resettlement

The resettlement of refugees from the post-WWII period through the end of the 1980s was primarily a State-driven process with a specific focus on serving a broader geopolitical purpose. The first major multilateral resettlement effort came at the conclusion of WWII in response to the close to 1 million people remaining in displaced persons camps through Allied-occupied Germany. As described by Ben Shephard, they had "diverse and complicated wartime histories".[194]

Displaced people queue for resettlement opportunities coordinated through the International Refugee Organization established in 1947.
© IRO

There were around 250,000 Holocaust survivors. There were others too: Estonians; Latvians; Lithuanians; Ukrainians; and Yugoslavs. Among them were those who had been displaced and forced to work in Germany, prisoners of war and Nazi collaborators. Their most unifying characteristic was an inability or unwillingness to return to their former homes.[195]

Part of the remit of the International Refugee Organization (IRO) was to assist in finding solutions to this displacement. Persons of German ethnic origin, "whether German nationals or members of German minorities in other countries", were excluded from its mandate on the grounds that they were the responsibility of Germany.[196] This was not the only politicization of the IRO.

While the Soviet Union and its allies supported the idea of a humanitarian relief agency, they opposed it having anything to do with the resettlement of refugees. They demanded that their nationals be returned to help rebuild their countries and for Nazi collaborators to be returned to face prosecution.[197] The refusal of the Soviet Union to join the IRO left the solutions work it undertook largely steered by Western allies. It also marked the beginning of Cold War politics influencing international efforts for durable solutions more generally.

The United States funded 40 per cent of the IRO's budget of close to half a billion dollars. Along with over 16 voluntary agencies, the IRO helped to coordinate with States the voluntary repatriation and resettlement of the displaced persons camp populations.[198] The latter was more of an immigration exercise than a humanitarian one.

Countries across Western Europe, the Americas and Australia approached the displaced person camps as sources of much needed labour. Depending on the national economy, workers were required for farming, mining, logging, manufacturing, and domestic work. At one point, there were over 50 national missions in the displacement camps undertaking recruitment operations.[199]

Each resettlement country had its own selection criteria, tailored to meet its immigration needs. Competition for workers was so intense that many displaced people were in a position to choose from several resettlement offers. UNHCR urged States to stop the "continuous skimming processes" whereby the most skilled and employable were taken first and others rejected.[200]

Forty per cent of those resettled, 380,000 persons, went to the United States. Australia and Canada resettled approximately 170,000 and 160,000 displaced persons respectively. Western European countries accounted for an additional 170,000 more and close to 100,000 displaced persons were resettled in Latin America, over two thirds of whom went to Argentina, Brazil and Venezuela.[201]

But tens of thousands of unselected refugees were left in the camps, including many Jewish refugees. Resettlement countries tended to screen them out as inadmissible, keeping the closed-door immigration policies of the war years firmly in place. It would take several years before the displaced persons camps in Europe were empty. The majority of the Jewish camp population eventually resettled in Palestine.[202]

Among the legacies of the post-war push for solutions to displacement was the fact that refugees were not screened for their wartime records, and subsequent decades revealed Nazi collaborators and war criminals successfully resettled with impunity.[203] Some were able to immigrate by obscuring their identities and histories. Others – including leading scientists, military and political leaders – were deliberately selected for resettlement to countries, like the United Kingdom and the United States, for their skills and knowledge.[204]

And so the immediate post-war period revealed that Cold War politics and State self-interest dominated the calculus in regard to international efforts in support of refugee repatriation and resettlement.[205] These motivations would again come into play in the international response to the Hungarian crisis of 1956.

In the course of the Russian military intervention to suppress the 1956 Hungarian Revolution, some 20,000 Hungarians were killed and over 200,000 Hungarians fled, most to Austria. Over 140,000 Hungarian refugees were resettled within two years to the United States, Canada, the United Kingdom, West Germany, Australia, Switzerland, and France.[206]

The fact that the refugees were fleeing communism, and a large proportion were young, educated and skilled largely accounts for the relatively swift response from allied nations. There was also considerable public support in the resettlement countries for the programme.[207] There were relatively few refugees left behind.[208]

An international resettlement effort of significant size would not come again for close to 25 years. There was one notable exception in 1972: the resettlement of South Asian residents of Uganda who Idi Amin ordered to leave the country within 90 days. They numbered around 80,000 people, many having lived in Uganda for decades. Over half of them held British passports.

Despite initial reservations, the United Kingdom accepted close to 30,000 Ugandan Asians who were British citizens.[209] Those with Bangladeshi, Indian or Pakistani nationality went there. The United Kingdom appealed for other countries to come forward with resettlement offers for the others who were not recognized as nationals by any country. The response was quick. Eighteen other countries participated, and the crisis was resolved within two years.

The success came about because refugees were largely skilled and educated, allowing them to meet labour needs in receiving countries. The United Kingdom's call for help from other countries was also an important factor.[210] The response was the first multilateral effort of such size outside Europe. It was a prelude to the massive efforts undertaken at the end of the 1970s to respond to the Indochinese crisis.

Multilateral efforts to resolve mass displacement in Indochina resulted in the resettlement of an estimated 1.4 million refugees from 1979 to 1996.[211] It was the largest multinational resettlement exercise since WWII and, like then, was a reflection of the geopolitical interests of resettlement States.

The end of the Vietnam War in 1975 saw the steady exodus of refugees from the communist regimes of Vietnam, Cambodia and Laos. By 1979, 570,000 refugees had fled.[212] Vietnam was the source of the largest number. Individuals associated with the previous United States-backed government faced persecution as did religious leaders, journalists and intellectuals who were suspected of questioning the government's policies. Over 1 million people were sent to forced labour "re-education" camps where many died.[213]

Ethnic Chinese, primarily concentrated in south Vietnam, were also viewed as anti-government and their loyalty was suspect. Their situation grew more tenuous following a brief border war between China and Vietnam between the years of 1977 and 1979. Growing restrictions on their rights to work, be educated and own a business prompted up to 260,000 to leave for China.[214]

From Laos, the Hmong and other highland people took flight fearing government retribution for being allied with the United States throughout the war. They were joined by other educated and urban refugees from the lowlands, also associated with the United States Government. In Cambodia, the policies of the Khmer Rouge who were in power from 1975 to 1979 included widespread killings of intellectuals, massive compulsory population relocations, forced labour, and repressive surveillance. An estimated 1.5–2 million people died as a result of their policies and, by 1978, over 160,000 Cambodians had fled the country.[215]

Most refugee departures were clandestine, across treacherous overland routes and perilous voyages by sea. As today, the ones who departed by boat captured the greater part of the world's attention, so much so that the movement came to be known as the "boat people crisis".

The crisis was due not just to the large and increasing numbers of refugees, but also to the then British Territory of Hong Kong and neighbouring States that progressively refused refugees entry. Refugees attempting to land were pushed out to sea where they languished for weeks to months in overcrowded, unseaworthy vessels, lacking sufficient food and water and prey to repeated and vicious pirate attacks.[216] An estimate 30,000 people perished at sea during this period.[217]

To address the growing human calamity, the United Nations convened an international conference in 1979 to broker a burden-sharing solution. It included delegates from over 65 governments, as well as representatives from international agencies and non-governmental organizations. Industrialized countries agreed to resettle refugees.[218] Receiving countries in the region agreed to admit and temporarily protect refugees pending their resettlement. For its part,

Vietnam agreed to maintain an Orderly Departure Program in collaboration with UNHCR, to enable Vietnamese to leave legally without risking their lives in the process.[219]

These commitments bore results. Pushbacks largely ceased. Some 125,000 persons departed directly from Vietnam during the first eight years of the Orderly Departure Program.[220] More than 400,000 Indochinese refugees were resettled overseas from countries in the region, considerably outpacing new arrivals which also fell.[221] By the end of the decade, however, these trends

Vietnamese refugees on a boat off the Malaysian coast in 1978.
© UNHCR/ Kaspar Gaugler

were in jeopardy. The pace of arrivals picked up, resettlement places declined, and pushbacks commenced again.[222] The willingness of resettlement countries waned, as many were receiving more asylum-seekers directly at their borders and there was a growing perception that people were leaving Vietnam more for economic than protection reasons.

In 1989, a second international conference on Indochinese refugees resulted in a revised agreement: The Comprehensive Plan of Action (CPA).[223] Under the CPA, the Orderly Departure Program from Vietnam continued. As for those who were newly arrived in countries in the region, only those determined to be refugees would be resettled, while the others were returned to their home countries.[224] The CPA provided for Vietnam to receive financial support and assistance in reintegrating returnees and UNHCR would monitor their safety on return.[225] It also included provisions for a mass media and education campaign on the dangers of irregular travel by sea.

The CPA was implemented by UNHCR and steered by a Committee of participating governments. Countries largely met their commitments, pushbacks diminished, and the number of arrivals fell.[226] Close to 400,000 Vietnamese and Laotians were resettled from countries in the region, while about half a million departed directly from Vietnam.[227] Receiving countries in the region worked with UNHCR to put in place refugee status determination procedures to determine eligibility for resettlement.[228]

The implementation of the CPA was not without its challenges and, while it succeeded in delivering solutions to more refugees in a given situation than before or since that time, it also had its weaknesses. The refugee determination procedures in countries varied. Procedural protections were not uniformly applied, criteria were open to diverse interpretations, and different approaches were taken on determining credibility.[229] There were also extensive delays, with many asylum-seekers having to wait for long periods, including years, in detention facilities or refugee camps. These were often overcrowded with high levels of violence reported.[230]

The CPA was based on a shared view that many of the boat arrivals were not compelled to flee but, rather, were seeking better life prospects. Some authors claim that the CPA may have reinforced notions in the Asia Pacific region that people arriving irregularly on boats were not refugees but economic migrants and queue jumpers.[231] It has also been suggested that the CPA unhelpfully deflected responsibility for refugees outside the region, away from receiving States. Countries of the region increasingly came to see solutions as lying with resettlement nations abroad. This could have reinforced reticence in some countries to sign the 1951 Convention and assume responsibilities towards refugee resettlement.[232]

Generally, observers agree that the CPA was on balance an exceptionally successful international refugee responsibility-sharing initiative in the post-WWII period. The forging of this agreement among disparate States across both sides of the Cold War divide looks like a remarkable achievement today. It was possible because of the rather unique convergence of interests of the country of origin, the countries of first asylum and resettlement countries.

Vietnam sought to repair relations with its Association of Southeast Asian Nations (ASEAN) neighbours. It had started to pursue greater economic liberalization for which better relations with industrialized States were important. For receiving States in the region, the CPA enabled them to resolve a growing problem at their maritime borders without being responsible for the permanent settlement of refugees.

For the countries that resettled most of the refugees, the CPA was aligned with their foreign policy objectives. These included normalizing relations with Vietnam to further regional stability and serving their immigration priorities which favoured refugees from communist countries. The CPA also received considerable public support in resettlement States, which helped to ensure the robust resettlement quotas they assumed.[233]

Although the size of the resettlement programme was record-breaking, the size of the refugee situation was not. There were existing and emerging situations in Africa and other parts of Asia which eclipsed the number of Indochinese refugees and for which no similar multinational resettlement effort was made.[234] In fact, globally there was an immediate drop in annual resettlement places following the Indochinese resettlement effort.

By the close of the Indochinese programme, most resettlement governments expressed a sense of having met their commitments. The strong public support for resettlement fell off.[235] The end of the Cold War also removed one of the incentives that had underpinned past resettlement efforts. The number of refugees arriving directly in resettlement countries seeking asylum was on the rise, leaving the countries less inclined to significantly increase resettlement programmes, especially during the economic recession of the early 1990s.

Local Integration at the Periphery

Through the 1960s and 1970s across Africa, local integration as a solution was not embraced although refugees faced relatively fewer barriers to achieving self-reliance. Tanzania, Uganda and Zambia were among the countries at this time that allocated land to refugees to cultivate and opportunities to trade in local markets.[236] Uganda has maintained this approach in areas designated for refugee settlement, while also granting access to employment and relative freedom of movement in recent years.[237]

Prince Sadruddin Aga Khan, during his tenure as the United Nations High Commissioner for Refugees (1966–1977), advocated for more development approaches to refugee situations. Considering the growing numbers of refugees in Africa and Asia, he stressed that development assistance was critical to help refugees contribute to the economic and social development of their host countries and assist those countries who faced significant development challenges of their own.[238] This would also be pursued by subsequent High

Commissioners but, as discussed in Parts IV and V, only gained significant traction recently.

Meanwhile, refugees faced increasing barriers to local integration and restrictions on their ability to integrate socially and economically in their host communities. These barriers and restrictions became more prevalent in the 1980s as refugee numbers grew appreciably. Refugees were increasingly confined to camps and otherwise prevented from moving freely, working, accessing services or otherwise integrating.

There was also very little effort made to encourage host States to integrate refugees. This was, in part, based on the assumption that local integration would involve significant costs that host States should not have to bear. That view would only be tested in later years as the cost of protracted displacement grew, and the potential benefits of greater inclusion came to the fore in the new millennium.

New Millennium

The 20 years of the new millennium are bracketed by two initiatives to enhance international responses to refugees and improve the record on achieving durable solutions. The first was the Global Consultations on International Protection in 2001–2002 and the Agenda for Protection marking the 50th anniversary of the 1951 Convention. The second was the 2018 Global Compact on Refugees.

The Global Consultations took place over the course of two years. They aimed to address the many challenges that faced the implementation of the 1951 Convention and its 1967 Protocol, including new forms of persecution and conflict, complex mixed movements, the reluctance of many States to accept refugees, and restrictive interpretations of the 1951 Convention. A specific component was dedicated to solutions, highlighting what had been learned from past experience and ways to secure more. Among the understandings reached was the value in investing in education and skills development in displacement and the many factors that help sustain successful voluntary repatriation.[239]

The Global Consultations helped inform the Agenda for Protection, first published in 2002. A joint effort by UNHCR and States, the Agenda was a comprehensive programme of action, one goal of which focused on "redoubling the search for durable solutions".[240] It included a number of commitments such as improving conditions for safe and sustainable voluntary repatriation, expanding resettlement and using it more effectively, and examining where, when, and how to promote secure legal status and resident rights for refugees in host countries.

Over the next 15 years various initiatives were launched to reach these goals. While they failed to realize significantly more solutions for refugees, the efforts led to a deeper understanding of displacement dynamics. They showed that strengthening human capital is often critical to the success of any solution, and that there are opportunities for more solutions to displacement beyond the traditional three options of permanent return, resettlement or local integration.

The Global Compact on Refugees reflects this orientation. In addition to affirming the need to expand opportunities to realize the three traditional solutions, it emphasizes strengthening the human capital of refugees and host communities. It promotes investing in institutional capacities through inclusive development policies and looks at opening up migration pathways to refugees and facilitating labour mobility.[241] Also drawing from past experience, it recognizes the need for improved data and better use of evidence to underpin programmes for solutions.

Voluntary Return

The 21st century has seen an overall reduction in the number of refugee returns from the previous decade, chiefly due the protracted nature of the conflicts that account for most of the world's refugee population and a significant proportion of internally displaced persons.

The 1990s led to a greater appreciation of the complexities of repatriation. Among the lessons learned was the damaging consequences of premature return. Another was the importance of strong links between return and the peace and reconciliation processes.[242] There was more insight into the importance of political stability and security. Without it, heavy investment in reconstruction and reconciliation are often not sufficient to sustain returns.[243] Experience also showed that returnees can arrive in places and circumstances that have been significantly reshaped since they left. That, in turn, demonstrated why the acquisition of new skills and capital during displacement is often critical to the sustainability of return.[244]

The fluid nature of return was also evident between 2000 and 2020, provoking new thinking on when movements in a back-and-forth pattern should be supported. Afghanistan provides an example of this. Between 2002 and 2020, over 6 million refugee returns were recorded, with the largest numbers following the fall of the Taliban regime in 2002. A further spike was ex-

Percentage of refugees and internally displaced people finding a solution

2000-2020

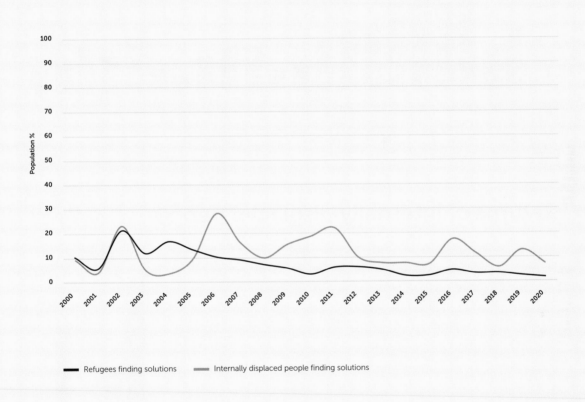

Refugee solutions

2000-2020

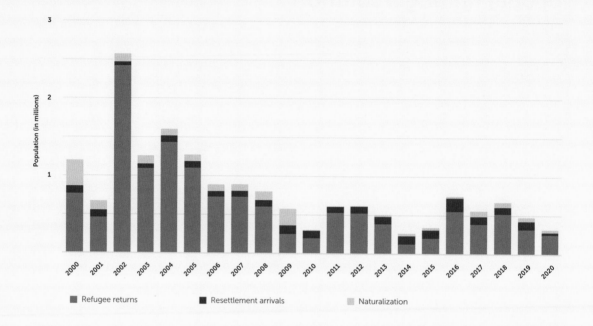

Population (in millions)

- Refugee returns
- Resettlement arrivals
- Naturalization

Returns of internally displaced people

2000-2020

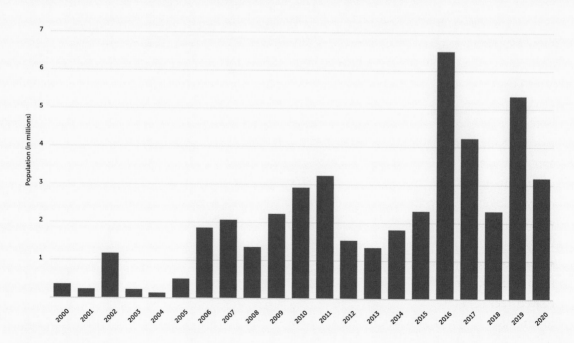

Population (in millions)

perienced in 2016 in the face of intensified pressure to return from Pakistan.[245]

Overall, however, Afghan refugee numbers remained relatively constant between 2002 and 2020, at 2–3 million persons.[246] At the end of 2020, 2.6 million Afghans remained refugees, more than 85 per cent of them hosted in Pakistan and Iran.[247] Overall, this points to persistently high levels of refugee displacement.

Available figures on internally displaced persons show a similar trend. Between 2002 and 2020, close to 1.3 million internally displaced persons reportedly returned to their places of origin. And, while the number of internally displaced persons initially fell after 2002, they began to rise annually again in 2007 reaching over 3.5 million people by mid-2021.[248]

Afghanistan has consistently ranked low on the Human Development Index afflicted by ongoing conflict, violence and extremely high rates of unemployment, weak State institutions and ongoing insecurity. These factors contribute to ongoing high levels of forced displacement.[249]

Studies of Afghan returnee populations demonstrated the precarious nature of their situations. They further highlighted the importance of acquiring skills and capital in exile and showed how robust return assistance can contribute positively to returnees' livelihoods and accommodation in certain contexts.[250] They also showed how return was not simply a one-way movement. Afghan returnees continued to move between Afghanistan and Iran and Pakistan, both in flight from violence as well as for employment and other commercial activities.[251]

The back-and-forth refugee flight and return pattern seen in Afghanistan is also apparent in other places. It comes as forcibly displaced people check on their families or landholdings and assess the prospects for longer return. It has been followed in recent decades by Congolese refugees in Uganda, Iraqi refugees in Jordan, and refugees from the conflicts in Sudan and South Sudan. These movements often predate periods of conflict and relate to seasonal and temporary labour opportunities as well as community and commercial ties.[252]

In Sudan, despite ongoing fragility, at least 750,000 refugees and internally displaced persons returned to the South between 2005 and 2010, many to participate in the 2011 independence referendum.[253] As noted in a 2008 study, they returned to an "impoverished and ill-prepared post-war social and economic environment", which came under further pressure from returning populations.[254] Returns were not all one-off movements. Some moved back and forth. Others opted for a staggered or partial process, such as maintaining links in the host country through employment, commercial activities or remaining family members, while seeking to secure a more stable foothold back home.[255] Maintaining these links was also important when renewed conflict caused some of the largest forced displacements of the past decade.[256]

Cyclical movements and significant forced displacement have marked the Democratic Republic of the Congo for many years. In the past decade refugee returns have remained relatively low, at just over 255,000. And while some 6.5 million internally displaced persons returned during the same period, as in Afghanistan, constant instability and insecurity led to further forced displacement. At the end of 2020, over 5 million people were internally displaced, up from 1.7 million in 2010.[257]

The Syrian civil war began in 2011 and, since then, over half its population of 22 million have been forced to flee, often multiple times. At the end of 2020, there were approximately 6.7 million Syrians internally displaced and 6.7 million Syrian refugees mostly residing in neighbouring countries of Turkey, Lebanon and Jordan.[258]

Internal forced displacements have remained both significant and fluid over the years. Families have repeatedly been forced to flee, as areas that had offered a modicum of safety come under fire and front lines shift. Many also move to seek humanitarian assistance and search for family members. Some have returned to their homes. Ongoing hostilities, however, have seen more people flee than return. In 2020 alone, close to 1.8 million internally displaced persons moved mostly due to conflict, while just under 450,000 were estimated to have returned home that year.[259]

The largest Syrian refugee movements occurred between 2011 and 2014, after which time neighbouring countries tightened their borders. Returns to Syria by refugees have been relatively modest. UNHCR has verified that, since 2016, some 280,000 refugees returned to Syria from Turkey, Lebanon, Jordan, Iraq and Egypt.[260] A World Bank analysis of returns of Syrian refugees between 2014 and 2018 reveals their complex nature.

It found that a lack of security inside Syria was a major deterrent to return. Other disincentives included destruction of the family home and the lack of employment, education, health and basic services.[261] This analysis mirrors the findings of a series of UNHCR Syrian Refugee Intention Surveys. These show that, while the majority of refugees want to return home eventually, fewer than 3 per cent wished to do so within the following 12 months, citing the same obstacles to return.[262]

Documented Syrian returns show a partial and staggered approach, as seen in other places. For example, it is not uncommon for some relatives of returning family members to remain behind, including those fearing reprisals for leaving or forced military service and those with insufficient capital and assets to restart their lives there.

Moreover, among those who do return, many do so to test the waters, as an interim approach to a decision to return permanently. This can help build confidence for eventual return. Many host States have been unwilling to facilitate this formally through the issuance of visas that would permit authorized cross-border movements. They have insisted that return should be one way. The result is that many refugees may be cautious about returning if it means giving up legal status in neighbouring countries.

There have been some notable State practices in the last 20 years that could provide useful precedents. Between 2007 and 2010, Nigeria regularized the status of 117,000 Liberian refugees and 18,000 Sierra Leonean refugees who did not wish to participate in the voluntary repatriation exercises at that time. They were permitted residency as migrants, on the condition that they also acknowledged they were no longer refugees.[263]

More recently, in 2017, Pakistan adopted a Comprehensive Policy on Voluntary Repatriation and Management of Afghan Affairs. It provides for a flexible visa regime for registered Afghan refugees that enables them to apply for visas from within Pakistan. While promising on its face, challenges remain. To qualify, a refugee must have an Afghan passport. Although the World Bank has provided funding for Afghanistan to issue passports within Pakistan, this has not yet occurred.[264] Additionally, a refugee who receives a visa must give up refugee status without being assured of reobtaining refugee status at the expiry of the visa. Finally, many eligible Afghans would have difficulty meeting the formal requirements for a visa.

If these challenges are overcome, a flexible visa system, like this and others elsewhere, could facilitate mobility between home and place of refuge. Such schemes may not be enough to signal an end to displacement, but they could regularize what is already a critical coping strategy and often a means to help prepare the way for future return. They could enhance security by revealing a more accurate picture of cross-border movement, not least for the host country and the country of origin. Some have even pointed out that a small fee for visas could raise substantial revenues.

Resettlement

Resettlement has moved between peaks and troughs in the first two decades of the 21st century, with little evidence to suggest that it will provide solutions for

Refugee resettlement

2000-2020

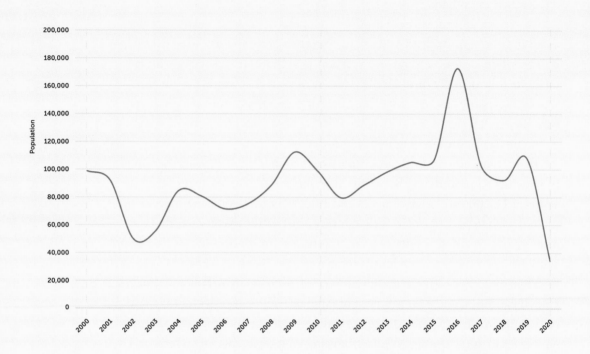

significantly more refugees in the future. But, more positively, resettled refugees increasingly have come from a broader range of countries.[265]

Annual resettlement levels fell by almost half following the 2001 terrorist attacks on the United States, to just 50,000 persons in 2002.[266] Not only did some major resettlement countries lower their annual quotas; most imposed more stringent security clearance tests which lengthened the processing times. It would take almost a decade before annual resettlement levels would rebound to approximately 100,000 persons.[267] Even after this recovery, resettlement served as a solution for a very limited number of refugees compared to the number of refugees globally.

Various efforts were made to improve resettlement processes. They included the 2004 Multilateral Framework of Understandings (MFU) on Resettlement. Endorsed by long-standing and emerging resettlement States, it was a compendium of good practices. Nonetheless, it underscored that the decision to use flexible selection criteria was entirely discretionary.[268]

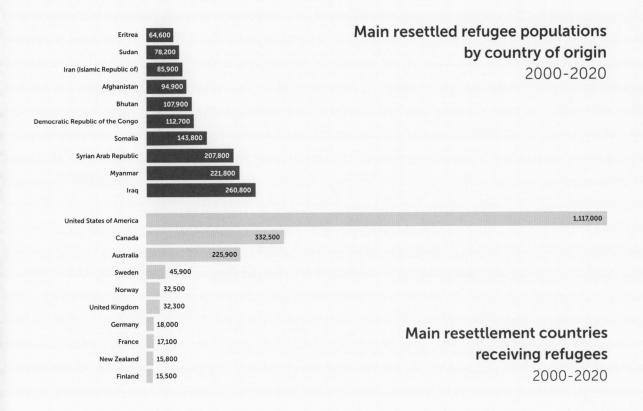

Main resettled refugee populations by country of origin
2000-2020

Country of origin	Population
Eritrea	64,600
Sudan	78,200
Iran (Islamic Republic of)	85,900
Afghanistan	94,900
Bhutan	107,900
Democratic Republic of the Congo	112,700
Somalia	143,800
Syrian Arab Republic	207,800
Myanmar	221,800
Iraq	260,800

Main resettlement countries receiving refugees
2000-2020

Resettlement country	Refugees
United States of America	1,117,000
Canada	332,500
Australia	225,900
Sweden	45,900
Norway	32,500
United Kingdom	32,300
Germany	18,000
France	17,100
New Zealand	15,800
Finland	15,500

An attempt to put the MFU to use as part of a Comprehensive Plan of Action for Somali refugees in 2004 fell through when the Plan did not materialize.[269] Aspects of the MFU, however, were used to facilitate expedited processing of refugees whose circumstances were so similar that individual processing was not necessary.[270] Rather than conduct individual interviews, they could be processed as a group.

Meanwhile, a parallel effort was underway to use resettlement more "strategically" to benefit not just resettled refugees but also other refugees. It envisaged, for example, agreements between resettlement and host countries whereby the former would increase the number of refugees it resettled and the latter would enact more favourable integration policies towards the majority of refugees remaining on its territory.

But, in practice, the strategic use of resettlement did not yield significant tangible benefits.[271] Instead, it led to some problematic results. Some European States considered it "strategic" to reduce offers of resettlement places in response to increased asylum applications, or to make resettlement conditional on the host country readmitting failed asylum-seekers.[272] Australia considered it was using resettlement "strategically" to benefit "worthy" refugees, while resorting to offshore processing and detention to deter asylum-seekers who were labelled "queue jumpers".[273]

Other initiatives achieved results more in line with their intentions, but for small numbers of refugees. In some instances, refugees who have already been selected for resettlement but are in imminent risk, are relocated temporarily to emergency transit facilities in Romania and the Philippines, pending the completion of resettlement processes.[274] Other facilities have since been set up in Niger and Rwanda for refugees evacuated from appalling detention conditions in Libya. Refugees in those centres are assessed for resettlement, although not all are selected by resettlement countries.

Beginning in 2016, there was an encouraging rise in annual resettlement figures, largely in response to the Syria situation. The number of resettlement States more than doubled between 2014 and 2017,[275] and resettlement departures rose to a 20-year high of 173,000 in 2016.[276] It was not to last. A significant reduction in United States resettlement places in 2017 led to a steep 41 per cent drop in the number of refugees annually resettled.[277] Refugee resettlement dropped to the lowest levels on record in at least two decades. Fewer than 35,000 refugees were resettled in 2020, representing a fraction of 1 per cent of refugees globally.[278]

In 2019, a set of goals for the decade ahead was agreed between UNHCR, resettlement countries and other partners. The aim is to facilitate the admission of 1 million refugees from 2019 to 2028 through resettlement, and an additional 2 million refugees through other immigration admission programmes, known as complementary pathways.[279]

The decline in annual resettlement quotas, however, is not encouraging, and neither is the level of firm multi-year pledges from States at the first Global Refugee Forum of 2019.[280] Most resettlement States pledged to continue their resettlement programmes, but there were no firm commitments to significantly increase them. While some countries pledged to start resettlement programmes, they provided few details on time frames or the numbers of refugees they would accept.[281] Meanwhile, calls to prioritize resettlement of refugees most at risk continue to clash with States determined to apply integration criteria relating to language or educational skills, religion, health and family size.

Resettlement has always provoked vigorous debate in receiving countries, especially during economically challenging times which also tend to correspond with increased populism and demands for fewer refugee admissions. Maintaining existing programmes, let alone increasing them, will likely continue to depend on public support. Evidence that resettled refugees do integrate into their communities and contribute to economic growth over time can help. Empirical evidence of what leads to better integration outcomes is improving.

There are costs in providing support to refugees, such as through financial assistance, language classes and help in accessing housing, health care, education and employment. However, recent findings show that the costs of

Syrian refugees, Abdel Qader and his sister, Ruha, are resettled to Germany in 2013. © UNHCR/ Elena Dorfman

these measures are more than compensated by economic gains that they generate in the medium and longer term.[282] The engagement of non-governmental organizations, local volunteers and diaspora also has been shown to improve integration outcomes and deepen understandings between refugees and host communities.[283]

Studies in the United States have demonstrated that employment rates of resettled refugees are on par with native-born citizens. Although they often experience lower wages and tend to be concentrated in unskilled sectors, they out-perform other migrants in terms of English language acquisition, labour market participation and earnings.[284] Over the course of their first 20 years in the United States, resettled refugees are estimated to pay on average $21,000 more in taxes than they receive in benefits.[285] Similar studies in the European Union also point to initial short-term economic costs that are estimated to be more than offset in the longer term.[286]

More generally, a recent review of available literature on the influx of refugees to high-income countries reveals that host countries are able to absorb large influxes into their labour markets with no adverse effects on average wages or overall employment.[287]

As long as there are immigrant-receiving countries and public support for refugees, government resettlement programmes will likely be around for some time to come. The 2020 drop in annual resettlement figures – largely on account of a global pandemic and policy change which has since been reversed in the largest resettlement country – is not likely to be permanent if past highs and lows are any guide.[288] Equally, however, we also are unlikely to see a significant increase in resettlement places beyond previous peak levels.

The resettlement strategy seems to reflect this. It calls for 1 million places over the next decade, a target consistent with the annual resettlement admissions of the past. There is one area where it looks for an increase: in the doubling of opportunities for refugees to access other immigration avenues referred to as "complementary pathways".

Complementary Pathways

Opening up more immigration channels to refugees and migrants appears among the commitments made by States in the New York Declaration in 2016. It is also found in two more recent compacts of 2018: the Global Compact on Refugees and the Global Compact for Safe, Orderly and Regular Migration.[289] Global migration trends point to the potential of complementary pathways. Immigration levels to high-income countries are increasing, and the national, economic, social and cultural backgrounds of immigrants are diverse.[290]

In 2021, UNHCR and the Organisation for Economic Co-operation and Development (OECD) examined the extent to which individuals from seven of the top refugee-producing countries were already benefiting from complementary pathways in 35 OECD member States and Brazil.[291] In particular, they looked at the granting of family, education and work visas between 2010 and 2019 to nationals from Afghanistan, Eritrea, Iran, Iraq, Somalia, Syria and Venezuela. The study produced three interesting pictures.

First, it found that 60 per cent more nationals from these countries came to the OECD and Brazil through family, education and work permits (1.5

million) than the number that arrived through resettlement (572,000).[292] Secondly, they made up a particularly small percentage of the total number of immigrant admissions through these categories overall.[293] The report concluded that more could be done to make these avenues more widely accessible to forcibly displaced populations.

Like many good intentions, commitments to expand complementary pathways systematically and significantly will take effort – and more than has been expended so far. That could include ensuring that forcibly displaced persons are aware of these options. Importantly, there is a need to ease barriers that obstruct access to them. The obstacles can be significant. They include a lack of needed documentation,[294] insufficient funds to pay processing and travel fees, evidence to show the person will not rely on public funds post-arrival and, in the case of temporary permits, guarantees that the person can return to their previous place of residence.

Furthermore, visa application processes can be complicated, and they are not uniform across countries. Knowing how to navigate them can take specialized knowledge not readily available in many forced displacement contexts. There are efforts to help refugees navigate these processes. But they have not yet reached the scale needed for States to meet their commitments for increased access to complementary pathways.[295]

Measures to widen access to family immigration schemes could include broadening the definition of family beyond the nuclear family, waiving processing fees, and easing some financial requirements that resident family members must demonstrate to show they can support applicants.[296]

Efforts to help forcibly displaced people access education pathways also need significant expansion to fulfil the ambitions of the Global Compact on Refugees. The existing programmes designed for this purpose are also relatively few in number and small in scale. Expansion could occur through broader outreach to refugee communities, greater engagement from education institutions, and financial support to refugees selected. They could also be complemented by further access to online education opportunities.

The situation with labour mobility schemes is arguably more complex. Migrant workers make up some 18 per cent of the workforce in high-income countries, according to the International Labour Organization. Over 45 per cent are concentrated in North America and Northern, Southern and Western Europe.[297] This points to opportunity. However, the OECD-UNHCR study demonstrated that only 4 per cent of all work permits issued to foreigners in the OECD went to nationals of the seven major refugee-producing countries under review. Positively, the number of work permits granted steadily increased throughout the decade and more than doubled by 2019.[298]

Some economists have voiced doubts about the prospects of labour migration to high-income countries becoming a viable option for refugees. Among the noted obstacles is that most labour programmes are set up on a temporary basis, which is a problem for refugees who cannot return home. If the work is in a third country, return to the country from which the refugee was selected, requires agreement of that State.[299] Experience has shown that host and transit countries are reluctant to enter readmission agreements. Without that, States with temporary worker programmes may be reluctant to offer labour market access if they believe the refugees will never leave.[300]

While others recognize the challenges in bringing labour mobility schemes to scale, they maintain that there is potential for them to be of significant benefit. Talent Beyond Boundaries (TBB), which matches displaced people with job opportunities around the world, holds this view. It points to Canada, where an initial agreement with the Government to match 10–15 refugees with employers has now expanded to 500 refugees and their families between 2021 and 2022.[301]

Kris Braun, a representative of Canada's technology industry observes that the programme has helped fill skills gaps. He notes that it works for refugees trying to "get their life moving forward again" and for Canada's growing tech industry that is in need of their skills.[302] Australia has initiated a scheme with a current quota of 100 refugees and their families.[303] The United Kingdom is considering a similar commitment.[304]

Private sponsorship programmes are another form of complementary pathways whereby private groups identify and sponsor refugees, undertaking responsibility for their care after arrival and for a specified period. Refugees benefiting from these programmes are identified independently by the sponsoring group or State and not by UNHCR, and not necessarily prioritized by critical need. While the number of these programmes is gradually expanding, they have not yet generated significant increases in overall refugee admissions.

Canada's private sponsorship programme is the largest and has been in place the longest. Through it, 327,000 refugees have been admitted to Canada over 40 years.[305] Most assessments conclude that community engagement improves reception and helps advance refugee integration. But some have also argued that, in certain cases, private sponsorship programmes can come at the expense of a reduction in State resettlement programmes.[306]

Taken together, the potential of complementary pathways is not yet clear.

State commitments over the past five years to expand their availability to forcibly displaced persons are a start. But much more work is needed to make these promises a reality. And, to repeat a recurring theme of this publication, better data collection is needed to assess progress against the ambitious target that has been set.

The Canadian example has demonstrated the value in starting with a pilot scheme in labour mobility. Since it was facilitated through a central ministry, it featured the ability to convene other government authorities, and the opportunity to assess what works, helping build support.

The OECD-UNHCR study reveals that immigration avenues are being used by populations affected by conflict, including those from the countries generating the largest displacements in the world.[307] Further study is needed to identify how those who benefited were able to access these pathways, notably whether refugees were able to access them autonomously, the obstacles they faced and how those were overcome.

Meanwhile, some academics have suggested that one way of opening more mobility for refugees is to facilitate their movement to a country of their choice by reviving the Nansen passport. A determination of refugee status by a recognized authority, such as UNHCR, could be followed by the granting of a Nansen passport recognized by States participating in refugee protection. The passport would entitle a refugee to move for work, to join family and/or to find a community beyond the country where the refugee first finds refuge. Recognizing that this idea is likely to meet opposition among States, the authors suggest that States could determine how many refugees they would accept in this way and make it conditional on factors, such as job offer, and proven means to be self-supporting upon arrival.[308]

Integrating Locally

Local integration figured rather timidly as a solution in the 2002 Agenda for Protection. In it, States committed only to "examining" the circumstances in which it could be supported. However, strengthening human capital in displacement – through education, skills and opportunities for self-reliance – was expressed more definitively.

Several initiatives followed over the next decade but, globally, the picture did not appreciably change.[309] There was ongoing resistance to the economic and social inclusion of refugees and serious challenges regarding the integration of internally displaced persons.[310] A significant shift finally emerged around 2015: At this time, the world's attention was focused on the mass movement of Syrian refugees from the Middle East to Europe.[311]

The relative impact the Syria crisis had on approaches to forced displacement will continue to be debated for some time to come. The growing reach of the Syrian exodus focused attention more clearly on the worsening situation faced within the country and its neighbours. Bordering countries hosting 5.5 million Syrian refugees – or 90 per cent of the global total – felt the strain on their already fragile infrastructure and economies. This was compounded by the loss of trade, tourism and investment due to the conflict. As middle-income countries, their calls stood out for development grants and concessional lending to help ease the burdens they were carrying.

As for Syrian refugees, their displacement was becoming protracted. Refugee poverty deepened as initial savings dried up, and mobility and employment restrictions limited their ability to provide for themselves. Humanitarian assistance was insufficient to meet all needs. Most children remained out of school, living conditions were overcrowded and frequently lacked adequate sanitation and protection from the elements. Access to health services was often restricted. While constituting a small minority, refugees with financial means sought a way out, willing to risk their lives in perilous journeys to Europe.

The realities in the region, the political challenges, and the sudden increase in refugee arrivals in Europe shifted the conversation. Investing in refugee-hosting areas, through substantial development funding, became a priority of many large bilateral and multilateral development donors. New funding instruments were introduced to support this.[312]

Strengthening human capital in displacement moved more into focus. It was supported through increased development investments to improve access to employment, education and health services for forcibly displaced and host communities.[313] The inclusion of forcibly displaced persons in efforts to achieve the Sustainable Development Goals was also more integrated into United Nations multisectoral development work.[314]

This orientation is reflected in the objectives of the Global Compact on Refugees and its Programme of Action. A significant part of it is dedicated to strengthening access to education, jobs and livelihoods, accommodation and health services for host communities and refugees.[315] The emphasis is not just on States opening these avenues to refugees, but also on the international community providing additional financial, material and technical support to reinforce such changes.

This had already begun. As discussed in more detail in Part V, from 2016, new international funding instruments came on stream and were specifically designed for low- and middle-income countries with large forcibly displaced populations.[316] They feature both concessional loans and grants to promote and support the socioeconomic inclusion of refugees. Objectives include improving infrastructure and inclusive service delivery to both forcibly displaced and host communities. There are efforts to enhance livelihoods in host community areas and measures to relieve government finances from the strains of their hosting responsibilities.

The range of development and financial institutions engaged in this work has grown significantly, as have the beneficiary countries over the past five years. Billions of dollars have been committed to strengthen the human capital of forcibly displaced and host communities.[317]

Increased financing opportunities also highlighted the need for better data. A recurrent theme of the Global Compact on Refugees is that efforts to enhance social and economic inclusion of refugees and support State institutions and services must be informed by improved, reliable, comparable and timely data.[318] Until recently, there were no agreed criteria to determine the socioeconomic conditions of refugees and internally displaced persons as compared to local hosts, an important building block to any inclusion strategy. Significant efforts are being made to close this information gap.

In 2018, the Expert Group on Refugee and Internally Displaced Persons Statistics (EGRIS)[319] developed guidance on refugee statistics including how to measure and quantify integration in a way that is comparable and consistent across different contexts.[320] A complementary exercise was subsequently concluded for internally displaced persons.[321] Both sets of indicators are designed to assess the situation of host and displaced communities in a simultaneous manner, that makes sound comparisons possible. Many are also useful for reporting progress on the Sustainable Development Goals.

Having comprehensive indicators is an important step. Data for them can be sourced from surveys, censuses, administration records and polling. But processes in which they are used are equally important. Studies have shown that integration assessments have a greater chance of influencing policy outcomes if they are collaborative from start to finish. In other words, they should engage all interested parties: humanitarian and development actors; donors; local and State authorities; forcibly displaced; and host communities.[322] It helps to achieve a consensus on methodology, findings and policy prescriptions. It is useful to find out from both forcibly displaced people and their hosts what they perceive as obstacles, and the potential for these to be overcome.

Two recent studies demonstrate the benefits of such an approach. One examined the situation in Ethiopia for refugees and the other examined the situation of internally displaced persons across four countries.

Ethiopia hosts over 800,000 refugees. In 2017, the Government agreed to make far-reaching legislative changes to facilitate the integration of long-term refugees. This included permitting refugees greater mobility and improved access to services, especially education. It also sought to improve livelihoods by expanding access to jobs and land. In February 2019, the Ethiopian Parliament passed a proclamation to strengthen these pledges via enabling legislation and administrative frameworks.

To inform this work, the World Bank conducted a study to determine the social impact of refugees on host communities in Ethiopia, the extent to which refugees were integrated, the obstacles they faced, and the impact more inclusive policies could have on host communities. Its findings are important, for their observations and the policy implications derived from them.

It highlighted the importance of local conditions to the prospects for greater refugee integration. In some areas of the country, improving the self-reliance of refugees could increase competition with host communities, risking the escalation of tensions between the two groups. Elsewhere, the creation of better opportunities for interaction and exchange between the communities could help build trust in tandem with improving livelihood opportunities. Policies and programmes have to be tailored to these different realities.[323]

Another World Bank study profiled the populations of internally displaced persons and host communities in Nigeria, Somalia, South Sudan and Sudan.[324] This study also found that the obstacles to integration varied across regions, highlighting the need for strategies to be tailored to the specific context.

In northern Nigeria, this meant prioritizing "security and improvements to living conditions in host areas". In Somalia, it included strengthening human capital by expanding access to education, health, skills training and cash transfers as well as enhancing living conditions of host communities. In South Sudan, the study found that security services and humanitarian assistance remain critical. As the security situation stabilizes, continuing to invest in human capital "through nutrition, health, and education programs" was also considered necessary along with expanding access to employment and helping host communities support new arrivals. In Sudan, improving security and enhancing employment opportunities were also identified as key priorities along with improved living conditions and reduced gender-based vulnerabilities.[325]

The studies show that successful local integration strategies are specifically designed for their contexts. They also build on any promising circumstances where integration already exists and address challenges that inhibit it. These observations apply to both durable and interim solutions, and there are other studies with similar policy implications.[326]

Economic and social inclusion for refugees is far preferable to ongoing marginalization, but it often does not constitute a full solution to displacement. There are many situations in the world where refugees have been displaced for generations, with younger people having few to no ties to their country of origin and therefore identifying more closely with their respective host country.

States hosting most of the world's refugee population are reluctant to provide a progressive path to citizenship for various political, social and economic reasons. This applies even when refugees comprise a relatively small proportion of total populations. Recent policy changes in Colombia are a dramatic and notable exception.

As discussed in Part II, in February 2021, Colombia announced that it will provide Temporary Protection Status (TPS) to all Venezuelans residing in the country who register with the Government within a certain period, as well as to prospective regular arrivals over the next two years. At the time of the announcement, over 1.7 million displaced Venezuelans were in Colombia and new arrivals were ongoing. The TPS will be valid for 10 years during which time permit holders will be able to work, attend school and access health services. During the 10-year period, they will be able to apply for permanent residency.

In announcing the policy, President Duque made clear that its aim was to provide Venezuelans the opportunity to make a positive contribution to Colombia, that he hoped other countries would do the same and he called on the international community to increase funding for the Venezuelan crisis.[327] Within five months, Ecuador, host to an estimated 450,000 Venezuelans, announced a new regularization policy for Venezuelans in the country. In communicating the news, President Lasso said the new policy would be complemented by economic integration and labour market access "to be an effective, lasting and permanent policy".[328]

José Soto and María José left Venezuela two years ago with their three sons and now live in Ibarra, Ecuador. They express the views of many Venezuelans who see regularization of their situation as removing the deep anxieties they have faced on account of their uncertain status. María José describes the impediments they face without a national identity document. They are unable to establish and grow their business, and their children cannot obtain their education diplomas. "Regularization is vital", she remarks, "it's what we need to find stability and calm."[329]

Other countries may follow these two examples. A positive outcome for Colombia and Ecuador will no doubt be important. Similarly, studies that demonstrate the benefits of offering permanent residence and citizenship could also be important.

Regularizing large numbers of migrants is already common in high-income countries, with a record of success. Research demonstrates how immigrants contribute to economies and communities, with rising productivity helping to reinforce social cohesion.[330] Regularization is often based on criteria, including length of residency, ties to the community, and proof of good conduct. For example, in 2017, the World Bank noted that Italy regularized 1.2 million migrants in 2012 accounting for 2 per cent of its population. In the first 15 years or so of the 21st century, the United States on average regularized 700,000 foreigners annually. That took the total to over 10 million people, roughly equivalent to the number of refugees hosted in low- and middle-income countries.[331] If these experiences are any guide, extending more opportunities for full citizenship to long-term refugees may also be of benefit to other host communities.

Lessons Learned

Seventy years of experience in the search for solutions to displacement reveal the following six main points.

First – Politics has often defined the level of support and attention solutions receive. They have been realized – or prematurely pushed – due to the geopolitical interests of States rather than based on acute need or sustainability. While States will continue to be motivated by geopolitical priorities, agencies working on behalf of displaced and affected communities must seek protection for those most at risk and insist that repatriation only be promoted when it is voluntary, safe and sustainable.

Second – There has been a traditional emphasis on voluntary return as the "preferred solution". And, while returning home is a fundamental right, it may not always be preferred, especially if the underlying causes of displacement are not resolved. Political stability, security and ability to sustain livelihoods are among the key requirements for it to succeed which, in many contexts, remain elusive.

Third – The resettlement solution has never reached more than a small proportion of the world's refugees. The potential to broaden third-country settlement for refugees depends on making fresh avenues more accessible, including through labour and education migration means.

Fourth – When development investment targets host communities alongside refugees, it can be of mutual benefit among communities. Programmes to improve the skills and employment opportunities of hosts and refugees alike help overcome resistance to the socioeconomic inclusion of forcibly displaced people. So do infrastructure and service delivery efforts, which also help reduce the poor health and multi-generational poverty associated with long-term displacement and dependence on humanitarian aid.

Fifth – Allowing back-and-forth movements across borders may amount to a solution in some areas of displacement. Solutions are not simply bestowed on forcibly displaced persons but are ones they seize based on their calculation of what will be best for them. Refugees may choose to return permanently or temporarily. Families may choose to move together or in a staggered manner to minimize risks. These assessments can change over time, especially when displacement has occurred for longer periods. Some refugees may move back and forth between the country of origin and displacement as the best means of securing a foothold back home. Facilitating such cross-border movements in some contexts may be the most appropriate solutions strategy.

Sixth – A shift in approach is essential for meaningful improvement in the life prospects of most refugees. The traditional durable solutions – sustainable return, resettlement and/or local integration – only provide a solution for a small proportion of the forcibly displaced. More people face a long-term wait between displacement and attaining a solution. Widening access to education, services and employment during displacement provides net benefits in the immediate term. It also lays important foundations for the success of any solution that may arise in the future.

The operational shifts that may be needed to do this more effectively are the subject of Part IV.

PART IV

Improving
Life Prospects

Table of Contents

Improving
Life Prospects

Improving lives and advancing human development for forcibly displaced persons is a global ambition. It is part of the international community's Sustainable Development Goals (SDGs), agreed by 193 States in 2015.[1]

This set of 17 goals and 169 targets aims at ensuring inclusive economic development and growth. They are due to be met by 2030[2] and apply to all nations, for the benefit of all people, regardless of status.[3] States have pledged that "no one will be left behind" in the efforts to meet the Sustainable Development Goals and to endeavour to reach "the furthest behind first".[4]

The 2030 Agenda, which outlines the goals, explicitly recognizes refugees and internally displaced persons as among the most vulnerable, and States resolve to remove all obstacles and strengthen support for their empowerment.[5]

But the fact that refugees and internally displaced persons *should* be included in these landmark development efforts does not mean that they *are*. While major international development donors increasingly take an inclusive approach, national practice lags behind. Although State practice is improving, internally displaced persons are not always included in national development plans.[6] Refugees are largely left out, regardless of how long they have lived in the country.[7]

The exclusion of internally displaced persons is striking, as they are nationals of the country in which they are displaced.[8] And, while their exclusion can be intentional, it also can arise because they are in remote areas, less visible, and/or their needs not prioritized given the many challenges their countries face. It is also the case that data on internally displaced populations is often insufficient to obtain a clear understanding of their socioeconomic status and poverty levels – important for development plans, as noted in Part III.[9]

Refugees are not nationals of host countries, and 83 per cent reside in low- and middle-income countries, which struggle to meet the needs of their own populations.[10] Receiving large numbers of refugees places additional strains on their infrastructure, environment and social services.[11] To include refugees in their development programmes, States need to be convinced that this will not only help refugees but also benefit their own communities.

This consideration is crucial to policy decision-making and is influenced by many factors. Local political considerations can be definitive. There may be insufficient public support for more inclusive policies. States may also not want to appreciably improve the lives of refugees if they think that, in doing so, refugees may be more inclined to remain. Governments may not be convinced that inclusive development will lead to better outcomes for local communities.

And so, the move towards more *progressive* and *inclusive* policies depends on persuasive evidence that doing so will not come at the cost of political support and will help to improve socioeconomic conditions for everyone. For this, sound evidence and additional technical and financial support are needed.

In Part IV, we look at the essentials required to improve lives by strengthening human capital in displacement – the skills, knowledge and experience that enable individuals to realize their potential as productive members of society. We focus on low- and middle-income countries, which are home to more than 90 per cent of the world's forcibly displaced populations. Investing in people through health care, education, skills, and jobs helps them develop their human capital. It is key to reducing poverty and to stimulating economic growth.[12] It provides the foundation for building sustainable solutions, as we saw in Part III.

Conflict and Displacement Impacts

It is often assumed that receiving large numbers of refugees invariably has negative impacts on host communities. The reality is more complex. Conflict itself often has knock-on effects internally and in neighbouring countries that exist independently of the impact of forced displacement. Conflict often disrupts and distorts economic and commercial performance and activities. For example, it can lead to disruptions in supply chains and higher costs of transport, goods and services, falling demand and diminished production. Knock-on effects include higher unemployment, reduced purchasing power, shrinking markets and declining investment and trade.[13]

It is difficult to disentangle the economic impact of the conflict from that of forced displacement. Other relevant factors are the size and composition of the displacement, pre-existing conditions in the place of displacement, government policies and development and humanitarian responses.[14]

For most host countries, refugees comprise considerably less than 1 per cent of their total population. There are a few notable exceptions, such as Jordan and Lebanon, where refugees constitute a much larger share: close to 30 per cent and 20 per cent respectively.[15] In most countries, however, the effects of receiving refugees are experienced locally, with only modest nationwide effects. The impact of internal displacement also tends to be experienced mostly at the local level.[16]

Many hosting areas confront significant development challenges. The sudden or sustained influx of forcibly displaced persons can place a strain on public services, like education and health care to the detriment of hosts. Infrastructure that may have been fragile before the influx can be further taxed by a larger population. That can include water and electricity and sanitation services. Environmental impacts can also be severe, with trees and shrubs cleared for firewood, water levels reduced, or waste improperly disposed. In countries with large subsidies on essential commodities, a sizeable influx can also lead to increased public expenditures.[17]

Even when the arrival of large numbers of forcibly displaced persons creates economic challenges, there are also opportunities. It can benefit employers by providing more workers and lift demand for goods and services, helping producers and suppliers. At the same time, however, new workers can also increase competition and lead to job losses among those who have similar skills. Prices for land and housing can rise, helping owners but hurting renters. Price movements for food and other commodities depend more on local contexts and can either rise or fall.

The negative impacts can lead to declining welfare, especially among the most vulnerable in the host community. That can worsen if public services, like health and education, become strained and lack increased investment to expand capacity. Even when household welfare actually improves, individuals may still *perceive* themselves to be worse off due to the presence of more forcibly displaced persons.[18]

Understanding the differential impact of a large influx of forcibly displaced persons requires a detailed and nuanced analysis that also examines the effect of government policies. Government policies can exacerbate the negative impacts or, conversely, responsive policies can mitigate losses and maximize potential gains from the socioeconomic changes of an influx.

In Part IV, we examine these issues in relation to education, health and employment opportunities. Traditionally, humanitarian assistance has been delivered through parallel health and education systems, in part due to government policies that did not encourage socioeconomic inclusion. Investments made to encourage self-reliance have been relatively modest.

This pattern is beginning to change, in step with the influences which informed the Sustainable Development Goals, and their commitment to *inclusive* development. We look at the opportunities this presents for meaningful change, which humanitarian and development partners have begun to accelerate.

Education

Context

"If your plan is for one year, plant rice. If your plan is for ten years, plant trees. If your plan is for one hundred years, educate children." Those words set the tone for the World Bank's 2018 World Development Report on education. They date back to the 7th century (BCE) Chinese philosopher and politician, Kuan Chung.[19]

To this day, they capture a centuries-old understanding of the importance of education to human development, which is also embedded in the foundational documents of the United Nations. Article 26 of the 1948 Universal Declaration of Human Rights begins quite simply with the phrase: "Everyone has the right to education." It goes further, recognizing education's intrinsic value, specifying that elementary education shall be both free and compulsory.[20]

Ever since, evidence consistently points to the crucial importance of education to human development. It is essential to the reduction of poverty. For individuals, education leads to enhanced earnings,[21] better health[22] and lower risks of gender-based violence,[23] all of which affect overall quality of life. For nations, it drives economic growth.[24]

Education targets have been central to every major global development

Syrian refugee children attend school in north Lebanon.
© UNHCR/ Andrew McConnell

initiative since the 1980s, not least because of its enormous development dividends. In 1987, the United Nations published *Our Common Future*, with recommendations to improve international cooperation on the environment and development with education playing a central role.[25] Achieving universal primary education was one of the eight Millennium Development Goals (MDGs) launched by the United Nations in 2000.[26] An expanded ambition for education followed in 2015, with the Sustainable Development Goals calling for inclusive and equitable quality education and lifelong learning opportunities for all by 2030.[27]

International efforts to achieve universal primary education by 2015 had some success. Global net enrolment rates in developing countries increased from 83 per cent in 2000 to 91 per cent by 2015.[28] But the gains were not experienced equally.

Children in the poorest households were "four times as likely to be out of school as those in the richest households": over 34 per cent of the poorest children did not complete primary school. In conflict-affected countries, the proportion of children not in school increased from 30 per cent in 1999 to 36 per cent in 2012.[29] This was a worrisome trend since the number of conflict-affected countries was also increasing.

And, while the rising *enrolment* of students overall was positive, this did not necessarily translate into good learning *outcomes*. Assessments showed that, in many developing countries, half of all children who completed primary school were unable to read simple texts or to perform basic arithmetic.[30] By the time the Sustainable Development Goals were adopted in 2015, there was widespread appreciation that "schooling is not the same as learning".[31] Attendance is important but learning while in school is critical.[32]

The Sustainable Development Goals' target for education was informed by these realities. It aims at expanding universal, free, equitable and quality primary and secondary education by 2030. It also focuses on early childhood education, eliminating gender disparities and enhancing access to affordable technical and tertiary education. It seeks to substantially increase the number of youth and adults with relevant skills for wage or self-employment. Among the targets are increased support for education facilities, strengthened teaching capacity and a substantial expansion in the global number of scholarships available for developing countries, particularly the least developed.[33]

Eliminating what is now known as "learning poverty" is widely acknowledged to be an urgent development priority. Global enrolment rates remain far from the Sustainable Development Goal target, and ensuring quality education will also take longer than the 2030 goal.[34] Positively, increased development resources are being invested in enhancing quality and equitable access to education.[35]

As we will see, COVID-19 has increased the challenges. Mandated school closures affected 1.6 billion children. The impacts are particularly severe in low-income and conflict-affected countries.[36] Working around COVID-19 restrictions has also led to the expansion of remote and home-based learning that may help education systems cope, recover and become more inclusive in the future.[37] But, as discussed below, this will require addressing the absence of connectivity to digital or broadcast networks faced by many forcibly displaced persons and the communities in which they live.

Evolution

Forced displacement is disruptive on many levels, especially for children. It generally involves the loss of home, friends, loved ones and quite literally all the things that make life familiar and predictable in childhood. For children who were in school, forced displacement marks the beginning of an extended period out of school – on average three-to-four years for refugees – and many do not remain in school.[38]

Each year of lost learning makes it difficult to catch up and leads to economic losses over time. Children out of school are more vulnerable to child labour, forced recruitment, sexual exploitation and child marriage.[39]

Education is often mentioned by forcibly displaced persons as their chief priority, regardless of how dismal their shelter, how insecure the environment, and even how irregular their access to food. That is not surprising given the benefits it provides. Even very young displaced children, unlikely to appreciate the links between learning and income, will frequently mention being able to go to school at the top of their wish list. School can provide a place of stability, friendship and learning. It helps to overcome trauma and loss.[40]

Or, in the words of an eight-year-old Syrian refugee boy in Lebanon, school "is like the difference between the earth and the sky".[41] Ahmed fled Syria with his parents in 2011, when he was just five years old. Initially, he was not admitted to school and had to work to supplement tight family finances. After two years of serving as a "tea boy" in Tripoli, he joined a local school. When asked to describe the change this had made to his life, Ahmed's poignant answer was given with his arms open wide.

UNHCR estimates that there are over 7 million school-age refugee children.[42] The enrolment rates of refugee children fall considerably short of global averages. There are an estimated 14.1 million school-age children who are internally displaced due to conflict and violence, many of whom also face significant challenges in securing an education.[43]

In 2019, 77 per cent of all refugee children were enrolled in primary school, compared to the global average of 91 per cent. The gap in secondary school was even starker: 31 per cent compared to 76 per cent globally, with refugee boys disproportionately represented compared to refugee girls. The rates for tertiary education fall to just 3 per cent enrolment for refugees compared to 38 per cent globally.[44]

As relevant as these statistics are, they provide only part of the picture. As mentioned, *enrolment* does not necessarily translate to *learning outcomes*. Many people forced to flee are in countries where access to quality education remains out of reach for many local people.[45] Here, improving learning opportunities for the forcibly displaced must go hand-in-hand with improving education opportunities for other poor and marginalized groups.

This inclusive approach has not always been made. For most of the 20th century, refugee education was predominately organized and delivered by refugee communities themselves with nominal support from UNHCR.[46] In the mid-1980s, in line with the growing international push for "education for all", UNHCR refocused its education efforts on supporting primary education for refugees.[47] It concentrated on programmes delivered to refugees in camps, often distant from local communities and cut-off from national institutions.[48] With a view to helping refugees prepare for eventual return, the content and language of instruction was aligned as closely as possible to their countries of origin.[49]

In this parallel system, the education refugees received was not nationally accredited, either by the country of origin or the host country. That created a barrier to transitioning into post-primary and secondary education and in recognizing qualifications for employment purposes.

As refugee numbers and the length of displacement grew, maintaining parallel education systems was not only costly but also failed to respond to refugee learning needs. Many refugees had no foreseeable prospect of living in their country of citizenship, so using its language and materials of instruction had significant drawbacks. Parallel education did not help with the social and economic inclusion of refugees and did not contribute to improved education outcomes for host communities.[50]

Including refugees in national education systems is increasingly recognized as the most sustainable and equitable approach.

In 2012, UNHCR launched a new global Education Strategy which focuses on the integration of refugee learners within national systems.[51] This remains the cornerstone of UNHCR's education efforts.[52] States also endorsed the approach in the 2018 Global Compact on Refugees. The Compact calls for additional support to host countries to expand and enhance the quality and inclusiveness of national primary, secondary and tertiary education systems.[53]

Inclusion Challenges

Meeting the Sustainable Development Goals' education targets for forcibly displaced children depends on being able to access school and learn there. In many countries, there are significant challenges to both.

Access

The fact that primary school enrolment of refugees reached 77 per cent in 2019 was promising.[54] But these figures reveal only part of the reality. As UNHCR's statistics show, the likelihood of a refugee child progressing to the next academic grade drops sharply with every year of education.[55]

The drop is particularly significant between primary and secondary school. Fewer than half of refugee children who start primary school end up in secondary school, with proportionately more refugee girls falling out of school than refugee boys. In 2019, 36 per cent of refugee boys were enrolled in secondary education compared to just 27 per cent of refugee girls.[56] This is further exacerbated by COVID-19. The Malala Fund estimates that half of all refugee girls in secondary school will not return when classrooms reopen.[57]

The loss is staggering, especially considering that women with secondary school education on average earn almost twice as much as those with no education at all.[58] The links between a lack of education and child marriage are similarly telling.[59]

Comparable figures for internally displaced persons are not available. As nationals, they have a right to attend public schools. Yet, they face many of the same challenges that confront refugee children.[60] Financial pressures can be prohibitive. Families often do not have resources to pay for fees, uniforms or school supplies. Forcibly displaced children are frequently located at significant distances from schools, with no available or affordable means of transport. There are added pressures for food-insecure families, whose survival often depends on every possible means of additional income, including through the work of their children. In addition, many internally displaced persons are in countries experiencing ongoing conflict and violence and at risk of persistent insecurity and repeated displacement. The public provision of education may not be a government priority.

In conflict areas, schools are often damaged or destroyed and teachers and students deliberately targeted. Between 2015 and 2019, the Global Coalition to Protect Education from Attack reported 11,000 incidents of education facilities being attacked or used for military purposes, harming over 22,000 students, teachers, and education workers. Over 8,000 children and education personnel were directly targeted with killing, injury, abduction, and threats of harm.[61]

Many forcibly displaced persons have fled their homes suddenly and do not have the documentation needed to place children in the right class. Even when they have appropriate certificates, some schools may not recognize them.

This can lead to the child not being accepted into the institution or receiving an inappropriate grade placement.[62]

For those who have completed secondary school, further education is often simply unobtainable. High tuition fees, pressures to earn an income to support themselves and their families, distance from education institutions and language barriers are among the multiple obstacles.[63]

Rez Gardi, an international lawyer and former refugee recounts the difficulties in overcoming these obstacles and the self-doubt that accompanied her

Ten-year-old Kamala (right) with her friend in 2016 in Golzow, on the German-Polish border, where her family's arrival from Syria helped the village school survive by reaching the minimum class size.
© UNHCR/ Gordon Welters

pursuit of a higher education. "People like me did not finish school, let alone end up at university." She recalls that wanting "more than safety and survival seemed ungrateful". Yet, it was also essential to reclaim "control of our lives". She set her sights on being a lawyer, to one day be able to influence the laws that apply to people who are displaced, as she once was.[64]

Learning

Access to school is a huge step but, as mentioned, it is not a guarantee to learning. In most cases of forced displacement, there are significant challenges, many of which are also shared by local students.

The list is long and led by the lack of financial resources. High-income countries account for 65 per cent of global education spending, while low-income countries make up just 0.5 per cent,[65] and both groups have approximately the same number of school-age children.

Insufficient financing means poor facilities, a lack of education materials, low teacher remuneration and large class sizes. Other persistent weaknesses include a lack of trained teachers, and the absence of strong school leadership and engagement of parents.[66] These contribute to weak education outcomes overall.[67]

In addition, forcibly displaced children often face other specific and daunting constraints. When they attend classes delivered in a language they do

Venezuelan children sit alongside their Colombian hosts in a school in Paraguachon in 2019. © UNHCR/ Vincent Tremeau

not understand, they may need additional support to learn. Many have been out of school for some time and need help catching up.[68] Trauma can also affect learning, requiring psychological support. Discrimination and bullying at school further contribute to low enrolment and require concerted efforts by schools to establish understanding among students and a safe learning environment.[69]

Sometimes, the attitudes of local children reflect deeper frustrations within the community. These can be particularly evident at the outset of forced displacement crises. For example, schools are sometimes used to shelter new arrivals, which interrupts classes of local children. Sudden increases in class sizes can also raise concerns of education quality being diminished.[70] National and local leadership is required to overcome these challenges, supported by strengthened technical and financial capacity.[71]

Supporting Sustainable Inclusion

Positive developments are in evidence over the last several years, not least with a number of countries opening their public schools to refugees.

In 2017, the eight countries which form the Intergovernmental Authority on Development (IGAD), pledged to ensure that every refugee, returnee, and member of host communities has access to quality education in a safe learning environment without discrimination.[72] Several have implemented laws and policies to give effect to their promise with some positive results already achieved.

In Uganda, primary school enrolment rates for refugees grew to 76 per cent in 2020, up from 73 per cent the previous year, although secondary school enrolment rates fell slightly and remained low at 11 per cent in 2020.[73] In Ethiopia, primary school enrolment has seen a progressive trend upward over the years, with primary and secondary school enrolment rates averaging 62 per cent and 13 per cent respectively in 2020.[74] In Ethiopia, however, education is provided to refugees in schools separate from local children and run by a different ministry.

In Kenya, refugees in urban areas have access to public schools. Those in camps have access to the national curriculum and are able to sit national exams, with schools managed and funded with international support.[75] In Rwanda, refugee children have equal access to the same schools as nationals.

There are some 3.7 million refugees in Turkey: host to the largest number of refugees globally.[76] Close to 3.6 million are from Syria. Turkey prioritized education early in the refugee emergency, investing in preparing Syrian refugee children to transition from temporary education centres into the Turkish public school system.

Additional help to refugees included Turkish language classes, remedial learning, school materials and transportation assistance. The Government also strengthened teacher capacity. The achievements are particularly striking. By 2020, 64 per cent of Syrian children were enrolled in formal education programmes, up from 30 per cent in 2014.[77] Similarly, Egypt has also facilitated the integration of Syrian refugee students, with some 95 per cent registered in mostly formal education.[78]

Lebanon opened its public schools to Syrian refugee children in 2012. Over time, the number of enrolled Syrian refugee children increased, stretching the capacity of the public education system and leading to the introduction of an afternoon shift in which a second set of children could be taught. At the end of 2020, some 197,000 Syrian refugee children were enrolled in Lebanese public schools.[79] Challenges remain in reaching the 57 per cent of Syrian refugee children in Lebanon who are out of school.[80]

Jordan has also pursued an inclusive education policy which aims to improve access to, and the quality of, education for Jordanians and refugees. The Jordan Education Strategic Plan (2018–2022) prioritizes resources to address the barriers and outstanding education needs of Jordanian and refugee children. At the end of 2020, 61 per cent of school-age Syrian refugee children were enrolled in school, nearly all in the formal system.[81]

In Iraq, refugees with legal residency have free access to public primary and secondary schools. The country integrates data on Syrian refugee children into its national education information management system. Yet, 34 per cent remain outside the formal and non-formal system.[82] Among the reasons are: limited availability in the public system; insufficient non-formal education options; financial pressures leading children to work to contribute to family income; and concerns regarding security on the way to and from school.[83]

In Latin America, several countries like Brazil, Chile, Colombia, Costa Rica and Ecuador have inclusive education policies for public primary and secondary education. Attending school, however, can be difficult for many displaced children and youth. In Brazil and Colombia, for example, Venezuelan children are much less likely to be in school than local children.[84] Among the practical barriers hindering access to education are: inability to pay for incidentals; pressures to earn an income; discrimination; language barriers; overcrowding of schools; and limited access to computer devices and the internet.[85] A lack of necessary personal documentation can also be an obstacle.[86]

The efforts of a number of States to include forcibly displaced children in national education programmes is a significant leap forward from just a decade ago. Maintaining momentum depends on improving evidence-based decision-making and sustained funding in support of inclusive policies.

Evidence-based decision-making

There are significant data gaps in forced displacement contexts which, if bridged, can help to inform government policy options, design effective programmes, raise money for them, measure progress and make adjustments, as necessary. The education sector is no exception.

Data collection generally needs to be strengthened, as discussed in Part V. For education programmes, better data would provide area-specific information concerning host and displaced children, with respect to their age, gender, special needs and education achieved. It should include information on household income since the costs of sending children to school or retaining them in school can be prohibitive.[87] The capacity of local institutions must also be assessed to determine how best to accommodate displaced children, and where efforts to strengthen capacities are needed.[88]

Host countries generally have education management systems, but most are not required to include refugees or internally displaced persons. And many do not.[89] This can be due to the lack of political will. But it can also be due to limited resources, difficulties in collecting data, especially in remote and conflict-affected areas, weak infrastructure for storing and analysing data, a lack of sufficient enumerators, and inherent difficulties in maintaining updated data on populations that must move frequently due to conflict or climate.[90]

Faced with many competing priorities, the inclusion of refugees and internally displaced persons in education management systems may need to be part of broader efforts to support national statistical capacities. Determining what areas of data improvement are most impactful would help. Improvement needs a context-specific approach, led by national education authorities, with engaged schools and local communities. There should be international support, as needed, with technical and financial assistance.

The United Nations Educational, Scientific and Cultural Organization (UNESCO), with other specialized partners, is working with education ministries in fragile States and those affected by conflict to strengthen education management information systems.[91] There may be further potential for other donors to strengthen data-inclusive systems as part of their funding for education in crisis-affected countries.[92]

Clear evidence on the impact of interventions helps to ensure programmes are efficient and effective. It is necessary for accountability to those they aim to benefit and to those who fund them. Impact evaluations of education programmes are common in non-conflict contexts.[93] In forced displacement situations, where tight resources tend to be directed at expanding or initiating programmes, such analysis is often lacking.[94] This leaves an absence of rigorous evidence on what works and what does not.[95]

Bridging the gap can improve programme design. It can also help to address anxieties that including forcibly displaced persons inevitably leads to worse outcomes for local students. A study in Jordan revealed that an influx of Syrian refugee students did not affect school enrolment or the retention of local Jordanian students.[96] Meanwhile, an assessment of maths, science and reading scores of Turkish youths revealed that they had improved following the arrival of Syrian refugees.[97] The results of these studies can help ease tensions in communities. Where studies find more negative trends, they can also be important in making adaptations to interventions.

Financing and partnerships

Humanitarian and development financing for educating people forced to flee is improving, although it remains far from meeting the need.[98] The World Bank and UNHCR recently estimated that close to $5 billion annually would be needed to support inclusive education for all refugee children and young people in low-, lower-middle, and upper-middle-income host countries,[99] from pre-school through grade 12. That is less than one day of global military expenditure.[100] It is six times what is available currently for refugee education.

To date, most education for refugees has come from humanitarian funding. As mentioned, for many years it went to fund parallel education systems. More recently it is increasingly prioritizing support for inclusive national programmes. Humanitarian funding is raised and disbursed much more quickly than development funding. But it is short-term, unpredictable and often tightly targeted to specific interventions and situations. It is not designed to provide the longer-term institutional support that inclusive and quality education through national systems requires. To maximize impact, humanitarian funding should complement development funding.

Development programmes are years in the making, through a process of engagement and agreement between donors and national governments. Their focus is on strengthening public systems. To maximize their benefits for forcibly displaced and local children alike, it is vital to support this transformational shift to inclusive, quality education in national systems.

Positively, funding for education in forced displaced contexts has risen in recent years. In 2016, the Education Cannot Wait fund was launched to support education in emergencies. Its funding has increased in successive years, with over $138 million disbursed across 34 countries in 2020.[101] A number of long-standing global funding agencies for education have also introduced new financing to address the needs of forcibly displaced and host communities.[102]

For example, through the World Bank's International Development Association (IDA) special mechanisms for host communities and refugees, approximately $330 million has been approved for education projects as of February 2021.[103] The International Finance Facility for Education could also prove to be important in forced displacement contexts. It aims to unlock at least $10 billion in new funding by 2030 for lower-middle-income countries, using innovative financing mechanisms.[104]

The Global Compact on Refugees calls for financing to be predictable, flexible, and multi-year and supportive of national inclusive education.[105] Predictable funding is essential to plan and deliver strategies over more than the short term. Flexibility is necessary to respond to new and challenging circumstances, brought on by sudden crises, such as large-scale displacement or the COVID-19 emergency. It also must be designed in a way that supports the move from short-term humanitarian strategies to longer-term development initiatives.

This transition is vital to meet the ambitions of the Sustainable Development Goals and the Global Compact on Refugees for education. The task ahead is enormous. Strong and informed partnerships will be critical. Currently, the mechanisms for planning and advocacy are diffuse. They include separate forums for: development partners; partners supporting refugee education; and partners supporting internally displaced populations. There are few cross linkages between them. Moreover, there is no means of comprehensively tracking what partners receive for education, or where the funds are allocated.[106]

This complexity is not conducive to well-coordinated approaches or to the mobilization of resources needed to maintain the advance towards those important ambitions. It can lead to serious gaps in critical areas, creating difficulty in understanding what works best to improve learning in a given context.[107]

Progress will be best served by country-led responses, where partners contribute based on their comparative advantages, seeking agreed results that can only be achieved in cooperation with each other.[108] Partners with a comparative advantage include those with technical expertise in education for development as well as those with operational knowledge of forcibly displaced communities and their education needs.

Sustainable change is more likely with leadership from State authorities. The aim should be to support governments to set priorities, coordinate the work of others and implement inclusive policies. Donors and specialized agencies need to work more on unified advocacy, gathering evidence and efforts to strengthen local capabilities.[109]

Humanitarian programmes will remain necessary in various circumstances. They include the immediate period of a displacement crisis, given that development funding generally has a much longer response time. But humanitarian programmes should be designed as much as possible to facilitate the eventual transition to the national system.

Education delivery through non-government systems may also be needed when legal and policy barriers prevent access to national systems, or in contexts where assistance cannot be channelled impartially and accountably through national institutions. They also can be of added benefit for services to children with specific needs.

In all contexts, however, consolidated approaches are required, supported by partners with the right expertise and comprehensive understanding of the specific needs, including those of refugees.[110]

The effects of the COVID-19 pandemic further show the need for robust, well targeted and coordinated responses for education. COVID-19 has had a disproportionate impact on poor and marginalized communities. Increased financial pressures put added strains on children who may be compelled to work.[111] Additionally, many remote learning options are not available. The United Nations Children's Fund (UNICEF) estimates that 31 per cent of schoolchildren around the world cannot be reached by digital or broadcast remote learning.[112] COVID-19 has brought to the fore the urgency of closing the digital divide given the potential of online learning.

The task is challenging, especially in remote underserviced areas. The Government of Kenya partnered with Alphabet Inc. and Telkom Kenya in deploying Google Balloons carrying 4G base stations to remote areas without internet access. But, after several years, the project was discontinued as it was not possible to bring costs down to a sustainable level. In commenting on the closure of the initiative, its chief executive observed that the "arc of innovation is long and unpredictable". He noted that, although they did not reach their goal, the project had value in that it pioneered new software, enhanced existing technologies, and strengthened cross-cutting partnerships.[113]

Some projects for enhancing internet connectivity have been able to reach their intended goal. For example, UNHCR and mobile operators worked successfully to introduce 3G and 4G coverage in northwest Uganda and there are plans to implement similar programmes in other countries.[114]

The remote delivery of education materials mitigates learning losses during school disruptions but is not a substitute for parental engagement, which is known to improve outcomes. Given that home-based learning is likely to be used more in the post-COVID-19 world, efforts to encourage and support parental involvement are also needed as part of the path to improve quality learning.

Overall, financing a holistic approach to education is needed,[115] not least to guarantee teachers. Shortages of trained teachers often occur in forced displacement settings. More efforts are required to expand the supply of qualified teachers including through appropriate salary structures, improved teacher training and recognition of teaching qualifications of refugees to address capacity gaps.[116]

The challenges ahead in reaching the education target of the Sustainable Development Goals are significant, and particularly so for forcibly displaced communities. But these should not detract from the significant gains achieved over the past decade.

Education for all is globally recognized as essential to individual well-being and national economic growth. A number of host countries have taken steps for the inclusion of refugees and internally displaced persons in public education systems and new financing instruments now support this. If governments have the data and evidence needed to make informed policy choices, the financing to implement and sustain them, and reliable partners, this positive trajectory has a strong chance of continuing.

Health

Context

Health promotes learning, and poor health seriously compromises it. Ensuring healthy lives and promoting well-being is the third goal of the Sustainable Development Goals.[117]

Poverty is a major cause of ill health, and ill health is a significant cause of poverty. A lack of financial resources can prevent a person from being able to afford quality food or from seeking and receiving health care when needed. A lack of proper nutrition in children affects mental and physical growth.[118] Poor health not only inhibits learning but also the ability to find and hold a job, maintain strong social relations and work towards a better future.[119]

In situations of conflict, poor health is not as visible a killer as bullets and bombs. Yet, a lack of access to food, water, sanitation and medical care in these contexts can lead to high levels of mortality.[120] Thousands of forcibly displaced persons die or are incapacitated each year due to the spread of communicable diseases, such as diarrhoea, and acute respiratory infections.[121] As the COVID-19 pandemic has made abundantly clear, communicable diseases can sweep through large communities with devastating force.[122]

Deaths due to non-communicable diseases are more insidious. Among their causes are respiratory, cardiac, renal and neurological conditions as well as forms of cancer. Many are treatable. Yet, in most forced displacement contexts, care is often unavailable, inaccessible and/or unaffordable, which can lead to severe disability and premature death.

Providing adequate health care to forcibly displaced persons is an enormous challenge and often at best only partially met. Health interventions can be relatively expensive compared to other forms of assistance, like food and shelter. Some treatments are simply unaffordable, especially ones that require a referral to specialists and/or the hospital. There are simply not enough funds to meet needs, leaving humanitarian health programmes to make very difficult choices. This means a life and death decision cannot always be made in favour of life.

Health care for refugees has mainly been delivered outside national systems. But this parallel provision is not sustainable, as the number of displaced persons increases and most live among local populations. Over time, the health-care needs of forcibly displaced populations become more similar to those of their hosts, and less specific to the immediate circumstances of their flight.[123]

In recent years, inclusivity and integrated service delivery through national systems have become the focus. With it, economies of scale can be realized in merged services. Delivering health care through existing public systems can improve it for displaced and local communities alike.[124]

The importance of inclusive health systems also forms part of a 2021 policy brief submitted by several academics to the High-Level Panel on Internal Displacement.[125] It is also the approach promoted in the Global Compact on Refugees, which recognizes the importance of ensuring health care is supported by expertise and resources from States and other relevant partners.[126] That could mean building and equipping health facilities, strengthening service delivery, and investing in disease prevention and immunization services. Other examples include support for adequate supplies of affordable medicines, vaccines, medical supplies and diagnostics.[127]

It has taken many decades to develop such clear and high-profile acknowledgments of the value of inclusive health care in displacement situations, and they are important. But, while inclusivity in health care shares its significance with inclusivity in education, there has been comparatively less study of it, and fewer comprehensive efforts to support it. This is only beginning to change.

Evolution

Health interventions for forcibly displaced persons from the 1960s to the 1990s were concentrated in camps, set up to respond to mass influx situations. Health programmes were focused on two imperatives. The first was food assistance, to stave off starvation and illness.[128] The second was the prevention of diseases, notably malaria, respiratory tract infections and diarrhoeal diseases.

As displacement numbers grew in the 1980s, the efficacy of the established

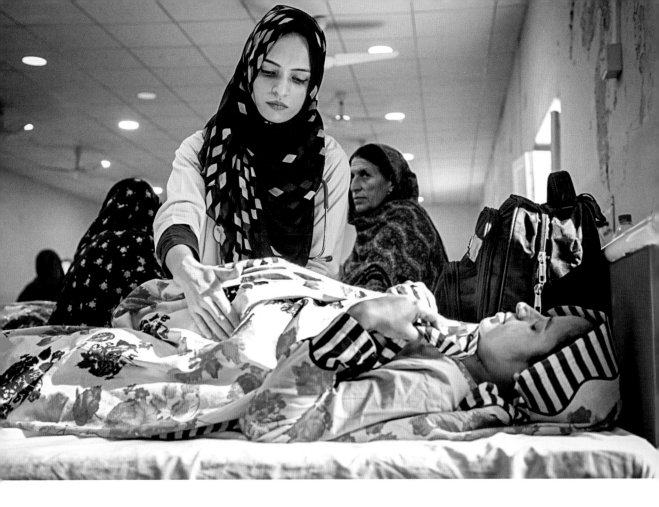

health interventions was brought into question, especially due to the relatively high mortality rates within the first year of an emergency. Evidence from refugee situations in Somalia, Sudan and Thailand and internal displacement in Ethiopia between 1979 and 1985 showed significantly high deaths among refugees and internally displaced persons. Mortality rates were between 7 and 45 times higher than local populations.[129]

In 1990, a review published in the Journal of the American Medical Association suggested that relief programmes were failing in too many cases. The authors observed several systemic problems, including deficiencies in the dietary composition of food rations, inadequate water and sanitation systems as well as insufficient immunizations.

In addition to addressing these lapses, the authors argued for policy objectives that eventually became standard. These included health information monitoring systems, increased engagement of forcibly displaced persons in preventive health measures, using financial resources to strengthen host countries' capacities and identifying alternatives to closed camps for displaced people.[130]

At the time the 1990 review was published, the global health community had already embraced a preventive approach to health care, drawing in part on

Saleema Rehman, a 28-year-old Afghan refugee in the final year of medical training, works on the postnatal ward at Holy Family Hospital in Rawalpindi, Pakistan in 2019. © UNHCR/ Roger Arnold

the experience in rural China.[131] It focuses on good health and full engagement of the community in its promotion. It covers nutrition, water and sanitation, accommodation, environment, stress and lifestyle.

Known as the Primary Health Care model, it was launched globally at an international conference in Kazakhstan in 1978. Convened by the World Health Organization (WHO) and UNICEF and attended by delegates from 134 States, and health experts from around the world, it resulted in the Alma-Ata Declaration that remains relevant to this day.[132] The Declaration stresses the importance of primary health care to "physical, mental and social well-being". Over 40 years later, it is recognized as the most cost-efficient and effective health delivery mechanism, including in forced displacement contexts.[133]

Advances and Ongoing Challenges

Primary health care

The value of the primary health-care approach was evident in some of the initial efforts to understand and remedy the relatively high rate of death and overall poor health of female refugees. Their comparably inferior health conditions were a focus at the International Consultation on Refugee Women in 1988 and of a 1994 study by the Women's Refugee Commission (WRC).

Among the main causes of poor health were inequitable food distribution practices, preferential feeding practices that discriminate against women and girls, and food aid which did not account for women's specific nutritional requirements. Additionally, inaccessible health services, lack of comprehensive sexual and reproductive health care, and sexual abuse and family violence were other contributory factors of poor health.[134]

Recommendations from the conference and from the WRC report included a broad range of actions to ensure better physical and mental health and psychosocial interventions. These ranged from tailored guidance on diet, comprehensive maternal and reproductive health services, safe accommodation, clean water and sanitation, and the engagement of women in project design and implementation.[135] They were acted upon in subsequent years.

An important element for the success of preventive efforts is community involvement. Greater understanding and acceptance of habits and practices to promote good health can often avoid the need for costly therapeutic interventions. Achieving this can be difficult in forced displacement contexts. Experience has shown that preventive measures may not be seen of value since the benefits are not immediate. Engaging community members to provide outreach on the importance of diet, clean water, sanitation, vaccines and reproductive care can help to overcome barriers.

The COVID-19 pandemic illustrated the value of community engagement. Across several countries, forcibly displaced people engaged in responses. These included delivering food, medical and other support to vulnerable refugees and host families.[136] In some countries they formed part of national and local government efforts.[137]

Gender-based violence and reproductive health responses

In the 1990s, a greater awareness developed of the prevalence of gender-based violence in displacement contexts. Sexual assault, human trafficking, harm-

A Colombian refugee survivor of sexual and gender-based violence receives help in 2019 at the Fundación Casa de Refugio Matilde in Ecuador, a local women's rights organization. © UNHCR/ Jaime Giménez

ful traditional practices, forced and early marriage, and increases in domestic and intimate partner violence were more widely documented, notably in the context of conflicts in Africa, the refugee exodus from Vietnam, and the Balkan Wars.[138]

Over time, expanded efforts to prevent and respond to gender-based violence and a focus on reproductive health needs became permanent features of primary health-care services. The objective is timely treatment for survivors of gender-based violence, comprehensive reproductive health services and community-based prevention efforts.[139] The extent of coverage in forced displacement contexts continues to be driven by available resources, which are often insufficient.

Alongside these responses, measures to prevent violence and discrimination based on gender, sexual orientation and identity, have been integrated into all aspects of humanitarian interventions beyond health services.[140] For example, accommodation and settlement areas are designed and equipped in a manner that reduces risks, such as providing lighting at night and secure places to shower, clean clothes and collect water. Other measures include working with community leaders to stop harmful practices, engaging authorities to prosecute crimes, providing income support to avert child marriage, and facilitating means for survivors to securely report incidents and receive immediate care.[141]

Communicable disease prevention

Measures to prevent the spread of communicable diseases were among the first to show inclusivity in health care. An example in the 1980s involved efforts to combat the spread of tuberculosis.[142] Since then, refugees and internally displaced persons have been covered by a number of host community testing and treatment programmes.[143] In later years, the same approach was applied in the prevention and treatment of HIV/AIDS.

Early studies found that population movements during conflict could in certain circumstances contribute to the spread of HIV/AIDS as could blood transfusions and the use of non-sterilized implements and procedures in these contexts.[144] Further studies showed that refugees were often incorrectly assumed to be more infected when, in fact, they generally had lower or similar HIV prevalence as compared to host populations. This misconception exacerbated discrimination.[145]

In 1994, the United Nations established the Joint United Nations Programme on HIV/AIDS (UNAIDS) to expand resources for combatting the spread of the disease and to consolidate approaches within United Nations participating agencies and the World Bank.[146] States are part of its governance structure. This work helped HIV/AIDS prevention and treatment become part of health responses in situations of forced displacement.[147]

Nonetheless, the inclusion of forcibly displaced populations in national strategies to combat HIV/AIDS, malaria and tuberculosis remains uneven. This was the finding of the UNHCR/United Nations Foundation study that reviewed applications for funding to The Global Fund to Fight AIDS, Tuberculosis and Malaria (the Global Fund).[148] The Global Fund provides a significant proportion of international funding for HIV/AIDS, malaria and tuberculosis.

The review revealed that, even among countries with large internally displaced populations, references to them for malaria and tuberculosis prevention and response had dropped dramatically from 2014 to 2019.[149] Similarly, proportionately fewer mentioned refugees or internally displaced persons in their HIV/AIDS-related activities. The report was careful to point out that failure to mention these groups specifically did not necessarily mean that they were excluded.[150] However, it did recommend that United Nations country teams press for forcibly displaced populations to be included and that Global Fund technical teams make this a consideration in their funding decisions.[151]

The COVID-19 pandemic has presented similar, yet more far-reaching, challenges. Worldwide, it has disrupted access to regular health services.[152] Key preventive measures, such as masks, handwashing testing, and social distancing, are not available in many displacement contexts. As one senior official in Yemen lamented, displaced communities often live in close quarters with many to a room, have no access to clean water or soap and cannot afford to miss work.[153]

More encouragingly, most States are working to include refugees and internally displaced persons in their vaccination strategies.[154] Yet, massive global disparities in access to vaccines are leaving middle- and low-income countries behind, heightening their risks and deepening their COVID-19-related losses.[155]

Mental health

Attention to mental health support for displaced persons has significantly increased over the past two decades. In the health field, there is growing evidence of how mental health affects physical health, learning and job retention.

Forcibly displaced persons have sustained enormous losses: their homes, assets, communities and livelihoods. Many have experienced severe violence or torture, witnessed family members killed or disappeared, and seen explosions shatter their houses and neighbourhoods.[156]

Their trauma can be exacerbated by the stresses of displacement: lack of income; barriers to education; loss of family or social networks; inadequate accommodation; discrimination; and uncertainty for the future.[157] These pressures are often compounded for individuals with specific needs, such as those who have experienced abuse, unaccompanied children, former child soldiers, and persons with physical and mental disabilities.[158]

Two comprehensive reviews of epidemiological studies in the refugee mental health field were conducted in 2005 and 2009. They revealed that refugees had an elevated risk of post-traumatic stress and depression, although the prevalence and rates varied considerably across contexts. This was due, in part, to the different methodological approaches used.

Nevertheless, they all were largely consistent in identifying post-flight stressors that impact mental health and in illustrating that post-traumatic stress and depression were higher among refugees exposed to torture or severe trauma as compared to non-refugee populations.[159] Similar findings emerged in studies

Rohingya refugee Shahina Begam, 45, in Bangladesh in 2014 holding the shirt of her son, Mohammad Unus, 18, who is imprisoned in Myanmar. © UNHCR/ Saiful Huq Omi

involving internally displaced populations.[160] Based on available data, a 2019 study co-funded by WHO estimated that approximately one in five people living in conflict-affected areas suffers from a mental health condition.[161]

Unfortunately, there remains limited data and analysis on important areas of mental health in displacement contexts. These include psychosis, substance use/abuse and age-related disorders, such as dementia and degenerative conditions.

More positively, mental health has been integrated into primary health-care approaches. For over a decade, there has been considerable effort in aligning approaches to mental health in emergencies and humanitarian contexts. In 2007, the Inter-Agency Standing Committee issued guidelines for addressing mental health and the provision of psychosocial support in emergencies.[162]

In 2013, UNHCR published operational guidelines on programmes for mental health and psychosocial support.[163] This was followed by joint WHO and UNHCR guidance for addressing and managing acute and post-traumatic stress and grief in settings where there is no specialized care.[164] The guidance is inclusive of addressing "mental, neurological and substance abuse conditions".

Recognition of the importance of mental health in forced displacement situations and agreed guidance for humanitarian agencies are important developments. But serious challenges in comprehensively treating mental health problems remain in many contexts and there is a need for rigorous assessments of the impact of current programme methodologies. There is also a need for accompanying education to help remove stigmas that can prevent people from seeking help when available.

Broadly speaking, there are a few dominant methodologies. Counselling and psychotherapy are the common methods accompanied by the use of specific medications for severe mental illnesses.[165] Social programmes are also a means to establish connections, foster support and help in overcoming displacement losses.[166] Programmes have also been designed to help those with specific needs, such as survivors of gender-based violence and former child soldiers.[167]

These treatments and humanitarian programmes very much depend on the availability of resources and trained professionals. As Hippocrates is reported to have said: "Healing is a matter of time but also of opportunity."[168]

Where there is a scarcity of trained medical professionals, efforts have been made to train lay or community workers, including displaced persons in the treatment of common mental disorders, such as post-traumatic stress, anxiety and depression. There is potential to build on these initiatives and integrate the approach where possible in public health systems.[169] This, as well as other mental health interventions, requires ongoing supervision and mentoring of front-line workers. This can be difficult in many locations where even remote supervision is stymied by intermittent or nonexistent internet or phone service.[170]

To date, there have been few long-term impact assessments in forced displacement contexts to determine the effectiveness of approaches to mental health and the treatment of mental illness in these contexts. Similarly, there is not enough evidence to know the extent to which mental health problems associated with flight and displacement become chronic and disabling over time.[171] These are evidentiary gaps that require prioritization in the coming years.

The more comprehensive approaches taken through the primary health-care model have led to broader health coverage in forced displacement situations.

Yet, the impact very much depends on the resources available for their implementation, which are always stretched. So, even when emergency and primary
health care are prioritized, the content and quality of care can vary.

Specialized care

Global health data reveals that deaths from non-communicable diseases are
responsible for 74 per cent of all deaths worldwide.[172] In contrast, communicable diseases are among the chief causes of excess morbidity of refugees and
internally displaced persons in low-income countries.[173] However, recent
years have also seen an increased prevalence of non-communicable diseases,
especially among older forcibly displaced populations in middle-income
countries.[174]

Globally, cardiovascular diseases, cancer, diabetes, and respiratory disease
are among the leading causes of death.[175] Major risk factors include unhealthy
diets, smoking, physical inactivity and mental health conditions.[176] Many
common risk factors are often present among forcibly displaced populations.
And, for those who already suffer from non-communicable diseases, these
factors can exacerbate their illness. Without proper care, these illnesses lead
to premature death.[177]

Primary health-care interventions can help to manage certain non-
communicable diseases, like diabetes and hypertension, by assisting those
afflicted to mitigate the risk factors that aggravate their disease.[178] Other
disorders, however, such as renal and cardiovascular disease and cancer,
may require treatments or complex surgeries that can be unavailable in remote
forced displacement settings. Even when offered in urban environments,
they can be prohibitively expensive. Humanitarian health budgets are
generally insufficient to cover these costs.

UNHCR confronted these challenges during the Kosovo crisis of the 1990s,
and the Iraq crisis of the following decade. In both situations, a high proportion
of refugees suffered from chronic diseases.[179] Refugees were largely displaced
in urban areas where treatment was available but costly.

UNHCR and partners had to decide how to best honour the long-held prioritization of emergency and primary care in the face of compelling requests for
more costly specialized treatments. It was a stark dilemma: how to maximize the
health of the greatest number of individuals, while permitting equitable exceptions for those with specific needs?[180] Guidelines were developed on how to
make these tough choices, and Exceptional Care Committees set up to do so.[181]

The first Exceptional Care Committees were established in Iraq. On the basis of predetermined guidance and criteria, such as prognosis and cost, the Committees consider individual cases and make independent decisions on whether to refer the individual for treatment.[182] The Committees are comprised of medical professionals and engage refugees with medical backgrounds to communicate and facilitate understanding of the process and constraints with refugee communities.[183]

This is not to suggest that an Exceptional Care Committee removes all ethical dilemmas in determining who gains access to specialized care. What it does is try to assure that tough choices are guided by a set of clear criteria, implemented consistently and transparently, communicated and discussed with affected communities. They are not yet in widespread use because, in many operational contexts, there are insufficient resources to support even a minimum number of chronic care interventions.[184]

Other responses are required, especially since displacement situations are more protracted, populations in displacement are ageing, and the incidence of chronic diseases is likely to increase in the future. It has led some to explore alternative funding models, including subsidized insurance schemes, as a possible means to respond to ongoing needs.[185]

Supporting Sustainable Inclusion

Evidence-based decision-making

In camps, where health services are provided by UNHCR and/or non-governmental partners, health data is relatively easy to collect. In these situations, health tracking systems and disaggregated data collection help achieve better health assessments, more targeted interventions and improved decisions on where scarce resources should be allocated first.

For example, improved epidemiological tracking systems can quickly detect disease outbreaks when they initially occur, leading to early treatment, isolation of cases and general protection of the non-infected populations. Yet, most forcibly displaced people do not live in camps. Many are located in urban or adjacent areas, relying on local health services, or a combination of those and humanitarian services. That makes systematic monitoring and data collection more complicated.

In many contexts, there is no local capacity for detailed data tracking and analysis for host communities let alone internally displaced persons and refugees. Many national health registries do not have a detailed tracking of diverse sub-categories of populations. In these contexts, household surveys are a tool to assess the health of displaced and host communities and obstacles they face in accessing health care.

UNHCR has employed Health Access and Utilization Surveys in Lebanon and Jordan and started to roll these out in other urban situations.[186] The surveys provide insight into how refugees access health services over time, the costs of accessing them and the barriers faced. This, in turn, informs advocacy and interventions aimed at overcoming challenges. It is a promising development, but far short of what is needed for strengthened and inclusive health systems overall.

Financing

In several countries, States report including refugees in their national health policies and systems. However, many refugees are unable to access them due to their inability to pay the fees for services, as well as due to discrimination, language barriers and, in some cases, long distances to health facilities.[187] Few countries include refugees in their national insurance schemes, and these often require the payment of a premium which can be beyond the abilities of refugees and internally displaced persons to pay.[188]

Low- and middle-income countries are not in a strong position to ensure refugees have access to basic services without additional funding to support their effective inclusion. Comprehensive information on increased financing to support inclusive health systems in displacement is not readily available. The World Bank, however, reports on some of its major and innovative contributions in this regard.

After the major influx of Rohingya refugees to Bangladesh in 2017, the World Bank set aside $50 million for health programmes in Cox's Bazaar where some 870,000 refugees are residing.[189] The programmes include health tracking and data systems, education materials and medical supplies for the benefit of both refugee and host communities.

The World Bank has similarly approved $36 million in grants and credit for Pakistan, to support district health services in regions with high numbers of refugees. Other host countries that are receiving additional support include Cameroon, Djibouti, and Mauritania.[190] Overall, 15 per cent of the over $2 billion which the World Bank has provided in support of refugees and host communities since 2017 under its International Development Association's special mechanisms has been approved for health services.[191]

Proposals have also been put forward to complement financing schemes with innovative tools which distribute risks among a wider group of stakeholders (including private sector investors) and utilize mechanisms, such as catastrophe bonds, to cover crisis-affected countries in case of an emergency.[192] Financing forced displacement responses is discussed more in Part V.

Good health is recognized as a key element in strengthening human capital which, in turn, supports sustainable solutions for displacement. Despite the progress made, there remain areas where further health advancements are necessary. They include expanding community approaches to preventive health and treatment, improving efforts to ensure mental health is systematically covered, and effectively including the forcibly displaced in national health services.

Research and academic interest in health in displacement are expanding[193] which, together with improved data systems and analysis, promises to enrich the evidence base for enhancing programme design, delivery and impact. This should help promote the consensus that moving from providing displaced people with parallel health systems to including them in the wider national care services is a more effective, equitable and sustainable approach.

Economic Inclusion

Context

The right to work is enshrined in the Universal Declaration of Human Rights,[194] the 1951 Convention, and the International Covenant on Economic Social and Cultural Rights.[195] But, once again, it is often respected more in theory than practice in regard to forcibly displaced persons.

Work is important for survival, to restore a sense of dignity and acquire skills that can improve life prospects. It also reduces dependency on aid. The inability to work legally can also drive individuals to cope in ways that are harmful to themselves or to others. These include resorting to survival sex, requiring children to earn wages, and marrying off daughters at a young age. In the absence of formal work, forcibly displaced persons are driven to the informal sector. There, they compete with low-skilled local workers, often disproportionately affecting less educated and female workers.[196]

Many refugees and internally displaced persons face challenges in finding work. Common difficulties include a lack of employment opportunities, especially in remote or conflict areas. They also may have lost productive assets, such as livestock, tools, vehicles, and documentation needed to earn a livelihood.[197] Discrimination by local officials and employers, language barriers and disruption of social networks can also hinder the ability to find employment.[198] And, those who are displaced from rural to urban environments, or vice versa, may find their skills are not in demand.[199]

Forcibly displaced persons tend to have lower levels of physical and mental health than host communities. As discussed, this can be due to the experiences they endured prior and during flight, and the conditions in which they reside, such as insecure residence, a lack of adequate accommodation, food and health care. This can negatively impact their ability to find and retain work.

Many displaced families have lost their wage earner, with households headed by women often disproportionally represented. Human capital can be diminished for those who have been out of work for some time. They may not be favourably considered by employers due to their long unemployment.[200]

Additionally, and most commonly, refugees face legal barriers which restrict their ability to move and their right to work. In fact, 70 per cent of refugees reside in countries where they face restrictions on their right to work, including countries with relatively few refugees.[201] This limits their ability to use their skills and entrepreneurship to benefit local economies.

Even where refugees have the right to work, this can be seriously limited. For example, where legal work is conditional on obtaining a work permit, permits can be subject to conditions and costs that refugees are unable to meet.[202] A lack of recognition of education certificates and professional quali-fications can be additional obstacles.[203] And the inability to access language or skills training can also impede the ability of forcibly displaced persons to improve their employment prospects.

Forcibly displaced persons also encounter serious difficulties in starting their own enterprises. Refugees can be prohibited by law from engaging in business. Even when legally permissible, a lack of individual documentation can be a limiting factor. This can leave individuals unable to open bank accounts, receive money transfers or benefit from loans.[204]

As noted earlier, in most host countries, refugees comprise less than 1 per cent of the population.[205] Yet, governments often assert that legal limitations on refugees' right to employment and ability to move freely are necessary to protect the local labour market and welfare of host populations.[206] The effects, discussed later in this section, can exacerbate existing disparities. Restrictions can drive refugees to concentrate in the local informal sector, often under more exploitative conditions than nationals.[207] Depending on the size of the influx, this may result in lower wages and unemployment of local workers in the sector – consequences the restrictions exacerbate rather than avoid. When refugees are permitted to work, they tend to work in more diverse occupations.[208]

While most refugees do not have the means to move elsewhere, the lack of opportunities can lead those who have some financial capital to move further afield. This generally means engaging smugglers and traffickers to help them move to other countries, risking their lives in the process.[209]

Many host countries are also concerned that measures that improve the lives of refugees, such as legal work, will inevitably reduce their readiness to return home, prolonging their displacement. This is a pervasive perception even though multi-generational restrictive policies in host countries have not led to significant refugee returns.[210] This is because conditions in the country of origin, notably safety and security, are what attracts refugees to return home, as noted in Part III. Negative drivers, such as dismal and unforgiving living conditions in exile, can be push factors but without peace and security, return is generally unsustainable and further displacement follows.

Security is another frequently cited reason for constraining refugee movement and employment and for the reticence to receive internally displaced persons favourably. There is often a presumption that an influx of forcibly displaced persons will lead to increased crime and conflict in host communities. A review of situations between 1991 and 2014 suggests that this has only been the case in exceptional situations, as a result of a mix of factors.

The risks are less when refugees are not confined to camps which can be infiltrated by armed individuals and groups. It is the responsibility of the government to ensure that camps are for civilians only and weapons-free: a responsibility that some host governments have been unwilling or unable to meet.[211] In internal displacement situations, threats to national security tend to emanate from the conflict with evidence suggesting that it generally has not spread to hosting areas.[212]

Perceptions that underpin host countries' reluctance to accept the economic inclusion of refugees persist. But these are being tested as more studies are undertaken to reliably assess the economic impact of forced displacement on host communities. This is an encouraging trend. It should support more context-specific policy advocacy and self-reliance strategies than has previously been possible.

Evolution

For most of recorded history, refugees given safety in regions beyond their own were expected to fend for themselves and make an economic contribution.

Examples in Europe from the 12th century through World War II (WWII) show how economic potential was a major consideration of States granting refuge, as discussed in Part I.

The drafting deliberations for the 1951 Convention also reveal that, for the United Nations, the aim was to ensure that refugees could rebuild their lives and become independent and integrated into their new societies.[213] The 1951 Convention itself commits States to facilitate as far as possible the assimilation and naturalization of refugees. It recognizes the rights of refugees to move freely and to individual identity and travel documents. It provides minimum standards for the treatment of refugees, such as access to the courts, to education, and to work.[214]

In the decades following the 1951 Convention, many host countries encouraged and enabled refugees to be self-reliant, especially in Africa.[215] Rising refugee numbers, however, were also met with increasing restrictions on employment. Where self-employment was permitted, it was often confined to specific areas or subject to restrictions limiting refugees' ability to work in the formal sector.

Humanitarians have long advocated for host States to recognize the right to work for refugees. Meanwhile, interventions to improve livelihoods for refugees and internally displaced persons focused on skills development or lending mechanisms to support small self-employment enterprises. They aimed more at improving access to jobs than on development interventions needed to create jobs. There has been little in the way of quantitative evidence of their impact.[216]

In fact, the evidence available on vocational and skills training points to many of these interventions falling short of their ambition.[217] Until relatively recently, they were not systematically informed by an assessment of the legal environment, the skills in demand, and the ability and willingness of forcibly displaced persons to attend the training.[218]

There is also limited evidence on the impact of interventions to strengthen self-employment and entrepreneurship among forcibly displaced populations. In their comprehensive review, Schuettler and Caron found that, in a few cases, loans to refugees led to increased incomes.[219] Similar positive outcomes have been noted in qualitative studies concerning internally displaced persons in Azerbaijan and Uganda, who benefited from microfinance.

However, the authors note that these examples are not necessarily indicative of positive outcomes overall. Most microfinance in low- and middle-income countries has not led to increased profits because of short and inflexible repayment periods.[220] They point to evidence that suggests that graduation-type programmes that include cash grants to help build assets, business or entrepreneurship training, as well as coaching and financial inclusion, are more likely to yield positive results for refugees and internally displaced persons.[221]

As discussed in Part III, efforts to attract development investments in forced displacement contexts had limited success. In the 1980s and 1990s, these included the International Conferences on Assistance to Refugees in Africa (ICARA I and II) and the International Conference on Central American Refugees (CIREFCA). In the new millennium, several other initiatives were launched, such as Development Assistance for Refugees, Development through Local Integration, and an integrated relief to development approach for sustainable repatriation.[222]

There were some modest results, but these initiatives did not mark a significant change in global orientation or resource allocation. That has come only relatively recently, and largely in the wake of the Syria crisis that began in 2011. Since then, strengthening human capital in displacement and significantly increasing development assistance to countries hosting large numbers of forcibly displaced persons became more of a shared global priority.

This is reflected throughout the Global Compact on Refugees. Drawing on the Sustainable Development Goals, the Compact recognizes the need for "shared and inclusive economic growth in refugee-hosting areas from which all can benefit", through additional development support and contributions from the private sector.[223]

Jobs and entrepreneurship are among the specific areas where the Global Compact on Refugees seeks to improve outcomes for host communities and refugees.[224] They are also areas where more development financing is being directed, supported by a growing body of evidence regarding economic impacts on host communities of receiving large numbers of forcibly displaced persons.

This expanding evidence base is helping to inform what kinds of policies are beneficial in a given context, and what types of interventions are needed to improve economic prospects for forcibly displaced persons and their hosts.[225]

Local Labour Market Impacts

High-income countries

There are many studies on the effects of refugee influxes on wages, productivity and economic growth in high-income countries. They include examinations of some of the major refugee influxes from the 17th century to the present day. Zara Sarzin's study provides a comprehensive review of these.[226] While debate is ongoing, there seems to be an emerging consensus that, by and large, host countries have been able to absorb large numbers of refugees with little to no effect on average wages or overall employment of native workers.

For example, the arrival of over 125,000 Cubans to Miami during the Mariel Boatlift of 1980 has been found not to have negatively affected local employment. Similarly, the arrival of over 1 million Jewish refugees and migrants from the former Soviet Union to Israel in the 1990s also is reported to have had no adverse impact on local wages or employment. [227]

Tim Julian, the Mayor of Utica in New York State, credits refugees with saving "entire neighbourhoods" of the US city in 2005. "We can't put a price on this," he said. © UNHCR/ Vincent Winter

Decades later, the influx of asylum-seekers to Germany between 2015 and 2016[228] was found not to have negatively affected host workers. Initially, refugees had difficulties in finding jobs. However, within five years, they integrated faster than previous influxes. Approximately half have reportedly found work, around 50,000 were doing apprenticeships, over 10,000 were enrolled in university, and three quarters of the arrivals lived in their own accommodation and felt welcome in Germany. The financial cost to the German Government is reported to be likely recovered in taxes sooner than anticipated.[229] According to a report commissioned by the Government, more than half of all Germans are reported to have supported the arrivals in some way.[230]

There have been a few documented exceptions to the general findings noted above. Ethnic Germans who fled or were expelled from East and Central

Europe to Germany in the wake of WWII were largely absorbed by the local labour market but did have a negative effect on the employment of host communities in some areas. These were areas where the refugees exceeded 15 per cent of the native population.[231]

This was also the case when over half a million Portuguese citizens moved to Portugal from its former colonies during the colonial wars of the 1970s. Their arrival coincided with a significant reduction in military employment at the time. The combined effect of these two events led to an increase in the labour force by 15 per cent, and a consequent fall in labour productivity and wages of native workers.[232]

Conversely, in other contexts, evidence suggests that employment and wages for native workers improved following the arrival of a large number of refugees. This was the case in Denmark in 1986 and 1998. Refugees concentrated in low-skilled employment, and less educated native workers moved from manual intensive occupations to more cognitive ones.[233]

Many studies point to the fact that the negative effects dissipate over time and positive effects take hold over the longer term. Among the factors that contribute to this is when forcibly displaced populations introduce new skills, production expands and/or workers of the host communities move to more skilled and higher wage-earning employment.[234]

These findings are important and can help to inform broader discussions concerning the impact of the refugees on high-income countries. This is particularly important in countering populist claims that refugees are a drain on these societies. Yet, while some 17 per cent of refugees are located in high-income countries, the remainder are hosted in low- and middle-income countries.[235] These contexts are very different.

High-income countries overall receive far fewer refugees than low- and middle-income countries and have greater capacity to absorb them. They have lower rates of unemployment, more effective labour market regulations, better working conditions, favourable business and investment climates and refugees are generally able to work legally and move to areas where they are more likely to find employment. They are also often assisted with other integration services, such as language classes, support to find accommodation, and job-seeking assistance.[236]

Low- and middle-income countries

There is a growing body of literature on the labour market consequences of forced displacement in low- and middle-income countries.[237] It points to several factors that influence how communities are impacted by the arrival of large numbers of forcibly displaced persons. As the following examples illustrate there can be both positive and negative consequences which, as with other impacts, can depend on pre-existing conditions, the size and composition of the influx, and the policy choices of the government.

Middle East

Turkey

The majority of recent empirical analyses in this area has been in the context of Syrian refugees in Turkey. Between 2012 and 2020, over 3.6 million Syrians fled to Turkey.[238] The arrival of Syrians led to some market changes in receiving communities. Demand for goods and services increased, as did labour competition in the informal sector, particularly in construction and agriculture.[239]

Several studies found that this concentration in the informal sector led to job losses of local workers while findings on wages are mixed.[240] Evidence of job losses were particularly pronounced in regions where refugees were more highly concentrated, such as border areas.[241] Local workers with low education levels, younger and female were most negatively affected.[242]

At the same time, employment in the formal sector increased slightly for local workers and highly educated Turkish workers moved from manual to more complex occupations.[243] It has also been suggested that the positive effect on formal employment did not last beyond the initial years and was reversed once the initial set-up of reception facilities was over, and Syrians began to disperse throughout the country.[244]

Several studies point to a sizable increase in small- and medium-sized enterprises started by Syrian refugees. In 2018, the Economic Policy Research Foundation of Turkey reported that approximately 10,000 companies had been established by Syrians since 2011, providing a living for an estimated 250,000 Syrians: 7 per cent of the Syrian population in Turkey.[245]

Overall, the influx of Syrian refugees to Turkey had both negative and positive effects on the economic outcomes of host communities. In areas where Syrian refugees were concentrated, there was a decline in employment of local workers, particularly in the informal sector. Meanwhile, prices of housing, transportation and some goods increased.[246]

More positively, production expanded to meet increased demand for goods and services,[247] new enterprises emerged, average consumer prices fell,[248] and wages of local workers overall remained largely unaffected.[249]

Lebanon

The Syrian conflict had a massive effect on Lebanon. It led to a considerable loss of trade and tourism, and interrupted capital flows – mainstays of the Lebanese economy.[250] Together with internal political insecurity, this led to investor uncertainty and weakened economic activity.[251] In addition, the conflict provoked mass displacement, with Lebanon receiving over 1 million Syrian refugees by 2014.[252]

A welfare study of Syrian refugees published by the World Bank in 2016 found that Syrian refugees lived in precarious situations and 70 per cent were poor.[253] Unable to work legally, unemployment rates of Syrian refugees were far higher than Lebanese.[254] Employed Syrians concentrated in the informal low-skilled sector, which led to job losses among vulnerable Lebanese. This negative effect was partially compensated by the increased economic activity driven by rising consumption and international aid.[255]

Lebanon was therefore faced with a struggling economy, political uncertainty and growing vulnerability among impoverished Lebanese and refugees. As a middle-income country, Lebanon was not eligible for concessional finance granted to low-income countries by multilateral development banks. New financing instruments, such as the Global Concessional Financing Facility established in 2016, were designed to help countries impacted by a refugee crisis, such as Lebanon, address the associated challenges by providing support to infrastructure and service delivery and helping stimulate economic growth.[256]

Jordan

In Jordan, the number of Syrian refugees also steadily increased from 2012 and, within two years, reached 600,000 persons.[257] Today, some 81 per cent of Syrian refugees in Jordan live among Jordanian communities, with the remainder living in three large refugee camps in the north of the country.[258]

Two economic studies reviewed the impact of Syrians on the Jordanian labour market through 2016.[259] Jordan experienced economic challenges prior to the Syria conflict. These were related to the global financial crisis of 2008–2009 and the economic impact of the Arab Spring.[260] The Syrian conflict also affected trade and tourism. Economic growth rates declined and poverty rates increased.[261] The influx of Syrian refugees compounded the challenges. Government expenditures increased to meet additional demands on water, electricity and sanitation, as well as health and education services, which were each made available to Syrian refugees.

The two studies found that the influx of Syrians had no significant negative effect on wages or employment of Jordanian workers. Syrians were prohibited from working, and those who found work in the informal sector largely competed with migrant labourers. Refugees were not entitled to move freely, which may have also limited the ability of Syrian workers to access jobs. Moreover, improved employment opportunities for Jordanians, as a result of the presence of international agencies and increased spending on health and education, may have increased the demand for Jordanian workers.[262]

A recent World Bank study examining the regional consequences of the Syrian conflict reached similar conclusions. In Jordan, it found that while labour force participation of Jordanians decreased and unemployment increased between 2010 and 2016, it was not on account of the Syrian influx. In fact, Jordanian unemployment rates were lower in areas with high refugee concentrations.[263]

Moreover, research conducted for the World Bank Group's Refugee Investment and Matchmaking Platform (RIMP) found that Syrian businesses contributed to the Jordanian economy, particularly in the areas of food processing, chemicals and pharmaceutical manufacturing, trade, real estate and hospitality. In 2019, there were over 1,600 Syrian-owned businesses in Jordan and over 10,000 with at least 50 per cent Syrian ownership. It was also estimated that capital invested by Syrians in Jordan had reached $240 million in 2017.[264]

In 2016, Jordan reached an agreement with several donors to improve education and employment opportunities for refugees and provide needed financial support to Jordan. Known as the Jordan Compact, the European Union (EU) and multilateral development banks[265] pledged over $2 billion in grants and low interest loans to Jordan and Jordan agreed to facilitate access to employment and education of Syrian refugees.[266] As with other compacts of its kind, it involves multi-year commitments by the parties in areas of policy reform and financial investments.[267]

The $700 million in grants and $1.9 billion in concessional loans were linked to specific targets, such as the granting of 200,000 work permits to Syrian refugees in certain sectors and measures to ensure Syrian children were able to attend public schools. The European Union agreed to provide Jordanian companies in special economic zones with easier access to European markets provided they met a hiring target of 15 per cent Syrian refugees.[268] Business reforms to help formalize Syrian businesses were also among the terms.[269]

Access to education improved under the Compact. However, the work permits were initially slow to be put in place due to a number of factors including lack of knowledge among refugees and employers. Fees and restrictions on applicable sectors also created disincentives for both.

It was difficult for businesses in the special economic zones to ensure 15 per cent of the workforce were Syrian refugees. The zones were far from where most Syrian refugees lived, had poor transportation links, and wages were often lower than could be earned in the informal sector. It was anticipated that Syrian job gains in these zones would benefit women garment workers. This expectation was not realized due to the remoteness of the zones, lack of required skills, social norms that did not encourage Syrian women to work outside the home, and the absence of childcare.[270]

For employers, the Compact initially did not result in significant benefits. Many employers preferred to maintain their largely migrant workforce rather than hire Syrian refugees. They were also often unable to meet EU export standards, and some were not incentivized to do so because they already had a market in the United States.[271] Measures to improve access for Syrians to open businesses also did not initially deliver intended outcomes as the conditions to register a business remained too onerous for most Syrians to meet.

Several adjustments were subsequently made, such as waiving work permit fees, de-linking permits from specific employer sponsorship, expanding the sectors in which refugees are permitted to work and increasing the flexibility of work permits to enable workers to move jobs within specific sectors.[272]

By the end of 2020, over 200,000 work permits were issued to Syrians,[273] with research indicating that possessing a work permit had a positive impact on income, sense of security and overall socioeconomic conditions.[274] Tariff reductions were extended to firms outside the special economic zones and the Government made it easier for Syrians to run home-based businesses without the necessity of having a Jordanian partner.[275] This approach aimed to lower barriers for women to formally engage in business opportunities.[276] Further analysis will be needed to assess the full impact of the changes.[277]

The experience pointed to the importance of a thorough contextual analysis. This includes a market analysis, an understanding of the skills and constraints facing refugees in employment and business creation, as well as the ability of firms to meet qualification standards of intended markets.[278] Ensuring critical stakeholders, notably refugees and employers, are consulted early on can help avoid potential implementation difficulties.[279]

The Jordan Compact continues to be regarded as an important initiative that has resulted in more Syrians entering the formal labour market and providing needed support to Jordan affected by the crisis in Syria. It is seen as an innovative departure from previous approaches, not least because it linked financing to meet agreed protection targets and shifted the focus from short-term responses to sustainable investments aimed to be of economic benefit to both Jordanians and refugees. It marked a shift in Jordanian Government policy, enabling agencies for the first time to expand livelihoods and skills programmes for Syrian refugees.[280]

Latin America

Colombian internal displacement

In 2016, the Parliament of Colombia approved the peace agreement between the Government and the Revolutionary Armed Forces of Colombia (FARC), bringing the over 50-year civil war to a formal conclusion. The conflict, which began in the 1960s, saw rising levels of internal displacement, with some 7.4 million persons internally displaced by the time of the peace agreement, according to Government statistics.[281]

A number of studies have examined the wage and employment impact of internally displaced persons in receiving municipalities. Several have pointed to adverse effects concentrated in the informal sector, with a fall in wages in the short term, especially in regard to low-skilled jobs.[282] After several years, there is no overall effect on wages, which could be due to an increase in local residents moving to other areas. However, the negative effect on low-skilled women was found to be more prolonged. Among the reasons for this is that while they can adapt to a new labour market, they face more competition and tend to have less flexibility to move elsewhere than others.[283]

Venezuelan displacement

Since 2013, millions of Venezuelans have left their country mostly for other countries in the region. At the end of 2020, there were some 5.4 million Venezuelan refugees and migrants globally, the majority of whom were hosted in the region.[284] This has been in response to a severe economic crisis, political instability, chronic shortages of basic goods and services, criminality, and violence.[285]

A number of studies have examined the economic impact of displaced Venezuelans in host countries. One examined the short-term impact and found that, between 2013 and 2017, Colombian host communities witnessed a decline in local wages in the low-skilled informal sector, with young workers and low-skilled men particularly affected. Lower wages also corresponded to higher poverty levels. The effect was concentrated in urban areas.[286]

In 2018, Colombia enacted a new policy: to regularize over 400,000 undocumented Venezuelans. Over 60 per cent of those eligible applied and received a renewable two-year visa, *Permiso Especial de Permanencia* (PEP), which entitled them to work and access public services.[287] An economic study on the impact of the programme found that it had no significant effect

Carmen Sánchez, a Colombian refugee in Ecuador, shows the bread she is baking at her home to sell it in the local Esmeraldas area in 2021.
© UNHCR/ Jaime Giménez

on hours worked, monthly wages, employment and labour participation of Colombians in the formal or informal sectors. It also found a small positive impact on the formal employment of Venezuelan workers.[288]

Ecuador has received over 400,000 Venezuelans who comprise over 2 per cent of the population. Their arrival corresponded to a difficult economic period induced by the 2014 fall in oil prices. This led to a decrease in government revenues, a reduction in spending and economic growth. GDP stagnated and, by 2016, had fallen.[289]

Most Venezuelans moved beyond the border areas to high-income regions of the country.[290] A study of the labour market effects reveals that employed Venezuelans were concentrated in the informal sector. While overall their presence did not affect employment prospects of local workers, there were negative impacts on the quality of employment and income of young, less educated Ecuadorians. They experienced lower wages and/or fewer hours of work compared to similar workers in areas of the country that had far lower concentrations of Venezuelan workers.[291]

Depending on the policy choices of the Ecuadorian Government, the authors noted that the inflow of workers could spur investment, the creation of new businesses, and economic opportunities over time. They recommended the consideration of granting formal labour market access to Venezuelans to help lessen the concentration in the informal sector, while contributing to increased productivity of Venezuelan workers and entrepreneurs.[292]

In 2021, Ecuador announced a new regularization policy for Venezuelans in the country, to be complemented by economic integration and labour market access.[293]

Africa

The examples from the Middle East and Latin America examined the labour market outcomes as a result of the influx of forcibly displaced persons. The case studies presented below from Africa examine the effect on livelihoods and welfare.[294]

The policy context in each host country varies. In Kenya and Tanzania, governments have restrictive refugee policies, requiring refugees to reside in camps and limiting legal work. In contrast, Rwanda and Uganda have promoted the social and economic integration of refugees and host communities.

Tanzania

In 1993–1994, Tanzania experienced two large influxes of refugees. In 1993, over 250,000 Burundian refugees fled to western Tanzania, followed by a similar number of Rwandan refugees the next year.[295] Numbers continued to grow and, by 1995, there were 830,000 refugees in Tanzania, over 90 per cent from Burundi and Rwanda.[296] The refugees were concentrated in the northwest Kagera region, one of the poorest in the country, with a local population of some 1.5 million persons at the time.[297]

Refugees were accommodated in camps and had to seek permission to leave them to work or trade. To benefit from services, they had to return to the camps in the evening.[298] Several studies have looked at the impact of the refugee influx on local communities, showing both positive and negative effects.[299]

The settlement of so many refugees led to environmental degradation, with trees and shrubs cut mainly for firewood. Various water sources were depleted.[300] Some casual workers were paid less due to increased competition from refugees.[301] Prices of certain commodities increased, benefiting suppliers but hurting Tanzanians on low fixed incomes.[302] And, while child labour initially decreased following the influx, likely due to an increase in household welfare, the rates increased again after 10 years. This could be a result of increased demand for agricultural labour.[303]

At the same time, increased demand led to expanded local markets, helping suppliers in and beyond the camp areas.[304] New businesses were created,[305] and infrastructure, health and sanitation services in the region improved largely as a result of the increased presence of international organizations. Additionally, farmers benefited from lower labour costs and increased prices for their commodities. Non-agricultural workers experienced an increase in job opportunities and higher wages, principally in humanitarian organizations.[306]

On balance, the refugee presence had a persistent positive economic effect on the local population,[307] but it was not evenly distributed. The more vulnerable Tanzanians did not benefit equally. Several studies concluded that education and microfinance opportunities could support those most negatively impacted to cope and adapt to the new conditions.[308]

Kenya

For over three decades, Kenya has been one of the largest host countries on the African continent. Today, the country hosts more than 500,000 refugees and asylum-seekers, with some 84 per cent living in camps in its northwest and eastern areas.[309] A joint World Bank-UNHCR socioeconomic survey in 2018, found that in Turkana County in the remote northwest, refugees and local residents "are among the worse off in Kenya".[310] It is susceptible to extended periods of drought and consequent famine.[311]

Two studies published in 2016 and 2018 examined the economic impact of refugees in Turkana County.[312] It hosts some 216,000 refugees or about 40 per cent of the national total. Refugees comprise approximately one fifth of Turkana County's population.[313] In a refugee camp near the town of Kakuma, more than 50 per cent of the people are from South Sudan, with most of the others coming from Somalia and the Democratic Republic of the Congo.[314]

Receiving permits to work outside the camps is extremely difficult, which means that refugees within them depend on food aid, remittances, and any income they earn from their own businesses or employment opportunities within the camp.[315]

A long-established community of Burundian refugees thrives in the Tanzanian village of Lukama in 2008 and hopes to do even more when granted citizenship. © UNHCR/ Brendan Bannon

The studies found that Kakuma's refugee camp has a more vibrant market than the town itself and is better connected to other major markets than most towns in the wider county. Goods come from other regions, often through Somali firms located in Kakuma town. The camp market is open to the host community, who come to both buy and sell goods and services.[316]

Within the camp, Turkana workers are employed in security and domestic service, construction, maintenance and clerical work. Members of the Turkana community also supply basic necessities, such as charcoal, firewood[317] and livestock.[318] The studies observed that members of the Turkana community who lived near the camp benefited from the presence of refugees overall in terms of income, employment and nutrition.[319]

The benefits to the local community, however, were unevenly distributed.

Farmers and wage earners, for example, experienced long-term asset growth which was not the case for those who raised livestock. They did not benefit from rising prices, largely because they sell through brokers who charge a commission.[320] The studies concluded that further economic integration, alongside targeted interventions to assist local populations, would help.[321]

In 2015, the Kalobeyei settlement was established within close proximity to Kakuma, with the aim of promoting refugee self-reliance and social cohesion. In it, land is allocated for homes and household gardens. Cash is provided directly to residents, enabling them to purchase materials for housing and other goods. To help build good relations, members of the local community also live within the settlement.[322]

There were relatively fast and broad positive outcomes, some of which

Ishimagizwe Eliana, a 23-year-old pregnant refugee from Burundi, in the shop she runs in Kalobeyei village in Kenya in 2020. © UNHCR/ Samuel Otieno

became evident within the first 15 months of Kalobeyei's operation.[323] A study undertaken in 2017 found refugees there had improved nutrition and sense of autonomy compared with residents in the Kakuma camp. But improvements in self-reliance were curtailed by the same constraints experienced by refugees in Kakuma: an absence of access to financing, and laws restricting the right to work and to move.[324] This suggests that the impact of efforts to improve self-reliance is diminished when such basic limits remain.

This is consistent with findings of the 2018 UNHCR-World Bank socio-economic survey of conditions of refugees and host communities around Kalobeyei. It concluded that improving programmes and interventions for both refugees and hosts could enhance their well-being. Examples provided include more investments in building and maintaining human capital and programmes to improve agricultural self-reliance for better food security. Increased work possibilities and more favourable business environments could be supported by partnerships with financial institutions as well as the private sector to promote refugee-led business and create employment opportunities.[325]

Uganda

Uganda stands apart from most host countries. Its policies support the self-reliance of refugees with a range of long-established open and inclusive measures.[326]

It hosts over 1.4 million refugees, most from South Sudan.[327] Refugees are allowed to move freely, work, own property and businesses and can access national services. In dedicated settlements, they receive a plot of land to live on and cultivate.[328] The settlements are remote, but people are free to move out to find employment, although they then lose access to almost all humanitarian assistance, which the Government limits to the settlements.[329]

A study of the economic impact of refugees on the population of Uganda between 2002 and 2010, found that poverty levels among Ugandans living near refugee settlements declined.[330] During this time, Uganda hosted on average 209,000 refugees, the majority from the Democratic Republic of the Congo.[331] Households also benefited from improved education services and infrastructure, findings which when published in 2016,[332] showed similarities to studies undertaken in Tanzania.

But it also found that host communities *perceived* that they were worse off. They felt that, compared to refugees, they had been neglected by the Government.[333] Thus, while the overall effects were positive, they were unevenly experienced. Some groups faced competition from refugee labour, and increased demand for health services came without deeper Government investment.

Such findings highlight the importance of helping members of the host community adversely affected by an influx and making efforts to foster better understanding between the local community and the displaced.[334]

Rwanda

A study published in 2019 examined the influence that Congolese refugees had on the labour market activity and household welfare of host communities in Rwanda. It is based on data from 2016, when Rwanda hosted 156,000 refugees of whom 73,000 were from the Democratic Republic of the Congo.[335] They resided primarily in five camps throughout the country. The study analysed household survey data collected from three Congolese refugee camps and surrounding areas.[336]

It observed that refugees had access to basic health care, water and sanitation. Refugee children attended school in local communities or exceptionally in camp-based schools which follow the national curriculum.[337] Refugees also had the right to move and to be employed. However, the right to move out of the camps and work was subject to formal procedures and costs that can be difficult for refugees to meet.[338] This was found to increase their dependence on assistance for prolonged periods of time.

Rwandans living near refugee camps were more likely to have moved from subsistence agriculture into wage employment. This may have been due to their being better able to hire low-skilled labour to maintain farming or livestock production and take up other opportunities. Local women living near the camps had a higher likelihood of being self-employed, and proximity to the camps also correlated with greater household asset ownership.[339]

Overall, host communities near the camps did not perceive their situation to be worse than before the refugees arrived. Nonetheless, neither did they perceive a net benefit, despite evidence to the effect that there was.[340]

Another related study found that, in relation to education, school attendance and education outcomes for local children living near the camps were higher than for those elsewhere. Locals living near the camp positively viewed the effects of refugees on education and appreciated the Government's investments in education in these areas.[341]

Sudan

In 2003, armed groups in the Darfur region rebelled against Government policies that disadvantaged the non-Arab population. Repression by

Government forces and the Janjaweed militia led to tens of thousands of deaths and mass forced displacement. By 2011, the number of internally displaced persons reached over 2.4 million persons, rising to 3.2 million in 2015.[342]

Most lived in camps adjacent to major cities and were heavily dependent on food assistance. In many areas, the number of internally displaced persons was larger than that of local populations.[343]

The conflict caused the collapse of rural economic activities. And, while demand for goods and services rose in internal displacement areas affected by conflict, so too did competition for low-skilled jobs, according to a study published in 2015. The urban economies were not able to easily absorb the increase, and recently arrived internally displaced persons faced unemployment.[344] However, local residents had a higher probability of being employed in skilled sectors compared to those in cities outside conflict areas, and a lower likelihood of being unemployed.[345]

To help address the impact on the host areas, the authors suggested preferential employment opportunities for the most vulnerable or heavy investments in securing the periphery of cities to allow for more agricultural production. This would be a source of employment for low-skilled and unemployed workers and help reduce food shortages.[346]

Consolidated Findings

The findings of these country studies are consistent with a broader review published by the World Bank in 2019. It found that there are long-term positive effects from the arrival of forcibly displaced persons, while the negative impact dissipates over time. It puts the chances of an overall negative impact for host communities at less than 20 per cent.

The review examined the results of studies on the economic impact of forced displacement on host communities conducted over the previous 29-year period. It examined 762 results related to employment, wages, prices and household well-being.[347] Measures of well-being included levels of income, consumption, accommodation, assets and poverty. In regard to well-being, the results pointed to positive or insignificant change over 80 per cent of the time.[348]

As country-specific studies show, prices can increase or decrease. Those for food and rent tend to rise, while those for labour-intensive services or products fall. Employment and wages showed similar variation, with close to two thirds of results showing no significant changes. Positive and significant improvements are documented in up to 20 per cent of the results, with up to 25 per cent of the cases pointing to negative and significant results, mostly experienced by young and informal workers.[349]

While the research suggests that, over time, the positive effects remain relatively constant, and the negative impacts wane, longer-term work is needed to better understand the prevalence of these trends.[350] More in-depth reviews are also needed to determine the extent to which forcibly displaced persons are socially and economically integrated over time.[351]

For refugees, the findings are clear on the benefits of legal employment: It removes the insecurity of being fined, detained or arrested for working. Formal work tends to be higher paid. Incomes increase over time and opportunities to be self-reliant are enhanced. It can also encourage further investment in personal development because it increases the likelihood of acquired skills being put to use.

Refugees who are productive and have improved incomes support the economy through their spending and payment of taxes.[352] They are better able to provide for themselves and their families and build the human capital essential for sustainable solutions.

Legally recognizing the right to work removes a disincentive some employers may have in employing those who are not authorized to work. This could help raise refugee employment rates.[353] However, because informal markets in low- and middle-income countries tend to be large, refugees and internally displaced persons may remain in the informal sector, especially those with fewer skills.[354]

Loss of wages or employment for local workers needs to be addressed through skills training or social protection programmes, integrated into national poverty-reduction strategies and supported internationally as a meaningful form of burden-sharing.

Achieving socioeconomic inclusion and improved outcomes for host and forcibly displaced communities is complex. It requires deep appreciation of the *local* context, including the structure of the economy, related laws and policies, economic trends and potential for growth. It also requires information on the economic impact of conflict and forced displacement, and the relative skills and capacities of displaced and host populations. Interventions to improve human capital in displacement need to be based on reliable, context-specific data, analysis and "evidence of what works and at what cost".[355]

The 2030 Ambition

International cooperation frameworks for responding to forced displacement are focused on more than ensuring safety. They also seek dignified lives and improved futures for people forced to flee. That has often been elusive.

National policies and practices have frequently undermined the ability of displaced persons to overcome their losses, improve their lives and make a contribution to the communities in which they live. Global recognition that forced displacement is as much a development imperative as a humanitarian one has only come recently.

The explicit inclusion of refugees and internally displaced persons in the Sustainable Development Goals is a significant and promising turning point reflected in two of the four objectives of the Global Compact on Refugees: easing the pressures on host countries and enhancing refugee self-reliance.

These objectives are more likely to be met if education and health services are inclusive and economic growth is facilitated.

In less than a decade, significant and financially supported policy changes have already facilitated improved access to education for forcibly displaced populations. Improved and inclusive public education can provide powerful benefits for displaced and host communities. Consolidating gains and the experience and evidence they provide may be the best way of ensuring that this approach spreads. Progress is usually incremental with global policy initiatives.

Compared to education, inclusive health-care provision has seen fewer global initiatives and investment. Nonetheless, progress in preventive and community health care has been significant. Communicable diseases are best controlled by national and local health strategies that do not discriminate between displaced and local communities.

Considerable and recent economic study into the labour market effects of forcibly displaced persons also provides clarity. It should help set a new direction for national policy: to facilitate lawful work, rather than inhibit it. Most of the time, this brings net benefits. But measures may also be necessary to mitigate the impact for some within host communities.

This path to inclusivity in education and health care and openness in labour markets depends on context-specific data, analysis and evidence. We need considerably more of these. The countries most affected by conflict-driven displacement face pre-existing economic and development challenges, which can be exacerbated by the arrival of large numbers of forcibly displaced persons. These countries need evidence of the benefits offered by a broad and inclusive development agenda – and how its risks can be mitigated – before they can be expected to embrace it. This requires strengthened technical capacity and additional development support.[356]

PART V

Bridging
The Gap

Table of Contents

Bridging the Gap

"Don't let me become a beggar" was the simple plea from a recently arrived Tigrayan refugee in an emergency displacement camp in eastern Sudan. Speaking to a visiting delegation, he mentioned his education, skills and desire to independently support himself and his family.[1] He did not want to be relegated to a path of dependency and despair, but to be able to use his skills to provide for himself and his family.

A large number of forcibly displaced people have been trapped on that dependency path, as this book has shown. Many have reached safety but struggle to restore dignified lives or hope for better futures. This book has focused on that gap in outcomes, and the changes needed to close it. There is significant work ahead to ensure that the Tigrayan refugee in eastern Sudan, and so many like him, have opportunities to become self-reliant, contribute to the community and invest in the future. His ambition was simple, but fulfilling it is not easy.

A significant shift in policy orientation is needed. For many years, most governments receiving large numbers of forcibly displaced persons have viewed their arrival as a security issue, and a temporary phenomenon which needs to be contained until the people leave. Camps have been erected and other restrictions have prohibited social and economic inclusion with host communities.

Humanitarian agencies have adapted to these situations. Facing short-term and limited funding, agencies do what they can to ensure people are safe and their basic subsistence needs are met. Their development counterparts, focused on more sustainable development-oriented responses, are engaging more in forced displacement contexts. But they often arrive after the initial architecture has been established, which is difficult to dislodge.

Mihret Gerezgiher, 25, fled from Ethiopia and is a trained construction engineer and teacher, volunteers with UNHCR in Sudan's Tunaydbah camp in 2021, overseeing construction and helping other refugees access medical care. © UNHCR/ Ahmed Kwarte

The 1951 Convention relating to the Status of Refugees (1951 Convention) was written with a view to refugees having agency over their futures. The Global Compact on Refugees seeks to realize this. To improve self-reliance in displacement, the full support of host governments is definitive. They need evidence that changing the decades-old approach of containment will benefit their communities.

This requires deep and context-specific analysis. It needs to cover the likelihood of displacement being protracted, the socioeconomic status of displaced and host communities, as well as the economic impact on different members of affected communities. It should outline the opportunities if the right policy frameworks are in place.

In Part V, we look at some of the factors necessary for this change. Financing needs to be much more robust, predictable and broader based. Improvements are needed in data, evidence and analysis. Better use should be made of the comparative advantages of the wider group of stakeholders that are now engaged. Part V ends by looking at accountability, another important aspect of improving responses to forced displacement.

Financing

Meeting the needs of forcibly displaced people requires significant financial resources for both humanitarian assistance and development support. They have different objectives yet are complementary.

Humanitarian assistance sets out to "save lives, alleviate suffering and maintain dignity during and in the aftermath of man-made crises and natural disasters".[2] It helps to meet immediate needs, such as safety, food, water, shelter, and health care. Increasingly, it has been relied on to support lives and welfare over protracted periods of time. Long durations have strained its reach and effectiveness. It is not designed to provide medium- and longer-term support for forcibly displaced persons or the communities in which they live. Neither is it sufficient for it.

The level of humanitarian funding has increased in the last decade, but so too has the global level of humanitarian needs. United Nations entities and their partners often make requests to donors for humanitarian funds jointly, through consolidated humanitarian appeals. These grew by 300 per cent between 2011 and 2020, from just under $10 billion to close to $39 billion. Contributions also rose but never by enough: On average, 60 per cent of consolidated humanitarian appeals were funded from 2011 to 2019, falling to 52 per cent in 2020 with the emergence of COVID-19.[3]

Over 95 per cent of humanitarian funding for a number of years has come from 20 donors, and three of them contributed over half of the total.[4] The need for additional high-income States to contribute more remains a pressing one. More positively, humanitarian financing from private sources has increased in recent years. Individuals, businesses and philanthropic foundations are becoming strong partners in supporting relief efforts. As of 2019, 22 per cent of international humanitarian funding was from private sources.[5] Over two thirds of this came from individuals, with 14 per cent provided by corporations and trusts.[6] These sources of funding are expected to grow.

Because of the COVID-19 pandemic, an additional 19 million more people were in need of humanitarian assistance in 2020, but funding did not keep pace.[7] The financial repercussions of COVID-19 will continue. This makes the shift away from a heavy dependance on humanitarian assistance towards more sustainable development responses more urgent.

Development support focuses on reducing the poverty among forcibly displaced persons and their host communities. Development financing aims to advance sustainable socioeconomic improvements in lives over the medium and long term. This work includes advising host countries on policy options for inclusive development. Development financing can support reforms necessary to: foster economic growth and job creation; invest in infrastructure; strengthen service delivery and skills training; and support measures to help offset the risks that can be an obstacle to greater private sector engagement.

Forced displacement crises tend to require complementary humanitarian and development approaches, because they are rarely short in duration. Yet, their funding is typically dominated by humanitarian interventions. The move towards using a development approach has gained traction only in recent years, after decades of advocacy.

There are several reasons for the traditional reliance on short-term humanitarian funding. For many years, forced displacement situations were regarded as temporary. Refugees were expected to return to their countries. Many host countries and donors were reluctant to acknowledge the protracted nature of displacement and the need to shift to longer-term funding.

Additionally, development financing is oriented towards sustainable approaches, including support for forcibly displaced persons to become economically self-reliant. Many host countries have legal impediments to refugee self-reliance, including restrictions on their right to move freely and/or to work. Given the acute needs of their own citizens, low- and middle-income countries often are reluctant to support the inclusion of refugees in development programmes. They have also been concerned that refugee employment will come at the expense of locals and will discourage refugees from returning home, as discussed in Part IV.

As a consequence, the costs of forced displacement have been largely calculated on the basis of what was needed to meet short-term humanitarian needs. The full costs to host States of protracted displacement were not systematically captured.[8] The cost to refugees and their home countries, in terms of their human development losses, was neglected.

This began to change in 2015, with the Syria situation, and the increased refugee arrivals in Europe. It was then that the exceptional scale and costs of a major refugee emergency became more fully visible. The financial architecture for forced displacement began to shift in a meaningful way. This section looks at this potentially transformative change, shown by the rapid growth of financing instruments, new partnerships and approaches.

Increased humanitarian and development funding is crucial to improve responses to forced displacement. So too is using resources effectively and efficiently. Both are priorities within the Global Compact on Refugees.[9]

Humanitarian Financing

The need to expand humanitarian funding and diversify funding sources was a central focus of the 2016 World Humanitarian Summit, convened by then United Nations Secretary-General, Ban Ki-moon. The aim of the Summit was to improve international humanitarian action for people caught in crises and to improve the financial architecture. Nearly all United Nations member States participated along with some 9,000 delegates. It resulted in the Agenda for Humanity, including a Platform for Action and some 3,500 commitments.[10]

By this time the High-Level Panel on Humanitarian Financing, appointed by the Secretary-General in 2015, had issued its report and recommendations. Although it focused on humanitarian funding, it also acknowledged the need for deeper use of development approaches.

The Panel called for a "Grand Bargain" between donors and humanitarian organizations, a term which found resonance. Donors agreed in principle to provide more predictable, multi-year and unearmarked humanitarian funding, with reduced reporting burdens. In exchange, humanitarian organizations agreed to cut duplication and management costs and work more closely with development partners. They would also enhance the capacity of local partners while making greater space for them. Humanitarian organizations agreed to improve joint and impartial needs assessments and to be more transparent on funding received.[11]

The Panel predicted that these reforms would lead to greater efficiencies, eliminating certain costs and freeing significant resources for frontline delivery. The New York Declaration of 2016 reflected the Grand Bargain's ambition of ensuring adequate, flexible, predictable financing for the immediate humanitarian response and longer-term development needs.[12] It was picked up again in the Global Compact on Refugees of 2018.[13]

To date, the $1 billion in projected savings from the Grand Bargain have not been realized.[14] Annual independent reports on progress reveal that ownership and accountability for the commitments have varied among signatories. The bulk of engagement has been driven by a core group, although the latest report indicates that, in some areas, more signatories have increased their efforts.[15]

On the donor side, humanitarian funding remains unpredictable,[16] although there has been some progress in increasing multi-year financing and reducing the restrictions or "earmarks" placed on financing.[17] A simplified reporting template has been agreed, but it is not used by most donor signatories.[18] There has also been little progress in securing new bilateral donors.[19]

Humanitarian organizations have expanded the use of a method widely recognized as cost-efficient: multipurpose cash-based programming. As well, implementation has increasingly been delegated to local partners, although at levels below the original goal for the overall share of funds.[20] There has been greater transparency for the funding received by humanitarian entities, and they have improved the quality and frequency of joint needs assessments, eliminating duplication and helping align priorities.[21] Independent reviews also point to the need to further build the capacities of local implementers and to reduce duplication and management costs.[22]

Financing for Development

International development assistance to low-income countries is provided on "concessional terms", through grants and low-interest loans to State and local government actors. Funding largely comes through international financial institutions (IFIs), including multilateral and regional development banks,[23] and bilaterally from high-income countries. It is negotiated through a lengthy process of assessment and dialogue with recipient countries, with a multi-year implementation time frame. It aims to support interventions to sustainably alleviate poverty, generate economic growth and reduce reliance on external aid.

The World Bank has helped to lead the shift to increased development support to forced displacement situations. In 2009, it established a Global Program on Forced Displacement (GPFD) Trust Fund which, for several years, focused on how to bring development approaches to forced displacement contexts. In 2017, it published *Forcibly Displaced: Toward a Development Approach Supporting Refugees, the Internally Displaced, and Their Hosts*.[24] This was the first comprehensive articulation of specific challenges faced by these communities as well as a guide on how development actors can support policies and interventions to overcome them. In step with its publication, the World Bank opened a new financing mechanism for that purpose.

International Development Association (IDA) specific mechanisms

The new mechanism is part of the International Development Association (IDA). Through the IDA, the World Bank provides grants and low-interest loans to the world's poorest countries. The loans have an extended repayment period of 30–40 years. It is one of the largest sources of development assistance of its kind. In recent years, annual commitments averaged over $29 billion in the past three years.[25] IDA priorities include support to policy and institutional reform, investment in human capital in the areas of education, health, water and sanitation, as well as infrastructure to help economic growth, job creation, poverty reduction and better living conditions.[26]

IDA has been in operation since 1960. A new IDA mechanism, IDA18 Regional Sub-window for Refugees and Host communities, is a means to provide additional support to low-income countries hosting large numbers of refugees. The funding is on top of IDA regular allocations and is designed to create medium- and long-term development opportunities for both refugees and hosts. Through it, the World Bank provides $2 billion in concessional development financing.[27] A second, IDA19 Window for Host Communities and Refugees, will finance up to $2.2 billion in operational support, close to half of which will address the impacts of COVID-19.[28] These mechanisms also have facilities to encourage private sector investments in concert with other institutions of the World Bank Group (WBG).[29]

The funding is contingent on countries adhering to an adequate framework of protection for refugees and agreeing to take concrete steps to advance solutions of benefit to them and the communities in which they live. This includes efforts to facilitate the socioeconomic inclusion of refugees.

So far, 14 countries have benefited from the first mechanism for refugees and host communities.[30] In Ethiopia, as discussed later in this Part, it is supporting the Government's new policy towards greater socioeconomic inclusion of refugees.[31] It has similarly been supportive in the development and implementation of the Strategic Plan for Refugees in Rwanda which includes increased access to services and economic opportunities. In several other countries, such as Cameroon, Chad, the Republic of the Congo, Mauritania, Niger, and Uganda, the financing supports the inclusion of refugees in various national health, education and social protection progammes.[32]

IDA funding is not available to middle-income countries. Yet, as the last decade has illustrated, they too have been hard hit by displacement crises. In 2016, some 58 per cent of refugees and asylum-seekers were in middle-income countries.[33]

Global Concessional Financing Facility

To assist these countries, in 2016, the United Nations, the Islamic Development Bank (IsDB) and the World Bank created the Global Concessional Financing Facility (GCFF).[34] It provides low cost, long-term loans to middle-income-countries hosting large numbers of refugees. It achieves this by mobilizing grants from donors and then uses the financing to provide loans at rates that are lower than normal for middle-income countries. In this way, every $1 in grants can unlock $3–4 in low-interest loans. The Facility now has

The Soto family from Venezuela on World Refugee Day in 2021 in Ecuador as the announced regularization of an estimated 300,000 Venezuelans is about to make their stay official. © UNHCR/ Santiago Escobar-Jaramillo

nine supporting country donors and the European Commission. The implementation is supported by four multilateral development banks (MDBs) and the United Nations.[35] At the end of 2020, the facility had disbursed close to $660 million in funding, unlocking $4.8 billion in concessional support for projects in Colombia, Ecuador, Jordan and Lebanon.[36]

The financing focuses on improving infrastructure, job creation and service delivery for the benefit of host communities and refugees. It was a source of financing for the Jordan Compact, discussed in Part IV, which helped to improve education, employment and entrepreneurial opportunities for Syrian refugees while supporting the Jordanian Government in the process.[37]

In Colombia, the financing helped to support the Government's adaptation of policies towards displaced Venezuelans. In 2021, Colombia initiated the granting of 10-year Temporary Protection Status (TPS) and a path to permanent residency, with attendant rights to work, as well as access to school and health services.[38] Similar positive results have accompanied the funding to Ecuador. It has provided budget support across several ministries for inclusive service provision as Ecuador too revises its policies to regularize Venezuelans and for their economic integration and labour market access.[39]

Multilateral Development Bank Coordination Platform

Another significant milestone was the 2018 launch of the Multilateral Development Bank Coordination Platform on Economic Migration and Forced Displacement. Its members include six major regional MDBs and the World Bank. At the 2019 Global Refugee Forum, they endorsed the vision of the Global Compact on Refugees for additional development financing in support of inclusive socioeconomic growth of refugees and host communities.[40]

Members pledged to increase financing that benefits forcibly displaced and host communities, with a focus on resilience and social cohesion, provide financial support more rapidly and foster the engagement of the private sector in situations of forced displacement.[41] Among the priority areas for the Coordination Platform are: a common framework for engagement; sharing of data, evidence and knowledge; and strategic coordination with governments, United Nations agencies and other partners.[42]

OECD International Network on Conflict and Fragility (INCAF)

The Organisation for Economic Cooperation and Development (OECD) was founded in 1961. It is an inter-governmental organization and forum for policy dialogue and the sharing of promising practices. Its stated ambition is to support resilient, inclusive sustainable growth and economic progress worldwide.[43] It currently has 38 members, mostly high-income countries.

Within the OECD, the Development Assistance Committee (DAC) is the leading international forum for aid and development policy.[44] For the first time, in 2019, a network of DAC members adopted a Common Position on supporting comprehensive responses in refugee situations. It contains several principles, including to: promote the inclusion of refugees in national and/or local service delivery and development strategies; support interventions of benefit to host communities and refugees tailored to specific contexts; and expand flexible financing mechanisms for timely and sustainable responses. The Common Position acknowledges the benefits of blending humanitarian, development and peace interventions early on as a crisis unfolds.[45] The collective adoption of these principles forms a basis to launch coordinated action with the aim to put them in practice.

These efforts are a significant signal of how major development donors have recognized their comparative advantage and relevance in forced displacement contexts. Before this, their involvement was episodic. Now it is expected that they will engage governments and partners more systematically, providing guidance and operational support in a coordinated manner.

Application

In addition to the World Bank, other multilateral development banks are demonstrating their commitment in tangible ways. For example, the

In Aysaita in the Afar region of Ethiopia, refugees and host community members live and farm together as part of an agricultural project.
© UNHCR/Helle Degn

European Bank for Reconstruction and Development (EBRD) focuses on private sector growth. It has invested €268 million in Jordan, Lebanon and Turkey and mobilized €160 million of grants to support projects that benefit refugees and host communities.[46] This too complements additional development support from bilateral and MDB donors.[47]

The benefits of these cooperative efforts are also evident in Ethiopia. In 2016, the Government signed the "Jobs Compact" with a number of bilateral donors, notably the United Kingdom, the European Union, the European Investment Bank (EIB) and the World Bank Group. The Jobs Compact aims to generate 100,000 sustainable jobs and economic opportunities for

Ethiopians and refugees.[48] Under the Compact, the Ethiopian Government agrees to make policy changes to permit refugees to work, improve their access to legal documentation, social services and freedom of movement.

For their part, donors have approved $500 million in financing. Of this, the World Bank and the United Kingdom have committed nearly $300 million in concessional financing available through the Ethiopia Economic Opportunities Program to improve the business environment, increase productivity and enhance the sustainability of industrial parks. Disbursements are contingent on several targets being met, such as the number of refugees with access to economic opportunities.[49]

In 2019, the Ethiopian Government passed a new refugee law, which permits refugees to: obtain work permits; access primary education, health and banking services; transfer property, register births, deaths and marriages in civil registries; and obtain drivers' licenses.[50] Supplementary legislation and administrative measures to advance these provisions are under development. The new policy is a major shift to inclusivity after decades of camp-based policies.

In 2019, the Inter-American Development Bank (IADB) announced the provision of $100 million non-reimbursable resources from its Grant Facility to support countries receiving large and sudden inflows of refugees and/or migrants.[51] The funds are to help receiving countries provide better access to security and public services and improve infrastructure, such as clean water, sanitation and housing. The funds will be combined with a regular IADB loan of $800 million.

In announcing the financing, the IADB noted the need to ensure necessary policy frameworks are in place to help mitigate the negative impacts that a sudden large influx can have on services, infrastructure and fiscal budgets. The funding aims to support local and national governments to implement comprehensive development programmes, facilitating the social integration of refugees and migrants benefiting them and the communities in which they live.[52]

The IADB's work also includes expanding the evidence base through research, sharing experiences and promising practice, and engaging in training to strengthen public sector capacities to integrate migrants and refugees into their host communities.[53]

The African Development Bank (AfDB) set up a Transition Support Facility (TSF) to assist member countries in "fragile settings or in transition". It aims to strengthen institutions and economies and to consolidate peace.[54] Support to forced displacement situations has been limited but with potential for growth.[55] According to an independent evaluation of the Facility, further growth may depend on a number of factors including adjusting criteria and deepening its resource base.[56]

Multilateral development banks and bilateral donors rely on different means for providing funds. The most common mechanism in forced displacement situations entails grants and low-interest loans to finance specific activities – *investment project financing*. Another means is to provide funds directly to the host government – *budget support*, to improve a particular sector or national policies. It is a common form of general development funding for countries that have the required level of financial management capacity. This mechanism is being used by the World Bank in programmes to support the Jordanian energy and water sectors, which face increased demand due to the presence of Syrian refugees, and to facilitate job creation and economic growth in Colombia, Ecuador, Jordan and Lebanon.[57]

Another mechanism that is becoming more common is *outcome funding*. As the name suggests, funding is provided when certain targets are reached. For example, in a number of the concessional financing agreements between the World Bank and refugee-hosting governments, the latter agree to implement programmes through their own systems, like health, education and employment, and funding is provided when certain agreed targets on refugee inclusion are met. These can include increased access to health services, improved access and quality of education and enhanced employment and entrepreneurship opportunities. This is the funding mechanism used, for example, in the Ethiopia Economic Opportunities Program.[58]

Private Sector Investments

In recent years, there has been increased interest in the role that private, profit-driven enterprises can play in contributing to economic growth and job creation in forced displacement contexts and, by extension, in promoting the self-reliance of refugees and internally displaced persons (IDPs). The private sector can complement, but not replace, indispensable public sector interventions and/or humanitarian assistance targeting displaced and host communities alike.

Its potential for improving the lives of forcibly displaced and host communities is recognized in the Global Compact on Refugees as well as the report of the High-Level Panel on Internal Displacement. Areas noted include: job creation and job placement; mentorship; expanding access to financial products; infrastructure improvements; improving internet access; enhancing data collection and use; financing; mentorship and solutions strategies.[59]

In 2019, the International Chamber of Commerce published the Charter of Good Practice on the Role of the Private Sector in Economic Integration of Refugees. Recognizing the importance of empowering refugees as economic agents, the Charter sets out standards and guidelines to facilitate their economic integration, including expanding financial inclusion for refugees and host communities.

The Charter was co-sponsored by the World Bank Group, the European Investment Bank and the Confederation of Danish Industry. It grew via an international meeting of hundreds of practitioners, with participation from the International Chamber of Commerce, UNHCR and the World Economic Forum, and draws on their collective experience.[60] Its principles support entrepreneurship, employment and investment and highlight enabling factors, such as legal frameworks, technical advice, financing, skills development, market viability and financing.

Another initiative with broad application is the Humanitarian and Resilience Investing (HRI) Initiative. It was launched in 2019 at the World Economic Forum and seeks to leverage private capital in support of vulnerable individuals and fragile communities.[61] This includes investing in opportunities that improve resilience and self-reliance. It promotes collaboration among donors, development banks, development finance institutions and humanitarian-development organizations to share knowledge, build expertise and promote feasible projects to improve resilience. It also aims to mitigate uncertainty for prospective investors through the provision of guarantees and other risk financing.[62]

Application of these guidelines and principles are in the early stages. Many private sector job creation initiatives in forced displacement contexts have only recently come on stream. They have tended to be of relatively small size.[63] A number are part of broader, multilateral job creation efforts.[64] Although it is too soon to discern long-term impact, these initiatives are providing lessons.

Chief among them is that context matters. In some situations, there are significant obstacles to increased private sector investments. Many host countries rank in the lower half of the World Bank's Ease of Doing Business index.[65] Their regulatory frameworks may not be conducive to establishing businesses, enforcing contracts or registering property. Tax laws may not be favourable and cross-border trade can be challenging. Political instability or relatively high security threats can also dampen investor confidence.

Forcibly displaced populations are often located in remote and under-developed areas, with limited transportation, access to water, electricity and the internet. This increases the cost of doing business and makes access to larger markets difficult. For example, successful Nairobi entrepreneurs cited poor transportation routes as the reason for their lack of investment in Kakuma and Kalobeyei refugee camps in the remote Turkana County.[66] Ensuring links with markets is a key determinant of success for livelihood interventions, as is long-term planning for their sustainability in the design phase.[67]

To stimulate inclusive economic development, forcibly displaced persons must be able to benefit from employment or entrepreneurial opportunities. Yet, often, refugees are not able to work legally, or employment is restricted to only a few sectors. Companies seeking access to camps may need a special permit to operate there, a further disincentive.[68]

Restrictions on the right to move freely or to access financial services can prevent refugees from starting their own enterprises. If confined to camps, refugee-owned businesses are reliant on paid intermediaries to source supplies from outside. This increases costs to refugee business owners and can lead to higher prices. It also means that refugee owners cannot ensure the safe transport or quality of products.[69]

Refugees who do not have government-issued identification, or who are by law prohibited from opening a bank account or accessing other financial services, are often unable to grow their businesses.[70] Other restrictions, like prohibitions on owning property or entering contracts, are further limiting. To bypass these barriers, refugees may partner with local businesses but, without enforceable rights, they are vulnerable to exploitation.[71]

In some cases, the qualifications of refugees and internally displaced persons can be limiting factors. Many have had their education interrupted or have been unable to maintain their skills due to protracted periods of unemployment. Businesses that rely on qualified or skilled workers may not see displacement areas as being able to meet their labour needs.[72]

Further, commercial enterprises may not be aware of the business opportunities in large forced displacement contexts. This is another reason data, evidence and analysis are so important.

Market studies

Development actors are undertaking more studies in forced displacement contexts to help bridge the knowledge gap. Among them is the International Finance Corporation (IFC).

The IFC is one of the five institutions that form the World Bank Group.[73] Started around the same time as UNHCR, the IFC is the largest global development institution focused on the private sector. The IFC invests in private enterprises that contribute to development, promotes investment opportunities to investors, and stimulates private capital flows. In tandem with the creation of the new World Bank financing mechanisms for host communities and refugees, the IFC has also focused part of its work on how private investment can improve lives in forced displacement situations.

In 2018, the IFC published *Kakuma as a Market Place*[74], which analysed revenues, consumption patterns, consumer preferences and financial transactions in the refugee camp and neighbouring town. It was the first comprehensive study of its kind aimed at examining the potential for greater private sector engagement in a refugee context.

The study found that there was potential to attract new private sector players to the area, expand existing firms and support local entrepreneurs. Expected positive impacts included increased employment opportunities for hosts and refugees, reduced prices, improved services and general advancement in regional development.

Banks, microfinance institutions, telecommunications companies, and small- and medium-sized enterprises were all identified as potential beneficiaries of operating there. The study also pointed to the opportunities for social enterprise[75] as well as for local host and refugee entrepreneurs. Among its recommendations were: vocational skills training for refugees and hosts; expanded business services and microfinance; and technical assistance, seed capital and de-risking support to encourage commercial firms, social enterprises and local entrepreneurs.[76]

In Rwanda, a market study in 2018 identified significant opportunities for financial service providers in refugee areas.[77] The following year, UNHCR and the International Labour Organization (ILO) published a report on a market analysis conducted in Dadaab refugee camp. It identified job creation and private sector business opportunities in vegetable and fruit production, waste management and recycling. To realize the potential, the study highlighted that initial financial or technical support from development actors will be required, and legal and policy restrictions on freedom of movement and access to land would need to be eased.[78]

In 2018, another study in Cox's Bazaar, Bangladesh, revealed a range of business opportunities in areas as diverse as clean energy, seafood, non-timber forestry products (such as honey or fruits) and handicrafts. These opportunities could be better realized with policy reforms enabling refugees to become self-reliant and measures to improve the business environment.[79]

These studies have all shown that removing existing obstacles to private sector engagement has the potential to provide economic benefits to refugees and host communities.

Application

An investment from the IKEA Foundation in the Dollo Ado refugee camps in Ethiopia revealed both the opportunities and challenges of market-based initiatives in isolated areas. The camps accommodate some 200,000 Somali refugees.[80] Between 2012 and 2018, the IKEA Foundation provided nearly $100 million in grants, including over $37 million prioritized investments in education and incomes for refugees and host communities.[81] Income generation focused on improving irrigation to expand agricultural production, commercially developing the livestock sector, expanding access to renewable energy, and providing microfinance support.[82] Most interventions involved setting up cooperatives consisting of refugees and members of the host community.[83]

Among the positive outcomes, incomes increased alongside consumption. However, the gains were unequal, links to wider markets remained a challenge, and most refugees continued to depend on humanitarian aid. The project showed that access to larger markets is important in ensuring the viability of efforts to achieve self-reliance.[84]

Vodacom is an African company that provides connectivity and digital and financial services. Over 60 per cent of its shares are owned by the United Kingdom's multinational Vodafone. Both have been active in forced displacement contexts. In 2016, Vodacom erected a 3G tower to bring cell phone connection to the Nyarugusu refugee camp in Tanzania,[85] where around 130,000 refugees reside.[86] Within months, the tower operated at full capacity. The evident demand and proven economic viability of the tower led other mobile network operators to invest in the area.[87]

Turkcell has also benefited from increased subscribers due to the Syrian influx in Turkey. It developed a mobile app, which provides users with speech translation from Arabic to Turkish and information on public services, bus stops and automated teller machines (ATMs), as well as a newsfeed. Turkcell reports around 2 million Syrian customers.[88]

Finance leveraging mechanisms

A number of financing mechanisms are being used to help attract private sector investments in viable enterprises in forced displacement contexts. They include the following.

Blended financing is a way to help mitigate some of the risks often associated with investing in fragile and conflict-affected settings. The World Bank's IDA programme, discussed earlier, incorporates this type of financing, working with the IFC and the Multilateral Investment Guarantee Agency (MIGA).[89] The use of relatively small amounts of concessional donor funds can help mitigate specific investment risks for pioneering investments that might be otherwise unable to proceed on strictly commercial terms. It can offer a means to de-risk private sector investments in forced displacement contexts and help leverage third-party financial resources for new projects that target refugees.[90]

A Dutch Development Bank, FMO,[91] also works in this area. FMO seeks to maximize the development impact of private sector investments, focusing on supporting job and income generation through long-term financing for projects in countries where commercial investors are unlikely to invest. One of its programmes, NASIRA, prioritizes projects which empower young, female and COVID-19 affected entrepreneurs, including refugees and internally displaced persons. By utilizing "risk-sharing", NASIRA reduces the perceived and real risks of lending to vulnerable and underserved parts of the population. It does this by guaranteeing loans provided by local lenders to these populations to support micro-, small- and medium-sized enterprises, including those owned by Syrian refugees in Jordan.[92]

Risk insurance: The Multilateral Investment Guarantee Agency is one of the five institutions that make up the World Bank Group. It was established in 1988 to encourage private sector investment in low- and middle-income countries by providing risk guarantees on cross-border investments[93] that advance development and meet high social and environmental standards. MIGA insures against political risks, such as expropriation, war, terrorism, civil disturbance, breach of contract by the host government, or inability to convert local currency into hard currency or transfer hard currency out of the country.[94] The coverage extends to equity and debt up to a limit of $250 million per project for up to 15 years.

Matching: In 2018, the World Bank Group launched a Refugee Investment and Matchmaking Platform (RIMP) with support from the United Kingdom. The Platform matches private sector investors with opportunities in refugees-hosting areas to promote the growth of small- and medium-sized enterprises.

The Platform's work in Jordan has shown early promise. It introduced 267 businesses registered in Jordan to over 480 global businesses and investors. This has helped attract over $64 million in investments in Jordan-based businesses, owned by both Jordanians and refugees. Related sales reached $115 million, with the creation of close to 2,000 new jobs of which 17 per cent were occupied by refugees. It has also helped strengthen Jordanian institutions through the creation of Jordan Exports (JE). JE connects Jordanian exporters with market opportunities abroad, and facilitates the formation of partnerships between JE, the Jordan Investment Commission and the Jordan Enterprise Development Corporation.[95] The Platform is taking this approach to Djibouti and Iraq.[96]

Trade preferences: Trade preferences are part of the Jordan Compact, aimed at supporting Jordan's economic development and increasing economic opportunities for Syrian refugees. The European Union agreed to ease the access of Jordanian exports to the European market for Jordanian firms located in special economic zones whose workforce included at least 15 per cent Syrian refugees. The Jordan Compact has proved to be an important initiative, both for what it has achieved and lessons learned that can be applied to other, similar efforts. It has provided needed support for Jordan and led to some 200,000 work permits provided to Syrians, allowing them to enter the formal labour market and work legally.[97]

It has also pointed to the importance of ensuring initiatives span a significant period of time, are attractive to businesses for new or scaled-up investments, and will improve their competitiveness in the longer term. To be of benefit to refugees, they should also focus on sectors where refugees have the necessary skills, and are located in accessible geographic areas with working conditions that are favourable to their participation. Another important observation from the Jordan Compact is the need for governments to ease work permit regulations or employment quotas that impede progress against agreed objectives.[98]

Other Innovative Financing

Zakat is one of the five pillars of Islam. It is an obligation to donate a proportion of individual wealth to those in need. UNHCR estimates that Zakat donations have the potential to reach $350 billion globally,[99] and has encouraged a greater proportion of Zakat to be allocated to forced displacement responses, given displaced persons meet several eligibility criteria and an estimated 60 per cent of all forcibly displaced persons are Muslim.[100]

In 2018, some $76 million of Zakat was donated globally. In 2019, a dedicated Zakat Fund was established for forcibly displaced persons.[101] Although its global target has not been reached, close to $62 million was contributed to the

Fund in 2020, benefiting 2 million forcibly displaced persons in 13 countries.[102]

Crowdfunding involves raising modest sums from a large number of individuals, usually over the internet, for projects, charities and businesses. The crowdfunding market is estimated to be approximately $17 billion,[103] mostly concentrated in North America and Europe. It is expected to double by 2026.[104] It has been used to finance a variety of COVID-19 responses[105] and is an emerging potential source for increased funding in forced displacement contexts.

One crowdfunder, Kiva, has helped expand financial access to underserved communities, including forcibly displaced persons and their hosts.[106] It uses crowdfunding to provide small loans to borrowers, and has reportedly provided $14 million in loans to nearly 18,000 refugees and internally displaced persons. The largest number of borrowers were in Colombia, Lebanon and Palestine. Kiva reports a 95.5 per cent repayment rate, which is consistent with non-displacement settings.[107] It aims to expand its work further through the launch of its Refugee Investment Fund, to reach up to 200,000 borrowers.[108]

Other financing mechanisms could perhaps provide new sources of funding for forced displacement responses, although further study may be needed to assess their costs and benefits. For example, taxes and levies have been suggested as a potential new source of additional financing.[109] They have been used to raise money for climate and health initiatives. In 2005, France initiated a "solidarity levy" on airline tickets to raise funds in support of international efforts for the prevention and treatment of HIV/AIDS, and to support global immunization programmes. Other countries have also followed.[110] It has been a significant source of funding for Unitaid, a global health agency working on disease prevention, diagnosis and treatment in low- and middle-income countries.[111]

The *frozen assets* of States and individuals responsible for forced displacement may be a potential source of funds for humanitarian relief, according to some scholars.[112] The Security Council can call for collective economic sanctions under Article 41 of the United Nations Charter, including for the protection of civilians. Currently, there are 14 Security Council sanctions regimes.[113] It also has the authority to set up compensation funds, as was done after Iraq occupied Kuwait. It required Iraq to pay a percentage of its oil revenues to the fund. In the event that Iraq failed to do so, the Council authorized States holding Iraqi funds from petroleum sales to transfer them to a United Nations account.[114]

Outside the Security Council, national jurisdictions have also enacted laws which permit the imposition of sanctions, including asset freezes, against foreigners accused of serious human rights violations and/or corruption. They are often referred to as Magnitsky laws, after Sergei Magnitsky, a Russian financial auditor who uncovered extensive theft and corruption implicating members of the Russian police, judiciary, tax officials as well as politicians and members of organized crime. Arrested in 2009 and held in worsening conditions in a Moscow prison for nearly a year, Magnitsky died from deprivation and injuries inflicted on him while incarcerated. His death was widely condemned and led the United States Congress to pass sanctions against Russian officials claimed to be implicated.

Since then, the mechanism in the United States has been broadened beyond the circumstances of the Magnitsky case.[115] Similar legislation has been enacted by the European Union and by countries and territories, such as Canada, Estonia, Gibraltar, Jersey, Latvia, Lithuania, and the United Kingdom.[116] Corresponding legislation is under consideration in Australia.[117]

So far, most have focused on asset seizure, but some commentators see a potential use for seized assets to fund humanitarian relief. Switzerland has returned seized assets to the country of origin. Since the 1980s, it has seized and confiscated assets of political figures believed to have been illicitly stolen from their countries. It has returned some $2 billion dollars to Angola, Kazakhstan, Nigeria, Peru and the Philippines, among others, for the purpose of improving living conditions and strengthening the rule of law.[118]

Impact bonds typically involve private investors funding projects designed to provide positive social outcomes, such as improved social services. They operate over a defined period and the rate of return to investors depends on the programme outcome achieved. If the project meets its objectives, traditional donors, including both government and private entities, pay the investors at a pre-determined rate of return. If the project does not meet its objectives, the investors can lose some or all of their investment.[119] They can be structured so that the implementing agency pays some of the cost if the project fails, thereby incentivizing results.[120] Their use has grown in recent years, although largely outside humanitarian settings.[121]

In 2017, the International Committee of the Red Cross (ICRC) launched a five-year humanitarian impact bond aiming to raise 26 million Swiss francs (approximately $27.3 million) to fund medical centres in the Democratic Republic of the Congo, Mali and Nigeria for people wounded in conflict.[122] In 2021, a United Kingdom-funded evaluation of the projects showed the potential of impact bonds in humanitarian settings, as well as their possible drawbacks.

On the positive side, because impact bonds pay returns based on programme outcomes, this creates an incentive for improved monitoring and performance management, as well as accountability from implementors. They attract new sources of philanthropic capital focused on paying for results, while sharing the risk of unsuccessful outcomes with investors. They also incentivize innovation to achieve intended goals.[123]

Further study may be needed to determine the wider potential of impact bonds in forced displacement settings, as they tend to be relatively complex to set up and the legal, monitoring and advisory services are costly. It is not yet clear whether they could be more effective and cost-efficient compared with other alternative mechanisms.[124]

In the meantime, Kois, an impact investing firm, is developing impact bonds to finance organizations working to improve education and employment outcomes for Syrian refugees in Jordan and Lebanon. The IKEA Foundation has pledged to be one of the outcome funders.[125] This provides a further opportunity to test the practicality of impact bonds in forced displacement settings.

Perspectives

Improving financing for people forced to flee means increasing the number of contributors, enlarging the volume of funds available, expanding the use of development approaches and ensuring an efficient and effective use of resources.

Increasing volume and donor base: When the OECD was established in 1961, the question of how much high-income economies should spend on foreign aid had circulated for decades. In 1969, the Pearson Commission on International Development proposed a target for donors that stuck: 0.7 per cent of Gross National Product (GNP). The aim for this Official Development Assistance (ODA) target was for it to be reached between 1975 and 1980;[126] since then, it has been revised to 0.7 per cent of Gross National Income (GNI). It was passed in a United Nations resolution and taken up by the OECD's Development Assistance Committee (DAC).[127]

The target was reached by just four donor countries by 1980. Only a handful more achieved it in subsequent years, and then only temporarily.[128] Nevertheless, the ambition was again endorsed at the 2005 United Nations World Summit.[129] That same year, European Union members agreed to reach the target, this time by 2015.[130]

Combined humanitarian and development assistance has not come close to the 0.7 per cent target for most members of the OECD. In 2020, only six DAC members reached or exceeded the 0.7 per cent ODA target (Denmark, Germany, Luxembourg, Norway, Sweden and the United Kingdom).[131] The United Kingdom has since announced its intention to reduce 2021 ODA funding to 0.5 per cent of GNI, a reduction of some £4.5 billion (approximately $6.2 billion).[132]

The target set in the 1960s and endorsed in the new millennium, therefore, remains aspirational. But, given the number of times States have endorsed it, it should be achievable. For years, the largest contributions of foreign aid have been made by a relatively small group of high-income countries; this funding base needs to be more diverse.[133]

Systematic and comparable data: There is also a need for improved mechanisms to more accurately capture funding that is provided to forced displacement contexts. Currently, available information on humanitarian and development funding towards forced displacement responses is neither comprehensive nor comparable. ODA indicators are available for humanitarian and development financing globally, including but not restricted to forced displacement contexts. They are also not inclusive of all donors.[134]

There is also no comparable means to measure what host countries spend on responses to forced displacement. High-income countries have provided estimates through the DAC, based on their agreed methodology of their *in-country* spending on refugees and asylum-seekers.[135] Turkey has done the same. However, there is no universally agreed methodology.

Important efforts are underway to remedy this gap. The OECD has undertaken two surveys: one of DAC members; and another of non-DAC members and multilateral development banks.[136] These have shed light on spending on refugee situations. To ensure relevant data is systematically captured, the OECD has adapted its tracking systems to identify support to refugee situations specifically for reporting against Global Compact on Refugees indicators.[137] This work is furthering an OECD pledge made at the 2019 Global Refugee Forum and will help to measure progress against financial commitments made in support of the Compact. [138]

Yet, gaps remain, including in tracking funding to situations of internal displacement. Also, most developing countries, home to the vast majority of forcibly displaced persons, do not have the capacity to track spending associated with forced displacement across ministries. Efforts to agree on a common methodology are ongoing.[139] And while the new OECD tracking mechanism has the potential to be expanded in this manner, no firm plans are yet in place.

Potential of private sector: The last several years have seen the potential of private sector funding and income generation in forced displacement contexts. Private giving now accounts for close to 22 per cent of international humanitarian funding.[140] And new partnerships are developing to bring more sustainable livelihood opportunities to forcibly displaced and host communities. Partnerships between the private sector, national and local governments and business organizations can help to foster the needed policy and regulatory reforms for inclusive economic development.

New financial instruments, that include concessional financing and de-risking mechanisms to encourage private sector investments, are positive developments. So too is the work underway by investors, multinational companies, business associations, and humanitarian and development organizations to provide enterprise support to small- and medium-sized enterprises, including those owned by refugees.

Focus on development: The expansion of development-centred approaches to forced displacement contexts has been the most significant change, rewarding long years of advocacy. And it has gathered speed. The change over the past several years is astonishing. Large donors are linking their humanitarian and development efforts. International financial institutions have developed and are applying new financing models in support of socioeconomic development for forcibly displaced persons and their hosts. They are deepening the analytics used to inform policy recommendations, and incentivizing host countries to take a more inclusive approach through the provision of additional development funding.

These shifts are potentially transformational if sustained and supported through sound and effective programme implementation. They also need to be supported with good data and analytics, subjects to which we now turn.

Enhancing the Evidence Base

Data, evidence and analysis play a key role in responding to forced displacement. In addition to helping to measure progress related to financing, data also provides necessary information on the size of displacement situations. Data and analysis illuminates the needs and capacities of forcibly displaced persons, and their impact on host communities. They provide the foundation for designing effective programmes, assessing their impact over time, and measuring progress towards solutions. Well-analysed data is essential to understand the impact of conflict and displacement on local communities, as well as how government policies can mitigate losses and capitalize on opportunities associated with receiving large numbers of forcibly displaced persons.

For these reasons, improving data collection, quality, and interoperability is a primary aim of the Global Compact on Refugees. The Compact makes frequent mention of the need for improved data, including to enhance the socioeconomic conditions of refugees and host communities, assess impact and plan and realize solutions.[141]

Improving lives during displacement and preparing and sustaining solutions rests in part on addressing key data and knowledge gaps, and strengthening the capacity of host governments to collect, securely store and utilize data pertaining to forcibly displaced populations.

Content and Collection

Population data
The public face of forced displacement is generally large numbers of individuals being forced to flee their homes in dangerous circumstances and across perilous routes. Individual stories help to shed light on the very human challenges and tragedies of these movements.

The scale of displacement is often communicated in aggregate terms and measured using different collection methods.[142] Aggregate figures, however, tell only part of the story. Personal and household data is also critical to ensure individuals are protected and assisted and that efforts are made to resolve their displacement.

Individual biodata
As non-citizens, refugees must often establish their right to be in the host country. Individual registration is a first step. Many middle- and low-income countries request UNHCR to register refugees, which it does on an individual and confidential basis.[143] It includes the recording of basic information: name; age; gender; place of origin; address; and reasons for flight. Registration by UNHCR and generally by States[144] is accompanied by a document attesting to the fact that the person has claimed asylum or is recognized as a refugee. This document helps to protect the person from being arrested, detained or returned to potential harm.

Registration also provides an opportunity to determine an individual's specific protection and assistance needs, help locate family members, and keep track of the services provided and interventions made on the individual's behalf. In most refugee contexts, registration is done with biometric technology, such as iris scans or fingerprints, preventing the person's identity from being stolen and fraudulently re-used.[145]

There is no single international institution responsible for registering internally displaced persons, as most are citizens of the country in which they are displaced and fall within national systems. Many States lack capacity or are not willing to identify and meet the needs of internally displaced persons.[146]

Two-month-old Syrian refugee Mohammad is registered at UNHCR Khalda Refugee Registration Centre in Amman in 2018.
© UNHCR/Annie Sakkab

The task of identifying internally displaced persons and ascertaining their needs often falls on international and national partners. The absence of systematic coordination and consistent use of agreed methodologies can make it difficult to arrive at a consistent and comprehensive picture.[147] There is also a definitional challenge, including determining when internal displacement ends and whether it is passed on to successive generations.[148]

Socioeconomic data

Socioeconomic data includes information on education, skills and specific needs, as well as living conditions, consumption levels, sources of income and assistance, and access to basic services.[149] It is collected at the individual or household level and also through representational surveys.[150] When the collection includes both forcibly displaced and host communities, it has multiple important uses.

It helps to assess the relative poverty and vulnerabilities of forcibly displaced persons and host communities to ensure assistance and development programmes are designed and implemented equitably. Socioeconomic data also helps to assess the degree to which forcibly displaced persons are integrated into communities and to identify any obstacles to inclusion and to the realization of solutions. Such data is important for evaluating the impact of programmes on forcibly displaced and affected communities.[151]

Collecting more than basic biographical data is rarely considered in emergency situations for several reasons. For example, when many thousands of individuals are fleeing into an area daily, the imperative is to register individuals as quickly as possible in order to gain an understanding of overall numbers and immediate needs. Adding time to that process, by collecting additional information, can seem unnecessary and too resource-intensive when basic survival needs have not yet been met.[152]

However, adding a few more questions to the data collection – notably in the fields of education, health and employment – can be informative for more targeted interventions later on. And there may be few further opportunities to reach the same individuals in as short a period of time. On balance, investing in expanded data collection at the outset of an influx is merited, helping to design household surveys more rapidly. These are important for identifying where measures are most needed to alleviate household poverty and promote inclusion in education and health services.[153]

Harmonized collection

Despite some improvements in certain regional and country operations,[154] significant parts of the current data collection landscape remain in need of attention.

Humanitarian agencies collect individual data on displaced populations to inform their protection and assistance programmes.[155] But this is not always undertaken in a coordinated manner or systematically using agreed standard indicators. There is also often an absence of longitudinal data,[156] which tracks the situation of individuals or households over time. This data is important to understand how situations may or may not have changed over a specific period.

A lack of coordination can lead to the same data being gathered multiple times, using different methodologies for collection, and employing dissimilar analytical tools.[157] This can be frustrating for the persons surveyed, who are asked similar questions multiple times by different agencies with no discernable impact on their situations. Also importantly, results may be neither consistent nor comparable.

Joint needs assessments were a key commitment of States and humanitarian agencies made during the 2016 World Humanitarian Summit.[158] And, they are a means to overcome disjointed practice and provide consolidated inform-ation that governments need in making their policies.[159]

In recent years, several joint socioeconomic assessments of displaced and host communities have helped demonstrate their value. Examples included studies conducted across Ethiopia, Nigeria, Somalia, South Sudan and Sudan, which examined the socioeconomic conditions of forcibly displaced persons and host communities, as seen in Part III.[160]

The studies identified common and distinct vulnerabilities among both communities and also shed light on the extent to which forcibly displaced persons were integrated into host communities, the obstacles to integration and the prospects for overcoming them, taking into account prevailing political, social and economic conditions. Importantly, these studies were conducted in consultation with government authorities and other stakeholders, enhancing the opportunity to influence policy and practice.[161]

Uganda presents another interesting example. In 2018, the Govern-ment partnered with the World Bank to conduct a joint household survey of refugees and host communities, to better inform government policies. The report and recommendations were published the following year.

The survey found that food insecurity was high for both refugees and hosts in the Southwest and West Nile regions of the country and, thus, maintaining poverty reduction and food security measures in these regions was important. Refugees had relatively larger rates of unemployment but had the potential to benefit the local economy with additional investment in agricultural and non-agricultural skills training.[162]

In some areas, refugees had relatively better access to health services. There-fore, eliminating existing gaps in access to services by strengthening institu-tional capacity and providing financial support was critical. The results of the study are material to the World Bank's subsequent allocation of additional financing to support the socioeconomic development of refugees and host communities.[163]

Strengthening Capacities

Ideally, data on forcibly displaced populations would be integrated into national data collection systems, including those at the level of ministries, such as those responsible for education and health. Official statistics provide the basis for informing decision-making processes, determining priorities and establishing budgets at the national and sub-national levels. This data informs government development plans and implementation.

Official statistics are also relied on by development organizations in their analysis and investment decisions.[164] However, data on forcibly displaced populations is often not integrated into these systems, and refugees and internally displaced persons are not systematically included in efforts to achieve the Sustainable Development Goals (SDGs).[165]

In 2018, the World Bank and WHO reported that over 100 developing countries have deficient civil registration and vital statistics systems.[166] There are several reasons for this. These countries face many other development challenges, meaning improving data systems is often not prioritized. National systems often lack adequate funding and administrative capacity. Civil registries, health and education information management mechanisms and vital statistics are often not linked. This leads to different sets of data being stored in various locations with insufficient technical capacity to maintain and integrate them.[167] Given these constraints, it is not surprising that specific data on forcibly displaced persons is often not integrated into national systems.

The Expert Group on Refugee and Internally Displaced Persons Statistics (EGRIS) is a multi-stakeholder group with membership from United Nations and non-governmental specialized agencies, national statistical offices, regional bodies and international financial institutions.[168] It was formed in 2016 by the United Nations Statistical Commission to improve the quality and use of statistics on forced displacement by national and non-State partners.

Since 2018, it has published two sets of detailed guidance for States and non-State actors to improve the quality of refugee and internal displacement statistics and build the capacity of national statistical offices and services. The guidance relates to data collection methodologies, disaggregation, coordination and reporting.[169]

In parallel, the World Bank and UNHCR established the Joint Data Center on Forced Displacement (Joint Data Center) in 2019 to improve the availability and accessibility of high-quality socioeconomic data on those affected by forced displacement. It collaborates with EGRIS as well as with host country governments, affected populations, other international organizations, civil society, academia and the private sector.[170]

A number of States are also taking important steps towards including internally displaced persons and refugees in their national systems.[171] These are important initiatives; yet funding to strengthen State capacities has not appreciably increased, despite international commitments, notably in the Sustainable Development Goals.[172]

While the aim is for more inclusive national data systems, in the interim, there are other opportunities to include forcibly displaced persons in government data initiatives, such as through planned census or survey activities. These can be supported with initial seed funding and technical support to ensure the inclusion of samples of displaced populations.[173]

Accessibility

There is growing consensus around the benefits of making population and socioeconomic microdata on displaced and host communities more accessible to policymakers, humanitarian and development partners, academics and researchers. At the same time, there is also a need to protect individuals from the release of certain personal data that could jeopardize their safety.

This is particularly the case in forced displacement contexts, where individual or group persecution and violence has not only provoked flight but prohibits their safe return. Their security depends on their personal data not being accessible to those intending to harm them or others seeking to exploit their vulnerabilities.

Removing individual identifiers from microdata – anonymizing data – is a means to share it in a safe manner. Secure platforms for collecting, safely storing and disseminating data are also required. Important steps are being made in this regard, although some challenges in achieving full buy-in among agencies still need to be overcome. There can be competition among them, which can hinder full collaboration and be a disincentive to investing in anonymizing and disseminating relevant datasets.[174]

The World Bank has an open Microdata Library and UNHCR has recently adopted its own.[175] Prior to this, UNHCR shared aggregate socioeconomic and microdata only in specific contexts and subject to bilateral agreements. Through its new Microdata Library, it can securely store diverse anonymized microdata collected by UNHCR and its partners for others to use. Both microdata libraries are important resources of information to inform policy, design humanitarian and development interventions and assess their impact.

The work of the Joint Data Center is also centred on encouraging safe dissemination and analysis of microdata and facilitating broad collaboration in academic research and policy design. In addition to country-specific efforts, the Joint Data Center publishes regular literature reviews and convenes conferences and workshops on the application of microdata and evidence accumulated across various fields, including economics, education, health and integration.

The High-Level Panel on Internal Displacement, appointed by the Secretary-General in 2019, has provided policy recommendations for improved data collection, analysis and use relevant to internal displacement.[176] These include calling on governments to put in place processes and systems to securely collect, analyse and manage internal displacement data, and for international donors to provide financial assistance where necessary for this purpose. In recognition of the importance of data for the programmes of international and national partners, the Panel also recommends that governments provide the space for them to collect and analyse data relevant to their operations.[177]

Impact Evaluations

Designing a programme based on sound data is important. Equally critical is knowing that the programme is being implemented efficiently and is targeted to the needs it was designed to address, and that it results in the desired impact.

In humanitarian contexts, monitoring and evaluation are important aspects of programme design and implementation. Traditionally, these have focused on whether programmes were implemented as planned, how well they were delivered, whether recipients received what was intended and if objectives were met. These focused exercises are important in ensuring the integrity of programmes and learning lessons for further work.

Impact evaluations probe further. They seek to determine the impact of a policy, project or progamme by considering what the outcome would have been had the intervention not occurred. This is achieved by comparing the circumstances of those who received it with those of similar characteristics who did not.[178]

Widely used in the development field, impact evaluations in low- and middle-income countries have proved extremely useful and have positively shaped policy and practice beyond the specific intervention reviewed.[179] For example, in the area of education, deworming programmes in Kenya were found to improve school attendance of children who received deworming medication as well as classmates who did not, by decreasing infection rates overall.[180] This was a significant finding, given the relative low cost of the programme, its impact, and its relevance beyond Kenya.[181]

In the health sector, impact evaluations established that the free provision of insecticide treated bed nets increased their use substantially. This resolved an ongoing debate on whether it is preferable to freely distribute bed nets or require co-payment. These findings reportedly led many organizations globally to adjust their policies and practice.[182]

Efforts to improve self-reliance, including through cash transfers, micro-credit lending and skills and vocational training, have been subject to extensive impact evaluations. They have illustrated what has and has not been effective and what has yielded positive impact combined with other interventions.[183] The results have profoundly informed the design and application of these programmes.[184]

There were over 2,000 impact studies published between 2000 and 2012, primarily in the areas of health, education, social protection and agriculture in low- and middle-income countries.[185] In contrast, a very small proportion focus specifically on programmes for forcibly displaced persons, with fewer than 25 related randomized impact evaluations published between 2001 and 2019.[186]

There are a number of reasons for this. Humanitarians often work with short time frames and limited budgets, neither of which is easily adapted to impact evaluations, which take time and money to execute. Programmes are often initiated at an early stage of a crisis and when generally only basic biodata on the displaced populations is collected and is insufficient to support an impact assessment or comparison with host communities. Also, highly volatile situations, from which displaced populations are likely to move, can also make impact evaluations more difficult to carry out, as such evaluations entail measuring impact on the same group of individuals over time.[187]

However, the demonstrated usefulness of impact evaluations is helping to expand their application in forced displacement contexts. Major donors are supporting their implementation, and some have made them a condition of funding agreements. In addition, new financial instruments are increasingly linking funding to achievement of the desired impact.[188] And, a growing number of international humanitarian agencies are investing more in them to evaluate their progammes for forcibly displaced persons.

UNHCR, the United Nations Children's Fund (UNICEF), the World Food Programme (WFP) and the International Rescue Committee (IRC) are among the organizations that are increasing their technical capacity in this area. They also partner with multilateral development institutions and specialized agencies engaged in impact evaluations in forced displacement contexts.[189]

The results are clear. At the end of 2020, there were 40 documented randomized impact evaluations taking place in forced displacement contexts, close to double the number published over the past 20 years.[190] These include evaluations of the engagement of refugees in productive activities in Bangladesh, health and education support programmes in the Horn of Africa, cash reintegration assistance for returning Afghan refugees, teacher training efforts in Lebanon, pedagogical and socio-behavioural programmes for youth in Jordan, food distribution programmes in Iraq, an entrepreneurship support programme in Niger and programmes to reduce gender-based violence in Cameroon.[191]

This number continues to grow, a significant development itself.

The Global Compact on Refugees seeks to mobilize timely, predictable, adequate and sustainable public and private funding. It also emphasizes the importance of "maximizing the effective and efficient use of resources".[192] Improving the quality, collection and comparability of data are important steps in this direction. So too are efforts to better assess the impact of programmes delivered.

Together, they should improve the effectiveness of interventions for forcibly displaced persons and host communities. And, in meeting expectations for greater efficiency, transparency and optimal resource use, they should also help spur greater public and private financing called for in the Global Compact on Refugees.

Partnerships

The challenges to improving the futures of forcibly displaced persons and host communities may seem insurmountable. Yet, today, more than ever before, individuals and groups across a broad and needed spectrum of expertise are firmly engaged in overcoming them.

The Global Compact on Refugees recognizes this. It has set out a blueprint for more sustainable, inclusive responses that take a "whole-of-society" approach, engaging a wide range of stakeholders. It acknowledges their added value, informed by contributions they have already made, some for many decades.

This section tracks that evolution and the impact that different partners are having in advancing responses to forced displacement. It also looks at where efforts are needed to make multi-stakeholder approaches more meaningful and systematic.

Forcibly Displaced People

Most major humanitarian initiatives over the past 20 years have called for the greater engagement of refugees and internally displaced persons in the design of programmes that affect their lives.[193] And, most would say that this call has only been partially met. Generally, policies are set and programmes are designed and delivered "on behalf" of forcibly displaced persons, without their regular and active engagement.

This has not always been the case. There have been periods in history where refugees had much greater agency than they do today, as discussed in Part I. In Ancient Greece as well as in Europe from as far back as the 13th century, various refugee groups were able to negotiate the terms of their settlement and were accorded autonomy to provide for themselves and their families and to contribute to the broader community. In later periods, as States enacted immigration legislation, refugees who met selection criteria were admitted as immigrants and expected to integrate and contribute to the growth of their adopted countries.[194]

The Great Wars of the 20th century led to a new dynamic. Significant international relief efforts were mobilized to respond to the needs of the massive number of people displaced by war. And as we saw in Part III, at the conclusion of the conflicts, solutions for refugees who had no State to safely return to, were part of the negotiations between nations.

Refugees and those with lived refugee experiences played important roles in relief operations,[195] and some were engaged in the drafting of pivotal international agreements, notably the 1951 Convention.[196] Yet overall, most refugees then and now have had limited opportunities to set their own futures. Local integration opportunities have been limited, return often not possible, and resettlement determined through the application of selective criteria set by receiving States.

Today's emphasis on moving from humanitarian to more development-focused responses is intended to depart from the decades-old approach that inhibited refugees from becoming self-reliant and being able to forge better futures for themselves. The response must be accompanied by improved engagement with those it seeks to serve.

It has long been known that consulting with refugees and internally displaced persons on programmes to meet their needs will result in interventions that better address their priorities and are implemented in ways that are likely to have the most impact. Forcibly displaced persons are also calling for greater room to implement programmes and set policy priorities.

While important initiatives have tried to make consultation more systematic, participatory and accommodating to those of different ages, genders and diversity, these are neither widespread nor systematic.[197] Engaging refugees and internally displaced persons in policy and programme implementation remains largely aspirational. Consistent engagement with forcibly displaced communities in programme design, implementation and assessment is not standard practice among service agencies.

The High-Level Panel on Internal Displacement found, in its survey of

Syrian refugees Ahmad, 29, and his wife, Lazmiah, 18, UNHCR volunteers in Tripoli, Lebanon, 2014. Ahmad lost his legs due to a bomb blast in Syria. Since recovering, Ahmad helps other refugees. He says that when refugees see him continuing to work despite his injury, "it gives them strength and hope and that makes a difference."
© UNHCR/ Andrew McConnell

affected communities across 22 countries, that many internally displaced persons and host community members do not feel heard by their governments nor often by response organizations.[198] Several refugee-led consultations and surveys have reached similar conclusions. Common observations are that forcibly displaced persons are consulted on an ad hoc basis, generally excluded from the prioritization of interventions, and often not involved in their implementation or assessments of their effectiveness.[199] As Najeeba Wazefadost, a former refugee from Afghanistan observed, refugees want to be involved in the design, implementation and evaluation of programmes in their own communities "because", she asks rhetorically, "who knows better than them?"[200]

We looked at some inter-agency efforts to reverse this trend in Part III. Socio‑economic household surveys and assessments that include forcibly displaced and host communities in the design and surveying process are valuable for designing inclusion strategies. They have a greater chance of influencing policy outcomes if they are collaborative throughout the process, from the beginning to end. For example, in addition to engaging humanitarian and development partners and donors, it is also vital to involve local and State authorities, as well

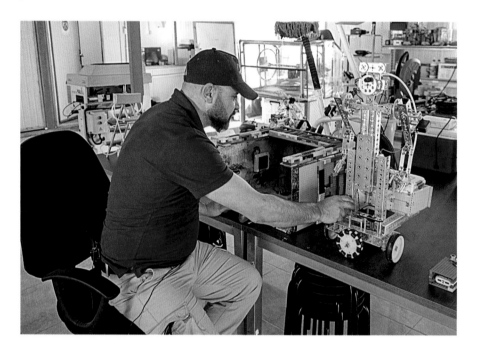

Marwan, a Syrian refugee and engineer, works as a robotics trainer and computer programming teacher helping young people in the Innovation Lab in Za'atari Camp, Jordan in 2021.
© UNHCR/ Shawkat Alharfoush

as forcibly displaced and affected communities.[201] This can be key to achieving a consensus on methodology, findings and policy prescriptions.[202]

Much still needs to be done, including in efforts to launch innovative approaches and new technologies in forced displacement responses. Strengthening innovation has gained prominence in the past decade and is often included in the strategic priorities of organizations working in the field.[203] Collaboration between agencies, civil society and private sector partners has helped bolster innovation. However, as Dragana Kaurin, a former refugee and founder of Localization Lab,[204] has observed, there is a lack of systematic involvement of forcibly displaced "end-users". This means that many innovations fail to solve the problems intended or are not useful to those they are meant to serve.[205]

Involving forcibly displaced persons in the design, development and testing of new approaches and projects can help to ensure that they are user-friendly, accessible and secure. Efforts to support the transition from the use of firewood for cookstoves in forced displacement settings provide telling examples.

The burning of firewood for fuel often has adverse environmental and respiratory effects and exposes women and girls to serious risks of gender-based violence in collecting it.[206] Over the years, alternatives to firewood, including solar-powered cookstoves, have been introduced in various settlements and many have not been successful. Some observers attribute this to a lack of sufficient community engagement. They note the positive results that have been achieved in addressing the same problem through more meaningful community participation.[207]

Beyond programme design, better engagement of forcibly displaced communities in implementing programmes also helps to support more sustainable responses. National, regional and global networks of refugees are bringing greater attention to the work of refugee organizations in forced displacement situations and the contributions they are making, as well as their need for more recognition and support to continue and expand upon their work.

Refugee and internally displaced persons organizations[208] are both formal and informal groups created by forcibly displaced persons to advocate for and serve their communities. The support they provide is varied and can include: psychosocial, education and legal assistance; language and skills training; sports and artistic endeavours; and mentorship. A number also provide services for members of host communities, helping not only to address their needs but also to foster good community relations. There is no comprehensive registry but, as of 2019, there were 130 groups known to be active in refugee displacement situations around the world.[209]

Organizations by and for forcibly displaced persons have the advantage of being intimately aware of their community needs and being known and trusted by them. They can, and do, disseminate public information messages, serve as community health care workers, help monitor programme delivery and impact, and help address harmful behaviours through dialogue and engagement.

The work and added value of these organizations became more visible in the context of the COVID-19 pandemic. As lockdowns prevented many humanitarian agencies from moving freely, community-based organizations were active in delivering food, rental assistance, medicines and other support to vulnerable forcibly displaced and host families.[210] They also helped disseminate messages in languages spoken by their communities through social media and radio broadcasts on risk mitigation and updates on lockdown and quarantine regulations. Some also provided education materials and remote learning during school closures.[211]

Most refugee organizations are informal, because of the legal and/or bureaucratic barriers to registering as non-governmental organizations (NGOs).[212] Such restrictions prevent them from being relied upon by humanitarian agencies to implement programmes. But even in situations where they can formally operate, lack of training or demonstrated capacity in financial, audit, performance and programme management can be additional barriers that prevent them from accessing international funding.[213] Mechanisms to ensure compliance in these areas are often part of donor grant agreements. Investments in strengthening capacities in these areas are warranted.[214]

Other suggestions that have been made for improvement include the development of policies to guide humanitarian agencies in increasing the involvement of refugee and internally displaced persons organizations. This could include updated knowledge of which ones are active in a specific situation to identify possible areas of partnership, capacity-building, and selection measures to ensure the fair and impartial delivery of services.[215]

Refugee experience positively influenced the drafting of the 1951 Refugee Convention. Specific provisions, now understood as foundational for refugee protection, were introduced and promoted by former refugees who knew first-hand what helps achieve safety.[216] The importance of experience on policy is no less significant today.

It is why the Global Refugee-led Network has called on governments, donors and hosts alike to see lived refugee experience as among the desirable employment qualifications for policy positions within relevant departments and ministries. Equally, it has called on service providers to do the same. It is another element to effect a "systemic transformation" for more meaningful participation and better informed policies.[217]

Local Actors and Authorities

Centuries before the creation of the first intergovernmental humanitarian agencies, *civil society groups* welcomed, protected, assisted and led advocacy and fundraising efforts for forcibly displaced persons, as noted in Part I. Often organized on the basis of religious, national or ethnic affiliation, they also were involved in the discussions that shaped the modern refugee protection regime.[218]

There is no established definition of civil society, although they are commonly considered to be self-governed, non-profit groups that are neither set up nor affiliated with a State. [219] Today, there are thousands of civil society organizations that work in whole or in part to benefit forcibly displaced persons. They include civic, cultural and sports organizations, legal advocates and faith-based groups. They work variously to advance protection, assistance and solutions for refugees and internally displaced persons and are recognized as essential partners in the Global Compact on Refugees.[220]

Venezuelan conductor Simón Arias leads the Music for Integration Foundation Orchestra at an auditorium in Santiago, Chile, in 2019.
© UNHCR/
Eduardo Beyer

Some civil society groups operate *internationally*, others are nationally or locally based. And while this section focuses on the latter, it is important to acknowledge the deep and long-standing engagement of many international civil society partners. These have been instrumental in advocacy, policy design and implementation of programmes for refugees and internally displaced persons around the world. Many international humanitarian non-governmental organizations implement a large proportion of in-country programmes either independent of the United Nations, and/or as its implementing partners. They have also formed global networks and participate actively in international and national fora on forced displacement issues.[221]

The range of *local civil society* partners is broad. Some are long-standing;

others are organized to respond to an influx. They too have set up networks to foster regional and international engagement on policies and programmes related to forced displacement.[222] Their contributions can vary, with some specializing in certain areas, like legal and social protection, health, education, skills development and livelihoods support. Many also engage in advocacy. They know their communities and countries well, and their perspectives may carry particular weight with government counterparts compared with international partners, which may be seen as outsiders. Conversely, local civil society actors can also be more susceptible to intimidation by the State.[223]

A mother at work in Yemen in 2021 helping displaced people weave coverings for shelters with local materials. She earns a daily wage for her work.
© UNHCR/Shadi Abusneida

Local authorities are centrally engaged in forced displacement responses, and their involvement predates – by many centuries – the creation of the modern State system.[224] Today, they continue to play a vital role as approximately four out of five forcibly displaced persons live in local communities, two thirds of which are in urban areas.[225] Yet local authorities have often been overlooked by humanitarian actors.[226] And central authorities do not always provide sufficient financial support to them to manage the increased demands placed upon them.[227]

Local authorities face significant challenges with the arrival of large numbers of forcibly displaced persons. New arrivals can add pressure to housing, sanitation, health, education, policing and energy services, often without additional funding from national budgets.[228] And efforts to integrate newcomers through language and skills training frequently fall on local authorities.[229]

Humanitarian funding, which accounts for most financing for responding to forced displacement, goes largely to international organizations and international non-governmental organizations that have grown steadily over the decades.[230] They have become professionalized, with processes in place to meet the administrative, programmatic, financial and ethical standards set by the United Nations as well as required by the donors that fund them. But this growth has also overshadowed the role of local actors, government and national non-governmental organizations in responding to humanitarian crises taking place within their own countries.

Local partners can have significant comparative advantages.[231] These include language skills, familiarity and understanding of local politics, economies, cultural values and communities. They may have greater acceptance among local society and can often access areas where international organizations and agencies may be prevented from going, either by law or their own security regulations. Local authorities and organizations can have legal standing in cases brought before national courts. Their operations are often smaller and less costly to run than international organizations.[232]

This does not mean that they are perfect substitutes for international organizations.[233] The latter bring global experience, established operational practices, and programme, fiscal and accountability management systems accepted and trusted by donors. They can also mobilize quickly, at scale and over protracted periods, which is often beyond the ability of local actors. In certain circumstances, they can be perceived by refugees and internally displaced persons as more independent, especially in contexts where there is great mistrust between displaced and local communities.

The issue is one of understanding where international organizations bring the most added value and where their role should be reduced in favour of local responders. This was a consideration of the 2016 World Humanitarian Summit, where there was widespread agreement that the heavy reliance on international agencies was not always justified and often not optimal, particularly from a cost and sustainability perspective.[234]

Implementation through local partners

That conclusion was shared by the High-Level Panel on Humanitarian Financing in its 2016 report to the Secretary-General. It observed that only 0.2 per cent of reported humanitarian funding was channelled directly to national and local partners who complained of being treated as sub-contractors rather than equal partners by international organizations. It advised that the preparedness and response be more centred at the national and local levels: "putting responsibility in the hands of people most affected by crisis".[235] This would not only be more efficient but would "promote local ownership, strengthen local civil society more generally, and increase that society's capacity to manage future shocks".[236]

Recommendations in this regard included strengthening capacities to "manage funds and navigate the complexities of the humanitarian system" and putting in place a shared system of certification so that, if a local partner is certified by an international agency, the certification would be accepted by others as well.[237] The move to what is now known as "localization" is included in the Grand Bargain, as discussed earlier. Signatories agreed to improve engagement with local and national responders, strengthen their institutional capacity and, by 2020, achieve a global, aggregated target of "at least 25 per cent of humanitarian funding" going to them "as directly as possible".[238]

Five years on, the results are mixed, according to an independent review commissioned by the Facilitator Group responsible for steering progress on the Grand Bargain commitments. The reviewers acknowledged that important actions had been taken, including the development of comprehensive guidance[239] and more strategic engagement by and with local actors. In addition, a number of signatories had made significant efforts to support institutional development and make funding available to local and national responders.[240] But, in all of these areas, it was found that significant ongoing work was required to bring about the desired level of transformational change.

For example, just 13 of the 53 grant-giving signatories reported meeting the target of at least 25 per cent of humanitarian funding being allocated to local and national responders and, globally, this had reached only 4.7 per cent of humanitarian funds.[241] Donor reluctance to fund more through local partners had not been overcome and the strengthening of local capacities has not been undertaken systematically.[242] This is due, in part, to the fact that enhancing capacities incurs overhead costs and there is no standardized agreement as to how these should be incorporated into funding instruments.[243] The independent review advised narrowing this gap.[244]

Establishing the capacity of local responders means more than involving them in policy dialogue and funding them to implement programmes. It also means recognizing their leadership. Here too the review found much work was required. Policy dialogue at headquarters and in the field had improved, but empowering local leadership lagged. The review pointed out that local non-governmental organizations were leading or co-leading just 8 per cent of inter-agency coordination mechanisms at national and sub-national levels. It welcomed the Inter-Agency Standing Committee (IASC) efforts to develop formal guidance on this.[245]

Network of cities

Cities have mobilized their own networks to ensure their voices are heard in global and national policies and that this translates into action on the ground.

Syrian refugee chef Nadeem Khadem Al Jamie prepares dishes from home in the kitchen of Hôtel d'Angleterre in Geneva for the Refugee Food Festival in 2017. © UNHCR/Mark Henley

The Mayors Migration Council is reflective of this change. Today, it represents close to 100 cities around the world, including most major urban centres, accounting for over 700 million people.

At its December 2018 launch, it issued the Mayors Declaration in Marrakech. This is a clear and detailed declaration of its members' commitment to advance the objectives of the Global Compact for Safe, Orderly and Regular Migration and the Global Compact on Refugees. The Declaration also called on the international community to consider the expertise and priorities of the cities in policymaking, to learn from their expertise, implement local or joint programmes, and create mechanisms to secure funding for cities and regional governments.[246] The work of the Mayors Migration Council has gained momentum, engaging in extensive knowledge exchange between member cities and on global advocacy.

The Cities Alliance, formed over 20 years ago, is another global network of cities that works to address migration and forced displacement challenges in urban areas. The Alliance operates around the world and provides technical support and funding for policy development, city planning and the strengthening of institutions for universal access to essential services. It is expanding research to advance inclusive development and share promising practices in relation to urban responses to migration and forced displacement.[247]

United Cities and Local Governments too is a large global alliance of cities and local, regional and metropolitan governments working to address global challenges. Among its priorities is "reshaping the narrative" on migrants and refugees including highlighting their contributions to local communities.[248]

Regionally, over 200 cities across Europe have formed their own network that also seeks to foster inclusive sustainable urban development through advocacy, knowledge exchange and training. Its work includes promoting and sharing promising practices in welcoming, receiving and integrating refugees into European communities.[249] The recent European Commission Action Plan on Integration and Inclusion 2021–2027 recognizes the role of local actors and the importance of their having access to funding for integration.[250]

Global and regional acknowledgements of the importance of local authorities and actors in forced displacement responses need to be matched by a tangible shift in how programmes are delivered in their communities. There is still a long way to go. Emergency international humanitarian capacity may be needed at the outset of a large influx but, for most situations, there should be a much clearer transition point to more locally delivered and sustainable responses. In the coming years, success will be measured by the extent that local capacities are strengthened and funding channeled to enable local implementation of inclusive and sustainable responses.

Private Sector

The role of the private sector in contributing to economic growth and job creation in forced displacement contexts was discussed in the financing section earlier in this Part. There are many other areas of private sector engagement in forced displacement responses.

Here, we look at: the importance of private sector partnerships for the provision of goods and services; inclusive hiring practices, mentoring of entrepreneurs; investments in skills development; and support to innovation and advocacy.[251] While the importance of private sector business partnerships in humanitarian settings has been promoted for some time, the global displacement crises of recent years have accelerated the calls for it.[252]

The 2016 World Humanitarian Summit recognized the need for innovative partnerships with the private sector in emergency humanitarian responses, as well as for preparedness, risk reduction and longer-term recovery.[253] The New York Declaration for Refugees and Migrants[254] of that same year has no less than 12 references to the importance of the private sector. Similarly, the private sector is noted many times as a critical stakeholder throughout both the Global Compact on Refugees[255] and the Global Compact for Safe, Orderly and Regular Migration.[256]

The private sector has responded to these calls. At the 2019 Global Refugee Forum, private sector organizations made pledges worth more than $250 million and included commitments for job creation, support to entrepreneurs, innovations, advocacy, and the provision of pro-bono legal support.[257]

In 2016, the founder and CEO of the United States food company Chobani, Hamdi Ulukaya, established the Tent Partnership for Refugees. It is a non-profit organization with over 170 major companies committed to the integration of refugees in host communities. Together, they have pledged to hire at least 39,000 refugees, support 5,000 or more refugee entrepreneurs and tailor products and services, such as financial services to refugees.[258]

Tent also engages and supports policy research, including country- and industry-specific studies and produces guidance for companies wishing to engage with refugees.[259] One of its studies of European consumers showed that many consumers, particularly millennials, are more likely to purchase from companies that hire refugees, invest in refugee enterprises, and deliver services to refugees.[260]

Among Tent's recently announced achievements were the employment of over 2,000 refugees in Colombia, support to around 200 refugee entrepreneurs in Europe, and the identification of temporary accommodations for over 20,000 refugees through Airbnb's Open Homes programme.[261] In 2021, some Tent members also committed to help address root causes of displacement in the countries of northern Central America by enhancing income generation, including through access to financial services, the internet and entrepreneurial support.[262]

Regional and local business coalitions have also been formed to support the objectives of the Global Compact on Refugees. And, each year at the annual meeting of the World Economic Forum in Davos, Switzerland, there are dedicated discussions on the means and partnerships needed for more sustainable and resilient responses to forced displacement.[263] Many non-governmental organizations and United Nations organizations have private sector engagement strategies and dedicated departments or divisions to advance them.[264]

Research shows that investors and consumers are increasingly interested in the social and environmental commitments of businesses and corporations.[265] As interest in forced displacement has increased, more businesses and corporations have become involved in responses to forced displacement as a part of their core business activities.[266]

Areas of operational engagement

The private sector has always been a major supplier of goods and services in forced displacement settings. This includes food, fuel, vehicles, agricultural implements, construction materials, hygiene and medical supplies, communications equipment, and security, freight, transport, property and financial services. In 2020, UNHCR purchased over $1.37 billion in goods and services, comprising close to 30 per cent of its overall expenditures.[267]

While this aspect of private sector engagement has remained steady over the decades, other areas have increased. Corporations are working with humanitarian partners in bringing their skills and expertise to address specific problems and improve human capital in forced displacement contexts. Education has been one key area of focus.

For example, UNHCR has partnered with Vodafone Foundation in six countries across Africa to introduce Instant Network Schools. These provide access to digital learning content and the internet. They are benefiting over 125,000 refugee and local students and their teachers. By 2025, Vodafone Foundation and UNHCR aim to expand access to quality digital education to reach 500,000 refugees and host community children.[268]

The LEGO Foundation, in partnership with a number of leading development and environmental actors, has committed hundreds of millions of dollars towards learning through play initiatives.[269] Adversity causes stress and anxiety and can affect the brain's development in young children. Play-based learning is a means to help develop cognitive and socio-emotional skills needed to mitigate the harm and improve learning.

The Mastercard Foundation is also supporting education through a Scholars Program that provides over 15,000 higher education scholarships, 70 per cent for young women. It has committed to award one quarter of these to refugees and forcibly displaced youth.[270] In 2020, the Foundation provided support to local partners to help medium- and small-sized enterprises in Rwanda recover from the COVID-19 pandemic. One thousand entrepreneurs in refugee communities were included in the support.[271]

Various corporate and business coalitions have also supported refugee skills development and entrepreneurship in recent years. In 2015, the German Chambers of Industry and Commerce (DIHK) and the Federal Ministry for Economic Affairs and Energy initiated a network of companies across

Students learn at the Instant Network School in Maratane Refugee Settlement in Mozambique in 2021. Photo courtesy of Vodafone Foundation © UNHCR/ Vodafone Foundation/Sala Lewis

Germany to facilitate the integration of refugees into the workforce.[272] As of mid-2021, over 2,700 companies formed part of the network to build and share information and experiences on employing refugees and expanding opportunities for them.[273]

In 2016, another network of German companies was established to help integrate the large number of refugees that had arrived in Germany. Starting with 36 companies, the network grew to over 230 companies and reported the successful integration of more than 33,000 refugees in the German labour market at the closure of its activities in 2019. Some of Germany's largest corporations played a part.[274]

The Tent Partnership for Refugees has also created guides for employers on how to hire, mentor and foster the integration of refugees.[275] And refugee job training and language skills development are offered by the Ingka Group, of which the majority of IKEA stores are a part.[276]

Improving energy sources in forced displacement contexts is also attracting business and corporate engagement. The Clean Energy Challenge was launched at the 2019 Global Refugee Forum and attracted many commitments to bring affordable, reliable and sustainable energy to forced displacement situations by 2030. Over 200 partners are working towards this goal, including companies such as Deloitte, Schneider Electric, IKEA Foundation, Accenture and Kube Energy.[277]

Companies have also introduced important technologies that are improving the delivery of assistance. One of them is a biometric iris scan software, developed by IrisGuard, which is being used in displacement situations in the Middle East.[278] This as well as other biometric identity software, such as fingerprints and facial scans, mitigate the risk of corruption and identity theft compromising assistance delivery. They have facilitated the secure delivery of services, food, medicine and cash-based assistance and remittances to the individuals intended.

As of 1 July 2021, UNHCR had biometrically enrolled more than 9.3 million individuals across 79 country operations. This represents more than seven in every 10 refugees over 5 years of age currently registered by UNHCR.

Advocacy

Many businesses and corporations have stepped up efforts to advocate on behalf of refugees and counter negative narratives. They have done this through their online platforms, in-store awareness-raising, and the sponsorship of discussions, conferences, campaigns, as well as through their business networks, including the World Economic Forum and the International Chamber of Commerce.

One particularly visible effort was IKEA's Brighter Lives for Refugees campaign (2014–2015) which, in addition to raising over €30.8 million from the sale of light bulbs and lamps, brought the needs of refugees directly to IKEA's considerable consumer base.[279] The campaign funded the construction of a solar farm in Azraq refugee camp in Jordan. This brought stable, sustainable power generation and light to the camp. Among the valued benefits is that it enabled food refrigeration, and lighting at night that enabled children and youth to read and study and gave added protection to women and girls. In the words of Asmahan, a Syrian refugee and mother of four, the transition was like moving from ancient times into the modern century.[280]

Other companies have also launched fundraising and awareness campaigns for forced displacement, including TikTok, UNIQLO, Careem, Twitter and H&M Foundation.[281] In Colombia, private sector partners are supporting the Somos Panas (We are Friends) campaign designed to promote solidarity between Colombians and Venezuelans through radio, digital ads, social media, print communications, public events and workshops for journalists.[282]

Opening up more immigration channels for refugees and migrants are among the elements of the Global Compact on Refugees and the Global Compact for Safe, Orderly and Regular Migration. Education and labour complementary pathways are two areas where private sector advocacy and engagement are important and needed to bring current programmes to scale.[283]

These are just a sample of private sector initiatives aimed to generate public support for forcibly displaced persons, improve the delivery of humanitarian programmes, and support the education and skills development of forcibly displaced persons.

Most major humanitarian partners have dedicated microsites on their web pages highlighting areas where they are working in partnership with the private sector.[284] There is fertile ground for further study and analysis on how the numerous initiatives cumulatively impact the lives of forcibly displaced persons and how they are shaping the wider response.[285]

Academics

Prior to 2000, academic literature on forced displacement was focused primarily on the fields of anthropology, sociology, health and legal studies.[286] Beginning in 2000, additional disciplines began to engage more, including in the fields of political science, geography, urban studies, economics and education. In the last decade, there has been a significant upsurge in publications concerning forced displacement across nearly all disciplines.

The number of published economics papers on forced displacement grew sixfold in the period, those in the health field nearly tripled and those in the field of education more than doubled.[287] Cumulatively, between 2000 and 2019, over 7,000 papers on forced displacement were published across economics, sociology, health and legal studies. This represents a more than 50 per cent increase from the previous decade.[288]

The publications have largely originated in high-income countries. Not surprisingly, the focus has mainly been on forced displacement affecting low- and middle-income countries, given that this is where the vast majority of the world's forcibly displaced persons reside. However, beginning in 2015, corresponding to the European refugee influx, the proportion of papers focused on refugees in high-income countries increased.[289]

Economic studies can be particularly relevant in the design and implementation of policy and operational responses across all forced displacement contexts. There has been a stream of studies examining the effects of refugee employment on the wages and jobs of host communities, as outlined in Part IV. Generally, these have pointed to positive gains for both over time while also recognizing that some people may not benefit equally, thus necessitating measures to mitigate or compensate for losses.

Similarly, there has been an increase in studies on the local context of forcibly displaced situations, including the structure of the economy, related laws and policies, economic trends, household welfare and potential for growth. This evidence and analysis is critical for effective humanitarian and development interventions. It can highlight the costs and benefits of various policy interventions available to the government and help in promoting social and economic policies that are inclusive of forcibly displaced persons. Detailed socioeconomic studies inform the design of programmes to support those who have suffered losses, strengthen the delivery of public services, and facilitate self-reliance for displaced and local communities.

This work is ongoing and needs to be continued. Additionally, it will be important in the coming years to understand how cities are managing to cope with larger numbers of forcibly displaced populations and the elements of effective strategies designed to support them. The Refugees in Towns initiative at the Feinstein International Center at Tufts University has started to explore this.

Since 2017, it has completed 34 case studies by local researchers, many of whom have been forcibly displaced or are members of the host communities. The objective is to create a global database to better understand the integration process of refugees and migrants in the cities where they live. They illustrate both the differences and the similarities in the factors that can enable or impede integration.[290]

For many years, legal studies have focused largely on the extent to which States have met their obligations under international, regional and national frameworks and whether those frameworks are sufficient. The discussion in Part II draws heavily on this significant body of work. In recent years, there has also been a marked increase in efforts to better understand, document, and respond to internal forced displacement. This is vital, given the growing number of internally displaced persons, the need to ensure more predictable, comprehensive responses and the importance of resolving unsettled issues, such as how best to determine when internal displacement ends.[291]

There has also been a growing focus in legal, political science and sociological literature on the ongoing problems encountered when refugees and migrants move together along unsafe routes, generally facilitated by smugglers and traffickers.[292] Potent images of refugees and migrants abandoned at sea, wading across rivers, scaling walls and fences are prevalent in the media. But the deeper issues of addressing root causes, creating safe pathways, acknowledging the obligations of States along transit routes, and recognizing the rights of refugees and migrants require further analysis.

Both the Global Compact on Refugees and the Global Compact for Safe, Orderly and Regular Migration sparked considerable academic commentary on their relevance and potential. We can expect the academic literature of the future to take stock of how well their aims are being achieved.

Social media is now ubiquitous. It can be an important information medium, helping forcibly displaced persons access safety and assistance. However, it also has been used in exploitative ways and as a platform to spread false narratives that can endanger security. Greater study of the role of social media and how to mitigate its harmful impact on refugees and internally displaced persons would be of value.

The voices and perspectives of forcibly displaced persons, and the actual and potential contributions they make to their own communities and host countries, are more prominently reflected in academic work. Their involvement has been shown to be of significant importance in shaping policies and programmes that affect them. More studies documenting this impact and providing actionable recommendations for their systematic engagement would be worthwhile.

Health studies concerning forced displacement have been largely concerned with refugees living in refugee camps, where health data is more readily accessible.[293] There is comparatively less on refugees outside camp contexts and even less on internally displaced persons. COVID-19 has attracted attention to pandemic-related issues, such as mitigating its transmission in forced displacement contexts and ensuring equitable access to treatment and vaccines.

Given the large and increasing number of internally displaced persons, much more research is needed to understand their health conditions and necessary interventions. And academic support and guidance is needed on how best to meet the health needs of displaced people through existing national systems in specific contexts as well as how to systematically engage effectively with them and host communities in improving services and health outcomes.

Published academic studies concerning education in forced displacement contexts have grown considerably, although the studies are predominantly concentrated on emergency responses and other situations where education is provided outside national systems. Areas canvassed include the legal and practical obstacles to accessing education, the completion rates of those enrolled in school, and the factors that help enable refugees and internally displaced persons to remain in school. There also has been work on the legal and practical barriers that limit refugee access to public schools and on the finances required to support inclusive education for refugees from preschool through grade 12. Since the COVID-19 pandemic, articles have also addressed the impact of the pandemic on refugee learning and efforts that have been made to mitigate losses.[294]

There remain large areas in need of further inquiry to improve education responses in forced displacement contexts. While there is growing consensus on the value of including refugees in national systems, there is relatively little context-specific analysis on how this may impact host communities. Nor is there much commentary on what will contribute to positive impacts for forcibly displaced and host communities alike.[295]

Similarly, there is a limited number of qualitative studies on difficulties that forcibly displaced students face in host community schools, including discrimination, bullying and physical violence. More work is needed to understand how widespread this behaviour is to inform measures to prevent and mitigate it.[296]

While we know what helps and hinders access to school, there is relatively little evidence on literacy and numeracy among forcibly displaced children and youth. Addressing this gap is hugely important, as is greater evidence on the effectiveness of interventions aimed to improve learning.

For example, there have been some studies on the use of technology for learning, such as tablets and smart phones, but these tend to be focused on specific projects. There is a need to broaden and deepen this work so that the impact of technology can be isolated from other influences on learning outcomes. Moreover, the effect of trauma on learning and social and emotional skills is important. Studies of it have largely occurred outside forced displacement contexts.[297]

Dropout rates are particularly pronounced when forcibly displaced students transition from primary to secondary school and when they move on to colleges and universities. Operational responses would also be strengthened with studies that can help determine the causes underlying low retention rates.

Building Evidence on Forced Displacement is a research partnership established in 2016 by the United Kingdom Foreign, Commonwealth and Development Office (FCDO), the World Bank and UNHCR. It is focused on expanding high-quality and policy-relevant research, principally in the areas of poverty, education, social protection, health, jobs, social cohesion and gender. To date, it has undertaken seven global studies, with over 50 background papers, 15 impact evaluations, over 10 focus papers, and research support to over 24 scholars.[298]

Similar collaboration is taking place to address an imbalance whereby most such studies originate in the better-resourced academic centres of high-income countries, which are more remote from areas of forced displacement.[299] Efforts include improved financing of research studies by academics working in countries most affected by forced displacement and creating stronger linkages between institutions across all regions. Many established academic networks and specialist centres covering refugee and migration issues are involved.

There is also a need for more robust interchange between academics and those delivering programmes on the ground. The Global Compacts on refugees and migration have helped encourage this, and more interdisciplinary work is underway. But there is considerable potential for this to be improved.[300]

It requires both a practical shift and a change in attitudes. An appreciation by academics of political and operational realities can help ensure that their studies are of greater practical benefit. Likewise, operational agencies need to overcome their perceived and occasional tendency to assume they know best. They must be open to the expertise that academics in relevant fields can provide.

Efforts by humanitarian organizations are heading in the right direction in recent years, including moves to partner with academics and specialized institutions on context analysis, surveys and impact evaluations. So too are greater efforts to centrally engage forcibly displaced populations in this work. Academics are also teachers and educators of those who may be involved in setting policies, delivering operations and contributing financing to forced displacement responses in the future – a further motivation to reinforce collaboration today.

Accountability

International Criminal Prosecution

Lidia Yusupova survived two Chechen wars between 1994 and 2009 but witnessed great brutality and experienced the loss of family and friends. It marked her and motivated her to become a human rights advocate working to bring perpetrators of human rights abuses to justice.

In describing the importance of the work, her sentiments are similar to many who have survived atrocities and are willing to come forward as witnesses. Giving up is not an option: "There is still our conscience, there is still the memory of the victims… there is still our duty to prevent further bloodshed."[301]

This call to end impunity, and many others like it, have gained greater resonance in recent years. As forced displacement numbers soared in the last decade, there has been a significant increase in efforts to hold accountable those directly responsible for the serious crimes they have committed.

This section focuses on criminal prosecutions of individuals accused of serious human rights violations.[302] It traces the historic path of post-World War II (WWII) international criminal prosecutions and increasing national ones. The record is patchy and often disappointing. But there is clear movement towards greater accountability and justice for survivors.

It is also important to keep in mind that those who have perpetrated the human rights violations causing flight *cannot benefit* from international protection. The 1951 Convention explicitly does not protect those suspected of grave international crimes, serious non-political crimes or acts contrary to the principles of the United Nations.[303]

International and national efforts to criminally prosecute those responsible for the abuses that often lead to mass flight can be part of broader transitional justice measures in countries emerging from periods of conflict or serious repression. These can include efforts to establish accountable institutions, ensure access to justice, sustain peace and promote reconciliation, such as through truth and reconciliation commissions.[304]

International Military Tribunals

"The wrongs which we seek to condemn and punish have been so calculated, so malignant, and so devastating, that civilization cannot tolerate their being ignored, because it cannot survive their being repeated." [305]

These were the words of Robert H. Jackson, Chief Prosecutor for the United

States at the International Military Tribunal (IMT) in Nuremberg. It was established by the Allies in December 1945 to criminally prosecute leaders of the Nazi regime.[306] A similar entity was set up several months later in Tokyo, for the trial of Japanese military and other leaders: the International Military Tribunal for the Far East (IMTFE).[307]

While the kind of wrongs to which Jackson referred would be repeated, these international tribunals marked a powerful turning point in international law: holding leaders and other officials specifically to account for causing egregious and widespread harm. They provided a detailed record of atrocities committed by the Axis powers, as well as recognition and retribution for survivors. Significantly, they recognized the international crimes that would collectively come to be known as "atrocity crimes" – war crimes, crimes against peace and crimes against humanity.[308]

The Charters establishing the tribunals defined crimes against peace as the planning, preparation, initiation or waging of war in violation of international treaties, agreements or assurances. War crimes are violations of the laws or customs of war. Crimes against humanity include murder, extermination, enslavement, deportation, inhumane acts against the civilian population before or during war, and/or persecution on political, racial, or religious grounds.[309]

In October 1946, the International Military Tribunal convicted 19 defendants and acquitted three.[310] The International Military Tribunal for the Far East concluded in 1948 with 25 convictions.[311] Those convicted by both tribunals received sentences ranging from death to long-term imprisonment. They represented military leaders and prominent members of the political, diplomatic and economic establishments.[312]

At the time the tribunals were created, the United Nations General Assembly passed a resolution recommending that States take all necessary measures to arrest suspected war criminals and return them to countries where their alleged crimes were committed for prosecution.[313] And on 11 December 1946, within months of the Nuremberg verdicts, the United Nations General Assembly passed a resolution recognizing *genocide* as an international crime, defining it as the denial of an entire group's right to exist.[314] It called on the Economic and Social Council to draft a convention to prevent it and to punish the perpetrators.

Nearly two years later to the day, the Convention on the Prevention and Punishment of the Crime of Genocide (Genocide Convention) was unanimously adopted by United Nations member States. It confirmed that genocide, whether committed in times of peace or in times of war, is a crime under international law which the signatory States undertake to prevent and punish. It defines the offence, and it obliges all signatories to enact legislation to implement the Convention and to prosecute perpetrators be they constitutional rulers, officials or individuals. It also provides for trials by competent national tribunals of the State where the act was committed, or by an international penal tribunal.[315]

The following year, a further set of four treaties was signed in Geneva. They set out standards of conduct *during armed conflict* and laid the foundations for the investigation and prosecution of those violating them. Known collectively as the *Geneva Conventions*, along with their Additional Protocols, they form the major components of international humanitarian law. Serious violations of them constitute *war crimes*.[316] They govern the treatment of civilians, medical and religious personnel, aid workers and troops no longer participating in hostilities during times of war.[317]

The first three concern the treatment of sick or wounded combatants in the field or at sea, and of prisoners of war, respectively. The fourth covers the protection of civilians.[318] International humanitarian law also contains specific provisions for the protection of refugees in the territory of a party to an international armed conflict.[319]

Thus, within several years of the conclusion of WWII, major officials were tried and convicted of atrocity crimes, the Genocide Convention was passed, the Geneva Conventions consolidated international humanitarian law treaties, and jurisprudence regarding war crimes and crimes against humanity was developed. In addition, the Universal Declaration of Human Rights was ratified in 1948, and the 1951 Convention established an international refugee protection regime.[320]

It was a strong start. But the hopes raised for a permanent international tribunal dedicated to the prosecution of genocide and other international crimes was a long way from being realized.[321] For several decades thereafter, not a single person was internationally held to account for war crimes or crimes against humanity. It took until the 1990s for the next international judicial response, after the atrocities committed in the former Yugoslavia[322] and in Rwanda. This time it was by international criminal tribunals set up under the auspices of the United Nations, and not military tribunals of the victors over the vanquished.[323]

Ad hoc international criminal tribunals

International Criminal Tribunal for the Former Yugoslavia
The International Criminal Tribunal for the former Yugoslavia (ICTY) was

created by a Security Council resolution in 1993 to prosecute war crimes and specifically: genocide; crimes against humanity; and breaches of laws or customs of war, including the Geneva Conventions.[324] It was located in The Hague, the Netherlands. Among the accused was Slobodan Milošević, President of Serbia, and the first serving head of State to be indicted in an international prosecution for war crimes.[325]

During its 24 years of operation, the ICTY indicted 161 individuals, mostly Serbs and Bosnian Serbs as well as Croats, Bosnian Muslims and Kosovo Albanians. It secured 90 convictions.[326] Among its many findings was that: the mass murder of over 7,000 men and boys in Srebrenica was a genocide; rape was used as an instrument of terror; and massive and "hellish" persecution was inflicted on those detained in the camps in northwestern Bosnia.[327] The judgments of the tribunal furthered the jurisprudence on genocide, war crimes and crimes against humanity.

International Criminal Tribunal for Rwanda

Shortly after the ICTY was set up, the United Nations Security Council established the International Criminal Tribunal for Rwanda (ICTR), mandated to prosecute those responsible for genocide and other serious violations of international law committed in Rwanda and neighbouring States in 1994.[328] The Tribunal was located in Arusha, Tanzania with offices in Kigali, Rwanda and its appeal chamber in The Hague. Its specific focus was on the killing of approximately 800,000 to 1 million persons, most within a 100-day period in 1994.

The work of the ICTR extended over 21 years. It indicted 93 individuals, of whom 62 were convicted, including high-ranking military and government officials, politicians and businessmen, as well as religious militia and military leaders.[329] It too furthered the jurisprudence on genocide, crimes against humanity and war crimes, and was the first international tribunal to convict individuals for the crime of genocide, as established in the 1948 Genocide Convention. It also found that rape was a means of perpetrating genocide. Among the other precedents it established was that members of the media could be prosecuted and convicted of incitement to commit genocide.[330]

The remaining cases of the Yugoslavia and Rwanda tribunals were eventually transferred to the International Residual Mechanism for Criminal Tribunals (IRMCT). Created by the Security Council in 2010, the IRMCT was established to assume several functions of the former Tribunals, including hearing appeals and prosecuting the remaining fugitives from justice.[331]

International Criminal Court

From the end of WWII, advocates called for the creation of a permanent international criminal court. The road to its realization, however, was long. In 1947, the United Nations General Assembly requested that the International Law Commission (ILC)[332] write a *Draft Code of Offences Against the Peace and Security of Mankind*. In parallel, the United Nations General Assembly also established a committee to prepare a draft statute for an international criminal court. Within a few years, both a draft code and draft statute were submitted to the General Assembly[333] but were not acted upon, due to a lack of political consensus aggravated by the Cold War.[334]

It would take several decades before progress towards a permanent international criminal court gained traction. In 1989, the General Assembly requested the International Law Commission to draft a statute for such a court, which it subsequently presented in 1994.[335] It was then considered by an Ad Hoc Committee, followed by a Preparatory Committee both established by the General Assembly.[336]

The Preparatory Committee consulted widely within and outside the United Nations system. Among those active in the work was the Coalition for the International Criminal Court (CICC) whose members included legal human rights and international justice organizations from around the world.[337]

The result of these efforts culminated in the Rome Statute on the International Criminal Court (the Rome Statute), adopted by 120 countries in 1998.[338] The treaty came into effect in 2002. Currently, 123 countries are party to it, including most countries in Africa, Europe and Latin America. Three Security Council members, China, Russia and the United States are not party to it.[339] Many countries in Asia and the Middle East are also not signatories.

The International Criminal Court is an independent permanent tribunal. Its jurisdiction extends to crimes committed after 2002 and over war crimes, crimes against humanity and genocide. It can also prosecute those who interfere with the administration of justice, for example, by giving false testimony, tampering with a witness, or improperly interfering in the duties of Court officials.[340]

The International Criminal Court may only exercise jurisdiction where national legal systems fail to do so, including when they purport to act but do not genuinely carry out proceedings. This is known as the principle of complementarity. The rationale is both to respect the primary jurisdiction of States and to serve the interests of efficiency and effectiveness since States are often best placed to access evidence and witnesses.[341]

Genocide is defined in the Rome Statute as in the Genocide Convention. It includes acts committed *with intent to destroy*, in whole or in part, a national, ethnical, racial or religious group. To establish the crime, it must be proved that the perpetrator intended to destroy the group in whole or in part.[342]

The Rome Statute also provides a detailed and precise definition of crimes against humanity, war crimes and crimes of aggression.

Crimes against humanity are those "committed as part of a *widespread or systematic attack* directed against any civilian population" and executed as part of a State or organizational plan or policy. They include murder, extermination, enslavement, deportation and forcible transfer, torture, severe sexual violence, persecution, apartheid, enforced disappearance and "other inhumane acts of a similar character intentionally causing great suffering, or serious injury to body or to mental or physical health".[343] Perpetrators need not have knowledge "of all characteristics of the attack or the precise details of the plan or policy". Intent is satisfied "if the perpetrator intended to further such an attack".[344]

War crimes under the Rome Statute include grave breaches of the Geneva Conventions and other serious violations of international law applicable in international armed conflict. They include the killing of civilians, torture, inhumane treatment, willfully causing great suffering, or serious injury to body or health. Also included is militarily unnecessary and wanton destruction of property. Other actions that can be so severe as to constitute war crimes include forced recruitment of prisoners of war or civilians into hostile forces, denial of a fair trial, unlawful deportation or transfer, unlawful confinement or hostage-taking.[345]

The *crime of aggression* refers to the planning, preparation, initiation or execution of an act of aggression which, by its character, gravity and scale, constitutes a manifest violation of the Charter of the United Nations. Culpability extends to any person in a position to exercise control or to direct the political or military action of a State. It includes acts by armed forces of a State against the territory of another State, such as military occupation, bombardment, blockade of the ports or coasts, attacks by land, sea or air, and the use of armed groups to carry out grave acts against another State.[346]

The International Criminal Court's jurisdiction is limited to situations where the alleged perpetrator is a national of a State Party or where the crime was committed in the territory of a State Party. The only exceptions to these two criteria are if the Security Council refers the case to the Court, or the relevant non-State signatory consents to the Court's jurisdiction.[347] Of note is the 2019 decision of the Court, that its remit can extend to situations engaging a non-State party to the Court, if at least part of the criminal conduct takes place within the territory of a State party.[348]

This decision was in regard to the Prosecutor's request to authorize an investigation into the deportations, acts of persecution and other inhumane acts committed against the Rohingya population of Myanmar (non-State Party), which has precipitated the flight of close to 700,000 Rohingya refugees to Bangladesh (State Party) since 2016. The decision is of import as the reasoning could be applied in other situations of significant forced displacement, provided one of the receiving States is a party to the Rome Statute.[349]

The International Criminal Court also has the power to issue reparations to the victims, including monetary compensation, return of property, rehabilitation or symbolic measures, such as apologies or memorials. A Trust Fund for Victims has been established to raise the funds necessary to comply with an order for reparations if the convicted person does not have sufficient resources to do so.[350]

Since it was established in 2002, the Court has brought charges against 46 individuals, of which 10 have been convicted.[351] Five persons were convicted for administration of justice offences, such as witness tampering.[352] Of the five convicted of atrocity crimes, three involve leaders of armed groups in the Democratic Republic of the Congo. Thomas Lubanga was convicted by the Court in 2012 of the war crimes of enlisting and conscripting children under 15 years of age and sentenced to 14 years imprisonment.[353] In 2014, Germain Katanga was found guilty of murder, attacking a civilian population, destruction of property and pillaging, and sentenced to 12 years in prison.[354] Five years later, the Court found Bosco Ntaganda guilty of 18 counts of war crimes and crimes against humanity and sentenced him to 30 years in prison.[355]

The fourth convicted war criminal is Ahmed Al-Mahdi, a Tuareg militia member who pled guilty to destroying historical and religious monuments in Timbuktu, Mali. He received a nine-year prison sentence.[356] And, in 2021, Dominic Ongwen, a commander in the Lord's Resistance Army (LRA) was found guilty of crimes against humanity and war crimes, committed in Northern Uganda between 1 July 2002 and 31 December 2005. He was sentenced to 25 years imprisonment.[357]

As of October 2021, the Internal Criminal Court was carrying out 15 investigations, 10 of which are in Africa. Close to all are situations that have involved mass forced displacement.[358] There were three trials underway and one appeal in process.[359] Thirteen accused remain at large and their trials pending.[360]

The Court has faced criticism over the years, including that it has been partial in the selection of situations to investigate and cases to pursue.[361]

Situations in Africa have largely been the focus of the Court's attention. More cases have been brought against rebel leaders than serving government officials and commanders of government troops. Notable exceptions include the 2009 and 2011 indictments of the former President of Sudan, Omar Al-Bashir, and the then Kenyan Deputy Prime Minister Uhuru Kenyatta, respectively.

African leaders' frustrations with the Court led the 2015 Summit of the African Union to pass a conclusion that serving heads of State should not be put on trial. This is among the reasons why Omar Al-Bashir remained at large after the warrant for his arrest.[362] Kenyatta, however, surrendered himself to the Court, and denied the charges, which were eventually dropped amid difficulties in obtaining evidence due to a lack of cooperation from witnesses and concerns of witness tampering.[363]

Disappointment with the Court has been broad, even reaching within the Court itself and its strongest backers. As one commentator noted in 2012, the International Criminal Court is a Court of "unfulfilled aspirations".[364] It took seven years for it to begin its first trial, and it consistently failed to meet its own strategic targets. Dissatisfaction over the small number of convictions, time-consuming prosecutions, and lack of cooperation by some States led the President of the Court, in 2019, to request an independent review.

States parties to the Rome Statute mandated a group of nine independent experts to undertake the review.[365] In September 2020, they issued their final report: close to 350 pages of detailed findings and recommendations.[366]

While emphasizing the commitment of most of the Court's personnel and the important role of the Court, the experts found serious failings in the work culture and observed that cumbersome bureaucratic processes, a lack of strategic planning, and delayed judgments contributed to inefficiencies. The experts prioritized their recommendations, and States parties have since created a mechanism for follow-up.[367] The work is ongoing. The relevance of the International Criminal Court will no doubt depend on how well and how fast it moves on the implementation.

Other international tribunals

Special Court for Sierra Leone

At the time the International Criminal Court was established, another ad hoc international criminal tribunal was created in a forced displacement context. The Special Court for Sierra Leone was established in 2002, following the conclusion of the 11-year civil war in which tens of thousands were killed, and over 1 million forcibly displaced at the peak of the crisis.[368] Widespread atrocities were committed, including mass murder, mutilation, rape, forced marriage, sexual slavery, and extensive and brutal forced recruitment of children.[369]

The Court was set up by a treaty agreement between the United Nations and the Government of Sierra Leone, and endorsed by the Security Council.[370] It included judges and prosecutors from Sierra Leone and the international community. Unlike the international criminal tribunals for the former

Charles Taylor's trial for war crimes and crimes against humanity is televised from the Hague in 2012. The former president of Liberia was found guilty of all 11 charges and sentenced to 50 years in prison.
© Lee Karen Stow/Alamy

Yugoslavia and Rwanda, which were funded by the United Nations, the Special Court for Sierra Leone relied on voluntary contributions. Its jurisdiction was limited to prosecuting those "bearing the greatest responsibility" for war crimes, crimes against humanity, or serious violations of international humanitarian law or Sierra Leonean law.[371] It was based in the country's capital, Freetown.

Within its 11 years of operation, 10 people were tried for atrocity crimes, and all were convicted, with the exception of one who died before the end of the proceedings.[372] The last judgment was issued in 2013 by the Appeals Chamber, upholding the conviction of the former President of Liberia, Charles Taylor, whose forces were engaged in the war.

He was the first sitting head of State to be convicted of war crimes by an international tribunal since the Nuremberg trials.[373] The Special Court for Sierra Leone set a series of other precedents. It found that forced marriage was a war crime, attacks against United Nations peacekeepers were war crimes, and crimes against humanity included the recruitment, enlistment and use of child soldiers.[374]

The War Crimes Chamber in Bosnia and Herzegovina

The 1995 General Agreement for Peace in Bosnia and Herzegovina, also known as the Dayton Accords provided for an international High Representative to oversee the civilian implementation of the agreement. The High Representative maintains broad powers, including to enact laws.[375]

In 2000, the High Representative issued a proclamation for the creation of the Court of Bosnia and Herzegovina, which was subsequently established through an Act of Parliament in 2002. The War Crimes Chamber forms part of the Court. It is accountable for prosecuting persons responsible for serious violations of international humanitarian law committed in the former Yugoslavia since 1991, including genocide, crimes against humanity, war crimes, and violations of the laws and practices of war.[376] It began its work in 2005, and international judges and personnel formed part of the Court as a transitional means to strengthen national capacity.

Between 2005 and 2020, the Chamber concluded over 240 cases and convicted 269 individuals who received a range of sentences, with 12 years imprisonment being the average length of incarceration imposed.[377] Capacity issues have led to some difficulties, including in strategic planning, which has meant that many cases have been pursued but the most important have not been prioritized.

Delays have been incurred due to procedural errors that had to be remedied before indictments could proceed. These are among the reasons why the Chamber is behind in meeting its 2023 case completion target.[378] Observers have noted that, notwithstanding some deficiencies, fairness has largely been observed in the judicial process and rulings issued.[379]

National Criminal Prosecution

There have been significant prosecutions of atrocity crimes in national courts. The following examples concern situations where the criminal acts have also been responsible for significant forced displacement. They illustrate difficulties often encountered in ensuring timely, fair and independent proceedings.

Cambodia

Justice was delayed for the victims of the Cambodian genocide committed during the Khmer Rouge regime between 1975 and 1979. It was not until 2001 that the Cambodian National Assembly created the Extraordinary Chambers in the Courts of Cambodia (ECCC) to prosecute senior leaders and those most responsible for grave violations of national and international law during the Khmer Rouge period.[380]

During the four years that the Khmer Rouge were in power under Pol Pot, 1.5 to 2 million people are estimated to have died from starvation, torture, executions and forced labour.[381] More than 2 million were forcibly displaced within the country and close to 200,000 fled to neighbouring countries.[382] Following their ouster from power, the Khmer Rouge continued an insurgency that lasted until the late 1990s.

The Cambodian law establishing the Extraordinary Chambers provided for both national and international personnel and was supported by the United Nations through a special agreement.[383] Because of the support received from the United Nations and the fact that it engages a mix of international judges and prosecutors, the Chambers is sometimes characterized as a "hybrid" international tribunal. But, since it was created and can be dissolved by the law of Cambodia, it is a national tribunal.[384]

The Extraordinary Chambers in the Courts of Cambodia commenced work in 2006. The Court has indicted nine individuals and, by mid-2021, had convicted three. In 2010, Kaing Guek Eav was found guilty of crimes against humanity and war crimes for his actions while leading a special branch of the Khmer Rouge security and operating prison. In 2014, two other high officials, Khieu Samphan and Nuon Chea were found guilty of crimes against humanity.

Khieu Samphan was a high official in the Khmer Rouge who eventually succeeded Pol Pot as President of the State Presidium. Nuon Chea was the party's chief ideologist, Deputy Secretary of the Party, and President of the National Assembly. In 2018, both men were also convicted of genocide. Among the acts that formed the basis of their convictions was the forced displacement of over 2 million people, enforced disappearances and attacks against human dignity.[385]

Among the other cases before the Extraordinary Chambers, one accused person died during the proceedings. One case was dismissed because of the mental health of the accused.[386] The prosecution of four others did not proceed beyond the pre-trial phase due to disagreements between the Cambodian and international judges on whether the cases should go to trial.[387] In August 2020, one of the cases was terminated due to a lack of an enforceable indictment.[388]

The decade-long deadlock has been attributed to political pressure on the Cambodian judges.[389]

The Extraordinary Chambers in the Courts of Cambodia is considered to have mixed results. Positively, it has delivered a degree of accountability and justice for the atrocities committed under the Khmer Rouge and provided victims with stronger participatory rights than comparable courts and tribunals. But its reputation has been tarnished amid reports of political pressure, alleged corruption of some court officials, and failure to adhere systematically to due process.[390] Also, while it did provide a greater measure of victim parti-

Nuon Chea
during the Trial
Chamber hearing
in Case 002.
ECCC Handout/
Nhet Sok Heng/
Wikimedia
Commons

cipation, the practice has been uneven.[391] And, because the Government took so long to pursue prosecutions, many perpetrators lived freely for years, and some either died or were too infirm to be tried.

Bangladesh

Bangladesh's prosecution of atrocity crimes has also received mixed reactions. One year following the creation of Bangladesh in 1972, legislation was passed to prosecute and punish persons "responsible for committing genocide, crimes against humanity, war crimes and other crimes under international law".[392] However, immediate post-war efforts to hold perpetrators to account were quickly abandoned, and it was only in 2010 that Bangladesh's International

Crimes Tribunal was established, based on a revised version of the 1973 law.[393] Special tribunals were constituted and indictments issued, including of leaders of the Jamaat-e-Islami, accused of genocide and other international crimes arising from the events in 1971.[394]

By 2020, several had been convicted and received sentences ranging from death to life imprisonment.[395] While the creation of the national tribunal was viewed positively,[396] legal scholars and human rights groups have since registered concern over the proceedings. Some have observed that the Bangladesh Constitution has been interpreted to deny constitutional protections to those detained or charged of international crimes. In addition, provisions in the enabling legislation of the International Crimes Tribunal are seen as undermining the rights of the accused and the independence and fairness of the proceedings.[397]

Guatemala

In Guatemala, prosecution for gross human rights abuses during the country's civil war from the 1960s through the 1990s was also delayed. It was not until 2012 that José Efraín Ríos Montt, former President of Guatemala and previous high official in the armed forces, was arrested. Montt was charged with genocide against Ixil indigenous communities and crimes against humanity committed during the 36-year civil war from 1960 to 1996.

As a member of Congress until 2012, he had been protected by legislative immunity. In 2013, he was found guilty of genocide and crimes against humanity. Only days later, the conviction was overturned by the Constitutional Court of Guatemala on the grounds that he had been denied a fair trial. He died in 2018 before his retrial was completed.[398]

Chad

Chad took a long time to prosecute senior officials for atrocity crimes, which took place during the eight-year Presidency of Hissène Habré, between 1982 and 1990. Following his ouster by Idriss Déby in 1990, Habré fled to Senegal. Chad did not seek to extradite him. It also waited many years before prosecuting members of his regime.

It was not until 2013, after close to 25 years of victims' advocacy, that arrest warrants were issued against his former officials.[399] In 2015, a Chadian criminal court convicted 21 men of serious offences, including crimes against humanity. Seven of them received life imprisonment. Among them were Saleh Younous, the former director of the political police, and Mahamat Djibrine, chief of police charged with illegal detention, torture and "acts of barbarism".[400]

Some of the above cases reveal how political reluctance can mean perpetrators are not prosecuted in their national courts. This may be motivated by an intention to leave the past behind and move forward, and/or not to bring to light evidence that could implicate current office holders.

There are other reasons preventing domestic courts from hearing cases of international crimes. Prosecutions are often complex, necessitating detailed evidence gathering, and multiple layers of processing, requiring a level of resources and judicial infrastructure that many countries lack. So, even if a country is willing to prosecute, it may lack the means to do so.[401]

Universal Jurisdiction

The principle of universal jurisdiction applies to the offences that are so serious that States may prosecute them under national legislation, even when the crimes are not committed on their territory or by their citizens.[402] In 1961, Israel relied on universal jurisdiction to convict Adolf Eichmann of offences including crimes against humanity and war crimes.[403] Eichmann's status as a senior German officer of the Third Reich established his responsibility for the forced deportation of Jews and other detainees to extermination camps.

Augusto Pinochet was the first former head of State to be indicted for crimes against humanity under universal jurisdiction. In 1973, he led the military coup that overthrew the democratically elected government of Salvador Allende. His dictatorship lasted until 1990 and is known for its brutal repression of suspected leftists, activists and political opponents. More than 3,000 are known to have been killed or disappeared during his regime, some 40,000 are estimated to have survived torture and political imprisonment,[404] and many thousands of persons fled the country.[405]

In 1998, Pinochet was arrested in London, under an international arrest warrant issued by Spain. The charges included torture and other international crimes. Pinochet fought his extradition to Spain, claiming that, as a former head of State, he was immune from prosecution. His claim was rejected by the House of Lords, then the highest court of appeal[406] on the grounds that Chile was a party to the Convention Against Torture (CAT) and the CAT is clear that no immunity can be claimed for the crime of torture.[407] Pinochet, therefore, could be extradited to Spain.[408]

However, the United Kingdom's Home Secretary decided not to extradite Pinochet on the grounds that he was in ill health. Pinochet was returned to

Chile. After several Court rulings there on his capacity to stand trial, he was eventually criminally charged under Chilean law, but died before the trial commenced.[409]

Pinochet was not held accountable for his crimes. But the decision of the United Kingdom House of Lords to refuse him immunity and recognize universal jurisdiction is regarded as important. From that point, use of universal jurisdiction began to increase, supported by persistent advocacy and casework by victims' groups, and human rights and legal advocates.

Senegal's prosecution of Hissène Habré, the former President of Chad, is an example. Although Chad did not prosecute him, Senegal was willing to do so and, in 2014, passed a Statute of the Extraordinary African Chambers to prosecute genocide, crimes against humanity, war crimes and torture committed in Chad during his government. It was the first application of universal jurisdiction in Africa.[410] The Court was supported by the African Union and had a mix of Senegalese and international judges.

Accusations against Habré included targeted killings of civilian populations and suspected political opponents, mass arrests and systematic use of torture by State security and armed forces under Habré's command. The Court found him responsible for mass sexual slavery and for ordering the killing of 40,000 people. In 2016, he was convicted of crimes against humanity and sentenced to life in prison.[411] He was the first former head of State convicted under universal jurisdiction for atrocity crimes, making Habré's high-profile case a landmark conviction.

The last decade has seen an increase in universal jurisdiction cases, the majority concerning events beyond Africa.[412] Between 2008 and 2017, there were over 800 new universal jurisdiction cases globally, a 60 per cent increase over the previous decade.[413] Twenty-nine universal jurisdiction cases were completed between 2010 and 2017, close to the same number completed over the previous 49 years.[414]

As of April 2021, estimates suggest that 144 persons were reported under investigation or charged with a serious international crime in universal jurisdiction proceedings globally. Thirty trials were underway in 18 countries. The cases involved crimes committed in 21 countries across Africa, Asia, Latin America and the Middle East.[415]

Several reasons have been advanced for the increased number of universal jurisdiction cases. One is that countries have passed domestic legislation recognizing crimes against humanity, war crimes and genocide, and authorizing their prosecution. According to Amnesty International, 147 United Nations member

States have provided for universal jurisdiction over one or more of the international crimes of genocide, war crimes, crimes against humanity and torture.[416]

Several countries have also established special units within their national institutions for the investigation and prosecution of international crimes.[417] This has not only brought specialized expertise to the task but has also helped ensure that links are in place with other national law enforcement, immigration and intelligence branches of government.[418]

Countries have gained experience in exercising universal jurisdiction, which has helped in effectively selecting, investigating and conducting prosecutions. The same is true for non-governmental organizations and legal advocates who have been instrumental in documenting and advocating for the prosecution of international crimes. They provide legal assistance to victims, litigation support, and training on evidence gathering and strengthening local capacity.[419]

Technology has also helped. It has made the collection of evidence easier, not least when carried out far away from the prosecuting State, and it has lowered costs. The widespread use and sharing of audio and visual materials have helped document atrocity crimes and provide evidence. Sharing platforms are available to governments and non-governmental organizations. The publication of evidence of gross human rights violations is believed to contribute to increased public support and demand for accountability.[420]

Forcibly displaced people themselves have played an important role in the growing use of universal jurisdiction. The rise in cases over the past decade coincided with the increased arrivals of refugees from Syria and Iraq in Western Europe, where the majority of universal jurisdiction cases have been lodged.[421] In some cases, individuals who have claimed asylum have been investigated for serious international crimes.[422] At times, asylum-seekers and refugees have reported people suspected of serious crimes to authorities.

Independent Fact-Finding

Collecting evidence to support prosecutions is generally very difficult and time-consuming. It often involves gathering evidence in remote and insecure areas, locating and protecting witnesses, and tracking down suspects. Each step is long and complex, and the process can be costly, especially given the distance between the location of the alleged crimes and the country of prosecution.[423] Successful prosecutions are often hard-won, given these challenges.[424] In recognition, various United Nations mechanisms have been increasingly relied upon to investigate possible atrocity crimes.

In 2016, the General Assembly created the International, Impartial and Independent Mechanism on Syria (IIIM).[425] It was sponsored by over 50 States reportedly frustrated by the deadlock in the Security Council in regard to the conflict in Syria. The mandate of the Mechanism is to assist in the investigation and prosecution of those responsible for the most serious crimes under international law committed in Syria since March 2011. It collects, consolidates, analyses and preserves evidence to facilitate independent criminal proceedings in national, regional or international courts.[426] In its annual report to the General Assembly in 2021, the Mechanism noted it had received close to 100 requests for assistance from 11 jurisdictions and supported 36 domestic investigations.[427]

In parallel, the Human Rights Council (HRC) also mandates fact-finding missions, commissions of inquiry and independent investigations into serious human rights abuses and related crimes, with a view to avoid impunity and ensure accountability.[428] Since 2015, these have included investigations and fact-finding into situations in Belarus, Burundi, Democratic Republic of the Congo, Lake Chad Basin, Libya, Myanmar, Palestine/Israel, South Sudan, Syria, Venezuela and Yemen.[429]

In 2018, the HRC showed a willingness to link investigations directly to prosecutions. It came as it established the Independent Investigative Mechanism for Myanmar. Its mandate provides for the collection of evidence of the most serious international crimes and violations of international law and preparation of files for criminal prosecution.[430]

The Security Council also has the authority to mandate investigations into serious international crimes. It has used it sparingly. The Office of the High Commissioner for Human Rights documents just five such Security Council authorizations since 1963, four of which were prior to 2000.

However, in 2017, unanimity was reached in regard to a request by Iraq for the United Nations' assistance in holding the Islamic State in Iraq and the Levant (ISIL) accountable for atrocities committed when it was in control of large parts of Iraq (2014–2017). The Council established UNITAD, the Investigative Team to Promote Accountability for Crimes Committed by Da'esh/ Islamic State in Iraq and the Levant. It is mandated to work with Iraqi authorities and other stakeholders in the *collection, preservation and storage of evidence* in Iraq of acts that might amount to war crimes, crimes against humanity and genocide.[431]

In his 2021 Annual Report to the Security Council, Karim A. A. Khan, the Special Adviser who then led the work of the Investigative Team, reported that it had identified close to 1,500 potential ISIL perpetrators of attacks against Yazidis. It completed core investigations into two of the most prominent attacks prioritized in its mandate.[432] It confirmed the repeated deployment of chemical weapons by ISIL against civilian populations. Khan also reported on advances in evidence-gathering, including the innovations in digital platforms, artificial intelligence and data analysis. Ongoing capacity-building of the Iraqi authorities to collect, store and preserve evidence and establish a legislative framework for future prosecutions was ongoing.[433]

UNITAD also works closely with survivors and, in 2021, supported the return of the remains of those killed by ISIL and buried in mass graves of Kocho. Nadia Mourad, Nobel Laureate and Yazidi survivor of sexual slavery under ISIL, spoke to the Security Council of the deep significance that event had on her community as part of the work to press ahead in holding ISIL accountable.

She reminded the Council that 200,000 Yazidis remain in displacement camps, a few hours from their homes "hoping for justice and restoration", while 2,800 women and children are still captives of ISIL.[434] She urged the Council to create a special international tribunal or refer the situation to the International Criminal Court for the prosecution of ISIL. To do less, she warned, denies hundreds of thousands of Yazidis justice and invites future groups to commit such crimes.[435]

Ongoing international efforts to strengthen the prosecution capacities of national and regional institutions may also help further accountability for international crimes.[436] They not only could expand the number of fora in which accountability can be pursued and allow for proceedings to take place closer to affected communities and in languages more accessible to them. They could help provide real and perceived impartiality in the adjudication of what are often highly politicized cases.[437]

There are countless testimonials from those who have survived atrocity crimes of the importance of criminal prosecution of their perpetrators. In his evidence before the Extraordinary African Chambers in Senegal, Souleymane Guengueng described his imprisonment, the cries of fellow detainees being tortured, and the disappearance and death of other prisoners.

He also spoke of the promise he made to himself during that dismal time that was being realized in the courtroom in which he now sat:

"From the depths of my soul, from the depths of that madness, I took an oath before God that if I got out alive, I would fight for justice."

He did, and we should do no less.

Reflecting Back and Facing Forward

Reflecting Back and Facing Forward

The history of responding to forced displacement has a positive overall trajectory, but one that has always been uneven.

From the earliest periods of civilization, people forced to flee have found protection and even longer-term solutions to their plight from others. Although these responses were typically ad hoc and localized, they reflected broader values of safety, solidarity and self-reliance. The 1951 Convention relating to the Status of Refugees and its 1967 Protocol gave them global reach.

In its 70 years, the 1951 Convention has been central to successful efforts to improve the lives of some of the world's most vulnerable people. Millions of refugees have been protected and realized solutions to their displacement. The Convention has also helped inspire international protection responses for internally displaced persons, as well as for those displaced due to the adverse effects of climate change and disasters.

But history also reveals how often national and international responses have fallen short. This book shows how that pattern persists. Lasting solutions have remained elusive for millions of people forced to flee. The absence of conditions that enable safe and sustainable return has contributed to increasing protracted displacement. Resettlement has only ever been provided to a small proportion of refugees. And forcibly displaced people often face significant obstacles to sustainable local integration.

Countries hosting the vast majority of forcibly displaced persons have been left without sufficient support to address the impact of conflict and forced displacement on their institutions, infrastructure and economies. And too few efforts have been made to strengthen human capital in displacement – the skills, knowledge and experience that enable individuals to realize their potential as productive members of society. This has left many forcibly displaced persons unable to overcome the initial vulnerabilities of their displacement.

Loss of assets, poor health and trauma linger when restrictions leave people unable to move freely and they lack access to education, health services and employment. Many are unable to provide for themselves, or to prepare or even hope for a better future. In the words of one Syrian refugee mother, asked what keeps her family going in their greatly diminished circumstances, "we live for lack of death".[1]

Her words came as her chances of returning to Syria receded, her savings were depleted, her children remained out of school and her family was prevented from working legally. It is a scenario replicated millions of times over. It is one that the 2018 Global Compact on Refugees seeks to remedy, with polices designed to ease pressures on host countries, and promote new avenues for dignified living and solutions to displacement.

This long-awaited approach is as significant as the challenges it aims to address. It recognizes that supporting host countries and helping forcibly displaced people is a development imperative as well as a humanitarian concern.

The call for integrated *development and humanitarian responses* to forced displacement is many decades old. But earlier development efforts did not take root. These were neither widespread nor sufficient in the specific situations to which they were applied. Much more development support was, and continues to be, needed to help host governments cope with the challenges of receiving large numbers of forcibly displaced persons. In the last decade alone, the global number of forcibly displaced persons has more than doubled to over 82 million. Over 90 per cent are in middle- and low-income countries. Pressure on limited humanitarian financing has mounted.

The increased arrival of refugees to Europe in 2015 was a catalyst for change. It exposed the fact that humanitarian funding was insufficient to combat deepening poverty in protracted forced displacement contexts. And it gave greater visibility to the reality that most of the world's forcibly displaced populations fled from, and reside in, countries deeply affected by fragility, conflict and violence, with limited capacities to respond.[2] The impacts of climate change and the COVID-19 pandemic have also added to the pressing need for more effective and sustainable responses.

Development approaches have expanded in forced displacement contexts and seek to support host countries and displaced populations based on a shared vision of inclusive development. They provide support to host countries and communities to address the challenges involved in receiving large numbers of forcibly displaced persons, and to seize the economic opportunities these movements provide. Development approaches depend on national agreement and ownership supported by enabling legislation and policy frameworks, and commitment to strengthen institutions, accountability and governance.

These conditions are not always present, especially in situations where conflict is ongoing or unstable conditions undermine economic growth, or where there is a lack of national ownership. New or renewed conflict can be disruptive, leaving commitments only partially executed. In these situations, reliance on humanitarian programmes may be needed for the foreseeable future.

Even so, we have a better appreciation today of how humanitarian programmes can be designed to help lay the groundwork for more development-focused responses, not least by strengthening the human capital of both the forcibly displaced and host communities.

Boosting their health, education and skills improves lives during displacement. Improved social and economic capital also helps sustain solutions.

Advocacy is also needed for recognition of the range of rights that enable people to live in dignity: legal status; freedom to move; civil registration; right to work; access to education; health; justice and financial services without discrimination. Humanitarian programmes need to be designed in a manner that reduces competition in access to services between refugees, internally displaced persons and hosts. Effective humanitarian responses support community relations through local mediation and conflict resolution mechanisms to de-escalate intra- and inter-communal conflicts.

Traditionally, responses to new crises have been met with the immediate deployment of emergency humanitarian assistance to save lives. This is critical in the first weeks and months. But those early days are also important for setting up a more sustainable response. This requires timely engagement with development partners and plans for such a transition to take place.

Donors can help by writing these expectations into their financing agreements.

Where more development-focused responses are suitable, humanitarian and development actors need to recognize how they complement each other and identify how their work can be mutually reinforcing. This is not always as simple as it may sound. There are long traditions of working in parallel. Objectives may be shared, but funding mechanisms, operational expertise and focus are often different.

Development actors have extensive socioeconomic analytical capacities. They liaise across government ministries, including those responsible for economic and financial policy. They can provide significant medium-term funding to governments to improve their capacities, help which is often crucial to support change. Humanitarian actors have a large and diverse field presence, which affords direct access to and knowledge of forcibly displaced communities. They have well-developed emergency response capacities and expertise in understanding protection risks and how they can be mitigated through law and practice.

The need to bridge the humanitarian-development divide is now one of the strategic priorities of the main responders to forced displacement. And, as documented throughout this book, it has taken root in an increasing number of places, many of them situations of protracted displacement. This has supported changes in government policies for inclusive development, which should bring benefits to displaced people and the communities in which they live.

These positive steps need *predictable and sustainable financing*. This is critical. The expansion of such funding instruments is among the most remarkable changes in recent years. Their focus on the socioeconomic development of displaced and host communities comes with methodologies that support the design and implementation of sustainable programmes. They have helped shine more light on the importance of government-led processes, a shared approach to context and risk analysis, the value of better data and the importance of evaluation and impact assessments.[3]

High-income countries need to demonstrate *greater solidarity*. There should be tangible improvements in the sharing of burdens and responsibilities with other nations, an area where progress consistently falls short. This requires more than increasing humanitarian and development support to countries most affected by forced displacement crises. Honouring international commitments to protect refugees who arrive at their borders is also necessary.

This means improving reception and asylum systems, rather than restricting access to them. The current practice to deter, resist and push back displaced

people undermines the foundations of the international protection regime. Resettlement opportunities require meaningful expansion. Safe and orderly alternative pathways for refugees and migrants to high-income countries need to be widened. Repeated expressions of solidarity with countries of much scarcer resources that host most of the world's forcibly displaced populations are not enough.

History teaches us that patience and perseverance is needed for progressive shifts to take hold. We will need both, as the world turns towards more sustainable responses to forced displacement. Situations can change and so too can political commitment. Development, by definition, takes time and many years can pass before outcomes improve and achievements become visible.

Similarly, *institutional change* does not occur overnight. Accounting for the different perspectives and approaches of development and humanitarian partners, private and civil society actors is challenging. Engaging forcibly displaced people to contribute meaningfully to policy and implementation also needs more effort.

But the grounds for cautious optimism are clear. They appear in the firmer links being made between humanitarian and development programming and funding streams in support of them. They are evident in the gradual widening of inclusive government responses. They are there in the greater global willingness to hold criminally liable individuals whose actions are at the root of so much forced displacement.

There is also a broader base of *committed and active stakeholders* seeking improved responses to forced displacement than at any other time. This brings more comparative expertise to help improve lives and realize solutions. It includes forcibly displaced persons themselves, who continue to show, including during the COVID-19 pandemic, how quickly and effectively they can mobilize support for their own and for host communities.

As we saw at the beginning of this book, this "whole-of-society" approach was emblematic of the first Global Refugee Forum of 2019. Hafsar Tameesuddin, a Rohingya human rights activist and former refugee who attended it, was asked if it met her expectations. She replied that she anticipated more visibility for refugees and more say in the decisions that affect their lives: "We are the ones who know what we have experienced we need to move forward with our lives."[4]

as not yet confident that the voices of forcibly displaced persons would ly heard when it really matters. Nonetheless, she was reassured by the here were so many people engaged in the issue, representing many constituencies.

er knew there were so many people who cared so much and stood nake a difference," she said.

umber of people is growing, and with it the possibility of lasting hange, which brings us back to how this book began. The ambition e safety, solidarity and solutions for people forced to flee is timeless. s of the Lebanese man offering help to his Syrian neighbours give it sonance. It is both "a matter of history and a matter of heart".

Deng Awuol, 76, first fled his home around 1969, during the First Sudan War. He did so again during the Second Sudan War, which started in 1983. He was then displaced again and is pictured here with his grandchild in Mingkaman, South Sudan in 2014.
© UNHCR/ Andrew McConnell

Endnotes

...Introduction...

Introduction

1   UN General Assembly, Global Compact on Refugees (2 August 2018), UN Doc A/73/12 (Part II).

2   For more on these perspectives and other commentary on the GCR, see the special issue: 'The 2018 Global Compacts on Refugees and Migration', *The International Journal of Refugee Law* 30, no. 4 (December 2018).

3   UNHCR, 'Pledges & Contributions Dashboard', *The Global Compact on Refugees Digital Platform*.

4   UNHCR, *Outcomes of the Global Refugee Forum 2019*, Conference Report, 2020. For more on the 2019 Global Forum, see: '2019 Global Refugee Forum', *UNHCR* website.

5   UNHCR, 'Pledges & Contributions Dashboard'.

6   UNHCR, 'Mandate of the High Commissioner for Refugees and His Office: Executive Summary', Document, *UNHCR* website.

7   For example, statistics on internally displaced persons during the last century are sparse, improving steadily from the 1990s. Refugee statistics are available since the 1950s and have been improved since the 1990s through more disaggregation. In recognition that international attention to internal displacement has been insufficient, and in response to a UN Member State's request, the Secretary-General established a High-Level Panel on Internal Displacement in 2019 to examine the matter. It issued its report in September 2021 with recommendations on how to better respond to internal displacement, in particular where it is protracted, and achieve government-led durable solutions. UN Secretary-General's High-Level Panel on Internal Displacement, *Shining a Light on Internal Displacement: A Vision for the Future*, Report (September 2021).

8   For the mandate of UNRWA, see: 'Who We Are', *UNRWA* website.

9   Institute on Statelessness and Inclusion, *The World's Stateless: Deprivation of Nationality*, Report (March 2020); Institute on Statelessness and Inclusion, *The World's Stateless*, Report (December 2014); Rosa-Luxemburg-Stiftung, *Atlas of the Stateless−Facts and figures about exclusion and displacement* (Berlin: Rosa-Luxemburg-Stiftung, 2020).

10   Convention relating to the Status of Refugees (adopted 25 July 1951), UN Doc A/CONF.2/108.

11   In his closing speech to the Conference of Plenipotentiaries, where the 1951 Convention was negotiated and approved, the President of the Conference, Mr. Larsen, noted that the

All online sources referenced in this book were last accessed in September 2021

outcome may not meet all the 'wishes and ideals' of refugees but it also did not serve 'only the interests of States'. But, he said, it did establish 'a fairly good legal standard and legal status' for refugees. He also predicted it would be the object of study, examination and also criticism. 'Closing Speech of Mr Larson, President of the Conference Plenipotentiaries on the Status of Refugees' made at the 35th meeting, July 1951, *UNHCR* Archives, 'Conference of Plenipotentiaries on Draft Convention Relating to the Status of Refugees, 1951', 4/1/1-G1/12/1/10. For more on the conference, see: 'Conference of Plenipotentiaries on the Status of Refugees and Stateless Persons: Summary Record of the Thirty-Fifth Meeting', UN Doc A/CONF.2/SR.35 (3 December 1951).

12 UNGA, Agenda for Protection (26 June 2002), UN Doc A/AC.96/965/Add.1; UNGA, 'World Humanitarian Summit 2005 Outcome' (24 October 2005), UN Doc A/RES/60/1; UNGA, 'Outcome of the World Humanitarian Summit 2016: Report of the Secretary-General' (23 August 2016), UN Doc A/71/353; UNGA, New York Declaration for Refugees and Migrants (3 October 2016), UN Doc A/RES/71/1; UNGA, Global Compact on Refugees (2018).

13 This includes: 48 million IDPs; 20.7 million refugees under UNHCR's mandate; 5.7 million Palestine refugees under the mandate of UNRWA; 4.1 million asylum-seekers; and 3.9 million Venezuelans displaced abroad. UNHCR, *Global Trends:Forced Displacement in 2020*, Annual Report (2021), p. 2.

14 Ibid., pp. 7, 24.

15 Ibid., p. 20; UNHCR, Refugee Data Finder.

16 UN Security Council, 'Thirteenth report of the Secretary-General on the threat posed by ISIL (Da'esh) to international peace and security and the range of United Nations efforts in support of Member States in countering the threat' (27 July 2021), UN Doc S/2021/682.

17 For updates on global terrorism and measures to address it, see: the United Nations Counter-Terrorism Strategy and other documents available on the websites of the United Nations Office of Counter-Terrorism as well as that of the United Nations Security Council Counter-Terrorism Committee.

18 'Forced displacement growing in Colombia despite peace agreement', Briefing, *UNHCR News* (10 March 2017); David James Cantor, *Returns of Internally Displaced Persons during Armed Conflict: International Law and Its Application in Colombia* (Leiden: Brill Nijhoff, 2018), pp. 186–192.

19 Amelia Cheatham, 'Central America's Turbulent Northern Triangle', Article, *Council on Foreign Relations* website (1 July 2021); David James Cantor, 'As deadly as armed conflict? Gang violence and forced displacement in the Northern Triangle of Central America', *Agenda Internacional* 23, no. 34 (September 2016): pp. 79–89.

20 Many donors now include counter-terrorism clauses in their funding documents to prevent their funding from supporting, even indirectly, terrorist groups. Financial institutions have sought to minimize their risks by refusing to provide financial services to humanitarian agencies operating in areas where terrorist organizations are active. For a review of the legal regime, the tension in the application of counter-terrorism law vis-à-vis international humanitarian law and the dilemmas this poses for humanitarian action, see: David McKeever, 'International Humanitarian Law and Counter-terrorism: Fundamental Values, Conflicting Obligations', *International & Comparative Law Quarterly* 69, no. 1 (January 2020): pp. 43–78.

21 'Counter-terrorism measures must not restrict impartial humanitarian organizations from delivering aid', Statement, *International Committee of the Red Cross* website (12 January 2021); InterAction, 'Detrimental Impacts: How Counter-Terrorism Measures Impede

...Introduction...

Humanitarian Action', Review (April 2021); Fionnuala Ní Aoláin, Special Rapporteur, 'Promotion and protection of human rights and fundamental freedoms while countering terrorism' (3 September 2020), UN Doc A/75/337.

22   UNSC, Res. 2462 (28 March 2019), UN Doc S/RES/2462 (2019); UNSC, Res. 2482 (19 July 2019), UN Doc S/RES/2482 (2019).

23   IPCC, 'Summary for Policymakers', in *Special Report: Global Warming of 1.5ºC* (2018), p. 17.

24   Janani Vivekananda et al., *Shoring up Stability: Addressing Climate and Fragility Risks in the Lake Chad Region*, Report, (Adelphi, May 2019); Saheed Babajide Owonikoko and Jude A. Momodu, 'Environmental degradation, livelihood, and the stability of Chad Basin Region', *Small Wars & Insurgencies* 31, no. 6 (August 2020): pp. 1295–1322.

25   Robert Malley, 'Climate Change Is Shaping the Future of Conflict', Speech, UN Security Council's virtual Arria session on climate and security risks (22 April 2020); Ibrahim Yahaya Ibrahim (ICC), 'Role of climate change in Central Sahel's conflicts: not so clear', *The Africa Report* website (24 April 2020).

26   See discussion in Part II on Climate, conflict and sustaining peace. David G. Timberman, *Violent Extremism and Insurgency in the Philippines: A Risk Assessment*, Report, USAID, (January 2013); Karolina Eklöw, and Florian Krampe, *Climate-related security risks and peacebuilding in Somalia*, Policy Paper, Stockholm International Peace Research Institute (SIPRI) (October 2019); International Crisis Group, *The Insurgency in Afghanistan's Heartland*, Asia Report no. 207 (June 2011); Vivekananda et al., *Shoring up Stability*.

27   Peter Tinti and Tuesday Reitano, *Migrant, Refugee, Smuggler, Saviour* (London: C. Hurst & Co, 2016), pp. 5–6, 264.

28   Julia Litzkow, Bram Frouws, and Roberto Forin, *Smuggling and mixed migration: Insights and key messages drawn from a decade of MMC research and 4Mi data collection*, Briefing Paper (Mixed Migration Centre, June 2021); Philippe Fargues and Marzia Rango, *Migration in West and North Africa and across the Mediterranean: Trends, risks, development and governance* (Geneva: International Organization for Migration (IOM), 2020).

29   Tinti and Reitano, *Migrant, Refugee, Smuggler, Saviour*, p. 273.

30   UNGA, Global Compact for Safe, Orderly and Regular Migration (19 December 2018), UN Doc A/RES/73/195; Duncan Breen, *'On This Journey, No One Cares If You Live or Die' Abuse, protection, and justice along routes between East and West Africa and Africa's Mediterranean coast*, Report, UNHCR and MMC (2020).

31   UNHCR, 'Temporary Measures and Impact on Protection', *COVID-19 Platform* website (2020).

32   UNHCR, *Global Trends: Forced Displacement in 2020*, pp. 5, 47. Arrivals of refugees and asylum-seekers were reduced by an estimated 1.5 million, and only 34,400 refugees out of an estimated 1.4 million in need of resettlement were resettled.

33   Over 4.6 million deaths reported to the World Health Organization as of 16 September 2021.

34   World Bank Group, *Global Economic Prospects: June 2021*, Flagship Report (2021), p. 5. 'Global Recovery Strong but Uneven as Many Developing Countries Struggle with the Pandemic's Lasting Effects', Press Release, *World Bank* News (8 June 2021).

35   World Bank Group, *Global Economic Prospects: June 2021*, p. 30.

36   Ibid., p. 28.

37   Ibid., p. 6.

38 Ibid.; 'Data points to negative impacts of COVID-19 for forcibly displaced women and children', *UNHCR* News (5 June 2021).

39 'United to Reform', *UN* website.

40 UNGA and UNSC, 'Peacebuilding and sustaining peace: Report of the Secretary-General' (30 July 2020), UN Docs A/74/976, S/2020/773; UNGA, 'Review of the implementation of the peace and security reform: Report of the Secretary-General' (20 July 2020), UN Doc A/75/202; Secretary-General's Peacebuilding Fund, *Investing in Peacebuilding Leadership: Strategic Plan Results 2017—2019*, 3 Year Report, (February 2021); UN and World Bank, *Partnership in Crisis-Affected Situations: 2020 UN-WB Partnership Monitoring Report* (February 2021). In addition, the Peacebuilding Commission also reports annually. It is an intergovernmental body, established in 2005 by resolutions of the General Assembly and the Security Council (UN Docs A/RES/60/180 and S/RES/1645(2005)) of December 2005 to advise on integrated strategies for post-conflict peacebuilding and recovery. UNGA and UNSC, 'Report of the Peacebuilding Commission on its fourteenth Session' (12 January 2021), UN Docs A/75/747, S/2021/139; IPCC, *Climate Change 2021: The Physical Science Basis*, Report (August 2021); UN Economic and Social Council, 'Progress towards the Sustainable Development Goals – Report of the Secretary-General' (30 April 2021), UN Doc E/2021/58. See also the Secretary-General's recent report including how to address root causes of displacement: UN, *Our Common Agenda*, Report (2021), p. 41.

41 UNGA, Global Compact on Refugees (2018), paras. 17–19.

42 To be attended by senior government officials and senior representatives of key stakeholder groups, including: international organizations; humanitarian and development actors; international and regional financial institutions; regional organizations; local authorities; civil society, including faith-based organizations; academics and other experts; the private sector; media; host community members and refugees. See: UNHCR, 'What is the High-Level Officials Meeting?', website.

PART I: **The Roots of Asylum**

1 Universal Declaration of Human Rights (adopted 10 December 1948), UN General Assembly Resolution 217(III), Article 14(1). UN Doc A/RES/217(III).

2 Russell Howard Tuttle, 'Human Evolution', *Encyclopædia Britannica* online (3 February 2020); Yuval Noah Harari, *Sapiens: A Brief History of Humankind* (NY: HarperCollins, 2015), pp. 21–22.

3 W. Hilton Johnson, 'Pleistocene Epoch: Pleistocene fauna and flora', *Encyclopædia Britannica* online (30 July 2018).

4 Intergovernmental Panel on Climate Change, *Special Report on the Ocean and Cryosphere in a Changing Climate* (September 2019). The range depends in part on greenhouse gas emissions. The lower rise is if greenhouse gases are sharply reduced and global warming limited to below 2°C, and the larger rise if they continue to increase. IPPC, 'Choices made

...PART I: **The Roots of Asylum...**

now are critical for the future of our ocean and cryosphere', Press Release (25 September 2019).

5   Preslav Peev et al., 'Bulgaria: Sea-Level Change and Submerged Settlements on the Black Sea', in Geoff Bailey et al. (eds.), *The Archaeology of Europe's Drowned Landscapes* vol. 35 (Cham: Springer, 2020), pp. 393–412; Cynthia Stokes Brown, *Big History; From the Big Bang to the Present* (New York: The New Press, 2012), p. 66. She notes that "this astonishing flood became seared in the memory of its survivors as the myth of the world flood; accounts of floods are included in about 500 of the world's mythologies".

6   Anne H. Osborne et al., 'A humid corridor across the Sahara for the migration of early modern humans out of Africa 120,000 years ago', *Proceedings of the National Academy of Sciences of the United States of America* 105, no. 43 (October 2008): pp. 16444–16447; Cynthia Stokes Brown, *Big History*, p. 66.

7   See: Mark Allen, and Terry Jones (eds.), *Violence and Warfare among Hunter-Gatherers* (Abingdon, UK: Routledge, 2014).

8   Harari, *Sapiens*. Harari notes that empires have been "the world's most common form of political organization for the last 2,500 years" and that maintaining them has "usually required the vicious slaughter of large populations and the brutal oppression of everyone who was eft", pp. 191, 193.

9   Linda Rabben, *Sanctuary and Asylum: A Social and Political History* (WA: University of Washington Press, 2016), p. 32; Philip Marfleet, 'Understanding "Sanctuary": Faith and Traditions of Asylum', *Journal of Refugee Studies* 24, no. 3 (July 2011): p. 443; Jan Hallebeek, 'Church Asylum in Late Antiquity, Concession by the Emperor or Competence of the Church?', in E. C. Coppens (ed.), *Secundum Ius. Opstellen aangeboden aan prof. mr. P.L. Nève* (Nijmegen: Gerard Noodt Instituut, 2005), pp. 167, 172–174.

10 For example, churches and religious organizations in Kenya worked with UNHCR and the Red Cross to provide safe spaces for internally displaced persons during the violence following the Kenyan elections 2007–2008. See: Berkley Center for Religion, Peace & World Affairs, *Refugees in Kenya: Role of Faith* (November 2015), p. 34. Churches in Europe have been offering sanctuary from deportation to asylum-seekers in recent years, most famously the Bethel Church in The Hague, Netherlands which held a service for 96 days to protect a family from deportation. Patrick Kingsley, '96 Days Later, Nonstop Church Service to Protect Refugees Finally Ends', *The New York Times* (30 January 2019).

11 Trevor Bryce, *Kingdom of the Hittites* (Oxford: Oxford University Press, 2005), pp. 263–265.

12 Westbrook notes that the granting of asylum did not always guarantee a person's safety, as illustrated in the case of the Mittani chariot commander who in the 14th century BCE received asylum from the Babylonian King who later tried to assassinate him. Raymond Westbrook, 'Personal Exile in the Ancient Near East', *Journal of the American Oriental Society* 128, no. 2 (2008): pp. 317–323.

13 Westbrook, 'Personal Exile in the Ancient Near East': pp. 318–319.

14 Garrett Galvin, *Egypt as a Place of Refuge* (Tübingen: Mohr Siebeck, 2011).

15 Benjamin Gray, 'Exile, Refuge and the Greek Polis: Between Justice and Humanity', *Journal of Refugee Studies* 30, no. 2 (June 2017): p. 190. Gray notes that refugees from beyond the Greek world, although sympathetically portrayed in Greek myths, likely "slipped relatively invisibly into the subordinate categories of metics (resident, registered foreigners) or even

slaves in their host Greek cities, without leaving many marks on the historical record". Benjamin Gray, 'Citizenship as Barrier and Opportunity for Ancient Greek and Modern Refugees', *Humanities* 7, no. 3 (September 2018): p. 3.

16 Gray, 'Exile, Refuge and the Greek Polis': p. 191.

17 Ibid.: pp. 205, 207.

18 Ibid.: pp. 209–211.

19 For example, Acarnanian refugees fled to Athens in the mid-4th century BCE and were afforded the rights to own property, be exempt from foreigner taxes, bring legal suits and, otherwise, generally were protected by the Athenian State. P.J. Rhodes and Robin Osbourne (eds.), *Greek Historical Inscriptions 404–323 BC* (Oxford: Oxford University Press, 2007), pp. 382–383; Gray, 'Exile, Refuge and the Greek Polis: Between Justice and Humanity': p. 197. The practice in Athens was not unique but also apparent in many other city-states of the period, see: Gray, 'Exile, Refuge and the Greek Polis: Between Justice and Humanity' and Gray, 'Citizenship as Barrier and Opportunity'.

20 Ibid.: pp. 8–9.

21 Gray, 'Exile, Refuge and the Greek Polis': p. 202.

22 Ibid.: pp. 193–194. This was a morality play reflecting ideological issues discussed at the time, and other parts of the play reflect additional issues related to asylum debated at that time. In practice, women could be compelled to marry the person chosen by their guardians.

23 Peter J. Heather, 'Refugees and the Roman Empire', *Journal of Refugee Studies* 30, no. 2 (June 2017): pp. 220–242. According to Heather, Imperial Rome received tens of thousands of refugees. Bernard S. Bachrach, 'The Barbarian Hordes That Never Were', *Journal of Military History* 74, no. 3 (July 2010): pp. 901–904.

24 Heather, 'Refugees and the Roman Empire'. Heather examines patterns from the 4th to the 5th centuries describing evidence in the latter period of formal agreements Rome made with refugee groups (which themselves could be multi-ethnic) for settlement in large blocks "with overall political and military leaders intact" (p. 233). These advantageous terms reflected the relative military strength of the refugees, and the Roman motivation to forge alliances on Roman soil.

25 Yuval Noah Harari contends that polytheistic societies, which dominated the ancient world, expected and demanded their gods be venerated but did not require subjected people to give up their own. He contrasts this with the emergence of monotheistic societies more inclined to violently suppress other faiths. Harari, *Sapiens*, pp. 215–216.

26 Scholars do not agree on the number. Jane S. Gerber puts the number at 175,000 in Gerber, *Jews of Spain: A History of the Sephardic Experience* (NY: Simon and Schuster, 1994), p. 140; Jonathan S. Ray suggests the number was closer to 80,000 in Ray, *After Expulsion: 1492 and the Making of Sephardic Jewry* (NY: New York University Press, 2013), p. 39; Henry Kamen suggests it was 40,000–50,000 in Kamen, 'The Mediterranean and the Expulsion of Spanish Jews', *Past & Present* 119, no. 1 (May 1988): p. 1. Susanne Lachenicht notes that Jews were persecuted and expelled from many parts of Europe from the 11th century onward. Lachenicht, 'Refugees and Refugee Protection in the Early Modern Period', *Journal of Refugee Studies* 30, no. 2 (2016): p. 263.

27 Benjamin J. Kaplan, *Divided by Faith: Religious Conflict and the Practice of Toleration in Early Modern Europe* (Cambridge, MA: Bellknap Press, 2007), p. 310. Kaplan states that over 300,000 Muslims were expelled between 1609–1614. Lachenicht, 'Refugees and Refugee Protection': p. 263.

28 This was from a combination of hunger, disease, and violence. For more on this period, see: Philipp Ther, *The Outsiders* (Princeton, NJ: Princeton University Press, 2019), pp. 28–35.

29 Concessions granted by King Henry IV in 1598 and revoked by the Edict of Fontainebleau of 1685. Ibid., p. 28.

30 Aristide R. Zolberg, Astri Suhrke, and Sergio Aguayo, *Escape from Violence: Conflict and the Refugee Crisis in the Developing World* (NY: Oxford University Press, 1989), p. 6.

31 Lachenicht, 'Refugees and Refugee Protection': p. 264.

32 Ibid.: p. 263.

33 Ther, *The Outsiders*, pp. 24–27.

34 Lachenicht, 'Refugees and Refugee Protection': pp. 266–269; Susanne Lachenicht, 'Refugee "nations" and Empire-Building in the Early Modern Period', *Journal of Early Modern Christianity* 6, no. 1 (April 2019): p. 102. In some cases, the privileges refugees enjoyed were commensurate not only with their perceived usefulness but also improved the further distance they were from the capital region. Regarding Russia's welcoming of foreigners, see: Roger P. Bartlett, *Human Capital: The Settlement of Foreigners in Russia 1762–1804*, (Cambridge: Cambridge University Press, 2008), pp. 29, 97.

35 Susanne Lachenicht, 'Refugee "nations" and Empire-Building': p. 102; Lachenicht,' Refugees and Refugee Protection': p. 265. Ther, *The Outsiders*, p. 32, notes that many German states granted specific privileges for Huguenots, such as citizenship, tax abatements and startup loans.

36 Francesca Bregoli and David B. Ruderman, *Connecting Histories: Jews and Their Others in Early Modern Europe, Jewish Culture and Contexts* (Philadelphia, PA: University of Pennsylvania Press, 2019), p. 2; Carl H. Nightingale, *Segregation: A Global History of Divided Cities* (Chicago, IL: University of Chicago Press, 2012), p. 36; Susanne Lachenicht, 'Early modern German states and the settlement of Jews: Brandenburg—Prussia and the Palatinate, sixteenth to nineteenth centuries', *Jewish Historical Studies* 42 (2009): pp. 9–10.

37 Lachenicht, 'Refugees and Refugee Protection': p. 275. Ther also notes instances where they received assistance, such as the support Burghers of Erlangen were compelled to provide to Huguenot refugees in the late 17th century as well as the relief Swiss cantons and churches provided. Ther, *The Outsiders*, p. 32.

38 Lachenicht, 'Refugees and Refugee Protection': p. 265. See also: Ther, *The Outsiders*, pp. 35–36, who also describes the concessions afforded to Sephardi Jews by the Ottomans, p. 32.

39 Lachenicht, 'Refugees and Refugee Protection': p. 267; Susanne Lachenicht, 'Refugee "nations" and Empire-Building': pp. 99–109.

40 Ther writes that the "Sephardim were allowed to continue practicing their faith and operating their own schools and courts". They and many Christians were required to pay their taxes and remain loyal, and this system "functioned well from the fifteenth through the eighteenth centuries". Ther, *The Outsiders*, p. 24.

41 These include "Moravians in Sarepta, Mennonites on the river Volga, Salzburg Lutherans and Calvinists in Transylvania, Jews in Russia, the Balkans and Galicia", Lachenicht, 'Refugees and Refugee Protection': pp. 268–269; Susanne Lachenicht, 'Refugee "nations" and Empire-Building': p. 102.

42 Philipp Blom, *Nature's Mutiny: How the Little Ice Age of the Long Seventeenth Century*

Transformed the West and Shaped the Present (New York: Liveright, 2019), pp. 10–11. There is some controversy on how long it lasted, although there is consensus that the most precipitous and sustained drop was from the late 16th through the late 17th century. While Blom's book focuses on the effects in Europe, he notes that the consequences were also felt across North America, China, India and the Ottoman Empire.

43 Lachenicht, 'Refugees and Refugee Protection': p. 266.

44 Geert Janssen, 'The Republic of Refugees: Early Modern Migrations and the Dutch Experience', *The Historical Journal* 60, no. 1 (November 2016): pp. 1–20. Freedom of conscience and religion were guarantees written into the Union Treaty of 1579, uniting the Dutch northern provinces. Full independence was secured in 1648 with the Treaty of Westphalia.

45 Janssen, 'The Republic of Refugees': p. 15. He also notes that between 30 and 40 per cent of the population in Dutch urban areas were foreign-born.

46 Tamira Combrink and Matthias van Rossum, 'Introduction: the impact of slavery on Europe – reopening a debate', *Slavery & Abolition* 42, no. 1 (2021): pp. 2–3; Filipa Ribeiro da Silva, *Dutch and Portuguese in Western Africa: Empires, Merchants and the Atlantic System, 1580–1674* (Leiden: Brill, 2011), ch. 6.

47 For a review of the British, French, Dutch and Portuguese slave trades, see: Richard B. Allen, 'Satisfying the "Want for Labouring People": European Slave Trading in the Indian Ocean, 1500–1850', *Journal of World History* 21, no. 1 (March 2010): pp. 45–73. For genocides in German Africa, Australia, and North America, see: Dirk Moses and Dan Stone, *Colonialism and Genocide* (Abingdon, UK: Routledge, 2007).

48 Discussed in Phil Orchard, 'It's Always Darkest before the Dawn: Displacement, Institutional Development and the Normative Environment. The Case of the League of Nations and the United Nations', paper presented at the International Conference on Refugees and International Law, Oxford, 15–16 December 2006.

49 This was a motivation for many minority religious groups who settled in the United States and Canada in the 17th to 19th centuries. See: Ninette Kelley and Michael Trebilcock, *The Making of the Mosaic* (Toronto: University of Toronto Press, 2010); David A. Weir, *Early New England: A Covenanted Society* (Grand Rapids, MI: William B. Eerdmans Publishing Co., 2005); Mark Häberlein, 'German Migrants in Colonial Pennsylvania: Resources, Opportunities, and Experience', *The William and Mary Quarterly* 50, no. 3 (1993): pp. 555–574.

50 Coined by historian Eric Hobsbawm, *The Age of Revolution: Europe: 1789–1848* (London: Weidenfeld & Nicolson, 1962).

51 Maya Jasanoff, 'The Other Side of Revolution: Loyalists in the British Empire', *The William and Mary Quarterly* 65, no. 2 (2008): p. 208.

52 Jasanoff, 'The Other Side of the Revolution': p. 220.

53 Friedemann Pestel, 'French Revolution and Migration after 1789', *European History Online* (11 July 2017), para. 1.

54 Ibid., para. 9.

55 Philip Laure and Juliette Reboul (eds.), *French Emigrants in Revolutionised Europe: Connected Histories and Memories, War, Culture and Society, 1750–1850* (London: Palgrave Macmillan, 2019), p. 208; Pestel, 'French Revolution and Migration after 1789', paras. 12–4.

56 Pestel, 'French Revolution and Migration after 1789', para. 26.

57 Laure and Reboul, *French Emigrants in Revolutionised Europe*, p. 6.

58 Parliament of Great Britain, Aliens Act 1793, 33 Geo 3 c 4.

59 Phil Orchard, *A Right to Flee: Refugees, States and the Construction of International*

...PART I: **The Roots of Asylum...**

Cooperation (Cambridge: Cambridge University Press, 2014), p. 83. Orchard also notes that refugees continued to be "lumped within the broader aliens category".

60 Congress of the United States of America, Naturalization Act; Aliens Act; Alien Enemies Act; Sedition Act (1798), Sess. II, Ch. 58, Fifth Congress.

61 Aristide R. Zolberg, 'The Roots of American Refugee Policy', *Social Research: An International Quarterly* 55, no. 4 (Winter 1988): pp. 649–650; R. R. Palmer and David Armitage, *The Age of the Democratic Revolution: A Political History of Europe and America, 1760–1800* (Princeton, NJ: Princeton University Press, 2014), pp. 767–768; Ken Drexler, 'Alien and Sedition Acts: Primary Documents in American History', Research Guide, *Library of Congress* website (27 September 2019); Orchard, *A Right to Flee*, pp. 94–95.

62 Congress of the United States, Aliens, Alien Enemies, Sedition and Naturalization Acts (1798).

63 Theophilus C. Prousis, 'Russian Philorthodox Relief During The Greek War Of Independence', *History Faculty Publications* 17 (University of North Florida, 1985): pp. 33–52. Prousis also points out that while the Tzarist regime did not wish to encourage rebellion, as the "protector of Orthodoxy", there was considerable popular clamoring for the Greeks to be assisted, p. 34.

64 For more on the Greek War of Independence as well as on the factors behind the engagement of regional powers, see: William St Clair, *That Greece Might Still Be Free: The Philhellenes in the War of Independence* (Cambridge: Open Book Publishers, 2008), pp. 29–34, 51–65, 312–317.

65 Ther, *The Outsiders*, pp. 145–146.

66 '"Great" Polish Political Emigration (1831–1870)', in *Encyclopedia of 1848 Revolutions* online (19 October 2004).

67 Ther, *The Outsiders*, pp. 149–156.

68 According to Ther, this marked the end of an "almost sixty-year tradition as a country of exile", ibid., p. 152.

69 Helena Toth, '"Out of Pure Patriotism I Have Taken up this Service": Political Refugees in the American Civil War', *Muster* blog (14 July 2017).

70 Orchard, *A Right to Flee*, pp. 99–100.

71 Başak Kale, 'Transforming an Empire: The Ottoman Empire's Immigration and Settlement Policies in the Nineteenth and Early Twentieth Centuries', *Middle Eastern Studies* 50, no. 2 (2014): p. 262.

72 György Csorba, 'Hungarian Emigrants of 1848–49 in the Ottoman Empire', in Hasan Celâl Güzel, C. Cem Oguz, Osman Karatay (eds.), *The Turks* vol. 4 (Ankara: Yeni Türkiye, 2002), p. 225.

73 Orchard, *A Right to Flee*, p. 96. David FitzGerald notes as well that by the end of the 19th century, while variable in law and practice, "an incipient principle of not returning people into the arms of their enslavers was becoming established among the Western powers". David FitzGerald, 'Refugee Regimes', in Marcelo J. Borges and Madeline Y. Hsu (eds.), *Cambridge History of Global Migrations* vol. II (Cambridge: Cambridge University Press, forthcoming).

74 Article 16 provides that "Political refugees shall be afforded an inviolable asylum; but it is the duty of the nation of refuge to prevent asylees of this kind from committing within its territory any acts which may endanger the public peace of the nation against which the offense was committed." Treaty on International Penal Law, adopted by the First South American Congress on Private International Law in Montevideo (23 January 1889), art. 16. For more on the treaty, see: Anders B. Johnsson, 'Montevideo Treaty on International Penal Law: 1889–1989 – 100 years of Treaty Making on Asylum Issues,' *International Journal of Refugee Law* 1, no. 4 (1989): pp. 554–574.

75 Ther, *The Outsiders*, pp. 152–153.

76 In the 18th century, non-Muslims were organized into three millets: Greek Orthodox; Armenian; and Jewish. See: Efrat Aviv, 'Millet System in the Ottoman Empire', *Oxford Bibliographies* (28 November 2016).

77 Hakan Kirimli, 'Emigrations from the Crimea to the Ottoman Empire during the Crimean War', *Middle Eastern Studies* 44, no. 5 (2008): p. 766; Kale, 'Transforming an Empire': p. 258. For more on the experience of those who were displaced, see: Vladimir Hamed-Troyansky, 'Circassian Refugees and the Making of Amman, 1878–1914', *International Journal of Middle East Studies* 49, no. 4 (November 2017): p. 9.

78 Which could not be sold for 20 years. Kale, 'Transforming an Empire': p. 258.

79 Tax concessions could vary depending on whether one was Muslim and also by location of settlement. Hamed-Troyansky, 'Circassian Refugees': pp. 608, 619; Kirimli, 'Emigrations from the Crimea': p. 766.

80 See: Vladimir Hamed-Troyansky, 'Imperial Refuge: Resettlement of Muslims from Russia in the Ottoman Empire, 1860–1914', PhD Dissertation, Stanford University, 2018, pp. 14–16.

81 Nesim Şeker, 'Forced Population Movements in the Ottoman Empire and the Early Turkish Republic: An Attempt at Reassessment through Demographic Engineering', *European Journal of Turkish Studies* 16 (2013): pp. 4–5. Kemal H. Karpat, 'Ottoman Population Records and the Census of 1881/82–1893', *International Journal of Middle East Studies* 9, no. 3 (1978): p. 246; Stanford Shaw and Ezel Kural Shaw, *History of the Ottoman Empire and Modern Turkey* (Cambridge: Cambridge University Press, 1976), p. 116. The treaty that concluded the Russian-Turkish war redrew the map of the Balkans: It accorded independence to Romania, Serbia and Montenegro, diminished Ottoman territory in Europe, expanded Austria-Hungary, and left many of the participants with simmering grievances that contributed to further conflicts in the next century.

82 Kale, 'Transforming an Empire': p. 254.

83 Dawn Chatty, 'Refugees, Exiles, and Other Forced Migrants in the Late Ottoman Empire', *Refugee Survey Quarterly* 32, no. 2 (June 2013): pp. 42–44. Prior to this time, the settlement of refugees was largely ad hoc and left to the care of local authorities with assistance provided by local, social and religious associations. Fuat Dündar, 'How Migration Institutions "Think"?: The Ottoman-Turkish Case', *Anatoli* 9 (2018): p. 169. Seker describes how the Ottomans approached the settlement of these groups to meet their military, strategic and political interests. Seker, 'Forced Population Movements': p. 5.

84 Kale, 'Transforming an Empire': p. 264. In his review of immigration/refugee institutions of the period, Dündar argues that they were often inefficient in part because they were erected and disbanded frequently (leading to instability), heavily dependent on charismatic leaders, and insufficiently equipped. At the same time, he acknowledges that they helped the Empire receive newcomers on a massive scale and contributed to the building of the modern State. See: Dündar, 'How Migration Institutions "Think"?': pp. 169–182. Violent clashes between refugees and local communities perpetrated by both sides were not infrequent.

85 Dündar, 'How Migration Institutions "Think"?': pp. 171–174, 177–178; Kale, 'Transforming an Empire': p. 265; Chatty, 'Refugees, Exiles, and Other Forced Migrants': p. 44.

...PART I: **The Roots of Asylum...**

86   Hamed-Troyansky's study reveals how refugees in the Ottoman Empire utilized the 1858 Land Code and that it generated market opportunities. He notes that: "The allotment of land to refugees unfolded within the framework of the 1858 Ottoman Land Code, which provided an updated and centralized system governing land ownership." Hamed-Troyansky, 'Circassian Refugees': p. 608. Dündar, 'How Migration Institutions "Think"?': p. 170–172.

87   Dündar, 'How Migration Institutions "Think"?': pp. 181–182.

88   Hamid Troyansky notes that in the northern Balkans, there was lower State support for land and subsidies, which contributed to Muslim-Christian clashes and eventually led to the Russo-Ottoman War. In central Anatolia, there was also lower State investment, resulting in economic stagnation. In contrast, among successful settlements were those of the Circassians whose villages in the southern Levant flourished and whose industry boosted regional trade and attracted outside investment. He also credits the Ottoman support for refugee settlement as enabling refugees to establish three of the four major cities in modern Jordan, including the capital city of Amman. Hamed-Troyansky, 'Imperial Refuge', pp. iv–v, 3; Hamed-Troyansky, 'Circassian Refugees': p. 606.

89   Ther, *The Outsiders*, p. 44. Ther also notes that Jewish refugees had great difficulty finding a State that was willing to accept them. In regard to the United States, Jewish organizations supported the difficult resettlement procedures, which required good health, the ability to care financially for themselves and payment for the journey. Many could not meet these strict requirements and, absent a port of refuge, eventually had to return to Russia.

90   Charles Keely examines how States with more than one national group have approached nation-building and identifies four ways: i) creating a supranational identity that is separate from any constituent group; (ii) creating a national identity based on one dominant group and requiring others to conform; (iii) expelling or transferring those not of the dominant group; (iv) making confederation arrangements. He notes that, while all four patterns include the possibility of conflict among groups, which can lead to conflict and forced displacement, those that require the destruction or suppression of national identity are most likely to be met with resistance and a high risk of conflict. Charles B. Keely, 'How Nation-States Create and Respond to Refugee Flows', *The International Migration Review* 30, no. 4 (1996): pp. 1053–1054.

91   Mark Biondich, 'The Balkan Wars: violence and nation-building in the Balkans, 1912–13', *Journal of Genocide Research* 18, no. 4 (2016): pp. 389–400. Greece, Serbia and Montenegro expanded appreciably, the Balkan League collapsed, and the Serbia/Russia alliance deepened, to the alarm of Austria-Hungary and Germany.

92   The number of Muslim refugees following the First Balkan War (1912) is estimated at 400,000 in Biondich, 'The Balkan Wars': p. 392. See also: Berna Pekesen, 'Expulsion and Emigration of the Muslims from the Balkans', *European History Online* (7 March 2012), para. 7; Nedim İpek, 'The Balkans, War, and Migration', in M. Hakan Yavuz and Isa Blumi (eds.), *War and Nationalism: The Balkan Wars, 1912–1913, and their Sociopolitical Implications* (Salt Lake City, UT: University of Utah Press, 2013), p. 649.

93   Peter Gatrell, *The Making of the Modern Refugee* (Oxford: Oxford University Press, 2013), p. 24.

94   Gatrell, *The Making of the Modern Refugee*, p. 23.

95   İpek, 'The Balkans, War, and Migration', pp. 645–646.

96 According to İpek, the Ottoman State's policies to incentivize refugee return were designed to result in returnees' self-reliance and contribution to the state treasury as well as to populate certain areas more densely. Returnees would farm state owned land and unoccupied or abandoned territories and generate taxable income for the state. İpek, 'The Balkans, War, and Migration', pp. 650–652.

97 İpek, 'The Balkans, War, and Migration', pp. 651–652; Eyal Ginio, 'Mobilizing the Ottoman Nation during the Balkan Wars (1912–1913): Awakening from the Ottoman Dream', *War in History* 12, no. 2 (2005): pp. 165–167.

98 Gatrell, *The Making of the Modern Refugee*, p. 25.

99 Steven Mintz, 'Historical Context: The Global Effect of World War I', *Gilder Lehrman Institute of American History* website.

100 Peter Gatrell, 'Refugees', *1914–1918 Online: International Encyclopedia of the First World War* (8 October 2014); Zolberg, Suhrke, and Aguayo, *Escape from Violence*, p. 18.

101 See, for example: Harald Wixforth, 'The Economic Consequences of the First World War', *Contemporary European History* 11, no. 3 (August 2002): pp. 477–488; John Singleton, '"Destruction...and misery": the First World War' in Michael J. Oliver and Derek H. Aldcroft (eds.), *Economic Disasters of the Twentieth Century* (Cheltenham, UK: Edward Elgar, 2007); Apocalypse: 10 Lives, 'The Consequences of the First World War'.

102 Including Austria, Czechoslovakia, Estonia, Hungary, Latvia, Lithuania, Poland and Yugoslavia.

103 Included in these forced relocations were Jews, Poles, Germans, and Baltic farmers. Gatrell, *The Making of the Modern Refugee*, p. 30.

104 Peter Gatrell, 'War, refugeedom, revolution: understanding Russia's refugee crisis, 1914–1917', *Cahiers du Monde Russe*, 58, 1/2 (2017): pp. 123–146. The Russian Civil War broke out just as WWI came to an end and created further waves of refugee movements, as well as conflicts between factions — the White Army fought the Red Army, and nationalist groups across the Baltic fought both, as well as further struggles across the Caucasian and Asiatic regions of Russia. Ibid., p. 138.

105 Gatrell estimates that the number of internally displaced persons in Russia reached 3–7 million people between 1915 and 1917 alone. Peter Gatrell, 'Refugees and Forced Migrants during the First World War', *Immigrants & Minorities* 26, no. 1/2 (March/July 2008): p. 86. Skran notes that Russian refugee numbers are hard to determine, but that by 1922 there were an estimated 900,000 concentrated in European countries bordering the former Russian Empire. There were over a hundred thousand in the Far East. Skran, *Refugees in Inter-War Europe: The Emergence of a Regime* (Oxford: Oxford University Press, 2011), pp. 35–36.

106 Regarding displacement during WWI, see: Ther, *The Outsiders*, p. 57.

107 Martin Gilbert, 'Twentieth-Century Genocides', in Jay Winter (ed.), *America and the Armenian Genocide of 1915* (Cambridge: Cambridge University Press, 2004), p 19; Jay Winter, 'The Armenian Genocide in the context of total war' in *America and the Armenian Genocide of 1915*, p. 48; Henry Morgenthau, *Ambassador Morgenthau's Story* (Garden City, NY: Doubleday, Page & Company, 1918). Armenian lands were used to resettle the refugees from the Balkan Wars.

108 Skran, *Refugees in Inter-War Europe*, p. 45. Syria, Greece and France were among the main receiving countries.

109 Gatrell notes that they built "on the foundations of a common sense of loss and the need for collective effort to regain what has been forfeited in wartime", *The Making of the*

...PART I: **The Roots of Asylum...**

Modern Refugee, p. 43. For difficulties faced by refugees in Italy, see: Matteo Ermacora, 'Assistance and Surveillance: War Refugees in Italy, 1914–1918', *Contemporary European History* 16, no. 4 (November 2007).

110 Gatrell, *The Making of the Modern Refugee*, p. 40. Gatrell notes, for example, "Arthur Ringland who was instrumental in the creation of CARE, and Maurice Pate, who helped to found UNICEF". In regard to those who became political leaders, see: Gatrell, 'Refugees and Forced Migrants': p. 103.

111 Skran, *Refugees in Inter-War Europe*, p. 38.

112 Skran, *Refugees in Inter-War Europe*, pp. 38–39. Skran writes that of the estimated 900,000 Russian refugees in 1922, nearly half remained in an insecure status 20 years later.

113 At the end of the War, and on behalf of the League, Nansen was in charge of the exchange of over 400,000 prisoners of war between the former Austria-Hungary, Germany and Russia. In 1921, he coordinated relief efforts for the millions of people facing death by starvation during the famine in the Soviet Union. For all his efforts, he was awarded the Nobel Peace Prize in 1922, The Nobel Prize, 'Fridtjof Nansen: Facts', website. On his character, see: Skran, who writes that his "personality embodied the humanitarian principle of the international refugee regime" in *Refugees in Inter-War Europe*, p. 288.

114 States were reluctant to extend refugee status beyond specified groups. See: Skran *Refugees in Inter-War Europe*, pp. 114–116.

115 Katy Long, *The Point of No Return: Refugees, Rights, and Repatriation* (Oxford: Oxford University Press, 2013), p. 55.

116 Skran, *Refugees in Inter-War Europe*, pp. 152–154. Only 6,000 Russian refugees were repatriated. Long, *The Point of No Return*, p. 56.

117 In the 19th century, Argentina, Australia, Brazil, Canada, and the United States were among the main immigrant-receiving countries. For a comparative review, see: Ashley S. Timmer and Jeffrey G. Williamson, *Racism, Xenophobia or Markets? The Political Economy of Immigration Policy Prior to the Thirties*, NBER Working Paper Series: Working Paper 5867 (Cambridge, MA: National Bureau of Economic Research, 1996); Kelley and Trebilcock, *The Making of the Mosaic*; Skran, *Refugees in Inter-War Europe*, pp. 22–23, National Museum of Australia, 'White Australia Policy', website; Diego Acosta Arcarazo, 'Immigration and wealth in 19th century South America', Expert Comment, DOC Research Institute (29 November 2018); Diego Acosta Arcarazo, *The National versus the Foreigner in South America: 200 Years of Migration and Citizenship Law* (Cambridge: Cambridge University Press, 2018), pp. 92–101.

118 Among the major immigration-receiving countries, attracting immigrants was initially critical to settling the land and there were sizable inducements to foreigners and relatively few barriers. Tighter restrictions emerged due to a number of factors. Available land for settlement was diminishing and growing industrialization was tempering the former large demand for labour. Trade unions were also growing in strength and insisted on preventing foreign workers from undermining wages. Additionally, countries saw immigration as helping to define the national character and build a homogeneous society based on common values, traditions and institutions.

119 See, for example: League of Nations, Arrangement Relating to the Legal Status of Russian and Armenian Refugees (signed 30 June 1928), League of Nations Treaty Series vol. LXXXIX, no. 2005.

120 Susan Martin discusses some of these barriers, while noting the passport's significance in recognizing that refugees had a specific juridical status. Susan F. Martin, *International Migration: Evolving Trends from the Early Twentieth Century to the Present* (New York: Cambridge University Press, 2014), pp. 51–56. See also: James Hathaway, 'The Evolution of Refugee Status in International Law: 1920–1950', *International & Comparative Law Quarterly* 33, no. 2 (April 1984): pp. 351–352.

121 Thompson wrote this in 1938 and is quoted in Skran, *Refugees in Inter-War Europe*, p. 122.

122 Ibid., p. 105.

123 Ibid., p. 192. These are those the ILO directly placed. It claimed to have reduced the unemployment of able-bodied Armenian and Russian refugees directly and indirectly by 50 per cent: from 400,000 to 200,000, p. 192.

124 Skran, *Refugees in Interwar Europe*, pp. 43–44; League of Nations, The Settlement of the Greek Refugees: Scheme for an International Loan. Protocol (30 October 1924), C. 524. M. 187. 1924. II, p. 8.

125 Ellinor Morack, 'Refugees, Locals and "The" State: Property Compensation in the Province of Izmir Following the Greco-Turkish Population Exchange of 1923', *Journal of the Ottoman and Turkish Studies Association* 2, no. 1 (2015): pp. 147–166.

126 The Convention concerning the Exchange of Greek and Turkish Populations formed part of the 1923 Treaty of Lausanne signed between the British Empire, France, Greece, Italy, Japan, Romania, and the Serb-Croat-Slovene State on the one side, and Turkey on the other "to bring to a final close the state of war which has existed in the East since 1914". Convention Concerning the Exchange of Greek and Turkish Populations (signed 25 August 1923), LNTS vol. XXXII, no. 806.

127 Skran, *Refugees in Interwar Europe*, pp. 44. A similar exchange took place between Greece and Bulgaria under the Treaty of Neuilly, whereby 45,000 Greeks inside Bulgaria left for Greece and 92,000 of 139,000 Bulgarians in Greece left for Bulgaria.

128 Convention Concerning the Exchange of Greek and Turkish Populations (1923); Al Jazeera World, 'The Great Population Exchange between Turkey and Greece', Video (10:43) (28 February 2018).

129 Gatrell, *The Making of the Modern Refugee*, pp. 67–70; Kontogiorgi, *Population Exchange in Greek Macedonia: The Rural Settlement of Refugees, 1922–1930* (Oxford: Oxford University Press, 2006), pp. 166–168, 338.

130 Gatrell, *The Making of the Modern Refugee*, pp. 64, 70.

131 The loan was for GDP 10 million. The RSC was not permitted to carry out "relief" or charity assistance unless it served the core goal of self-reliance of the refugee population. League of Nations, 'The Settlement of the Greek Refugees' (1924), art. XV, p. 26.

132 Martin Hill, 'The League of Nations and the Work of Refugee Settlement and Financial Reconstruction in Greece, 1922–1930', *Weltwirtschaftliches Archiv* 34 (1931): p. 269.

133 Elie Murard and Seyhun Orcad Sakalli, 'Mass Refugee Inflow and Long-run Prosperity: Lessons from the Greek Population Resettlement', Discussion Paper 11613, IZA Institute of Labor Economics (June 2018), p. 5. Refugees in urban areas, comprising approximately 50 per cent of the refugee population, were assisted with housing but no other means of support. They were expected to find work, particularly in the industrial sector. Murard and Sakalli, 'Mass Refugee Inflow and Long-run Prosperity', p. 8.

134 John Hope Simpson, 'The Work of the Greek Refugee Settlement Commission', *Journal of the Royal Institute of International Affairs* 8, no. 6 (1929): pp. 590–591, 596; Gatrell, *The Making of the Modern Refugee*, p. 66. Lack of ongoing investments in the health sector, however, meant that the positive impact was not sustained beyond several years. Kontogiorgi, *Population Exchange in Greek Macedonia*, p. 276.

135 Simpson, 'The Work of the Greek Refugee Settlement Commission': pp. 599–600.

136 Skran, *Refugees in Inter-War Europe*, p. 164.

137 Indicated by higher earnings, higher levels of household wealth, greater educational attainment, as well as larger financial and manufacturing sectors, see: Murard and Sakalli, 'Mass Refugee Inflow and Long-Run Prosperity'.

138 Ibid., pp. 3, 36–38. The study acknowledges empirical challenges in measuring impact. In 2017, the United Nations General Assembly requested UNHCR to "coordinate an effort to measure the impact arising from hosting, protecting and assisting refugees, with a view to assessing gaps in international cooperation and promoting burden- and responsibility-sharing that is more equitable, predictable and sustainable, and to begin reporting on the results to Member States in 2018". UN General Assembly, Resolution 72/150, Office of the United Nations High Commissioner for Refugees (19 December 2017), UN Doc A/RES/72/150, para 20. This was further taken up in: UN General Assembly, Global Compact on Refugees (2 August 2018), UN Doc A/73/12 (Part II), para. 103. UNHCR issued its first report on 1 July 2020. UNHCR, 'Measuring the Impact of Hosting, Protecting and Assisting Refugees', Progress Report, 1 July 2020.

139 See discussion in Part IV.

140 Skran, *Refugees in Inter-War Europe*, pp. 167–170.

141 Skran, *Refugees in Inter-War Europe*, pp. 177–82. In regard to the loans, they were more successful with urban-based refugees. Farmers had difficulties meeting the repayments in part due to crop failures in the mid-1930s and some political unrest in certain areas. (p. 181) An initial proposal to support loans to Armenians within Russian territories failed to gain traction as allied countries were not keen to invest in areas under Soviet control. Ibid., pp. 171–176.

142 The Office was established following the death of High Commissioner Nansen in 1930. It was responsible for supervising the implementation of the League's work in regard to specific groups of refugees, namely Russian refugees and Christian refugees from the former Ottoman Empire. It eventually was merged into the Office of the High Commissioner for Refugees in 1938. On the representation of refugees, see: Ibid., pp. 83–84.

143 Louise W. Holborn, 'The Legal Status of Political Refugees, 1920–1938', *The American Journal of International Law* 32, no. 4 (1938): p. 689.

144 League of Nations, Convention relating to the International Status of Refugees (signed 28 October 1933), LNTS vol. CLIX, no. 3663.

145 Convention relating to the International Status of Refugees (1933), arts. 2, 3, 6, 7, respectively. The United Kingdom did not agree to the prohibition on expulsion at the border and applied a reservation in this regard. Gilbert Jaeger, 'On the History of the International Protection of Refugees', *International Review of the Red Cross* 83, no. 843 (September 2001): p. 730.

146 Convention relating to the International Status of Refugees (1933) arts. 8, 10, and 12 respectively.

147 Convention relating to the International Status of Refugees (1933), art. 15.

148 Tristan Harley, 'Refugee Participation Revisited: The Contributions of Refugees to Early

International Refugee Law and Policy', Reference Paper for the 70th Anniversary of the 1951 Refugee Convention, UNHCR (October 2021) .

149 Russians, Armenians, Assyrians, some Turks, and Assyro-Chaldeans.

150 Belgium, Bulgaria, Czechoslovakia, Denmark, France, Italy, Norway, and the United Kingdom. Convention relating to the International Status of Refugees (1933).

151 'Spanish Civil War (1936–39)', in *Dictionary of World History* (Oxford: Oxford University Press, 2006).

152 Gatrell estimates 300,000 refugees fled to France alone by October 1937 in: *The Making of the Modern Refugee*, p. 73.

153 At this point France had received 70,000 refugees from Spain. Skran, *Refugees in Inter-War Europe*, p. 58. Vicki Caron, 'Unwilling Refuge: France and the Dilemma of Illegal Immigration, 1933–1939', in Frank Caestecker and Bob Moore (eds.), *Refugees from Nazi Germany and the Liberal European States* (New York: Berghahn Books, 2010).

154 Gatrell, *The Making of the Modern Refugee*, p. 73.

155 Scott Soo, *The routes to exile: France and the Spanish Civil War refugees, 1939–2009* (Manchester, UK: University of Manchester Press, 2013), pp. 26–27, 35, 59; Ther, *The Outsiders*, p. 164. Geneviève Dreyfus-Armand, 'When Spain's Refugees Turned to France', *Le Monde Diplomatique* (May 2017).

156 Dreyfus-Armand, 'When Spain's Refugees Turned to France'. According to Soo, the camp populations had been reduced from 275,000 to 5,000 by the close of 1940. Soo, *The routes to exile*, p. 126.

157 Ther, *The Outsiders*, pp. 165-166. Among those who remained, many fell under German occupation during WWII, were detained in concentration camps and used as forced labour. 'Spanish Civil War', *Holocaust Encyclopedia website*; Dreyfus-Armand, 'When Spain's Refugees Turned to France'; Soo, *The routes to exile*, pp. 80–81. Gatrell describes how following the war their situation remained precarious. Gatrell, *The Making of the Modern Refugee*, pp. 75–76.

158 Rosy Rickett, 'Refugees of the Spanish Civil War and those they left behind: personal testimonies of departure, separation and return since 1936', PhD diss., University of Manchester, 2014, pp. 53, 59; Ther, *The Outsiders*, pp. 165–166.

159 Alicia Alted Vigil, 'Repatriation or Return? The Difficult Homecoming of the Spanish Civil War Exiles', in Sharif Gemie, Scott Soo and Norry LaPorte (eds.), *Coming Home? Vol. 1: Conflict and Return Migration in the Aftermath of Europe's Twentieth-Century Civil Wars* (Newcastle upon Tyne: Cambridge Scholars Publishing, 2013), pp. 22–26; Soo, *The routes to exile*, pp. 22–26; Gatrell, *The Making of the Modern Refugee*, p. 74; Karl D. Qualls, 'From Niños to Soviets? Raising Spanish Refugee Children in House No 1, 1937–1951', Paper 43, *Dickinson College Faculty Publications* (2014), p. 2.

160 Skran, *Refugees in Inter-War Europe*, pp. 48–53.

161 Ibid., p. 27.

162 His office was separate from the League, and he reported to the Commission's Governing body and not the League. For more on this and McDonald, see: Skran, *Refugees in Inter-War Europe*, pp. 197–198, 230.

163 Greg Burgess, *The League of Nations and the Refugees from Nazi Germany: James G. McDonald and Hitler's Victims*, (London: Bloomsbury Academic, 2016), pp. 32–33.

164 James G. McDonald, *Refugees and Rescue: The Diaries and Papers of James G. McDonald, 1935–1945*, eds. Richard Breitman, Barbara McDonald Stewart, and Severin Hochberg (Bloomington, Washington, D.C: Indiana University Press, 2009); Greg

Burgess, *The League of Nations and the Refugees from Nazi Germany*, pp. 161–162.

165 Skran, *Refugees in Inter-War Europe*, p. 200.

166 Ibid., p. 214.

167 Holborn, 'The Legal Status of Political Refugees, 1920–1938': pp. 694–695.

168 League of Nations, Convention concerning the Status of Refugees coming from Germany (signed 10 February 1938), LNTS vol. CXCII, no. 4461. For example, it had a qualified non-expulsion provision "without prejudice to the measures which may be taken within any territory", art. 5.2. It afforded refugees access to the courts, the right to work under specific conditions, and the most favourable treatment accorded to foreign nationals in regard to industrial accidents, social welfare and access to education, arts. 8, 9, 11, 14, respectively.

169 Belgium and the United Kingdom. Convention concerning the Status of Refugees coming from Germany (1938), Appendix.

170 Yad Vashem. The World Holocaust Remembrance Center, 'Decisions taken at the Evian Conference on Jewish Refugees, July 1938', website; Closed Borders, 'The International Conference at Evian', website.

171 Skran, *Refugees in Inter-War Europe*, pp. 209–214. At a conference in Bermuda in 1943, the Intergovernmental Committee's mandate was broadened from seeking resettlement for refugees from Nazi Germany to all European refugees. As Susan Martin notes, however, no renewed effort to lower barriers to entry for Jewish refugees was made by the allied powers. They refused to negotiate with Germany to seek the release of Jewish refugees because they did not want to be flooded by refugees nor take any action that would interfere with the war effort. Susan F. Martin, *International Migration*, p. 60.

172 As one Berlin publication, *Der Weltkampf* observed: "We are saying openly that we do not want the Jews while the democracies keep on claiming that they are willing to receive them – then leave the guests out in the cold. Aren't we savages better men after all?" Quoted in Kelley and Trebilcock, *The Making of the Mosaic*, p. 256.

173 Skran, *Refugees in Inter-War Europe*, p. 222. Skran estimates that half of those who immigrated from Germany were assisted by private organizations. Emma Haddad, *The Refugee in International Society: Between Sovereigns* (Cambridge: Cambridge University Press, 2008); Ronald C. Newton, 'Indifferent Sanctuary: German-Speaking Refugees and Exiles in Argentina, 1933–1945', *Journal of Interamerican Studies and World Affairs* 24, no. 4 (November 1982): pp. 395–420; Gao Bei, 'The Chinese Nationalist Government's Policy toward European Jewish Refugees during World War II', *Modern China* 37, no. 2 (March 2011): pp. 202–237. See also: 'Refugees', *Holocaust Encyclopedia* website.

174 Stephen MacKinnon, 'Refugee Flight at the Outset of the Anti-Japanese War' in Diane Lary and Stephen MacKinnon (eds.), *Scars of War: The Impact of Warfare on Modern China* (Vancouver, Canada: UBC Press, 2001), p. 122.

175 Steven I. Dutch, 'The Largest Act of Environmental Warfare in History', *Environmental and Engineering Geoscience* 15, no. 4 (November 2009): pp. 287–297; Gatrell, *The Making of the Modern Refugee*, p. 181.

176 Gatrell, *The Making of the Modern Refugee*, p. 181.

177 MacKinnon, 'Refugee Flight at the Outset of the Anti-Japanese War', p. 122; Gatrell, *The Making of the Modern Refugee*, p. 178. According to Gatrell, "upwards of 30 million [were] displaced by 1939", p. 180.

178 For more on the organizing in Wuhan and the legacy, see: Ibid, pp. 127–133. For information on local relief efforts and Chinese charitable organizations, see: Hanna B. Krebs, 'Responsibility, legitimacy, morality: Chinese humanitarianism in historical perspective', HPG Working Paper, Overseas Development Institute (September 2014), pp. 9, 13; Pichamon Yeophantong 'Understanding humanitarian action in East and Southeast Asia: a historical perspective', HPG Working Paper, Overseas Development Institute (February 2014), p. 9.

179 Skran, *Refugees in Inter-War Europe*. She provides a summary in the final chapter, pp. 261–296.

180 Emma Haddad, *The Refugee in International Society*, p. 129. Gatrell estimates over 40 million, Gatrell, *The Making of the Modern Refugee*, p. 89.

181 Haddad, *The Refugee in International Society*, p. 129. Haddad recounts that the civilian refugees fled advancing German armies including from Poland, Belgium, the Netherlands, Luxembourg, France, Yugoslavia, and the Soviet Union.

182 Ther, *The Outsiders*, p. 79.

183 Haddad, *The Refugee in International Society*, p. 129. Ther writes that overall the Germans "uprooted at least two million people, and deported three million Poles as forced laborers. Russians, Ukrainians and Serbs suffered similar fates". Ther, *The Outsiders*, p. 80.

184 Gatrell, *The Making of the Modern Refugee*, p. 92.

185 Rebecca Manley, 'The Perils of Displacement: The Soviet Evacuee between Refugee and Deportee', *Contemporary European History* 16, no. 4 (November 2007): pp. 495–509.

186 Mark Wyman, *DPs: Europe's Displaced Persons, 1945–51* (Ithaca, NY: Cornell University Press, 1998), p. 17.

187 Notably Egypt, Palestine, Syria, Iran as well as Uganda, Tanzania and India, among others. See, for example: Ishaan Tharoor, 'The forgotten story of European refugee camps in the Middle East', *The Washington Post* (2 June 2016); Evan Taparata and Kuang Keng Kuek Ser, 'During WWII, European refugees fled to Syria. Here's what the camps were like', *The World* (26 April 2016).

188 William I. Hitchcock, *The Bitter Road to Freedom: A New History of the Liberation of Europe*, (New York: Free Press, 2009), Ch. 7 and 9; David Nasaw, *The Last Million* (New York: Penguin Press, 2020), pp. 9–12.

189 Wyman, *DPs: Europe's Displaced Persons*, pp. 22–23, 34–35.

190 For more on displacement in Burma and to and within India, see: Yasmin Khan, *India at War: The Subcontinent and the Second World War* (New York: Oxford University Press, 2015).

191 Richard Overy, *The Oxford Illustrated History of World War Two* (Oxford: Oxford University Press, 2015), pp. 35, 322 and 337.

192 UNHCR, *The State of The World's Refugees 2000: Fifty Years of Humanitarian Action* (Oxford: Oxford University Press, 2000), p. 59.

193 Prashant Bharadwaj, Asim Ijaz Khwaja, and Atif R. Mian, 'The Big March: Migratory Flows after the Partition of India', *Economic and Political Weekly* 43 (August 2008): pp. 1–5; L. A. Kosinski and K. M. Elahi (eds.), *Population Redistribution and Development in South Asia* (Heidelberg: Springer, 2013).

194 The exact death toll is disputed, but most scholars place the range at 0.2–2 million people. For a discussion of the different estimations, see: Gyanendra Pandey, *Remembering Partition: Violence, Nationalism and History in India* (Cambridge: Cambridge University Press, 2003), pp. 89–91.

195 Bharadwaj, Khwaja, and Mian, 'The Big March'.

196 Its initial budget in 1943 was $2 billion of which the United States agreed to pay $1.3 billion. Contributions reached close to $4 billion by 1946. Ben Shephard, *The Long Road Home:*

...PART I: **The Roots of Asylum...**

The Aftermath of the Second World War (New York: Anchor Books, 2012), pp. 154–157; UNRRA, *50 Facts about UNRRA* (New York: UNRRA, 1947).

197 The vast bulk of UNRRA's resources were spent in central, eastern and southern Europe. Over $2.5 billion of shipments were directed there, as compared to just $500 million to the rest of the world. Jessica Reinisch, '"Auntie UNRRA" at the Crossroads', *Past & Present* 218, suppl. 8 (2013): p. 73. On this as well as UNRRA's development work in China, Reinisch cites George Woodbridge, *UNRRA: The History of the United Nations Relief and Rehabilitation Administration* vol. 3 (New York: Columbia University Press, 1950), pp. 103, 413–414.

198 Colin Bundy, 'Migrants, refugees, history and precedents', *Forced Migration Review* 51 (January 2016): p. 6.

199 Louise W. Holborn, *The International Refugee Organization: A Specialized Agency of the United Nations: Its History and Work, 1946–1952* (London: Oxford University Press, 1956).

200 USA and USSR, Agreement Relating to Prisoners of War and Civilians Liberated by Forces Operating Under Soviet Command and Forces Operating Under United States of America Command (signed 11 February 1945). The agreement provided that all Soviet citizens liberated by force under United States command and all United States citizens liberated under Soviet command "will, without delay after their liberation, be separated from enemy prisoners of war and will be maintained separately from them in camps or points of concentration until they have been handed over to the Soviet or United States authorities", art. 1. According to Hitchcock, the United States was so keen to see its nationals home that it agreed to the Soviet insistence that the return of Soviet citizens be with or without their consent. Hitchcock, *The Bitter Road to Freedom*, Ch. 7. As one lawyer for the British Foreign Office noted: "In due course, all those with whom the Soviet authorities desire to deal must be handed over to them, and we are not concerned with the fact that they may be shot or otherwise more harshly dealt with than they might be under English law." Shephard, *The Long Road Home*, p. 80.

201 Ibid., p. 80.

202 Shephard, *The Long Road Home*, p. 85; Ther, *The Outsiders*, p. 175.

203 Reinisch also notes that Central and Eastern European countries also began to resent the dominance of the United States and the United Kingdom and, in particular, their control over relief supplies. Jessica Reinisch, 'Internationalism in Relief: the Birth (and Death) of UNRRA', *Past & Present* 210, suppl. 6 (2011): pp. 283–284.

204 Reinisch, '"Auntie UNRRA" at the Crossroads': pp. 87–88. Reinisch elaborates further on the change of policy and also notes how many United States citizens who worked for UNRRA were later made to appear at hearings of the House Un-American Activities Committee (p. 97). Evidence that the Communist Governments of Yugoslavia and Poland were privileging pro-government supporters for the UNRRA aid further underscored mistrust of the institution, especially within Republican circles. So too did the fact that some UNRRA provisions were being sold to fund other needs. See also: Shephard, *The Long Road Home*, pp. 148–9, 263.

205 It provided that "the transfer to Germany of German populations, or elements thereof, remaining in Poland, Czechoslovakia and Hungary, will have to be undertaken". Protocol of the Proceedings of the Potsdam Conference (1 August 1945), art. XII.

206 Enmity was deeper than the war. Ben Shephard notes that in Czechoslovakia for example, there was a feeling among Czechs that they had long been treated as second-class citizens, subordinated to German culture and religion and all but dominated by a German elite dating back hundreds of years. Shephard, *The Long Road Home*, p. 123.

207 Shephard, *The Long Road Home*, p. 125.

208 R. M. Douglas, *Orderly and Humane: The Expulsion of the Germans after the Second World War*, (New Haven, CT: Yale University Press, 2012), p. 1; Federal Ministry for Expellees, Refugees and War Victims, *Facts Concerning the Problem of the German Expellees and Refugees* (Bonn: Federal Ministry for Expellees, Refugees and War Victims, 1966).

209 Philipp Ther and Ana Siljak (eds.), *Redrawing Nations: Ethnic Cleansing in East-Central Europe 1944–1948* (Lanham, MD: Rowman & Littlefield Publishers, 2001), pp. 53–57; Theodora Dragostinova and David Gerlach, 'Demography and Population Movements' in Irina Livezeanu and Árpád von Klimó (eds.), *The Routledge History of East Central Europe since 1700* (Routledge Handbooks Online, 2017) pp. 155–156. According to Gatrell, 250,000 ethnic Turks were expelled from Bulgaria. Gatrell, *The Making of the Modern Refugee*, pp. 92–93.

210 According to Hitchcock, within two years of the conclusion of the war, around 250,000 Jewish refugees travelled west to Austria, Germany and Italy, mostly from Poland and many with the hope of eventually reaching Palestine. Hitchcock, *The Bitter Road to Freedom*, Ch. 9.

211 Gatrell, *The Making of the Modern Refugee*, p. 97.

212 United Nations, Constitution of the International Refugee Organization, (Opened for signature 15 December 1946), UNTS vol. 18, no. 283.

213 Ibid.

214 Hathaway, 'The Evolution of Refugee Status in International Law': pp. 374–376.

215 Post-war resettlement is discussed in Part III.

216 In 1945, United States President Harry Truman commissioned a fact-finding mission to Europe. It was headed by Earl G. Harrison, the dean of the University of Pennsylvania Law School and a former commissioner of immigration and naturalization. Harrison reported that "as matters now stand, we appear to be treating the Jews as the Nazis treated them except that we do not exterminate them. They are in concentration camps in large numbers under our military guard instead of SS troops". Hitchcock, *The Bitter Road to Freedom*, Ch. 9. Hitchcock provides a detailed account of the conditions in the displaced persons camps during the immediate aftermath of the war. See also: Wyman, *DPs: Europe's Displaced Persons*, pp. 43–44.

217 Hitchcock, *The Bitter Road to Freedom*, ch. 9; David Nasaw, *The Last Million*, pp. 358–360; Gatrell, *The Making of the Modern Refugee*, p. 122.

218 UN, 'The Declaration by the United Nations', in *United Nations Yearbook 1946–1947* (Lake Success, NY: United Nations Department of Information, 1947), part I, sec. 1,ch. A, p. 1.

219 UN, Charter of the United Nations (26 June 1945).

220 ECOSOC was specifically asked to form a Committee to consider the issue of refugees and write a report for presentation to the GA. UNGA, 'Question of refugees' (12 February 1946), UN Doc A/RES/8(I); UNGA, Constitution of the International Refugee Organization, and Agreement on Interim Measures to be taken in respect of refugees and displaced persons, (15 December 1946), UN Doc A/RES/62(I).

221 Universal Declaration of Human Rights (1948).

222 Ibid., art. 14(1).

223 It excluded refugees assisted by other United Nations agencies. The United Nations Relief and Works Agency for Palestine Refugees in the Near East (UNRWA) was created by: UNGA, 'Assistance to Palestine refugees' (8 December 1949), UN Doc A/RES/302 (IV); the United Nations Korean Reconstruction Agency (UNKRA) was created by:

UNGA, 'Relief and rehabilitation of Korea' (1 December 1950), UN Docs A/RES/410(V).

224 UNGA, Statute of the Office of the United Nations High Commissioner for Refugees (UNHCR Statute) (14 December 1950), UN Doc A/RES/428(V), ch. 1, art. 1.

225 ECOSOC was also given the opportunity in the Statute to have an advisory committee of States, elected on the basis of "their demonstrated interest in and devotion to the solution of the refugee problem", UNHCR Statute (1950), ch. 1, art. 4. This became the Executive Committee of UNHCR.

226 The United States was not in favour of UNHCR having a role in providing relief, while several European countries, as well as India and Pakistan thought it was vitally important. See: Alexander Betts, Gil Loescher and James Milner, *The United Nations High Commissioner for Refugees (UNHCR): The Politics and Practice of Refugee Protection*, (Abingdon, UK: Routledge, 2011), p. 14.

227 UNHCR, *The State of the World's Refugees 2000*, p. 22.

228 His budget was soon augmented by an over $3 million contribution from the Ford Foundation to assist refugee integration in Europe, see: *State of the World's Refugees 2000*, p. 22. The creation of the United Nations Refugee Fund followed in 1955, a year before van Heuven Goedhart's untimely death. It grew to over $16 million by 1958, when it was fully incorporated into UNHCR's annual programmes. UNHCR, *Forty Years of International Assistance to Refugees* (Geneva: Public Information Services, 1962), p. 26.

229 Harley, 'Refugee Participation Revisited'. In his study of refugee contributions to early 20th century refugee law and responses, Harley describes how Van Heuven Goedhart's own refugee experiences profoundly affected his leadership of UNHCR. He formed steady and appreciative partnerships with voluntary organizations, believing they deserved his "heartfelt tribute" for the contributions they made. Convinced that the Office could only be effective if it had direct access to refugees wherever there was a need, he established country offices not only in Europe but also in other geographic areas including Bogota, Cairo and Hong Kong. See: Gerrit Jan van Heuven Goedhart, 'Speech Made by Dr. Gerrit Jan van Heuven Goedhart, United Nations High Commissioner for Refugees', at the Meeting of Swiss Aid to Europe in Berne, 19 February 1953.

230 ECOSOC Res. 248 (IX)B (8 August 1949), UN Doc E/RES/248(IX). It became known as the Ad Hoc Committee. The committee was instructed to consider whether a consolidated convention was necessary and, if it was, to prepare a draft text.

231 Belgium, Brazil, Canada, China (Taiwan), Denmark, Israel, Poland, the Soviet Union, Turkey, the United Kingdom, the United States and Venezuela. The members from Poland and the Soviet Union officially resigned, however, because they did not consider Taiwan to be a legitimate United Nations member State.

232 Harley, 'Refugee Participation Revisited'.

233 Harley, 'Refugee Participation Revisited'; Irial Glynn, 'The Genesis and Development of Article 1 of the 1951 Refugee Convention', *Journal of Refugee Studies* 25, no. 1 (2011): p. 136. Harley also notes, however, that Robinson was successful in arguing for its non-applicability to persons fleeing environmental disasters.

234 Now codified in arts. 32 and 33 of the Convention relating to the Status of Refugees (adopted 25 July 1951) (1951 Convention), UN Doc A/CONF.2/108; Harley, 'Refugee Participation Revisited'.

235 Terje Einarsen, 'Drafting History of the 1951 Convention and the 1967 Protocol', in Andreas Zimmermann (ed.), *The 1951 Convention Relating to the Status of Refugees and Its 1967 Protocol: A Commentary* (Oxford: Oxford University Press, 2011), C: IV: 4 para. 42.

236 Ibid., paras. 46–50.

237 Australia, Austria, Belgium, Brazil, Canada, Colombia, Denmark, Egypt, France, Federal Republic of Germany, Greece, Holy See, Iraq, Israel, Italy, Luxembourg, Monaco, Netherlands, Norway, Sweden, Switzerland (the Swiss delegation also represented Liechtenstein), Turkey, United Kingdom, United States, Venezuela, Yugoslavia. United Nations Conference of Plenipotentiaries on the Status of Refugees and Stateless Persons, 'Final Act and Convention Relating to the Status of Refugees' (25 July 1951) UN Doc A/CONF.2/108.

238 Congo, Madagascar, Monaco and Turkey. Turkey maintained its declaration of geographical limitation upon accession to the 1967 Protocol.

239 Text is available at UNHCR, *Convention and Protocol Relating to the Status of Refugees* (UNHCR, 2010).

240 James C. Hathaway, *The Law of Refugee Status* (Toronto, Vancouver: Butterworths Canada Ltd, 1991), p. 8. Hathaway writes that "by mandating protection for those whose (Western-inspired) civil and political rights are jeopardized, without at the same time protecting persons whose (socialist-inspired) civil and socio-economic rights are at risk, the Convention adopted an incomplete and politically partisan human rights rationale."

241 Terje Einarsen suggests that it is likely that this ground was aimed to include those who had suffered under the Third Reich for being "undesirable", such as "hereditarily ill", "asocial persons" and "homosexuals", Einarsen, 'Drafting History', C: V: 2.

242 The only exception is for a person for whom there are reasonable grounds "for regarding as a danger to the security of the country in which he is, or who, having been convicted by a final judgment of a particularly serious crime, constitutes a danger to the community of that country". The Refugee Convention (1951), art. 33.

243 Other non-derogable Articles in the Convention are those pertaining to the definition, non-discrimination, freedom of religion and access to the courts. 1951 Convention, arts. 1, 3, 4 and 16(1) respectively. Regarding the non-refoulement as a principle of customary international law, see: UNHCR, 'Advisory Opinion on the Extraterritorial Application of Non-Refoulement Obligations under the 1951 Convention relating to the Status of Refugees and its 1967 Protocol'.

244 Aleinikoff and Zamore write that this was a means to deal with those remaining in the displaced persons camps. States "that had been funding the IRO (as well as broader development programs, most notably the Marshall Plan) and resettling hundreds of thousands of refugees came to the conclusion that the remaining populations would need to be integrated into the states in which they were residing". Leah Zamore and T. Alexander Aleinikoff, *The Arc of Protection: Toward a New International Refugee Regime* (Redwood City, CA: Stanford University Press, 2019), p. 44.

245 1951 Convention, arts. 16, 23, 20, 22, 14, 29 and 24.

246 1951 Convention, arts. 17 and 15.

247 1951 Convention, arts. 18, 21 and 22.

248 1951 Convention, art. 34. The Ad Hoc Committee was informed by an initial draft of the Convention provided by the Secretary-General who, in conveying it to the Committee, emphasized that the aim was for refugees to be integrated into the economic system of the countries of asylum, to provide for their own needs and to be fully integrated into the national community. UN Ad Hoc Committee on Refugees and Stateless Persons, 'Ad Hoc

Committee on Statelessness and Related Problems, First Session: Summary Record of the Twenty-Second Meeting' (2 February 1950), UN Doc E/AC.32/SR.22.

249 Article 35 of the 1951 Convention and para 8 of the UNHCR Statute. States undertake to cooperate with the Office and provide it with information and statistical data on the condition of refugees, the implementation of the Convention and laws and decrees relating to refugees. On the ways UNHCR exercises this responsibility, see: Volker Türk, 'UNHCR's Supervisory Responsibility', Working Paper 67, *New Issues in Refugee Research*, UNHCR (October 2002): pp. 6–16.

250 For examples, see: Volker Türk and Rebecca Dowd, 'Protection Gaps', in Elena Fiddian-Qasmiyeh, Gil Loescher, Katy Long, and Nando Sigona (eds.), *The Oxford Handbook of Refugee and Forced Migration Studies* (Oxford: Oxford University Press, 2014).

251 Discussed further in Part II.

252 Some examples of the commentary are: Betts, Loescher, and Milner, *The United Nations High Commissioner for Refugees*; Guy S. Goodwin-Gill, 'The Movements of People between States in the 21st Century: An Agenda for Urgent Institutional Change', *International Journal of Refugee Law* 28, no. 4 (December 2016): pp. 679–694; Volker Türk and Madeline Garlick, 'From Burdens and Responsibilities to Opportunities: The Comprehensive Refugee Response Framework and a Global Compact on Refugees', *International Journal of Refugee Law* 28, no. 4 (December 2016): pp. 656–678; Zamore and Aleinikoff, *The Arc of Protection*.

253 'Closing Speech of Mr Larson, President of the Conference of Plenipotentiaries on the Status of Refugees' made at the 35th meeting, July 1951, *UNHCR* Archives, 'Conference of Plenipotentiaries on Draft Convention Relating to the Status of Refugees, 1951', 4/1/1-G1/12/1/10.

254 'The 1951 Refugee Convention', *UNHCR* website.

255 UNHCR, *Global Trends: Forced Displacement in 2020, Annual Report* (2021), pp. 5, 19.

PART II: **Protecting More Broadly**

1   Convention relating to the Status of Refugees (adopted 25 July 1951) (1951 Convention), UN Doc A/CONF.2/108, arts. 35 and 36.

2   UNHCR's Statute provides: "The High Commissioner shall provide for the protection of refugees falling under the competence of his Office by: (a) promoting the conclusion and ratification of international conventions for the protection of refugees, supervising their application and proposing amendments thereto", para 8. UNGA, Statute of the Office of the United Nations High Commissioner for Refugees (14 December 1950), UN Doc A/RES/428(V). For more on UNHCR's supervisory responsibilities, see: Volker Türk, 'UNHCR's supervisory responsibility', Working Paper No. 67, *New Issues in Refugee Research*, UNHCR (October 2002).

3   Refugees, asylum-seekers, returnees, stateless persons, and internally displaced persons. For more on UNHCR's mandate, see: UNHCR, 'Note on the Mandate of the High Commissioner for Refugees and His Office' (October 2013).

4   *Sepet and Another v. Secretary of State for the Home Department* (2003) UKHL 15 (UK), para. 6. Similarly recognized in other jurisdictions, see: *Suresh v. Canada* (2002) 1 SCR 3 (Canada), para. 87; *A. v. Minister for Immigration & Ethnic Affairs* (1997) 190 CLR 225 (Australia), para. 22; *AC (Syria)* (2011) NZIPT 800035 (New Zealand), para. 62.

5   As part of its supervisory responsibilities for refugees under the 1951 Convention, UNHCR issues Guidelines on International Protection which provide interpretative and procedural guidance, reflecting updated legal jurisprudence. UNHCR, 'Handbook for Determining Refugee Status and Guidelines on International Protection', Collected Documents, *UNHCR* website.

6   For a legal analysis of persecution by non-State actors, see: James C. Hathaway and Michelle Foster, *The Law of Refugee Status* (Cambridge: Cambridge University Press, 2014), pp. 292–332; UNHCR, 'Guidance Note on Refugee Claims Relating to Victims of Organized Gangs' (31 March 2010).

7   For a legal analysis of how the understanding of persecution for reasons of membership of a particular social group (e.g. due to gender, sexual orientation and/or gender identity, family, age, and disability) has evolved over time, see: Hathaway and Foster, *The Law of Refugee Status*, pp. 423–461; Guy S. Goodwin-Gill and Jane McAdam, *The Refugee in International Law* (Oxford: Oxford University Press, 2007), pp. 73–86; UNHCR, *Handbook on Procedures and Criteria for Determining Refugee Status under the 1951 Convention and the 1967 Protocol relating to the Status of Refugees* (Geneva: UNHCR, 2019); UNHCR, 'Persons in need of international protection', Factsheet (June 2017); UNHCR, 'Guidelines on International Protection No. 2: "Membership of a particular social group" within the context of Article 1A(2) of the 1951 Convention and/or its 1967 Protocol relating to the Status of Refugees' (7 May 2002), p. 2.

8   UNHCR was called to assist, initially by Tunisia and later by the UN General Assembly. It was the beginning of a much more expansive engagement in Africa. UNHCR, 'Chapter 2: Decolonization in Africa', in *The State of The World's Refugees 2000: Fifty Years of Humanitarian Action* (Oxford: Oxford University Press, 2000), pp. 38–44.

9   In 1954, Africa was almost entirely under colonial rule except for Egypt, Ethiopia, Liberia

...PART II: **Protecting More Broadly...**

and Libya, which were sovereign States, and South Africa which had Dominion status. For a list of dates of independence of African States, see: Alistair Boddy-Evans, 'Chronological List of African Independence', *ThoughtCo.* website (25 January 2020).

10   John Parker and Richard Rathbone, *African History: A Very Short Introduction* (Oxford: Oxford University Press, 2007).

11   UNGA, Declaration on the granting of independence to colonial countries and peoples (14 December 1960), UN Doc A/RES/1514(XV).

12   For example, art. 1 (2) "equal rights and self-determination of peoples" and ch. XI ('Declaration regarding Non-Self-Governing Territories', arts. 73 and 74), UN, Charter of the United Nations (26 June 1945). The Charter was signed on 26 June 1945 and came into force on 24 October 1945.

13   Basil Davidson, 'The Struggle for Independence of 'Portuguese' Africa: 15 million Africans in Angola, Mozambique and Guinea (Bissau) in search of a new identity', *The UNESCO Courier: a window open on the world* XXVI, 11 (1973): pp. 5–10.

14   Guinea-Bissau gained independence in 1973, Mozambique in 1974, and Angola in 1975. By this time, the Government in Portugal had been overthrown. Growing fatigue with the colonial wars, which by 1970 exacted 40 per cent of the Portuguese annual national budget, contributed to the downfall of the Government. See: Peter Abbott and Ronald Volstad, *Modern African Wars: Angola and Mozambique 1961–74* vol. 2 (Oxford: Osprey Publishing, 1988), pp. 34–35.

15   Between 1960 and 1975, the numbers of refugees from Angola, Guinea-Bissau and Mozambique fluctuated but reached a peak in 1974 when close to 670,000 were recorded of which 450,000 were from Angola, the majority of whom had sought refuge in what is today the Democratic Republic of the Congo. Rebel groups set up command and logistical capacities in neighbouring countries, with Marxists drawing support from China, Cuba and the Soviet Union and those that favoured more free market democratic systems supported by the United States. Thomas H. Henriksen, 'People's War in Angola, Mozambique, and Guinea-Bissau', *The Journal of Modern African Studies* 14, no. 3 (1976): pp. 377–399; Aristide Zolberg, Astri Suhrke, and Sergio Aguayo, *Escape from Violence: Conflict and the Refugee Crisis in the Developing World* (New York: Oxford University Press, 1989), pp. 75–79; UNHCR, Refugee Data Finder.

16   UNHCR, Refugee Data Finder.

17   UNHCR, Refugee Data Finder. The formation of Tutsi militia intending to regain power in Rwanda, and the support of some for local insurgencies in what is now the Democratic Republic of the Congo, precipitated the Government to demand that Rwandan refugees be settled elsewhere. About half of those in Congo moved to Burundi and Uganda. For more on the crisis in the region, see: Philip Gourevitch, *We Wish To Inform You That Tomorrow We Will Be Killed With Our Families* (New York: Picador, 2000); Gérard Prunier, *The Rwanda Crisis, 1959–1994: History of a Genocide* (London: C. Hurst & Co. Publishers, 1995).

18   This is the region in Africa most commonly around the following lakes: Lake Albert; Lake Edward; Lake Kivu; Lake Malawi; Lake Tanganyika; and Lake Victoria. It is often used to refer to the countries that border these lakes: Burundi; Democratic Republic of the Congo; Kenya; Rwanda; Tanzania; and Uganda. The mass displacement of the 1990s is discussed in Part III.

19 Mark Fathi Massoud, *Law's Fragile State: Colonial, Authoritarian, and Humanitarian Legacies in Sudan* (New York: Cambridge University Press, 2013), p. 91 and, for more, see: pp. 88–92.

20 Ibid., p. 94.

21 UNHCR, Refugee Data Finder.

22 Zolberg, Suhrke and Aguayo, *Escape from Violence*, p. 52. According to UNHCR data, the highest number of Sudanese refugees during this time was recorded in 1968 at 175,500 persons. Internal displacement numbers are from Zolberg, Suhrke and Aguayo, *Escape from Violence*.

23 UNHCR operations in Africa constituted 70 per cent of its budget by the end of the 1960s. Zolberg, Suhrke and Aguayo, *Escape from Violence*, p. 38. On the numbers of known refugees at the time, see: UNHCR, Refugee Data Finder.

24 It was also influenced by the fact that newly formed governments were threatened by counter-insurgency efforts from neighbouring States. The OAU Convention has provisions to ensure that asylum not be used for this purpose, obliging States to prohibit refugees from attacking any member State by "any activity likely to cause tension" and as far as possible settling refugees at a reasonable distance from the border of their country. Organization of African Unity (OAU), Convention Governing the Specific Aspects of Refugee Problems in Africa (10 September 1969) (OAU Convention), arts. 3(2) and 2(6). On this motivation in general, see: Tamara Wood, 'In search of the African Refugee: A principled interpretation of Africa's expanded refugee definition', PhD thesis, University of New South Wales, 2018, pp. 30–31; Marina Sharpe, *The Regional Law of Refugee Protection in Africa* (Oxford: Oxford University Press, 2018), pp. 22–23.

25 OAU Convention (1969), Preamble.

26 Ibid., arts. 2(3), 2(4), 2(1), 5 respectively.

27 Ibid., art. 1(2).

28 Bonaventure Rutinwa, 'Relationship between the 1951 Refugee Convention and the 1969 OAU Convention on Refugees: A Historical Perspective', in Volker Türk, Alice Edwards, and C. W. Wouters (eds.), *In Flight from Conflict and Violence: UNHCR's Consultations on Refugee Status and Other Forms of International Protection* (New York: Cambridge University Press, 2017), pp. 108–109.

29 This has been done, for example, in 2010 and 2011 in Ghana, Guinea, Liberia and Togo for individuals fleeing the Ivory Coast. Sharpe, *The Regional Law of Refugee Protection in Africa*, p. 47. In Ethiopia, a prima facie approach is used for persons fleeing South Sudan and Somalia. Tsion Tadesse Abebe, Allehone Abebe, and Marina Sharpe, 'The 1969 OAU Refugee Convention at 50', *Africa Report* 19 (2019): p. 5. On prima facie, see: endnote 38.

30 Tamara Wood, 'Protection and Disasters in the Horn of Africa: Norms and Practice for Addressing Cross-Border Displacement in Disaster Contexts', Technical paper (Nansen Initiative, January 2013), pp. 23–30; Sharpe, *The Regional Law of Refugee Protection in Africa*, pp. 49–51. Guy Goodwin Gill and Jane McAdam note that, while this interpretation is possible, the prevailing view among States is that there must be a link with conflict and violence in the country concerned, as was the case when countries in the Horn of Africa accepted Somali refugees on a prima facie basis during the 2011–2012 drought. Guy S. Goodwin-Gill and Jane McAdam, *UNHCR & Climate Change, Disasters and Displacement* (Geneva: UNHCR, 2017), p. 32. On prima facie, see: endnote 38.

31 This work is expected to begin in the last quarter of 2021. African Union, 'Addis Ababa Declaration of The Continental Commemorative Meeting on The Implementation and Supervision of the 1969 OAU Refugee Convention' (20 June 2019).

...PART II: **Protecting More Broadly...**

32 The States that have signed but not ratified are Eritrea, Madagascar, Mauritius, Namibia, Sao Tomé and Principe, Somalia and Western Sahara. Madagascar, Namibia, Sao Tomé and Principe and Somalia are party to the 1951 Convention.

33 Marina Sharpe, 'Regional Refugee Regimes: Africa', in Cathryn Costello, Michelle Foster, and Jane McAdam (eds.), *The Oxford Handbook of International Refugee Law* (Oxford: Oxford University Press, 2021), p. 293. For more on the domestic application of the OAU Convention, see also: Tamara Wood, 'Who Is a Refugee in Africa? A Principled Framework for Interpreting and Applying Africa's Expanded Refugee Definition,' *International Journal of Refugee Law* 31, no. 2–3 (2019): p. 295.

34 Colloquium on the International Protection of Refugees in Central America, Mexico and Panama, Cartagena Declaration on Refugees and the Protection of People Fleeing Armed Conflict and Other Situations of Violence in Latin America (22 November 1984) (Cartagena Declaration).

35 Asian-African Legal Consultative Organization, '"Final Text of the AALCO's 1966 Bangkok Principles on Status and Treatment of Refugees" as adopted on 24 June 2001 at the AALCO's 40th Session, New Delhi' (24 June 2001) (Bangkok Principles).

36 African Union, Convention for the Protection and Assistance of Internally Displaced Persons in Africa (23 October 2009) (Kampala Convention).

37 OAU Convention (1969), Preamble.

38 This is an approach that is used when the evidence makes it readily apparent that the refugees are at risk of harm for 1951 Convention grounds and need not establish this in an individual assessment process. UNHCR, 'Guidelines on International Protection No. 11: Prima Facie Recognition of Refugee Status' (24 June 2015), p. 11.

39 Including at its 50th Anniversary in 2019, declared "The Year of Refugees, Returnees and Internally Displaced Persons". See: Tadesse Abebe, Abebe, and Sharpe, 'The 1969 OAU Refugee Convention at 50'. It is also noted as one of the core regional refugee protection instruments in the Global Compact on Refugees. UN General Assembly, Global Compact on Refugees (2018), UN Doc A/73/12 (Part II), I. B. 5.

40 Also of note is that in 2017 the Intergovernmental Authority on Development (IGAD) adopted the Djibouti Declaration on Education in which member States commit to ensure that "every refugee, returnee and members of host communities have access to quality education in a safe learning environment within [their] respective countries without discrimination". IGAD, 'Djibouti Declaration on Regional Conference on Refugee Education in IGAD Member States' (14 December 2017); UNHCR, 'Implementing the Djibouti Declaration: Education for refugees, returnees & host communities', Global Compact on Refugees Digital Platform (25 March 2020).

41 Marina Sharpe and others note the following situations as illustrative: refugees fleeing Liberia in 1996, from Sierra Leone in 1999, and from Angola in 2000; and the forced returns of Somalis from Kenya in 2010, 2013, and 2014; of Rwandans from Uganda in 2010; of Nigerians from Cameroon beginning in 2015; of northern Nigerians from Niger in 2015; and of Eritreans from Sudan in 2016. Sharpe, *The Regional Law of Refugee Protection in Africa*, pp. 75–76; Tadesse Abebe, Abebe, and Sharpe, 'The 1969 OAU Refugee Convention at 50': p. 7. For earlier examples in the 1990s, see: George Okoth-Obbo, 'Thirty years on: a legal review of the 1969 OAU Refugee Convention', *African Yearbook of International Law*

8 (2000): p. 84 and Sharpe, *The Regional Law of Refugee Protection in Africa*, p. 74. More recent examples include forced returns of Nigerians from Cameroon in 2018 and 2019 and push-backs of Mozambicans from Tanzania in 2021. UNHCR, 'UNHCR alarmed by continuing forced returns of Nigerians by Cameroon', Press Release (20 April 2018); UNHCR, 'UNHCR deplores forced refugee returns from Cameroon', Press Release (18 January 2019); UNHCR, 'UNHCR appeals for Mozambicans fleeing violence to be given access to asylum in Tanzania', Press Release (18 May 2021).

42 See the study commissioned by UNHCR: Marina Sharpe, 'The 1969 OAU Refugee Convention and the Protection of People fleeing Armed Conflict and Other Situations of Violence in the Context of Individual Refugee Status Determination', Research Paper (January 2013). See also: Wood, 'Who Is a Refugee in Africa?': p. 301 and Rutinwa, 'Relationship between the 1951 Refugee Convention and the 1969 OAU Convention on Refugees', pp. 109–110.

43 Uganda, for example, has long had progressive policies which it maintained even in the face of increased numbers of refugees, discussed more in Part III.

44 For more on encampment and restrictions on integration, see: Part III. Due to its complementarity, the OAU Convention does not enumerate social and economic rights like the 1951 Convention, although it is considered to extend refugees the same rights by virtue of its recognition of the 1951 Convention as the universal source of refugee rights. OAU Convention (1969), Preamble, para 9. For a more thorough discussion of the legal commentary in this regard, see: Marina Sharpe, 'The 1969 African Refugee Convention: Innovations, Misconceptions, and Omission', *McGill Law Journal* 58, no. 1 (September 2012): pp. 124–129.

45 Rutinwa, 'Relationship between the 1951 Refugee Convention and the 1969 OAU Convention on Refugees', p. 113.

46 Global Compact on Refugees (2018).

47 Barry Sen, 'Protection of Refugees: Bangkok Principles and After', *Journal of the Indian Law Institute* 34, no. 2 (1992): p. 187.

48 Asian-African Legal Consultative Organization, 'About AALCO', website, part A. 'Origin' and part C. 'Member States'.

49 Six of the 10 main refugee-hosting States are members of the AALCO: Turkey (3.7 million); Pakistan (1.4 million); Uganda (1.4 million); Sudan (1 million); Lebanon (0.9 million); and Bangladesh (0.9 million). UNHCR, *Global Trends: Forced Displacement in 2020*, Report (2021), p. 8. Of them, Sudan, Turkey, and Uganda are States parties to the 1951 Convention and Protocol.

50 Susan Kneebone, 'ASEAN and the Conceptualization of Refugee Protection in Southeastern Asian States', in Ademola Abass and Francesca Ippolito (eds.), *Regional Approaches to the Protection of Asylum Seekers: An International Legal Perspective* (Aldershot, UK: Ashgate Publishing, 2014), p. 315.

51 As in the OAU Convention and the Cartagena Declaration. Bangkok Principles (2001), arts. I(1) and I(2).

52 Ibid., art. V.

53 Ibid., arts. VII, IX, X. The reference to burden-sharing was added in 1987 when total displacement numbers in Asia and Africa had grown exponentially, principally on account of the increased number of Afghan refugees who fled following the Soviet invasion of Afghanistan. AALCO, 'Addendum to the Status and Treatment of Refugees' (13 January 1987).

54 Sara E. Davies, 'Legitimising Rejection: International Refugee Law in Southeast Asia', *Refugees and Human Rights* 13 (2007): p. 4; Hui-Yi Katherine Tseng, 'Protect the Unprotected:

...PART II: **Protecting More Broadly...**

the escaping North Korean issue and China's dual dilemma of theoretical enlightenment and operational trial', *The Pacific Review* 32, no. 4 (2019): pp. 513–517; Merrill Smith, 'The Bangkok Principles on the Status and Treatment of Refugees', *Rights in Exile* 18 (December 3, 2011). Solutions are discussed further in Part III.

55   Pia Oberoi, 'Developments. Regional Initiatives on Refugee Protection in South Asia', *International Journal of Refugee Law* 11, vol. 1 (1999): pp. 197–201 and Smith, 'The Bangkok Principles'.

56   First South American Congress on Private International Law, Montevideo Treaty on International Penal Law (23 January 1889), art. 16. For more on the treaty, see: Anders B. Johnsson, 'Montevideo Treaty on International Penal Law: 1889–1989 – 100 years of treaty making on asylum issues', *International Journal of Refugee Law* 1, no. 4 (1989): pp. 554–574.

57   Organization of American States (OAS), Convention on Political Asylum (26 December 1933); OAS, Treaty on Asylum and Political Refuge (4 August 1939); OAS, Convention on Diplomatic Asylum (28 March 1954), OAS Treaty Series, No. 19, UN Registration: 03/20/89 No. 24377; OAS, Convention on Territorial Asylum (28 March 1954), OAS Treaty Series, No. 19, UN Registration: 03/20/89 No. 24378.

58   José H. Fischel de Andrade, 'The 1984 Cartagena Declaration: A Critical Review of Some Aspects of Its Emergence and Relevance', *Refugee Survey Quarterly* 38, no. 4 (2019): p. 345. The author notes that there is no precise account of the numbers of forcibly displaced people as a result of the conflicts in the late 1970s and early 1980s in Central America but that some 2 million people are estimated to have been displaced in total. The majority of those displaced by the conflicts were internally displaced. Numbers known to, and recorded by, UNHCR at the time did not include internally displaced persons. UNHCR, *The State of The World's Refugees 2000*, p. 124.

59   For example, Mexico—which, according to UNHCR records, hosted about 170,000 refugees in the early 1980s—and Honduras were not parties to the 1951 Convention at that time. UNHCR, Refugee Data Finder. For States parties, including reservations and declarations, to the 1951 Convention and its 1967 Protocol, see: 1951 Convention.

60   Zolberg, Suhrke and Aguayo, *Escape from Violence*, pp. 204–205.

61   For more on US concerns regarding the social and agrarian reform movements in Central America during this period and on support to right-wing governments and insurgencies, see: UNHCR, The State of the World's Refugees 2000, pp. 121–123. The United States was opposed to the socialist ideology of the Sandinistas, their economic policies, the close relations they forged with Cuba and the support they provided Salvadoran and Guatemalan rebels.

62   UNHCR, Refugee Data Finder. According to UNHCR data, there were 52,650 Nicaraguan refugees in 1985, of whom 35,000 were in Honduras and 15,200 in Costa Rica. UNHCR, Refugee Data Finder. In 1989, this number had increased to a total of 97,700, of whom 41,590 were in Honduras and 38,560 in Costa Rica. UNHCR, Refugee Data Finder. Following the signing of the peace agreements, returns started to increase and the number of Nicaraguan refugees dropped to 53,000 in 1990. UNHCR, Refugee Data Finder.

63   Five of these movements coalesced in the Farabundo Marti National Liberation Front (Frente Farabundo Martí para la Liberación Nacional or FMLN). Estimates place the number of civilian deaths between 30,000 and 70,000. For more on these estimates and the atrocities, see: World Peace Foundation, 'El Salvador', *Mass Atrocity Endings* website (7

August 2015); Amelia Hoover Green, *The Commander's Dilemma: Violence and Restraint in Wartime* (Ithaca, NY: Cornell University Press, 2018); UNHCR, *The State of The World's Refugees 2000*, p. 123.

64 Zolberg, Suhrke, and Aguayo, *Escape from Violence*, pp. 206–207; Megan Bradley, 'Unlocking Protracted Displacement: Central America's "Success Story" Reconsidered', *Refugee Survey Quarterly* 30, no. 4 (December 2011): p. 90; María Cristina García, *Seeking Refuge: Central American Migration to Mexico, the United States, and Canada* (Berkeley, CA: University of California Press, 2006), p. 35. UNHCR records from this time do not include IDPs and refugee figures are much lower possibly due to low registration and recognition rates. UNHCR, Refugee Data Finder.

65 With several groups united in the Guatemalan National Revolutionary Unity (Unidad Revolucionaria Nacional Guatemalteca or UNRG).

66 UNHCR records from this time do not include IDPs and the number of Guatemalan refugees known to UNHCR at the time was much lower, staying below 54,000 even during peak years. This discrepancy may be due to a comparatively low level of official registration. UNHCR, Refugee Data Finder.

67 Fischel de Andrade, 'The 1984 Cartagena Declaration': p. 348; UNHCR, *The State of The World's Refugees 2000*, p. 124.

68 Rebecca Bodenheimer, 'The Guatemalan Civil War: History and Impact', *ThoughtCo.* website (22 March 2020). As part of the Guatemala Peace Process a Commission for Historical Clarification was established through an accord signed by the parties in Oslo, Norway in 1994. It reviewed the underlying causes of the war and documents the widespread gross human rights violations committed. The Committee found state forces and related paramilitary groups were responsible for "93% of the violations documented by the CEH, 92% of the arbitrary executions and 91% of forced disappearance". It records in detail the particular cruelty of the State forces and that "in the majority of massacres were multiple acts of savagery". Historical Clarification Commission, *Guatemala: Memory of Silence*, Report (1999), paras. 15, 87.

69 UNHCR, *The State of the World's Refugees 2000*, pp. 128–131.

70 UNHCR, *The State of the World's Refugees 2000*, pp. 124.

71 Ten governments were represented from Belize, Colombia, Costa Rica, El Salvador, Guatemala, Honduras, Mexico, Nicaragua, Panama and Venezuela. Experts from countries in the region also participated.

72 Cartagena Declaration, arts. III(5) and III(12).

73 Ibid., arts. III(6), II (h), II(i).

74 Ibid., art. III(11).

75 Ibid., art. III(3).

76 Argentina, Bolivia, Chile, El Salvador, Guatemala, Mexico and Nicaragua have adopted the definition in its entirety. Belize, Brazil, Colombia, Ecuador, Honduras, Paraguay, Peru and Uruguay have adopted it in modified form. Luisa Feline Freier, Isabel Berganza, and Cécile Blouin, 'The Cartagena Refugee Definition and Venezuelan Displacement in Latin America', *International Migration* 58, no. 6 (2 December 2020): pp. 15–19. On the extent to which countries in the region have or have not incorporated its provisions and/or modified them in their national laws, see: Michael Reed-Hurtado, 'The Cartagena Declaration on Refugees and the Protection of People Fleeing Armed Conflict and Other Situations of Violence in Latin America' in Türk, Edwards, and Wouters (eds.), *In Flight from Conflict and Violence*, pp. 158–161.

...PART II: **Protecting More Broadly...**

77 Colombia, Costa Rica, Ecuador, and Mexico. Juan Ignacio Mondelli, 'Reshaping Asylum in Latin America as a Response to Large-Scale Mixed Movements: A Decade of Progress and Challenges (2009–2019)', Reference Paper for the 70th Anniversary of the 1951 Refugee Convention, UNHCR (October 2021), p. 5.

78 *Pacheco Tineo Family v. Plurinational State of Bolivia* (2013) IACHR, paras. 137–140; *Advisory Opinion OC-25/18* (2018) IACHR, paras. 112, 113, 131 and 132; *Advisory Opinion OC-21/14* (2011) IACHR, paras. 102–123. The Court considered State obligations under Article 22 of the American Convention on Human Rights, which came into force in 1978. That Article provides for the right of every person "to seek and be granted asylum" in accordance the "the legislation of the state and international conventions". OAS, American Convention on Human Rights (Pact of San José) (1969).

79 For a review of these, see: Mondelli, 'Remodeling Asylum in Latin America' pp. 7–11.

80 This includes the 1994 San José Declaration (Cartagena +10) which, among other things, agreed on principles to respond to internal displacement, years before the International Guiding Principles on Internal Displacement were formulated. The Cartagena Declaration is also a foundational document for the 2004 Mexico Declaration (Cartagena +20) that included an Action Plan for sustainable solutions and advanced regional cooperation in regard to border management, refugee solutions and cooperation among cities. The 2014 Brazil Declaration also reaffirmed the Cartagena Declaration and included an ambitious Plan of Action for the 2015–2024 period. For the first time, the Caribbean countries have joined as full members of the process. Carlos Maldonado Castillo, 'The Cartagena Process: 30 Years of Innovation and Solidarity', *Forced Migration Review* 49 (2015): p. 90; Mondelli, 'Remodeling Asylum in Latin America', p. 7.

81 Reed-Hurtado, 'The Cartagena Declaration on Refugees', p. 162.

82 R4V, 'Key Figures', Inter-Agency Coordination Platform for Refugees and Migrants from Venezuela, website.

83 UNHCR, 'Guidance Note on International Protection Considerations for Venezuelans – Update I' (May 2019), para. 5.

84 Argentina, Bolivia, Brazil, Mexico, Paraguay and Uruguay.

85 Of the over 1 million asylum claims filed, just 170,000 had received a positive decision as of the end of 2020. R4V, 'Key Figures'.

86 UNHCR, 'UNHCR welcomes Brazil's decision to recognize thousands of Venezuelans as refugees', Press Briefing (6 December 2019). As of the end of 2020, Brazil had accepted 46,700 Venezuelan refugees on a prima facie basis. UNHCR, Refugee Data Finder.

87 Blouin, Berganza, and Freier, 'The Spirit of Cartagena?': p. 66.

88 R4V, 'Residence and Stay Permits', Inter-Agency Coordination Platform for Refugees and Migrants from Venezuela, website. Argentina, Brazil, Chile, Colombia, Ecuador and Peru, for example, have used Temporary Stay Permit programmes and/or simplified require-ments in their visa/migration schemes to facilitate the access of Venezuelans to legal stay alternatives and documentation.

89 Grupo Interagencial sobre Flujos Migratorios Mixtos (GIFMM) and R4V, 'Venezuelans in Colombia', Factsheet (November 2020).

90 Ministry of Foreign Affairs, Republic of Colombia, 'Decree No. 216: Temporary Protection Statute for Venezuelan Migrants under Temporary Protection' [Spanish] (1 March 2021).

91 BBC News, 'Colombia to grant legal status to Venezuelan migrants', website (9 February 2021).

92 UNHCR, 'UN High Commissioner for Refugees praises Latin America for its commitment to the inclusion of all those in need of protection', Press Release (23 June 2021); Luc Cohen, 'Ecuador to start new "normalization process" for Venezuelan migrants', *Reuters* (17 June 2021).

93 UNHCR, Refugee Data Finder. At the end of 2020, forcibly displaced populations from El Salvador, Guatemala and Honduras included close to 105,000 refugees under UNHCR's mandate and nearly 445,000 asylum-seekers. There were an additional 319,000 IDPs, the vast majority in Honduras (some 77 per cent) and the remainder in El Salvador. UNHCR, Refugee Data Finder.

94 For more, see: UNHCR, 'The MIRPS', Global Compact on Refugees Digital Platform.

95 UNHCR, Refugee Data Finder and UNHCR, Refugee Data Finder. Most of the recognitions have been in Costa Rica, Mexico, Spain and the United States. UNHCR, Refugee Data Finder.

96 See: endnote 76.

97 Discussed further in Part III.

98 Discussed further in this Part.

99 As noted in the preamble to the 1951 Convention. The commitment is also found in Article II(4) of the OAU Convention (1969): "where a Member State finds difficulty in continuing to grant asylum to refugees, such Member State may appeal directly to other Member States and through the OAU, and such other Member States shall in the spirit of African solidarity and international cooperation take appropriate measures to lighten the burden of the Member State granting asylum".

100 UNHCR, *A Thematic Compilation of Executive Committee Conclusions (7th Edition)* (June 2014), pp. 44 and 42–61.

101 Ibid. See, for example: No. 100 (LV) 2004 'International Cooperation and Burden and Responsibility Sharing in Mass Influx Situations', which reaffirms that "respect by States for their protection responsibilities towards refugees is strengthened by international solidarity involving all members of the international community and that the refugee protection regime is enhanced through committed international cooperation in a spirit of solidarity and responsibility and burden sharing among all States", p. 56.

102 UNHCR, *Global Trends 2020*, p. 2.

103 UNHCR, 'Resettlement', website.

104 See, for example: Barnaby Willitts-King and Alexandra Spencer, *Reducing the humanitarian financing gap: review of progress since the report of the High-Level Panel on Humanitarian Financing*, HPG Commissioned Report, Overseas Development Institute (April 2021); UNHCR, 'UNHCR's engagement in the Grand Bargain: Summary of the progress made per workstream', External Update (November 2020). The reports show that overall funding has increased in recent years, but the gap between needs and resources has not narrowed while high levels of tight earmarking persist.

105 See: Part V.

106 Hathaway and Gammeltoft-Hansen refer to this as a "schizophrenic attitude towards international refugee law" because they remain formally engaged with refugee law yet simultaneously try to avoid related responsibilities. James C. Hathaway and Thomas Gammeltoft-Hansen, 'Non-Refoulement in a World of Cooperative Deterrence', *Columbia Journal of Transnational Law* 53, no. 2 (2015): p. 282.

107 And following two years of global consultations aimed to address the many challenges that faced the implementation of the 1951 Convention and its 1967 Protocol, including new forms of persecution and conflict, complex mixed movements, the reluctance of many States to accept refugees, and the restrictive interpretation of the 1951 Convention. For the papers and the conclusions resulting from the Global Consultations, see: Erika Feller, Volker Türk, and Frances Nicholson, *Refugee Protection in International Law: UNHCR's Global Consultations on International Protection* (New York: Cambridge University Press, 2003).

108 UNHCR, 'Declaration of States Parties to the 1951 Convention and/or Its 1967 Protocol Relating to the Status of Refugees' (16 January 2002), UN Doc HCR/MMSP/2001/09; UNHCR, 'Report of the Ministerial Meeting of States Parties to the 1951 Convention and/ or Its 1967 Protocol Relating to the Status of Refugees' (18 January 2002), UN Doc HCR/ MMSP/2001/10.

109 UNHCR, *Agenda for Protection (Third Edition)* (October 2003).

110 UN, 'Ministerial Communiqué' (8 December 2011), UN Doc HCR/MINCOMMS/2011/6. 153 United Nations member States participated in the intergovernmental event at the ministerial level of member States of the United Nations on the occasion of the 60th anniversary of the 1951 Convention relating to the Status of Refugees and the 50th anniversary of the 1961 Convention on the Reduction of Statelessness, held in Geneva (7–8 December 2011), which culminated in the issuance of the Communiqué. UNHCR, 'Ministerial Meeting: List of Participants' (22 December 2011), UN Doc HCR/MINCOMMS/2011/09.

111 See later in this Part.

112 Informed by the Secretary-General's Report to the UNGA, 'In safety and dignity: addressing large movements of refugees and migrants' (21 April 2016), UN Doc A/70/59.

113 UNGA, New York Declaration for Refugees and Migrants (19 September 2016), UN Doc A/ RES/71/1.

114 181 United Nations member States voted in favour of adopting the Global Compact on Refugees, Hungary and the United States voted against it, and the Dominican Republic, Eritrea and Libya abstained. 152 UN member States voted in favour of adopting the Global Compact for Safe, Orderly and Regular Migration, five (Czech Republic, Hungary, Israel, Poland, United States) voted against it, and 12 abstained. Global Compact on Refugees (2018); UNGA, Global Compact for Safe, Orderly and Regular Migration (GCM) (19 December 2018), UN Doc A/RES/73/195.

115 Global Compact on Refugees (2018), paras. 60–61; Global Compact for Safe, Orderly and Regular Migration (2018), objective 7, para 23. The GCM also makes specific reference to this in regard to search and rescue efforts. Objective 8, para 24.

116 Global Compact on Refugees (2018), paras. 13, 57–58, 94–96; Global Compact for Safe, Orderly and Regular Migration (2018), objective 10. This is consistent with the Palermo Protocols that are supplementary to UNGA, Convention against Transnational Organized Crime (15 November 2000), UN Doc A/RES/55/25: UNGA, 'Protocol to Prevent, Suppress and Punish Trafficking in Persons, Especially Women and Children, Supplementing the United Nations Convention against Transnational Organized Crime' (15 November 2000); UNGA, 'Protocol against the Smuggling of Migrants by Land, Sea and Air, Supplementing the United Nations Convention against Transnational Organized Crime' (15 November 2000).

117 UNHCR, *Agenda for Protection*, pp. 46–52; UNHCR, 'The 10-Point Plan in Action: 2016 Update' (December 2016).

118 Convention against Transnational Organized Crime (2000); 'Protocol against the Smuggling of Migrants by Land, Sea and Air'; 'Protocol to Prevent, Suppress and Punish Trafficking in Persons, Especially Women and Children'.

119 Risks that give rise to a need for international protection include persecution, threats to life, freedom or physical integrity arising from armed conflict, serious public disorder, certain situations of violence, or other risks. Refugees have a right to international protection as may others who are outside their own country and unable to return home because they would be at risk there and their country is unable or unwilling to protect them. For more on this and a list of international and regional agreements which include the non-refoulement principle, see: UNHCR, 'Persons in Need of International Protection'.

120 Mathias Czaika, Hein De Haas, and Maria Villares-Varela, 'The Global Evolution of Travel Visa Regimes', *Population and Development Review* 44, no. 3 (2018): p. 592.

121 Czaika, De Haas, and Villares-Varela, 'The Global Evolution of Travel Visa Regimes'. The authors show how visas have been the rule rather than the exception over the past 40 decades, see: pp. 591–592 and 601.

122 Ibid.: p. 594. They note that there are at least 20 economic unions and communities around the world and they usually but not exclusively liberalize trade, investment, travel and migration among the member States, see: p. 597.

123 On the use of visas, see: Ibid.: p. 610. For examples of countries that use visa requirements to reduce asylum claims, see: David Scott FitzGerald, *Refuge beyond Reach: How Rich Democracies Repel Asylum Seekers* (New York: Oxford University Press, 2019). For example, Canada imposed visa requirements in response to increasing claims from refugees arriving from Haiti in the late 1970s, from Central and Latin America in the 1970s and 1980s, from Czech Republic in the 1990s (re-increased claims from Roma), from Hungary and Zimbabwe in the early 2000s, pp. 60–61. The EU has also used visas in response to increased refugee flows. In 1987, the European Community agreed on a list of 50 countries for visas which expanded to over 100 countries in the new millennium. Additional airport transit visas were imposed on nationals of some of the largest refugee movements. Ibid., p. 165. Most nationalities require a visa to enter the United States, a requirement which is not aimed exclusively at asylum-seekers but equally does not provide exemptions for them, pp. 60–61.

124 1951 Convention, arts. 31, 33.

125 Hathaway and Gammeltoft-Hansen, 'Non-Refoulement in a World of Cooperative Deterrence': pp. 238–239.

126 Canada: The Immigration Act (1869), arts. 3–4 and 11; Australia: Immigration Restriction Act (1901), para. 9. This Act was the foundation of Australia's "white only" policy. USA: Immigration Act (1924), sec. 16. UK: British Aliens Act (1793), secs. II and VII.

127 Astri Suhrke and Kathleen Newland, 'UNHCR: Uphill into the Future', *The International Migration Review* 35, no. 1 (2001): p. 290.

128 Bernard Ryan and Valsamis Mitsilegas, *Extraterritorial Immigration Control: Legal Challenges* (Leiden: Brill Nijhoff, 2010), p. 20. Hathaway and Gammeltoft-Hansen, 'Non-Refoulement in a World of Cooperative Deterrence': p. 253.

129 Paula Hancocks, 'Israel starts installing barrier on its Egyptian border', *CNN News* (22 November 2010).

130 For numbers of refugees and asylum-seekers in Israel in 2012, see: UNHCR, Refugee Data Finder. Hadas Yaron, Nurit Hashimshony-Yaffe, and John Campbell, '"Infiltrators" or Refugees? An Analysis of Israel's Policy Towards African Asylum-Seekers', *International*

Migration 51, no. 4 (2013): pp. 4–5; Ron Friedman, 'Netanyahu: Migrants threaten our national identity', *The Times of Israel* (20 May 2012).

131 UNHCR, 'UNHCR's position on the status of Eritrean and Sudanese nationals defined as "infiltrators" by Israel' (November 2017), para. 3. For a chronology of legislative developments from 2010 to date impacting asylum-seekers and asylum procedures in Israel, see: UNHCR Israel, 'Legislation', website. On recognition rates in Israel compared with the EU, see: endnote 138.

132 UNHCR, 'UNHCR's position on the status of Eritrean and Sudanese nationals defined as "infiltrators" by Israel'.

133 UNHCR, 'UNHCR is concerned at new Amendment to Israel's Law on the Prevention of Infiltration', Briefing Notes (10 January 2014).

134 The Court issued its judgment on 12 September 2014. Reuven Ziegler, 'Second Strike and You are (Finally) out? The Quashing of the Prevention of Infiltration Law (Amendment No. 4)', *Israel Democracy Institute* (29 September 2014).

135 UNHCR Israel, 'Legislation'; UNHCR, 'UNHCR concerned over Israel's refugee relocation proposals', Press Release (17 November 2017).

136 The suspension of deportations was ordered by the Israeli High Court in March 2018. At the end of 2018, there were around 32,000 Eritreans and Sudanese left in Israel, down from some 48,000 in 2012. UNHCR, Refugee Data Finder. Some 4,500 had been relocated under the Government's forced relocation policy. UNHCR, 'UNHCR and Israel sign agreement to find solutions for Eritreans and Sudanese', Press Release (2 April 2018).

137 The Times of Israel, 'Some 200 asylum seekers cross into Israel despite Sinai fence' (6 December 2015); Gili Cohen, 'Israel Raising Height of Egypt Border Fence to Keep out Asylum Seekers', *Haaretz* (15 March 2018); Human Rights Watch (HRW), 'UN: Egypt to Chair Refugee Agency's Governing Body – Highlights Urgency for Cairo to End Abuses Against Refugees and Asylum Seekers', *HRW* News (8 October 2010); HRW, 'Egypt/Israel: Egypt Should End "Shoot to Stop" Practice at Sinai Border Crossings', *HRW* News (11 December 2008); Patrick Strickland, 'Sudanese refugees shot dead on Egypt-Israel border', *Al Jazeera* (15 November 2015); Rachel Humphris, 'Refugees and the Rashaida: human smuggling and trafficking from Eritrea to Sudan and Egypt', Research Paper No. 254, *New Issues in Refugee Research*, UNHCR (March 2013), p. 4.

138 For numbers up until 2017, see: 'UNHCR's position on the status of Eritrean and Sudanese nationals defined as "infiltrators" by Israel', p. 3. Between 2018 and 2020, recognition rates for Eritreans in Israel were on average below 2 per cent. No Sudanese were granted refugee status in Israel during this time. Some 600 Sudanese received complementary protection status. For Sudanese numbers, see: UNHCR, Refugee Data Finder and for Eritreans, see: UNHCR, Refugee Data Finder. In 2018 and 2019, EU recognition rates for Eritreans were around 80 per cent, and for Sudanese fluctuated between 54 and 62 per cent. In 2020, the recognition rate of Eritreans in the EU stood at 82 per cent and preliminary data for Sudanese indicates a recognition rate of approximately 46 per cent. European Commission, 'First instance decisions on applications by citizenship, age and sex – annual aggregated data (rounded)', *Eurostat* Data Browser (6 March 2021).

139 Keno Verseck, 'How Hungary is violating EU law on refugees', *Deutsche Welle* (2 August 2021); UNGA, Human Rights Council, 'Visit to Hungary: Report of the Special Rapporteur on

the human rights of migrants' (11 May 2020), UN Doc A/HRC/44/42/Add.1, pp. 7–8; UNHCR, 'Hungary as a Country of Asylum: Observations on restrictive legal measures and subsequent practice implemented between July 2015 and March 2016', Report (May 2016), pp. 8–12.

140 *European Commission v. Hungary* (17 December 2020), CJEU, C-808/18, para. 175.

141 *European Commission v Hungary*, para. 266.

142 On 9 June 2021, the European Commission initiated a non-compliance procedure against Hungary under art. 260(2) of the Treaty on the Functioning of the European Union (TFEU) for failing to comply with the CJEU judgment of 17 December 2020 (C-808/18). The Commission may consider referring the case back to the CJEU with a proposal for financial sanctions. European Commission, 'June Infringements Package: Key Decisions', website (9 June 2021).

143 UNHCR, 'UNHCR Position on Hungarian Act LVIII of 2020 on the Transitional Rules and Epidemiological Preparedness related to the Cessation of the State of Danger' (June 2020).

144 Ibid.; UNHCR, 'Access to asylum further at stake in Hungary', Press Release (29 June 2020). On other reactions to the legislations, see, for example: European Parliament, 'Parliamentary questions: Access to asylum in Hungary', (7 July 2020), E-004020/2020; 'Answer to Parliamentary Question' (19 November 2020), E-004020/2020(ASW). The Commission noted in its answer that it "has serious concerns as regards the compatibility of the new system with obligations under EU asylum law to ensure effective access to the asylum procedure, including at the border, and has already raised the matter with the Hungarian Government at several occasions".

145 The EU reported that the arrivals were being facilitated by Belarus "as a political tool to destabilize the European Union and its Member States". European Commission, 'Communication from the Commission to the European Parliament, the Council, the European Economic and Social Committee and the Committee of the Regions on the Report on Migration and Asylum' (29 September 2021), COM(2021) 590 final, pp. 1, 3, 10. The agencies called for the situation to be managed "in accordance with international legal obligations", and that "asylum-seekers and migrants should never be used by States to achieve political ends". UNHCR, 'UNHCR and IOM shocked and dismayed by deaths near Belarus-Poland border', Press Release (21 September 2021). Poland had previously announced measures to build a fence and increase its military presence along its border. Kasper Pempel, 'Poland to build fence, double troop numbers on Belarus border', *Reuters* (23 August 2021). Two cases are currently before the European Court of Human Rights (ECHR) filed by applicants at the borders of Latvia and Poland seeking admission. In an interim ruling the Court decided to request Polish and Latvian authorities to provide aid to the applicants without prejudice to its decisions on the merits of the applications. ECHR, 'Court indicates interim measures in respect of Iraqi and Afghan nationals at Belarusian border with Latvia and Poland', Press Release (25 August 2021).

146 Christopher Giles, 'Trump's wall: How much has been built during his term?', *BBC News* (12 January 2021); Lauren Giella, 'Fact Check: Did President Trump Build the "Big, Beautiful" Border Wall He Promised?', *Newsweek* (12 January 2021).

147 UNHCR, 'UNHCR deeply concerned about new U.S. asylum restrictions', Press Release (15 July 2019).

148 US Department of Homeland Security, 'Migrant Protection Protocols', Archived Content (24 January 2019).

149 Under this practice, 70,000 asylum-seekers were returned to Mexico until the practice was discontinued in February 2021. By May 2021, more than 11,200 asylum-seekers with active

...PART II: **Protecting More Broadly...**

cases in the programme were allowed to return to the United States to await rulings. Kristy Siegfried, 'The Refugee Brief', UNHCR website (4 June 2021). Among the criticisms of the policy are the unsafe conditions in which migrants and refugees have to wait in Mexico. HRW, '"Like I'm Drowning" - Children and Families Sent to Harm by the US 'Remain in Mexico' Program', Report (January 2021).

150 UNHCR, Refugee Data Finder. In 2016, 96,900 refugees were resettled to the United States. This number dropped to 33,400 in 2017 and further to 22,900 in 2018. In 2019, the number slightly increased again but was still only at 27,500. In 2020, the total number was at a historic low of 9,900 in the context of the COVID-19 pandemic during which access to asylum was further curtailed.

151 Ariel G. Soto Ruiz, 'One Year after the U.S.-Mexico Agreement Reshaping Mexico's Migration Policies', Policy Brief, Migration Policy Institute (June 2020). Mexico was reported to have acted over concerns that it would otherwise face escalating trade tariffs. Makini Brice, 'Trump threatens more tariffs on Mexico over part of immigration deal', *Reuters* (10 June 2019); BBC News, 'US-Mexico talks: Agreement to avoid tariffs reached, says Trump', website (9 June 2019).

152 U.S. Customs and Border Protection, 'Southwest Border Migration FY 2019', website. Inadmissibility metrics include: "individuals encountered at ports of entry who are seeking lawful admission into the United States but are determined to be inadmissible, individuals presenting themselves to seek humanitarian protection under our laws, and individuals who withdraw an application for admission and return to their countries of origin within a short timeframe".

153 Asylum-seekers are either placed in formal immigration proceedings or expedited removal proceedings. In the latter, the person can express a fear of persecution or torture in their country of origin, and a United States asylum official assesses whether there is a "significant possibility" that this claim would be recognized in a formal hearing. If so, the person is sent to the formal hearing process. Those denied can request a review of the decision by an immigration judge. If the judge confirms the negative decision, the person is removed. Prior to 2013, 4–8 per cent of asylum-seekers from Central America were placed in expedited processing. This increased to over 40 per cent. Ben Harrington, 'The Law of Asylum Procedure at the Border: Statutes and Agency Implementation', Congressional Research Service Report R46755 (4 September 2021), pp. 10–13, 17–18, 20–25, 27–28; U.S. Department of Homeland Security, 'Assessment of the Migrant Protection Protocols (MPP)' (28 October 2019), p. 7.

154 The most controversial being the separating of children from their parents and their detention. United Nations human rights experts declared the practice illegal under international law. This policy was terminated by President Trump in June 2018. OHCHR, 'UN experts to US: "release migrant children from detention and stop using them to deter irregular migration"', *OHCHR* News (22 June 2018). In an April 2021 filing with the District Court of Southern California, the US Justice Department and the American Civil Liberties Union (ACLU) reported that there remained over 445 separated children not yet reunited with their parents. The majority of the parents had been deported. *Ms. L. v. U.S. Immigration and Customs Enforcement* (2018) S.D. Cal., 3:18-cv-00428; Aishvarya Kavi, 'A court filing says parents of 445 separated migrant children still have not been found', *The New York Times* (8 April 2021).

155 Eleanor Acer, 'Criminal Prosecutions and Illegal Entry: A Deeper Dive', *Just Security* website (18 July 2019); American Immigration Council, 'Prosecuting People for Coming to the United States', Factsheet (23 August 2021).

156 Department of Homeland Security, 'Statement on the Suspension of New Enrollments in the Migrant Protection Protocols Program', website (20 January 2021). This decision has subsequently been subject to court challenges. In August 2021, a district judge in Texas ruled that the Government had to reinstate the Migrant Protection Protocols. The Biden administration then lodged an emergency appeal with the United States Supreme Court to stay the order. The Court refused, requiring the Biden administration to make a "good faith" effort to implement the policy while the court case proceeds. *Biden v Texas* (2021) USSC, 21-10806. The administration has also suspended and initiated the process to terminate the Asylum Cooperative Agreements (ACA) with the Governments of Guatemala, Honduras and El Salvador. Under the agreements, a person could be denied the right to seek asylum at the United States border and sent to any of these countries. US Secretary of State Antony J. Blinken, 'Suspending and Terminating the Asylum Cooperative Agreements with the Governments of El Salvador, Guatemala and Honduras, Press Release (2 June 2021); Aaron Reichlin-Melnick, 'Biden Administration Ends "Safe Third Country" Agreements', *Immigration Impact* (8 February 2021).

157 Centers for Disease Control and Prevention (CDC), Department of Health and Human Services (HHS), 'Order Suspending the Right To Introduce Certain Persons From Countries Where a Quarantinable Communicable Disease Exists', *Federal Register* (13 October 2020); UNHCR representative to the United States and the Caribbean Matthew Reynolds, 'UNHCR concerned over U.S. expulsion flights under COVID-19 asylum restrictions', Press Release (11 August 2021).

158 UN, 'UNHCR chief calls on US to end COVID-19 asylum restrictions at the Mexico Border', *UN* News (20 May 2021); UNHCR, 'News Comment by UN High Commissioner for Refugees Filippo Grandi on conditions and expulsions at US Border', Press Release (21 September 2021). The Biden Administration had just a few months earlier extended temporary protection to Haitians that had come to the United States in the wake of the 2010 earthquake. US Citizenship and Immigration Services, 'Temporary Protected Status Designated Country: Haiti' (May 2021).

159 Including at airports. Regina Jefferies, Daniel Ghezelbash, and Asher Lazarus Hirsch, 'Assessing Protection Claims at Airports: Developing procedures to meet international and domestic obligations', Policy Brief 9, Kaldor Centre for Refugee Law (September 2020).

160 Persons entering Australia at airports with visas and presenting an asylum claim or suspected of later doing so have also faced detention. Ibid., p. 8.

161 According to Australia's official records, the number of unauthorized arrivals by sea steadily increased over the preceding years: It stood at 200 persons in 1998, over 3,700 persons in 1999, close to 3,000 in 2000 and over 5,500 in 2001. Janet Phillips and Harriet Spinks, 'Boat Arrivals in Australia since 1976', Research Paper, Parliament of Australia, Department of Parliamentary Services: Social Policy Section (2013), Appendix A; Parliament of Australia, Senate Select Committee, 'Chapter 10 - Pacific Solution: Negotiations and Agreements', A Certain Maritime Incident, Report (2002); Kaldor Centre for International Refugee Law, 'The Tampa affair: 20 years on', website (10 August 2021).

162 Ariane Rummery, 'Australia's "Pacific Solution" draws to a close: The last 21 Sri Lankan refugees on Nauru leave for Australia, signalling the end of Australia's "Pacific Solution"', *UNHCR* News (11 February 2008).

...PART II: **Protecting More Broadly...**

163 Janet Phillips, 'Boat arrivals and boat "turnbacks" in Australia since 1976: a quick guide to the statistics', Research Paper, Parliament of Australia, Department of Parliamentary Services: Social Policy Section (2017), table 1; Bob Douglas, Claire Higgins, Arja Keski-Nummi, Jane McAdam and Travers McLeod, 'Beyond the boats: building an asylum and refugee policy for the long term', Report following high-level roundtable (November 2014), p. 17.

164 There were an estimated 1,400 deaths at sea between 2001 and 2014. See: Douglas et al., 'Beyond the boats', p. 13; Kenneth McLeod, 'Deadly voyages: Border related deaths associated with Australia', Interactive Charts, *SBS News* (23 April 2015).

165 They were predominately from Afghanistan, Iran, Iraq, Pakistan or Sri Lanka or were stateless. Janet Phillips, 'Asylum seekers and refugees: what are the facts?', Research Paper, Parliament of Australia, Department of Parliamentary Services: Social Policy Section (2015).

166 Refugee Council of Australia, 'Offshore processing statistics - How many people are on Nauru and PNG?', website (30 August 2021).

167 As part of larger measures to remove incentives for people to attempt to come to Australia without prior authorization. See: Government of Australia, 'Report of the Expert Panel on Asylum Seekers' (13 August 2012); Janet Phillips, 'A comparison of Coalition and Labor government asylum policies in Australia since 2001', Research Paper, Parliament of Australia, Department of Parliamentary Services: Social Policy Section (2 February 2017); Elibritt Karlsen, 'Australia's offshore processing of asylum seekers in Nauru and PNG: a quick guide to statistics and resources', Research Paper, Parliament of Australia, Department of Parliamentary Services: Law and Bills Digest Section (19 December 2016).

168 Department of Home Affairs, Australian Government, 'Operation Sovereign Borders', website.

169 UNHCR, 'Returns to Sri Lanka of individuals intercepted at sea', Press Release (7 July 2014); UN Committee on the Rights of the Child, 'Concluding observations on the combined fifth and sixth periodic reports of Australia' (1 November 2019), UN Doc CRC/C/AUS/CO/5-6, pp. 12–13; UN Committee on the Elimination of Discrimination against Women, 'Concluding observations on the eighth periodic report of Australia' (25 July 2018), UN Doc CEDAW/C/AUS/CO/8, p. 16; Committee on the Elimination of Racial Discrimination, 'Concluding observations on the eighteenth to twentieth periodic reports of Australia' (26 December 2017), UN Doc CERD/C/AUS/CO/18-20, p. 7; Zeid Ra'ad Al Hussein, 'Statement by UN High Commissioner for Human Rights Zeid Ra'ad Al Hussein at the Interactive Dialogue on the Human Rights of Migrants at the 29th session of the Human Rights Council', Speech reported on OHCHR website (15 June 2015).

170 Human Rights Council, 'Report of the Special Rapporteur on the Human Rights of Migrants on his mission to Australia and the regional processing centres in Nauru' (24 April 2017), UN Doc A/HRC/35/25/Add.3, paras. 72–79.

171 Ibid., paras. 80–82.

172 *Namah v. Pato* (2016) PNGSC, SC1497; Kelly Buchanan, 'Australia/Papua New Guinea: Supreme Court Rules Asylum-Seeker Detention Is Unconstitutional', *Global Legal Monitor*, Library of Congress website (2 May 2016).

173 Joseph Lew, 'Photos of Nauru's (Now) Mostly Empty Immigration Detention Centre', *VICE World News* (22 October 2020); Refugee Council of Australia, 'Seven Years on: An Overview of Australia's Offshore Processing Policies', Report (July 2020), p. 7. The Nauru Regional

Processing Centre (in 2015) and Manus Island Regional Processing Centre (in 2016) had previously been transitioned to more open facilities. UNHCR, 'UNHCR appeals to Australia to act and save lives at immediate risk', Press Release (23 October 2018).

174 Kaldor Centre for Refugee Law, 'Offshore Processing: An Overview', Factsheet (11 January 2021); Refugee Council of Australia, 'Seven Years on: An Overview', p. 11.

175 Refugee Council of Australia, 'How many people are on Nauru and PNG?'.

176 Australian Human Rights Commission, 'Tell Me About: Bridging Visas for Asylum Seekers', Factsheet (17 April 2013).

177 Department of Home Affairs, Australian Government, 'Immigration Detention and Community Statistics Summary', Report (30 April 2021). See also: UNHCR, 'Australia: UNHCR Submission for the Universal Periodic Review - Australia - UPR 37th Session' (July 2020), p. 4.

178 Claire P. Gutekunst, 'Interdiction of Haitian Migrants on the High Seas: A Legal and Policy Analysis,' *The Yale Journal of International Law* 10, no. 1 (1984): pp. 152–154. For more on the economic and human rights situation, see: David Nicholls, 'Haiti: the rise and fall of Duvalierism', *Third World Quarterly* 8, no. 4 (1986): pp. 1243–1244; HRW, *Haiti's Rendezvous with History: The Case of Jean-Claude Duvalier*, Report (2011), p. 2.

179 Claire P. Gutekunst, 'Interdiction of Haitian Migrants on the High Seas': pp. 156–158 and 164. Practices, such as expedited hearings and mass exclusion hearings behind closed doors, were found to violate United States constitutional and statutory rights in several court cases. Subsequent individual hearings were also found not to comply with procedural safeguards. See also: Gil Loescher and John Scanlan, 'Human Rights, U.S. Foreign Policy, and Haitian Refugees', *Journal of Interamerican Studies and World Affairs* 26, no. 3 (1984): pp. 333, 335, 339–341, 345.

180 Niels Frenzen, 'Responses to "Boat Migration": A Global Perspective – US Practices', in Violeta Moreno-Lax and Efthymios Papastavridis (eds.), *'Boat Refugees' and Migrants at Sea: A Comprehensive Approach* (Leiden: Brill Nijhoff, 2017): p. 287. The only way a Haitian could gain access to a screening interview was to call out or use gestures to show a "manifestation of fear". This came to be known as the "shout test". Eleanor Acer, 'A System Designed to Fail Haitians', *Human Rights First* website (10 February 2010). FitzGerald, *Refuge beyond Reach*, pp. 79–82.

181 Niels Frenzen, 'Responses to "Boat Migration"', pp. 282–283, 288–292, 296–297.

182 Homeland Security and United States Coast Guard, 'Maritime Law Enforcement Assessment – Fiscal Year 2020 Report to Congress', Report (9 December 2020), pp. 5–7. The report refers to an Executive Order that states that the Government's obligations under the 1967 Protocol do not extend to persons located outside the territory of the United States. It also refers to the Executive Order authorizing the Attorney General to "maintain custody, at any location he deems appropriate, of any undocumented aliens he has reason to believe are seeking to enter the United States and who are interdicted or intercepted in the Caribbean region". George Bush, Executive Order 12807, Interdiction of Illegal Aliens (1992), Homeland Security Digital Library; George W. Bush, Executive Order 13276, Delegation of Responsibilities Concerning Undocumented Aliens Interdicted or Intercepted in the Caribbean Region (2002), Homeland Security Digital Library.

183 Frenzen, 'Responses to "Boat Migration"', pp. 299–302; Azadeh Dastyari, *United States Migrant Interdiction and the Detention of Refugees in Guantánamo Bay* (Cambridge: Cambridge University Press, 2015), pp. 161–171, 207–214; Bill Frelick, Ian M. Kysel, and Jennifer Podkul, 'The Impact of Externalization of Migration Controls on the Rights of

Asylum Seekers and Other Migrants,' *Journal on Migration and Human Security* 4, no. 4 (December 2016): p. 200.

184 *Sale v. Haitian Centers Council, Inc.* (1993) USSC, 509 U.S. 155.

185 Hathaway and Gammeltoft-Hansen, 'Non-Refoulement in a World of Cooperative Deterrence': pp. 247–248. For an analysis of *Sale v. Haitian Centers Council*, see: Dastyari, *United States Migrant Interdiction and the Detention of Refugees in Guantánamo Bay*, pp. 106–112; FitzGerald, *Refuge beyond Reach*, pp. 84–91.

186 Hathaway and Gammeltoft-Hansen, 'Non-Refoulement in a World of Cooperative Deterrence': p. 247.

187 *Hirsi Jamaa and Others v. Italy* (2012) ECHR, 27765/09.

188 Council of Europe, Convention for the Protection of Human Rights and Fundamental Freedoms (4 November 1950), UNTS vol. 213, no. 2889, art. 3.

189 *Hirsi Jamaa and Others v. Italy*, paras. 82, 123.

190 For more commentary on the case, see: Meltem Ineli-Ciger, *Temporary Protection in Law and Practice* (Leiden: Brill Nijhoff, 2018), p. 56.

191 UNHCR, 'UNHCR warns against "exporting" asylum, calls for responsibility sharing for refugees, not burden shifting', Press Release (19 May 2021); UNHCR, 'Observations on the Proposal for amendments to the Danish Alien Act (Introduction of the possibility to transfer asylum-seekers for adjudication of asylum claims and accommodation in third countries)' (8 March 2021), para 16.

192 As of 2021, the United States has appropriated about $3.3 billion to the Mérida Initiative since 2008. Clare Ribando Seelke, 'Mexico: Evolution of the Mérida Initiative, 2007–2021', Congressional Research Service Report IF10578 (13 January 2021), p. 1; Clare Ribando Seelke and Kristin Finklea, 'U.S.-Mexican Security Cooperation: The Mérida Initiative and Beyond', Congressional Research Service Report R41349 (29 June 2017), pp. 11–12. Other investments in the region have come through the Central America Security Initiative (CARSI) and as of 2014 the Strategy for Engagement in Central America to improve conditions in the region as also a means to reduce unauthorised arrivals. Disbursements of approved funding slowed down during the Trump administration which some have said may have contributed to increased arrivals. In 2021, the Biden administration announced a $4 billion comprehensive strategy for the region. Peter J. Meyer, 'U.S. Strategy for Engagement in Central America: Policy Issues for Congress', Congressional Research Service Report 44812 (12 November 2019), pp. 4–5, 12, 18–20, 22–23; Mark L. Schneider, 'Six Months On: Changes in U.S. Policy toward the Northern Triangle', Commentary, Center for Strategic and International Studies (CSIS) (20 July 2021).

193 Including through the training of border officers, the provision of patrol boats and surveillance equipment. Hathaway and Gammeltoft-Hansen, 'Non-Refoulement in a World of Cooperative Deterrence': pp. 254; Human Rights Law Centre, *Can't flee, can't stay: Australia's interception and return of Sri Lankan asylum seekers*, Report (March 2014), pp. 24–25, 27–33. These measures have been criticized by human rights activists including on the basis that they prevent those at risk in Sri Lanka from fleeing. Ibid., pp. 4–7 and 14–18.

194 Hathaway and Gammeltoft-Hansen, 'Non-Refoulement in a World of Cooperative Deterrence': p. 254.

195 More than €800 million have been mobilized since 2015 by the North of Africa window of the EU Emergency Trust Fund alone for 38 programmes implemented in Algeria, Egypt, Libya, Morocco and Tunisia. Over half goes to protection, community stabilization and socio-economic support, while one third goes to border management and the rest to migration governance and labour migration. EU, 'EU Emergency Trust Fund for Africa: Improving Migration Management in the North of Africa Region', Factsheet (September 2020). There are other bilateral arrangements as noted in the case of Morocco noted below.

196 Hathaway and Gammeltoft-Hansen, 'Non-Refoulement in a World of Cooperative Deterrence': p. 251.

197 This was reportedly approved just after Morocco relaxed its border controls allowing 12,000 migrants and asylum-seekers to enter within two days. Spanish officials had accused Morocco of using migrants as a means to exert leverage over Spain, amidst political tensions over Spain permitting a leader of the Polisario Front to access medical treatment in Spain. Nicholas Casey and José Bautista, '"Come On In, Boys": A Wave of the Hand Sets Off Spain-Morocco Migrant Fight', *The New York Times* (2 June 2021).

198 Ibid.

199 Hathaway and Gammeltoft-Hansen, 'Non-Refoulement in a World of Cooperative Deterrence': p 250.

200 Funding is channelled through the facility, with only part of it provided as direct grants to government ministries. European Commission, 'The EU Facility for Refugees in Turkey', Factsheet (September 2021).

201 EU, Council of the European Union, 'EU-Turkey Statement' (18 March 2016); Kyilah Terry, 'The EU-Turkey Deal, Five Years On: A Frayed and Controversial but Enduring Blueprint', Article, Migration Policy Institute (8 April 2021); Berkay Mandiraci, 'Sharing the Burden: Revisiting the EU-Turkey Migration Deal', Commentary, International Crisis Group (13 March 2020).

202 UNHCR, 'UNHCR's reaction to Statement of the EU Heads of State and Government of Turkey', Press Briefing (8 March 2016); UNHCR, 'UNHCR expresses concern over EU-Turkey plan', *UNHCR* News (11 March 2016); UNHCR, 'Legal considerations on the return of asylum-seekers and refugees from Greece to Turkey as part of the EU-Turkey Cooperation in Tackling the Migration Crisis under the safe third country and first country of asylum concept' (23 March 2016); UNHCR, 'Legal considerations regarding access to protection and a connection between the refugee and the third country in the context of return or transfer to safe third countries' (April 2018). See also: Lisa Haferlach and Dilek Kurban, 'Lessons Learnt from the EU-Turkey Refugee Agreement in Guiding EU Migration Partnerships with Origin and Transit Countries', *Global Policy* 8, no. S4 (2017): pp. 85–93; Jesuit Refugee Service, 'The EU-Turkey Deal: Analysis and Considerations', Europe Policy Discussion Paper (30 April 2016).

203 Turkey may grant non-Europeans a "conditional refugee status", which provides for a lesser protection status and is intended to be temporary with the only durable solution being resettlement to another country. Since 2011, Turkey grants Syrians fleeing the civil war temporary protection. Ineli-Ciger, *Temporary Protection in Law and Practice*, pp. 168–170.

204 European Commission, 'EU-Turkey Statement: Three Years On' (March 2019), p. 1; UNHCR, 'Mediterranean Situation', UNHCR Operational Data Portal - Refugee Situations.

205 Over 34,180 refugees were resettled from Turkey to Europe from 2016 to 2021, far short of the agreed maximum of 72,000. UNHCR, Resettlement Data Finder (RDF); European Commission, 'EU-Turkey Statement: Three Years On', p. 2; Terry, 'The EU-Turkey Deal'.

206 This may have contributed to Turkey's decision to relax its controls in early 2020. Terry, 'The

EU-Turkey Deal'; Mandiraci, 'Sharing the Burden'; UNHCR, 'UNHCR statement on the situation at the Turkey-EU border', Press Release (2 March 2020). Some observers say that other factors were also thought to play a role, including securing additional funding and seeking EU support for Turkey's military strategy in Idlib, Syria. Mandiraci, 'Sharing the Burden'.

207 Frontex, 'Migration flows: Eastern, Central and Western routes', Infographic; Frontex, 'Eastern Mediterranean Route', website.

208 The Central Mediterranean route connects Sub-Saharan Africa through central north Africa (Algeria, Libya and Tunisia) with Europe (Italy and Malta). The Western Mediterranean route connects north-west Africa (Morocco and western Algeria) with Spain. UNHCR, 'Routes towards the Western and Central Mediterranean Sea: Working on Alternatives to Dangerous Journeys for Refugees', Updated Risk Mitigation Strategy and Appeal (January 2021), p. 5.

209 European Union, 'EU Emergency Trust Fund for Africa: Strategy in the North of Africa', website; Mixed Migration Centre, *Mixed Migration Review 2020*, Annual Report (18 November 2020), pp. 19–25.

210 The International Organization for Migration (IOM) estimates that, even though almost 800,000 migrants left Libya in 2011, the country continues to host over 570,000 migrants mostly working in sectors that pose higher risks to health and safety and provide less protection against violence, exploitation and abuse (such as construction, water supply, electricity and gas sectors, agriculture, pastoralism, the food industry, and manual craft). IOM estimates that around 22 per cent of migrants are unemployed. Emma Borgnäs, Linda Cottone, Tassilo Teppert, 'Labour Migration Dynamics in Libya', in Philippe Fargues et al. (eds.), *Migration in West and North Africa and across the Mediterranean: Trends, Risks, Development and Governance* (IOM, 2020), p. 303; Displacement Tracking Matrix (DTM) and IOM, 'Libya's Migrant Report', Mobility Tracking Round 33 (September–October 2020), p. 6; DTM and IOM, 'Libya's Migrant Report', Mobility Tracking Round 35 (January–February 2021), p. 4. At the end of 2020, there were some 44,000 refugees and asylum-seekers registered with UNHCR, and several hundred thousand persons estimated to be internally displaced by the conflict. UNHCR, Refugee Data Finder.

211 Salah Sarrar, 'Gaddafi and Berlusconi sign accord worth billions', *Reuters* (30 August 2008); Ian Traynor, 'EU keen to strike deal with Muammar Gaddafi on immigration', *The Guardian* (1 September 2010).

212 Katie Kuschminder, 'Once a Destination for Migrants, Post-Gaddafi Libya Has Gone from Transit Route to Containment', Article, Migration Policy Institute (5 August 2020); IOM, *Living and Working in the Midst of Conflict: The Status of Long-Term Migrants in Libya* (2019), pp. 1–2.

213 In 2016, Italy received some 181,400 arrivals, most of whom arrived from Libya (some 163,000). Spain received some 8,200. UNHCR, 'Mediterranean Situation'; UNHCR, 'Italy Country Update - December 2016', Situation Report (9 February 2017).

214 UNHCR, 'Mediterranean Situation'; Deutsche Welle, 'Thousands of African migrants saved off Italian coast', website (5 October 2016); Phillip Connor, 'Italy may surpass Greece in 2016 refugee arrivals', Article, *Pew Research Center* website (2 November 2016); Steve Scherer, 'Record 2016 pushes migrant arrivals in Italy over half million', *Reuters* (30 December 2016); Louise Hunt, 'Cracks widen in "impossible" Italian asylum system', *The New Humanitarian* (15 August 2016).

215 Relocations were based on quotas with only asylum-seekers of nationalities having an average EU asylum recognition rate of 75 per cent or higher eligible for transfer. An audit concluded that, out of a total of a close to half a million qualifying asylum-seekers in Greece and Italy, just 35,000 (some 22,000 from Greece and close to 13,000 from Italy) were relocated to 22 member States and three associated countries (Liechtenstein, Norway and Switzerland). The United Kingdom and Denmark exercised their opt-out rights and Hungary and Poland refused to relocate any asylum-seekers. European Court of Auditors, 'Special report No 24/2019: Asylum, relocation and return of migrants: Time to step up action to address disparities between objectives and results' (13 November 2019), pp. 8 and 20–22.

216 Such as through port closures, refusals of disembarkation and legal repercussions for staff on rescuing vessels. UNHCR, 'UNHCR and IOM call for urgent disembarkation of rescued migrants and refugees in Central Mediterranean Sea', Press Release (29 August 2020); Crispian Balmer, 'Italian magistrates set to level charges against sea rescuers, NGOs', *Reuters* (3 March 2021); Médecins Sans Frontières (MSF) International, 'Lives on the line as legal appeal lodged to free the Sea-Watch 4', Press Release (23 October 2020).

217 OHCHR, '"Lethal Disregard": Search and rescue and the protection of migrants in the central Mediterranean Sea', Report (May 2021), p. 21.

218 According to the European Union Agency for Fundamental Rights (FRA), "in some cases, rescue vessels were blocked in harbours due to flag issues or the inability to meet maritime safety-related and other technical requirements". FRA, 'December 2020 update - NGO ships involved in search and rescue in the Mediterranean and legal proceedings against them', website (18 December 2020).

219 UNHCR and IOM have consistently objected to the criminalization of saving lives at sea, noting the crucial role that NGOs have played in it. They have also urged that commercial vessels not be requested to transfer rescued persons to the Libyan Coast Guard or otherwise have them disembark in Libya. UNHCR, 'Joint Statement: UN High Commissioner for Refugees Filippo Grandi and IOM Director General António Vitorino welcome consensus on need for action on Libya, Mediterranean' (22 July 2019). In September 2020, the European Commission presented a proposal for a New Pact on Asylum and Migration (New EU Pact). The proposals include for example new border and return procedures, preparedness and solidarity measures, promoting legal pathways to the EU and enhancing search and rescue operations. Positively, it recognises that "there is a need to avoid criminalisation of those who provide humanitarian assistance to people in distress at sea". European Commission, 'Commission Recommendation (EU) 2020/1365 of 23 September 2020 on cooperation among Member States concerning operations carried out by vessels owned or operated by private entities for the purpose of search and rescue activities', *Official Journal of the European Union* 63 (October 2020), para. 5.

220 In total, the EU has funded around €700 million in support to Libya from 2014 to 2020 under various funding instruments. The EU Emergency Trust Fund for Africa has invested thus far €455 million in community stabilization, protection and border management projects in Libya under the North Africa window. Of this, 13 per cent € 57.2 was allocated for border management projects, which included technical trainings for members of the Libyan Coast Guard as well as logistical and infrastructure support. EU Emergency Trust Fund for Africa, 'EU Support on Migration in Libya', Factsheet (October 2020); EU Trust Fund for Africa, 'DEC: Support to Integrated border and migration management in Libya – First phase', website (27 July 2017); EU Trust Fund for Africa, 'DEC: Support to Integrated border and migration management in Libya – Second phase', website (13 December 2018). Italy has also provided additional assistance to Libyan authorities. Charlotte Oberti, 'Agreement between Italy and the Libyan coastguard renewed for three years', *InfoMigrants* (7 February 2020); Anja Palm, 'The Italy-Libya Memorandum of Understanding: The baseline of a policy approach aimed at closing all doors to Europe?', EU Migration and Asylum Law and Policy blog (2 October 2017).

221 Search and Rescue (SAR) regions are established in accordance with the International Convention on Maritime Search and Rescue to ensure that the rescue of persons in distress at sea is coordinated and that assistance is provided. International Maritime Organisation (IMO), 'SAR Convention', website (27 April 1979). They are acknowledged by the International Maritime Organization. See: Alarm Phone et al., *Remote Control: The EU-Libya Collaboration in Mass Interceptions of Migrants in the Central Mediterranean*, Report (17 June 2020), pp. 2 and 8–10.

222 The New EU Pact includes proposals to enhance the search and rescue operations of EU member States, to provide for predictable disembarkation arrangements based on solidarity mechanisms within the EU and to strengthen the cooperation with countries of origin and transit. European Commission, 'Communication from the Commission to the European Parliament, the Council, the European Economic and Social Committee and the Committee of the Regions on a New Pact on Migration and Asylum' (23 September 2020), COM/2020/609, pp. 13–14. For more on the New EU Pact, see: European Commission, 'New Pact on Migration and Asylum: A fresh start on migration in Europe', website; European Commission, 'Migration and Asylum Package: New Pact on Migration and Asylum documents adopted on 23 September 2020', Collected Documents. For an update on the proposals, see: European Commission, 'Report on Migration and Asylum' (29 September 2021).

223 Tom Kington, 'Turkish ships muscle in on Europe's role in Libyan waters', *The Times* (21 May 2021); Emma Wallis, 'Are Turkish ships working with the Libyan coastguard in the central Mediterranean?', *InfoMigrants* (30 January 2020).

224 UNHCR, 'UNHCR Position on the Designation of Libya as a Safe Third Country and as a Place of Safety for the Purpose of Disembarkation Following Rescue at Sea' (September 2020), paras. 10 and 13.

225 The estimated number of detainees in official detention centres constantly fluctuates and forced disappearances are reported. As of 30 July 2021, UNHCR estimated that some 5,400 individuals were detained in Libya, of whom 1,000 were persons of concern to UNHCR (refugees, asylum-seekers, IDPs, returnees and stateless persons). UNHCR, 'Libya Update', Situation Report (30 July 2021).

226 Amnesty International, *'Between life and death': Refugees and Migrants trapped in Libya's cycle of abuse*, Report (2000), pp. 21–32; HRW, *No Escape from Hell: EU Policies Contribute to Abuse of Migrants in Libya*, Report (2019), pp. 30–57.

227 UNHCR/IOM, 'IOM and UNHCR condemn the return of migrants and refugees to Libya', Joint Press Release (16 June 2021).

228 United Nations Secretary-General, 'UN Secretary-General's video remarks to the Berlin II Conference on Libya', Transcript (23 June 2021); Permanent Representative of Germany to the United Nations, 'Letter Dated 22 January 2020 from the Permanent Representative of Germany to the United Nations addressed to the President of the Security Council', Annex l: 'The Berlin Conference on Libya: Conference Conclusions' (22 January 2020), UN Doc S/2020/63; UNHCR, 'Position on the Designation of Libya', paras. 33 and 34; UNSC, Res. 2510 (12 February 2020), UN Doc S/RES/2510; Zeid Ra'ad Al Hussein, 'UN human rights chief: Suffering of migrants in Libya outrage to conscience of humanity', *OHCHR* News (14 November 2017).

229 Julia Litzkow, Bram Frouws, and Roberto Forin (Mixed Migration Centre), 'Smuggling and mixed migration: Insights and key messages drawn from a decade of MMC research and 4Mi data collection', Briefing Paper (June 2021), p. 5; The Danish Refugee Council and the MMC, 'Countering Human Smuggling: No Silver Bullet for Safer Mobility - Evidence based recommendations towards a protection-sensitive approach to actions against Human smuggling', Position Paper (July 2021), p. 3.

230 UNHCR, 'Mediterranean Situation'. The number of arrivals across the Central Mediterranean increased in 2020 possibly as a result of the impact of COVID-19 measures in Northern Africa and other African countries. UNHCR, 'Routes towards the Western and Central Mediterranean Sea', pp. 9–11. See also: Frontex, 'Migration Flows'.

231 UNHCR, 'Mediterranean Situation'; Frontex, 'Migration Flows'.

232 UNHCR, 'Spain - land and sea arrivals - December 2019', Factsheet (23 January 2020); UNHCR, 'Spain - land and sea arrivals - December 2020', Factsheet (19 January 2021).

233 Most refugees and migrants on this route transit through The Gambia, Mauritania, Morocco, Senegal and Western Sahara. UNHCR, 'Routes towards the Western and Central Mediterranean Sea', pp. 4, 10–11; European Council and Council of the European Union, 'Western Mediterranean and Western African routes', website.

234 Some 1,750 people may have died along these land routes between 2018 and 2019, with an average of at least 72 deaths per month. UNHCR and MMC, *'On this journey, no one cares if you live or die.' Abuse, protection, and justice along routes between East and West Africa and Africa's Mediterranean coast*, Report (July 2020), pp. 7, 14.

235 Ana-Maria Murphy-Teixidor (MMC), 'Mixed migration and migrant smuggling in Libya: The role of non-Libyan smuggler intermediaries', Briefing Paper (June 2021), p. 2.

236 Litzkow, Frouws and Forin, 'Smuggling and mixed migration: Insights and key messages', p. 4; DRC and MMC, 'Countering Human Smuggling: No Silver Bullet for Safer Mobility', p. 5.

237 Ioanna Kotsioni, 'Detention of Migrants and Asylum-Seekers: The Challenge for Humanitarian Actors', *Refugee Survey Quarterly* 35 (2016): pp. 41–55.

238 Shin-wha Lee, 'South Korea's Refugee Policies: National and Human Security Perspectives', in Carolina G. Hernandez et al. (eds.), *Human Security and Cross-Border Cooperation in East Asia* (Cham, Switzerland: Palgrave Macmillan, 2019), pp. 227–248. In Japan, asylum-seekers fleeing situations of armed violence and conflict are denied 1951 Convention status on the grounds that they were not individually targeted but suffered indiscriminate violence. Brian Aycock and Naoko Hashimoto, 'Complementary Protection in Japan: To What Extent Does Japan Offer Effective International Protection for Those Who Fall Outside the 1951 Refugee Convention?', *Laws* 10, no. 16 (2021): pp. 6, 9, 19. See also: Naoko Hashimoto, 'Why does Japan recognise so few refugees?', Refugee Law Initiative blog (1 May 2018).

239 From 2010 to 2020, South Korea recognized nearly 700 refugees, rejected 31,700 applications, and accorded complementary protection status to 2,200 persons. Japan recognized nearly 200 refugees, rejected 77,700 applications, and accorded complementary protection to 1,300 persons. UNHCR, Refugee Data Finder. See also: Lee, 'South Korea's Refugee Policies'.

...PART II: **Protecting More Broadly...**

240 Between 2010 and 2019. UNHCR, *Global Trends: Forced Displacement in 2019*, Report (2020), p. 43.

241 Lee, 'South Korea's Refugee Policies'; Aycock and Hashimoto, 'Complementary Protection in Japan': pp. 18–23.

242 Ademola Abass and Francesca Ippolito, 'Establishing the Common European Asylum System: "It's a Long, Long Way to Tipperary"', in *Regional Approaches to the Protection of Asylum Seekers*, pp. 114–124.

243 UNHCR, Refugee Data Finder and UNHCR, Refugee Data Finder.

244 European Council on Refugees and Exiles (ECRE), 'Making the CEAS Work, Starting Today', Policy Note #22 (2019).

245 UK House of Commons, 'Nationality and Borders Bill', Bill 141 of 2021–2022.

246 Government of the United Kingdom, 'New Plan for Immigration', Policy Statement (24 March 2021).

247 UNHCR, 'Observations on the New Plan for Immigration policy statement of the Government of the United Kingdom' (May 2021); UNHCR, 'UK asylum bill would break international law, damaging refugees and global co-operation', Press Release (23 September 2021).

248 Martin Lemberg-Pedersen, 'Op-ed: Danish Externalization Desires and the Drive Towards Zero Asylum Seekers', *ECRE* website (12 March 2021).

249 UNHCR, Refugee Data Finder.

250 Government of Denmark, 'Forslag til lov om ændring af udlændingeloven og hjemrejse-loven (Indførelse af mulighed for overførsel af asylansøgere til asylsagsbehandling og eventuel efterfølgende beskyttelse i tredjelande)' [Proposal for amendments to the Danish Alien Act and Return Act (Introduction of the possibility to transfer asylum-seekers for asylum proceedings and possible subsequent protection in third countries)] (3 June 2021), L 226, The Danish Parliament website.

251 Jan M. Olsen, 'Danes tap migration envoy as EU eyes asylum system reforms', *AP News* (10 September 2020).

252 UNHCR, 'Observations on the Proposal for amendments to the Danish Alien Act (Introduction of the possibility to transfer asylum-seekers for adjudication of asylum claims and accommodation in third countries)' (8 March 2021), para. 11.

253 Lemberg-Pedersen, 'Op-Ed: Danish Externalization Desires and the Drive Towards Zero Asylum Seekers'.

254 UNHCR, 'UNHCR deeply concerned at discriminatory two-tier UK asylum plans, urges rethink', Press Release (10 May 2021); John Cosgrave et al., *Europe's refugees and migrants - Hidden flows, tightened borders and spiralling costs*, Report (ODI, September 2016).

255 Peter Tinti and Tuesday Reitano, *Migrant, Refugee, Smuggler, Saviour* (London: C. Hurst & Co, 2016), p. 5.

256 They make the important point that: "In each hub, and along each major route, the smuggling market needs to be analysed for its unique political economy in order to understand the motivations of those moving through the route, those engaged in trade, those who protect it, and those who are profiting". Ibid., p. 273.

257 The adverse effects of climate change refer to "changes in the physical environment or biota [...] which have significant deleterious effects on the composition, resilience or productivity of natural and managed ecosystems or on the operation of socio-economic systems or on human health and welfare", United Nations Framework Convention on Climate Change (UNFCCC) (1992), UNTS vol. 1771, no. 30822, art. 1.

258 A disaster is a "serious disruption of the functioning of a community or a society" involving widespread "human, material, economic and environmental losses and impacts", which exceeds the ability of the affected community or society to cope using its own resources. See: United Nations Office for Disaster Risk Reduction, 'Terminology: Glossary - Disaster', website. They include but are not limited to those related to climate change impacts. See: UNHCR, 'Key Concepts on Climate Change and Disaster Displacement', Factsheet.

259 Data from the Internal Displacement Monitoring Centre (IDMC) shows that new internal displacements due to disaster have exceeded new internal displacements due to conflict every year since 2011. IDMC, *Global Report on Internal Displacement: Internal displacement in a changing climate 2021* (GRID 2021), Report (May 2021), p. 8.

260 Phil Orchard, *Protecting the Internally Displaced: Rhetoric and Reality* (NY: Routledge, 2019), pp. 63–64.

261 Ibid, pp. 64–72. He also recounts that UNRRA's mandate was expanded to include assistance to those displaced within and outside their countries, while the subsequent IRO's definition of refugee was limited to those who were outside their countries.

262 Ibid., pp. 75–79.

263 Eleanor Roosevelt, quoted in Orchard, *Protecting the Internally Displaced*, p. 74.

264 UNGA, 'Statute of the Office of the United Nations High Commissioner for Refugees' (1950), para. 9.

265 Samuel Cheung, 'Internal Displacement, UNHCR and the International Community', Reference Paper for the 70th Anniversary of the 1951 Refugee Convention, UNHCR (October 2021), pp. 3–4; UNGA, 'Office of the United Nations High Commissioner for Refugees' (26 April 1993), UN Docs A/RES/47/105, para. 14; Executive Committee of the High Commissioner's Programme, 'Internally Displaced Persons No. 75 (XLV)' (7 October 1994).

266 Samuel Cheung, 'Internal Displacement, UNHCR and the International Community', pp. 5–8. See also: Susan Martin, 'Making the UN Work: Forced Migration and Institutional Reform', *Journal of Refugee Studies* 17, no. 3 (2004): pp. 301–318.

267 UNGA, 'New International Humanitarian Order' (14 December 1981), UN Doc A/RES/36/136.

268 ECOSOC, Commission on Human Rights, 'Study on Human Rights and Massive Exoduses' (1981), UN Doc E/CN.4/1503.

269 Independent Bureau for Humanitarian Issues (formerly Independent Commission for International Humanitarian Issues), 'Purpose', website.

270 Independent Commission on International Humanitarian Issues, *Winning the Human Race? The Report of the Independent Commission on International Humanitarian Issues* (London: Zed Books, 1988), pp. 97–107.

271 In the meantime, two international conferences also discussed the need for improved international and institutional responses to IDPs: UNGA, 'International Conference on Central American Refugees' (16 December 1991), UN Doc A/RES/46/107; UN Secretary-General, 'International Conference on the Plight of Refugees, Returnees and Displaced Persons in Southern Africa (SARRED)', Report (19 October 1988), UN Doc A/43/717.

272 ECOSOC, 'Note by the Secretary-General pursuant to Economic and Social Council resolution 1990/7, Addendum: Report on refugees, displaced persons and returnees prepared by Mr. Jacques Cuénod, Consultant' (27 June 1991), UN Doc E/1991/109/Add.1.

273 UNGA, 'Strengthening of the coordination of humanitarian emergency assistance of the

...PART II: **Protecting More Broadly...**

United Nations' (19 December 1991), UN Doc A/RES/46/182. See section on International Co-ordination in this Part.

274 This was approved by the Economic and Social Council on 20 July 1992. As part of his mandate, he was to consider international norms applicable to IDPs. The position continued until 2010, when the Human Rights Council appointed a Special Rapporteur on the human rights of IDPs.

275 Francis M. Deng, 'Comprehensive study prepared by Mr. Francis M. Deng, Representative of the Secretary-General on the human rights issues related to internally displaced persons, pursuant to Commission on Human Rights Resolution 1992/73' (21 January 1993), UN Doc E/CN.4/1993/35.

276 UNGA, 'Protection of and assistance to internally displaced persons' (11 March 1996), UN Doc A/RES/50/195 and UN Commission on Human Rights, 'Internally Displaced Persons' (19 April 1996), UN Doc E/CN.4/RES/1996/52. Deng worked with a team of international legal scholars in developing the Guiding Principles on Internal Displacement. UN Commission on Human Rights, 'Report of the Representative of the Secretary-General, Mr. Francis M. Deng, submitted pursuant to Commission resolution 1997/39, Addendum: Guiding Principles on Internal Displacement' (11 February 1998), UN Doc E/CN.4/1998/53/Add.2, para 12.

277 Francis. M. Deng, 'Report of the Representative of the Secretary-General, Mr. Francis M. Deng, Submitted Pursuant to Commission Resolution 1997/39, Addendum: Guiding Principles on Internal Displacement' (Guiding Principles on Internal Displacement), para. 9.

278 Guiding Principles on Internal Displacement, Introduction, para. 2.

279 Ibid., Principles 1, 8, 12 and 14.

280 Ibid., Principle 6.

281 Ibid., Principle 7.

282 Ibid., Principles 18–20 and 23.

283 Roberta Cohen and Francis M. Deng, 'Reflections from Former Mandate Holders: Developing the Normative Framework for IDPs', *International Journal of Refugee Law* 30, no. 2 (2018): pp. 310–311.

284 International Conference on the Great Lakes Region (ICGLR), 'Protocol to the Pact on Security, Stability and Development in the Great Lakes Region on the Protection and Assistance to Internally Displaced Persons' (30 November 2006).

285 Kampala Convention (2009). The Kampala Convention expands on the Guiding Principles. For example, it elaborates on the protections afforded to IDPs in situations of armed conflict, the prohibitions related to armed groups (Article 7), the obligations of States beyond those specified in the Guiding Principles (Article 9), and the prevention of displacement induced by projects (Article 10).

286 UNGA, '2005 World Summit Outcome' (16 September 2005), UN Doc A/RES/60/1, para. 132.

287 See, for example: UN Human Rights Council 'Mandate of the Special Rapporteur on the human rights of internally displaced persons' (11 July 2019), UN Doc A/HRC/RES/41/15; UNSC, 'Report of the Secretary-General to the Security Council on the protection of civilians in armed conflict' (8 September 1999), UN Doc S/1999/957, Recommendation 7; UNGA, 'Protection of and assistance to internally displaced persons' (18 January

2019), UN Doc A/RES/74/160. To mark the 20th anniversary of the Guiding Principles, the Special Rapporteur, jointly with UNHCR and OCHA, launched the GP20 Plan of Action based on the Guiding Principles with the objective to reduce and resolve internal displacement through prevention, protection and solutions. Human Rights Council, 'Report of the Special Rapporteur on the human rights of internally displaced persons' (11 April 2018), UN Doc A/HRC/38/39; Human Rights Council, 'Global and national activities under the twentieth anniversary of the Guiding Principles on Internal Displacement' (12 June 2019), UN Doc A/HRC/40/41/Add.1.

288 See, for example: OAS, 'Internally Displaced Persons' (3 June 2008), AG/RES. 2417 (XXXVI-II-O/08). See also: Council of Europe, Committee of Ministers, 'Recommendation Rec (2006)6 of the Committee of Ministers to member states on internally displaced persons' (5 April 2006).

289 David J. Cantor, '"The IDP in International Law"? Developments, Debates, Prospects', *International Journal of Refugee Law* 30, no. 2 (2018): pp. 199–200. He draws examples from the treaty bodies that interpret the following: "1966 International Covenant on Civil and Political Rights (ICCPR); 1950 European Convention on Human Rights (ECHR) and its 1952 Protocol No 1 (ECHRP1) and 1963 Protocol No 4 (ECHRP4); 1969 American Convention on Human Rights (ACHR); 1981 African Charter on Human and Peoples' Rights (ACHPR)".

290 Cohen and Deng, 'Reflections from Former Mandate Holders: Developing the Normative Framework for IDPs': p. 312.

291 UN Office on Genocide Prevention and the Responsibility to Protect, 'About: Responsibility to Protect', website; Ivan Šimonović, 'The Responsibility to Protect', *UN Chronicle*.

292 Phil Orchard, *Protecting the Internally Displaced,* pp. 225–226. He notes, for example: Kyrgyzstan where the definition only includes citizens whose homes were destroyed during a certain period of time and in specific areas; Kosovo which adopted a broad definition but whose policy is limited to those displaced within a fixed time period between 1998 and 2004; and Bosnia whose law only covered citizens displaced after 1991. In all of these contexts, the specific limitations set by the governments excluded some IDPs in need.

293 This was the case for example in early laws and policies adopted by Angola and Kosovo, although Adeola and Orchard note that, in recent years, most IDP legislation includes all possible solutions and engages IDPs in planning and decision-making. Romola Adeola and Phil Orchard, 'The Role of Law and Policy in Fostering Responsibility and Accountability of Governments Towards Internally Displaced Persons', *Refugee Survey Quarterly* 39, no. 4 (2020): pp. 416–418. See also: Daniel MacGuire, 'The Relationship between National Normative Frameworks on Internal Displacement and the Reduction of Displacement', *International Journal of Refugee Law* 30, no. 2 (2018): pp. 276–277.

294 According to Adeola and Orchard, as of 2020, 43 States with conflict-induced displacement have laws and policies on internal displacement. Of the 72 laws and major policies, the Guiding Principles are mentioned in less than half of them (32), and the definition of an internally displaced person is endorsed in 21. Adeola and Orchard, 'The Role of Law and Policy in Fostering Responsibility and Accountability': p. 414. For a database with national laws and policies, see: Global Protection Cluster, 'Global Database on IDP Laws and Policies', website.

295 Orchard, *Protecting the Internally Displaced*, pp. 196–199, 211–213. He cites several examples between the 1990s and 2018, such as Burundi following the Arusha Accords that brought an end to the 7-year civil war, Guatemala's commitments to facilitate IDP return and reintegration at the conclusion of its 36-year civil war in the mid-1990s, and

...PART II: **Protecting More Broadly...**

South Sudan's failure to fulfil its obligations for IDPs set out in the 2011 transitional Constitution. In regard to the latter, promising efforts to draft a new IDP law in line with the Kampala Convention have been made since 2018 that include the views of IDPs. See: GP20, 'Working Together Better to Prevent, Address and Find Durable Solutions to Internal Displacement: GP20 Compilation of National Practices', Report (23 November 2020), pp. 181–182.

296 For example, in situations where they face discrimination or are unable to access needed documentation health services, employment, education and shelter. Orchard, *Protecting the Internally Displaced*, pp. 170–171; HRW, 'Struggling Through Peace – Return and Resettlement in Angola', Report, vol. 5, no. 16(A) (August 2003).

297 These were some of the main findings of a stocktaking exercise carried out by the International Committee of the Red Cross (ICRC), which examined experiences in eight African States that had implemented IDP laws and policies. ICRC, 'Translating the Kampala Convention into Practice: A Stocktaking Exercise', *International Review of the Red Cross* 99, no. 904 (2017): pp. 404–405. See also: UN Secretary-General's High-Level Panel on Internal Displacement, *Shining a Light on Internal Displacement: A Vision for the Future*, Report (September 2021), pp. 5, 9, 18–20.

298 Orchard, *Protecting the Internally Displaced*, pp. 144–145, 152–153, 159.

299 Adeola and Orchard, 'The Role of Law and Policy in Fostering Responsibility and Accountability', pp. 421–422; Orchard, *Protecting the Internally Displaced*, p. 228.

300 Human Rights Council, 'Internal displacement and the role of national human rights institutions: Report of the Special Rapporteur on the rights of internally displaced persons' (17 April 2019), UN Doc A/HRC/41/40, pp. 9–11, 13–15.

301 Ministry of Refugees and Repatriation, Islamic Republic of Afghanistan, 'The National Policy of the Islamic Republic of Afghanistan on Internal Displacement' (2013).

302 Orchard, *Protecting the Internally Displaced*, pp. 193–196, 213.

303 GP20, 'Working Together Better to Prevent, Address and Find Durable Solutions to Internal Displacement', pp. 133–138.

304 ECOSOC, 'Note by the Secretary-General pursuant to Economic and Social Council resolution 1990/78, Addendum: Report on refugees, displaced persons and returnees, prepared by Mr. Jacques Cuénod, Consultant', para. 125.

305 Abby Stoddard et al, 'Cluster Approach Evaluation', Humanitarian Policy Group, Overseas Development Institute (November 2007); Julia Steets et al., 'Cluster Approach Evaluation 2 Synthesis Report', Groupe Urgence Réhabilitation Développement, Global Public Policy Institute (April 2010); Simon Bagshaw and Diane Paul, *Protect or Neglect? Toward a More Effective United Nations Approach to the Protection of Internally Displaced Persons - An Evaluation* (The Brookings-SAIS Project on Internal Displacement and The UN Office for the Coordination of Humanitarian Affairs, November 2004); Elizabeth Ferris, 'Ten Years After Humanitarian Reform: How Have IDPs Fared?', Study, Brookings-LSE Project on Internal Displacement (December 2014).

306 Ferris, 'Ten Years After Humanitarian Reform'.

307 Walter Kälin, 'Innovative Global Governance for Internally Displaced Persons', World Refugee Council Research Paper No. 10, Centre for International Governance Innovation (April 2019): pp. 9–12.

308 UN Secretary-General's High-Level Panel on Internal Displacement, *Shining a Light on Internal Displacement*, pp. 64–70.

309 Ibid.

310 The Advisory Group on Climate Change and Human Mobility notes that human mobility encompasses the following: i) displacement: "situations where people are forced to leave their homes or places of habitual residence"; ii) migration: "movements that are predominantly voluntary"; and iii) planned relocation: "an organized relocation, ordinarily instigated, supervised and carried out by the state with the consent or upon the request of the community". The Advisory Group on Climate Change and Human Mobility, 'Human Mobility in the Context of Climate Change', Report (March 2014), p. 3. The Advisory Group is composed of ILO, IOM, NRC/IDMC, Refugees International, Sciences Po-CERI, UNDP, UNHCR and UNU-EHS. This definition was among its recommendations on Human Mobility in the Context of Climate Change made to the COP20 in Lima, Peru.

311 See: Part I.

312 Pastoralism, for example, "developed 7,000 years ago in response to long-term climate change. It spread throughout Northern Africa as an adaptation to the rapidly changing and increasingly unpredictable arid climate". FAO, *Pastoralism in Africa's drylands: Reducing risks, addressing vulnerability and enhancing resilience* (October 2018): p. ix. Today, the effects of climate change can also have a positive effect, "allowing new economic activities such as agriculture or tourism". Sarah Opitz Stapleton et al., *Climate change, migration and displacement: The need for a risk-informed and coherent approach*, Report (ODI and UNDP, November 2017), p. 7.

313 United Nations Office for Disaster Risk Reduction, 'Terminology: Glossay – Disaster', website.

314 Intergovernmental Panel on Climate Change (IPCC), *Climate Change 2021 – The Physical Science Basis*, Report (7 August 2021), pp. 4–41.

315 IDMC, *GRID 2021*, pp. 11–12. For a definition of hazards, see: World Meteorological Organization, 'Natural Hazards and Disaster Risk Reduction', website.

316 Out of those, 9.8 million were displaced internally and 1.4 million externally. UNHCR, *Global Trends 2020*, p. 6.

317 According to Etienne Piguet, this was due to a belief "that modernity implies a decreasing impact of nature on societies". Etienne Piguet, 'Mobility, Migration and Climate Change' [Video], Global Migration Lecture, Graduate Institute of Geneva, 2 March 2021.

318 Piguet provides seven reasons for this. Etienne Piguet, 'From "Primitive Migration" to "Climate Refugees": The Curious Fate of the Natural Environment in Migration Studies', *Annals of the Association of American Geographers* 103, no. 1 (2013): pp. 153–154. In 1992, the United Nations convened an International Conference on Environment and Development (Earth Summit). Participants included political leaders, diplomats, scientists, representatives of the media and NGOs from 179 countries. The focus was on the impact of human socioeconomic activities on the environment in which States agreed on the need for a Climate Convention. UN 'United Nations Conference on Environment and Development, held in Rio de Janeiro, Brazil, 3–14 June 1992: Background', website. This would eventually lead to the United Nations Framework Convention on Climate Change (UNFCCC) and the creation of the UNFCCC Task Force on Climate Displacement discussed further in this Part. For more on how research developments informed UNFCCC deliberations and led to migration and displacement being formally recognized in the UNFCCC process, see: Koko Warner, 'Climate Change Induced Displacement: Adaptation Policy in the Context of the UNFCCC Climate Negotiations', Background Paper for UNHCR's Expert Roundtable on Climate Change and Displacement (May 2011).

319 IPCC, 'Climate Change: The IPCC 1990 and 1992 Assessments', Report (June 1992), pp. 89, 103.

320 Norman Myers, 'Environmental Refugees', *Population and Environment* 19, no. 2 (1997): p. 175.

321 Piguet, 'From "Primitive Migration" to "Climate Refugees"', pp. 154–155. In 2007, the High Representative and the European Commission to the European Council warned of "millions of 'environmental' migrants by 2020" as one of the risks facing the continent. Javier Solana and Benita Ferrero-Waldner, 'Climate Change and International Security: Paper from the High Representative and the European Commission to the European Council' (14 March 2008), S113/08, p. 4.

322 Piguet, 'From "Primitive Migration" to "Climate Refugees"', p. 154.

323 Ibid., p. 155. See also: François Gemenne, 'Why the numbers don't add up: A review of estimates and predictions of people displaced by environmental changes', *Global Environmental Change* 21, no. 1 (2011): pp. 41–49; Caroline Zickgraf, 'Climate Change and Migration: Myths and Realities', *Green European Journal* (20 January 2020).

324 Opitz Stapleton et al., *Climate Change, Migration and Displacement*, pp. 12–14; The Government Office for Science, London, *Foresight: Migration and Global Environmental Change*, Final Project Report (2011), pp. 11–12; K.K. Rigaud et al., *Groundswell: Preparing for Internal Climate Migration*, Report, (World Bank Group, 2018), pp. 19–20.

325 Viviane Clement et al., *Groundswell Part 2: Acting on Internal Migration*, Report, (World Bank Group, 2021). p. xxxi; Rigaud et al., 'Groundswell', pp. 19–29.

326 Janani Vivekananda et al., *Shoring up Stability: Addressing Climate & Fragility Risks in the Lake Chad Region* (Adelphi, 15 May 2019); Saheed Babajide Owonikoko and Jude A. Momodu, 'Environmental Degradation, Livelihood, and the Stability of Chad Basin Region', *Small Wars & Insurgencies* 31, no. 6 (17 August 2020): pp. 1295–1322.

327 For a review of global estimates of sea level rise and migration trends, see: Celia McMichael et al., 'A Review of Estimating Population Exposure to Sea-Level Rise and the Relevance for Migration', *Environmental Research Letters* (28 September 2020). According to Piguet's estimate, five island States (Kiribati, the Maldives, the Marshall Islands, Nauru and Tuvalu) are at risk of being submerged by the end of the century to the point that they will be uninhabitable. This would potentially leave the more than half a million inhabitants stateless. Etienne Piguet, 'Climatic Statelessness: Risk Assessment and Policy Options', *Population and Development Review* 45, no. 4 (2019): p. 871. Also see: Etienne Piguet, 'Mobility, Migration and Climate Change'.

328 In 2018, the IPCC reported that: "Climate-related risks to health, livelihoods, food security, water supply, human security, and economic growth are projected to increase with global warming of 1.5°C and increase further with 2°C". IPCC, 'Summary for Policymakers', in *Special Report: Global Warming of 1.5°C* (2018), p. 9. In 2021, it reported that "unless there are immediate, rapid and large-scale reductions in greenhouse gas emissions, limiting warming to close to 1.5°C or even 2°C will be beyond reach". IPCC, 'Climate change widespread, rapid, and intensifying', Press Release (9 August 2021). IPCC, *Climate Change 2021 – The Physical Science Basis*.

329 Clement et al., 'Groundswell Part 2'; Rigaud et al., 'Groundswell'.

330 Clement et al., 'Groundswell Part 2', pp. xxii, 3. Specifically, its modelling estimates the following possible internal displacement scenarios: approximately 86 million people in Sub-Saharan Africa, 49 million in East Asia and the Pacific, 40 million in South Asia; 19 million in North Africa, 17 million in Latin America and 5 million in Eastern Europe and Central Asia, pp. xv, xxii. See also: Graham Watkins and Andrea Garcia Salinas, 'The climate crisis could drive massive human displacement in Latin America and the Caribbean', Inter-American Development Bank blog (30 October 2020).

331 Clement et al., 'Groundswell Part 2', pp. xxvii, xxviii; Rigaud et al., 'Groundswell', p. 181.

332 The World Bank Group, 'Action Plan on Climate Change Adaptation and Resilience: Managing Risks for a More Resilient Future' (2019), p. 5.

333 Sustainable Development Goal 13, from: UNGA, Transforming our world: The 2030 Agenda for Sustainable Development (25 September 2015), UN Doc A/RES/70/1.

334 See, for example: Guy J. Abel et al., 'Climate, Conflict and Forced Migration', *Global Environmental Change* 54 (2019): pp. 239–249. In their study of the countries affected by the Arab Spring during 2010–2012 and of some Sub-Saharan countries during the same period, they conclude that the assertion that climate change will lead to conflict and, in turn, to displacement is too simplistic. This scenario can occur but depends on other variables and is most likely if the effects of climate change coincide with political instability and inadequate government responses. See also: Asha Amirali, 'Migration and the risk of violent conflict and instability', K4D Helpdesk Report (18 March 2020), pp. 5–8.

335 Guy J. Abel et al., 'Climate, Conflict and Forced Migration'; François Gemenne et al., 'Forced displacement related to the impacts of climate change and disasters', Reference Paper for the 70th Anniversary of the 1951 Refugee Convention, UNHCR (October 2021), pp. 9–14; Government Office for Science, *Foresight: Migration and Global Environmental Change*, pp. 20–21.

336 ICRC, *When Rain Turns to Dust: Understanding and Responding to the Combined Impact of Armed Conflicts and Climate and Environmental Crisis on People's Lives*, Report (2020), pp. 5, 8, 10. For example, it notes that 60 per cent of the 20 countries considered to be most vulnerable to climate change are ones affected by armed conflict. Similarly, the Stockholm International Peace Research Institute (SIPRI) reported in February 2021 that "6 of the 10 biggest UN peace operations (by total international personnel) were in countries ranked most exposed to climate change". Florian Krampe, 'Why United Nations Peace Operations Cannot Ignore Climate Change', SIPRI website (22 February 2021).

337 Laura Heaton, 'The Key to Saving Somalia Is Gathering Dust in the British Countryside', *Foreign Policy* (31 May 2017).

338 Sanjula Weerasinghe, 'In Harm's Way: International protection in the context of nexus dynamics between conflict or violence and disaster or climate change', UNHCR Report (December 2018), pp. 36–37.

339 Karolina Eklöw, and Florian Krampe, 'Climate-related security risks and peacebuilding in Somalia', Policy Paper No. 53, SIPRI, (23 October 2019), pp. 26–27.

340 UNHCR, *Global Trends: Forced Displacement in 2011*, Report (2012), p. 12.

341 See: Eklöw and Krampe, 'Climate-related security risks and peacebuilding in Somalia'; Giovanna Kuele, and Ana Cristina Miola, 'Climate change is feeding armed conflict in Somalia', *Institute for Security Studies (ISS)* website (6 April 2018). Shalle Hassan Abdirahman described how the drought and Al-Shabaab's confiscation of the little assets they had affected the whole community. Fearful of Al-Shabaab, he said, they "force us to produce what we did not have". Katie Nguyen, 'As drought compounds security woes, Somalis flee to Ethiopia', *UNHCR* News, 2019. For an earlier example of how policies of the colonial power in the Sahel have contributed to famine, see: Piguet, 'From "Primitive Migration" to "Climate Refugees"', p. 157.

342 Robert Malley, 'Climate Change Is Shaping the Future of Conflict', Transcript, speech given to the UN Security Council at the Arria session on climate and security risks (22 April 2020). Other examples include well-intentioned policies in Mali during the 1970s that inadvertently led to competition among communities. At that time, new wells in central Mali were constructed to benefit Fulani herders. The wells not only improved pastoral areas but made previous arid areas more attractive to farmers. Dogon farmers settled in central Mali initially with the permission of Fulani herdsmen. Over time, tensions between herders and farmers increased as farmers asserted more rights over land. In the absence of effective land use settlement mechanisms, conflicts escalated corresponding to the rise of jihadist and self-defense groups. Ibrahim Yahaya Ibrahim, 'Role of climate change in Central Sahel's conflicts: not so clear', *The Africa Report* (24 April 2020).

343 FAO, *Pastoralism in Africa's Drylands*, pp. ix, 4-7; FAO, 'Resilience analysis of pastoral and agropastoral communities in South Sudan's cross-border areas with Sudan, Ethiopia, Kenya and Uganda', FAO resilience analysis report No. 17 (2019), pp. v, ix, 1-2, 7.

344 FAO, *Pastoralism in Africa's Drylands*, pp. 4–17; UNOWAS, 'Pastoralism and Security in West Africa and the Sahel: Towards Peaceful Coexistence' (2018), pp. 13–14; Robert Malley, 'Climate Change Is Shaping the Future of Conflict'. Other examples can be found in ICRC, *When Rain Turns to Dust*.

345 Relevant Security Council resolutions in regard to root causes include UNSC, Res. 2558 (2020), S/RES/2558; UNSC, Res. 2282 (2016), S/RES/2282. Security Council resolutions in 2020 regarding adverse effects of climate change within risk management strategies include: UNSC, Res. 2552, S/RES/2552; UNSC, Res. 2524, S/RES/2524; UNSC, Res. 2556, S/RES/2556; UNSC, Res. 2531, S/RES/2531; and UNSC, Res. 2540, S/RES/2540. Climate Security Expert Network, 'Climate Security at the UNSC – A Short History', website. However, there is disagreement within the Security Council as to whether the adverse effects of climate change are a matter of international peace and security and, therefore, of concern to the Council. Russia and China are of the view that the adverse effects of climate change are development issues and, therefore, best addressed in the related international fora. In contrast, France, the United Kingdom and, most recently, the United States take the position that climate change is a threat to collective security and, therefore, a matter for the Security Council's attention and action. Stéphanie Fillion, 'Can the Issue of Climate-Induced Wars Stick to the UN Security Council Agenda? The UK Tries It Out', *PassBlue* (18 February 2020). See also: Security Council Report, 'The UN Security Council and Climate Change', Research Report (21 June 2021).

346 Janani Vivekananda, Adam Day and Susanne Wolfmaier, *What Can the UN Security Council Do on Climate and Security?*, CSEN Policy Paper (21 July 2020), p. 5.

347 Rigaud et al., 'Groundswell', pp. xxii, 5–7 and 184–187.

348 Refugees International, 'Hindou Oumarou Ibrahim, Refugees International's Richard C. Holbrooke Awardee 2020', blog (21 April 2020).

349 The Government of Fiji, 'Planned Relocation Guidelines: A framework to undertake climate change related relocation' (2018). Other important policies are: The Government of Fiji, 'Displacement Guidelines: In the context of climate change and disasters' (2019); The

Government of Fiji, 'The Republic of Fiji National Climate Change Policy 2018–2030' (2019); The Government of Fiji, 'Republic of Fiji National Adaptation Plan: A pathway towards climate resilience' (2018).

350 These and other practices are documented in: GP20, 'Working Together Better to Prevent, Address and Find Durable Solutions to Internal Displacement', pp. 89–94.

351 T. Alexander Aleinikoff, 'Environmental Mobility: The Responsibility of the International Community', *International Migration* 58, no. 6, Commentary (2020): p. 256. A report by Oxfam and the Stockholm Environment Institute (SEI) found that "the richest 10 per cent of the world's population (c.630 million people) were responsible for 52 per cent of the cumulative carbon emissions" and "the poorest 50 per cent (c.3.1 billion people) were responsible for just 7 per cent of cumulative emissions". Tim Gore, 'Confronting carbon inequality', Report Summary (21 September 2020). For an example of reducing greenhouse gas emissions through making the polluter pay for its pollution, see: Hillary Aidun, Daniel J. Metzger and Michael B. Gerrard, 'Principles of International Law and the Adoption of a Market Based Mechanism for Greenhouse Gas Emissions from Shipping', Report, Sabin Center for Climate Change Law (February 2021), pp. 4–13.

352 There are currently 197 parties to the UNFCCC (196 States and 1 regional economic integration organization). United Nations, 'Status of Ratification of the Convention', UNFCCC website.

353 Each year, the Conference of Parties (COP) reviews progress and agrees on future work. In 2015, 21 years after the first meeting, the parties signed the Paris Agreement to strengthen the global response. The Paris Agreement commits States to limit the increase in climate temperature by mid-century to well below 2 degrees Celsius above pre-industrial levels, and to pursue efforts to limit the temperature increase even further to 1.5 degrees Celsius. UNFCCC, Paris Agreement, in 'Report of the Conference of the Parties on its twenty-first session, held in Paris from 30 November to 13 December 2015' (29 January 2016), UN Doc FCCC/CP/2015/10/Add.1, Annex, art. 2.1.(a).

354 UNFCCC, 'Addendum: Part two: Action taken by the Conference of the Parties at its twenty-first session', in 'Report of the Conference of the Parties on its twenty-first session, held in Paris from 30 November to 13 December 2015' (29 January 2016), UN Doc FCCC/CP/2015/10/Add.1, para. 49.

355 UN World Conference on Disaster Risk Reduction, Sendai Framework for Disaster Risk Reduction 2015–2030 (18 March 2015). It was adopted by the General Assembly in 2015 and will be in place through 2030.

356 Michelle Yonetani, 'Positioned for Action: Displacement in the Sendai Framework for disaster risk reduction', Briefing Paper, IDMC (16 February 2017).

357 Many States report annually. As of September 2019, 47 least developed countries had started reporting and over 100 countries reported that they have national strategies in place. Relatively few country strategies are fully aligned with the Sendai Framework principles. Mami Mizutori, 'Reflections on the Sendai Framework for Disaster Risk Reduction: Five Years Since Its Adoption', *International Journal of Disaster Risk Science* 11, no. 2, Commentary (2020): p. 148. UNDRR, 'Measuring Implementation of the Sendai Framework', *Sendai Monitor* website.

358 Mizutori, 'Reflections on the Sendai Framework': p. 148; Yonetani, 'Positioned for Action: Displacement in the Sendai Framework', pp. 4, 9.

359 Global Compact for Safe, Orderly and Regular Migration (2018), paras 18(a), 18(h)–18(l), 21(h). The United Nations Network on Migration includes in its workplan policy and analysis in support of States to meet the objectives of the Global Compact for Safe, Orderly, and Regular Migration. United Nations Network on Migration, 'Network Workplan: 2021-2022 Priorities' (28 April 2021), p. 14.

360 See: UNHCR, 'Legal considerations regarding claims for international protection made in the context of the adverse effects of climate change and disasters' (1 October 2020).

361 The Nansen Initiative, *Agenda for the Protection of Cross-Border Displaced Persons in the Context of Disasters and Climate Change*, Vol. 1 (December 2015), para. 56; Weerasinghe, 'In Harm's Way', pp. 2–4; UNHCR, 'Legal considerations regarding claims for international protection made in the context of the adverse effects of climate change and disasters', pp. 7–10.

362 OAU Convention (1969), art. 1(2); Cartagena Declaration (1984), art. III (3); Sharpe, *The Regional Law of Refugee Protection in Africa*, pp. 48–49.

363 Goodwin-Gill and McAdam, *Climate Change, Disasters and Displacement*, pp. 35–36.

364 Wood, 'Who Is a Refugee in Africa?': p. 307; Sharpe, *The Regional Law of Refugee Protection in Africa*, pp. 48–49; UNHCR, 'Legal considerations regarding claims for international protection made in the context of the adverse effects of climate change and disasters', pp. 8–9.

365 For example, UNGA, International Covenant on Civil and Political Rights (ICCPR) (16 December 1966), UN Doc A/RES/2200(XXI)A, arts. 6, 7. See also: UNHCR, 'Legal considerations regarding claims for international protection made in the context of the adverse effects of climate change and disasters', para 19.

366 The Human Rights Committee (HRC) is a body of independent experts that monitors implementation of the ICCPR by its States parties. *Ioane Teitiota v. New Zealand* (2020), HRC, No. CCPR/C/127/D/2728/2016.

367 Ibid., para. 9.11. Para 61 of the Global Compact on Refugees also calls for "fair and efficient determination of individual international protection claims" made in accordance with the State's "applicable international and regional obligations". Global Compact on Refugees (2018).

368 Ama Francis, 'Free Movement Agreements & Climate-Induced Migration: A Caribbean Case Study', Sabin Center for Climate Change Law (September 2019), p. 18; David Cantor, 'Environment, Mobility, and International Law: A New Approach in the Americas', *Chicago Journal of International Law* 21, no. 2 (2021): p. 302. According to Susan Martin, the exercise of discretion on humanitarian grounds can be found in the laws and practices of Argentina, Bolivia, Brazil, Canada, Chile, Costa Rica, Ecuador, El Salvador, Guatemala, Honduras, Jamaica, Mexico, Nicaragua, Panama, Peru, and the United States. Several laws make specific reference to their use in circumstances of natural disasters, such as Argentina, Mexico and Peru. Susan Martin, 'Climate Change', UNHCR (unpublished), pp. 9–10.

369 IGAD, 'Protocol On Free Movement Of Persons Endorsed At Ministerial Meeting', Press Release (26 February 2020).

370 Sectoral Ministerial Meeting on the Protocol on Free Movement of Persons in the IGAD Region, Khartoum, Republic of Sudan, 'Communiqué' (26 February 2020). See also: Tamara Wood, 'Opinion: New pact offers innovative solutions to climate displacement', *Reuters* (28 February 2020).

371 See: Tamara Wood, 'The Role of Free Movement of Persons Agreements in Addressing Disaster Displacement: A Study of Africa', *Platform on Disaster Displacement* Report (May 2018).

372 For examples of those who have advanced this point of view, see: Jane McAdam, 'Swim-

ming against the Tide: Why a Climate Change Displacement Treaty is Not the Answer', *International Journal of Refugee Law* 23, no. 1 (2011): pp. 5–6. See also: François Gemenne et al., 'Forced displacement related to the impacts of climate change and disasters', p. 5.

373 Guy Goodwin-Gill and Jane McAdam, 'UNHCR and Climate Change, Disasters, and Displacement', *UNHCR* Report, (May 2017): pp. 13–18.

374 Cantor, 'Environment, Mobility, and International Law': pp. 320–322.

375 See, for example: Jane McAdam, 'Swimming against the Tide'; Simon Behrman and Avidan Kent, *Climate Refugees: Beyond the Legal Impasse?* (Abingdon, UK: Routledge, 2018); Cantor, 'Environment, Mobility, and International Law': pp. 280–282, 320–322; Alexander Betts, 'Towards a "soft law" framework for the protection of vulnerable migrants', Research Paper No. 162, *New Issues in Refugee Research*, UNHCR (August 2008).

376 McAdam specifically cites responses that "may enable people to remain in their homes for as long as possible (which is the predominant wish among affected communities), or to move safely within their own countries, or to migrate in a planned manner over time". McAdam, 'Swimming against the Tide', pp. 5–6.

377 Goodwin-Gill and McAdam, 'UNHCR and Climate Change, Disasters, and Displacement', pp. 14–19.

378 Nansen Initiative, 'Agenda for the Protection of Cross-Border Displaced Persons in the Context of Disasters and Climate Change'.

379 Ibid., pp. 45–48.

380 Ibid., pp. 24–29. See also: Koko Warner et al., 'Integrating Human Mobility Issues within National Adaptation Plans', UNU-EHS Policy Brief no. 9 (June 2014). Pages 18–24 of this report describe how National Adaptation Plans in Kiribati, Tuvalu and other countries, like Bangladesh and Kenya, link climate change and human mobility and include reskilling and other development programmes to better manage and support different types of mobility caused by climate change.

381 Nansen Initiative, 'Agenda for the Protection of Cross-Border Displaced Persons in the Context of Disasters and Climate Change', pp. 36–39. As for prevention, the Agenda examines approaches to risk-mapping and risk reduction, including the ways that States are reducing vulnerabilities and building resilience to risks, pp. 34–36.

382 It was established in 2016 and is State-led and based in Geneva. Platform on Disaster Displacement, 'About Us' *website*.

383 Nansen Initiative, 'Guide to Effective Practices for RCM Member Countries: Protection for persons moving across borders in the context of disasters' (2016). Adopted by Belize, Canada, Costa Rica, the Dominican Republic, El Salvador, Guatemala, Honduras, Mexico, Nicaragua, Panama, and the United States.

384 Cantor, 'Environment, Mobility, and International Law': p. 318.

385 South American Conference on Migration (CSM), International Organization for Migration (IOM), Platform on Disaster Displacement (PDD), *Regional Guidelines on Protection and Assistance of Persons Displaced across Borders and Migrants in Countries Affected by Disasters of Natural Origin* [Spanish] (2019). These provide guidance tailored to the region on risk reduction, admission, temporary stay arrangements and durable solutions for those who cannot return to their respective countries of origin. The guidelines also include migrants who are affected by disaster in their respective countries of residence or transit.

386 PDD, 'Report - Advisory Committee Workshop 2019' (February 2019), p. 12.

387 Nansen Initiative, 'Agenda for the Protection of Cross-Border Displaced Persons in the Context of Disasters and Climate Change', pp. 6 and 50.

...PART II: **Protecting More Broadly...**

388 United States Congress, Immigration Act (1990), Pub. L. 101-649, 104 STAT. 4978, art. 244 A(b).

389 Cantor, 'Environment, Mobility, and International Law': pp. 294–295. He provides several examples. Although only used infrequently, TPS were of benefit to nationals of countries affected by the following disasters: the 1998 Hurricane Mitch (El Salvador, Honduras and Nicaragua), the 1997 volcanic eruption in Montserrat and the 2000 earthquake in El Salvador. Following the 2010 earthquake in Haiti, Haitian nationals received protection under a separate TPS provision. This was extended in May 2021. U.S. Citizenship and Immigration Services, 'Temporary Protected Status Designated Country: Haiti', website. More generally, see: Jill H. Wilson, 'Temporary Protected Status and Deferred Enforced Departure', Congressional Research Service Report RS20844 (9 August 2021).

390 Cantor, 'Environment, Mobility, and International Law': p. 296. Jamaica used these for Haitians following the 2010 earthquake.

391 Ibid., p. 300.

392 Ibid., p. 298. Costa Rica, for example, regularized 150,000 disaster-affected migrants from Hurricane Mitch.

393 United Nations Global Compact for Safe, Orderly and Regular Migration (2018), Objective 5.

394 Susan Martin, 'Climate Change', pp. 16–17. See also: Holly Lawton, 'Pacific Labour Scheme: expanding while borders are closed', Development Policy Centre blog (27 May 2021); Hikina Whakatutuki, 'Pacific Migrants Trends and Settlement Outcomes Report', New Zealand Ministry of Business, Innovation and Employment (MBIE) (December 2018).

395 Brookings Institution, University of Bern 'Addressing Internal Displacement: A Framework for National Responsibility' (April 2005). This is a State obligation in the Kampala Convention, which States must then operationalize through national laws and practice. Kampala Convention (2009), art. 13.1. The importance of governments putting in place "processes and systems to collect, analyse and manage internal displacement data" and be supported in their efforts was also stressed by the High-Level Panel on Internal Displacement. High-Level Panel on Internal Displacement, *Shining the Light on Internal Displacement*, pp. 37–39.

396 Ibid.; Natalia Baal and Laura Ronkainen, 'Obtaining representative data on IDPs: challenges and recommendations', UNHCR Statistics Technical Series (April 2017).

397 Gabriel Cardona-Fox, 'The Politics of IDP Data', *Refugee Survey Quarterly* 39, no. 4 (2020): pp. 626–627.

398 Cardona-Fox observes that in Ukraine, the Government "will only recognise IDPs that are officially registered with the authorities and have thus overcome several restrictive hurdles, such as the production of documentation, which is not always possible". Ibid., pp. 624–625. For a more in-depth review of the challenges in Ukraine, see: IDMC, 'IDP Registration in Ukraine: Who's In? Who's Out? And Who's Counting?', Expert Opinion (March 2015).

399 Cardona-Fox, 'The Politics of IDP Data': pp. 626–629.

400 Ibid.: p. 623.

401 Kira Vinke and Roman Hoffmann note that most climate-related migration is internal, yet this is difficult to count and no monitoring mechanisms are in place for regularly capturing population mobility within and between countries. For this and other data challenges, see:

Vinke and Hoffman, 'Data for a difficult subject: Climate change and human migration', *Migration Policy Practice* 10, no. 1 (2020): pp. 16–20.

402 Efforts to improve coordinated data collection is discussed further in Part V.

403 Natalia Krynsky Baal, 'Forced Displacement Data: Critical gaps and key opportunities in the context of the Global Compact on Refugees', Reference Paper for the 70th Anniversary of the 1951 Refugee Convention, UNHCR (October 2021), pp. 10–11.

404 Actors currently involved in collecting data on IDPs include UNHCR, IDMC, IOM, NGOs and the Joint IDP Profiling Service (JIPS). For more on their roles, see: Eurostat, *Technical Report on Statistics of Internally Displaced Persons* (17 October 2018), pp. 64–66. The challenges in data collection and quality are regularly noted by UNHCR and IDMC. Since 1998, IDMC annually provides consolidated and multi-sourced estimates of IDPs displaced by conflict and violence as well as by disasters. See: IDMC, *GRID 2021*. In regard to UNHCR and data availability, see: UNHCR, 'Refugee Data Finder: Methodology', website.

405 Debora Gonzalez Tejero, Lorenzo Guadagno, Alessandro Nicoletti, 'Human mobility and the environment: Challenges for data collection and policymaking', *Migration Policy Practice* 10, no. 1 (January–March 2020): p. 5. Even when migrants are asked why they move, they are frequently asked to cite the main reason, which omits the contributing ones. This could be improved through the use of ranked scales. Cantor and Apollo make a similar observation in regard to internal displacement generally. David James Cantor and Jacob Ochieng Apollo, 'Internal Displacement, Internal Migration, and Refugee Flows: Connecting the Dots', *Refugee Survey Quarterly* 39, no. 4 (2020): pp. 647–664. They note that internal displacement "cannot always be neatly separated off from other forms of movement", p. 660. In addition to conflict, patterns of displacement including decisions on when, where and how long to move can be influenced by other factors, such as labour opportunities, and family or social connections elsewhere in the country. Movement can reflect broader trends, such as migration from rural to urban areas. Ibid., pp. 648–649.

406 EGRIS is part of the United Nations Statistical Commission, which was created in 1947 to set global standards for the collection and use of statistics. Among the relevant areas of measurement are: legal and civil status; education, health and economic status; and social inclusion. Indicators of progress include: citizenship, civil documentation and travel documents; family status; language proficiency; income and consumption; rights to work, move freely, own property, open a bank account, and access benefits and justice.

407 EGRIS, *International Recommendation on Refugee Statistics (IRRS)* (March 2018); EGRIS, *International Recommendations on Internally Displaced Persons Statistics (IRIS)* (March 2020). Endorsed in 2020 by the UN Statistical Commission, they provide an internationally agreed framework for the production and dissemination of quality statistics comparable between regions and countries.

408 World Bank Group, 'Global Civil Registration and Vital Statistics: Abut CRVS', website (20 March 2018).

PART III: **Solutions — An Uneven Record**

1   While these sources enable us to see general trends and the lessons learned, significant gaps remain in the data. These are discussed further in this Part in relation to each of the solutions.

2   Exceptions were during the years 1971–1972, 1991–1992, 1994, 1996 and 2002–2005 when annual returns exceeded 10 per cent of the total refugee population. See: UNHCR, Refugee Data Finder.

3   The collection of data on internal displacement commenced in 1993 and on return of internally displaced persons in 1997.

4   UNHCR, Refugee Data Finder. In 13 of the past 23 years (i.e., since data first became available), annual return rates remained below 10 per cent. In seven of these 23 years, annual returns ranged from 11 to just under 20 per cent. In just three years, return rates ranged from 21 to 26 per cent of the global total of conflict-induced internal displacement.

5   In each of the past 20 years, between one third and two thirds of forcibly displaced persons in the world were from these countries. Since 2013, Syria has been the main country of origin, consistently producing one fifth or more of all forcibly displaced persons globally. See: UNHCR, Refugee Data Finder.

6   World Bank Group, *Forcibly Displaced: Toward a Development Approach Supporting Refugees, the Internally Displaced, and Their Hosts* (Washington, D.C: World Bank, 2017), p. 105.

7   Ibrahim Elbadawi, Linda Kaltani, and Klaus Schmidt-Hebbel, 'Post-Conflict Aid, Real Exchange Rate Adjustment, and Catch-up Growth', Working Paper 4187, The World Bank (April 2007), pp. 5–6, 18–20.

8   World Bank Group, *Forcibly Displaced*, p. 107.

9   Surveys conducted since 2018 by IDMC among returnees in Afghanistan, Colombia, Iraq, Myanmar, Nigeria and South Sudan found that nearly 77 per cent were living outside their respective areas of origin at the time of the research. While some opted to settle elsewhere in pursuit of new livelihood opportunities, many of these returning refugees were unable to return to their areas of origin or were displaced again. See: Bina Desai et al., 'On This Side of the Border — The Global Challenge of Internal Displacement: Scale, Impacts and Solutions', Reference Paper for the 70th Anniversary of the 1951 Refugee Convention, UNHCR (October 2021), pp. 6–8.

10 For examples, see: Victoria Metcalfe, Simone Haysom, and Ellen Martin, 'Sanctuary in the City? Urban Displacement and Vulnerability in Kabul', Humanitarian Policy Group Working Paper, Overseas Development Institute (June 2012): p. 39. And for the need for new approaches, see: Simone Haysom, 'Sanctuary in the city? Urban displacement and vulnerability', HPG Final Report 33, ODI (June 2013).

11 World Bank Group, *Forcibly Displaced*, p. 101.

12 Niels Harild, Asger Christensen, and Roger Zetter, *Sustainable Refugee Return: Triggers, Constraints and Lessons on Addressing the Development Challenges of Forced Displacement*, Report (The World Bank Group, 2015), pp. x, xv, 10, 12, 13, 14, 35, 110, 127–128.

13 Fear of forced conscription is among the concerns young Syrian male refugees note in

contemplating return. Young Somali refugees cite a similar fear in relation to forced recruit-ment by Al-Shabaab. See: DRC et al., *Unprepared for (Re)Integration: Lessons Learned from Afghanistan, Somalia and Syria on Refugee Returns to Urban Areas*, Report (Novem-ber 2019), pp. 19, 21.

14 Desai et al., 'On This Side of the Border – The Global Challenge of Internal Displacement', p. 6.

15 Rez Gardi, 'The Future of Solutions', Reference Paper for the 70th Anniversary of the 1951 Refugee Convention, UNHCR (October 2021). They were eventually resettled in New Zealand.

16 Generally, the decision is taken following a personal interview to determine whether the refugee under consideration meets the State's own priorities and the validity of the docu-ments provided is assessed.

17 As will be discussed further in this Part, it is noteworthy that the annual refugee resettle-ment numbers exceeded 100,000 in only 21 of the 61 years since 1959 when data first became available. See: UNHCR, Refugee Data Finder.

18 This includes persons who are in danger of being forcibly returned to their countries, or who are being seriously threatened by others. It also may include persons who have specific health needs that cannot be adequately treated in the country of refuge, including life-saving treatments or psychological interventions for those who have survived torture or extreme violence. It may also include children who are at risk of being forced to work or to marry, or of being trafficked. See: UNHCR, *The Resettlement Handbook* (2011).

19 In cases of extreme urgency regarding refugees at immediate risk, some States provide more rapid processing which can be completed within seven days of the UNHCR referral.

20 Commonly experienced by UNHCR resettlement staff in field locations. This can create conflicting incentives. For example, some refugees might be less inclined to accept meas-ures to overcome their vulnerabilities if they believe it could hurt their ability to be selected for resettlement based on their specific needs.

21 Discussed further in this Part.

22 For statistical purposes, UNHCR refers to naturalization as the legal process by which non-citizens may acquire citizenship. See: UNHCR, *Global Trends: Forced Displacement in 2019*, Annual Report (2020), pp. 68–69.

23 Available data on naturalization remains limited. The number of countries reporting on naturalization for the purpose of the UNHCR 2020 Mid-Year Review was 25; UNHCR, therefore, considers available data to underestimate the extent to which refugees are in fact naturalized.

24 The Netherlands, France, Belgium and Ireland each naturalized 26,700, 18,600, 14,800 and 4,900 refugees respectively in the decade. UNHCR, Refugee Data Finder.

25 UNHCR, *Global Trends 2019*, p. 54; UNHCR, Refugee Data Finder.

26 UNHCR, Refugee Data Finder.

27 World Bank Group, *Forcibly Displaced*, p. 112.

28 World Bank Group, *Forcibly Displaced*, p. 68. While there is believed to be a net positive gain, they may still displace other host community workers who may require further skills development and support. For more on this, see: Economic Inclusion in Part IV.

29 Zara Sarzin notes that these concerns "are often based on unsubstantiated perceptions rather than empirical evidence, and tend to focus on short run costs rather than long-term benefits arising from the economic inclusion of forced migrants". Zara Sarzin, 'The Impact of Forced Migration on the Labor Market Outcomes and Welfare of Host Communities',

...PART III: **Solutions – An Uneven Record...**

Reference Paper for the 70th Anniversary of the 1951 Refugee Convention, UNHCR (October 2021), p. 3. See also discussion on Economic Inclusion in Part IV.

30   UNHCR, 'Livelihoods and Economic Inclusion', website.

31   Roger Zetter and Héloïse Ruaudel, 'Refugees' Right to Work and Access to Labor Markets – An Assessment', Part I, KNOMAD (September 2016), p. 29.

32   For example, see: Utz Johann Pape and Ambika Sharma, 'Informing Durable Solutions for Internal Displacement in Nigeria, Somalia, South Sudan, and Sudan' Vol. A: 'Overview', Report, World Bank Group (2019), pp. ix, x, 4, 13, 27, 32.

33   World Bank Group, *Forcibly Displaced*, p. 111.

34   This is discussed in Part II. For example, several countries, including some with the largest numbers of internally displaced persons, such as Somalia, South Sudan and Afghanistan, have national laws and policies that reflect the criteria and principles in the IASC, 'Framework on Durable Solutions for Internally Displaced Persons' (April 2010). Additionally, see: Global Protection Cluster, '20th Anniversary of the Guiding Principles on Internal Displacement: A Plan of Action for Advancing Prevention, Protection and Solutions for Internally Displaced People 2018–2020' (23 May 2018).

35   The High-Level Panel on Internal Displacement addresses this problem in its recommendations. It calls for "a combination of positive incentives and accountability measures", including financial and other incentives, high-level diplomatic advocacy and criminal prosecutions for egregious abuse. See: UN Secretary-General's High-Level Panel on Internal Displacement, *Shining a Light on Internal Displacement: A Vision for the Future*, Report (September 2021), pp. 18–20.

36   ECOSOC, Ad Hoc Committee on Statelessness and Related Problems, Status of Refugees and Stateless Persons – Memorandum by the Secretary-General (3 January 1950), UN Doc E/AC.32/2.

37   UNHCR's Statute provides that it is to seek permanent solutions for refugees by assisting governments to "facilitate voluntary repatriation" or "assimilation within new national communities". See: UNGA, Statute of the Office of the United Nations High Commissioner for Refugees (14 December 1950) (UNHCR Statute), UN Doc A/RES/428(V), ch. 1, para. 1.

38   See: Part I. See also: Convention relating to the Status of Refugees (adopted 25 July 1951), UN Doc CONF.2/108, art. 34; T. Alexander Aleinikoff and Stephen Poellot, 'The Responsibility to Solve: The International Community and Protracted Refugee Situations', *Virginia Journal of International Law* 54 (March 2014).

39   Art. 33 of the 1951 Convention. The right to return is found in Article 13 of the Universal Declaration of Human Rights (adopted 10 December 1948), Article 14(1), UN Doc A/RES/217(III).

40   Organization of African Unity, Convention Governing the Specific Aspects of Refugee Problems in Africa (10 September 1969) (OAU Convention); Colloquium on the International Protection of Refugees in Central America, Mexico and Panama, Cartagena Declaration on Refugees and the Protection of People Fleeing Armed Conflict and Other Situations of Violence in Latin America (22 November 1984) (Cartagena Declaration); Asian-African Legal Consultative Organization, Bangkok Principles on the Status and Treatment of Refugees (31 December 1966) (Bangkok Principles); European Parliament and Council, 'On standards for the qualification of third-country nationals or stateless persons as beneficiaries of international protection, for a uniform status for refugees or for persons eligible for subsidiary protection, and for the content of the protection granted' (13 December 2011), Directive 2011/95/EU; UN General Assembly, Global Compact on Refugees (2 August 2018), UN Doc A/73/12 (Part II).

41 In practice, this is through tripartite agreements between the country of asylum, the country of origin, and UNHCR.

42 The engagement of States and of intergovernmental agencies, as well as the rights of returnees and non-penalization for having left are found in the OAU Convention, art. V with respect to refugees in Africa. The Bangkok Principles stipulate a right to return in art. VI, the voluntariness of return and non-penalization for having left in art. VII, the promotion of comprehensive solutions including voluntary repatriation, local settlement and third country resettlement in art. VIII, and the right to compensation in art. IX.

43 See: Part I.

44 Twenty-nine States have made reservations on art. 17 (wage-earning employment). Twenty States have made reservations in regard to labour legislation and social security (art. 24).

45 The Refugee Convention (1951), art. 34. The Ad hoc Committee was informed by an initial draft of the Convention provided by the Secretary-General who, in conveying it to the Committee, emphasized that the aim was for refugees to be integrated into the economic system of the countries of asylum, to provide for their own needs and be fully integrated into the national community. ECOSOC, 'Ad Hoc Committee on Statelessness and Related Problems, First Session' (14 February 1950), UN Doc E/AC.32/SR.22.

46 OAU Convention (1969), art. II (1).

47 Ibid., Preamble.

48 Economic Community of West African States (ECOWAS), 'Protocol Relating to Free Movement of Persons, Residence and Establishment' (29 May 1979), A/P 1/5/79. It was revised and updated in 1993. The objective of the protocol is to permit community citizens to enter, reside and economically engage in the territory of a member State. This is to be automatic within the first 90 days and extended through established processes thereafter.

49 Aderanti Adepoju, Alistair Boulton, and Mariah Levin, 'Promoting integration through mobility: free movement and the ECOWAS Protocol', Working Paper 150, *New Issues in Refugee Research,* UNHCR (2007). They also note other barriers, including costs of visas, which were prohibitive for many refugees. Nigeria is a notable exception: Between 2007 and 2010, it provided migration status to 117,000 Liberian refugees and 18,000 Sierra Leoneans, discussed later in this Part. For more on the Protocol and how it has facilitated movement of some groups over others, see: Thomas Yeboah et al., 'The ECOWAS Free Movement Protocol and Diversity of Experiences of Different Categories of Migrants: A Qualitative Study', *International Migration* 59, no. 3 (June 2021).

50 Included in the Contadora Act on Peace and Co-operation in Central America. See: The Cartagena Declaration (1984).

51 Governments of Latin America and the Caribbean, 'A Framework for Cooperation and Regional Solidarity to Strengthen the International Protection of Refugees, Displaced and Stateless Persons in Latin America and the Caribbean (Brazil Declaration and Plan of Action)' (3 December 2014). For discussion on the impact of previous declarations on the current displacement crisis from Venezuela, see: Luisa Feline Freier, Isabel Berganza and Cécile Blouin, 'The Cartagena Refugee Definition and Venezuelan Displacement in Latin America', *International Migration* 58, no. 6 (December 2020).

52 UN, Global Compact on Refugees (2018); Brazil Declaration (2014), paras. 98–99.

53 See: Part I.

...PART III: **Solutions – An Uneven Record...**

54 For Global Refugee Forum pledges, see: UNHCR, 'Pledges & Contributions Dashboard', *The Global Compact on Refugees Digital Platform*.

55 Francis M. Deng, 'Guiding Principles on Internal Displacement', *International Migration Review* 33, no. 2 (June 1999): pp. 484–493.

56 Ibid.: p. 493.

57 African Union, Convention for the Protection and Assistance of Internally Displaced Persons in Africa (23 October 2009) (Kampala Convention), art. 2.

58 The humanitarian coordination forum of UN and non-UN humanitarian partners.

59 IASC, 'Framework on Durable Solutions for Internally Displaced Persons', p. 5.

60 Ibid., p. 27.

61 See, for example, some of the problems that the World Bank links to current definitions, discussed in this Part. World Bank, 'Issues for Consideration by the High-Level Panel on Internal Displacement', Submission, 2020.

62 GP20, 'Submission from the GP20 Initiative to the UN Secretary General's High-Level Panel on Internal Displacement' (8 May 2020), p. 7. The GP20 policy brief of 2021 also recognizes that, due to the generic character of the IASC definition, it should be applied considering the specific situation and context and complement more detailed operational guidance adopted by humanitarian and development actors or national and local authorities. GP20, 'Ten Years since the IASC Framework on Durable Solutions', Policy Brief (May 2021), p. 4.

63 Megan Bradley, 'Durable Solutions and the Right of Return for IDPs: Evolving Interpretations', *International Journal of Refugee Law* 30, no. 2 (2018): pp. 218–242.

64 The World Bank advocates for defining durable solutions "as the point where IDPs are living in conditions that are similar to the rest of the population". World Bank, 'Issues for Consideration by the High-Level Panel on Internal Displacement', p. 4. In some situations, government policies create incentives for continuing to be counted as displaced even after a solution has been reached. For example, a profiling exercise of internally displaced persons in the Luhansk Region in Ukraine observed that, while many internally displaced persons perceived that they were integrated, government policies required them to maintain their status as internally displaced persons in order to access pensions and other social services. Norwegian Refugee Council and Joint IDP Profiling Service, 'Profiling of IDP situation in Luhansk Region, Ukraine – Data-driven approach to durable solutions', Report (December 2020), p. 25.

65 UNHCR has estimated refugee numbers by region from 1950, with more precise annual numbers of refugees becoming available by countries of origin and asylum from 1980 onwards. Annual resettlement figures became available from 1959. From the 1980s, UNHCR datasets include government data on the annual number of refugees that governments have resettled including, but not limited to, refugees referred by UNHCR. Since 2003, UNHCR has maintained yearly statistics on UNHCR resettlement activities, such as submissions to resettlement countries and annual departures.

66 In 1998, the Internal Displacement Monitoring Centre (IDMC) was established as part of the Norwegian Refugee Council to provide comprehensive data and analysis on situations of internal displacement. IDMC provides a yearly Global Report on Internal Displacement (GRID), which includes a repository of data and analysis on internal displacement. The consolidation of UNHCR data collected through its annual statistical activities, data provided by the United Nations Relief and Works Agency for Palestine Refugees in the Near East (UNRWA) and data provided by IDMC on persons displaced within their country due to conflict or violence is available at: UNHCR, Refugee Data Finder. For further information on data availability, see: UNHCR, 'Methodology', website.

67   Among the challenges is that national definitions for internally displaced persons are not uniform and can be politically motivated (e.g. recognizing only persons displaced by certain actors and not others). Additionally, there are significant data collection challenges in fragile and conflict-affected areas that can lead to both under- and over-reporting. See: World Bank, 'Issues for Consideration by the High-Level Panel on Internal Displacement'. Generally, compiling refugee and internal displacement return statistics is complex due to differences in the availability, timeliness, quality and comparability of the statistics received from different sources. For further information on data availability, see: UNHCR, 'Methodology'; UNHCR, *Statistical Yearbook 2010* (2011), pp. 15–20.

68   UNHCR, *Global Trends 2019*, p. 54.

69   Ibid., p. 54.

70   Although not formally binding, Conclusions on International Protection are relevant to the interpretation of the international protection regime. They constitute expressions of opinion which are broadly representative of the views of the international community.

71   UNHCR, *A Thematic Compilation of Executive Committee Conclusions* (7th Edition) (June 2014). The Executive Committee is comprised of 104 States elected to the Committee by the United Nations Economic and Social Council.

72   UNHCR, Refugee Data Finder.

73   Sadako N. Ogata, *The Turbulent Decade: Confronting the Refugee Crises of the 1990s* (New York: W.W. Norton & Co, 2005), p. 277.

74   UNHCR, Refugee Data Finder. The available data on refugee returns during this period is likely an underestimation as data on returns only became available in 1965 and was only partially available until the 1990s. As mentioned earlier, the number of internally displaced persons who returned in this period is not known.

75   See: Part I.

76   UNHCR, *The State of The World's Refugees 2000: Fifty Years of Humanitarian Action* (NY: Oxford University Press, 2000), pp. 41–42.

77   According to Gil Loescher, this helped garner the trust of African States that were then open to UNHCR normative guidance. Gil Loescher, *The UNHCR and World Politics: A Perilous Path* (Oxford: Oxford University Press, 2001), pp. 107–109.

78   After the Dayton Accords that concluded the Bosnian War, refugee returns did not feature prominently in peace agreements. Peace agreements are the culmination of negotiations. Return and sustainable reintegration are continuing processes that are subject to many variables over indeterminate lengths of time. The parties to a peace agreement may not be the same parties necessary to set terms and conditions for refugee returns.

79   For more on the Algerian crisis, see: UNHCR, *The State of The World's Refugees 2000*, pp. 41–43.

80   Loescher, *The UNHCR and World Politics*, pp. 107–108.

81   For the different perceptions and terminology on the war, see: Anam Zakaria, 'Remembering the War of 1971 in East Pakistan', *Al Jazeera* (16 January 2016).

82   Willem van Schendel, 'Pakistan Falls Apart', in *A History of Bangladesh* (Cambridge: Cambridge University Press, 2009), pp. 121–130.

83   As described by Gary Bass in his book on these events and the US response, it was a

...PART III: **Solutions – An Uneven Record...**

"slaughter" that in "the dark annals of modern cruelty... ranks as bloodier than Bosnia, and by some accounts, in the same league as Rwanda". Gary J. Bass, *The Blood Telegram* (NY: Penguin Random House, 2014), p. xiii.

84   UNHCR, *The State of The World's Refugees 2000*, p. 61. Estimates of the number of deaths vary. The official Bangladesh figure is 3 million although the United States Department of State estimated 200,000 which according to Gary Bass is a conservative one. Gary Bass, 'Looking Away from Genocide', *The New Yorker* (19 November 2013).

85   Loescher, *The UNHCR and World Politics*, pp. 159–160.

86   UNHCR also coordinated on behalf of the United Nations humanitarian efforts in support of the exchange of populations between Pakistan, India and Bangladesh. This repatriation exercise was encompassed in the New Delhi Agreement signed in 1993 by Pakistan, India and Bangladesh. It provided for the repatriation of Pakistani prisoners of war and civilian internees in India, all Bengalis in Pakistan, and non-Bengalis in Bangladesh who chose to move to Pakistan. Over 230,000 people benefited from this agreement. For more on this and the refugee influx to India, see: UNHCR, 'Rupture in South Asia', in *The State of The World's Refugees 2000*, pp. 59–74.

87   UNHCR and ICRC also supported the transfer of over 200,000 people who found themselves "stranded in states of which they no longer wanted to be a part". These included Bengalis in Pakistan and Biharis in Bangladesh. UNHCR, *The State of The World's Refugees 2000*, pp. 71–74.

88   Note, however, that Urdu speakers from Bangladesh who had comprised a privileged minority before the war, were confined to camps in the 40 years following the war, without recognition of their legal identity and associated rights. For more on the resolution of their situation through the conferral of recognized citizenship, see: Ninette Kelley, 'Ideas, Interests, and Institutions: Conceding Citizenship in Bangladesh', *The University of Toronto Law Journal* 60, 2 (2010): pp. 349–371.

89   UNHCR, *The State of The World's Refugees 2000*, p. 75; Katy Long, *The Point of No Return: Rights, Refugees, and Repatriation* (Oxford: Oxford University Press, 2013), pp. 90–91; Loescher, *The UNHCR and World Politics*, pp. 224–225.

90   Long, *The Point of No Return*, pp. 90–91; Loescher, *The UNHCR and World Politics*, pp. 224–225.

91   Discussed later in this Part.

92   Discussed further under Resettlement in this Part.

93   Loescher, *The UNHCR and World Politics*, pp. 210–211.

94   Ibid., p. 213.

95   Ibid., pp. 210–13.

96   Other post-independence return movements during the 1970s that were similarly assisted but on a much smaller scale, were to Guinea-Bissau (51,000 persons), Angola (86,000 persons), and Mozambique (59,000 persons). UNHCR, Refugee Data Finder.

97   UNHCR, Refugee Data Finder. Loescher, *The UNHCR and World Politics*, pp. 149–150.

98   The conflict between the south and north would wage on until the south achieved independence in 2011. Peace, however, was short-lived: Within two years the new country was plunged into a prolonged civil war causing mass forced displacement. Elsewhere in Sudan, another rebellion in Darfur erupted in 2003, also leading to mass displacement and ongo-

ing fragility requiring the continued presence of an African Union and UN peacekeeping operation until the end of 2020.

99 UNHCR, Refugee Data Finder.

100 UNHCR, 'Chapter 5: Proxy Wars in Africa, Asia and Central America' in *The State of The World's Refugees 2000*, pp. 106–107.

101 Ibid., p. 110.

102 Jeff Crisp, 'The Politics of Repatriation: Ethiopian Refugees in Djibouti, 1977–83', *Review of African Political Economy* 30 (1984): pp. 73–82.

103 UNHCR, *The State of the World's Refugees 2000*, p. 115. The circumstances leading to this exodus are discussed in Part II.

104 Long, *The Point of No Return*, pp. 98–99.

105 In Barbara Hendrie's review of the return movement, she writes that UNHCR did not formally participate because of the absence of agreement to it from the Ethiopian Government, the lack of support for it from the United States, and because UNHCR did not have sufficient information or access to areas of return nor full appreciation of the coping skills of the Tigrayans. Barbara Hendrie, 'The Politics of Repatriation: The Tigrayan Refugee Repatriation 1985–1987', *Journal of Refugee Studies* 4, no. 2 (1991): pp. 200–218.

106 UNHCR, 'Handbook of Selected Lessons Learned from the Field: Refugee Operations and Environmental Management' (December 2002), p. 12; Hendrie notes that initially men returned and their families followed as agricultural production improved. Hendrie, 'The Politics of Repatriation': p. 204.

107 Amnesty International, 'Ethiopia: Tepid International Response to Tigray Conflict Fuels Horrific Violations over Past Six Months', Press Release (4 May 2021).

108 Prior to the conflict, the Tigray region was host to some 100,000 Ethiopian internally displaced persons. By March 2021, the number of internally displaced persons in Tigray had increased to an estimated 1 million persons. Some suggest that this is only an estimate, as access to the region has been restricted. In addition, over 63,000 Ethiopians had fled to Sudan as of April 2021. UNHCR, 'Ethiopia Situation (Tigray Region) Regional Update #15', Situation Report (5 May 2021), pp. 1, 3; UNHCR, ' Ethiopia Situation – Tigray Emergency Response', Operational Data Portal.

109 UNHCR, Refugee Data Finder. By 1989, the number of Ugandan refugees in Sudan had decreased to just over 9,000.

110 Jeff Crisp, 'Ugandan Refugees in Sudan and Zaire: The Problem of Repatriation', *African Affairs* 85, no. 339 (1986): p. 174. He notes that food assistance had been cut in southern Sudan, and that hunger and lack of medical care were among the reasons for return. He also writes that more returned from Zaire (Now Democratic Republic of the Congo) than from Sudan.

111 IDMC, 'Uganda: Focus shifts to securing durable solutions for IDPs', Internal Displacement Profile (3 November 2008), p. 9.

112 Between 1980 and 1989, nearly 568,000 Ugandan refugees returned, according to UNHCR data. UNHCR, Refugee Data Finder. However, several sources indicate that accurate data collection was difficult at the time and numbers should therefore be considered indicative only. On this issue, see, for example: Crisp, 'Ugandan Refugees in Sudan and Zaire'. For more on Uganda displacement at this time, see: Lucy Hovil, 'Uganda's Refugee Policies: The History, the Politics, the Way Forward', Policy Paper, International Refugee Rights Initiative (October 2018): pp. 4–5.

113 UNHCR, Refugee Data Finder.

114 Penelope Mathew and Tristan Harley, *Refugees, Regionalism and Responsibility* (Cheltenham, UK: Edward Elgar Publishing Ltd, 2016), p. 165.

115 Alexander Betts notes that the "only significant donor contributions made were done on the basis of wider strategic and foreign policy interests, with the United States, for example, targeting most of its contributions towards "its strategic allies in African Cold War proxy conflicts". Alexander Betts, *Protection by Persuasion: International Cooperation in the Refugee Regime* (Ithaca, NY: Cornell University Press, 2009), pp. 65–66. Mathew and Harley note that these allies included Angola and Sudan, Mathew and Harley, *Refugees, Regionalism and Responsibility*, p. 172.

116 UN General Assembly, Resolution 37/197, 'International Conference on Assistance to Refugees in Africa' (18 December 1982), UN Doc A/RES/37/197, para. 5.

117 Kate Milner recalls how major donors were criticized for their slow initial response to assist a communist regime the policies of which contributed to the massive crisis. Kate Milner, 'Flashback 1984: Portrait of a Famine', *BBC News* (6 April 2000).

118 This and the following assessment can be found in Robert F. Gorman, *Coping With Africa's Refugee Burden: A Time for Solutions* (Leiden: Martinus Nijhoff Publishers, 1987), pp. 24–30.

119 In 2017, the General Assembly requested UNHCR to "coordinate an effort to measure the impact arising from hosting, protecting and assisting refugees, with a view to assessing gaps in international cooperation and promoting burden-and-responsibility sharing that is more equitable and sustainable, and to begin reporting on the results to Member States in 2018". Affirmed the next year in the Global Compact on Refugees, para. 103.

120 Robert F. Gorman, *Coping With Africa's Refugee Burden*, pp. 24–25; Robert F. Gorman, 'Beyond ICARA II: Implementing Refugee-Related Development Assistance', *International Migration Review* 20, no. 2 (March 1986): p. 288.

121 The General Assembly requested UNHCR to coordinate efforts to measure the impact arising from hosting, protecting, and assisting refugees as part of the larger commitments of the Global Compact on Refugees towards enhanced burden-sharing. To that end, UNHCR, with support from the World Bank and in consultation with a range of member States, has been working to develop a common approach and methodology to measure impact. There are many challenges, not least of which is the availability of comparable sound data and the difficulty in isolating the impacts caused by refugees on host communities from other causes, including neighbouring conflict. For more on this ongoing work, see: UNHCR, 'Measuring the Impact of Hosting, Protecting and Assisting Refugees', Progress Report (1 July 2020).

122 Robert F. Gorman, 'Beyond ICARA II': pp. 288–289.

123 Evident in the Global Compact on Refugees and discussed in more detail in Part V.

124 UNHCR, Refugee Data Finder.

125 UNHCR, Refugee Data Finder.

126 Ogata, *The Turbulent Decade*, pp. 285–286.

127 UNHCR, 'Going Home: Voluntary Repatriation', in *The State of The World's Refugees 1993: The Challenge of Protection* (NY: Penguin, 1993), p. 104.

128 UN Security Council, 'Final Act of the Paris Conference on Cambodia' (30 October 1991), UN Doc S/23177, art. 20.

129 Long, *The Point of No Return*, p. 123; Loescher, *The UNHCR and World Politics*, pp. 281–282.

130 A number of factors helped to stabilize the country, including a resumption in international aid after the United Nations supervised elections in 1993, which helped attract foreign direct investment and economic recovery. The return of Prince Sihanouk to Cambodia was a stabilizing influence, helping heal the trauma of previous decades. Although he was removed by a coup d'état in 1997 by Prime Minister Hun Sen, the country has not experienced renewed internal armed conflict. Sokty Chhair and Luyna Ung, 'Economic History of Industrialization in Cambodia', Working Paper No. 2013/134, UNU-Wider (2013); Hal Hill and Jayat Menon, 'Cambodia: Rapid Growth with Institutional Constraints', Working Paper 331, Asia Development Bank (January 2013). Scholars have examined the impact of the peace agreement and, specifically, lessons learned that may have a bearing on the evolution of one-party rule and political unrest in more recent times. See, for example: United States Institute for Peace, 'Lessons from Cambodia's Paris Peace Accords for Political Unrest Today', Brief (16 May 2017). See also: Hal Hill and Jayat Menon, 'Cambodia: Rapid Growth with Institutional Constraints'.

131 Loescher, *The UNHCR and World Politics*, pp. 284–286; UNHCR, Refugee Data Finder.

132 UNHCR, Refugee Data Finder.

133 Loescher, *The UNHCR and World Politics*, pp. 224–225; Long, *The Point of No Return*, pp. 123–25.

134 UN, 'Rohingya Refugee Crisis a "Human Rights Nightmare", UN Chief Tells Security Council', *UN* News (28 September 2017).

135 UNHCR, Refugee Data Finder.

136 UNHCR, *The State of The World's Refugees 2000*, p. 212.

137 Ogata, *The Turbulent Decade*, p. 28.

138 UN Security Council, Resolution 688 (5 April 1991), UN Doc S/RES/688(1991).

139 The Coalition was established further to a 1990 Security Council resolution authorizing States to use "all necessary measures" to compel Iraq's withdrawal from Kuwait. UNSC, Res. 678 (29 November 1990), UN Doc S/RES/678(1990).

140 According to UNHCR's Refugee Data Finder, a total of 1.3 million persons returned to Iraq in 1991. See also: UNHCR, *The State of The World's Refugees 2000*, pp. 213–218.

141 UNHCR, *The State of The World's Refugees 2000*, p. 213; Long, *The Point of No Return*, pp. 107–109.

142 In his book, Gil Loescher also notes that the experience led UNHCR to improve its preparedness and emergency response mechanisms, including supply chain and stockpiling. Given the influence of the media during this period, it also led to greater investments in public communication. Loescher, *The UNHCR and World Politics*, pp. 290–291.

143 UNHCR, Refugee Data Finder.

144 The Great Lakes region in Africa includes Burundi, the Democratic Republic of the Congo, and Tanzania.

145 Ogata, *The Turbulent Decade*, p. 176.

146 A total of 1.2 million refugees returned to Rwanda from Burundi, Tanzania, Uganda and Zaire in 1994. UNHCR, Refugee Data Finder. For more on this movement, see: UNHCR, *The State of The World's Refugees 2000*, pp. 245–273.

147 Those who crossed borders to flee went to Zaire, Tanzania, Burundi and Uganda. Ogata, *The Turbulent Decade*, p. 189.

148 Long, *The Point of No Return*, p. 127.

...PART III: **Solutions – An Uneven Record...**

149 A UNHCR commissioned report by Robert Gersony to assess the conditions for repatriation and reintegration found that between 5,000 and 10,000 persons were killed each month from late April through July 1994. Ogata, *The Turbulent Decade*, pp. 190–195.

150 UNHCR, *The State of The World's Refugees 2000*, p. 250.

151 In 1994, an estimated 12,000 Rwandan refugees died in Goma in eastern Zaire. A. K. Siddique et al., 'Why Treatment Centres Failed to Prevent Cholera Deaths among Rwandan Refugees in Goma, Zaire', *The Lancet* 345, no. 8946 (1995): p. 359.

152 An initial attempt to support the deployment of a special Zairian security force within the camps brought a modicum of order. But this was relatively short-lived for a variety of reasons, including political divisions and corruption, and impunity within the camps continued.

153 Kisangani N. F. Emizet, 'The Massacre of Refugees in Congo: A Case of UN Peacekeeping Failure and International Law', *The Journal of Modern African Studies* 38, no. 2 (2000): pp. 168–169.

154 Ibid.: pp. 168–169.

155 UNGA, 'Report of the Joint Mission Charged with Investigating Allegations of Massacres and Other Human Rights Violations Occurring in Eastern Zaire (Now Democratic Republic of the Congo) since September 1996' (2 July 1997), paras. 38–76; Emizet, 'The Massacre of Refugees in Congo': p. 163.

156 Ray Wilkinson, 'Cover Story: Heart of Darkness', *Refugees Magazine* 110 (Crisis in the Great Lakes), UNHCR (1997).

157 UNHCR, Refugee Data Finder. In May 1997, the Mobutu government fell.

158 By the end of that year, over half a million refugees had returned from Tanzania to Rwanda. UNHCR, Refugee Data Finder. For more on this return movement, see: Ogata, *The Turbulent Decade*, pp. 253–255; Long, *The Point of No Return*, pp. 130–131.

159 The Kibeho camp held over 80,000 Hutu refugees fearful that they would be killed in revenge attacks should they return home. According to the Rwandan Government, the camp sheltered those responsible for the genocide. It announced that the camp would be closed and all camp residents screened for possible culpability in the genocide. Tensions intensified and food and water supplies ran thin. Gérard Prunier, *Africa's World War: Congo, the Rwandan Genocide, and the Making of a Continental Catastrophe* (Oxford: Oxford University Press, 2009), pp. 37–72. According to the account of journalist, Joshua Hammer, gunfire broke out when some tried to flee the screening. Joshua Hammer, 'He Was the Hero of "Hotel Rwanda". Now He's Accused of Terrorism', *The New York Times* (2 March 2021).

160 Successive killings of international aid workers and the response also illustrated the precarity of the situation. Three Spanish humanitarian workers were killed by Hutu militia men in northwest Rwanda in January 1997. Three hundred people were killed by the Rwandan army in attempts to arrest the suspects. The following month, five UN human rights observers were assassinated in Cyangugu, leading the UN to pull out its relief workers from the western region. Amnesty International, *Rwanda: Ending the Silence*, Report (25 September 1997), p. 19.

161 Human Rights Watch, *Uncertain Refuge: International Failures to Protect Refugees*, Report (April 1997), p. 4; Amnesty International, 'Rwanda: human rights overlooked in mass repatriation', Report (January 1997); Amnesty International, 'Great Lakes region: Still in need of

protection: repatriation, refoulement and the safety of refugees and the internally displaced', Report (January 1997); Amnesty International, 'Rwanda: Amnesty delegates back from Rwanda report new wave of human rights abuses', Press Release (19 February 1997).

162 In 1997, UN High Commissioner for Refugees, Sadako Ogata, recognized as much when she acknowledged that: "UNHCR faces increasing pressures to support repatriation which is neither strictly voluntary nor strictly safe. Either safety in the country of asylum cannot be guaranteed, because of armed conflict or insecurity, or because asylum is being withdrawn by the host government. Although there 'may be problems at home, returning home in such circumstances may be better than staying'." Quoted in UNHCR, *The State of The World's Refugees: A Humanitarian Agenda 1997–1998*, (New York: Oxford University Press, 1997), p. 91.

163 Alexander Betts, Gil Loescher, and James Milner, *The United Nations High Commissioner for Refugees (UNHCR): The Politics and Practice of Refugee Protection* (Abingdon, UK: Routledge, 2011), p. 51.

164 Loescher, *The UNHCR and World Politics*, pp. 282–283; UNHCR, Refugee Data Finder.

165 UNSC, General Peace Agreement for Mozambique (8 October 1992), UN Doc S/24635.

166 United Nations Operations in Mozambique (ONUMOZ, Portuguese: Operação das Nações Unidas em Moçambique), which ended in January 1995.

167 Jeff Crisp et al., 'Rebuilding a War-Torn Society: A Review of the UNHCR Reintegration Programme for Mozambican Returnees', *Refugee Survey Quarterly* 16, 2 (1997): pp. 24–71.

168 Crisp et al., 'Rebuilding a War-Torn Society', pp. 24–25. They also found that UNHCR's presence throughout the country helped build confidence in return as well as play a role in resolving local disputes, pp. 38, 54.

169 Crisp et al., 'Rebuilding a War-Torn Society', p. 31.

170 UNHCR had indicated previously that they be recognized on a prima facie basis, but receiving States were reluctant to do so. The numbers are best estimates. Aristide R. Zolberg, Astri Suhrke, and Sergio Aguayo, *Escape from Violence: Conflict and the Refugee Crisis in the Developing World* (New York: Oxford University Press, 1989), p. 212; José H. Fischel de Andrade, 'The 1984 Cartagena Declaration: A Critical Review of Some Aspects of Its Emergence and Relevance', *Refugee Survey Quarterly* 38, no. 4 (1 December 2019): pp. 345, 348; UNHCR, *The State of The World's Refugees 2000*, p. 136.

171 CIREFCA, Declaration and Concerted Plan of Action in Favour of Central American Refugees, Returnees and Displaced Persons (30 May 1989), CIREFCA 89/13/Rev.1, I: Declaration, para. 22.

172 CIREFCA, Declaration and Concerted Plan of Action, II: Plan of Action, paras. 21–23.

173 Alexander Betts, 'Comprehensive Plans of Action: Insights from CIREFCA and the Indochinese CPA', Working Paper 120, *New Issues in Refugee Research*, UNHCR (2006), p. 15.

174 Ibid., pp. 10–11.

175 The European Economic Community contributed $115 million. In addition, Italy was the largest bilateral donor providing over $115 million for development projects, followed by Sweden who pledged $60 million. The United States, so prominent in the CPA, chose to favour its bilateral process over the multilateral processes. This was driven, in part, by its political alliances, with support to Nicaragua picking up after the Sandinistas lost the 1990 election. UNHCR, 'Review of the CIREFCA Process', Evaluation Report (1 May 1994); Betts, 'Comprehensive Plans of Action', pp. 11, 27–28, 52–53; Mathew and Harley, *Refugees, Regionalism and Responsibility*, p. 178.

176 UNHCR, Refugee Data Finder.

...PART III: **Solutions – An Uneven Record...**

177 Ron Redmond, 'The Human Side of CIREFCA', *Refugees Magazine* 99, UNHCR (1995). NGOs gained more prominence and implemented close to 40 per cent of all project funding received. See: Betts, 'Comprehensive Plans of Action', p. 15. According to Betts, this was important because States in the region had traditionally been reluctant to acknowledge the role of civil society or non-State actors.

178 Part of this failing was laid at the feet of the main international organizations: UNHCR and UNDP. At the time, UNHCR did not consider itself to have a mandate for internally displaced persons and UNDP's approach was geographically based, focusing on areas of high vulnerability and needs, which did not always include internally displaced persons. See: Betts, 'Comprehensive Plans of Action', pp. 8–10, 12, 18. See also: Megan Bradley, 'Forced Migration in Central America and the Caribbean', *The Oxford Handbook of Refugee and Forced Migration Studies* (NY: Oxford University Press, 2014) p. 106; Arafat Jamal, 'Refugee repatriation and reintegration in Guatemala: Lessons learned from UNHCR's experience', Evaluation Report, UNHCR-EPAU (2000); Paula Worby, 'Security and Dignity: Land Access and Guatemala's Returned Refugees', *Refuge* 19, No 3 (2021): pp. 17–24.

179 Betts, 'Comprehensive Plans of Action', p. 14. According to Betts, meeting normative protection conditions was not a condition of the development funding that UNDP coordinated and the Italian Government supported. An opportunity to use the leverage of financing to improve refugee policies was lost as restrictive policies remained in some countries.

180 The 1993 report of the UN-approved Commission for El Salvador implicated the State as responsible for 85 per cent of the human rights abuses of the war, including named individuals in the military, civil service and judiciary. Reinaldo Figueredo Planchart, Belisario Betancur, and Thomas Buergenthal 'From Madness to Hope: The 12-Year War in El Salvador: Report of the Commission on the Truth for El Salvador' (1 April 1993) UN Doc S/25500, Annex, p. 43. The UN-sponsored Truth Commission for Guatemala similarly found that 93 per cent of the widespread human rights violations in Guatemala were perpetrated by the State, principally the army, and that over 83 per cent of the victims were indigenous Maya. Commission for Historical Clarification, *Guatemala: Memory of Silence*, Report (1999), pp. 20, 85.

181 Jose Miguel Cruz, 'The Root Causes of the Central American Crisis', *Current History* 114, no. 769 (February 2015): pp. 43–48.

182 Ibid, pp. 46–48. Additional economic stresses have also contributed to migration from the region. Some have been brought on by the adverse effects of climate change, which have led to increased storms and floods in recent years. Together with other political, social and economic factors, they have influenced decisions to migrate abroad. More recently, the COVID-19 pandemic has led to further economic losses and, in 2020, two successive hurricanes that hit Central America and Mexico displaced an estimated 3 million people. International Rescue Committee (IRC), 'Migration search trends point to growing displacement from Central America due to COVID, climate change and conflict', Press Release (16 March 2021); The Nansen Initiative, 'Disasters and Cross-Border Displacement in Central America: Emerging Needs, New Responses', Background Paper (2013); World Meteorological Organization, 'Natural Hazards and Disaster Risk Reduction', website; Gena Steffens, 'Changing Climate Forces Desperate Guatemalans to Migrate', *National Geographic* (23 October 2018).

183 UNHCR, Refugee Data Finder.

184 For more on the status of Kosovo, see: UNSC, Res. 1244 (10 June 1999), UN Doc S/Res/1244 (1999).

185 UNHCR, Refugee Data Finder. Some earlier statistics suggested that the numbers were higher with some 700,000 displaced to Western European countries and 500,000 to 800,000 displaced to neighbouring countries. Ogata, *The Turbulent Decade*, pp. 112, 167; UNHCR, *The State of The World's Refugees 2000*, p. 219.

186 In reporting on the 25th anniversary of the Dayton Peace Agreements, The Economist described how the country remained deeply ethnically divided and the impact of the political structure on deepening divides and hindering economic development. The Economist, 'Dayton at 25: After a Quarter of a Century of Peace, Bosnia Remains Wretched' (21 November 2020).

187 The Republic of Bosnia and Herzegovina, the Federation of Bosnia and Herzegovina, and the Republika Srpska, Dayton Peace Agreement (21 November 1995), Annex 7: Agreement on Refugees and Displaced Persons.

188 For example, according to Long, nationalist authorities "create[d] economic incentives for 'their' people to relocate through the often illegal distribution of building plots and business premises". Intimidation and harassment of minorities with impunity, the ongoing presence of war criminals and three education systems that taught different histories were among the many ongoing challenges. Long, *The Point of No Return*, pp. 113–114; Loescher, *The UNHCR and World Politics*, p. 323.

189 Maria Derks-Normandin, *Linking Peace, Security and Durable Solutions in a Multi-Ethnic Society: The Case of Kosovo*, Report (Brookings Institution, 2014) p. i; World Bank, 'Population Total: Kosovo', DataBank. Ogata writes that by mid-May 1999, 800,000 had fled externally and 600,000 were internally displaced. Ogata, *The Turbulent Decade*, pp. 153 and 161. The UNHCR Refugee Data Finder shows lower figures because it does not account for shorter-term displacement within the year.

190 The international presence was to monitor the withdrawal of Serbian forces, demilitarize the Kosovo Liberation Army and other armed groups and establish "a secure environment in which refugees and displaced persons can return home in safety, the international civil presence can operate, a transitional administration can be established, and humanitarian aid can be delivered", UNSC Res. 1244.

191 Derks-Normandin, *Linking Peace, Security and Durable Solutions in a Multi-Ethnic Society*, pp. 19–23.

192 Ogata, *The Turbulent Decade*, pp. 159–162.

193 In October 2020, the United Nations Interim Mission in Kosovo reported that "there remain 16,052 displaced persons within Kosovo", as well as "69,627 persons with displacement-related needs across the Western Balkans". UNSC, 'United Nations Interim Administration Mission in Kosovo: Report of the Secretary-General' (1 October 2020), UN Doc S/2020/964.

194 Ben Shephard, *The Long Road Home: The Aftermath of the Second World War* (NY: Penguin Random House, 2012), p. 5.

195 Ibid., pp. 4–5. See also: Part I.

196 UNGA, Constitution of the International Refugee Organization (15 December 1946), UN Doc A/RES/62(I), Annex I, Part 1, Section D4 and Annex III. This exclusion covered Germans who had been evacuated from Germany during the war, as well as those who were being expelled from countries in Europe.

197 For more on the position of the Soviet Union and the work of the IRO: Shephard, *The Long Road Home*, pp. 264, 339, 384; George Ginsburgs, 'The Soviet Union and the Problem of

Refugees and Displaced Persons 1917–1956', *American Journal of International Law* 51, no. 2 (April 1957): pp. 325–361.

198 It also facilitated the return of 73,000 displaced persons. UNHCR, *The State of The World's Refugees 2000*, p. 17.

199 Shephard, *The Long Road Home*, p. 343. He notes that countries that agreed to resettle the refugees "tried to extract only those people who suited their labour needs and philosophy of immigration", and the outcome determined whether a refugee ended up in "Chile, or Chicago, Manitoba or Melbourne", p. 5.

200 Auguste Lindt, who was the United Nations High Commissioner for Refugees from 1956 to 1960, pressed hard for this to stop, saying it was a tragedy so many were left behind. Statement by Dr. Auguste R. Lindt, United Nations High Commissioner for Refugees, at the Special Meeting on World Refugee Year, Tenth Session, Council of the Intergovernmental Committee for European Migration (ICEM), 9 April 1959. It would take several more years beyond the expiration of his tenure before solutions to the residual camp population was resolved.

201 Shephard, *The Long Road Home*, p. 383 (United States), p. 340 (Western Europe), p. 347 (Latin America). In Canada, arrivals took place over several years. See: Government of Canada, 'The Arrival of Displaced Persons in Canada, 1945–1951', website. With respect to Australia, see: National Archives of Australia, 'Refugees Displaced by World War II' (1947), website.

202 David Nasaw, *The Last Million: Europe's Displaced Persons from World War to Cold War* (NY: Penguin Random House, 2020), pp. 358–434.

203 Nasaw, *The Last Million*, pp. 10–13 and 36–38; Adina Hoffman, 'How a Million Refugees Became Postwar Pawns of the Allies', *The New York Times* (15 September 2020); Judy Feigin, 'The Office of Special Investigations: Striving for Accountability in the Aftermath of the Holocaust', Justice Department Report (December 2006), published online by *The New York Times*.

204 Shephard, *The Long Road Home*, p. 346.

205 The United States was, by far, the largest resettlement country. Beginning in the 1950s, its Escapee Programme had three key objectives: Help people fleeing the Sino-Soviet bloc, encourage others to do so, and provide the United States with vital intelligence. 'Circular airgram No. 72: The Secretary of State to Certain Diplomatic and Consular Offices', in David M. Baehler et al. (eds.), *Foreign Relations of the United States, 1952 to 1954, Eastern Europe; Soviet Union; Eastern Mediterranean* vol. VIII (Washington D.C.: United States Government Printing Office, 1988), published online by *The Office of the Historian*; Deutsche Welle, 'US Cold War Resettlement Program Used for Propaganda, Spying' (29 December 2008).

206 UNHCR, *The State of The World's Refugees 2000*, pp. 29, 32.

207 That support, together with the advocacy of UNHCR, also helped to ensure that family members were resettled with selected refugees. Loescher, *The UNHCR and World Politics*, p. 88.

208 Among the refugee population were minors and young people who were separated from their families in Hungary. Believing in the importance of family unity, Lindt worked with the authorities in Hungary, Austria and Western asylum and resettlement States to enable their voluntary repatriation. According to Loescher, some 18,000 returned home. Loescher, *The UNHCR and World Politics*, p. 88.

209 Shezan Muhammedi, '"Gifts From Amin": The Resettlement, Integration, and Identities of Ugandan Asian Refugees in Canada', PhD Thesis, University of Western Ontario, 2017, pp. 101–102; Becky Taylor, 'Good Citizens? Ugandan Asians, Volunteers and "Race" Relations in 1970s Britain', *History Workshop Journal* 85 (January 2018): p. 121.

210 Muhammedi, '"Gifts From Amin"', pp. 3, 5 and 51. The South Asian population was heavily concentrated in the commercial, management and professional sectors. For further information on the resettlement of Ugandan Asians, see: Loescher, *The UNHCR and World Politics*, pp. 164–167.

211 This estimate includes some 650,000 Vietnamese who departed directly from their country of origin and some 800,000 Vietnamese, Cambodian and Laotian refugees who were resettled from countries in the region. Judith Kumin, 'Orderly Departure from Vietnam: Cold War Anomaly or Humanitarian Innovation?', *Refugee Survey Quarterly* 27, no. 1 (2008): p. 105. UNHCR, Refugee Data Finder. Earlier estimates were even higher than this. UNHCR, *The State of The World's Refugees 2000*, p. 85.

212 UNHCR, Refugee Data Finder.

213 UNHCR, *The State of The World's Refugees 2000*, p. 82.

214 For more on ethnic Chinese in Vietnam and the circumstances of this exodus, see: Pao-min Chang, 'The Sino-Vietnamese Dispute over the Ethnic Chinese', *The China Quarterly* 90 (June 1982): pp. 195–230. The total number who fled is found on p. 230; Kumin, 'Orderly Departure from Vietnam': pp. 107–109; UNHCR, Refugee Data Finder.

215 UNHCR, Refugee Data Finder; The Editors of Encyclopaedia Britannica, 'Khmer Rouge', *Encyclopædia Britannica* online.

216 Reports at the time detailed the brutality of the pirates who attacked refugees with clubs and knives, robbed them of their possessions, killed many and abducted women and girls. UNHCR, *The State of The World's Refugees 2000*, p. 87.

217 Barry Wain, *The Refused: The Agony of the Indochina Refugees* (New York: Simon and Schuster, 1981), p. 83; Other estimates put the total of those who died at sea throughout the crisis at about 200,000. See: Nghia M. Vo, *The Vietnamese Boat People, 1954 and 1975–1992* (Jefferson, N.C.: McFarland, 2006), p. 167.

218 Australia, Canada, France, Germany, the United Kingdom, and the United States collectively agreed to resettle 260,000 refugees, see: Mathew and Harley, *Refugees, Regionalism and Responsibility*, p. 145.

219 Ibid., pp. 145–146. Subsequent agreements included increased regional cooperation for rescue-at-sea operations and emergency relief to displaced Cambodians, p. 147.

220 Kumin, 'Orderly Departure from Vietnam': p. 105. Judith Kumin is the former head of UNHCR's programmes for orderly departure from Vietnam and for resettlement of Indochinese refugees.

221 UNHCR, Refugee Data Finder. UNHCR, *The State of The World's Refugees 2000*, p. 84.

222 Notably from Thailand and Malaysia.

223 UNGA, 'Declaration and Comprehensive Plan of Action of the International Conference on Indo-Chinese Refugees, Report of the Secretary-General' (22 September 1989), UN Doc A/44/523, Part II, D.

224 To accommodate differences among States, with some insisting the returns be voluntary and others refusing to specify this in the agreement, it was agreed that those refused refugee status would receive counselling for a period of three months to encourage their

voluntary return and would be monitored by UNHCR when returned. Betts, 'Comprehensive Plans of Action', pp. 35–36.

225 Mathew and Harley, *Refugees, Regionalism and Responsibility*, pp. 151–152. They note that between 1989 and 1995, UNHCR undertook over 18,000 returnee monitoring visits to Vietnam, p. 152.

226 Ibid., pp. 145–151. Two countries continued to bar new arrivals: Singapore no longer permitted rescue-at-sea cases or direct arrivals to disembark; and local authorities in Malaysia had orders to redirect boat arrivals back into international waters between 1989 and 1990. UNHCR, *State of the World's Refugees 2000*, pp. 83, 85.

227 UNHCR, Refugee Data Finder. Kumin, 'Orderly Departure from Vietnam': pp. 104–105.

228 This was significant since many of the States were not parties to the Refugee Convention (1951) or Refugee Protocol (1967).

229 Richard Towle, 'Processes and Critiques of the Indo-Chinese Comprehensive Plan of Action: An Instrument of International Burden-Sharing?', *International Journal of Refugee Law* 18, no. 3–4 (September/December 2006): pp. 537–570.

230 Mathew and Harley, *Refugees, Regionalism and Responsibility*, p. 155. Note however that Towle suggests that even with these challenges the CPA was important for it helped UNHCR, government officials, and advocates to develop experience and lessons learned in approaches to mass individualized refugee status determinations. Richard Towle, 'Processes and Critiques of the Indo-Chinese Comprehensive Plan of Action': p. 269.

231 Mathew and Harley, *Refugees, Regionalism and Responsibility*, pp. 157–158.

232 Sara Ellen Davies, *Legitimising Rejection: International Refugee Law in Southeast Asia* (Leiden: Brill, 2008), p. 226.

233 On United States policy interests, see: Betts, 'Comprehensive Plans of Action', pp. 42–43. In regard to Canada and the CPA, see: Ninette Kelley and Michael Trebilcock, *The Making of the Mosaic: A History of Canadian Immigration Policy* (Toronto: University of Toronto Press, 2010), pp. 397–398. The Vietnamese diaspora were particularly supportive, as were civil and faith-based groups.

234 For example, in 1980, there were close to 2 million Afghan refugees and over 2.5 million refugees from Ethiopia. In 1989, at the time of the second international conference for Indochinese refugees, there were over 5.5 million Afghan refugees, 1.4 million refugees from Ethiopia and 1 million refugees from Mozambique. UNHCR, *State of the World's Refugees 2000*, p. 314.

235 John Fredriksson and Christine Mougne, 'Resettlement in the 1990s: A Review of Policy and Practice', UNHCR (December 1994), pp. 5–6.

236 While these countries maintained an open door to refugees during this time, restrictive policies, such as the Refugees (Control) Act 1966 in Tanzania, the Control of Alien Refugees Act (CARA) 1960 in Uganda and the Refugee (Control) Act 1970 in Zambia were in place. Those, however, were not always fully implemented in practice.

237 Alexander Betts et al., *Refugee Economies in Uganda: What Difference Does the Self-Reliance Model Make?* (Oxford: Refugee Studies Centre, 2019), p. 6. Policy and practice became more restrictive in Tanzania in the 1990s, see: Michèle Morel, 'The lack of refugee burden-sharing in Tanzania: tragic effects', *Afrika Focus* 22, 1 (2009): pp. 111–112; James Milner, 'Two steps forward, one step back: understanding the shifting politics of refugee policy in Tanzania', Research Paper 255, *New Issues in Refugee Research*, UNHCR (July 2013): pp. 4–7. While having imposed some restrictions on refugees, particularly in terms of freedom of movement, Zambia is pursuing increasingly inclusive policies, particularly in recent years, see: 'UNHCR, 'Implementing a Comprehensive Refugee Response: The Zambia Experience', Report (December 2019).

238 See, for example: Sadruddin Aga Khan, 'Statement by Prince Sadruddin Aga Khan, United Nations High Commissioner for Refugees, to the Third Committee of the United Nations General Assembly at its 1519th Meeting, 20 November 1967' (20 November 1967).

239 Including civil documentation and the adjudication and enforcement of housing, land and property rights. UNHCR, *Agenda for Protection (Third Edition)* (October 2003), p. 77. The Global Consultations on International Protection and the Agenda for Protection are also discussed in Part II.

240 UNHCR, *Agenda for Protection*.

241 The Global Compact calls for increasing the pool of resettlement places, and more investment in robust reception and integration services. See: UNGA, Global Compact on Refugees (2018), paras. 91–92. See also: UNGA, Res. 73/151 (17 December 2018), UN Doc A/RES/73/151, para. 53.

242 Reflected in the Global Compact on Refugees with its emphasis on improved cooperation among political, humanitarian, development and peace actors. See: Global Compact on Refugees, paras. 8, 11, 24 and 48.

243 See, for example, the 2017 OECD study that observed that despite "more than 15 years of large-scale international efforts in Afghanistan, the country remains marred by weak rule of law, political fragility and persistent insecurity – circumstances that are likely to continue to discourage many Afghan refugees and migrants abroad to return home voluntarily", Susanna Morrison-Métois, 'Responding to Refugee Crises: Lessons from Evaluations in Afghanistan as a Country of Origin', OECD Development Co-Operation Working Paper (2017), p. 1.

244 Many refugees from rural areas, for example, do not return to their place of origin with many moving to urban areas. World Bank, *Forcibly Displaced*, pp. 101–103. See also the studies discussed in Jolien Tegenbos and Koen Vlassenroot, 'Going Home? A Systematic Review of the Literature on Displacement, Return and Cycles of Violence', Working Paper, LSE Conflict Research Programme (2018). Tegenbos and Vlassenroot conclude from their review that most studies of returning refugees and internally displaced persons are rather narrowly focused on specific groups and on development and humanitarian return policies. They identify areas in need of further research including: the experience of returnee populations who continue to be mobile and those that do not following return; how societal changes in areas of return affect the strategies and positions of those considering return and those who stayed behind; and the role of local government in regions where national institutions are absent, pp. 25–26.

245 UNHCR increased its return assistance substantially to assist the returnees and was criticized by some human rights organizations for assisting in coerced returns. For its part, UNHCR reported on the need to assist the returnees amidst growing insecurity in Pakistan. Gerry Simpson, 'Pakistan Coercion, UN Complicity: The Mass Forced Return of Afghan Refugees', Report, Human Rights Watch (13 February 2017); UNHCR, 'Repatriation of Afghan Refugees from Pakistan: Supplementary Appeal (Revised)' (28 October 2016).

246 UNHCR, Refugee Data Finder.

247 UNHCR, Refugee Data Finder.

...PART III: **Solutions – An Uneven Record**...

248 At the end of 2020, there were some 2.85 million Afghans internally displaced. UNHCR, Refugee Data Finder. This number rose precipitously in 2021. UNHCR, '"After the Airlift". News Comment Attributable to UN High Commissioner for Refugees Filippo Grandi', Press Release (30 August 2021).

249 United Nations Development Programme, 'Human Development Index' website. See also: UNDP, 'Human Development Reports: Afghanistan', website. David Turton and Peter Marsden, 'Taking Refugees for a Ride? The Politics of Refugee Return to Afghanistan', Working Paper, The Afghanistan Research and Evaluation Unit (December 2002), p. 20. In a December 2020 symposium, the UNDP Resident Representative in Afghanistan pointed to the fact that the country had a 70 per cent unemployment rate and significant economic growth would be necessary to support and sustain large-scale refugee returns. Center for Conflict and Humanitarian Studies Symposium, 'Placing Refugee Return and Reintegration at the Heart of International Development Policy', website (7 December 2020).

250 Although return assistance alone is not sufficient to ensure sustainability. For reflections on Afghan returns, see for example: Thea Yde-Jensen et al., 'Afghanistan's Displaced People: A Socio-Economic Profile, 2013–2014', Report (World Bank, 2018), pp. 4–5; and Hisham Esper, Nandini Krishan, and Christina Wieser, 'More Is Better: Evaluating the Impact of a Variation in Cash Assistance on the Reintegration Outcomes of Returning Afghan Refugees', Draft Paper, presented at 2020 Research Conference on Forced Displacement.

251 In 2012, UNHCR together with Afghanistan, Iran and Pakistan agreed on a Solutions Strategy for Afghan Refugees (SSAR) to facilitate repatriation and enable sustainable reintegration, including through community support projects. The idea was to encourage investment in infrastructure (schools, road rehabilitation, water points) and services (job placement, health services). A 2019 report by the Danish Refugee Council and other NGOs noted that expectations had not been met for a number of reasons, including a lack of State backing, lack of measures to safeguard protection principles, over-reliance on return as the preferred solution, and insufficient inclusion and consultation of civil society and refugees. DRC et al., 'Unprepared for (Re)Integration', p. 37. The strategy was revised in 2019 through the creation of a Support Platform to mobilize additional financial, technical and material support. Governments of the Islamic Republic of Afghanistan et al., 'SSAR Support Platform: Joint Communique', UNHCR Operational Data Portal (16 December 2019).

252 See: Katy Long, 'Rethinking "Durable" Solutions', *The Oxford Handbook of Refugee and Forced Migration Studies* (NY: Oxford University Press, 2014).

253 UNHCR, Refugee Data Finder and UNHCR, Refugee Data Finder. According to Lucy Hovil, 'Hoping for peace, afraid of war: the dilemmas of repatriation and belonging on the borders of Uganda and South Sudan', Research Paper 196, *New Studies in Refugee Research,* UNHCR (November 2010), p. 8, over 2 million returned in this period.

254 Sara Pantuliano et al., 'The Long Road Home: Opportunities and Obstacles to the Reintegration of IDPs and Refugees Returning to Southern Sudan and the Three Areas – Report of Phase II', HPG, ODI (2008), p. 1.

255 Ibid., pp. 9–15. She notes how some family members remained behind in Uganda to access health and education services, yet still considered themselves to have repatriated to Sudan.

256 In the following decade, the numbers of South Sudanese refugees and internally displaced persons would soar again to 2.2 million refugees and 1.6 million internally displaced persons in 2020, according to UNHCR data. UNHCR, Refugee Data Finder.

257 The number of refugees from the Democratic Republic of the Congo also increased from some 477,000 in 2010 to over 840,000 in 2020. UNHCR, Refugee Data Finder.

258 UNHCR, Refugee Data Finder. OCHA, 'Humanitarian Needs Overview: Syrian Arab Republic', Humanitarian Programme Cycle 2021 (March 2021).

259 OCHA, 'Syrian Arab Republic: Spontaneous IDP Returnee Movements Overview, Jan–Dec 2020 (As of 31 December 2020)', *ReliefWeb* (8 March 2021). In some cases, the same internally displaced person may have moved multiple times.

260 UNHCR, 'Syria Regional Refugee Response: Durable Solutions', Operational Data Portal (7 July 2021). The figures on returns are limited to those that UNHCR can verify; the actual number could be higher, although still dwarfed by the number who remain outside the country.

261 World Bank, *The Mobility of Displaced Syrians: An Economic and Social Analysis*' (World Bank, 2020).

262 UNHCR, 'Sixth Regional Survey on Syrian Refugees' Perceptions and Intentions on Returns to Syria', Report (March 2021).

263 Essentially by acknowledging that they were re-availing themselves of the protection of their countries. Katy Long, 'Rethinking 'Durable' Solutions', p. 483.

264 World Bank, 'Afghanistan: Eshteghal Zaiee-Karmondena (EZ-Kar) Project Grant Proposal', Project Appraisal Document (27 November 2018).

265 Between 2000 and 2009, nearly 50 per cent of resettled refugees came from Iraq, Myanmar, Somalia, Sudan, Iran and Afghanistan. The remaining 50 per cent came from various other countries around the world. In contrast, more than 50 per cent of resettled refugees in the 1990s came only from Vietnam and Russia. UNHCR, Refugee Data Finder.

266 UNHCR, 'Progress Report on Resettlement' (7 June 2004), UN Doc EC/54/SC/CRP.10; UNHCR, Refugee Data Finder.

267 Between 2002 and 2013 — with the exception of 2009 — annual resettlement numbers stayed below 100,000. The average for these years (except 2009) was below 80,000 per year. UNHCR, Refugee Data Finder.

268 The Framework was drafted and approved by the Core Group on Resettlement, comprised of States from both the developed and developing world, including States hosting refugees for protracted periods, as well as long-standing and emerging resettlement countries. The European Commission and the International Organization for Migration (IOM) were also members. UNHCR, 'Progress Report: Convention Plus', (8 November 2005), UN Doc FORUM/2005/6.

269 Several reasons have been advanced for this, including instability within Somalia which made voluntary return — a key component of the plan — premature, as well as the absence of a government authority in Somalia with recognized authority to act and insufficient buy-in within UNHCR and among donor States.

270 UNHCR, in some years, experienced difficulties meeting annual resettlement quotas. Group resettlement helped overcome this and could be applied to those coming from the same country, fleeing similar circumstances and having similar risk profiles in need of resettlement. Those who have benefited from this include specific groups of refugees from Afghanistan, Bhutan, Burundi, Democratic Republic of the Congo, Eritrea, Liberia, Myanmar, Somalia and Uzbekistan.

271 Situations in which it was successfully used were relatively modest. For example, an agreement was reached with India in 2015 whereby resettlement countries agreed to resettle 300 refugees in India in exchange for India agreeing to naturalize several thousand Sikh

...PART III: **Solutions – An Uneven Record...**

and Hindu refugees. Also in Asia, the resettlement of Burmese refugees from Thailand was said to have improved UNHCR's access to refugees and enabled UNHCR to set up an asylum process for new arrivals. Joanne van Selm, 'Great Expectations: A Review of the Strategic Use of Resettlement', Evaluation, UNHCR Policy Development and Evaluation Service (2013), pp. 18–20.

272 Prompting Erika Feller, then UNHCR's Director of International Protection, to caution in 2007 that "resettlement should not become a substitute for asylum within a State for spontaneous arrivals; nor should it become the quid pro quo for a functioning re-admission arrangement". van Selm, 'Great Expectations', p. 20.

273 UNHCR's concerns on the offshore processing were communicated to the Australian Minister for Immigration and Citizenship and are found in: António Guterres (Former United Nations High Commissioner for Refugees), 'Correspondence to the Hon. Chris Bowen MP, Former Minister for Immigration and Citizenship of Australia regarding Nauru Detention Centre' (5 September 2012), in 'United Nations Observations on Australia's transfer arrangements with Nauru and Papua New Guinea', UNHCR website.

274 These were established between 2008 and 2011. An additional one in Slovakia has since been closed.

275 Participating resettlement States grew from 14 in 2014 to over 30 in 2017.

276 Syria accounted for 20 per cent of all refugees resettled between 2010 and 2019, followed by Iraq and Myanmar, collectively representing 50 per cent of the over 1 million refugees resettled during that time. The remaining resettled refugees came from countries around the globe, largely influenced by UNHCR's annual assessment of needs.

277 The number of refugees departing for resettlement countries started to plummet by over 40 per cent from 173,000 in 2016 to 107,000 in 2019. For over 30 years, the United States had resettled more refugees than all other countries combined.

278 Pandemic-induced border closures and travel restrictions put a hold on many resettlement movements. UNHCR, 'UN Refugee Agency Releases 2022 Resettlement Needs', Press Release (23 June 2021); UNHCR, Refugee Data Finder.

279 UNHCR, 'The Three-Year Strategy (2019-2021) on Resettlement and Complementary Pathways' (June 2019), pp. 6, 10, 11, 12 and 14.

280 Global Compact on Refugees (2018), paras. 17–18; UNHCR, 'Outcomes of the Global Refugee Forum 2019', Report (2020), p. 38.

281 This could be related to the additional resources that can be needed to establish resettlement programmes such as to cover the costs to process submissions, provide for refugee integration and strengthen capacities of local partners to assist refugees upon arrival. See discussion further on regarding how these costs can be offset by the contributions resettled refugees make over time.

282 Philippe Legrain, *Refugees Work: A Humanitarian Investment that Yields Economic Dividends*, Report (Tent, 2021); Graeme Hugo et al., 'Economic, Social and Civic Contributions of First and Second Generation Humanitarian Entrants', Report, Department of Immigration and Citizenship (2011); William N. Evans and Daniel Fitzgerald, 'The Economic and Social Outcomes of Refugees in the United States: Evidence from the ACS', NBER Working Paper 23498 (June 2017); d'Artis Kancs and Patrizio Lecca, 'Long-term Social, Economic and Fiscal Effects of Immigration into the EU: The Role of the Integration Policy', JRC Working Papers

in Economics and Finance, 2017/4, (Publication Office of the European Union, 2017).

283 Louise Olliff, 'From Resettled Refugees to Humanitarian Actors: Refugee Diaspora Organizations and Everyday Humanitarianism', *New Political Science* 40, no. 4 (October 2018).

284 Kalena E. Cortes, 'Are refugees different from economic immigrants? Some empirical evidence on the heterogeneity of immigration groups in the US', *Review of Economics and Statistics* 86, no. 2 (2004): pp. 465–480.

285 Evans and Fitzgerald, 'The Economic and Social Outcomes of Refugees in the United States', pp. 7, 33.

286 OECD, 'How will the refugee surge affect the European economy?', *Migration Policy Debates* 8 (November 2015); European Commission, 'An Economic Take on the Refugee Crisis: A Macroeconomic Assessment for the EU', Institutional Paper 033 (July 2016).

287 See: Zara Sarzin, 'The Impact of Forced Migration on the Labor Market'.

288 In September 2021, for example, the United States announced the intention to raise the annual ceiling for refugee resettlement to 125,000 for the fiscal year 2022. UNHCR, 'UNHCR welcomes U.S. plan to increase refugee resettlement', Briefing (21 September 2021).

289 UNGA, New York Declaration for Refugees and Migrants (19 September 2016), UN Doc A/RES/71/1, paras. 77, 79; Global Compact on Refugees (2018), paras. 47, 94–96; UNGA, Global Compact for Safe, Orderly and Regular Migration (19 December 2018), UN Doc A/RES/73/195, Objective 5. For earlier efforts to expand such pathways, see: Long, 'Rethinking "Durable" Solutions'; Hovil, 'Hoping for Peace, Afraid of War', pp. 4–7.

290 Hein De Haas, Stephen Castles, and Mark J. Miller, *The Age of Migration: International Population Movements in the Modern World* (London: Red Globe Press, 2019), p. 9.

291 Two member States were not included in the study because of their different data collection methods (The Republic of Korea and Turkey). OECD and UNHCR, 'Safe Pathways for Refugees II – OECD-UNHCR Study on Third-Country Solutions for Refugees: Admissions for Family Reunification, Education, and Employment Purposes between 2010 and 2019', Report (March 2021).

292 Ibid., p. 14.

293 Of the three types of visas issued to nationals of the seven countries over the course of the decade, family permits accounted for 67 per cent, education permits made up 18 per cent, while labour permits accounted for just 13 per cent. When compared with the number of permits issued from these categories overall in 2019, the seven countries accounted for 9 per cent of family visas, 2 per cent of education visas and 4 per cent of employment visas. Ibid., p. 16.

294 Many people who flee do so suddenly and often without all their individual documents, such as birth, marriage, and education certificates, any or all of which can be essential to apply for an immigration visa. Even when they have documents, some have expired.

295 For examples, see: Tamara Wood, 'The Role of "Complementary Pathways" in Refugee Protection', Report, Kaldor Centre for International Refugee Law (November 2020), pp. 34–38. Among the examples Tamara Wood provides is: the World University Services of Canada, which has facilitated 2,000 refugees to immigrate on a permanent basis for study purposes in Canada since 1978; the Japan International Christian University Foundation, which has provided two refugee scholarships per year to Syrian refugees since 2017; and Talent Beyond Boundaries, which has matched 127 refugees with prospective employers in Australia and Canada since 2017, although not all have immigrated.

296 Statistics from the OECD-UNHCR study showed some promising signs in 2017 when the proportion of family visas to nationals of the countries under review rose. Since then, however, they have declined to previous levels. OECD and UNHCR, 'Safe Pathways for Refugees II', pp. 15–16.

297 International Labour Organization, *ILO Global Estimates on International Migrant Workers: Results and Methodology* (Third edition), (ILO, 2021), p. 14.

298 OECD and UNHCR, 'Safe Pathways for Refugees II', p. 16.

299 Martin and Ruhs, 'Labour Market Realism and the Global Compacts on Migration and Refugees', *International Migration* 57, no. 6 (2019): pp. 86. They also point out that many labour market schemes are subject to bilateral agreement between the source and the destination country. In the case of refugees, the country of origin cannot play the role and first countries of asylum are unlikely to do so. See: pp. 86–87.

300 Michael Lokshin and Martin Ravallion have proposed that citizens be entitled to rent their right to work to refugees enabling refugees to benefit. Such a scheme would arguably be subject to similar constraints as raised by Martin and Ruhs. Michael Lokshin and Martin Ravallion, 'The Missing Market for Work Permits', Policy Research Working Paper 9005, World Bank Group (September 2019).

301 The project is coordinated by the ministry responsible for immigration, refugees and citizenship and engages participating provincial governments, UNHCR and NGOs that recruit potential candidates for referral to Canada. Government of Canada, 'The Economic Mobility Pathways Project: Exploring Labour Mobility as a Complementary Pathway for Refugees', website (14 October 2020).

302 Quoted in Talent Beyond Boundaries, 'Hire displaced talent' [Video]: Kris Braun, former VP Engineering at Bonfire, Canada, shares his experience of hiring software developer, Mohammed via Talent Beyond Boundaries, Talent Beyond Boundaries website.

303 See: The Honourable David Coleman MP, 'Address to the Menzies Research Centre, Melbourne', Transcript (7 February 2020). "The Government is also rolling out a two-year Skilled Refugee Pilot to offer skilled employment in Australia to up to 100 skilled refugees, including in regional areas. We will be working with an experienced external provider to develop the pilot within our existing, permanent skilled visa framework".

304 See: 'Statement of Baroness Williams of Trafford to the House of Lords', *Hansard*, HC 806, columns 408–409 (5 October 2020); Kaldor Centre for International Refugee Law, 'Complementary Refugee Pathways: Labour Mobility Schemes', Factsheet (August 2020).

305 Government of Canada, 'By the Numbers: 40 years of Canada's Private Sponsorship of Refugees Program', website.

306 Shauna Labman, 'Private Sponsorship: Complementary or Conflicting Interests?', *Refuge: Canada's Journal on Refugees*, 32, no. 2 (2016): pp. 67–80; A. Hirsch, K. Hoang and A. Vogl, 'Australia's Private Refugee Sponsorship Program: Creating Complementary Pathways Or Privatising Humanitarianism?', *Refuge* 35, no. 2 (2019): pp. 109–122; Katherine Rehberg, 'The Future of Refugee Resettlement and Complementary Pathways', Report, CWS (12 October 2020).

307 OECD and UNHCR, 'Safe Pathways for Refugees II'.

308 T. Alexander Aleinikoff and Leah Zamore, *The Arc of Protection: Toward a New International Refugee Regime* (Redwood City, CA: Stanford University Press, 2019), pp. 81–83, 117.

309 As part of the 2002 Agenda for Protection, UNHCR advanced a Framework for Durable Solutions, which included securing development assistance to enable refugee self-reliance and to benefit host areas (Development Assistance for Refugees (DAR)), the 4R approach (Repatriation, Reintegration, Rehabilitation and Reconstruction) and the Development through Local Integration (DLI) approach. UNHCR, 'Framework for Durable Solutions for Refugees and Persons of Concern' (May 2003). On the Solutions Alliance, see: UNDP, 'The Solutions Alliance', website.

310 In 2010, the Transitional Solutions Initiative (TSI) was conceived as a renewed attempt to engage development actors more systematically and promote the inclusion of displaced persons in government development plans. See: UNHCR, 'Concept Note – Transitional Solutions Initiative UNDP and UNHCR in collaboration with the World Bank' (October 2010). A pilot project for internally displaced persons in Colombia was implemented as part of the TSI between 2012 and 2016 and was considered a success overall in terms of the regularization of informal settlements and securing land ownership. Challenges, however, remained, including persistently high poverty levels and obstacles in accessing basic services due to continuing land ownership issues. Greta Zeender and Bronwen James Crowther, 'Reducing Protracted Internal Displacement: A Snapshot of Successful Humanitarian-Development Initiatives', Occasional Policy Paper (Office for the Coordination of Humanitarian Affairs, June 2019), pp. 11–14; Econometría, 'External Assessment of the UNHCR-UNDP Joint Program "Transitional Solutions Initiative"', Final Report (31 October 2016), p. 85. As noted in a 2019 study by IDMC, long-standing legislation on internal displacement, humanitarian assistance, compensation and property restitution and the peace agreement had not resolved large-scale displacement. Chloe Sydney, 'Stuck in the Middle: Seeking Durable Solutions in Post-Peace Agreement Colombia', IDMC Report (March 2019).

311 UNHCR, *Global Trends: Forced Displacement in 2015*, Report (2016); UConn Today, 'Syrian Refugee Crisis Continues to Capture World's Attention', Discussion, website (12 November 2015).

312 These are discussed more in Part V.

313 The Syrian situation was the catalyst for these changes, as many refugees moved onward due to a loss of hope, an inability to work or a lack of access to health and education services. UNHCR, 'Seven Factors behind Movement of Syrian Refugees to Europe', Briefing Note (25 September 2015). Many donors targeted their policies and programmes to address these needs in the countries neighbouring Syria.

314 The Sustainable Development Goals are the core of the 2030 Agenda for Sustainable Development, adopted by all United Nations member States in 2015. They are 17 goals to end poverty, improve health and education, reduce inequality, spur economic growth, tackle climate change and protect the environment with the aim to "leave no one behind". UNGA, 'Transforming Our World: The 2030 Agenda for Sustainable Development' (25 September 2015), UN Doc A/RES/70/1.

315 Global Compact on Refugees, paras. 64–84 and 97–99. In addition, two of its four goals aim to: (i) ease pressures on host countries; and (ii) enhance refugee self-reliance, para. 7.

316 Internally displaced persons – as citizens of the country in which they are displaced – should be included in national development plans.

317 For further details, see: Doreen Kibuka-Musoke and Zara Sarzin, 'Financing for Forced Displacement Situations', Reference Paper for the 70th Anniversary of the 1951 Refugee

...PART III: **Solutions – An Uneven Record...**

Convention, UNHCR (October 2021). Criteria for World Bank concessional funds require, among others, that the receiving countries have in place policies and practices consistent with the principles of the 1951 Refugee Convention or its 1967 Protocol.

318 Paras. 45–48.

319 Expert Group on Refugee and Internally Displaced Persons Statistics (EGRIS) is part of the UN Statistical Commission, which was created in 1947 to set global standards for the collection and use of statistics.

320 EGRIS, *International Recommendation on Refugee Statistics (IRRS)* (March 2018), pp. 81–113. Among the relevant areas of measurement for integration are: legal and civil status; education, health and economic status; and social inclusion. Indicators of progress include: citizenship, civil documentation and travel documents; family status; language proficiency, income and consumption; rights to work, move freely, own property, open a bank account, and access benefits and justice.

321 Endorsed in 2020 by the UN Statistical Commission, they provide an internationally agreed framework for the production and dissemination of quality statistics comparable between regions and countries. EGRIS, *International Recommendations on Internally Displaced Persons Statistics (IRIS)* (March 2020). They build on the Interagency Durable Solutions Indicators and Guide for a systematic and collaborative analysis that engages all key stakeholders. See: Interagency Durable Solutions Indicator Library.

322 Karen Jacobsen and Therese Bjørn Mason, 'Measuring Progress Towards Solutions in Darfur', Review, UK Aid and Durable Solutions Working Group, (May 2020).

323 Varalakshmi Vemuru, Aditya Sarkar, and Andrea Fitri Woodhouse, *Impact of Refugees on Hosting Communities in Ethiopia: A Social Analysis*, Report, World Bank (2020).

324 Utz Johann Pape et al., Informing Durable Solutions for Internal Displacement in Nigeria, Somalia, South Sudan, and Sudan', Vol. B: 'Country Case Studies', Report, World Bank Group (2019)

325 Ibid., pp. viii–ix, 19 (Nigeria); pp. 19–22 (Somalia); pp. 29–30 (South Sudan); and p. 36 (Sudan).

326 Jacobsen and Bjørn Mason, 'Measuring Progress Towards Solutions in Darfur'; Zeender and Crowther, 'Reducing Protracted Internal Displacement'.

327 Ministry of Foreign Affairs, Republic of Colombia, 'Decree No. 216: Temporary Protection Statute for Venezuelan Migrants under Temporary Protection' [Spanish] (1 March 2021); BBC News, 'Colombia to grant legal status to Venezuelan migrants', website (9 February 2021); Julia Symes-Cobb, 'Colombia to give temporary protective status to Venezuelan migrants', *Reuters* (8 February 2021).

328 UNHCR, 'UN High Commissioner for Refugees Praises Latin America for Its Commitment to the Inclusion of All Those in Need of Protection', Press Release (23 June 2021); Luc Cohen, 'Ecuador to start new "normalization process" for Venezuelan migrants', *Reuters* (17 June 2021); UNHCR, 'Ecuador Monthly Update: May 2021', website.

329 Jaime Giménez and Ángela Méndez Triviño, 'For Displaced Venezuelans, Regularization is the Key to Building Productive Lives', *UNHCR* News (23 June 2021).

330 OECD, 'Boosting Immigrants' Contribution to Development and Promoting their Integration', in *Interrelations between Public Policies, Migration and Development* (Paris: OECD, 2017); Katy Long et al., 'Citizenship, migration and the 2030 Agenda for Sustainable Development', ODI Briefing Paper (September 2017); OECD/ILO, *How Immigrants Contribute to Developing Countries' Economies*, Report (Paris: OECD, 2018), pp. 62–71; Patrick A. Imam, and Kangni R. Kpodar, 'Does an Inclusive Citizenship Law Promote Economic Development?', Working Paper 19/3, International Monetary Fund (11 January 2019), p. 27.

331 World Bank Group, *Forcibly Displaced*, p. 113. See also: Albert Kraler, 'Regularization of Irregular Migrants and Social Policies: Comparative Perspectives', *Journal of Immigrant & Refugee Studies* 17, 1 (2019): pp. 94–113 for the experience of seven European countries between 2000 and 2014.

PART IV: **Improving Life Prospects**

1 They were developed through an extensive participatory process of global consultations with a wide array of partners. This included governments, civil society, academics, the private sector, and international and national humanitarian, development, peace and human rights organizations. UN General Assembly, 'The road to dignity by 2030: ending poverty, transforming all lives and protecting the planet: Synthesis report of the Secretary-General on the post-2015 sustainable development agenda' (4 December 2014), UN Doc A/69/700, paras. 36–47.

2 The Sustainable Development Goals (SDGs) are: 1. No Poverty; 2. Zero Hunger; 3. Good Health and Well-being; 4. Quality Education; 5. Gender Equality; 6. Clean Water and Sanitation; 7. Affordable and Clean Energy; 8. Decent Work and Economic Growth; 9. Industry, Innovation and Infrastructure; 10. Reducing Inequalities; 11. Sustainable Cities and Communities; 12. Responsible Consumption and Production; 13. Climate Action; 14. Life Below Water; 15. Life On Land; 16. Peace, Justice, and Strong Institutions; 17. Partnerships for the Goals.

3 In contrast to the Millennium Development Goals that targeted developing nations.

4 UNGA, 'Transforming our world: The 2030 Agenda for Sustainable Development' (25 September 2015), UN Doc A/RES/70/1.

5 Ibid., para. 23.

6 Some States, like Somalia and Colombia, have included internally displaced persons in their national development plans. Countries in the IGAD region, where internal displacement is a major concern, agreed in 2019 to integrate internal displacement in national development plans and policies. See: Devora Levakova, Adrián Calvo Valderrama, Jacques Ajaruvwa Wathum and Damien Jusselme, 'Using collaborative approaches to improve internal displacement data', *Forced Migration Review* 65 (November 2020): p. 11; GP20 Colombia, 'Prioritising the participation of IDPs in driving solutions', *Forced Migration Review* 65 (November 2020): pp. 14–15; Charles Obila and Ariadna Pop, 'Reflections on State experiences in the IGAD region', *Forced Migration Review* 65 (November 2020): p. 18.

7 States agreed to voluntarily report annually through Voluntary National Reviews (VNR) on their progress on achieving the SDGs. Of the 42 countries that completed VNRs in 2019, only 13 mentioned refugees as meriting specific attention and none provided refugee-related data in regard to meeting any of the SDGs. See: Allison Grossman and Lauren Post, *Missing Persons: Refugees Left Out and Left Behind in the SDGs*, Report, International Rescue Committee (September 2019).

8   The Guiding Principles on Internal Displacement refer to IDPs as persons or groups of persons who have been forced or obliged to flee or to leave their homes or places of habitual residence. The latter therefore can include persons who may not be citizens but who have resided in the country for some time, such as stateless persons. Brookings Institution, *Protecting Internally Displaced Persons: A Manual for Law and Policymakers* (October 2008), pp. 12–13.

9   See: Part II. Issues recognized in the report of the UN Secretary-General's High-Level Panel on Internal Displacement, *Shining a Light on Internal Displacement: A Vision for the Future*, Report (September 2021).

10   UNHCR, *Global Trends: Forced Displacement in 2020*, Annual Report (2021), p. 19. This number includes refugees, asylum-seekers and Venezuelans displaced abroad.

11   For example, in Iraq, Jordan and Lebanon, the arrival of Syrian refugees led to greater congestion and increased depreciation of the transportation infrastructure, aggravated existing structural problems in health services delivery, and led to rising fiscal costs of energy borne by the central governments due to increased demand. World Bank, *The Fallout of War: The Regional Consequences of the Conflict in Syria* (Washington, D.C.: World Bank, 2020), pp. 20–23.

12   World Bank, 'The Human Capital Project: Frequently Asked Questions', website.

13   See, for example: World Bank, *Forcibly Displaced: Toward a Development Approach Supporting Refugees, the Internally Displaced, and Their Hosts* (Washington, D.C: World Bank, 2017), pp. 49–51, 68.

14   World Bank, *Forcibly Displaced*, p. 51. The economic and social impact of the Syria conflict is examined in: World Bank, *The Fallout of War*. It notes how the economies of Iraq, Jordan and Lebanon were vulnerable. Lebanon and Jordan depended heavily on foreign and direct investment, which declined, and transit trades routes were disrupted. Iraq too experienced a decrease in net capital inflows and falling oil prices between 2015 and 2018, as well as increased instability due to the Islamic State insurgency. Additionally, each had low institutional resilience. See: pp. 4, 12, 27–29.

15   UNHCR, *Global Trends 2020*, p. 2; UNHCR, Refugee Data Finder. These proportions include Palestine refugees under UNRWA's mandate. Two smaller nations also have a high proportion of refugees in comparison to their respective populations: Aruba (1 in 6) and Curaçao (1 in 10).

16   World Bank, *Forcibly Displaced*, p. 57.

17   Ibid., p. 65.

18   See the example on Uganda.

19   World Bank, *World Development Report 2018: Learning to Realize Education's Promise* (2018), p. 3.

20   Universal Declaration of Human Rights (adopted 10 December 1948), UN Doc A/RES/217(III), art. 26. The International Covenant on Economic, Social and Cultural Rights also recognizes "the right of everyone to education" and that "primary education shall be compulsory and available free to all", UNGA, International Covenant on Economic, Social and Cultural Rights (ICESCR) (adopted 16 December 1966), UN Doc A/RES/2200(XXI), art. 13.

21 George Psacharopoulos and Harry Anthony Patrinos, 'Returns to Investment in Education: A Decennial Review of the Global Literature', Policy Research Working Paper 8402, World Bank (April 2018). The authors analysed data from 139 economies between 1950 and 2014. They found that, for each additional year of formal education, individual lifetime earnings increased by around 9 per cent on average. The return rates are highest in low-income countries and higher for girls than for boys. The authors note that future work will aim to include analyses on returns to school quality, which has only started to emerge in recent years. For an overview of studies on the return on education, see also: UNICEF, *The Investment Case for Education and Equity,* Report (January 2015), pp. 6−9.

22 Donald A. P. Bundy et al., *Disease Control Priorities: Child and Adolescent Health and Development* vol. 8 (Washington, D.C.: World Bank, 2017), pp. 423−435. This study links increased education with lower mortality rates. Female education, in particular, is linked to significant mortality reductions in low- and middle-income countries between 1970 and 2010. Summaries and references to further studies confirming the positive impact of education on health can be found in UNICEF, *The Investment Case for Education and Equity*, pp. 10−11.

23 Jeni Klugman et al., *Voice and Agency: Empowering Women and Girls for Shared Prosperity* (Washington D.C.: World Bank Group, 2014), p. 77. This study examines the key drivers and determinants of enhancing voice and agency of women and girls. Among its findings, based on extensive data and surveys, is that women who have a secondary education or partial secondary education respectively have an 11 and 36 per cent lower risk of experiencing violence, compared with women with no education. Additionally, a woman with a husband or partner with some education is at reduced risk of violence, although not as substantial a reduction as her having an education.

24 "Each additional year of education is linked to an increase in national GDP per capita of between 13 and 35 per cent." UNICEF and IDMC, 'Equitable access to quality education for internally displaced children', Report (2019), p. 4.

25 World Commission on Environment and Development, *Our Common Future* (Oxford: Oxford University Press, 1987).

26 The MDGs emerged from the 2000 United Nations Development Declaration which set out eight targets. UNGA, United Nations Millennium Declaration (18 September 2000), UN Doc A/RES/55/2.

27 UNGA, 'Transforming our world' (2015), Goal 4.

28 UN, *The Millennium Development Goals Report 2015* (2015), p. 4.

29 Ibid., pp. 24−26.

30 Lant Pritchett, *The Rebirth of Education: Schooling Ain't Learning*, Center for Global Development (Baltimore, MD: Brookings Institution Press, 2013); World Bank, *World Development Report 2018*, p. 5. See also: World Bank, Ending Learning Poverty: What will it take?, Report (2019), p. 16.

31 World Bank, *World Development Report 2018*, p. 3.

32 Eric A. Hanushek, 'The Role of Cognitive Skills in Economic Development', *Journal of Economic Literature* 46, no. 3 (2008): pp. 607−688. In Hanushek's view, the literature has focused heavily on education level and not sufficiently on cognitive skills development in examining the link between education and individual earnings.

33 UN General Assembly, 'Transforming our world', Goal 4.

...PART IV: **Improving Life Prospects...**

34   Manos Antoninis and Silvia Montoya, 'The World is Off Track to Deliver on its Education Commitments by 2030', UNESCO Institute for Statistics blog (9 July 2019).

35   See, for example: World Bank, 'Education: Overview', website. In 2016, an estimated $800 million was spent on refugee education, approximately funded in equal parts by humanitarian and development aid. This figure excludes funding provided for education of Palestine refugees, which amounted to an additional $453 million. UNESCO, *Global Education Monitoring Report 2019: Migration, displacement and education: Building Bridges, Not Walls* (2019), pp. xix, 250–251. Through the World Bank's International Development Association (IDA) special mechanisms IDA18 Sub-window for Refugee and Host Communities and IDA19 Window for Host Communities and Refugees around $330 million has been approved for education projects as of February 2021. World Bank, 'World Bank's Global Program on Forced Displacement – Brief for Partners Consultation' (25 March 2021).

36   Dina Abu-Ghaida and Karishma Silva, 'Educating the Forcibly Displaced: Key Challenges and Opportunities', Reference Paper for the 70th Anniversary of the 1951 Refugee Convention, UNHCR (October 2021), p. 21. See also: Samer Al-Samarrai et al., 'Education Finance Watch 2021', Report, World Bank, 2021, p. 2. The report highlights that "[t]wo-thirds of low- and lower-middle-income countries, included in the data collected for [Education Finance Watch] have cut their education budgets since the onset of the COVID-19 pandemic. In comparison, only a third of upper-middle and high-income countries have reduced their budget."

37   Abu-Ghaida and Silva, 'Educating the Forcibly Displaced: Key Challenges and Opportunities'.

38   UNHCR, *Missing Out: Refugee Education in Crisis*, Report (September 2016), p. 4.

39   UNHCR, 'Education Brief 1: Education and Protection' (July 2015), p. 2; UNHCR, 'Education Brief 2: Out-of-School Children in Refugee Settings' (July 2015), p. 1.

40   Abu-Ghaida and Silva, 'Educating the Forcibly Displaced: Key Challenges and Opportunities', p. 8. On the importance of education for the psychosocial well-being of displaced children, see also: UNESCO, 'Education as healing: Addressing the trauma of displacement through social and emotional learning', Policy Paper 38 (April 2019).

41   From the Arabic expression: '*Mitl al fare' bein al ard wa al sama*'. Interview with author, Ahmed's name is changed for reasons of confidentiality. In 2012, the Lebanese Ministry of Education and Higher Education opened the doors of public schools to Syrian refugee children. Second shifts were subsequently added as the number of enrolled Syrian refugee children increased. At the end of 2019, more than 200,000 Syrian refugee children were enrolled in Lebanese public schools. Yet, 44 per cent of the refugee children in Lebanon at compulsory school age remained out of formal school. Lebanon Inter-Agency Working Group, 'Education: End of Year 2019 Dashboard', Factsheet, UNHCR Operational Data Portal.

42   These are refugees under UNHCR's mandate. UNHCR, *Stepping Up: Refugee Education in Crisis*, Report (2019), p. 11. There are a further 1.3 million under UNRWA's mandate. UNHCR, Refugee Data Finder. UNHCR estimates that 80 per cent of refugees register with the Office. Note that UNHCR estimates that, out of the 79.5 million forcibly displaced people at the end of 2019, 30–34 million are children. UNHCR, *Global Trends: Forced Displacement in 2019,* Annual Report (2020), p. 14.

43   Ages 5 to 17 years inclusive. On the difficulties related to disaggregated data on IDPs, see:

IDMC, *Global Report on Internal Displacement* (May 2021), pp. 17–18. In their joint report of 2019, UNICEF and IDMC estimate that only 14 per cent of the countries and territories with data on conflict-related IDPs disaggregate by age, only a quarter of which doing so systematically. UNICEF and IDMC, *Equitable Access to Quality Education for Internally Displaced Children*, Report (July 2019), p. 4. Access challenges are discussed further in this Part.

44   UNHCR, *Coming Together For Refugee Education*, Report (2020), pp. 9, 23. Comparisons compiled by Abu-Ghaida and Silva, 'Educating the Forcibly Displaced: Key Challenges and Opportunities'. Using data from: World Bank, 'World Development Indicators', databank. Recently released UNHCR education data shows a drop in primary school indicators since 2019 with 68 per cent of refugee children enrolled in primary school as of March 2020, secondary enrolment having risen to 34 per cent and tertiary education enrolment up to 5 per cent. UNHCR, *Staying the Course: The Challenges Facing Refugee Education,* UNHCR Education Report 2021 (September 2021), pp. 6–7.

45   86 per cent of people displaced across borders are in developing countries. UNHCR, *Global Trends 2020,* p. 2. 98 per cent of IDPs are in developing countries (46.9 of 48.0 million). UNHCR, Refugee Data Finder (IDMC data).

46   Sarah Dryden-Peterson, 'Refugee Education: The Crossroads of Globalization', *Educational Researcher* 45, no. 9 (December 2016): p. 477. UNHCR support was primarily through funding a limited number of post-primary scholarships.

47   In 1990, the World Conference on Education adopted the World Declaration on Education for All and a Framework for Action. The launch of the global programme was a product of five leading international agencies: (United Nations Educational, Scientific and Cultural Organization (UNESCO), United Nations Children's Fund (UNICEF), United Nations Population Fund (UNFPA), United Nations Development Programme (UNDP) and the World Bank. Since then, the initiative has grown to represent a broad coalition, including national governments, civil society groups, development actors, and specialized NGOs. See: UNESCO, 'Education for All (EFA)', *International Bureau of Education* website.

48   During this period, refugee children in camps were more likely to go to school than other forcibly displaced children. Marc Sommers, 'Children, education and war: reaching Education for All (EFA) objectives in countries affected by conflict', CPR Working Paper 1, World Bank Group (30 June 2002), pp. 27–28. For more on the history of education interventions for refugees, see: Dryden-Peterson, 'Refugee Education'.

49   UNHCR, *Revised (1995) Guidelines for Educational Assistance to Refugees* (Geneva: UNHCR, 1995), Part III: 'Refugee Education in Large Scale Emergencies, Oriented to Durable Solutions'.

50   Dryden-Peterson, 'Refugee Education'.

51   UNHCR, *2012–2016 Education Strategy* (January 2012).

52   UNHCR, *Refugee Education 2030: A Strategy for Refugee Inclusion* (2019).

53   UNGA, Global Compact on Refugees (2 August 2018), UN Doc A/73/12 (Part II), para. 68. National education systems can be either formal or informal. Formal education refers to programmes recognized and certified by a Ministry of Education. Non-formal education programmes are not certified by a Ministry of Education, although they may take place in an educational institution. They include vocational and technical programmes as well as literacy, numeracy, life skills and recreational activities, which may not lead to a certificate. Abu-Ghaida and Silva, 'Educating the Forcibly Displaced: Key Challenges and Opportunities'.

54   UNHCR, *Coming Together For Refugee Education*, p. 9. The data is based on data from 12

countries that host more than half of the 20.4 million refugees under UNHCR's mandate, p. 10. This refers to the total number of children in primary school, regardless of age.

55 UNHCR, *Coming Together For Refugee Education*, p. 9; UNHCR, *Stepping Up*, p. 23.

56 UNHCR, *Coming Together For Refugee Education*, p. 9. Both rates were well below the global average of 76 per cent. World Bank, World Development Indicator. Further study is needed to compare these rates with local populations. This is part of overall commitments to improve responses to forced displacement in a manner that also benefits hosts.

57 UNHCR, *Coming Together For Refugee Education*, p. 5; UNHCR, *Staying the Course*, p. 32; Naomi Nyamweya, 'Displacement, Girls' Education and COVID-19', Global Partnership for Education blog (26 June 2020).

58 Quentin Wodon et al., *Missed Opportunities: The High Cost of Not Educating Girls*, Report, World Bank (July 2018), p. 4. The report notes that women with some level of primary education earn 14–19 per cent more than those with no education at all. Women with secondary education, however, earn on average double the amount of those with no education. The difference is even more pronounced for those with tertiary education, who earn nearly three times the income of those without any education.

59 Wodon et al., 'Missed Opportunities' p. 4; Klugman et al., *Voice and Agency*, pp. 2, 38, 49, 103, 107–111. This study cites many case studies to support this correlation. Moreover, women who marry early have a reduced chance of literacy, are more likely to experience intimate partner violence, have a higher incidence of HIV in some contexts, and have less human agency overall.

60 For an overview of challenges in education for internally displaced persons (IDPs), see: UNICEF, IDMC, 'Equitable Access to Quality Education for Internally Displaced Children'.

61 The GCPEA is a non-profit coalition of organizations that includes: co-chairs Human Rights Watch and Save the Children; the Council for At-Risk Academics (Cara); the Institute of International Education (IIE); UNHCR; the Education Above All Foundation; Plan International; UNICEF; and UNESCO. Global Coalition to Protect Education from Attack, GCPEA, *Education Under Attack: A Global Study of Attacks on Schools, Universities, Their Students and Staff, 2017-2019*, Report (2020), pp. 8–13. Over two thirds of the attacks directly targeted schools and included arson, improvised explosive devices (IEDs), airstrikes, ground strikes, raids and looting.

62 Abu-Ghaida and Silva, 'Educating the Forcibly Displaced: Key Challenges and Opportunities', pp. 8–9.

63 For those who have completed their secondary education prior to flight, a lack of official school certificates can be an additional barrier. UNHCR, *Refugee Education 2030*, p. 13; RRM for Higher Education in Emergencies and Global Platform for Syrian Students, 'Higher Education in Emergencies – On the Road to 2030', Report (January 2020).

64 Rez Gardi, 'Access to higher education for forcibly displaced persons: challenges, good practices and suggestions for the future', Reference Paper for the 70th Anniversary of the 1951 Refugee Convention, UNHCR (October 2021). Rez Gardi is a Kurdish New Zealander and spent the first six years of her life in a refugee camp in Pakistan.

65 UNESCO, *Global Education Monitoring Report 2019*, p. 235.

66 Abu-Ghaida and Silva, 'Educating the Forcibly Displaced: Key Challenges and Opportunities', p. 10.

67 Secondary and tertiary education are more expensive, requiring specialized teachers, and demand exceeds supply. In addition to not being able to afford the cost of post-primary education, forcibly displaced persons may not be able to forego working in order to attend school for financial reasons. For more on this, see: Abu-Ghaida and Silva, 'Educating the Forcibly Displaced: Key Challenges and Opportunities'.

68 Programmes designed for this purpose are often referred to as accelerated education programmes which UNHCR describes as "flexible, age-appropriate programmes, run in an accelerated timeframe, which aim to provide access to education for disadvantaged, over-age, out-of-school children and youth – particularly those who missed out on, or had their education interrupted due to poverty, marginalisation, conflict and crisis". UNHCR, 'Accelerated Education', website.

69 Abu-Ghaida and Silva, 'Educating the Forcibly Displaced: Key Challenges and Opportunities', p. 9.

70 Mohammed Al-Sabahi and Ghaidaa Motahar, 'Using public schools as shelter for IDPs in Yemen', *Forced Migration Review* 55 (June 2017); Mercy Corps, 'The promise of education brings Syrian and Jordanian girls together', blog (10 February 2015).

71 Financing of forced displacement responses is discussed in Part V.

72 IGAD is a regional intergovernmental platform in the East and Horn of Africa with the following members: Djibouti; Eritrea; Ethiopia; Kenya; Somalia; South Sudan; Sudan; and Uganda. For more on the initiative, see: UNHCR, *Refugee Education 2030*, p. 31.

73 The changes in the refugee gross enrolment ratio between 2018/19 and 2019/20 were from 73 per cent to 76 per cent for primary school and from 13 per cent to 11 per cent for secondary school. UNHCR Education statistics.

74 In Ethiopia, the changes in the refugee gross enrolment ratio between 2018/19 and 2019/20 were from 67 per cent to 66 per cent for primary school and from 11 per cent to 13 per cent for secondary school. UNHCR Education statistics.

75 UNHCR, 'Kenya: Education', website.

76 UNHCR, *Global Trends 2020*, p. 2.

77 Source: Jennifer Roberts, UNHCR Senior Education Officer in reference to Turkey's Ministry of Education data; No Lost Generation, *Continued Learning for All Syrian Children and Youth*, Report (2020), p. 6. The report provides a table showing trends 2017–2020.

78 Ibid., p. 5. Enrolment rates for refugee students overall are less. The most recent collection by UNHCR in Egypt reported primary and secondary enrolment rates of 58 per cent and 54 per cent respectively. UNHCR Education statistics. At the 2019 Global Refugee Forum, Egypt pledged to advance inclusion more uniformly across all refugee groups. UNHCR, 'Pledges & Contributions Dashboard', Global Refugee Forum Digital Platform.

79 No Lost Generation, *Continued Learning for All Syrian Children and Youth*, p. 6. This is a significant decline from 280,000 in 2019 and reflects reductions in global refugee enrolment experienced due to COVID-19 in 2020.

80 No Lost Generation, *Continued Learning for All Syrian Children and Youth*, p. 6.

81 Ibid., pp. 4, 6.

82 Ibid., pp. 4, 6. Access and retention of school-aged Syrian refugee children in the Kurdistan region remains a serious challenge despite efforts by the Kurdistan Regional Government Ministry of Education and education partners. Prior to the COVID-19 pandemic, primary school enrolment rates were just 51 per cent in camps and 29 per cent in urban areas. A substantial share was enrolled in non-formal education. A strategy to support the inclusion of refugees in the national system has been developed by education partners and the KRG

Ministry of Education, which is still to be formally adopted by the Council of Ministers. No Lost Generation, *Continued Learning for All Syrian Children and Youth*, pp. 4–6; Camille Le Coz et al., 'A Bridge to Firmer Ground: Learning from International Experiences to Support Pathways to Solutions in the Syrian Refugee Context', Research Report, Durable Solutions Platform and Migration Policy Institute (March 2021), p. 55.

83   Source: Jennifer Roberts, UNHCR Senior Education Officer. Limited availability in the public system refers to those schools where Arabic is the language of instruction.

84   In Brazil, the gross enrolment rate for grades 1–9 is around 74 per cent among Venezuelans compared to 100 per cent among Brazilians. In high school, it is 40 per cent for Venezuelans compared to 80 per cent for Brazilians. See: Mrittika Shamsuddin et al., 'Integration of Venezuelan Refugees and Migrants in Brazil', Policy Research Working Paper 9605, World Bank Group (March 2021), pp. 18–20. See also: UNHCR/World Bank, 'Brazil's policies boost inclusion of Venezuelans, but challenges remain', Joint Press Release (18 May 2021); On Colombia, see: UNHCR, *Staying the Course*, p. 12.

85   R4V Inter-Agency Coordination Platform for Refugees and Migrants from Venezuela, *Regional Refugee and Migrant Response Plan (RMRP) For Refugees and Migrants from Venezuela: January–December 2021* (December 2020), pp. 64–65, 88–89, 105–106, 129–130; Andrew Selee and Jessica Bolter, 'An Uneven Welcome: Latin American and Caribbean Responses to Venezuelan and Nicaraguan Migration', Report, Migration Policy Institute (February 2020), pp. 30–34.

86   Andrew Selee and Jessica Bolter, 'An Uneven Welcome', p. 31. The authors provide several examples, such as Peru, Trinidad and Tobago, and Uruguay. See also: Diana Rodríguez-Gómez, 'Bureaucratic Encounters and the Quest for Educational Access among Colombian Refugees in Ecuador', *Journal on Education in Emergencies* 5, no. 1 (2019): pp. 62–93.

87   Global Education Monitoring Report Team, *Global Education Monitoring Report 2019*, p. 236. This report estimates on the basis of available data that the share of household spending on education is approximately 18 per cent in high-income, 25 per cent in middle-income and 33 per cent in low-income countries.

88   For a more detailed discussion on data needed in the education sector and why, see: Abu-Ghaida and Silva, 'Educating the Forcibly Displaced: Key Challenges and Opportunities'.

89   As noted, most do not report systematically on IDPs. Of the 42 countries that reported progress on the SDGs in 2019, only 13 mentioned refugees as meriting specific attention and none provided refugee-related data in regard to meeting any of the Sustainable Development Goals' targets.

90   Johannes Hoogeveen and Utz Pape (eds.), *Data Collection in Fragile States: Innovations from Africa and Beyond* (Cham: Palgrave Macmillan, 2020): referenced in Abu-Ghaida and Silva, 'Educating the Forcibly Displaced: Key Challenges and Opportunities', p. 15.

91   UNESCO, 'Strengthening EMIS and Data for Increased Resilience to Crises – International Conference 2020', Concept Note. Conference held in UNESCO Headquarters, Paris, 21–23 April 2020. Together with Education Cannot Wait and NORCAP (Norwegian Refugee Council's pool of expert personnel, who support humanitarian, development and peacebuilding organizations). NRC, 'About NORCAP', website.

92   Abu-Ghaida and Silva, 'Educating the Forcibly Displaced: Key Challenges and Opportunities' p. 21.

93 World Bank, *World Development Report 2018*, p. 108. The report notes an example of this growth: "[T]he number of impact evaluations of interventions intended to improve learning outcomes in developing countries rose from 19 in 2000 to 299 by 2016."

94 As Abu-Ghaida and Silva explain, "data collection has generally been treated as a by-product of the intervention rather than a more deliberate activity to inform evidence-based policymaking". "Data collection is generally reflected through reporting to Education or Protection Clusters, or from individual organizations to donors. This data tends to be program-specific and not entirely adequate to respond to data requirement for policy design." Abu-Ghaida and Silva, 'Educating the Forcibly Displaced: Key Challenges and Opportunities', p. 17.

95 On the need for more impact evaluations in forced displacement contexts generally, see: Paola Elice, 'Impact Evaluations in Forced Displacement Contexts: A Guide for Practitioners', Reference Paper for the 70th Anniversary of the 1951 Refugee Convention, UNHCR (October 2021).

96 Ragui Assaad, Thomas Ginn, and Mohamed Saleh, 'Impact of Syrian Refugees on Education Outcomes in Jordan', Working Paper 1214, Economic Research Forum (September 2018).

97 Semih Tumen, 'The Effect of Refugees on Native Adolescents' Test Scores: Quasi-Experimental Evidence from Pisa', Working Paper 1356, Economic Research Forum (October 2019).

98 Abu-Ghaida and Silva, 'Educating the Forcibly Displaced: Key Challenges and Opportunities', pp. 27–28. The authors note that in 2016, combined humanitarian and developmental support to refugee education (excluding Palestine refugees) amounted to $800 million, which is six times less than what is required to support refugee children enrolment from kindergarten through grade 12. See also: Global Education Monitoring Report Team, *Global Education Monitoring Report 2019*, p. 252.

99 World Bank and UNHCR, *The Global Cost of Inclusive Refugee Education*, Joint Report (January 2021), p. 36. This does not include Palestine refugee children, for whom an estimated $443 million would be required in addition per year.

100 Stockholm International Peace Research Institute, 'Global military expenditure sees largest annual increase in a decade — says SIPRI — reaching $1917 billion in 2019', Press Release (27 April 2020). In 2019, global military expenditure stood at $1,917 billion, meaning that on average over $5 billion was spent on military each day.

101 Education Cannot Wait (ECW), *Winning the Human Race: 2020 Annual Results Report* (July 2021), p. 12.

102 This includes the Global Partnership for Education (GPE). Launched in 2002, GPE is a global fund dedicated to education in lower-income countries. It has made support to conflict-affected and fragile countries a priority area of focus. GPE, 'Education in Crisis Situations', website. Also beginning over nine years ago, Educate A Child (EAC), a programme of Education Above All, aims to trigger significant breakthroughs and a material difference in the lives of children who have no access to primary education. EAC has been helping millions of the hardest to reach out-of-school children (OOSC), including refugees, around the world realize their right to a quality education.

103 These relatively new funding mechanisms known as IDA18 Sub-window for Refugee and Host Communities and IDA-19 Window for Host Communities and Refugees are discussed more in Part V. The funding they have provided for education represents some 15 per cent of the $2.2 billion accessed so far. 'World Bank's Global Program on Forced Displacement — Brief for Partners Consultation, pp. 5–6.

...PART IV: Improving Life Prospects...

104 For middle-income countries that may have less access to development aid, it promotes reduced lending terms, and loan repayment guarantees to increase their access to financing. The Education Commission, 'International Finance Facility for Education', website; Abu-Ghaida and Silva, 'Educating the Forcibly Displaced: Key Challenges and Opportunities', p. 32.

105 Global Compact on Refugees (2018).

106 Abu-Ghaida and Silva, 'Educating the Forcibly Displaced: Key Challenges and Opportunities'.

107 Ibid.

108 World Bank Group, *World Bank Group Strategy for Fragility, Conflict, and Violence 2020–2025*, Board Report (February 2020), p. 11.

109 This was also one of the commitments made at the 2016 World Humanitarian Summit. The commitment was made by all those engaged in development and humanitarian fields to work based on the "comparative advantage among actors, whether local, national or international, public or private" towards collective outcomes which reinforce national and local systems. UNGA, 'One humanity: shared responsibility: Report of the Secretary-General for the World Humanitarian Summit', Annex: 'Agenda for Humanity' (2 February 2016), UN Doc A/70/709. The fact that many partners in education draw from the same donors also makes coordination essential, a role some have suggested UNESCO could possibly play. Abu-Ghaida and Silva, 'Educating the Forcibly Displaced: Key Challenges and Opportunities'.

110 Including those related to their legal status.

111 Isabel Arciniegas Guaneme et al., 'COVID-19 and Forcibly Displaced People: addressing the impacts and responding to the challenges', Reference Paper for the 70th Anniversary of the 1951 Refugee Convention, UNHCR (October 2021), pp. 28–31.

112 Such as through television, radio, and interactive text messaging. UNICEF, 'COVID-19: Are Children Able to Continue Learning During School Closures', Factsheet (August 2020). Another study estimates that 2.2 billion people aged below 25 years did not have internet access at home. UNICEF and International Telecommunication Union, *How Many Children and Young People Have Internet Access at Home? Estimating digital connectivity during the COVID-19 pandemic*, Report (2020).

113 Alastair Westgarth, 'Saying goodbye to Loon', *Medium* (21 January 2021).

114 Amy Lynn Smith (UNHCR Innovation Service), 'The Pursuit of Refugees' Inclusion in Digital Connectivity', *Medium* (6 August 2021).

115 Abu-Ghaida and Silva, 'Educating the Forcibly Displaced: Key Challenges and Opportunities'.

116 Ibid. The qualifications of refugee teachers are often not recognized by host governments. This as well as general prohibitions on refugees engaging in employment, means that they cannot help address teacher shortages. Some qualified refugee teachers can support education informally and can be paid nominal amounts of incentive pay by international and non-governmental organizations.

117 UN Department of Economic and Social Affairs, 'Sustainable Development Goals', website, Goal 3.

118 Mercedes de Onis and Monika Blössner, 'The World Health Organization Global Database on Child Growth and Malnutrition: methodology and applications', *International Journal of Epidemiology* 32, no. 4 (August 2003): pp. 518–526. Data shows that undernutrition impedes children's physical growth as well as their mental development. It also leaves them "more susceptible to infectious diseases, such as malaria, meningitis and pneumonia".

119 See, for example: World Bank, 'Poverty and Health', website.

120 Michael J. Toole and Ronald J. Waldman, 'Prevention of Excess Mortality in Refugee and Displaced Populations in Developing Countries', *Journal of the American Medical Association* 263, no. 24 (27 June 1990): pp. 3296–3302. A study of four large humanitarian crises in the mid–2000s occurring in the Democratic Republic of the Congo, Ethiopia, Somalia and Sudan found significantly higher mortality rates in IDPs than for refugees and host populations affected by the crises. The authors speculated that the reason for the differences could be that humanitarian programmes faced fewer obstacles in reaching refugee areas than areas of high IDP concentrations. Peter Heudtlass, Niko Speybroeck, and Debarati Guha-Sapir, 'Excess mortality in refugees, internally displaced persons and resident populations in complex humanitarian emergencies (1998–2012) – insights from operational data', *Conflict and Health* 10, no. 15 (2016): pp. 1–11.

121 Máire A. Connolly et al., 'Communicable diseases in complex emergencies: impact and challenges', *The Lancet* 364, no. 9449 (2004): pp. 1974–1983. In 2020, malaria was the single most common cause of morbidity reported among refugees (20 per cent), followed by upper and lower respiratory tract infections. UNHCR, *2020 Annual Public Health Global Review* (June 2021); Oluwakemi C. Amodu, Magdalena S. Richter, and Bukola O. Salami, 'A Scoping Review of the Health of Conflict-Induced Internally Displaced Women in Africa', *International Journal of Environmental Research and Public Health* 17, no. 4 (2020): pp. 16–17.

122 An adequate level of health care, including immunizations can help to mitigate this along with monitoring measures and control of infections. Angel N. Desai et al., 'Infectious disease outbreaks among forcibly displaced persons: an analysis of ProMED reports 1996–2016', *Conflict and Health* 14, no. 49 (2020): p. 8. ProMED is a programme of the International Society for Infectious Diseases (ISID), launched in 1994 to identify unusual health events related to emerging and re-emerging infectious diseases and toxins affecting humans, animals and plants. At the same time, there remains very little data or surveillance of tropical diseases, like Dengue, Zika, Chagas, Chikungunya, Trypanosomiasis, to which forcibly displaced populations are also exposed.

123 See, for example: WHO Regional Office for Europe, 'Health of refugees and migrants: Regional situation analysis, practices, experiences, lessons learned and ways forward', Report (2018), pp. 8–11. The report highlights that, despite differences in health needs resulting from displacement itself or the situation in countries of origin, many health needs of refugees and migrants in the EU are shared with those of the host population or the overall population in regions of origin more generally. For example, the report notes that chronic and non-communicable diseases are important contributors to refugee and migrant morbidity in Europe and are also increasingly prevalent among the general population globally and the population in low- and middle-income countries, in particular.

124 In some contexts, this is not possible as displacement is in remote underserviced areas or areas of ongoing conflict, and/or displaced populations distrust services provided by the State where the State is the cause of their displacement.

125 By Dr Jina Swartz (FMedSci), Professor David Cantor (Internal Displacement Research

Programme), and Professor Bayard Roberts (London School of Hygiene and Tropical Medicine). Their brief was based on discussions held at an interdisciplinary workshop in February 2021 on key health issues facing IDPs, gaps in knowledge and policy implications. 'IDP Health and How it can be Improved', workshop at Refugee Law Initiative, 'Panel Launch: Enabling Health Solutions for Internally Displaced Persons' (19 April 2021); UK Academy of Medical Sciences (AMS), Internal Displacement Research Programme (IDRP), and School of Advanced Study (University of London), 'Policy Brief: Internal Displacement and Health – Submitted to the UN Secretary General's High Level Panel on Internal Displacement' (April 2021).

126 Global Compact on Refugees (2018), para. 72. Specifically: "States and relevant stakeholders will contribute resources and expertise to expand and enhance the quality of national health systems to facilitate access by refugees and host communities."

127 Ibid., para. 73. Given the concern of host countries to not be compelled to adopt an inclusion strategy, the Global Compact on Refugees also provides that inclusion in health systems is subject to national health care laws and policies.

128 See, for example: G. B. Masefield, 'Food and nutrition procedures in times of disaster', *FAO Nutritional Studies*, no. 21 (1967): pp. 1–96. As it turns out, these were not always inclusive of the specific nutritional needs of women as discussed further in this Part.

129 Toole and Waldman, 'Prevention of Excess Mortality in Refugee and Displaced Populations in Developing Countries': p. 3297.

130 Ibid.: pp. 3329–3301.

131 Marcos Cueto, 'The ORIGINS of Primary Health Care and SELECTIVE Primary Health Care', *American Journal of Public Health* 94, no. 11 (November 2004): p. 1865.

132 International Conference on Primary Health Care, 'Declaration of Alma-Ata' (Alma-Ata, USSR: 1978).

133 See, for example: WHO, 'Building the economic case for primary health care: a scoping review' (2018).

134 Ninette Kelley, International NGO Working Group on Refugee Women, and International Consultation on Refugee Women (eds.), *Working with Refugee Women: A Practical Guide* (Geneva: International NGO Working Group on Refugee Women, 1989), pp. 26–27. Deirdre Wulf, *Refugee Women and Reproductive Health Care: Reassessing Priorities* (New York: Women's Commission for Refugee Women and Children, 1994), pp. 3, 8.

135 In regard to reproductive health, a 1999 review in forced displacement contexts found that, while reproductive health was on the agenda for agencies and more resources were going to support it, there were barriers to overcome. These included the hesitation of some organizations and "field workers to prioritize reproductive health". Celia Palmer, Louisiana Lush, and Anthony Zwi, 'The emerging international policy agenda for reproductive health services in conflict settings', *Social Science & Medicine* 49, no. 12 (December 1999): pp. 1689–1703.

136 Discussed in Part V under Partnerships.

137 See, for example, Jordan: Jordan Times, 'Refugee medics employed in Jordanian COVID-19 response' (4 September 2021). In Canada, the Canadian Government announced a special programme for asylum-seekers who have worked in the COVID-19 health-care response to be eligible to apply for permanent residency. However, advocates for frontline work-

ers, dubbed "guardian angels", have raised concerns about the low numbers approved for residency thus far. Standing Committee on Citizenship and Immigration (CIMM), 'Guardian Angels (Asylum Claimants Working on the Front Lines)', *Government of Canada* website (8 March 2021); Jacob Serebrin, 'Few Quebec "guardian angels" who worked in health care during pandemic granted residency', *The Canadian Press* (24 March 2021); Stefan Christoff, 'Canada is deporting its "guardian angels"', *Al Jazeera* (23 July 2021).

138 Liz Miller, 'The Irony of Refuge: Gender-Based Violence against Female Refugees in Africa', *Human Rights & Human Welfare: Minority Rights Digest* (2011): pp. 77–90. In regard to the Balkan Wars, see: Caroline Kennedy-Pipe and Penny Stanley, 'Rape in War: Lessons of the Balkan Conflicts in the 1990s', *The International Journal of Human Rights* 4, no. 3–4 (2000): pp. 67–84. The authors also review how rape has been a common feature of recorded histories of war generally. UNHCR, *The State of The World's Refugees 2000: Fifty Years of Humanitarian Action* (Oxford: Oxford University Press, 2000), p. 87; Amodu, Richter, and Salami, 'A Scoping Review of the Health of Conflict-Induced Internally Displaced Women in Africa': pp. 4–10.

139 Comprehensive reproductive health services were further advanced through adherence to the Minimum Initial Service Package to respond to reproductive health needs at the onset of a humanitarian crisis. See: United Nations Population Fund, 'Minimum Initial Service Package (MISP) for SRH in Crisis Situations', website (November 2020). Community-based prevention efforts can include strategies to promote positive behaviours, communication activities to increase awareness on relevant legal rights, empower women and girls and engage men and boys in understanding and promoting gender equality. For further examples and evaluations of recent community-based activities designed to prevent sexual- and gender-based violence, see: Teresa Hanley, 'SGBV response, risk mitigation and prevention in humanitarian crises: A synthesis of findings from evaluations of UNHCR operations 2019' UNHCR Report, September 2019, pp. 17–18; N. Glass et al., 'Evaluating the communities care program: best practice for rigorous research to evaluate gender based violence prevention and response programs in humanitarian settings', *Conflict and Health* 12, no. 5 (2018): p. 5.

140 Inter-Agency Standing Committee, 'Policy: Protection in Humanitarian Action' (October 2016).

141 Evidence shows that working with communities to combat sexual- and gender-based violence tends to lessen the incidence and improve safety overall. These can include strategies to promote positive behaviours, communication activities to increase awareness on relevant legal rights, empower women and girls and engage men and boys in understanding and promoting gender equality. For further examples and evaluations of recent community-based activities designed to prevent sexual- and gender-based violence, see: Hanley, 'SGBV response, risk mitigation and prevention in humanitarian crises, pp. 17–18; N. Glass et al., 'Evaluating the communities care program'; UNHCR, *How Night-Time Street Lighting Affects Refugee Communities – A population-based assessment of community lighting in Northern Uganda's Rhino Camp refugee settlement*, Evaluation Report (December 2017). The assessment found that the lighting prevented violence and stimulated productive night-time activity such as reading or studying. Equally important, the community engagement and management helped to ensure the success of the initiative.

142 Among the early examples are refugees who fled from Ethiopia's Ogaden region to Somalia in 1978–1980. They were included in national tuberculosis prevention and response strategies. Paul Shears, 'Tuberculosis Control in Somali Refugee Camps', *Tubercle* 65, no.

...PART IV: **Improving Life Prospects...**

2 (1984): p. 112. In subsequent years, this approach was systematically encouraged. WHO Global Tuberculosis Programme and UNHCR, *Tuberculosis Control in Refugee Situations: An Inter-Agency Field Manual* (Geneva: WHO, 1997). The manual and its successor edition also contain further examples of early government-led tuberculosis control programmes that include refugees. WHO and UNHCR, *Tuberculosis Care and Control in Refugee and Displaced Populations: An Inter-Agency Field Manual* (Geneva: WHO, 2007).

143 UNHCR maintains a dashboard that shows that almost all countries which receive funding from the Global Fund include refugees in tuberculosis responses through national systems. UNHCR, 'Public Health Services Survey – Inclusion of Refugees into National Health Systems', website.

144 See, for example: M. O. Santos-Ferreira et al., 'A Study of Seroprevalence of HIV-1 and HIV-2 in Six Provinces of People's Republic of Angola: Clues to the Spread of HIV Infection', *Journal of Acquired Immune Deficiency Syndromes* 3, no. 8 (1990): pp. 780–786.

145 Paul B. Spiegel, 'HIV/AIDS among Conflict-Affected and Displaced Populations: Dispelling Myths and Taking Action', *Disasters* 28, no. 3 (2004): pp. 322–339. Note: The UN General Assembly special session on HIV/AIDs in June 2001, made a declaration of commitment to support HIV/AIDS prevention and treatments of "populations destabilized by armed conflict [...]" including forcibly displaced persons. UNGA, 'Declaration of Commitment on HIV/AIDS' (2001), pp. 36–37. In their study of ProMed reports, Desai et al. found that, while the reported incidence of diseases in excess of what would normally be expected increased in forced displacement contexts between 1996 and 2016, the majority were locally acquired. Desai et al., 'Infectious Disease Outbreaks among Forcibly Displaced Persons': p. 8.

146 UNAIDS, 'About UNAIDS', website; UN, 'UNAIDS: Joint United Nations Programme on HIV/AIDS', website.

147 In regard to guidance for humanitarian agencies, see: Inter-Agency Standing Committee, 'Guidelines: HIV/AIDS Interventions in Emergency Settings' (2003); IASC, 'Guidelines for Addressing HIV in Humanitarian Settings' (2010). UNAIDS, *Global AIDS Strategy 2021–2026: End Inequalities. End AIDS.* (2021).

148 United Nations Foundation and UNHCR, 'Inclusion of Refugees and Internally Displaced Persons in 2016–2019 Global Fund Applications', Report (2020). Established in 2002, the Global Fund is an international financing instrument, which provides $4 billion each year to support programmes in over 100 countries. Global Fund, 'Overview', website.

149 The study looked at applications received 2017–2019 as compared to those received 2014–2016. United Nations Foundation and UNHCR, 'Inclusion of Refugees and Internally Displaced Persons in 2016–2019 Global Fund Applications'.

150 In March 2021, UNAIDS observed that there had been progress in the inclusion of refugees and IDPs in programmes in humanitarian settings. It also noted that "a survey of 48 refugee hosting countries found that in 90% of countries refugees living with HIV have the right to access ART through national health systems" and, in 82 per cent of host countries, refugees were "receiving certain HIV services through Global Fund grants". However, it also found that more work was needed to achieve equitable access to national programmes for refugees and IDPs. UNAIDS, *Global AIDS Strategy 2021–2026*, pp. 86–87.

151 United Nations Foundation and UNHCR, 'Inclusion of Refugees and Internally Displaced Persons in 2016–2019 Global Fund Applications'.

152 Isabel Arciniegas Guaneme et al., 'COVID-19 and Forcibly Displaced People', pp. 17–19.

153 UN, 'I Believe in Humanity – Jean-Nicolas Beuze Interviewed by Melissa Fleming', Awake at Night podcast, season 3, episode 18 (19 February 2021). He noted the tough choices people make daily — noting that, if you have limited income and if people need to choose between using their meagre resources to buy soap or rice — the choice was clear.

154 As of June 2021, UNHCR reported that "of the 126 countries with a refugee population of more than 500 people, [...] 123 have either explicitly included refugees in their vaccination plans or provided assurances that they will do so. [...] refugees and asylum-seekers have begun receiving COVID-19 vaccinations in 91 of the 162 countries monitored". UNHCR, 'UNHCR calls on states to remove barriers to access to COVID-19 vaccines for refugees', Press Release (24 June 2021).

155 The IMF estimated that a further 95 million people have joined the ranks of the extreme poor as a result of the pandemic. IMF, *World Economic Outlook: Managing Divergent Recoveries* (April 2021); World Bank, 'COVID-19 to Add as Many as 150 Million Extreme Poor by 2021', Press Release (7 October 2020).

156 For a review of health outcomes for populations exposed to torture and other trauma in conflict and displacement setting, see: Zachary Steel et al., 'Association of Torture and Other Potentially Traumatic Events With Mental Health Outcomes Among Populations Exposed to Mass Conflict and Displacement: A Systematic Review and Meta-Analysis', *Journal of the American Medical Association* 302, no. 5 (2009): pp. 547–548.

157 Some of these are discussed in the following: Derrick Silove, Peter Ventevogel, and Susan Rees, 'The contemporary refugee crisis: an overview of mental health challenges', *World Psychiatry* 16, no. 2 (June 2017): p. 132; Matthew Porter and Nick Haslam, 'Predisplacement and Postdisplacement Factors Associated With Mental Health of Refugees and Internally Displaced Persons: A Meta-analysis', *Journal of the American Medical Association* 294, no. 5 (2005): pp. 602–612; Amodu, Richter, and Salami, 'A Scoping Review of the Health of Conflict-Induced Internally Displaced Women in Africa': pp. 10–11; Maureen Seguin, 'Aspects of loss and coping among internally displaced populations: Towards a psychosocial approach', in Elena Fiddian-Qasmiyeh (ed.), *Refuge in a Moving World: Tracing refugee and migrant journeys across disciplines* (London: UCL Press, 2020), pp. 300–301; Elisa Van Ee, Trudy Mooren, and Rolf Kleber, 'Broken mirrors: Shattered relationships within refugee families', in Ruth Pat-Horenczyk, Danny Brom, Juliet M. Vogel (eds.), *Helping Children Cope with Trauma: Individual, Family and Community Perspectives* (NY: Routledge, 2014), pp. 146–147.

158 Silove, Ventevogel, and Rees, 'The contemporary refugee crisis': p. 134; Kenneth E. Miller and Andrew Rasmussen, 'War exposure, daily stressors, and mental health in conflict and post-conflict settings: Bridging the divide between trauma-focused and psychosocial frameworks', *Social Science & Medicine* 70, no. 1 (2010): pp. 7–16; Kenneth E. Miller and Andrew Rasmussen, 'The mental health of civilians displaced by armed conflict: an ecological model of refugee distress', *Epidemiology and Psychiatric Sciences* 26, no. 2 (April 2017): pp. 129–138.

159 Silove, Ventevogel, and Rees, 'The contemporary refugee crisis': pp. 131–132.

160 Porter and Haslam, 'Predisplacement and Postdisplacement Factors Associated With Mental Health of Refugees and Internally Displaced Persons'.

161 Fiona Charlson et al., 'New WHO prevalence estimates of mental disorders in conflict settings: a systematic review and meta-analysis', *The Lancet* 394, no. 10194 (20 July 2019): pp. 241, 245.

...PART IV: **Improving Life Prospects...**

162 IASC, 'Guidelines on Mental Health and Psychosocial Support in Emergency Settings' (2007). The guidelines linked the provision of psychosocial support and mental health in an integrated manner.

163 UNHCR, *Operational Guidance: Mental Health & Psychosocial Support Programming for Refugee Operations* (2013).

164 WHO and UNHCR, *mhGAP Humanitarian Intervention Guide (mhGAP-HIG)* (2015).

165 Such as depression, schizophrenia, and bipolar disorders.

166 Silove, Ventevogel, and Rees, 'The contemporary refugee crisis': p. 135.

167 In Silove, Ventevogel, and Rees, 'The contemporary refugee crisis'. The authors make the point that "special populations or vulnerable groups such as former child soldiers and survivors of gender-based violence may require specifically designed programs" (p. 136). Examples of special programmes for vulnerable groups can be found in the following: War Child, *Reclaiming Dreams: Prioritising the Mental Health and Psychosocial Wellbeing of Children in Conflict*, Report (2018); UNFPA, 'Healing when Crisis Strikes', Report (2019).

168 Hippocrates, 'Precepts', in *Hippocrates: Ancient Medicine. Airs, Waters, Places. Epidemics 1 and 3. The Oath. Precepts. Nutriment*, trans. W. H. S. Jones (Cambridge, MA: Harvard University Press, 1923), pp. 303–334.

169 See, for example: Silove, Ventevogel, and Rees, 'The contemporary refugee crisis': p. 134. In discussing the brief and structured cognitive behavioural therapies that have been devised for use amongst refugee and post-conflict populations, they note some of the advantages. These include that "a) they can be adapted to local cultures; b) they allow rapid training of front-line personnel; and c) they facilitate task-shifting, that is, the transfer of skills from professionals such as psychologists to lay or community workers, a vital provision to allow uptake and dissemination in settings where there is a severe lack of mental health specialists". They also note that they are time-limited and low cost which contributes to their dissemination and integration within routine public health or community centre settings. Rasheed Hussein Rasheed, 'Refugees deliver mental health services to locked down camps in Iraq', *UNHCR* News (8 July 2020); Victoria Thomas and Emily Álvarez, 'Venezuelan counsellors offer fellow refugees "Psychological First Aid"', *UNHCR* News (14 May 2020).

170 Silove, Ventevogel, and Rees, 'The contemporary refugee crisis': p. 135.

171 Ibid.: p. 132.

172 World Health Organization, 'The top 10 causes of death', website (9 December 2020).

173 See the following for research on this in conflict-affected settings: Paul B. Spiegel et al., 'Health-care needs of people affected by conflict: future trends and changing frameworks', *The Lancet* 375, no. 9711 (2010): p. 342. See also: UNHCR, *2020 Annual Public Health Global Review*; UNHCR, 'Access to Healthcare', website.

174 Jennifer Leaning, Paul Spiegel, and Jeff Crisp, 'Public health equity in refugee situations', *Conflict and Health* 5, no. 6 (2011): p. 3. In the Middle East, for example, both host and forcibly displaced populations suffer from a wide variety of non-communicable diseases, including hypertension, diabetes, heart disease and cancers. In 2014, a survey of Syrian refugees and host communities was conducted in Lebanon and identified the prevalence and responses to five non-communicable diseases: hypertension; cardiovascular disease; diabetes; chronic respiratory disease; and arthritis. Over half of the host community and refugee households (60.2 per cent and 50.4 per cent, respectively) reported a member

with one of the five non-communicable diseases. Shannon Doocy et al., 'Prevalence, care-seeking, and health service utilization for non-communicable diseases among Syrian refugees and host communities in Lebanon', *Conflict and Health* 10, no. 21 (2016).

175 WHO, 'Noncommunicable diseases', website (13 April 2021).

176 UNGA, Political declaration of the third high-level meeting of the General Assembly on the prevention and control of non-communicable diseases (17 October 2018), UN Doc A/RES/73/2, paras. 5, 11.

177 Paul B. Spiegel et al., 'Health-care needs of people affected by conflict': p. 343.

178 Ibid.: p. 343.

179 Leaning, Spiegel, and Crisp, 'Public health equity in refugee situations': p. 3. For displacement figures during the Kosovo crisis, see: Part III. In 2007, there were 2.3 million Iraqi refugees. UNHCR, Refugee Data Finder.

180 Leaning, Spiegel, and Crisp, 'Public health equity in refugee situations': p. 4.

181 UNHCR Public Health and HIV Section, *UNHCR's Principles and Guidance for Referral Health Care for Refugees and Other Persons of Concern* (2009).

182 Leaning, Spiegel, and Crisp, 'Public health equity in refugee situations': p. 6.

183 Ibid.: p. 6.

184 For example on the medical dilemmas confronting UNHCR in Lebanon during the Syria crisis and the use of Exceptional Care Committees, see: Karl Blanchet, Fouad M. Fouad, and Tejendra Pherali, 'Syrian refugees in Lebanon: The search for universal health coverage', *Conflict and Health* 10, no. 12 (2016). See also: UNHCR, 'Guidelines to Referral Health Care in Lebanon' (January 2014), pp. 11–16; UNHCR, 'Guidelines for Referral Health Care in Lebanon: Standard Operating Procedures' (June 2020), pp. 17–18.

185 Paul Spiegel, Rebecca Chanis, and Antonio Trujillo, 'Innovative health financing for refugees', *BMC Medicine* 16, no. 90 (15 June 2018).

186 UNHCR, 'Health Access and Utilization Survey: Access to Healthcare Services Among Syrian Refugees in Jordan', Report (December 2018); UNHCR, 'Health access and utilization survey among Syrian refugees in Lebanon', Report (October 2020). See also: Emily Lyles et al., 'Health service utilization and adherence to medication for hypertension and diabetes among Syrian refugees and affected host communities in Lebanon', *Journal of Diabetes & Metabolic Disorders* 19, no. 2 (2020): pp. 1245–1259.

187 Of the 48 refugee host States that participated in UNHCR's Public Health Inclusion survey, 29 have included refugees in their national health plan/policy; two more States have included refugees partially. Of the 33 countries which had national health insurance schemes at the time of the survey, nine reported that they include/cover refugees, and three additional countries reported that their national insurance schemes cover refugees partially. UNHCR, 'Inclusion of Refugees into National Health Systems'.

188 Subsidies can help cover the cost of premiums but are difficult to sustain. UNHCR, 'A Guidance Note on Health Insurance Schemes for Refugees and Other Persons of Concern to UNHCR' (March 2012); Spiegel, Chanis, and Trujillo, 'Innovative health financing for refugees': p. 4. The authors suggest that certain circumstances where the number of refugees paying the premiums is sufficiently high could allow for subsidizing or reducing the co-payments of those who have less financial means. Ibid.: p. 4.

189 Provided through the IDA18 Sub-window for Refugees and Host Communities and an additional $150 million for other parts of the country. World Bank, 'Health and Gender Support Project for Cox's Bazar district' (approved 31 March 2020), Project Overview, website. For refugee statistics in Bangladesh, see: UNHCR, Refugee Data Finder. See also:

...PART IV: **Improving Life Prospects...**

UNHCR, 'Bangladeshi authorities, aid agencies and refugee volunteers rush to respond as massive fire leaves some 45,000 Rohingya refugees without shelter', *UNHCR* News (23 March 2021).

190 See the following Project Overview websites from the World Bank: 'Balochistan Human Capital Investment Project'; 'Cameroon – Health System Performance Reinforcement Project'; 'Djibouti – Improving Health Sector Performance Project'; and 'Mauritania – Health System Support Project'.

191 World Bank, 'Global Program on Forced Displacement – Brief for Partners Consultation', pp. 5–6. These mechanisms, IDA18 Sub-window for Refugees and Host Communities and IDA19 Window for Host Communities and Refugees are discussed earlier under Education and in Part V.

192 For further details, see: Spiegel, Chanis, and Trujillo, 'Innovative health financing for refugees'.

193 Filippo Dionigi and Domenico Tabasso, 'Academic Trends in Forced Displacement', Reference Paper for the 70th Anniversary of the 1951 Refugee Convention, UNHCR (October 2021). See also health recommendations in the report of the High-Level Panel on Internal Displacement, *Shining a Light on Internal Displacement*.

194 Universal Declaration of Human Rights (1948), art. 23: "Everyone has the right to work, to free choice of employment, to just and favourable conditions of work and to protection against unemployment."

195 International Covenant on Economic, Social and Cultural Rights (16 December 1966), UN Doc A/RES/2200(XXI), art. 6: "The States Parties to the present Covenant recognize the right to work, which includes the right of everyone to the opportunity to gain his living by work which he freely chooses or accepts, and will take appropriate steps to safeguard this right." Articles 17–19 of the Convention relating to the Status of Refugees (adopted 25 July 1951) (1951 Convention), UN Doc A/CONF.2/108, obligate States to provide refugees the most favourable treatment accorded to foreigners in regard to wage employment and "treatment as favourable as possible and, in any event, not less favourable than that accorded to aliens generally" with respect to self-employment and engagement in liberal professions. The Guiding Principles on International Displacement underscore the right of IDPs to not be discriminated against in the enjoyment of their rights, including their right to seek employment and participate in economic activities. UN Commission on Human Rights, 'Report of the Representative of the Secretary-General, Mr. Francis M. Deng, submitted pursuant to Commission resolution 1997/39, Addendum: Guiding Principles on Internal Displacement' (11 February 1998), UN Doc E/CN.4/1998/53/Add.2.

196 World Bank, *Forcibly Displaced*, p. 68.

197 Many people forced to flee do so suddenly and without all of their civil documentation and education and skills certificates. Refugees generally face risks in retrieving documents from home. IDPs also can face administrative obstacles. Council of Europe Congress of Local and Regional Authorities, 'The role of local and regional governments in protecting internally displaced persons (IDPs)', Report (29 October 2019), p. 9.

198 Kirsten Schuettler and Laura Caron, 'Jobs Interventions for Refugees and Internally Displaced Persons', Jobs Group Working Paper 47, World Bank (2020), p. 12. Social networks can be helpful in finding jobs and referrals to employers.

199 Utz Johann Pape and Ambika Sharma, *Informing Durable Solutions for Internal Displacement in Nigeria, Somalia, Sudan, and South Sudan* vol. A: 'Overview', The World Bank Group (2019), pp. ix, x, 4, 21, 34.

200 Schuettler and Caron, 'Jobs Interventions for Refugees and Internally Displaced Persons', p. 8.

201 UNHCR, 'Livelihoods and Economic Inclusion', website. Articles in the 1951 Convention pertaining to wage-earning employment and labour legislation have also received some of the largest numbers of reservations from States parties. For more on States' restrictive approach to the right to work for refugees, see also: Roger Zetter and Héloïse Ruaudel, 'Refugees' Right to Work and Access to Labor Markets – An Assessment', Part 1, KNOMAD (September 2016).

202 Ibid., pp. 12–13.

203 Ibid., p. 18. Dina Nayeri, whose mother had been a doctor in Iran before she became a refugee, describes how she worked far below her skills level in the United States. She relates how difficult this was and how her accent was often enough for people to assume she was not intelligent. Dina Nayeri, 'The ungrateful refugee: "We have no debt to repay"', The Guardian (4 April 2017).

204 Zetter and Ruaudel, 'Refugees' Right to Work and Access to Labor Markets', p. 16. Alexander Betts et al., *Refugee Economies: Forced Displacement and Development* (Oxford: Oxford University Press, 2016), p. 52; see also: Joscha Albert et al., 'Reckoning with Reality: Five Key Findings from the Finance in Displacement Studies', Joint Study, Tufts University, International Rescue Committee and Katholische Universität Eichstätt-Ingolstadt (April 2021). Iran recently moved to formalize access to banking services – including debit cards, for Afghan refugees in the country. UNHCR, 'Iran policy change gives refugees access to banking services', *UNHCR* News (8 June 2021). The Economic and Research Policy Foundation of Turkey similarly found that "access to banking systems and access to finance are two of the foremost obstacles limiting Syrian entrepreneurs' inclusion into the Turkish economy". Economic Policy Research Foundation of Turkey, 'Syrian Entrepreneurship and Refugee Start-ups in Turkey: Leveraging the Turkish Experience', Final Report, Tepav and EBRD (2018), p. 9.

205 Jordan and Lebanon are notable exceptions as well as smaller host countries, like Aruba and Curaçao. UNHCR, *Global Trends 2020*, p. 2; World Bank, *Forcibly Displaced*, p. 57.

206 World Bank, *Forcibly Displaced*, p. 68.

207 Zetter and Ruaudel, 'Refugees' Right to Work and Access to Labor Markets'.

208 World Bank, *Forcibly Displaced*, p. 68.

209 Contributing factors and routes to Europe in 2015 are reviewed in OECD, 'Is this humanitarian migration crisis different?', *OECD Migration Policy Debates* 7 (September 2015). See also: Peter Tinti and Tuesday Reitano, *Migrant, Refugee, Smuggler, Saviour* (London: C. Hurst & Co, 2016).

210 See, for example: the responses of host countries to interviews conducted by the Word Bank as part of a quantitative study in 2015. World Bank, *Forcibly Displaced*, pp. 58–59.

211 Ibid., p. 61. There are a number of examples in the 1990s of the problem of armed groups in refugee camps. See, for example: Karen Jacobsen, 'A "Safety-First" Approach to Physical Protection in Refugee Camps', Working Paper 4 (May 1999).

212 World Bank, *Forcibly Displaced*, p. 61. The authors recognize that it can be empirically difficult to separate the presence of IDPs from the many factors that determine how conflict spreads during a war. However, they note that IDPs are a consequence and not the cause of conflict already existing in the country.

213 An ambition expressed by United Nations Secretary-General Trygve Lie in 1950. UN Economic and Social Council Ad Hoc Committee on Statelessness and Related Problems, Status of Refugees and Stateless Persons, 'Memorandum by the Secretary-General' (3 January 1950), UN Doc E/AC.32/2.

214 See discussion in Part I and Part III.

215 Discussed in Part III.

216 Schuettler and Caron, 'Jobs Interventions for Refugees and Internally Displaced Persons'.

217 Ibid., p. 26–27. A UNHCR evaluation also found that vocational trainings that were not linked to job markets did not deliver intended outcomes, see: UNHCR, 'Evaluation of UNHCR's Livelihoods Strategies and Approaches' (December 2018), p. 31.

218 Skills trainings offered without consideration of whether those who were to benefit from them had the time, or the means to attend. Women, for example, may have been restricted due to social norms or lack of childcare. Schuettler and Caron, 'Jobs Interventions for Refugees and Internally Displaced Persons', p. 27.

219 Schuettler and Caron, 'Jobs Interventions for Refugees and Internally Displaced Persons', p. 25. Specifically, in Costa Rica, Kenya and Serbia. The authors refer to the following sources: Michelle Azorbo, 'Microfinance and refugees: lessons learned from UNHCR's experience', Research Paper No. 199, *New Issues in Refugee Research*, UNHCR (January 2011); UNHCR, 'Microfinance Programmes in UNHCR Operations: Innovative Microlending in Kenya – Kiva Zip & RefugePoint', Factsheet (2018).

220 Schuettler and Caron, 'Jobs Interventions for Refugees and Internally Displaced Persons', p. 26. They note the following studies: Christopher Blattman and Laura Ralston, 'Generating Employment in Poor and Fragile States: Evidence from Labor Market and Entrepreneurship Programs', Social Science Research Network (2015); Abdul Latif Jameel Poverty Action Lab (J-PAL) and Innovations for Poverty Action (IPA), 'Where Credit Is Due', Policy Bulletin, (February 2015); Abhijit Banerjee, Dean Karlan, and Jonathan Zinman, 'Six Randomized Evaluations of Microcredit: Introduction and Further Steps', *American Economic Journal: Applied Economics* 7, no. 1 (2015): pp. 1–21.

221 Schuettler and Caron, 'Jobs Interventions for Refugees and Internally Displaced Persons', p. 26.

222 UNHCR, 'Framework for Durable Solutions for Refugees and Persons of Concern', Core Group on Durable Solutions (May 2003); Betsy Lippman and Sajjad Malik, 'The 4Rs: the way ahead?', *Forced Migration Review* 21 (2004): pp. 9–11.

223 Global Compact on Refugees (2018), paras. 32, 64.

224 Ibid., paras. 70–71. Note also that (i) easing pressures on host countries and (ii) enhancing refugee self-reliance are two of its four goals.

225 Paolo Verme and Kirsten Schuettler, 'The Impact of Forced Displacement on Host Communities: A Review of the Empirical Literature in Economics', Policy Research Working Paper 8727, World Bank (February 2019), p. 3. These authors note that, after 2011, the average number of studies per year increased tenfold.

226 Zara Sarzin, 'The impact of forced migration on the labor market outcomes and welfare of host communities', Reference Paper for the 70th Anniversary of the 1951 Refugee Convention, UNHCR (October 2021).

227 Ibid. The Mariel Boatlift refers to efforts of thousands of Cubans to enter the United States.

For more on this movement and the United States response, see: David Scott FitzGerald, *Refuge beyond Reach: How Rich Democracies Repel Asylum Seekers* (New York: Oxford University Press, 2019), pp. 104–109. For more on the causes of Jewish flight and migration to Israel, see: Larissa Remennick, 'The Two Waves of Russian-Jewish Migration from the USSR/FSU to Israel: Dissidents of the 1970s and Pragmatics of the 1990s', *Diaspora: A Journal of Transnational Studies* 18 (2015): pp. 8–13.

228 UNHCR, Refugee Data Finder.

229 Markus Gehrsitz and Martin Ungerer, 'Jobs, Crime, and Votes – A Short-run Evaluation of the Refugee Crisis in Germany', Discussion Paper No. 10494, IZA Institute for Labor Economics (January 2017), pp. 23–28; Thomas Rogers, 'Welcome to Germany', *The New York Review of Books* (29 April 2021); The Economist, 'Did they handle it? Five years after arrival, Germany's refugees are integrating' (29 August 2020). Rogers notes that the challenges included that many of the refugees arrived with skills but were working in jobs well below their qualifications. Women refugees were underrepresented in employment, in part because some come from traditions where work outside the home is not encouraged.

230 Including through monetary or in-kind donations, public support, and active help like teaching language classes or accompanying refugees to medical appointments. The report was commissioned by the Ministry for Family, Seniors, Women and Youth. Rogers, 'Welcome to Germany'; Bundesministerium für Familie, Senioren, Frauen und Jugend, 'Studie zeigt: Viele Menschen engagieren sich freiwillig für Flüchtlinge' [German] (7 February 2018); Bundesministerium für Familie, Senioren, Frauen und Jugend, 'Engagement für Geflüchtete' [German] (7 February 2018).

231 Sebastian Braun and Toman Omar Mahmoud, 'The Employment Effects of Immigration: Evidence from the Mass Arrival of German Expellees in Postwar Germany', *The Journal of Economic History* 74, no. 1 (2014): pp. 69–72. Among the reasons was that the refugees were highly skilled and spoke the same language. For further information on these movements, see: Philipp Ther, *The Outsiders: Refugees in Europe since 1492* (Princeton, NJ: Princeton University Press, 2019), ch. 3.

232 Erik Mäkelä, 'The effect of mass influx on labor markets: Portuguese 1974 evidence revisited', *European Economic Review* 98 (2017): pp. 240, 242–243, 256–257, 260.

233 Mette Foged and Giovanni Peri, 'Immigrants' Effect on Native Workers: New Analysis on Longitudinal Data', *American Economic Journal: Applied Economics* 8, No. 2 (2016): pp. 1–34.

234 See, for example: Sarit Cohen-Goldner and M. Daniele Paserman, 'The dynamic impact of immigration on natives' labor market outcomes: Evidence from Israel', *European Economic Review* 55, no. 8 (2011); Francine D. Blau and Christopher D. Mackie (eds.), *The Economic and Fiscal Consequences of Immigration* (Washington, D.C.: National Academies of Sciences, Engineering, and Medicine, 2017).

235 UNHCR, *Global Trends 2019*, p. 19.

236 Sarzin, 'The impact of forced migration on the labor market outcomes and welfare of host communities'.

237 See, for example the literature reviews by Sarzin, 'The impact of forced migration on the labour market outcomes and welfare of host communities'; Verme and Schuettler, 'The Impact of Forced Displacement on Host Communities'.

238 UNHCR, Refugee Data Finder.

239 In 2016, Syrians were permitted to apply for work permits. Don Murray, 'High Commissioner welcomes Turkish work permits for Syrian Refugees', *UNHCR* News (18 January

2016). Yet, the majority of Syrian workers continue to be concentrated in the informal sector. Luis Pinedo Caro, 'Syrian Refugees in the Turkish Labour Market', Report, International Labour Organization (March 2020), p. 12.

240 Onur Altindag, Ozan Bakis, and Sandra V. Rozo, 'Blessing or burden? Impacts of refugees on businesses and the informal economy', *Journal of Development Economics* 146 (2020): p. 17; Ximena V. Del Carpio and Wagner Mathis, 'The Impact of Syrians Refugees on the Turkish Labor Market', Policy Research Working Paper 7402, World Bank (August 2015); Evren Ceritoglu et al., 'The impact of Syrian refugees on natives' labor market outcomes in Turkey: evidence from a quasi-experimental design', *IZA Journal of Labor Policy* 6, no. 5 (2017): p. 4; Oğuz Esen and Ayla Oğuş Binatlı, 'The Impact of Syrian Refugees on the Turkish Economy: Regional Labour Market Effects', *Social Sciences* 6, no. 4 (2017): p. 11; Semih Tumen, 'The Economic Impact of Syrian Refugees on Host Countries: Quasi-experimental Evidence from Turkey', *The American Economic Review* 106, no. 5 (May 2016): p. 459.

241 Yusuf Kenan Bağır, 'Impact of the Syrian refugee influx on Turkish native workers: An ethnic enclave approach', *Central Bank Review* 18, no. 4 (2018): p. 139; Esen and Oğuş Binatlı, 'The Impact of Syrian Refugees on the Turkish Economy': p. 3.

242 Bağır, 'Impact of the Syrian refugee influx on Turkish native workers': p. 139; Ceritoglu et al., 'The impact of Syrian refugees on natives' labor market outcomes in Turkey', p. 5; Tumen, 'The Economic Impact of Syrian Refugees on Host Countries'.

243 Ceritoglu et al., 'The impact of Syrian refugees on natives' labor market outcomes in Turkey', p. 5; Ege Aksu, Refik Erzan, and Murat Güray Kırdar, 'The Impact of Mass Migration of Syrians on the Turkish Labor Market', Discussion Paper 12050, IZA Institute of Labor Economics (December 2018), p. 34–35. Del Carpio and Mathis, 'The Impact of Syrians Refugees on the Turkish Labor Market', pp. 12–13. They found that those with more than a high school education experienced a net increase in their employment rate, while the "net negative labour market consequences" were limited to "Turkish workers with at most a high school education". Yusuf Emre Akgündüz and Huzeyfe Torun, 'Two and a half million Syrian refugees, tasks and capital intensity', *Journal of Development Economics* 145 (2020): p. 12. The authors suggest that lower educated workers may have been less able to transition to tasks that were complementary to Syrian workers, which is why they were more negatively affected.

244 Esen and Oğuş Binatlı, 'The Impact of Syrian Refugees on the Turkish Economy': p. 10. These authors suggest that more studies are needed in this area.

245 Economic Policy Research Foundation of Turkey, 'Syrian Entrepreneurship and Refugee Start-ups in Turkey', p. 8; Selen Ucak, Jennifer P. Holt, and Kavya Raman (Building Markets), *Another Side to the Story: A Market Assessment of Syrian SMEs in Turkey*, Report (20 June 2017), p. 9; Michael Clemens, Cindy Huang, and Jimmy Graham, refer to Syrians hiring over 56,000 persons in formal enterprises, most of whom were hosts, in 'The Economic and Fiscal Effects of Granting Refugees Formal Labor Market Access', Brief, Center for Global Development and Tent, (October 2018), p. 19. For further information on jobs of refugees in Turkey, see: Turkish Red Crescent and World Food Programme, 'Refugees in Turkey: Livelihoods Survey Findings', Report, (25 July 2019).

246 Ucak, Holt, and Raman, 'Another Side to the Story', p. 17.

247 Supported by lower labour costs. Particularly in the construction, restaurant and hotel sectors. Altindag, Bakis, and Rozo, 'Blessing or Burden?', p. 3.

248 Binnur Balkan and Semih Tumen, 'Immigration and prices: quasi-experimental evidence from Syrian refugees in Turkey' *Journal of Population Economics* 29, issue 3, No 1 (2016): pp. 657–686; Tumen, 'The Economic Impact of Syrian Refugees on Host Countries': p. 459.

249 Del Carpio and Mathis, 'The Impact of Syrians Refugees on the Turkish Labor Market'. These authors found that average Turkish wages rose, although this was likely because those who would have experienced wage losses left the labour market, p. 19. Evren Ceritoglu et al., 'The Impact of Syrian Refugees on Natives' Labor Market Outcomes in Turkey': p. 3. Those who remained employed experienced a marginal increase in wages. Altindag, Bakis, and Rozo, 'Blessing or burden?', p. 2; Tumen, 'The Economic Impact of Syrian Refugees on Host Countries': p. 458.

250 IMF, 'Lebanon: 2014 Article IV Consultation Staff Report', Country Report No. 14/237 (July 2014).

251 Anda David et al., 'The economics of the Syrian refugee crisis in neighbouring countries: The case of Lebanon', *Economics of Transition and Institutional Change* 28, no. 1 (2020): p. 94. World Bank, *The Fallout of War*, pp. 25–27.

252 UNHCR, Refugee Data Finder.

253 Paolo Verme et al., *The Welfare of Syrian Refugees: Evidence from Jordan and Lebanon* (Washington, D.C.: World Bank, 2016), p. xvi.

254 David et al., 'The economics of the Syrian refugee crisis in neighbouring countries': p. 95. In 2014, 60 per cent of Syrians were unemployed compared to 11 per cent of the Lebanese population (for whom unemployment figures were only available for 2011).

255 Ibid., p. 104.

256 Ibid., p. 107. The Global Concessional Financing Facility was established by the United Nations, the Islamic Development Bank (IsDB) and the World Bank and is discussed more in Part V. See also: Doreen Kibuka-Musoke and Zara Sarzin, 'Financing for Forced Displacement Situations', Reference Paper for the 70th Anniversary of the 1951 Refugee Convention, UNHCR (October 2021), pp. 23–25.

257 UNHCR, 'Syria: Regional Refugee Response', Operational Data Portal. This represents Syrians registered with UNHCR.

258 According to UNHCR statistics, there are close to 700,000 Syrian refugees in Jordan: UNHCR, 'Jordan: Statistics for Registered Syrian Refugees', Operational Data Portal. Camp-based refugees are located in Zaatari, Azraq and the Emirati Jordanian camp. Official Government of Jordan statistics suggest there could be as many as 1.36 million Syrian refugees in Jordan, including those registered with UNHCR. The Hashemite Kingdom of Jordan Ministry of Planning and International Cooperation, *Jordan Response Plan for the Syria Crisis 2020-2022*, p. 69.

259 Ali Fakih and May Ibrahim, 'The impact of Syrian refugees on the labor market in neighboring countries: empirical evidence from Jordan', *Defence and Peace Economics* 27, no. 1 (2016): pp. 64–86; Belal Fallah, Caroline Krafft, and Jackline Wahba, 'The impact of refugees on employment and wages in Jordan', *Journal of Development Economics* 139 (2019).

260 Fakih and Ibrahim, 'The impact of Syrian refugees on the labor market in neighboring countries': p. 65.

261 World Bank, *The Fallout of War*, pp. 3, 14, 18, 26, 108.

262 Fakih and Ibrahim, 'The impact of Syrian refugees on the labor market in neighboring countries': pp. 71, 83–84; Fallah, Krafft, and Wahba, 'The impact of refugees on employment and wages in Jordan': p. 214.

...PART IV: **Improving Life Prospects...**

263 World Bank, *The Fallout of War*, pp. 115–21. The World Bank report does not find system-atic effects of refugee presence on wages. However, another study suggests that declining wages in the informal sector were associated with high refugee concentrations but also noted that Syrian refugees invested millions of dollars in the Jordanian economy, "boost-ing domestic output and employment". Salem Ajluni and Dorsey Lockhart, 'The Syrian Refugee Crisis and Its Impact on the Jordanian Labour Market', Report, WANA Institute (March 2019), p. 23.

264 World Bank Group, 'Refugee Investment & Matchmaking Platform (RIMP): Progress, Results & Opportunities', Report (15 January 2021), p. 6.

265 Notably the World Bank and the European Bank for Reconstruction and Development (EBRD).

266 Government of Jordan, 'The Jordan Compact: A New Holistic Approach between the Hashemite Kingdom of Jordan and the International Community to deal with the Syrian Refugee Crisis', statement given at Supporting Syria & the Region conference held in London (4 February 2016); World Bank, 'Economic Opportunities for Jordanians and Syrian Refugees – Questions and Answers', Brief, *World Bank* website (28 June 2016).

267 Center for Global Development and International Rescue Committee, *Refugee Compacts: Addressing the Crisis of Protracted Displacement*, Final Report of the Forced Displacement and Development Study Group (18 April 2017), p. 9.

268 For more on the Jordan Compact, see: Jennifer Gordon, 'Refugees and decent work: Lessons learned from recent refugee jobs compacts', Employment Working Paper 256, ILO (17 December 2019), pp. 1–23; For details on the Compact, see: European Commission, 'Joint Proposal for a Council Decision on the Union Position within the Association Coun-cil Set up by the Euro-Mediterranean Agreement establishing an association between the European Communities and their Member States, of the one part, and the Hashemite Kingdom of Jordan, of the other part, with regard to the adoption of EU-Jordan Partnership Priorities and annexed Compact' (19 September 2016), JOIN/2016/041 final-2016/0289 (NLE).

269 Veronique Barbelet, Jessica Hagen-Zanker, and Dina Mansour-Ille, 'The Jordan Compact: Lessons learnt and implications for future refugee compacts', Policy briefing, Overseas Development Institute (February 2018), p. 2; Cindy Huang and Kate Gough, 'The Jordan Compact: Three Years on, Where Do We Stand?', Center for Global Development, website (11 March 2019).

270 95 per cent of the Syrian permit holders were men. Gordon, 'Refugees and decent work', p. 12.

271 Ibid., p. 13.

272 Ibid., p. 18.

273 Government of Jordan Ministry of Labour Syrian Refugee Unit, 'Syrian Refugee Unit Work Permits Progress Report December and annual 2020' (January 2021).

274 ILO, *Lessons Learned and Emerging Good Practices of ILO's Syria Crisis Response in Jordan and Lebanon*, Report (2018), pp. 29–30.

275 Gordon, 'Refugees and decent work', p. 17; Huang and Gough, 'The Jordan Compact'.

276 Gordon, 'Refugees and decent work', p. 18.

277 In 2020, the World Bank's programme to improve employment opportunities for Jorda-nians and Syrian refugees, which forms part of the Jordan Compact, was extended for an additional two years. Meriem Ait Ali Shlimane et al., 'New economic opportunities for Jordanians and Syrian refugees', World Bank blog (29 July 2020).

278 Huang and Gough, 'The Jordan Compact'.

279 Barbelet, Hagen-Zanker, and Mansour-Ille, 'The Jordan Compact', p. 3.

280 The Hashemite Kingdom of Jordan, Ministry of Planning and International Cooperation 'Jordan Response Plan for the Syria Crisis 2016–2018' (2015). It has been a positive example of improving protection outcomes through partnerships between the international community and host countries.

281 UNHCR, Refugee Data Finder. Colombia continues to report the highest number of IDPs, with 8.3 million at the end of 2020, according to Government statistics. The Government has indicated its intention to review these numbers with technical support from UNHCR and partners, as the large number of registered IDPs comes from the total cumulative figure in the Government's Victims Registry, which commenced in 1985. UNHCR, *Global Trends 2020*, p. 24.

282 Valentina Calderón-Mejía and Ana María Ibáñez, 'Labour market effects of migration-related supply shocks: evidence from internal refugees in Colombia', *Journal of Economic Geography* 16, no. 3 (1 May 2016): pp. 695–713. This study examines the period between 2001 and 2005. Juan S. Morales, 'The impact of internal displacement on destination communities: Evidence from the Colombian conflict', *Journal of Development Economics* 131 (2017): pp. 132–150. This study concerns 1998–2005. For more on these and other studies, see: Sarzin, 'The impact of forced migration on the labor market outcomes and welfare of host communities'.

283 Morales, 'The impact of internal displacement on destination communities': pp. 133, 142.

284 UNHCR, *Global Trends 2020*, p. 3.

285 UNHCR, 'Guidance Note on International Protection Considerations for Venezuelans – Update I' (May 2019). See also: Dany Bahar and Meagan Dooley, 'Venezuela refugee crisis to become the largest and most underfunded in modern history', Brookings Institution blog (9 December 2019).

286 German Caruso, Christian Gomez Canon, and Valerie Mueller, 'Spillover effects of the Venezuelan crisis: migration impacts in Colombia', *Oxford Economic Papers* 73, no. 2 (April 2021).

287 On 1 March 2021, President Iván Duque signed a decree creating the Temporary Protection Status (TPS) for Venezuelans in Colombia to facilitate their socioeconomic inclusion. Venezuelans can apply for the TPS to regularize their stay in the country for a period of 10 years. Republic of Colombia, Ministry of External Affairs, 'Decree No. 216' [Spanish] (2021), p. 11. Andrew Selee and Jessica Bolter, 'An Uneven Welcome: Latin American and Caribbean Responses to Venezuelan and Nicaraguan Migration', Migration Policy Institute (February 2020), p. 16.

288 Dany Bahar, Ana María Ibáñez, and Sandra V. Rozo, 'Give me your tired and your poor: Impact of a large-scale amnesty program for undocumented refugees', *Journal of Development Economics* 151 (June 2021): pp. 1–24. The authors consider several explanations, including the possibility that Venezuelans may have taken up the permit to access services rather than seek employment. They discount this given that wages in the formal sector are relatively high but acknowledged that Venezuelans may have difficulty in finding formal employment. They also consider whether labour market outcomes could take longer to be observed than the 18-month time frame of the study. They concluded that, even if this were so, observable negative effects would be evident during the study time frame. Their

...PART IV: **Improving Life Prospects...**

overall conclusion is that their findings are consistent with other studies that show little to no effect of migrant inflows on labour outcomes of native populations.

289 Sergio Olivieri et al., 'The Labor Market Effects of Venezuelan Migration in Ecuador', Discussion Paper 13501, IZA Institute for Labor Economics (July 2020), p. 7.

290 Cantons with 10 per cent higher income received 5 per cent more Venezuelans than otherwise similar regions. Ibid., p. 3.

291 Olivieri et al., 'The Labor Market Effects of Venezuelan Migration in Ecuador', pp. 1, 3–4, 19.

292 Ibid., pp. 19–20.

293 UNHCR, 'UN High Commissioner for Refugees praises Latin America for its commitment to the inclusion of all those in need of protection', Press Release (23 June 2021); Luc Cohen, 'Ecuador to start new "normalization process" for Venezuelan migrants', *Reuters* (17 June 2021); For the number of those whose status was irregular at the time of the announcement, see: UNHCR, 'Ecuador Monthly Update: May 2021', p. 1. Discussed in Part III.

294 All of which are covered in more detail in Sarzin, 'The impact of forced migration on the labor market outcomes and welfare of host communities'.

295 For the total number of Burundian and Rwandan refugees in Tanzania during this time, see: UNHCR, Refugee Data Finder. Further breakdowns are provided by Jean-François Maystadt and Gilles Duranton, 'The development push of refugees: evidence from Tanzania', *Journal of Economic Geography* 19, no. 2 (March 2019): pp. 299–334.

296 UNHCR, Refugee Data Finder.

297 Maystadt and Duranton, 'The development push of refugees'. By the end of June 2021, there were 253,040 refugees and asylum-seekers in Tanzania, primarily consisting of Burundians and Congolese (DRC), most of whom are located in the Kigoma region, northwest Tanzania. The Kigoma region is one of the poorest regions of Tanzania. The refugee camps in the Kagera region have since been closed. UNHCR, 'Operational Update: United Republic of Tanzania', Brief (June 2021). For further up-to-date information, see also: UNHCR, 'Refugee Situations: Tanzania', Operational Data Portal.

298 Maystadt and Duranton, 'The development push of refugees': p. 304.

299 Ibid.; Chiara Kofol, and Maryam Naghsh Nejad, 'Child Labor and the Arrival of Refugees: Evidence from Tanzania', Discussion Paper 11242, IZA Institute for Labor Economics (December 2017); Isabel Ruiz and Carlos Varga-Silva, 'The impact of hosting refugees on the intra-household allocation of tasks: A gender perspective', *Review of Development Economics* 22, no. 4 (2018): pp. 1461–1488.

300 Maystadt and Duranton, 'The development push of refugees': p. 304; Beth Elise Whitaker, 'Refugees in Western Tanzania: The Distribution of Burdens and Benefits Among Local Hosts', *Journal of Refugee Studies* 15, no. 4 (2002): pp. 342.

301 Whitaker, 'Refugees in Western Tanzania': p. 348.

302 Ibid.: p. 347.

303 Kofol and Nejad, 'Child Labor and the Arrival of Refugees', p. 24.

304 Whitaker, 'Refugees in Western Tanzania': p. 342.

305 According to Maystadt and Verwimp, the local effect of this is ambiguous as there were more opportunities but some were seized by business operators from other parts of Tanzania, which may have led to the closure of some local businesses. Jean-François Maystadt and Philip Verwimp, 'Winners and Losers among a Refugee-Hosting Population', *Economic Development and Cultural Change* 62, no. 4 (July 2014): p. 777.

306 Maystadt and Verwimp, 'Winners and Losers among a Refugee-Hosting Population': pp. 776–777. Ruiz and Vargas-Silva, 'The impact of hosting refugees on the intra-household allocation of tasks': pp. 1463, 1479. This included women who could read and perform simple mathematical operations. However, this study also found that women were less likely to engage in outside employment than men. This was likely due to the environmental impact of refugees, which meant that women had to walk farther, spending more time to collect firewood and fetch water. Whitaker, 'Refugees in Western Tanzania': pp. 342–344, 347.

307 Overall, host communities experienced an increase in their welfare measured through their individual consumption. Maystadt and Verwimp, 'Winners and Losers among a Refugee-Hosting Population': pp. 778, 803; Maystadt and Duranton, 'The development push of refugees': p. 328

308 Maystadt and Verwimp, 'Winners and Losers among a Refugee-Hosting Population': p. 803; Kofol and Nejad, 'Child Labor and the Arrival of Refugees', p. 23.

309 UNHCR, Refugee Data Finder; UNHCR, 'Kenya: Registered Refugees and Asylum-Seekers', Operational Data Portal (31 July 2021).

310 Jedediah Rooney Fix et al., 'Understanding the Socioeconomic Conditions of Refugees in Kenya', vol. A: 'Kalobeyei Settlement: Results from the 2018 Kalobeyei Socioeconomic Profiling Survey', Joint Report, World Bank Group and UNHCR (2019) p. x.

311 Apurva Sanghi, Harun Onder and Varalakshmi Vemuru *"Yes" In My Backyard? –The Economics of Refugees and Their Social Dynamics in Kakuma, Kenya*, Joint Report, UNHCR and World Bank (2016), pp. 5–6.

312 Jennifer Alix-Garcia et al., 'Do refugee camps help or hurt hosts? The case of Kakuma, Kenya', *Journal of Development Economics* 130 (January 2018): pp. 66–83; Sanghi, Onder and Vemuru, *"Yes" In My Backyard?*; UNHCR, 'Kenya: Registered Refugees and Asylum-Seekers'.

313 UNHCR, 'Kenya: Overview', Operational Data Portal; Jennifer Alix-Garcia, Erhan Artuc, and Harun Onder, *The Economics of Hosting Refugees: A Host Community Perspective from Turkana*, World Bank (2017), p. 64.

314 UNHCR, 'Kakuma & Kalobeyei Population Statistics', Operational Data Portal, (31 December 2020).

315 Those who work tend to be engaged in small trades, have small- or medium-sized enterprises or are engaged as incentive workers. Income can also come from foreign cash remittances. UNHCR, 'Kakuma Refugee Camp and Kalobeyei Integrated Settlement', website; Refugees have expressed their frustrations at barriers to receiving work permits. Refugee Consortium of Kenya, 'Refugees and Asylum Seekers Lament Limited Access to Work Permits in Kenya', website (January 2019); UNHCR, 'Kenya: Livelihoods', website.

316 Alix-Garcia et al., 'Do refugee camps help or hurt hosts?': p. 68. Sanghi, Onder and Vemuru, *"Yes" In My Backyard?*, pp. 3, 8, 10.

317 From the invasive Prosopis trees. Indigenous trees are protected against charcoal and firewood use.

318 Sanghi, Onder and Vemuru, *"Yes" In My Backyard?*, p. 11.

319 Ibid., p. 54; Alix-Garcia et al., 'Do refugee camps help or hurt hosts?': p. 76.

320 Sanghi, Onder and Vemuru, *"Yes" In My Backyard?*, pp. 29, 32.

321 This could include skills acquisition and technical support to improve farm cultivation and livestock production for more sustainable development. Alix-Garcia et al., 'Do refugee camps help or hurt hosts?': p.76. Moving from short humanitarian emergency funding to more long-term development investment would be beneficial. Sanghi, Onder and Vemuru, *"Yes" In My Backyard?*, p. 55. A subsequent 2019 UNHCR-World Bank socio-economic survey of refugees and hosts in Kakuma found that, although 62 per cent of Turkana hosts are employed compared to just 20 per cent of working age refugees, both groups lived in overcrowded dwellings with little access to electricity and inadequate sanitation. Secondary school attendance was low for both groups and food insecurity high. It recommends targeted investments to address these shortfalls, as well as investments in skills training to match market needs, and eased access to financial services to improve employment prospects for both refugees and host populations. Utz Pape et al., 'Understanding the Socio-Economic Conditions of Refugees in Kenya', vol. B: 'Kakuma Camp : Results from the 2019 Kakuma Socioeconomic Survey', Joint Report, World Bank Group and UNHCR (March 2021).

322 UNHCR, 'Kenya: Kalobeyei Settlement', website. Planning figures expected a population of 20,000 host community members and 60,000 refugees. As of December 2020, the majority of the settlement's residents were refugees (40,000). See: UNHCR, 'Kakuma & Kalobeyei Population Statistics'; UN Habitat, *Kakuma and Kalobeyei: Spatial Profile,* Report (June 2021), p. 50.

323 Pascal Zigashane, a refugee from the Democratic Republic of the Congo who heads a refugee-led initiative, describes the positive changes in Kakuma. Examples include new initiatives, such as food catering businesses run by women, the provision of tools and seeds, and the operation of a greenhouse which economically benefited refugees and members of the host community. This helped foster social cohesion. Pascal Bahati Zigashane, 'Strengthening Refugee Human Capital in Displacement', Reference Paper for the 70th Anniversary of the 1951 Refugee Convention, UNHCR (October 2021), p. 9.

324 Alexander Betts, Naohiko Omata, and Olivier Sterck, 'The Kalobeyei Settlement: A Self-Reliance Model for Refugees?', *Journal of Refugee Studies* 33, no. 1 (March 2020): pp. 189–223. Zigashane, 'Strengthening Refugee Human Capital in Displacement', p. 10.

325 Fix et al., 'Understanding the Socioeconomic Conditions of Refugees in Kenya', vol. A.

326 The self-reliance strategy (SRS) was introduced in 1998 initially to assist Sudanese refugees who were primarily located in three districts in the West Nile Region. It was later adopted as the main policy framework for refugee assistance in the country. In 2004, following a review of the SRS which revealed successes but also several shortcomings, it started to be transitioned into a Development Assistance for Refugee-Hosting Areas (DAR) programme. Shortly thereafter, the 2006 Refugees Act was drafted, requesting the Ugandan Commissioner for Refugees to "promote self-reliance among refugees and sustainable development in the affected areas". A decade later, the Refugee and Host Community Empowerment (ReHoPE) strategy was devised to again build on lessons learned from the previous approaches and further strengthen self-reliance prospects of refugees and host communities. UNHCR, *Handbook for Planning and Implementing Development Assistance for Refugees (DAR) Programmes* (2005), p. 25; World Bank Group, 'An Assessment of Uganda's Progressive Approach to Refugee Management' (May 2016), pp. 20–25; Government of Uganda, 'The Refugees Act' (2006), Act 21, para. 44.4(b).

327 UNHCR, Refugee Data Finder.

328 Office of the Prime Minister of Uganda and UNHCR, 'Revised Inter-Agency Uganda Country Refugee Response Plan, July 2020–December 2021' (August 2020), p. 10.

329 See, for example: Alexander Betts et al., *Refugee Economies in Uganda: What Difference Does the Self-Reliance Model Make?*, Report, Refugee Studies Centre (21 January 2019), pp. 18, 36. Only very limited support is available for vulnerable refugees in Kampala.

330 Merle Kreibaum, 'Their Suffering, Our Burden? How Congolese Refugees Affect the Ugandan Population', *World Development* 78 (February 2016): pp. 262–287.

331 UNHCR, Refugee Data Finder.

332 The decrease in poverty was evidenced by an increase in consumption. Education services improved with the assistance of non-governmental and private agencies assisted by the Government. Kreibaum, 'Their Suffering, Our Burden?': pp. 270, 272.

333 Ibid.: p. 271.

334 Ibid.: p. 275. A study published a few years later found that refugee businesses were of value in providing goods and services to host communities. For example, in Nakivale settlement near the border with Tanzania, host community members reported buying and selling goods and services in the settlement. As found in earlier studies, the benefits were not equally distributed, however, with some local workers struggling to compete with refugee labour, while others benefited from their demand for specific goods and housing, and others found employment in refugee-run businesses or households. Betts et al., *Refugee Economies in Uganda*, pp. 29–33.

335 For all refugees in Rwanda at the time, see: UNHCR, Refugee Data Finder. For refugees from the Democratic Republic of the Congo, see: UNHCR, Refugee Data Finder.

336 Craig Loschmann, Özge Bilgili, and Melissa Siegel, 'Considering the benefits of hosting refugees: evidence of refugee camps influencing local labour market activity and economic welfare in Rwanda', *IZA Journal of Development and Migration* 9, no. 1 (2019): pp. 5–6.

337 Ibid.: p. 6. The exceptional instance of camp-based schooling is noted in a separate paper which the same scholars co-authored: Özge Bilgili et al., 'Is the Education of Local Children Influenced by Living near a Refugee Camp? Evidence from Host Communities in Rwanda', *International Migration* 57, no. 4 (2019): p. 295.

338 Loschmann, Bilgili, and Siegel, 'Considering the benefits of hosting refugees': p. 6.

339 Ibid.: p. 19.

340 Ibid.: pp. 1, 3, 19.

341 Bilgili et al., 'Is the Education of Local Children Influenced by Living near a Refugee Camp?': pp. 305–306.

342 IDP figures from UNHCR, Refugee Data Finder.

343 Jennifer Alix-Garcia and Anne Bartlett, 'Occupations under fire: the labour market in a complex emergency', *Oxford Economic Papers* 67, no. 3 (July 2015): p. 688.

344 Ibid.: pp. 687, 710.

345 Ibid.: p. 710.

346 Ibid.: p. 711.

347 Verme and Schuettler, 'The Impact of Forced Displacement on Host Communities', pp. 11–12.

348 Ibid., p. 13.

349 Ibid., p. 16. The authors note the range in which positive and significant results are found is from 12–20 per cent and that of negative and significant results from 22–25 per cent.

350 The authors explain that some of the positive results could be a consequence of "the inflow of international aid and its relative importance in a poor country". Ibid.

351 Ibid., pp. 16–17. Also noted in Part III – this could shed light to the extent to which IDPs for example have attained a solution.

352 Clemens, Huang, and Graham, 'The Economic and Fiscal Effects of Granting Refugees Formal Labor Market Access', p. 20.

353 Ibid., p. 15. However, the authors note that, in many countries, a lack of education, skills and social norms can prevent women from working in the formal sector causing them to benefit less.

354 Ibid., p. 18.

355 World Bank, *Forcibly Displaced*, p. 134.

356 This is reflected in paras. 33–37 of the Global Compact on Refugees which note the importance of engaging a broad coalition of stakeholders and the critical role of development actors and development support.

PART V: **Bridging the Gap**

1   World Bank-UNHCR assessment mission, June 2021.

2   It also includes helping to prevent and prepare for man-made crises. Good Humanitarian Donorship Initiative, '24 Principles and Good Practice of Humanitarian Donorship', website.

3   Contributions rose by 12 per cent annually between 2011 and 2019. They did not rise in 2020, despite the increased need due to COVID-19. Development Initiatives, 'Global Humanitarian Assistance Report 2021' (June 2021), pp. 33–35.

4   Ibid., pp. 49, 61–62. The top government donors in recent years have been the United States, Germany and the United Kingdom. The top 10 recipient countries in 2019–2020 were: Syria; Yemen; Lebanon; South Sudan; the Democratic Republic of the Congo; Somalia; Sudan; Ethiopia; Turkey; and Iraq.

5   Ibid., p. 32.

6   Ibid., pp. 52–53. Specifically for the years 2015–2019.

7   Bringing the total number in need to some 244 million people across 75 countries. Ibid., pp. 12–13, 33.

8   In the past, some host countries have tried to capture this. But there has not been an agreed methodology for doing so. In 2017, the United Nations General Assembly requested UNHCR to "coordinate an effort to measure the impact arising from hosting, protecting and assisting refugees, with a view to assessing gaps in international cooperation and promoting burden- and responsibility-sharing that is more equitable, predictable and sustainable, and to begin reporting on the results to Member States in 2018". UN General Assembly, (19 December 2017), UN Doc A/RES/72/150, para. 20. This was further taken up in UNGA, Global Compact on Refugees (2 August 2018), UN Doc A/73/12 (Part II), para. 103. UNHCR issued its first report 1 July 2020. UNHCR,

'Progress report: Measuring the impact of hosting, protecting and assisting refugees' (1 July 2020).

9   Global Compact on Refugees (2018), para. 32.

10 World Humanitarian Summit, 'FAQ', website. For previous efforts by UNHCR to engage more development responses, see: Part III. One of the earliest efforts was by High Commissioner, Sadruddin Aga Khan, pursued also by subsequent High Commissioners. Sadruddin Aga Khan, 'Statement by Prince Sadruddin Aga Khan, United Nations High Commissioner for Refugees, to the Third Committee of the United Nations General Assembly at Its 1519th Meeting' (20 November 1967), *UNHCR* website.

11 UN High-Level Panel on Humanitarian Financing, *Report to the Secretary-General: Too important to fail: addressing the humanitarian financing gap* (January 2016). The panel was co-chaired by Kristalina Georgieva, then European Commissioner for Humanitarian Aid and Crisis Management, and HRH Sultan Nazrin Shah, Ruler of Merak, Malaysia. The Grand Bargain has 63 signatories: 25 member States; 22 NGOs; 12 United Nations agencies; 2 inter-governmental organizations; and the International Committee of the Red Cross (ICRC) and International Federation of Red Cross and Red Crescent Societies (IFRC). The signatories represent over 80 per cent of all donor humanitarian contributions in 2019, and two thirds of humanitarian aid received by agencies. Inter-Agency Standing Committee, 'The Grand Bargain: A Shared Commitment to Better Serve People in Need' (23 May 2016).

12 UNGA, New York Declaration for Refugees and Migrants (3 October 2016), UN Doc A/RES/71/1, para. 38.

13 Global Compact on Refugees (2018), para. 32.

14 Victoria Metcalfe-Hough et al., 'Grand Bargain annual independent report 2020', Humanitarian Policy Group Commissioned Report, Overseas Development Institute (June 2020), p. 17.

15 Ibid.; Victoria Metcalfe-Hough et al., 'The Grand Bargain at five years: An independent review', HPG Commissioned Review, ODI (June 2021), pp. 47, 49, 57, 109. For example, more organizations are investing in the capacities of local and national responders and additional donors are providing flexible and predictable funding.

16 Metcalfe-Hough et al., 'Grand Bargain annual independent report 2020', p. 18.

17 Funding that is earmarked is provided for a specific purpose, programme and/or location. The agency cannot use the funds for other reasons, even for meeting more prioritized needs. For more on the role of earmarked funding and suggestions for improvement, see: Organisation for Economic Co-operation and Development, 'Earmarked funding to multilateral organisations: how is it used and what constitutes good practice?', Brief (October 2020).

18 Metcalfe-Hough et al., 'Grand Bargain annual independent report 2020', pp. 15, 18; Metcalfe-Hough et al., 'The Grand Bargain at five years', p. 113. As of March 2021, just nine of the 37 signatories that provide funds to international organizations or to implementing partners were using the common reporting template as the standard format.

19 Barnaby Willitts-King and Alexandra Spencer, *Reducing the humanitarian financing gap: review of progress since the report of the High-Level Panel on Humanitarian Financing*, HPG Commissioned Report, ODI (April 2020), p. 8.

20 Metcalfe-Hough et al., 'The Grand Bargain at five years', p. 47.

21 Ibid., pp. 38, 79–80.

22 Ibid., pp. 59, 69–70; Metcalfe-Hough et al., 'Grand Bargain annual independent report 2020', pp. 15, 34, 54–56, 68–71, 104. This is discussed later in this Part under the section on Partnerships.

...PART V: **Bridging the Gap...**

23   IFIs are established by more than one country and subject to international law. The most well-known, the World Bank and the International Monetary Fund, were established after World War II to assist in the reconstruction of Europe. The largest IFI is the European Investment Bank. See: European Investment Bank, 'Who we are', website.

24   World Bank, *Forcibly Displaced: Toward a Development Approach Supporting Refugees, the Internally Displaced, and Their Hosts* (Washington, D.C: World Bank, 2017).

25   As of the end of the fiscal year ending 30 June 2021, "IDA commitments totaled $36 billion, with about 70 percent going to Africa". International Development Association 'What is IDA?' website.

26   IDA, 'Information Statement: International Development Association', Report, World Bank (24 September 2020), p. 5; IDA, 'What is IDA?'.

27   World Bank Group, 'IDA18 Regional Sub-Window for Refugees and Host Communities', IDA-World Bank website.

28   'Window for Refugees and Host Communities', IDA-World Bank website. The COVID-19 funding is all in grants.

29   Notably, the International Finance Corporation (IFC) and the Multilateral Investment Guarantee Agency (MIGA), both of which are discussed under the section on private sector financing below. These are two of the five institutions of the WBG. The other three are: the International Bank for Reconstruction and Development (IBRD); the International Development Association (IDA); and the International Centre for Settlement of Investment Disputes (ICSID). The WBG is comprised of all five, while the World Bank is made up of the IBRD and IDA.

30   IDA, 'IDA18 Retrospective: Investing in Growth, Resilience, and Opportunity through Innovation', Report, IDA-World Bank (April 2021), pp. 16, 66.

31   Ibid., p. 16. Discussed further under Application.

32   Ibid. Social protection programmes comprise social assistance or safety nets, such as cash transfers and food assistance, as well as social insurance schemes, such as old-age pensions, disability pensions and unemployment insurance. World Bank Group, *Resilience, Equity, and Opportunity: Social Protection and Labor Strategy 2012–2022* (2012), Part IV.

33   Between 2016 and 2020, the proportion of refugees and asylum-seekers, excluding Venezuelans, displaced abroad in middle-income countries dropped from 58 per cent to 55 per cent. However, the proportion of all cross-border displaced persons of concern to UNHCR, including refugees, asylum-seekers and Venezuelans displaced abroad increased from 58 per cent to 59 per cent. UNHCR Refugee Population Statistics Database. Income groups are from the World Bank List of Economies (June 2020).

34   Global Concessional Financing Facility (GCFF), *GCFF Annual Report 2018–2019* (2019), p. 5; GCFF, 'Progress Report: 1 July–31 December 2020', December 2020.

35   The MDBs are: IsDB; European Bank for Reconstruction and Development; WBG; and the European Investment Bank. See: GCFF website.

36   GCFF, 'Progress Report: 1 July–31 December 2020', pp. 9–10. In addition, close to $130 million in grants from supporting countries were available or pledged for further projects.

37   Discussed in Part IV. See also: Doreen Kibuka-Musoke and Zara Sarzin, 'Financing for Forced Displacement Situations', Reference Paper for the 70th Anniversary of the 1951 Refugee Convention, UNHCR (October 2021).

38   Discussed in Part II and Part III. Weiyi Wang and Ozan Cakmak, 'Private Sector Initiatives

in Forced Displacement Contexts: Constraints and Opportunities for a Market-Based Approach', Reference Paper for the 70th Anniversary of the 1951 Refugee Convention, UNHCR (October 2021). UNHCR, 'UNHCR's support to the Temporary Protection Status in Colombia', Press Release (12 May 2021).

39 Ecuador is discussed in Part III: Solutions. In Lebanon, political and economic challenges as well as the COVID-19 pandemic have stalled progress on project approval and implementation. GCFF, 'Progress Report: 1 July–31 December 2020', pp. 15–19; GCFF, *Annual Report 2019–2020* (2021), pp. 12–13, 19–21.

40 Participating members of the Global Forum are: African Development Bank (AfDB); Asian Development Bank (ADB); European Bank for Reconstruction and Development (EBRD); European Investment Bank (EID); Inter-American Development Bank (IADB); and IsDB and the WBG.

41 African Development Bank Group et al., 'Joint Commitments by the MDB Coordination Platform on Economic Migration and Forced Displacement', Statement, Global Refugee Forum in Geneva, 17–18 December 2019.

42 World Bank Group, 'MDBs launch new platform to coordinate support for economic migration and forced displacement', Press Release (20 April 2018).

43 OECD, '60th Anniversary Timeline', website.

44 OECD, 'Development Assistance Committee (DAC)', website.

45 OECD DAC International Network on Conflict and Fragility (INCAF), 'INCAF Common Position on supporting comprehensive responses in refugee situations', Document (2019). The INCAF common position was based on: OECD, 'Financing for refugee situations', Development Policy Paper no. 24 (December 2019).

46 Nibal Zgheib, 'Multilateral development banks stepping up support for refugees', European Bank for Reconstruction and Development (EBRD) News (16 December 2019).

47 In its refugee response programme, the EBRD "promotes a strong role for the private sector" to boost employment for hosts and refugees alike and spur improvements to infrastructure, urban life, the environment and the overall economy. EBRD, 'Refugees: building host countries' resilience', website.

48 Senidu Fanuel, 'Ethiopia: Jobs Compact Project', Program-For-Results Information Document, World Bank (8 July 2017), pp. 2–3, 7.

49 World Bank, 'Ethiopia: World Bank Pledges $202 Million to Provide Better Economic Opportunities for Refugees and Host Communities', Press Release (26 June 2018); Ndiaye Jade Elena Garza, 'Ethiopia Economic Opportunities Program', Implementation Status and Results Report, World Bank (4 May 2021).

50 Federal Democratic Republic of Ethiopia, 'Refugees Proclamation' (27 February 2019), Proclamation No. 1110/2019; UNHCR, 'UNHCR welcomes Ethiopia law granting more rights to refugees', Press Release (18 January 2019).

51 Global Compact on Refugees, 'Development Actors', website (15 December 2020); IDB, 'IDB approves grant funds for countries receiving migrants in Latin America and Caribbean', IDB News (7 May 2019).

52 Ibid.

53 Ibid.

54 AfDB, 'Transition Support Facility: About the Facility', website (17 April 2019). The facility was previously known as the Fragile States Facility.

55 However, through its Africa Development Fund, the Bank has provided concessional financing to low-income countries including those with significant forcibly displaced

populations. This has supported energy for cooking and environmental restoration in refugee camps in Burundi; livelihoods in Zimbabwe; women's empowerment in East Africa; and a major regional COVID-19 support project in the G5 Sahel countries (Burkina Faso; Chad; Mali; Mauritania; and Niger). African Development Bank Group Data Portal, 2020.

56   Independent Development Evaluation, *Evaluation of the AfDB's Strategy for Addressing Fragility and Building Resilience in Africa (2014–2019),* Summary Report, AfDB Group (June 2020), pp. 14, 28; Transition Support Department (ORTS), 'African Development Bank Group Strategy for Addressing Fragility and Building Resilience in Africa (2014-2019)', AfDB Group (n.d.), p. 43.

57   Kibuka-Musoke and Sarzin, 'Financing for Forced Displacement Situations', pp. 27–28. Financing for these programmes comes from the GCFF.

58   See, for example: World Bank, 'Uganda Support to Municipal Infrastructure Development Program', Development Project, 2013; World Bank, 'Economic Opportunities for Jordanians and Syrian Refugees', Program for Results Project, 2016; World Bank, 'Ethiopia Economic Opportunities Program', Development Project, 2018; World Bank, 'Improving Quality of Health Care Services and Efficiency in Colombia', Development Project, 2020.

59   See, for example: Global Compact on Refugees (2018), paras. 32, 71; UN Secretary-General's High-Level Panel on Internal Displacement, *Shining a Light on Internal Displacement: A Vision for the Future*, Report (September 2021), pp. 17, 24–27, 30.

60   World Bank et al., 'The Role of the Private Sector in Economic Integration of Refugees: Charter of Good Practice' (2019).

61   World Economic Forum, 'Humanitarian Investing – Mobilizing Capital to Overcome Fragility', White Paper (September 2019).

62   Ibid., pp. 4, 11, 14–15. Among the areas of focus are: water and sanitation, agriculture and food security, health, energy, employment and education, financial inclusion and capital markets, and technology.

63   International Finance Corporation and The Bridgespan Group, 'Private Sector & Refugees—Pathways to Scale', Report (2019), p. 8. The report surveyed over 170 private sector initiatives in displacement contexts. Around half of those for whom detailed information was available invested less than $1 million and reached a maximum of 10,000 refugees, pp. 3, 7–8.

64   The Jordan Compact is an example discussed in Part IV and later in this Part.

65   The World Bank's "Ease of Doing Business" ranking scores countries in categories, such as "enforcing contracts", "trading across borders", "getting electricity", "registering a property" or "getting credit". The best score is one and the worst is 190. Among the 16 million refugees living in the largest host countries at the end of 2019, nearly 8 million lived in countries that scored 108–182 in the latest index. The situation is even worse in internal displacement situations. Among the 35 million internally displaced persons who were hosted in the top 10 largest host countries at the end of 2019, 27 million lived in countries which scored 131–190 with most IDPs in countries that are within the last 25 rankings in the list. Data from: World Bank, 'Ease of Doing Business Rankings', website; UNHCR, *Global Trends: Forced Displacement in 2019*, Report (2019).

66   Ibid. pp. 6, 10, 20, 22.

67   Wang and Cakmak, 'Private Sector Initiatives in Forced Displacement'.

68   Ibid., pp. 7–8.

69 See, for example, the situation in Dadaab, Kenya: UNHCR and ILO, *Doing Business in Dadaab Report: Market Systems Analysis for Local Economic Development in Dadaab, Kenya*, Report (January 2019), p. 17.

70 Many refugee businesses operate informally and, because they are not registered with the authorities, they cannot engage easily with medium or large legal enterprises. Wang and Cakmak, 'Private Sector Initiatives in Forced Displacement', pp. 7–10.

71 Ibid., p. 7–10.

72 Ibid., p. 10.

73 See: endnote 29.

74 IFC, *Kakuma as a Marketplace – A consumer and market study of a refugee camp and town in northwest Kenya*, Report (April 2018).

75 Firms that seek to maximize social and environmental objectives as well as profits.

76 IFC, *Kakuma as a Marketplace*, pp. 79–80.

77 BFA Global, UNHCR, and AFR, *Refugees and Their Money: The Business Case for Providing Financial Services to Refugees*, Report (March 2018), pp. 9–11. The study found that financial service providers are likely to generate similar levels of profit from serving refugees as from serving typical low-income Rwandan customers. The demand among refugee communities and access to banking yields the potential to improve income-generating opportunities through savings and microcredit options. It recommended that Rwanda's national bank issue a directive that expands the list of acceptable identity documentation to reduce access barriers.

78 UNHCR and ILO, *Doing Business in Dadaab*, pp. viii, 17–19, 42, 59–60.

79 Irene Yuan Sun and Cindy Huang, *Designing a Medium-Term Response to the Rohingya Refugee Crisis: Ideas for Bangladesh, the International Community, and the Private Sector*, Report, Center for Global Development (December 2019), pp. vii–x, 7–14, 21–24.

80 The number of Somali refugees in Dollo Ado reached and surpassed 200,000 in 2014 and remained on this level until mid-2019. UNHCR, 'Horn of Africa Somalia Situation', Operational Data Portal.

81 Alexander Betts et al., 'Building Refugee Economies: An evaluation of the IKEA Foundation's programmes in Dollo Ado', Report, Refugee Studies Centre (May 2020), pp. 23–24.

82 Ibid., pp. 10–14. The environment-friendly income-generating project intended to reduce reliance on firewood for energy, cooking and income. The aim was to reduce the negative impact on the environment, reduce risks for women who are traditionally relied upon to collect wood from remote locations, and establish a commercially viable production of an alternative energy source (Prosopis). However, the results of this particular intervention have been mixed.

83 The cooperatives function on a self-employment basis, whereby each member generates her/his own income but deposits an agreed share into a joint savings account. However, the savings are not yet sufficient to cover the cost of productive inputs for the cooperative. Alexander Betts and Raphael Bradenbrink, 'The IKEA Foundation and livelihoods in Dollo Ado: Lessons from the cooperatives model', *RSC Research in Brief* 17 (December 2020): pp. 1, 4.

84 Betts et al., 'Building Refugee Economies', pp. 10–12, 50–52, 139–140; Wang and Cakmak, 'Private Sector Initiatives in Forced Displacement Contexts', p. 19.

85 GSMA, *Mobile Is a Lifeline: Research from Nyarugusu Refugee Camp, Tanzania*, Report (2017), p. 2.

86 UNHCR, 'Tanzania Refugee Population Update', Factsheet (30 June 2021).

87 GSMA, *Mobile Is a Lifeline*, pp. 12–13; UNHCR Innovation Service, 'How to Work With

...PART V: Bridging the Gap...

Mobile Network Operators – Lessons from Tanzania', UNHCR website (10 November 2018). For more on Vodacom, see: Vodacom, 'About us', website.

88   Turkcell, 'Corporate Social Responsibility: Refugees', website.

89   World Bank, 'The World Bank Group's Experience with the IDA Private Sector Window: An Early-Stage Assessment', Report (July 2021). Recent findings point to: the possible need to adjust terms depending on the market context; the potential use of alternative approaches to mitigate non-financial risks; and the importance of technical assistance to the private sector in the implementation of projects.

90   See, for example: OECD, 'Blended Finance', website.

91   The acronym FMO stands for *Nederlandse Financierings-Maatschappij voor Ontwikke-lingslanden N.V.*

92   FMO, 'NASIRA: A new chance guaranteed', NASIRA/FMO News.

93   Investment made in one economy by the resident of another foreign economy with the aim to establish a lasting management interest there.

94   Multilateral Investment Guarantee Agency (MIGA), 'What We Do', website. Hard currency refers to United States Dollars, Euro or Yen. Inability to transfer refers to situations resulting from a government action or failure to act.

95   Wang and Cakmak, 'Private Sector Initiatives in Forced Displacement Contexts', p. 18.

96   World Bank Group, 'Refugee Investment & Matchmaking Platform (RIMP): Progress, Results & Opportunities', Report (15 January 2021), pp. 6–9, 67, 70. In Jordan, the RIMP studied the status of Syrian-owned businesses, their contributions to the Jordanian economy as well as potential for growth. Its methodology is to work closely with the Government in the preparation phase and to build local capacities to sustain the initiative, and improve transparency and accountability of joint enterprises.

97   The Jordan Compact is more fully covered in Part IV.

98   Kibuka-Musoke and Sarzin, 'Financing for Forced Displacement Situations'; Heliodoro Temprano Arroyo, 'Promoting Labour Market Integration of Refugees with Trade Preferences: Beyond the EU-Jordan Compact', EUI Working Papers, RSCAS 2018/42, European University Institute (2018), pp. 8–12, 25–27, 33; Kimberly Ann Elliott and Heliodoro Temprano Arroyo, 'Using Trade Preferences to Support Refugees and their Hosts', CDG Note (December 2019), pp. 3, 11.

99   UNHCR Zakat Program, 'Refugees: The Most in Need of Zakat Fund – Assessing How Zakat Can Drastically Improve the Lives of the World's Displaced Population', Launch Report (2019), p. 14.

100 Ibid., pp. 23–24. *Sadaqah* is also a form of Islamic charity, involving voluntary donations, and UNHCR has taken a similar approach in regard to its potential.

101 UNHCR Zakat Program, 'About The Refugee Zakat Fund', website.

102 UNHCR, 'Islamic Philanthropy: Transforming the Lives of the World's Displaced', Annual Impact Report (2021), p. 8.

103 Based on 2020 estimates. Market Data Forecast, 'Global Crowdfunding Market Research Report: Segmentation by Product (Awards-Based Crowdfunding, Crowdfunding Auctions, and others), End-users (Cultural Industries, Technology, Product, Healthcare, Others), Industry Analysis, Size, Share, Growth, Trends & Forecast To 2026' (April 2021).

104 Ibid.

105 Business Wire, 'Global Crowdfunding Market: Insights, Trends and Outlook 2020–2025 – ResearchAndMarkets.com', website (July 2020). For examples and information on crowd-funding campaigns related to COVID-19, see: Sameh Nagui Saleh, Christoph U. Lehmann, and Richard J. Medford, 'Early Crowdfunding Response to the COVID-19 Pandemic: Cross-Sectional Study', *Journal of Medical Internet Research* 23, no. 2 (February 2021): p. e25429; Ann Danaiya Usher, 'WHO Launches Crowdfund for COVID-19 Response', *The Lancet* 395, no. 10229 (March 2020): p. 1024; Greater London Authority, 'Mayor launches new fund to help local communities drive Covid recovery', website (3 December 2020).

106 Kiva, 'World Refugee Day', website; Kiva 'Our Impact', *Kiva Refugees* website.

107 Kiva 'Our Impact'.

108 Business Wire, 'Kiva to Scale Lending to Refugees with the Launch of the Kiva Refugee Investment Fund', website (20 June 2019).

109 Kibuka-Musoke and Sarzin, 'Financing for Forced Displacement Situations', p. 31.

110 Cameroon, Chile, Congo, Guinea, Madagascar, Mali, Mauritius, Niger and the Republic of Korea. Unitaid, 'About Us', website.

111 Unitaid, 'French levy on airline tickets raises more than one billion euros for world's poor since 2006', *Unitaid* News (25 January 2013).

112 Allan Rock, 'Using Frozen Assets to Assist the Forcibly Displaced: A Policy Proposal for Canada', Discussion Paper, World Refugee Council (10 April 2018); Selim Can Sazak, 'An Argument for Using Frozen Assets for Humanitarian Assistance in Refugee Situations', *Journal of International Affairs* 68, no. 2 (Spring/Summer 2015): pp. 305–318.

113 UN Security Council, 'Sanctions', website.

114 UNSC, Res. 778 (1992), UN Doc S/RES/778; UNSC, Res. 721 (1991), UN Doc S/RES/721; UNSC, Res. 706 (1991), UN Doc S/RES/706. For a discussion of the Security Council powers in this regard, as well as the potential for it to secure compensation in other untried means, see: Guy S. Goodwin-Gill and Selim Can Sazak, 'Footing the Bill: Refugee-Creating States' Responsibility to Pay', *Foreign Affairs* (29 July 2015); United Nations Charter (1945), Chapter VII, arts. 39, 41 and 42.

115 The Global Magnitsky Human Rights Accountability Act (2016) authorizes the US President to impose sanctions on, and deny entry to, foreign nationals who have engaged in significant corruption or engaged directly or indirectly in serious human rights abuses. In 2003, the United States confiscated $1.7 billion dollars in frozen Iraqi assets to assist in the reconstruction of Iraq. For more on this, see: Allan Rock, 'Using Frozen Assets to Assist the Forcibly Displaced', pp. 3–4, 9.

116 Phil Orchard, 'International, Regional, and Domestic Mechanisms to Hold States to Account for the Causes of Forced Displacement', Reference Paper for the 70th Anniversary of the 1951 Refugee Convention, UNHCR (October 2021), p. 24; Council of the European Union, 'concerning restrictive measures against serious human rights violations and abuse' (7 December 2020), Decision (CFSP) 2020/1999; Council of the European Union, 'EU adopts a global human rights sanctions regime', Press Release (7 December 2020).

117 Joint Standing Committee on Foreign Affairs, Defence and Trade, 'Criminality, corruption and impunity: should Australia join the Global Magnitsky movement?: An inquiry into targeted sanctions to address human rights abuses', Report, Parliament of Australia (December 2020); Reuters, 'Australia to adopt Magnitsky style sanctions law', website (5 August 2021).

118 The Swiss Confederation, Federal Act on the Freezing and the Restitution of Illicit Assets Held by Foreign Politically Exposed Persons (2015), SR 196.1, arts. 1–4 and art. 17; François

...PART V: **Bridging the Gap...**

Membrez and Matthieu Hösli, *How to Return Stolen Assets: The Swiss policy pathway,* Report, Centre for Civil and Political Rights and Anti-Corruption and Human Rights Initiative (February 2020); World Refugee Council, *A Call to Action: Transforming the Global Refugee System*, Report (January 2019), p. 64.

119 Ben Parker, 'Saving lives and making money: Can humanitarian impact bonds marry the two?', *The New Humanitarian* (15 August 2019).

120 Ibid. Under the terms of an ICRC bond to fund medical centres, if the project fails to meet its objectives, the outcome funders pay no interest and only pay back 50 per cent of the investor's principal, and ICRC must pay back a further 10 per cent of the investors' original stake. See also: Kibuka-Musoke and Sarzin, 'Financing for Forced Displacement Situations', p. 36.

121 According to the Brookings Institution, just 19 of 214 Impact Bonds contracted globally were in developing countries. Emily Gustafsson-Wright and Sarah Osborne, 'Brookings Impact Bonds Snapshot: August 1, 2021', Factsheet, *Brookings Institution* website. For more information on impact bonds, see: Government Outcomes Lab, 'Impact bonds', website.

122 Burton Bollag, 'ICRC launches world's first Humanitarian Impact Bond', Devex News, September 8, 2017. International Committee of the Red Cross, 'The world's first "Humanitarian Impact Bond" launched to transform financing of aid in conflict-hit countries', Press Release (6 September 2017); Parker, 'Saving lives and making money'.

123 Kay Lau et al., *Findings from the second research wave of the Independent Evaluation of the FCDO Development Impact Bonds Pilot Programme*, Report, Ecorys (February 2021).

124 See, for example: Parker, 'Saving lives and making money'. The United Kingdom-funded evaluation of the ICRC mechanisms included suggestions to lower transaction costs, while also recognizing that some of the benefits of impact bonds could be achieved through other well-defined grants. Kay Lau, et al., *Findings from the second research wave of the Independent Evaluation of the FCDO Development Impact Bonds Pilot Programme*, pp. 74, 87, 91; Kibuka-Musoke and Sarzin, 'Financing for Forced Displacement Situations'.

125 Refugee Investment Network, 'Kois Invest', website; Parker, 'Saving lives and making money'.

126 The Commission on International Development investigated the effectiveness of the World Bank's development assistance. Commission on International Development, *Partners in Development: Report of the Commission on International Development* (London: Pall Mall Press, 1969). In the 1990s, as part of the revised System of National Accounts, "gross national product was replaced by gross national income (GNI), an equivalent concept". OECD, 'The 0.7% ODA/GNI Target − a history', website.

127 UNGA, 'International Development Strategy for the Second United Nations Development Decade' (1970), A/RES/262 (XXV), para. 43.

128 The countries reaching it by 1980 were Denmark, the Netherlands, Norway and Sweden. Subsequently, Finland achieved it once, Luxembourg more continuously and, as of 2016, the United Kingdom for a period. But as of 2016, "no other DAC country has met the target since it was established, and the weighted average of DAC members' ODA has never exceeded 0.4% of GNP". DAC, 'History of the ODA Target', *DAC Journal* 3, no. 4 (2002): pp. III-9−III-11.

129 The 2005 World Summit was convened to take decisions in the areas of development, security, human rights and United Nations reform and was attended by 170 Heads of State and government actors. In its outcome document, the ambition to reach 0.7 per cent of GDP for official development assistance was reaffirmed. United Nations, 'The 2005 World Summit High-Level Plenary Meeting of the 60th session of the UN General Assembly', held in New York, 14–16 September 2005; UNGA, '2005 World Summit Outcome' (16 September 2005), UN Doc A/RES/60/1, para. 23 (a), (b).

130 G8, 'The Gleneagles Communiqué' (2005), Annex II.

131 OECD, 'COVID-19 spending helped to lift foreign aid to an all-time high in 2020 but more effort needed', *OECD* News (April 13 2021). Turkey, which is not among the DAC donors, reported that it provided aid equivalent to more than 1 per cent of its GNI.

132 Charley Coleman, 'Reduction in the UK's 0.7 percent ODA target', *House of Lords Library* website (18 June 2021).

133 For example, for much of the last decade, over 95 per cent of humanitarian funding came from 20 donors, and three of them contributed over half of the total. Kibuka-Musoke and Sarzin, 'Financing for Forced Displacement Situations', pp. 14–15; Development Initiatives, 'Global Humanitarian Assistance Report 2021', p. 49.

134 Similarly, most analyses on global humanitarian financing are based on United Nations coordinated appeals, which account for an estimated 66 per cent of all international humanitarian funding requests. They too provide only global amounts and are not specific to forced displacement contexts. They also do not include all donors. For more on the limitations of available data, see: Kibuka-Musoke and Sarzin, 'Financing for Forced Displacement Situations', pp. 8–9, 14.

135 The data is comparable, verified by the OECD and regularly collected (on a yearly basis). OECD, 'In-donor refugee costs', website.

136 OECD, 'Financing for Refugee Situations'; OECD, 'COVID-19 spending helped to lift foreign aid to an all-time high in 2020 but more effort needed'. Total Official Support for Sustainable Development (TOSSD) is designed to monitor all official resources flowing into developing countries for their sustainable development, as well as private resources mobilized through official means. See: TOSSD website.

137 DAC Working Party on Development Finance Statistics, 'Adjusting Development Cooperation Modalities to Track Support to Refugees in Developing Countries and Refugees Returning to Their Countries of Origin', Document, OECD (November 2020).

138 The relevant Global Compact on Refugees indicators are: number of donors providing ODA to, or for the benefit of, refugees and host communities in refugee-hosting countries (1.1.2); proportion of ODA provided to, or for the benefit of refugees and host communities, channelled to national actors in refugee-hosting countries (1.2.1); volume of ODA provided to, or for the benefit of, refugee returnees in the country of origin (4.1.1); number of donors providing ODA to, or for the benefit of, refugee returnees in the country of origin (4.1.2). UNHCR, 'Global Compact on Refugees: Indicator Framework', Report (July 2019), p. 10.

139 UNHCR, 'Elements of the oral update on UNHCR's coordination efforts to measure the impact arising from hosting, protecting and assisting refugees', 81st meeting of the Standing Committee, 5–7 July 2021; UNHCR, 'Oral update on UNHCR's coordination efforts to measure the impact arising from hosting, protecting and assisting refugees', 78th meeting of the Standing Committee, 7–9 July 2020.

140 Development Initiatives, Global Humanitarian Assistance Report 2021, p. 32.

141 Global Compact on Refugees (2018), paras. 45–47, 58, 82.

142 This includes registration, population movement tracking systems, national population censuses and population registrars, as well as sample and estimation methods for producing statistics when adequate and reliable data on individuals is unavailable. UN Economic and Social Council, 'Report of Statistics Norway and the Office of the United Nations High Commissioner for Refugees on Statistics on refugees and internally displaced persons' (8 December 2014), UN Doc E/CN.3/2015/9, pp. 6–7.

143 Registration is resource-intensive and many States do not have sufficient resources or technical expertise. In such situations, UNHCR supports the registration of refugees. This is recognized in UNHCR's Executive Committee Conclusions. See, for example: UNGA, 'Report of the Fifty-second Session of the Executive Committee of the High Commissioner's Programme', Conclusion on registration of refugees and asylum-seekers (5 October 2001), UN Doc A/AC.96/959, III B. Some of the world's largest refugee-hosting States, such as Iran, Pakistan and Turkey, register refugees, but many others rely on UNHCR.

144 The importance of identity documents has also been emphasized by UNHCR's Executive Committee. See, for example: UNGA, 'Addendum to the Report of the United Nations High Commissioner for Refugees', Conclusion of the Executive Committee of the High Commissioner's Programme on identity documents for refugees (5 November 1984) UN Doc A/39/12/Add.1, Part IV, para. 87 (3).

145 UNHCR, *Guidance on Registration and Identity Management*, chapter 3.2, 'Design a registration strategy'. UNHCR's Biometric Identity Management System (BIMS) is a centralized database that securely stores registration data. It allows real-time consolidation and verification of identity across all UNHCR operations. It provides a swift means to check identity and verify refugee numbers.

146 The value of national data management systems, current gaps and recommendations for remedying them are discussed in the report of the High-Level Panel on Internal Displacement. Recommendations include prioritizing State-led efforts, ensuring interoperability across government departments, aligning national with international reporting frameworks, and increased financial support from the international community. UN Secretary-General's High-Level Panel on Internal Displacement, *Shining a Light on Internal Displacement*, pp. 37–39.

147 See: Part II. See also: Natalia Krynsky Baal, 'Forced Displacement Data: Critical gaps and key opportunities in the context of the Global Compact on Refugees', Reference Paper for the 70th Anniversary of the 1951 Refugee Convention, UNHCR (October 2021), p. 8.

148 In its submission to the High-Level Panel on Internal Displacement, the World Bank commented on definitional ambiguity and specifically in regard to solutions. One of the criteria is "when people have an adequate standard of living and access to employment". According to the World Bank, this places the bar so high that it "is almost impossible to reach it in many developing countries", including for those who are not forcibly displaced. The World Bank recommended a durable solution to be defined as "the point where IDPs are living in conditions that are similar to the rest of the population, including in terms of progress towards key SDGs". World Bank, 'Issues for Consideration', Submission to the High-Level Panel on Internal Displacement, p. 4.

149 Specific needs can include: legal status; loss of assets; trauma experienced; as well as physical disabilities and other health vulnerabilities.

150 In some situations, it might not be necessary or possible to safely collect individual data due to protection, financial and/or time constraints. In such situations, collecting detailed data from a representative sub-group of the displaced population can provide relevant information about the overall population. To ensure the sample is representative, other data (for example from registration) may also be needed. Krynsky Baal, 'Forced Displacement Data', pp. 16–21.

151 Zara Sarzin, 'Stocktaking of Global Forced Displacement Data', Policy Research Working Paper no. 7985, World Bank (February 2017), p. 8. For examples on how socioeconomic data can inform evidence-based programming, policy and advocacy, see: UNHCR, *Using Socioeconomic Evidence for Action in Forcibly Displaced Contexts* vol. 1, Report (June 2021).

152 UNHCR's guidance makes a distinction between data to be collected in the context of an emergency, which is far less than more in-depth data collected in a more stable context. UNHCR, *Guidance on Registration and Identity Management*, chapter 3.4, 'Define the data set'.

153 UNHCR is also undertaking steps to expand data when refugees come to UNHCR subsequently or when UNHCR is notified of significant events, such as births, deaths and marriages. Verification exercises also provide an additional opportunity. Verification exercises are a means to determine whether those who originally registered have remained in the country, and to update their personal data and further ascertain their needs. They are a time-bound registration activity conducted in a specific area and/or for a specific population. This entails verifying and updating individual registration records and collecting additional information, as necessary, such as level of assets, health and employment status, and degree of access to safe water, sanitation and appropriate accommodation. UNHCR, *Guidance on Registration and Identity Management*, chapter 8.3, 'Verification exercises'.

154 Discussed earlier in Parts III and IV. Other examples include the annual inter-agency vulnerability assessments of Syrian refugees in Lebanon (VASyR) and Jordan (VAF). The VASyr has been carried out since 2013 and the VAF since 2014. Annual Reports available on: The VASyR Hub website; VAF Working Group available on UNHCR Operational Data Portal.

155 Krynsky Baal, 'Forced Displacement Data', p. 12.

156 Krynsky Baal, 'Forced Displacement Data', p. 7.

157 IASC, 'The Grand Bargain', p. 8. UN Secretary-General's High-Level Panel on Internal Displacement, *Shining a Light on Internal Displacement*, pp. 38–39; Krynsky Baal, 'Forced Displacement Data', p. 6.

158 IASC, 'The Grand Bargain', pp. 7–9.

159 In its 2019–2020 annual report, the JDC also provides additional examples of collaborative work on surveys and welfare studies in Bangladesh, Ethiopia and the Mashreq, as well as across multiple countries in regard to the impact of COVID-19. Joint Data Center on Forced Displacement, *Annual Report 2019–2020* (2021), pp. 4, 14–19, 22–23. The IASC has developed a 'Joint Intersectoral Analysis Framework (JIAF)' which is applied in 28 countries. Feedback received will inform further refinements to it. See: IASC, 'Workstream 5 on Joint Needs Analysis: Application of the Joint Intersectoral Analysis Framework underway', website (27 January 2021).

160 See: Part III. Karen Jacobsen and Therese Bjørn Mason, *Measuring Progress Towards Solutions in Darfur*, Review, UK Aid and Durable Solutions Working Group, (May 2020); Varalakshmi Vemuru, Aditya Sarkar, and Andrea Fitri Woodhouse, *Impact of Refugees on Hosting Communities in Ethiopia: A Social Analysis*, Report, World Bank (2020); Utz

Johann Pape and Ambika Sharma, *Informing Durable Solutions for Internal Displacement in Nigeria, Somalia, South Sudan, and Sudan vol.* A: 'Overview', World Bank Group (2019).

161   In 2018, a socioeconomic profiling exercise of refugees in Kalobeyei, Kenya was designed to align to Kenya's national household survey. This was important for it enabled comparisons to be made with Kenyan households in Turkana County. The exercise found that proportionately more refugee children were enrolled in school than host community children from Turkana County and both groups had lower levels of school enrollment and literacy than the Kenyan national average. In regard to economic activity, 35 per cent of non-refugee Turkana residents were out of work, compared to 26 per cent nationally. Refugees fell much further behind, with 59 per cent not engaged in economic activity. The profiling exercise was important to help guide humanitarian and development efforts. Jedediah Rooney Fix et al., 'Understanding the Socioeconomic Conditions of Refugees in Kenya', vol. A: 'Kalobeyei Settlement: Results from the 2018 Kalobeyei Socioeconomic Profiling Survey', Joint Report, World Bank Group and UNHCR (2019), pp. 13–17.

162   World Bank, 'Informing the Refugee Policy Response in Uganda: Results from the Uganda Refugee and Host Communities 2018 Household Survey', Factsheet (2019).

163   As part of its IDA18 Regional Sub-Window (RSW) for Refugees and Host Communities discussed earlier. For more on allocations within it, see: Kibuka-Musoke and Sarzin, 'Financing for Forced Displacement Situations'.

164   Joint Data Center and UN Statistical Division, 'Written Submission for the High-Level Panel on Internal Displacement from the Expert Group on Refugee and IDP Statistics' (February 2021), p. 4; Krynsky Baal, 'Forced Displacement Data', p. 8.

165   Refugees also often do not have access to civil registration systems.

166   World Bank and WHO, *Global Civil Registration and Vital Statistics: Scaling up Investment Plan 2015–2024* (May 2014, updated 2018), pp. xii, 8–9.

167   The need for interoperability across ministries is highlighted by the High-Level Panel on Internal Displacement. UN Secretary-General's High-Level Panel on Internal Displacement, *Shining a Light on Internal Displacement*, pp. 37–39.

168   EGRIS consists of statistical experts from national authorities of some 45 countries and territories and around 25 regional and international organizations. For more on its work and Steering Committee, see: Natalia Krynsky Baal, Emi Suzuki and Caroline Sergeant, 'World Bank's ongoing engagement through the Expert Group on Refugee and IDP Statistics (EGRIS)', World Bank Data blog (15 March 2021).

169   EGRIS, *International Recommendation on Refugee Statistics (IRRS)* (March 2018); EGRIS, *International Recommendations on Internally Displaced Persons Statistics (IRIS)* (March 2020).

170   Joint Data Center on Forced Displacement, 'Who We Are', website.

171   This includes Armenia, Central African Republic, Colombia, Ethiopia, Kenya, Mexico, Morocco, Somalia, Uganda and Ukraine. The Kurdistan Region of Iraq has also taken such measures. Krynsky Baal, 'Forced Displacement Data', p. 15. Joint Data Center and UN Statistical Division, 'Written Submission for the High-Level Panel on Internal Displacement', pp. 13–14.

172   Sustainable Development Goal 17: "Strengthen the means of implementation and revitalize the Global Partnership for Sustainable Development". Target 17.18 notes the need for

data disaggregation "by income, gender, age, race, ethnicity, migratory status, disability, geographic location and other characteristics relevant in national contexts". UNGA, Transforming our world: The 2030 Agenda for Sustainable Development (25 September 2015), UN Doc A/RES/70/1, pp. 14, 27. The Global Compact on Refugees calls for "the development of harmonized or interoperable standards for the collection, analysis, and sharing of age, gender, disability, and diversity disaggregated data on refugees and returnees". Global Compact on Refugees (2018), para. 46. See also: EGRIS and JIPs, Building Capacity to Improve Statistics on Forced Displacement, Conference Report (8 September 2020), p. 23.

173 Joint Data Center, *Annual Report 2019–2020*, p. 30. The report provides examples of such support in a range of countries, including the Central African Republic and Ethiopia.

174 Identified as an obstacle in the Joint Data Center, *Annual Report 2019–2020*, p. 8. A lack of awareness of the potential benefits can also play a part.

175 Ibid., p. 11. The World Bank supports the creation of UNHCR's Microdata Library through the Joint Data Center. The World Bank, Microdata Library; UNHCR, Microdata Library.

176 UN Secretary-General's High-Level Panel on Internal Displacement, 'Issues and Challenges before the Secretary-General's High-Level Panel on Internal Displacement', Concept Paper (12 February 2020), pp. 3, 10–11. The Panel also acknowledges and seeks to account for multiple displacements affecting the same persons, as well as vulnerabilities and capacities of displaced populations through the disaggregation of data and a shared understanding of risks and vulnerabilities.

177 UN Secretary-General's High-Level Panel on Internal Displacement, *Shining a Light on Internal Displacement*, pp. 7, 37–39.

178 There are several different types of impact evaluations. The most rigorous is a randomized control trial (RCT). In RCT, the group selected for the programme is randomly selected among a larger group of similarly situated individuals. This is to eliminate any unconscious bias in the selection. For more on impact evaluation methodologies, see: Nessa Kenny and Laura Benrey, 'Filling the Forced Displacement Evidence Gap: Taking Stock on World Refugee Day', Innovations for Poverty Action blog (18 June 2020).

179 Paola Elice, 'Impact Evaluations in Forced Displacement Contexts: A Guide for Practitioners', Reference Paper for the 70th Anniversary of the 1951 Refugee Convention, UNHCR (October 2021). See, in particular: Appendix 3 of this reference paper, which describes several ongoing impact evaluations and refers to the systematic reviews, such as those found here: International Initiative for Impact Evaluation (3ie), 'Evidence Use', website.

180 Edward Miguel and Michael Kremer, 'Worms: Identifying Impacts on Education and Health in the Presence of Treatment Externalities', *Econometrica* 72, No. 1 (January 2004): pp. 159–217.

181 For more on the impact of deworming in other countries, see: Evidence Action, 'Deworm the World', website.

182 Jessica Cohen and Pascaline Dupas, 'Free Distribution or Cost-Sharing? Evidence from a Randomized Malaria Prevention Experiment', *The Quarterly Journal of Economics* 125, no. 1 (February 2010): pp. 1–45; The Abdul Latif Jameel Poverty Action Lab (J-PAL), 'Free bednets to fight malaria', website.

183 Elice, 'Impact Evaluations in Forced Displacement Contexts'.

184 Micro-lending is an illustrative example, given the initial promise of these programmes, many of which were found not to have the desired impact. Abhijit Banerjee, Dean Karlan, and Jonathan Zinman, 'Six Randomized Evaluations of Microcredit: Introduction and Further Steps', *American Economic Journal: Applied Economics* 7, no. 1 (January 2015): pp. 1–21. For other examples of how impact evaluations have led to programme and

...PART V: Bridging the Gap...

policy changes, see: Elice, 'Impact Evaluations in Forced Displacement Contexts'; Kirsten Schuettler and Laura Caron, *Jobs Interventions for Refugees and Internally Displaced Persons*, Jobs Working Paper No. 47, World Bank Group, (2020).

185 Drew B. Cameron, Anjini Mishra, and Annette N. Brown, 'The growth of impact evaluation for international development: how much have we learned?', *Journal of Development Effectiveness* 8, no. 1 (January 2016): pp. 1–21. The authors documented 2,259 between 1981 and 2012 with a significant acceleration from 2008 onward. These were concentrated in South Asia, East Africa, South and Central America and Southeast Asia, p. 1. See also: Elice, 'Impact Evaluations in Forced Displacement Contexts', pp. 8–10.

186 Kenny and Benrey, 'Filling the Forced Displacement Evidence Gap'.

187 For a discussion of the challenges with impact evaluations and some methods for overcoming them, see: Elice, 'Impact Evaluations in Forced Displacement Contexts'.

188 Notably, the United Kingdom, the United States, as well as financial institutions like the World Bank.

189 Elice, 'Impact Evaluations in Forced Displacement Contexts'. For World Bank examples, see: World Bank, 'Building Evidence on Forced Displacement: Impact Evaluations', website. Other specialized agencies include the Abdul Latif Jameel Poverty Action Lab (J-PAL), Innovations for Poverty Action (IPA), Behavioural Insights Team (BIT), the International Initiative for Impact Evaluation (3ie) and ALNAP among others. The IRC, with support from the LEGO Foundation, leads a consortium of programmes for play-based learning in East Africa. Impact evaluation is a part of the roll-out of the work being undertaken as part of this partnership. BIT, 'BIT included in consortium to bring play to refugee children with $100 million grant from the LEGO Foundation', blog.

190 Kenny and Benrey, 'Filling the Forced Displacement Evidence Gap'. For impact evaluations more broadly in low- and middle-income countries, see: 3ie, 'Evidence use: Briefs', website.

191 Elice, 'Impact Evaluations in Forced Displacement Contexts', Appendix 3. See also: Innovations for Poverty Action, 'Published RCTs with Forcibly Displaced Populations in LMICs', Spreadsheet; World Bank, 'Impact Evaluations'. Also of note is that, in 2017, the Foreign Commonwealth Development Office (FCDO) of the United Kingdom commissioned the Abdul Latif Jameel Poverty Action Lab (J-PAL) and Innovations for Poverty Action (IPA) to conduct a review of RCTs examining strategies for reducing crime, violence and conflict. In 2019, the results of the review were published, highlighting the effective policies of J-Pal, IPA and UKAid. The review is a living document that is regularly updated to reflect recent changes. J-Pal, IPA and UKAid, 'Governance, Crime and Conflict Initiative Evidence Wrap-Up: Lessons from randomized evaluations on managing and preventing crime, violence, and conflict', Report (June 2021).

192 Global Compact on Refugees (2018), art. 3.1.

193 UNHCR, *Agenda for Protection (Third Edition)* (October 2003), Goal 3.4: "Refugee communities empowered to meet their own protection needs"; UNGA, 'Outcome of the World Humanitarian Summit' (23 August 2016), UN Doc A/71/353, paras. 28–32; New York Declaration for Refugees and Migrants (2016), paras. 15 and 31, Annex I 12d and 12e; Global Compact on Refugees (2018), paras. 13, 51, 75, 77, 84, 106.

194 See: Part I.

195 Tristan Harley, 'Refugee Participation Revisited: The Contributions of Refugees to Early International Refugee Law and Policy', Reference Paper for the 70th Anniversary of the 1951 Refugee Convention, UNHCR (October 2021); Claudena Skran, *Refugees in Inter-War Europe: The Emergence of a Regime* (Oxford: Clarendon Press, 1995), pp. 82–84; Peter Gatrell, *The Making of the Modern Refugee* (Oxford: Oxford University Press, 2013), p. 57; Paula Worby, 'Lessons Learned from UNHCR's Involvement in the Guatemala Refugee Repatriation and Reintegration Programme (1987–1999)', Evaluation, UNHCR (December, 1999).

196 See: Part I. See also: Harley, 'Refugee Participation Revisited'.

197 One of the means used in UNHCR is through participatory assessments. See: UNHCR, 'UNHCR Tool for Participatory Assessment in Operations', (May 2006).

198 UN Secretary-General's High-Level Panel on Internal Displacement, 'Summary of Key Trends from Consultations with IDPs and Affected Communities', Document (November 2020), p. 4. Feeling excluded was particularly prevalent among women, youth, indigenous, marginalized populations, host community members and lesbian, gay, bisexual, transgender and intersex persons. In its report, the High-Level Panel noted the need to recognize the rights and agency of internally displaced persons as citizens and residents of their country. This includes enabling them to be involved in setting policies related to displacement. UN Secretary-General's High-Level Panel on Internal Displacement, *Shining a Light on Internal Displacement*, pp. 11, 21.

199 For examples, see: Christa Kuntzelman and Robert Hakiza, 'Forging a new path, RLOs as Partners: Lessons from the Africa Refugee Leaders Summit', Reference Paper for the 70th Anniversary of the 1951 Refugee Convention, UNHCR (October 2021).

200 Asia Pacific Summit of Refugees (APSOR), 'Outcomes Report' (February 2019), p. 6. Najeeba Wazefadost is the Executive Director and one of the founding members of the Asia Pacific Network of Refugees (APNOR) and the Co-Founder of the Global Refugee-led Network (GRN) and the Global Independent Refugee Women Leaders (GIRWL).

201 Jacobsen and Bjørn Mason, *Measuring Progress Towards Solutions in Darfur*.

202 A number of studies that incorporate this methodology are discussed in Part III.

203 See, for example, the following strategy documents, all of which refer to innovation as part of their strategic efforts: UNHCR, *UNHCR's Strategic Directions: 2017–2021* (January 2017); World Food Programme, *WFP Strategic Plan (2017–2021)* (July 2017); UNICEF, *UNICEF Strategic Plan: 2018–2021*, Executive Summary (January 2018); Norwegian Refugee Council, *NRC Global Strategy 2018–2020* (December 2017).

204 The Localization Lab is an organization that supports the development of innovative technologies to ensure access, security, digital literacy and anonymity of individuals seeking safe avenues to access online information. Localization Lab, 'Homepage'.

205 Among the examples are many apps designed during the 2015 European refugee crisis. For these and other examples of challenges and lessons learned in involving "end-users" in innovations, see: Dragana Kaurin, 'Developments and Lessons Learned in Humanitarian Innovation for Forced Displacement', Reference Paper for the 70th Anniversary of the 1951 Refugee Convention, UNHCR (October 2021); Charles Martin-Shields, 'Digitalization in Displacement Contexts: Technology and the implementation of the Global Compact on Refugees', Reference Paper for the 70th Anniversary of the 1951 Refugee Convention, UNHCR (October 2021).

206 See, for example: UNHCR, *Sexual and Gender-Based Violence (SGBV) Prevention, Risk Mitigation and Response: Promising practices*, Report (December 2019), pp. 9, 26, 37;

...PART V: **Bridging the Gap...**

UNHCR, *Action against Sexual and Gender-Based Violence: An Updated Strategy* (June 2011), pp. 5, 17.

207 The Lorena stove, created by MIT D Lab, is one example. It was created with refugees in Burkina Faso who had previously not been able to adapt to a solar-powered stove, which had been introduced without their consultation and did not meet their needs. Dragana Kaurin, 'Developments and Lessons Learned in Humanitarian Innovation', pp. 21–22. For further examples on the importance of understanding user preferences and specific contexts in innovative cooking interventions, see: Laura Patel and Katie Gross, 'Cooking in Displacement Settings: Engaging the Private Sector in Non-wood-based Fuel Supply', Research Paper, Moving Energy Initiative (January 2019); Samer Abdelnour, Crispin Pemberton-Pigott, and Dirk Deichmann, 'Clean cooking interventions: Towards user-centred contexts of use design', *Energy Research & Social Science* 70 (December 2020); Global Alliance for Clean Cookstoves and D-Lab, *Handbook for Biomass Cookstove Research, Design, and Development: A Practical Guide to Implementing Recent Advances* (July 2017).

208 They are also known as Refugee/Internally Displaced Person Led Organizations or Refugee Community Organizations.

209 Global Refugee-led Network, 'Meaningful Refugee Participation As Transformative Leadership: Guidelines for Concrete Action' (2019), p. 5. On the value of organizations led by internally displaced persons, see: Delina Abadi, 'IDP-led Women's Assistance: New Roles for Traditional Groups', Article, Rethinking Refuge Platform (8 October 2021).

210 UNHCR, 'Awards honour refugee-led response to COVID-19 pandemic', *UNHCR* News (25 March 2021); Robert Hakiza et al., 'Refugee groups fill gaps in COVID-19 response, and they need support', *The New Humanitarian* (29 April 2020); Laura Angela Bagnetto, 'World Refugee Day: Grassroots groups support African refugees in COVID-19 struggle', *RFI* (20 June 2020); Amnesty International, 'Refugee-led organizations need support and funding so they can continue their vital work', *Amnesty International* News (19 August 2020); Fernando Duarte, 'The Burundian refugee soap maker who is fighting coronavirus in Kenya', *BBC World Service* (9 January 2021).

211 UNHCR, 'Awards honour refugee-led response to COVID-19 pandemic'; Kuntzelman and Hakiza, 'Forging a New Path, RLOs as Partners', p. 3. They make the point that refugees want to make similar contributions to regular programmes and contribute to policies at every stage "from design to implementation to monitoring and evaluation". Internally displaced persons also participated in the pandemic responses – see, for example, the work of the Jeel Albena Association for Humanitarian Development, 'Face Mask Making Project', website.

212 Kuntzelman and Hakiza, 'Forging a New Path, RLOs as Partners', p. 12.

213 Ibid., p. 12; Kate Pincock, Alexander Betts, and Evan Easton-Calabria, *The Global Governed?: Refugees as Providers of Protection and Assistance* (Cambridge: Cambridge University Press, 2020), pp. 2, 110–111.

214 This was among the recommendations at the 2019 African Refugee Summit, which brought together refugee leaders across Africa. For more, see: Kuntzelman and Hakiza, 'Forging a New Path, RLOs as Partners', pp. 12–15. Kuntzelman and Hakiza also point to a few NGOs that are investing in capacitating refugee organizations, like Oxfam and Urban Refugees.

215 This is a recommendation made by Pincock, Betts, and Easton-Calabria, but of relevance too for organizations led by internally displaced persons. Pincock, Betts, and Easton-Calabria, *The Global Governed?*, pp. 119–120. Some commentators have also noted the need to look closely at representation and consider how the leadership of these organizations are selected, and to whom they are accountable. Will Jones, 'Refugee Voices', Research Paper No. 8, World Refugee Council (February 2019), pp. 7–9.

216 Harley, 'Refugee Participation Revisited', pp. 10–15.

217 Global Refugee-led Network, 'Meaningful Refugee Participation As Transformative Leadership: Guidelines for Concrete Action' (2019), p. 6. The Network came out of the June 2018 Global Refugee Summit that was convened by the Australian National Committee on Refugee Women (ANCORW) and the Network for Refugee Voices (NRV). James Milner and Amanda Klassen, 'Civil Society and the Politics of the Global Refugee Regime', Reference Paper for the 70th Anniversary of the 1951 Refugee Convention, UNHCR (October 2021).

218 NGOs contributed to the work of the AdHoc Committee established by ECOSOC to draft the 1951 Convention. For more on the early role of civil society, see: Part I. See also: Skran, *Refugees in Inter-War Europe*; Gil Loescher, *The UNHCR and World Politics: A Perilous Path* (Oxford: Oxford University Press, 2001); Philipp Ther, *The Outsiders: Refugees in Europe Since 1492* (Princeton, NJ: Princeton University Press, 2019); Gatrell, *The Making of the Modern Refugee*; Milner and Klassen, 'Civil Society and the Politics of the Global Refugee Regime'; Elizabeth G. Ferris, 'The Role of Non-Governmental Organizations in the International Refugee Regime', in Mark Gibney, Gil Loescher, and Niklaus Steiner (eds.), *Problems of Protection: The UNHCR, Refugees, and Human Rights* (New York: Routledge, 2003), pp. 117–137.

219 For more on the definitions of civil society, and also suggestions to define them in a way that distinguishes between those working for a collective interest or good and those that may be set up to advance a political interest or the interest of a State, see: Milner and Klassen, 'Civil Society and the Politics of the Global Refugee Regime', pp. 2–3. For more on civil society actors in the Asia-Pacific region, see: Alice M. Nah, 'Networks and norm entrepreneurship amongst local civil society actors: advancing refugee protection in the Asia Pacific region', *The International Journal of Human Rights* 20, no. 2 (2016): pp. 223–240.

220 Global Compact on Refugees (2018), para. 33.

221 The International Council of Voluntary Agencies (ICVA) is a global network of 130 NGOs that protect and assist people in emergencies in 160 countries at global, regional, national and local levels. ICVA, *Annual Report 2020* (2021). See also: Milner and Klassen, 'Civil Society and the Politics of the Global Refugee Regime', pp. 4–5, 10.

222 For example, The Network for Empowered Aid Response (NEAR) is a collective of local and national organizations working in the humanitarian, development and peacebuilding fields. Formed in 2016, it now has a network of 96 organizations working across the Global South, advocating for systematic change in the international humanitarian and development aid systems. NEAR, *Strategic Plan 2021–2023* (2021), p.3. The Asia Pacific Refugee Rights Network (APRRN) consists of some 200 organizations and over 200 individual members committed to advance the rights of refugees in the Asia Pacific region, APRRN, *Annual Report 2018* (2019), p. 3; Nah, 'Networks and norm entrepreneurship amongst local civil society actors': pp. 10–16.

223 Milner and Klassen, 'Civil Society and the Politics of the Global Refugee Regime', pp. 3–4; Nah, 'Networks and norm entrepreneurship amongst local civil society actors': pp. 5–6.

224 As noted in Part I and accompanying references, this evidence stretches as far back as the ancient period, with consistent examples since then. Note as well the role of the cities was

...PART V: **Bridging the Gap...**

expressly acknowledged in the 2004 Mexico Plan of Action, marking the 20th anniversary of the Cartagena Declaration, discussed in Part II. One of the three pillars of the Plan, "Solidarity Cities", was established to foster coherent strategies and cooperation, including to enhance the self-sufficiency and local integration of forcibly displaced persons. On the 30th anniversary of the Cartagena Declaration, States acknowledged the work of the Solidarity Cities and the importance of incorporating the lessons learned in the promotion of inclusive service delivery and local integration. Mexico Declaration and Plan of Action to Strengthen the International Protection of Refugees in Latin America (16 November 2004); Brazil Declaration and Plan of Action: "A Framework for Cooperation and Regional Solidarity to Strengthen the International Protection of Refugees, Displaced and Stateless Persons in Latin America and the Caribbean" (3 December 2014).

225 UNHCR estimate, based on the demographic information available in the 2020 annual statistical report. This is consistent with larger global trends towards growing urbanization. By 2050, an estimated two thirds of the world's population will live in urban and peri-urban settings. UNDESA, *World Urbanization Prospects: The 2018 Revision*, Report (2019), pp. xix, 10.

226 This was the finding of a good practice review published in 2016. It also found that municipalities and local actors lacked resources and coordination mechanisms to adequately respond to crises. IMPACT and UCLG, 'Consultations on Humanitarian Responses in Urban Areas: Perspectives from Cities in Crisis', World Humanitarian Summit (May 2016), pp. 3, 7–8.

227 Evan Easton-Calabria, 'Urban Displacement, Local Engagement: Examining the past, current and future role of cities in forced displacement', Reference Paper for the 70th Anniversary of the 1951 Refugee Convention, UNHCR (October 2021), pp. 4–5, 8. Among the recommendations of the High-Level Panel on Internal Displacement is that States allocate funds for solutions from domestic budgets, including to support local and city authorities, and "ensure that funding allocations are based on current regional and municipality population figures (including IDPs) and the distinct service needs of IDPs". UN Secretary-General's High-Level Panel on Internal Displacement, *Shining a Light on Internal Displacement*, pp. 17, 64.

228 Evan Easton-Calabria, 'Urban Displacement, Local Engagement', pp. 4–5, 8. She notes, for example, that some municipal budgets are determined on the basis of censuses, which generally do not account for refugees. For a review of several examples of the ways cities around the world are responding to forcibly displaced persons in an inclusive manner, see: Special edition 'Cities and Towns', *Forced Migration Review* 63 (February 2020).

229 Bruce Katz and Luise Noring, 'In Europe, integrating refugees falls to cities', Brookings Institution blog (13 June 2016).

230 The 2016 Grand Bargain had the ambition of 25 per cent of humanitarian funds being allocated to local and national partners by 2020. By 2020, the goal had not been reached. See: IASC, 'The Grand Bargain'; Metcalfe-Hough et al., *The Grand Bargain at Five Years*, p. 47. The OECD also notes that: "Few actors channel aid through host governments in fragile contexts or refugee situations", OECD, 'Financing for refugee situations', Development Policy Paper 24 (December 2019), p. 21.

231 OECD, 'Localising the Response: World Humanitarian Summit', Policy Paper (2017), pp. 7–8.

232 The Red Cross and Red Crescent movement is a network of more than 190 national societies. Since its inception, it has stressed the importance of complementarity between national, regional and international humanitarian responses. In 2015, its Council of Delegates agreed to a resolution that included support for greater reliance on local partners. Council of Delegates of the International Red Cross and Red Crescent Movements, 'Message to the World Humanitarian Summit' (2015) Res. CD/15/R3.

233 The United Nations and international NGOs, both of which work across multiple countries globally.

234 UNGA, 'Outcome of the World Humanitarian Summit', paras. 36, 37, 51, 52. Already in 2003, it was a core principle of Good Humanitarian Donorship (an informal donor forum and network): "Strengthen the capacity of affected countries and communities to prevent, prepare for, mitigate and respond to humanitarian crises, with the goal of ensuring that governments and local communities are better able to meet their responsibilities and co-ordinate effectively with humanitarian partners." Good Humanitarian Donorship, '24 Principles and Good Practice of Humanitarian Donorship', Principle 8.

235 UN High-Level Panel on Humanitarian Financing, *Too Important to Fail*, pp. 3, 19.

236 Ibid., p. 20.

237 Ibid., p. 19.

238 IASC, 'The Grand Bargain', p. 5. Localization is also part of the European Commission's strategy. European Commission, 'Communication from the Commission to the European Parliament, the Council, the European Economic and Social Committee and the Committee of the Regions: Action Plan on Integration and Inclusion 2021–2027' (24 November 2020), COM(2020) 758 final, pp. 16–17, 19–20.

239 Metcalfe-Hough et al., *The Grand Bargain at Five Years*, pp. 46–47. Examples include guidance on capacity strengthening, financing, partnership, coordination, gender equality and the role of intermediaries, drawing on research, field consultations and good practice.

240 Ibid., pp. 18, 47.

241 Ibid., p. 52. They noted that this includes Christian Aid and the Catholic international development charity (CAFOD), with 73 per cent and 72 per cent of their respective humanitarian funding channelled to local partners in 2020. The other signatories are ActionAid, the Czech Republic, IFRC, New Zealand, OCHA (for CBPFs), Slovenia, Spain, UNFPA, UNHCR, UNICEF and WFP. They noted, however, that not all signatories track this in their financial systems and, among those that do, there is a lack of standardization.

242 Ibid., pp. 23–24. They noted good examples, including: a promising IRC strategy to significantly enhance the scale and quality of operational partners; positive practices funded by the European Civil Protection and Humanitarian Aid Operations (ECHO) and Germany for community-based initiatives in Turkey; and the work of the NRC through the expert pool NORCAP to strengthen local actors' capacities in the Lake Chad Basin. The latter includes training on monitoring and evaluation, programme and financial management and, in the areas of protection, gender-based violence and accountability to affected populations. Ibid., pp. 49–50.

243 Ibid., p. 51. They noted that some agencies had internal policies to standardize this, like Catholic Relief Services, UNFPA, UNHCR and the Rapid Response Facility (RRF) in the United Kingdom.

244 Ibid., p. 59. The reviewers also discussed the use and potential of pooled funds, such as those managed by OCHA to help mitigate risks, p. 55. The Global Protection Cluster also highlighted the importance of strengthening capacities in areas, such as human resources,

...PART V: **Bridging the Gap...**

finance and administration to advance localization. Anthony Nolan and Marie-Emilie Dozin, 'Advancing the Localisation Agenda in Protection Coordination Groups', Learning Paper, Global Protection Cluster (April 2019), p. 20. Save the Children and Street Child also pointed out that local actors required a level of core funding beyond project-based funds to develop their capacities. Save the Children and Street Child, 'Innovation for Localization: Exploring the impact of channelling unrestricted funding to NNGOs in Emergency Contexts', Research Report (October 2020), p. 7.

245 Led by UNHCR and the Somali NGO Consortia, the IASC Result Group 1 Sub-Group is developing the guidance. Metcalfe-Hough et al., *The Grand Bargain at Five Years*, pp. 47–48. As of 2021, national and local humanitarian actors constituted 8 per cent of leadership of cluster/sector coordination at the subnational level; this is exclusive of coordination mechanisms for refugee situations. Guidance was issued by the IASC in July 2021: IASC, 'Strengthening Participation, Representation and Leadership of Local and National Actors in IASC Humanitarian Coordination Mechanisms', Guidance Document (July 2021).

246 5th Mayoral Forum on Human Mobility, Migration and Development, 'Marrakech Mayors Declaration: Cities Working Together for Migrants and Refugees' (8 December 2018).

247 It was initially established to advance the development of cities and upgrading of slums. Among the initial large donors was the United Kingdom and the World Bank. It now has 29 members that provide strategic direction, finance the Fund, and engage in advocacy and operational activities. Independent Evaluation Group, 'Global Program Review: Cities Alliance', Report, (28 June 2007); COWI, 'Independent Evaluation of the Cities Alliance', Final Report (April 2012); Cities Alliance, 'Who We Are', website.

248 United Cities and Local Governments (UCLG), 'Join the #ItTakesACommunity global campaign for community-driven approaches to human mobility and diversity', UCLG News (23 April 2021). The UCLG reports working with over 240,000 "towns, cities and regional metropolises" and "175 local and regional government associations". UCLG, 'Who are We?', Factsheet.

249 Eurocities, 'Statement on asylum in cities' (2015); Eurocities, 'A better quality of life for all: strategic framework 2020–2030', website; Eurocities, 'About us', website.

250 European Commission, 'Action Plan on Integration and Inclusion 2021–2027', pp. 16–17 and 19–20; Eurocities, 'Cities rally for integration', *Eurocities* News (16 December 2020).

251 The sector encompasses a diverse array of groups, from private citizens, philanthropic foundations and trusts to corporate for-profit commercial enterprises and business associations and coalitions. There are many factors that motivate private sector actors to engage, and these are not mutually exclusive. They can include: sustaining or generating sales of goods and services; expanding markets; widening brand recognition and demonstrating good global citizenship. For the business case for working with and employing refugees, see: International Chamber of Commerce, 'Private Sector for Refugees (PS4R)', website; PwC Global Crisis Centre, 'Managing the refugee and migrant crisis: The role of governments, private sector and technology', Report (2017), pp. 16, 30; Somini Sengupta, 'Mark Zuckerberg Announces Project to Connect Refugee Camps to the Internet', *New York Times* (27 September 2015).

252 UNGA, 'World Summit Outcome' (2005), para. 22(e). It articulated areas including financing, investment, innovation, delivery of services and infrastructure support, paras. 23(d),

23(e), 24(d), 25(c). See also: OHCHR, 'Guiding Principles on Business and Human Rights: Implementing the United Nations "Protect, Respect and Remedy" Framework' (2011); World Economic Forum and the United Nations Office for the Coordination of Humanitarian Affairs (OCHA), 'Guiding Principles for Public-Private Collaboration for Humanitarian Action' (December 2007). Then, more recently: United Nations Global Compact, 'Guidelines on a Principle-Based Approach to the Cooperation between the United Nations and the Business Sector', Report (2015).

253 Stephen O'Brien, 'Coming of age for humanitarians and the private sector', *Devex* (5 July 2016); UNGA, 'One humanity, shared responsibility: Report of the Secretary-General for the World Humanitarian Summit', Annex 'Agenda for Humanity' (2 February 2016), UN Doc A/70/709.

254 New York Declaration for Refugees and Migrants (2016).

255 Including in the areas of: finance; job creation and commercial business ventures; infrastructure development and use of innovative technologies; access to financial services; national risk monitoring and preparedness measures; the expansion of complementary pathways. Global Compact on Refugees (2018), paras. 3, 27, 32, 42, 53, 71, 79.

256 Including in the areas of: migration governance; investment in sustainable development and human capital; information-sharing; skills-matching; promotion of decent work conditions; capacity-building of national authorities; and facilitation of remote work and learning. UNGA, Global Compact for Safe, Orderly and Regular Migration (19 December 2018), UN Doc A/RES/73/195, paras. 15(j), 18(d), 18(e), 19(e), 21(c), 22(e), 23(d), 34(e), 34(f), 34(h), 35(i), 35(j), 36, 39(d), 44.

257 UNHCR, 'Private sector steps up for refugees as Global Refugee Forum opens in Geneva', Press Release (16 December 2019); UNHCR, 'Outcomes of the Global Refugee Forum', Report (2019).

258 Tent Partnership for Refugees, 'Our Members', website.

259 Tent, 'Resources', website.

260 Tülin Erdem et al., 'How Helping Refugees Helps Brands: An Analysis of French, German, and Italian Consumer Perceptions', Report, NYU Stern and Tent (June 2019), pp. 17–19.

261 Tent, 'Airbnb.Org, DoorDash, IKEA, and Teleperformance recognized for their efforts to integrate refugees at first-ever awards', *Tent* News (17 June 2021); Tent, 'Major Dutch companies on track to fulfill commitments to support refugees', *Tent* News (8 April 2021).

262 Tent, 'Tent joins Vice President Harris's Call to Action in Support of the Northern Triangle', *Tent* News (27 May 2021).

263 The World Economic Forum is the 'International Organization for Public-Private Cooperation', established in 1971. The core group of stakeholders that it brings together are businesses, governments and international organizations, civil society, Young Leaders, academia and science communities, and media. World Economic Forum, 'Our Mission', website; World Economic Forum, *A Platform for Impact*, Brochure (2019). In 2016, the WEF Global Risks Report highlighted forced displacement as the highest risk affecting the world in terms of likelihood and the fourth highest in terms of impact after climate change-related risks, weapons of mass destruction and water crises. World Economic Forum, *The Global Risks Report 2016*, Insight Report (2016), pp. 11, 15–16.

264 See, for example: UNHCR et al., *Evaluation of UNHCR's Engagement with the Private Sector* (December 2019); UNICEF, 'UNICEF corporate partnerships', website; Norwegian Refugee Council, 'Corporate partnerships', website; Danish Refugee Council, 'Partner up', website.

265 As noted previously, a Tent European consumer study found that consumers, particularly

millennials, are more likely to purchase from companies that support refugees in differ-ent ways, such as hiring them, investing in refugee enterprises, and delivering services to refugees. Tülin Erdem et al., 'How Helping Refugees Helps Brands'.

266 Cindy Huang, 'Global Business and Refugee Crises: A Framework for Sustainable Engage-ment', Report, Center for Global Development and Tent Foundation (September 2017), pp. 9–10; The B Team, 'Refugees and Migrants: An Opportunity for Humanity', Report (2016), p. 19; Marta Martinez, 'More businesses commit to helping refugees thrive with new jobs, trainings, investment', *UNHCR* News (26 September 2018); Michael Levitin, 'Investing in people: how brands are stepping up to the refugee crisis', *Reuters* (7 August 2019). Other examples include: IKEA, *People & Planet Positive*, IKEA Sustainability Strategy (August 2020), pp. 16–17; UPS Foundation, *Humanitarian Relief & Resilience Program*, Overview (2019), pp. 2, 22–24; Starbucks, '2020 Global Environmental & Social Impact Report' (April 2021), p. 9; Unilever, 'Disasters and emergencies', website; Airbnb.Org, 'Opening homes in times of crisis', website.

267 UNHCR, 'Procurement in UNHCR', Brochure (2021), p. 22; UNHCR, *Global Report 2020* (2021), p. 19. In 2020, UNHCR's total expenditure amounted to $4.84 billion.

268 The Instant Network Schools project was set up in 2013 by the Vodafone Foundation and UNHCR. As of August 2021, the programme had reached over 126,456 students and 1,638 teachers in six African countries. For more, see: Vodafone, 'Instant Network Schools', website.

269 Including the International Rescue Committee (IRC), Sesame Workshop, Education Cannot Wait (ECW), and BRAC. The LEGO Foundation, 'Humanitarian', website. In March 2021, the LEGO Foundation and UNHCR came together to bring the power of learning through play to 37,500 refugee and host community children in Ethiopia.

270 Mastercard Foundation, 'Scholars Program', website; Mastercard Foundation, 'Master-card Foundation Scholars Program Commitment to Education for Refugees', website (17 December 2019).

271 Mastercard Foundation, '1,000 Entrepreneurs within Refugee Communities in Rwanda to Benefit from Economic Recovery Grants on World Refugee Day', website (19 June 2020).

272 *Netzwerk Unternehmen integrieren Flüchtlinge* translates as "Network Companies Inte-grate Refugees".

273 The network facilitates the exchange of information on relevant laws, as well as prom-ising practices, such as language training, skills development and ongoing mentorship. Eva Degler and Thomas Liebig, *Finding Their Way: Labour Market Integration of Refugees in Germany*, Report, OECD (March 2017), p. 62; NETZWERK Unternehmen integrieren Flüchtlinge, 'Netzwerk' [German], website.

274 Its work focused on promoting a more positive narrative on refugees, hiring refugees and encouraging their staff to engage in voluntary activities in support of refugees. Irina Mosel et al., 'Public narratives and attitudes towards refugees and other migrants: Germany coun-try profile', Briefing, ODI (November 2019), p. 8; Angeli Mehta, 'Refugee Crisis: German firms heed Merkel's plea for help', *Reuters* (26 June 2017); Wir zusammen, 'Integrations-Initiativen der deutschen Wirtschaft' [German], website.

275 Tent, 'Resources'.

276 Ingka Group, *Annual Summary & Sustainability Report FY20* (2020), p. 92.

277 UNHCR, 'Clean Energy Challenge', *UNHCR* website.

278 As of March 2021, some 2.7 million refugees had been registered using IrisGuard. IrisGuard, 'Iris biometrics facilitate change in aid sector worth hundreds of billions', website (March 2021); Alison Buckholtz and Andrew Raven, 'Eyeing a More Secure Future for Refugees', IFC Blogs (May 2019); Wang and Cakmak, 'Private Sector Initiatives in Forced Displacement Contexts', pp. 13–14.

279 UNHCR, 'IKEA Brighter Lives for Refugees Campaign raises 30.8 million euros for renewable energy sources for refugee families', *UNHCR* News (18 January 2016).

280 IKEA, 'Power for a brighter future' [Video], YouTube, 2017.

281 UNHCR, 'Join our TikTok challenge to show the world why #EveryoneCounts', *UNHCR* News (10 December 2019); UNHCR, 'Searching for Syria? Google and UNHCR offer answers to five top questions', Press Release (22 May 2017); Omer Elnaiem, 'UNHCR X CAREEM: Together We Can Make a Difference', Careem blog (22 April 2018); H&M Foundation, '$3.3 Million to education for refugee children', website (24 February 2017).

282 Private sector partners include WeWork, Sierra Nevada and Caracol Televisión. Somos Panas Colombia, 'Our Partners' [Spanish], website.

283 For more on complementary pathways, see: Part III.

284 A 2019 evaluation of UNHCR's engagement with the private sector found that, while it engages with over 250 private sector entities in over 60 countries on initiatives aimed to improve protection and overall well-being of forcibly displaced communities, improving engagement beyond fundraising objectives remains a challenge. For details, see: UNHCR et al., *Evaluation of UNHCR's Engagement with the Private Sector*. A first year report on WFP's 2020–2025 strategy for private sector partnerships and fundraising revealed progress on all key objectives and improved relationships with private sector partners. WFP, 'Private-sector partnerships and fundraising strategy (2020–2025): Cooperation with the private sector, foundations and individuals for the achievement of zero hunger', Strategy Document (14 November 2019); WFP, 'Quarterly report on private sector partnerships and fundraising strategy: Quarter 4: September to December 2020', Informal Consultation (March 2021).

285 Of note is that, while many initiatives say they are for the benefit of forcibly displaced persons, the majority of publicized examples are for refugees. Further efforts to raise their profile could contribute to a greater public understanding of the scale and impact of internal displacement.

286 Between 1990 and 1999, the approximate number of published studies concerning forced displacement in each of those subject areas was: sociology (700); anthropology (700); legal studies (500); and health (400). Filippo Dionigi and Domenico Tabasso, 'Academic Trends in Forced Displacement', Reference Paper for the 70th Anniversary of the 1951 Refugee Convention, UNHCR (October 2021), pp. 5–8, 32–34.

287 The increase in the number of published studies on forced displacement in each of those two decades in these fields was approximately: sociology from 1,500 to 2,700; economics from 90 to 570; and education from 180 to 460. Ibid. pp. 4–8.

288 Dionigi and Tabasso, 'Academic Trends in Forced Displacement', p. 8.

289 Ibid., p. 9.

290 Refugees in Towns, 'Refugees in Towns', website; Refugees in Towns, 'What Facilitates Refugee Integration? Report', Feinstein International Center (July 2020).

291 See: Part III.

292 For example, in 2018, the Danish Refugee Council (DRC) established the Mixed Migration Centre (MMC) as a platform for data collection, research and analysis with the objective to contribute to a more nuanced and balanced understanding of mixed movements and to

...PART V: **Bridging the Gap...**

contribute to evidence-based policymaking. The Centre also offers an external bibliography of research publications on mixed movements. Mixed Migration Centre, 'About MMC', website.

293 Overviews available at: Integrated Refugee Health Information System, 'iRHIS Home', website. See also: Part IV.

294 Some of this work is noted in the Education section of Part IV.

295 An unpublished literature review by UNHCR and partners in 2021 found a mere handful of studies examining the specific impact of inclusion on host communities.

296 Dina Abu-Ghaida and Karishma Silva, 'Educating the Forcibly Displaced: Key Challenges and Opportunities', Reference Paper for the 70th Anniversary of the 1951 Refugee Convention, UNHCR (October 2021); Joint Data Center on Forced Displacement, 'Forced Displacement and Educational Outcomes: Evidence, Innovations, and Policy Indications', *JDC Quarterly Digest* 2 (December 2020).

297 UNESCO, 'Social and Emotional Learning (SEL) in and through education: taking stock for improved implementation', Concept Note (February 2021).

298 World Bank, 'Building Evidence on Forced Displacement: Overview', website.

299 Dionigi and Tabasso, 'Academic Trends in Forced Displacement'. These include the following: Refugee Research Network (RRN) and International Association for the Study of Forced Migration (IASFM); Institute for the Study of International Migration (Georgetown University); Refugee Studies Centre (University of Oxford); Center for Migration and Refugee Studies (American University in Cairo); Colloquium for Refugees, Migrants, and Statelessness (Northwestern University); the Refugee Law Initiative (University of London); Kaldor Centre for International Refugee Law and the Forced Migration Network (University of New South Wales); Local Engagement Refugee Research Network (LERRN) (Carleton University); and Centre for Refugee Studies (York University). The High-Level Panel on Internal Displacement has called for more efforts to create and expand research networks in internal displacement, especially in displacement-affected countries. UN Secretary-General's High-Level Panel on Internal Displacement, *Shining a Light on Internal Displacement*, pp. 5, 22–23.

300 For reflections on how to enhance ethical and collaborative research of impact to policymakers, practitioners, and advocates, see: Susan McGrath and Julie E.E. Young (eds.), *Mobilizing Global Knowledge: Refugee Research in an Age of Displacement* (Calgary: Alberta University of Calgary Press, 2019).

301 AZ Quotes, 'Lidia Yusopova Quotes', website. Yusupova was the coordinator of the Grozny office of 'Memorial', a Moscow-based human rights organization. She is the recipient of the Martin Ennals award in 2003, the Rafto Prize in 2005, and a nomination for the Nobel Peace Prize in 2008. For more on her, see: Martin Ennals Award, 'Lidia Yusupova', website; Oslo Freedom Forum, 'Lidia Yusupova: Chechen lawyer and human rights activist', website; Rafto Prize, '2005 Laureate: Lidia Yusupova', website; European Parliament, 'Memorial human rights activist Lidia Yusupova on the "Virus" of fear', Article (16 April 2010).

302 It does not look at wider accountability of those whose actions less directly contribute to forced displacement, such as through the sale of arms. This book also does not cover issues pertaining to prevention, sustaining peace and transitional justice – all important and weighty topics but beyond the scope of this volume.

303 Convention relating to the Status of Refugees (adopted 25 July 1951) (1951 Convention), UN Doc A/CONF.2/108, art. 1(f).

304 International Center for Transitional Justice, 'What is Transitional Justice?', website; ICTJ Research Unit and Brookings-LSE Project on Internal Displacement, 'Transitional Justice and Displacement: Challenges and Recommendations', Report (June 2012).

305 Robert H. Jackson, 'Opening Statement before the International Military Tribunal', Palace of Justice at Nuremburg, Germany (21 November 1945).

306 Established by act of treaty initially with France, the Soviet Union, the United Kingdom, and the United States following the unconditional surrender of Germany. Other allies subsequently joined. William Schabas, *Unimaginable Atrocities: Justice, Politics, and Rights at the War Crimes Tribunals* (Oxford: Oxford University Press, 2012), p. 10.

307 It was not established by treaty but by a proclamation of General Douglas MacArthur, Supreme Allied Commander in the Pacific. M. Cherif Bassiouni et al. (eds.), *The Legislative History of the International Criminal Court: Second Revised and Expanded Edition* (Leiden: Brill Nijhoff, 2016), p. 29. As these authors explained, the allies also agreed to prosecute under their national laws and procedures persons believed to have committed "war crimes" and "crimes against humanity" and who were within their respective zones of occupation. France, Russia, the United Kingdom and the United States cumulatively prosecuted an estimated 15,000 persons. Similar arrangements were made in the Far East. Ibid.

308 For more on the Cold War and other reasons for the lack of State agreement for a permanent tribunal during this time, see: Schabas, *Unimaginable Atrocities*. Ethnic cleansing, while not defined as an independent crime under international law, includes acts that are serious violations of international human rights and humanitarian law that may themselves amount to one of the recognized atrocity crimes, in particular crimes against humanity. UN, 'Framework of Analysis for Atrocity Crimes: A Tool for Prevention' (2014), p. 1.

309 UN, Charter of the International Military Tribunal – Annex to the Agreement for the prosecution and punishment of the major war criminals of the European Axis (London Agreement) (8 August 1945), art. 6; Supreme Commander for the Allied Powers, Special Proclamation: Establishment of an International Military Tribunal for the Far East (19 January 1946), art. 5.

310 International Military Tribunal, *Trial of the Major War Criminals before the International Military Tribunal, Nuremberg, 14 November 1945–1 October 1946* vol. 1 (Nuremberg: IMT, 1947), pp. 179, 342, 365–367.

311 Charges were dropped for one defendant because he was found to be mentally unfit, and two died of natural causes during the trials. The National WWII Museum (New Orleans), 'Tokyo War Crimes Trial', website.

312 Twelve received the death penalty, including Hermann Göring who committed suicide prior to the execution of his sentence. IMT, *Trial of the Major War Criminals before the International Military Tribunal*, pp. 6, 365–367; International Court of Justice, *Nuremberg Trial Archives. The International Court of Justice: Custodian of the archives of the International Military Tribunal at Nuremberg*, Booklet (2018), pp. 12–14, 86. Of the 25 men convicted by the IMTFE, seven were executed, 16 received life imprisonment and two received lesser sentences. Edward Drea, 'Introduction', in *Researching Japanese War Crimes Records: Introductory Essays* (Washington, DC: National Archives and Records Administration for the Nazi War Crimes and Japanese Imperial Government Records Interagency Working Group, 2006), p. 6; The National WWII Museum, 'Tokyo War Crimes Trial'.

313 UNGA, 'Extradition and Punishment of War Criminals' (13 February 1946), UN Doc A/RES/3(I).

...PART V: **Bridging the Gap...**

314 UNGA, 'The Crime of Genocide' (11 December 1946), UN Doc A/RES/96(I).

315 UNGA, Convention on the Prevention and Punishment of the Crime of Genocide (9 December 1948), UNTS vol. 78, no. 1021, art. II. The offence includes any of the following acts committed with intent to destroy, in whole or in part, a national, ethnical, racial or religious group: killing members of the group; causing serious bodily or mental harm to members of the group; deliberately inflicting on the group conditions of life calculated to bring about its physical destruction in whole or in part; imposing measures intended to prevent births within the group; forcibly transferring children of the group to another group.

316 International Committee of the Red Cross, 'What Is International Humanitarian Law?', Factsheet (July 2004), p. 2.

317 ICRC, 'Geneva Conventions of 1949 and Additional Protocols, and Their Commentaries', Collected Documents, *ICRC* website.

318 The first three replaced earlier conventions and the fourth supplemented relevant provisions in the Hague Conventions. ICRC, 'Geneva Conventions of 1949 and Additional Protocols, and Their Commentaries'.

319 For example, the Fourth Geneva Convention contains two provisions expressly for the benefit of refugees. The first provides that refugees should not be treated as enemy aliens, solely on the basis of their nationality. The second addresses the situation where the State from which the refugee fled occupies the State of asylum. It provides that refugees may only be arrested, prosecuted, convicted or deported by the occupying power for offences committed after the outbreak of hostilities, and not punished for acts, such as political offences, which may have been the cause of their flight and recognition of their status as refugees. The Additional Protocol I also provides that refugees are "protected persons" within the meaning of the Fourth Convention. For a more in-depth analysis, see: Emanuela-Chiara Gillard, 'Humanitarian Law, Human Rights and Refugee Law – Three Pillars', Statement, ICRC (23 April 2005).

320 For more on the Universal Declaration of Human Rights and the 1951 Refugee Convention, see: Part I.

321 Schabas, *Unimaginable Atrocities*, pp. 2, 12–14.

322 "Including reports of mass killings, massive, organized and systematic detention and rape of women, and the continuance of the practice of 'ethnic cleansing', including for the acquisition and the holding of territory". UN Security Council, Res. 827 (1993) (25 May 1993), UN Doc S/RES/827, p. 1.

323 For an analysis of "victor's justice" at the International Military Tribunal, the International Military Tribunal for the Far East, the International Criminal Tribunal for the Former Yugoslavia, the International Criminal Tribunal for Rwanda, and the selection of situations at the International Criminal Court, see: Chapter 3: 'Victor's Justice? Selecting Targets for Prosecution', in Schabas, *Unimaginable Atrocities*, pp. 73–97.

324 UNSC, Statute of the International Tribunal for the Former Yugoslavia, adopted by Security Council Res. 827 (1993) of 25 May 1993 and amended by Security Council resolutions 1166 (1998) of 13 May 1998, 1329 (2000) of 30 November 2000, 1411 (2002) of 17 May 2002 and 1431 (2002) of 14 August 2002; UN, Updated Statute of the International Criminal Tribunal for the Former Yugoslavia (September 2009).

325 Philippe Sands, *East West Street: On the Origins of 'Genocide' and 'Crimes against Human-*

ity' (New York: Vintage Books, 2017), p. 363. Milosovic died in 2006 before the conclusion of his trial.

326 ICTY, 'ICTY Facts & Figures', Infographic.

327 ICTY, 'About the ICTY' and 'ICTY Remembers: The Srebrencia Genocide, website.

328 UNSC, Statute of the International Criminal Tribunal for Rwanda, as established by Security Council Res. 955 (1994) of 8 November 1994 and last amended by Security Council Res. 1717 (2006) of 13 October 2006.

329 International Residual Mechanism for Criminal Tribunals, 'About the ICTR', Legacy website for the International Criminal Tribunal for Rwanda.

330 Ibid.

331 International Residual Mechanism for Criminal Tribunals, 'Functions of the Mechanism', *ICTR* website.

332 The ILC was established by the UN General Assembly in 1947 for the promotion of the progressive development and codification of international law. It is comprised of independent legal experts whose numbers have grown from 15 to 34. UNGA, Establishment of an International Law Commission (17 November 1947), UN Doc A/RES/174(II). They are elected by the General Assembly every five years. ILC, 'Membership', website.

333 ILC, 'Draft Code of Offences against the Peace and Security of Mankind', *Yearbook of the International Law Commission* vol. II (1954), pp. 408–412; UN, Report of the 1953 Committee on International Criminal Jurisdiction, (27 July–20 August 1953), UN Doc A/2645.

334 Bassiouni et al., *The Legislative History of the International Criminal Court*, pp. 33–35.

335 UN, 'Report of the International Law Commission on the work of its forty-sixth session' (2 May–22 July 1994), UN Doc A/45/10.

336 Ad Hoc Committee on the Establishment of an International Criminal Court and Preparatory Committee on the Establishment of an International Criminal Court; Bassiouni et al., *The Legislative History of the International Criminal Court*, pp. 39–40.

337 Human Rights Advocacy and the History of Human Rights Standards, 'Individual Criminal Accountability', website; Coalition for the International Criminal Court, 'About the Coalition', website; Heidi Nichols Haddad, *The Hidden Hands of Justice: NGOs, Human Rights, and International Courts* (Cambridge: Cambridge University Press, 2018).

338 Seven countries voted against: China; Iraq; Israel; Libya; Qatar; the United States; and Yemen. Bassiouni et al., *The Legislative History of the International Criminal Court*, pp. 101; UN, Rome Statute of the International Criminal Court (17 July 1998), UNTS vol. 2187, no. 38544.

339 Rome Statute (1998). Both Russia and the United States initially signed the Rome Statute but neither ratified it. In 2002, the United States officially notified the UN Secretary-General that the United States did not intend to become a party. Under Secretary of State for Arms Control and International Security John R. Bolton, 'International Criminal Court: Letter to UN Secretary General Kofi Annan' (6 May 2002). In 2016, Russia also formally notified the Secretary-General of the same. The Ministry of Foreign Affairs of the Russian Federation, 'Statement by the Russian Foreign Ministry' (16 November 2016).

340 Rome Statute (1998), art. 70. In 2016, five persons were found guilty by the ICC of offences against the administration of justice. Their offenses included corruptly influencing witnesses and having solicited false witness testimonies in another case before the ICC. ICC, 'Situation in the Central African Republic: The Prosecutor v. Jean-Pierre Bemba Gombo, Aimé Kilolo Musamba, Jean-Jacques Mangenda Kabongo, Fidèle Babala Wandu and Narcisse Arido', Case Information Sheet (September 2018).

...PART V: Bridging the Gap...

341 International Centre for Truth and Justice, 'What Is Complementarity? National Courts, the ICC and the Struggle Against Impunity', website.

342 ICC, *Elements of Crimes*, Collected Documents (2013).

343 Rome Statute (1998), art. 7(1).

344 ICC, *Elements of Crimes*, p. 3. For further commentary, see: Chapter 13: 'Part 2 Jurisdiction, Admissibility, and Applicable Law: Compétence, Recevabilité, Et Droit Applicable, art. 10', in Schabas, *The International Criminal Court*.

345 Rome Statute (1998), art. 8.

346 Ibid.

347 Ibid., arts. 12 and 13. For an explanatory overview, see also: ABA-ICC Project, 'How the ICC Works', website.

348 ICC, Situation in the People's Republic of Bangladesh/Republic of the Union of Myanmar (14 November 2019) Pre-Trial Chamber III, Decision, ICC-01/19.

349 Orchard, 'International, Regional, and Domestic Mechanisms to Hold States to Account for the Causes of Forced Displacement', pp. 10–11.

350 The Trust Fund for Victims is independent of the Court, created in 2004 by the Assembly of States Parties, in accordance with Article 79 of the Rome Statute. The Trust Fund for Victims, 'Providing reparative value for victims and survivors', website.

351 ICC, 'About the Court', website; ICC, 'Defendants', website.

352 Administration of justice offences are set out in: Rome Statute (1998), art. 70.

353 Lubanga was released in 2020 having served his sentence, which included time served prior to sentencing. ICC, 'Situation in the Democratic Republic of the Congo: The Prosecutor v. Thomas Lubanga Dyilo', Case Information Sheet (July 2021).

354 Ibid.

355 Ibid.

356 International Criminal Court, 'Situation in the Republic of Mali: The Prosecutor v. Ahmad Al Faqi Al Mahdi', Case Information Sheet (July 2021).

357 ICC, 'Situation in Uganda: The Prosecutor v. Dominic Ongwen', Case Information Sheet (July 2021).

358 Afghanistan, Bangladesh/Myanmar, Burundi, Central African Republic, Central African Republic II, Côte d'Ivoire, Sudan (Darfur), Democratic Republic of Congo, Georgia, Kenya, Libya, Mali, State of Palestine, the Philippines and Uganda. ICC, 'Situations under Investigation', website. It was also conducting preliminary examinations to determine whether a full investigation was warranted in Bolivia, Colombia, Guinea, Nigeria, Ukraine and Venezuela. For further information on these, see: ICC, 'Preliminary examinations', website.

359 ICC, 'Cases', website.

360 Including Saif Al-Islam Gaddafi of Libya, Omar Al-Bashir, former President of Sudan, and the Ugandan rebel leader Joseph Kony of the Lord's Resistance Army. For the full list of defendants at large, see: ICC, 'Defendants at large', database.

361 See, for example: Schabas, *Unimaginable Atrocities*, pp. 83–89; Geoff Dancy et al., 'What Determines Perceptions of Bias toward the International Criminal Court? Evidence from Kenya', *Journal of Conflict Resolution* 64, no. 7–8 (August 2020): pp. 1443–1469; Chatham House, 'Beyond the ICC: The Role of Domestic Courts in Prosecuting International Crimes Committed in Africa', Meeting Summary (30 April 2010); Laurel Hart, 'The International Criminal Court: biased or simply misunderstood?', UNA-UK (28 October 2018). For a response from the ICC to these allegations, see for example: ICC, *Helping build a more just world: Understanding the International Criminal Court,* Booklet (The Hague: ICC, 2020), p. 15.

362 Since the ICC issued arrest warrants against Al-Bashir in 2009 and 2010, he travelled to several countries, including Chad, the Democratic Republic of the Congo, Djibouti, Jordan, Kenya, Malawi and Uganda. Despite several notifications from the ICC to the UN Security Council and the Assembly of States Parties to the Rome Statute, none of the countries he visited arrested him. See: ICC, 'Non-Cooperation', website. In 2019, he was convicted in Sudan of corruption and sentenced to imprisonment. Sudan has since announced it will transfer him to the ICC. Nima Elbagir, Hamdi Alkhshali, and Yassir Abdullah, 'Sudan to hand Ex-President Omar al-Bashir to ICC', *CNN* (11 August 2021).

363 *The Prosecutor v. Uhuru Muigai Kenyatta* (2015), ICC, No. ICC-01/09-02/11. In an analysis of the case, Daniel Mburu writes that the political campaign in Kenya and regionally against the ICC created a hostile and intimidating atmosphere for witnesses that led to their withdrawal from the case so that the collected evidence would not have been sufficient to establish guilt beyond a reasonable doubt against the new President Kenyatta. Daniel M. Mburu, 'The Lost Kenyan Duel: The Role of Politics in the Collapse of the International Criminal Court Cases against Ruto and Kenyatta', *International Criminal Law Review* 18, no. 6 (November 2018): pp. 1041–1046.

364 Schabas, *Unimaginable Atrocities*, p. 92.

365 ICC Assembly of States Parties, 'Review of the International Criminal Court and the Rome Statute system' (6 December 2019), ICC-ASP/18/Res.7.

366 Known as the Independent Expert Review (IER), ICC Assembly of State Parties, 'Independent Expert Review of the International Criminal Court and the Rome Statute System', Final Report (30 September 2020).

367 ICC Review Mechanism, 'Proposal for a Comprehensive Action Plan for the assessment of the recommendations of the Group of Independent Experts, including requirements for possible further action', Introductory Note (30 June 2021). Stakeholders included States parties, the Prosecutor, the International Criminal Court Bar Association, and civil society organizations. Ibid. I(5).

368 UNHCR, Refugee Data Finder. Estimates for the number of fatalities vary. See, for example: World Peace Foundation, 'Mass Atrocity Endings: Sierra Leone', website (8 July 2015); Mary Kaldor and James Vincent, 'Case Study: Sierra Leone – Evaluation of UNDB Assistance to Conflict-Affected Countries', UNDP Evaluation Office (2006), p. 4; Jennifer Pagonis, 'Refugee status for Sierra Leoneans to end', *UNHCR* News (6 June 2008).

369 UN Economic and Social Council, 'Situation of human rights in Sierra Leone: Report of the High Commissioner for Human Rights pursuant to Commission on Human Rights resolution 1999/1' (22 December 1999), UN Doc E/CN.4/2000/31; Rachel Kerr and Jessica Lincoln, 'The Special Court for Sierra Leone: Outreach, Legacy and Impact', Final Report, King's College, London (February 2008), p. 4.

370 Sierra Leone and United Nations, Agreement between the United Nations and the Government of Sierra Leone on the establishment of a Special Court for Sierra Leone (12 April 2002), UNTS vol. 2178; UNSC, Res. 1315 (2000), UN Doc S/RES/1315 (2000).

371 Limited to crimes committed after 30 November 1996, the date of the first peace agreement, the Abidjan Peace Accord, which failed. Residual Special Court for Sierra Leone, 'Homepage'.

372 The Court also conducted trials for the contempt charges which involved administration of justice offenses, such as tampering and threatening a witness. Ibid.

...PART V: Bridging the Gap...

373 *Prosecutor v. Charles Ghankay Taylor* (2013) Special Court for Sierra Leone, Appeals Chamber, SCSL-03-01-A.; 'Prosecutor welcomes UN-backed court's decision to uphold Charles Taylor conviction', *UN* News (26 September 2013).

374 RSCSL, 'Homepage'.

375 The Office of the High Representative has the status of a diplomatic mission. It is made up of diplomats seconded by the governments of the Peace Implementation Council (international body guiding the peace process) and nationals from Bosnia Herzegovina, international staff hired directly, and national staff from Bosnia and Herzegovina. Office of the High Representative, 'General Information'.

376 Initially, the War Crimes Chamber was responsible for trying lower to mid-level perpetrators referred to it by the ICTY, but its mandate was subsequently broadened.

377 The Court of Bosnia and Herzegovina, 'Statistics on judgements of the Court of Bosnia and Herzegovina for the period of 2004–2020', website.

378 Joanna Korner, 'Processing of War Crimes at the State Level in Bosnia and Herzegovina', Report, Organization for Security and Co-operation in Europe (2016), pp. 16, 24–25, 29–33, 39–41, 44; Joanna Korner, 'Improving War Crimes Processing at the State Level in Bosnia and Herzegovina: A Follow Up Report', British Embassy Sarajevo and Organisation for Security and Cooperation in Europe (2020), p. 54.

379 Bogdan Ivanišević, *The War Crimes Chamber in Bosnia and Herzegovina: From Hybrid to Domestic Court*, Report, International Center for Transitional Justice (2008), p. 1; James Meernik and Josue Barron, 'Fairness in National Courts Prosecuting International Crimes: The Case of the War Crimes Chamber of Bosnia-Herzegovina', *International Criminal Law Review* 18, no. 4 (November 2018): pp. 732–733.

380 Known formally as the Communist Party of Kampuchea (CPK). This period is discussed in Part III, with accompanying references.

381 Editors of the Encyclopedia Britannica, 'Khmer Rouge', *Encyclopedia Britannica* online.

382 *Prosecutor v. Nuon Chea and Khieu Samphan* 002/01 (2014) Trial Chamber, Extraordinary Chambers in the Courts of Cambodia, No. 002/19-09-2007/ECCC/TC. For further information on refugees from Cambodia during this time, see: Part III. Refugee data can be found here: UNHCR, Refugee Data Finder.

383 The Law on the Establishment of the Extraordinary Chambers in the Courts of Cambodia for the Prosecution of Crimes Committed during the Period of Democratic Kampuchea (2001) and the Agreement between the United Nations and the Royal Government of Cambodia concerning the prosecution under Cambodian law of crimes committed during the period of Democratic Kampuchea (ECCC Agreement) (2003). Both are available at: ECCC, 'Legal Documents: Agreements', Collection of Documents.

384 Schabas, *Unimaginable Atrocities*, p. 19.

385 *Prosecutor v. Nuon Chea and Khieu Samphan* 002/01, pp. 532, 556, 579; *Prosecutor v. Nuon Chea and Khieu Samphan* 002/02 (2018) Trial Chamber, Extraordinary Chambers in the Courts of Cambodia, No. 002/19-09-2007/ECCC/TC.

386 Ieng Thirith who had served as the Minister of Social Action under the Khmer Rouge regime was assessed as mentally unfit for trial and removed from the proceedings early on. Her husband, Ieng Sary, who has served as Minister of Foreign Affairs, died in 2013 less than one and a half years into the trial. Open Society Justice Initiative, *Performance and Perception:*

The Impact of the Extraordinary Chambers in the Court of Cambodia, Report (2016), p. 23.

387 ECCC, 'Accused/Charged Person: Ao An'; 'Accused/Charged Person: Meas Muth'; 'Accused/ Charged Person: Yim Tith'; 'Accused/Charged Person: Im Chaem', website.

388 ECCC, Decision on international Co-Prosecutors' immediate appeal of the trial chamber's effective termination of case 004/2 (October 2020), No. E004/2/1/1/2.

389 Open Society Justice Initiative, 'Recent Developments at the Extraordinary Chambers in the Courts of Cambodia: Deadlock Continues in Ao An Case', Briefing Paper (January 2020); Howard Varney and Katarzyna Zduńczyk, 'Advancing Global Accountability: The Role of Universal Jurisdiction in Prosecuting International Crimes', Research Report, International Center for Transitional Justice (December 2020), p. 5.

390 Open Society Justice Initiative, 'Performance and Perception', p. 16.

391 Ignaz Stegmiller, 'Legal Developments in Civil Party Participation at the Extraordinary Chambers in the Courts of Cambodia', *Leiden Journal of International Law* 27, no. 2 (June 2014), p. 473; Ken Gee-kin Ip, 'Fulfilling the Mandate of National Reconciliation in the Extraordinary Chambers in the Courts of Cambodia (ECCC) – An Evaluation through the Prism of Victims' Rights', *International Criminal Law Review* 13, no. 4 (November 2013), p. 886.

392 International Crimes Tribunal, Bangladesh, 'About ICT-BD', website.

393 Ibid.; Morten Bergsmo and Elisa Novic, 'Justice after decades in Bangladesh: national trials for international crimes', *Journal of Genocide Research* 13, no.4 (November 2011): pp. 503– 504; Caitlin Reiger, 'Fighting Past Impunity in Bangladesh: A National Tribunal for the Crimes of 1971', Briefing Paper, International Center for Transitional Justice (July 2010), pp. 3–4.

394 See: Part III.

395 As of September 2020, 74 cases had been investigated and judgments delivered in 42 cases. These involved 70 sentences. Six executions had been carried out. ICT-BD, 'Case Statistics', Chart. Examples include Mir Qasem Ali, a member of the Jamaat-e-Islaami party, who was sentenced to death by the ICT in November 2014, and Abdul Qader Mollah, another Jamaat-e-Islaami leader, who was sentenced to life imprisonment in February 2013 for war crimes and crimes against humanity. Human Rights Watch, 'Bangladesh: War Crimes Verdict Based on Flawed Trial', *HRW* News (22 March 2016); HRW, 'Bangladesh: Death Sentence Violates Fair Trial Standards', *HRW* News (18 September 2013).

396 HRW, 'Letter to Prime Minister Sheikh Hasina Re: International Crimes (Tribunals) Act', *HRW* News (8 July 2009); M. N. Schmitt, Louise Arimatsu, and T. McCormack, 'Correspondents' Reports', in *Yearbook of International Humanitarian Law 2010* (The Hague: T.M.C. Asser Press, 2011), p. 463; Anbarasan Ethirajan, 'Bangladesh finally confronts war crimes 40 years on', *BBC News* (20 November 2011); Lydia Polgreen, 'Bangladesh Faces Atrocities of Its Independence Era', *The New York Times* (3 May 2002).

397 Abdus Samad, 'The International Crimes Tribunal in Bangladesh and International Law', *Criminal Law Forum* 27, no. 3 (2016): pp. 276–277, 280–281, 286, 290; Surabhi Chopra, 'The International Crimes Tribunal in Bangladesh: silencing fair comment', *Journal of Genocide Research* 17, no. 2 (June 2015): pp. 212–214; UN, 'UN Human Rights experts urge Bangladesh to ensure fair trials for past crimes', *UN* News (2 July 2013); Amnesty International, 'Bangladesh: Fresh death sentences show urgent need to end executions', *Amnesty International* News (3 November 2013); HRW, 'Bangladesh: War Crimes Verdict Based on Flawed Trial'.

398 Open Society Justice Initiative, *Judging a Dictator: The Trial of Guatemala's Ríos Montt*, Report (November 2013); International Justice Monitor, 'Efrain Rios Montt & Mauricio Rodriguez Sanchez: Background', website; HRW, 'Guatemala: Rios Montt Convicted of

...PART V: **Bridging the Gap...**

Genocide', *HRW* News (5 October 2013); Hanna Bosdriesz and Sander Wirken, 'An Imperfect Success – The Guatemalan Genocide Trial and the Struggle against Impunity for International Crimes', *International Criminal Law Review* 14, no. 6 (December 2014): pp. 1067–1094. They argue that the fact "the trial was undertaken by the domestic justice system led to a societal impact more profound than any international trial could have had". For further information on the displacement resulting from the civil war in Guatemala, see: Part III.

399 This action was reportedly taken in response to the decision of Senegal to try Hissène Habré in Chad, discussed more fully under the section on universal jurisdiction in this Part.

400 BBC News, 'Mahamat Djibrine: Chadians hail ex-police chief's arrest' (16 May 2013); HRW, 'Q&A: The Case of Hissène Habré before the Extraordinary African Chambers in Senegal', *HRW* News (3 May 2016); HRW, 'Chad: Alleged Habré Accomplices to Stand Trial', *HRW* News (10 November 2014).

401 Theodor Meron, 'Closing the Accountability Gap: Concrete Steps Toward Ending Impunity for Atrocity Crimes', *American Journal of International Law* 112, no. 3 (2018): p. 434. For a further review of constraints, see for example: Antonio Cassese (ed.), 'Part A: Major Problems of International Criminal Justice, IV International Criminal Trials, The Rationale for International Criminal Justice', in *The Oxford Companion to International Criminal Justice* (Oxford: Oxford University Press, 2009), p. 125; Alex Obote-Odora, 'Transfer of cases from the International Criminal Tribunal for Rwanda to Domestic Jurisdictions', *African Journal of Legal Studies* 5, no. 2 (January 2012): pp. 154–159.

402 Orchard, 'International, Regional, and Domestic Mechanisms to Hold States to Account for the Causes of Forced Displacement', pp. 21–23. Máximo Langer and Mackenzie Eason, 'The Quiet Expansion of Universal Jurisdiction', *The European Journal of International Law* 30 no. 3 (2019): pp. 779–817. Langer and Eason consider a prosecuting state that does "not have a territorial, national or national interest link with a crime at the time of its commission" can have a jurisdictional claim "based on customary international law or a treaty", p. 789, footnote 22. For more on universal jurisdiction in general, see: Robert Cryer, Darryl Robinson, and Sergey Vasiliev, *An Introduction to International Criminal Law and Procedure* (Cambridge: Cambridge University Press, 2019), pp. 56–68; Antonio Cassese and Paola Gaeta, *Cassese's International Criminal Law* (Oxford: Oxford University Press, 2013), pp. 278–281. TRIAL International, *Evidentiary Challenges in Universal Jurisdiction Cases: Universal Jurisdiction Annual Review 2019* (March 2019).

403 In 1960, Eichmann was kidnapped by Israeli agents from Argentina where he had been living and transported to Israel undercover. Argentina raised the issue of the abduction in the UN Security Council on grounds of violation of its sovereignty. Israel held that the actions of the individuals who apprehended Eichmann had broken Argentinian law, but that this was not an act of the Israeli State. It further noted that the incident had to be viewed in "light of the exceptional and unique character of the crimes attributed to Eichmann". On 23 June 1960, the UNSC adopted a resolution in which it acknowledged the "concern of people in all countries that Eichmann should be brought to appropriate justice" while also noting that such acts "affect the sovereignty of a Member State and therefore cause international friction, may, if repeated, endanger international peace and security". The matter was declared closed in a joint statement issued by both countries on 3 August 1960. UNSC, 'Question Relating to the Case of Adolf Eichmann' (23 June 1960), UN Doc S/RES/138 (1960); UNSC,

'Chapter VIII: Consideration of Questions Considered by the Security Council under its Responsibility for the Maintenance of International Peace and Security', in *Repertoire of the Practice of the Security Council* (1959–1963), p. 161; *Attorney General v. Adolf Eichmann* (1962), District Court of Jerusalem, Israel, No. 40/61.

404 Amnesty International, 'Chile: 40 years on from Pinochet's coup, impunity must end', *Amnesty International* News (9 October 2013).

405 UNHCR, *The State of The World's Refugees 2000: Fifty Years of Humanitarian Action* (Oxford: Oxford University Press, 2000), pp. 126–127.

406 UK Courts and Tribunals Judiciary, 'The Supreme Court', website.

407 UNGA, Convention against Torture and Other Cruel, Inhuman or Degrading Treatment or Punishment (10 December 1984), UNTS vol. 1465, no. 24841, arts, 2 and 5.

408 *Regina v. Bartle and Regina v. Evans* (1999), House of Lords (On Appeal from a Divisional Court of the Queen's Bench Division). See also: Robert Dubler SC and Matthew Kalyk, *Crimes Against Humanity in the 21st Century: Law, Practice and Threats to International Peace and Security* (Boston, MA: Brill, 2018), pp. 1001–1002. Prior to the enactment of the Constitutional Reform Act 2005 and the resultant creation of the Supreme Court for the United Kingdom, the 12 most senior judges termed the Lords of Appeal in Ordinary or "Law Lords" sat in the House of Lords, making the House of Lords the highest court of appeal in the United Kingdom. UK Courts and Tribunals Judiciary, 'The Supreme Court'.

409 Jonathan Power, 'The Pinochet Case', in *Ending War Crimes, Chasing the War Criminals* (Leiden: Brill Nijhoff, 2017), pp. 90–92.

410 HRW, 'Q&A: The Case of Hissène Habré'.

411 *Ministère Public v Hissein Habré* (2016), Extraordinary African Chambers. A subsequent appeal was dismissed in 2017, and the Court confirmed the previous judgment. *The Prosecutor v Hissein Habré* (2017), Extraordinary African Chambers. Habré died in August 2021.

412 This includes complaints initiated and completed trials.

413 Langer and Eason, 'The Quiet Expansion of Universal Jurisdiction': p. 785. There were 503 cases between 1998 and 2007 and 342 cases between 1988 and 1997.

414 Ibid. Thirty-four universal jurisdiction cases were completed between 2008 and 2017.

415 TRIAL International, *Universal Jurisdiction Annual Review 2021: A year like no other? The impact of coronavirus on universal jurisdiction* (April 2021), p. 13. In terms of charges: 81 are for crimes against humanity; 76 for war crimes; 40 for torture; and 18 for genocide. By region of commission, there were 14 cases in West and Central Africa, 11 in East and Horn of Africa and Great Lakes, three in Southern Africa, three in the Americas, five in Asia and the Pacific, two in Europe, 30 in the Middle East and North Africa and one civil universal jurisdictional case prosecuted in the United States (Note: The case of Mahamat Nouri includes both Chad and Sudan as the "countries of commission").

416 Amnesty International, *Universal jurisdiction: A preliminary survey of legislation around the world, 2012 update*, Report (2012), p. 1. Some jurisdictions, however, impose limitations including reserving its application only to situations where the State is required by treaty law to exercise it, or only in circumstances where the State in which the crime was committed is unwilling or unable to prosecute. Kevin Jon Heller, 'What Is an International Crime? (A Revisionist History)', *Harvard International Law Journal* 58, no. 2 (Spring 2017): pp. 40–41.

417 Thirteen countries globally have specialized programmes established to investigate and prosecute war crimes, crimes against humanity and genocide, and deny a safe haven to perpetrators: Belgium; Canada; Croatia; Denmark; France; Germany; the Netherlands; Norway; South Africa; Sweden; Switzerland; the United Kingdom; and the United States.

...PART V: **Bridging the Gap...**

Devika Hovell, 'The Authority of Universal Jurisdiction', *European Journal of International Law* 29, no. 2 (23 July 2018): p. 448; Orchard, 'International, Regional, and Domestic Mechanisms to Hold States to Account for the Causes of Forced Displacement', p. 22. While the set-up of the units differs, some feature specialized police, prosecution, or immigration units, which are dedicated to international crimes. In some cases, such as Denmark and the United Kingdom, specific personnel are dedicated to grave international crimes. HRW, 'The Long Arm of Justice: Lessons from Specialized War Crimes Units in France, Germany, and the Netherlands', Report (September 2014).

418 Langer and Eason, 'The Quiet Expansion of Universal Jurisdiction': pp. 781–782.

419 Ibid.: pp. 781, 792–795.

420 Ibid.: pp. 793–796; Investigative Team to Promote Accountability for Crimes Committed by Da'esh/ISIL (UNITAD), 'Harnessing Technology to Deliver Justice for War Crimes, Crimes against Humanity and Genocide' [Video], UN, 12 May 2021.

421 TRIAL International, *Universal Jurisdiction Annual Review 2021*, pp. 46–51.

422 According to Langer and Eason, most defendants that have been tried on the basis of universal jurisdiction in recent years had sought asylum status in the prosecuting State prior to proceedings being initiated against them. Langer and Eason, 'The Quiet Expansion of Universal Jurisdiction': p. 797.

423 TRIAL International, *Universal Jurisdiction Annual Review 2019*, p. 9.

424 Ibid., p. 7.

425 Jenna B. Russo, 'R2P in Syria and Myanmar: Norm Violation and Advancement', *Global Responsibility to Protect* 12, no. 2 (May 2020): p. 219; UNGA, 'International, Impartial and Independent Mechanism to Assist in the Investigation and Prosecution of Persons Responsible for the Most Serious Crimes under International Law Committed in the Syrian Arab Republic since March 2011' (21 September 2016), UN Doc A/RES/71/248; IIIM, 'International, Impartial and Independent Mechanism', website. It was supported by a vote of 105 to 15, with 52 abstentions, Russo, 'R2P in Syria and Myanmar', p. 219.

426 IIIM, 'Mandate', website.

427 UNGA, 'International, Impartial and Independent Mechanism to Assist in the Investigation and Prosecution of Persons Responsible for the Most Serious Crimes under International Law Committed in the Syrian Arab Republic since March 2011', para. 30. This was the first General Assembly-mandated investigation since 1999, when the General Assembly asked the Secretary-General and the United Nations High Commissioner for Human Rights to investigate fully reports of mass killings of prisoners of war and civilians, rape and cruel treatment in Afghanistan. UNGA, 'Question of Human Rights in Afghanistan' (29 February 2000), UN Doc A/RES/54/185.

428 The number of such bodies has increased in the past decade. From 2006 to 2010, the HRC mandated seven commissions in four countries/territories. During the next decade, it mandated 32 commissions and missions in regard to events in 18 States/territories or regional situations. OHCHR, 'International Commissions of Inquiry, Fact-Finding Missions: Chronological List', OHCHR Library Database.

429 For more on these and related documents, see: OHCHR, 'International Commissions of Inquiry, Fact-Finding Missions: Mandating Authority', OHCHR Library Database.

430 OHCHR, 'Independent Investigative Mechanism for Myanmar', *HRC* website. The Mech-

anism is to make use of the information provided by the earlier mandated International Fact-Finding Mission on Myanmar. The explicit link to prosecutions stands in contrast with the mandate of other HRC resolutions mandating human rights examinations. See, for example: HRC, 'Situation of human rights in Belarus in the run-up to the 2020 presidential election and in its aftermath' (24 March 2021), UN Doc A/HRC/46/20.

431 UNSC, Res. 2379 (21 September 2017), UN Doc S/RES/2379 (2017).

432 Specifically, the attacks against the Yazidi community in the Sinjar region and the 2014 mass killing of unarmed cadets and military personnel at Tikrit Air Academy. UNSC, 'Sixth Report of the Special Adviser and Head of the United Nations Investigative Team to Promote Accountability for Crimes Committed by Da'esh/Islamic State in Iraq and the Levant', (3 May 2021), UN Doc S/2021/419, p. 2. In June 2021, Karim A. A. Khan was sworn in as the Prosecutor for the ICC.

433 Including with individual courts and investigating judges to strengthen national capacity in regard to the storage and preservation of evidence and the development of case files as a basis for future prosecutions. Ibid., pp. 15–17.

434 Nadia's Initiative, 'Nadia Murad Addresses UN Security Council at UNITAD Briefing' [Video], 10 May 2021.

435 Ibid.

436 These are among suggestions for improving accountability suggested by Theodor Meron, distinguished jurist and former judge of the international tribunals for the former Yugoslavia and Rwanda. Meron, 'Closing the Accountability Gap': pp. 434, 440, 450–451.

437 Ibid., p. 442.

438 Open Society Foundations, 'Talking Justice: The Long Road to the Extraordinary African Chambers' [Podcast] (26 April 2016).

CONCLUSION: **Reflecting Back and Facing Forward**

1 She and her husband had a fruit wholesale business before fleeing to Lebanon early in the civil war. By 2014, they had exhausted their savings and were living in an informal settlement in the Bekaa Valley. Their home, like that of so many others, was a tent that often leaked. She had lost hope in return and considered education for her children their most pressing need. Conversation with the author, 2014. They did not wish for their names to be identified.

2 Fragile States are those that are exposed to risks but do not have sufficient capacity to absorb and manage them. This can lead to violence, poverty, inequality, environmental degradation, political instability and forced displacement. In 2018, total bilateral ODA to fragile contexts amounted to $76 billion, over twice the level of foreign direct investment (FDI) and "two-thirds the value of remittances". For DAC members, 63 per cent of their net country-allocable ODA was spent on fragile contexts. OECD, *States of Fragility 2020*, Report (2020), Part I: 'The state of fragility in 2020'.

3 Discussed in Parts IV and V.

4 Conversation with author at the Global Refugee Forum held in Geneva, 16–18 December 2019.

Index

List of
visualizations

A